COURT FORMS

SECOND EDITION

VOLUME
23 (2)

1998 ISSUE

UNITED KINGDOM	Butterworths, a Division of Reed Elsevier (UK) Ltd, Halsbury House, 35 Chancery Lane, **London** WC2A 1EL and 4 Hill Street, **Edinburgh** EH2 3JZ
AUSTRALIA	Butterworths, a Division of Reed International Books Australia Pty Ltd, **Chatswood**, New South Wales
CANADA	Butterworths Canada Ltd, **Markham**, Ontario
HONG KONG	Butterworths Asia (Hong Kong), **Hong Kong**
INDIA	Butterworths India, **New Delhi**
IRELAND	Butterworth (Ireland) Ltd, **Dublin**
MALAYSIA	Malayan Law Journal Sdn Bhd, **Kuala Lumpur**
NEW ZEALAND	Butterworths of New Zealand Ltd, **Wellington**
SINGAPORE	Butterworths Asia, **Singapore**
SOUTH AFRICA	Butterworth Publishers (Pty) Ltd, **Durban**
USA	Lexis Law Publishing, **Charlottesville**, Virginia

ATKIN'S ENCYCLOPÆDIA OF

COURT FORMS

IN CIVIL PROCEEDINGS

SECOND EDITION

VOLUME

23 (2)

1998 ISSUE

Issues
Judicial Review
Land Charges
Land Registration

LONDON
BUTTERWORTHS
1998

Volume 23
Second Edition
First Published
1967
Revised and reissued
1978, 1988, 1993
Revised and reissued as Volume 23 (2)
1998
This reissue completely
supersedes all earlier
issues of this volume

©
Reed Elsevier (UK) Ltd

1967, 1978, 1988, 1993, 1998

All rights reserved. No part of this publication may be reproduced in any material form (including photocopying or storing it in any medium by electronic means and whether or not transiently or incidentally to some other use of this publication) without the written permission of the copyright owner except in accordance with the provisions of the Copyright, Designs and Patents Act 1988 or under the terms of a licence issued by the Copyright Licensing Agency Ltd, 90 Tottenham Court Road, London, England W1P 0LP. Applications for the copyright owner's written permission to reproduce any part of this publication should be addressed to the publisher.

Warning: The doing of an unauthorised act in relation to a copyright work may result in both a civil claim for damages and criminal prosecution.

A CIP Catalogue record for this book is available from the British Library.

Visit us at our website: http://www.butterworths.co.uk

ISBN
for complete set of volumes: 0 406 01020 X

Printed in Great Britain by
Clays Ltd, St Ives plc

Publication of the second edition of this work was commenced in 1961 under the Editorship-in-Chief of the late Rt Hon. the Lord Evershed, a Lord of Appeal in Ordinary 1962–1965, Master of the Rolls 1949–1962

Emeritus Editor

SIR JACK I. H. JACOB, Q.C., HON. LL.D. (BIRMINGHAM 1978, LONDON 1981, STAFFORDSHIRE 1994); DR. JUR. (WURZBURG 1982); FCI ARB; HONORARY BENCHER OF GRAY'S INN; FELLOW OF UNIVERSITY COLLEGE LONDON; HONORARY FELLOW OF THE UNIVERSITY OF WESTMINSTER; HONORARY FELLOW OF THE ACADEMY OF EXPERTS; FORMER DIRECTOR, INSTITUTE OF ADVANCED LEGAL STUDIES; FORMER SENIOR MASTER OF THE SUPREME COURT AND QUEEN'S REMEMBRANCER

Publisher

ELIZABETH HEATHFIELD, LL.B.

Publishing Manager

KARIN A. JONES, LL.B.
SOLICITOR OF THE SUPREME COURT

Editorial Managers

CATHERINE E. DOWLING, LL.B.
SOLICITOR OF THE SUPREME COURT

JONATHAN W. WOODS, B.Sc.
SOLICITOR OF THE SUPREME COURT

Advisory Editors

Chief Advisory Editor

ROBERT TURNER
THE SENIOR MASTER OF THE SUPREME COURT (QUEEN'S BENCH DIVISION) AND QUEEN'S REMEMBRANCER

Chancery Division

JONATHAN I. WINEGARTEN
A MASTER OF THE SUPREME COURT (CHANCERY DIVISION)

Queen's Bench Division

IAN FOSTER
A MASTER OF THE SUPREME COURT (QUEEN'S BENCH DIVISION)

Family Division

DISTRICT JUDGE G. B. N. A. ANGEL
SENIOR DISTRICT JUDGE OF THE SUPREME COURT (FAMILY DIVISION)

County Court and District Registries

HIS HONOUR JUDGE DAVID S. GEE
OF THE NORTHERN CIRCUIT

Commercial Matters

HIS HONOUR JUDGE MICHAEL KERSHAW Q.C.
OF THE NORTHERN CIRCUIT

Contributors to this Volume

Issues

PETER D. EMERY,
SENIOR COURT MANAGER, CENTRAL OFFICE AND CHANCERY
DIVISION OF THE SUPREME COURT

Judicial Review

LYNNE KNAPMAN, B. JUR (HONS), LL.M.
SOLICITOR OF THE SUPREME COURT; SOCIAL SECURITY
COMMISSIONER AND CHILD SUPPORT COMMISSIONER

Land Charges

M. P. WESTCOTT RUDD M.A.
SOLICITOR OF THE SUPREME COURT; ASSISTANT LAND
REGISTRAR H.M. LAND REGISTRY, LINCOLN'S INN FIELDS

Land Registration

M. P. WESTCOTT RUDD M.A.
SOLICITOR OF THE SUPREME COURT; ASSISTANT LAND
REGISTRAR H.M. LAND REGISTRY, LINCOLN'S INN FIELDS

Volume Editor

CATHERINE E. DOWLING, LL.B.
SOLICITOR OF THE SUPREME COURT

Editorial Staff

RANALD WATSON, M.A.
OF LINCOLN'S INN, BARRISTER

JANE FLYNN, B.A.
SOLICITOR OF THE SUPREME COURT

JOHN D. WALLACE, LL.B.
SOLICITOR AND BARRISTER OF THE SUPREME COURT OF SOUTH AUSTRALIA

SAMIRA MAHMOOD, LL.B.
OF LINCOLN'S INN, BARRISTER

THOMAS M. BRENAN, LL.B.
SOLICITOR OF THE SUPREME COURT

ALISON BLOOD, B.A.
OF GRAY'S INN, BARRISTER

ELIZABETH CHASEY, LL.B.
SOLICITOR OF THE SUPREME COURT

KAREN SCHRODER, M.A.
PRODUCTION EDITOR

YVONNE BRUCE
PUBLISHING ASSISTANT

B. BURKE, B.SC.
INDEXER

Contents

Table of Current Volumes	xi
Table of Statutes	xiii
Table of Rules and Regulations	xxv
Table of Cases	xxxv

Issues

PRACTICE	5
FORMS	37

Judicial Review

PRACTICE	75
PROCEDURAL TABLE	191
FORMS	197

Land Charges

PRACTICE	219
FORMS	233

Land Registration

PRACTICE	251
FORMS	291
Index	353

The Law stated in this Volume is that in force on
1 July 1998

Crown Copyright material is reproduced with the permission of the
Controller of Her Majesty's Stationery Office

TABLE OF CURRENT VOLUMES

Volume 1 (1992 Issue)
Actions
Accounts
Volume 2 (1994 Issue)
Administration of Estates
Volume 3 (1994 Issue)
Admiralty
Affidavits
Volume 4 (1995 Issue)
Agency
Agricultural Land
Animals
Volume 5 (1997 Issue)
Appeals
Volume 6 (1998 Issue)
Acknowledgment of Service
Auction
Bailment
Banking and Bills of Exchange
Volume 7 (1997 Issue)
Bankruptcy and Insolvency
Volume 8 (1) (1998 Issue)
Bills of Sale
Bonds
Building Contracts
Carriers
Civil Aviation
Commercial Court
Commons
Volume 9 (1995 Issue)
Companies—General
Volume 10 (1995 Issue)
Companies—Winding up
Volume 11 (1) (1997 Issue)
Construction Courts
Consumer Credit
Volume 11 (2) (1997 Issue)
Consumer Protection and
  Product Liability
Co-ownership of Property
Council Tax
Volume 12 (1) (1996 Issue)
Compromise and Settlement
Compulsory Acquisition
Computers
Contempt of Court
Volume 12 (2) (1996 Issue)
Contract
Copyright
Volume 13 (1992 Issue)
Coroners
Costs
County Courts
Volume 14 (1996 Issue)
Crown Practice
Crown Proceedings
Declaratory Judgments
Default
Volume 15 (1998 Issue)
Discontinuance and Dismissal
Discovery and Inspection
Distress
District Registries
Volume 16 (1994 Issue)
Divorce
Volume 17 (1997 Issue)
Easements
European Courts

Volume 18 (1996 Issue)
Ecclesiastical Law
Elections
Equitable Remedies
Evidence
Volume 19 (1) (1996 Issue)
Execution and Enforcement of
  Judgments and Orders
Volume 19 (2) (1997 Issue)
Financial Services
Volume 20 (1998 Issue)
Gaming and Wagering
Guarantee
Health and Safety at Work
Highways
Housing
Volume 21 (1) (1997 Issue)
Husband and Wife and
  Cohabitation
Volume 21 (2) (1997 Issue)
Infants (Part I)
Volume 21 (3) (1997 Issue)
Infants (Part II)
Volume 22 (1) (1996 Issue)
Inheritance
Injunctions
Insurance
Interim Orders
Interlocutory Proceedings
Interpleader
Interrogatories
Volume 22 (2) (1996 Issue)
Immigration and Extradition
Volume 23 (1) (1998 Issue)
Intoxicating Liquor
Judgments and Orders
Volume 23 (2) (1998 Issue)
Issues
Judicial Review
Land Charges
Land Registration
Volume 24 (1) (1995 Issue)
Landlord and Tenant (Part I)
Volume 24 (2) (1995 Issue)
Landlord and Tenant (Part II)
Lands Tribunal
Volume 25 (1998 Issue)
Legal Aid
Libel and Slander
Limitation of Actions
Local Government
Magistrates
Malicious Prosecution
Markets and Fairs
Volume 26 (1996 Issue)
Mental Health and Mental
  Incapacity
Volume 27 (1995 Issue)
Mines, Minerals and Quarries
Misrepresentation and Fraud
Money
Volume 28 (1997 Issue)
Mortgages
Motions
National Health Service
Ombudsmen
Volume 29 (1991 Issue)
Negligence
Nuisance and Rylands v Fletcher
Orders 14 and 14A
Originating Summonses

Volume 29 (2) (1996 Issue)
Pensions
Personal Injury
Professional Negligence
Volume 30 (1994 Issue)
Parties to Actions
Partnerships and Firms
Patents and Inventions
Volume 30 (1) (1995 Issue)
Partnerships and Firms—
  Insolvency
Volume 31 (1998 Issue)
Payment into and out of
  Court
Peerages and Dignities
Personal Rights
Petitions
Plant Breeders' Rights
Volume 32 (1996 Issue)
Pleadings
Probate
Public Health
Volume 33 (1997 Issue)
Rating
Receivers
References and Inquiries by
  the Court
Rentcharges and Annuities
Volume 34 (1) (1994 Issue)
Restrictive Covenants
Revenue
Royal Forces
Sale of Land
Volume 34 (2) (1998 Issue)
Sale and Supply of Goods and
  Services
Volume 35 (1995 Issue)
Sales under Court Direction
Service of Process
Volume 36 (1997 Issue)
Sheriffs and Bailiffs
Social Security and Pensions
Societies and Clubs
Solicitors
Volume 37 (1995 Issue)
Specific Performance
Stay of Proceedings
Stock Exchange
Theatres
Third Party Procedure
Volume 38 (1995 Issue)
Town and Country Planning
Trade, Labour and
  Employment
Trade Marks and Trade
  Names
Volume 39 (1995 Issue)
Transfer and Consolidation
Transport
Trespass to Goods
Trespass to Land
Volume 40 (1996 Issue)
Trespass to the Person
Trial and Juries
Tribunals and Inquiries
Volume 41 (1991 Issue)
Trusts and Settlements
Waters and Watercourses
Writs of Summons

Table of Statutes

	PAGE
Access to Health Records Act 1990	
s 3–5, 8	139
Access to Neighbouring Land Act 1992	
s 5	219
(1)	220, 227, 278, 286
(2)	274, 275
Administration of Estates Act 1925	
s 23(2)	259
Administration of Justice Act 1956	
s 53	252
Administration of Justice Act 1960	
s 1	180
(1)(a)	189
(2)	189
Administration of Justice Act 1977	
s 24	282
26(1)	274
Administration of Justice Act 1985	
s 50	259
65	214, 235, 298, 336, 352
Administration of Justice (Miscellaneous Provisions) Act 1933	
s 5	75
Administration of Justice (Miscellaneous Provisions) Act 1938	
s 7	75
Agricultural Holdings Act 1986	
ss 85, 86	221
Sch 11	
paras 26, 30	32
Agriculture (Miscellaneous Provisions) Act 1954	
s 6(1), (2)	32
Arbitration Act 1996	
s 107	32
(1)	221
Sch 3	
para 17	221
20	32
Sch 4	32
Asylum and Immigration Act 1996	118
s 3(1)(b)(i), (ii)	119
Sch 2	
paras 2, 4	119
Asylum and Immigration Appeals Act 1993	118, 119
s 8	119
British Law Ascertainment Act 1859	
s 1	34, 62, 63
2	34
3	34, 65
4	34
British Nationality Act 1981	
s 44(1)	119
(2)	158

	PAGE
British Nationality (Hong Kong) Act 1990	
s 1(5)	119
Building Societies Act 1986	
s 84(5)	32
Building Societies Act 1997	
s 43	32
46(2)	32
Sch 7	
para 36	32
Sch 9	32
Charging Orders Act 1979	227
s 2(1)(a)	272
(2)(a)	272
3(2)	220
Charities Act 1993	
s 37	276, 277
Children and Young Persons Act 1933	
s 39	90
Children (Scotland) Act 1995	
s 105(4)	139
Sch 4	
para 50(1)–(4)	139
Civil Defence Act 1939	
s 18(4)	221
19(1)	221
Civil Evidence Act 1995	13
Civil Procedure Act 1997	
s 10	5, 16, 223
Sch 2	
para 1(1)	5, 16
(3)	5
(6)	16
2(1), (4)	223
Coal Industry Nationalisation Act 1946	86
Commissioners for Oaths Act 1889	214, 235, 298, 336, 352
Commissioners for Oaths Act 1891	214, 235, 298, 336, 352
Common Law Procedure Act 1854	91
Companies Act 1948	
s 92(2)	158
Companies Act 1967	145
Companies Act 1985	
s 726(1)	179
Competition and Service (Utilities) Act 1992	144
Corn Rents Act 1963	
s 1(5)	221
County Courts Act 1984	
s 1	223
21	254
23	254
(c)	223
24	223
38(3)(a)	178
65	66

TABLE OF STATUTES

	PAGE
County Courts Act 1984—contd	
s 65(1)	67
(d)	35, 65
(3)	35
Courts and Legal Services Act 1990	
s 71(3)	252
113	214, 235, 298, 336, 352
125(7)	252
Sch 20	252
Courts-Martial (Appeals) Act 1968	
s 1(2)	89
Crime (Sentences) Act 1997	
s 49(1)	139, 143, 207
(2)	139, 207
(3)	139, 143
55	139
56(2)	139, 143
Sch 4	
para 12(1), (3)	139
Sch 6	139, 143
Criminal Justice Act 1948	
s 37(1)(b)(ii)	182
(d)	182
Criminal Justice Act 1988	
s 77	219, 220
(12), (13)	278
78, 79	220
170(1)	274, 275
(2)	226
Sch 15	
para 6	274, 275
Sch 16	226
Criminal Justice Act 1991	133
s 32(5)	134
80(1)	132
84	131
85(1)	131
(3)(a)	131
97(1), (3)	131
Crown Proceedings Act 1947	
s 23(3)(f)	258
Deeds of Arrangement Act 1914	
s 23	223, 288
Drug Trafficking Act 1994	
s 26	219, 220
(12), (13)	278
27	220
65(1)	274, 275
67(1)	274, 275
Sch 1	
para 1	274, 275
Sch 3	274, 275
Education Act 1944	
s 8	123, 126
55(1)	128
99	123
Education Act 1980	209, 210
s 6	126
(3)(a)	125
12(3), (5)	101
Education Act 1996	209
Pt IV (ss 312–349)	127
s 2(1), (2)	123, 126

	PAGE
Education Act 1996—contd	
s 14(1)–(3)	123, 126
(5)–(7)	123, 126
28	122
35(5)	123
(6)	122
36(1), (2), (4)	101
37(1), (3)	101
(5)	123
41(7)	123
(8)	122
43(2)	123
71	123
156	127
157(1), (2)	127
159	127
167(3)	123
(5)	122
168(1), (2), (4)	101
169(1), (3)	101
(5)	123
173(4)	122
175(1), (2)	122
218(4)	124
307A	127
312(4)	127
325	129
326	128
(3)	129
328(5)	129
367	126
409	125
411(1), (2)	126
(3)	125, 126
(4), (5)	126
413	126
423, 429	125, 210
470, 472	32
476(1)	32
496	124
497	123, 125
498	123
509(1), (2)	128
582(1)	32, 33, 129, 137
(2)	101, 122, 123, 125, 126, 128
Sch 16	127
Sch 22	124
Sch 23	
para 6	125
Sch 25A	127
Sch 34	32
Sch 37	
Pt I	
para 118(1), (2)	32, 33, 129, 137
(3)	32
Sch 38	
Pt I	101, 122, 123, 125, 126, 128
Education (No 2) Act 1986	
s 43	84
Education Reform Act 1988	122
s 206	129
Education Reform Act 1996	
s 409	122

TABLE OF STATUTES

	PAGE
Employment Rights Act 1996	
s 240	32, 129
Sch 1	
para 57	32, 129
Environment Act 1995	
s 98	221
120(1)	221
Sch 10	
para 14	221
Sch 22	
para 191	221
European Communities Act 1972	
s 1(2)	149
2(1)	167, 168
(2)	172
(4)	168, 169
3(1), (2)	169
Evidence Act 1938	13
Family Law Act 1996	
Pt IV (ss 30–63)	221, 222
s 15	219
30	222
31	222
(10), (11)	273
33	223
66(1)	220, 223, 230, 231, 246
(2), (3)	273
Sch 2	
paras 1, 6	219
Sch 4	
para 4(1)–(3)	230
Sch 8	
para 46	223, 230, 231, 246
47	220
Sch 9	
paras 11, 12	273
Sch 20	273
Finance Act 1986	
ss 100, 101	222
Sch 19	222
Finance (No 2) Act 1975	
ss 69, 70	145
Financial Services Act 1986	86
s 114	146
187	149
Sch 2	146
Foreign Compensation Act 1950	156
s 4(4)	157
Foreign Compensation Act 1969	
s 3(3)	157
Foreign Judgments (Reciprocal Enforcement) Act 1933	57, 58
Foreign Law Ascertainment Act 1861	34
Friendly Societies Act 1974	
s 83(7)	32
Further and Higher Education Act 1992	
Pt II (ss 62–81)	122
ss 36, 54–58	122
59(1)–(4)	122
60–62, 81	122
93(1)	126

	PAGE
Further and Higher Education Act 1992— *contd*	
Sch 8	
paras 75, 76	126
84, 85	126
Housing Act 1985	94, 95, 182
Housing Act 1996	
s 107(4)	219
182	120
184(3)	121
188	120
(1)	121
189	120
190(2)(a)	120
193, 202	120, 121
203	120
204	120
(1), (3), (4)	121
222, 227	33
Sch 10	
paras 1, 9	219
Sch 18	
Pt IV	
para 22(1)(a)	33
(2)	33
Sch 19	
Pt XIII	33
Income and Corporation Taxes Act 1970	
Pt XVII (ss 460–496)	148
Industrial and Provident Societies Act 1965	
s 60(9)	32
Industrial Tribunals Act 1996	
s 43	32, 129
Sch 1	
para 9(1), (2)	32, 129
Inland Revenue Regulation Act 1890	
s 13	147
Insolvency Act 1986	
s 340	331
375(2)	32
412	226
421	260
Interception of Communications Act 1985	
s 7(8)	158
Judicial Pensions and Retirement Act 1993	
s 26(10)	33
Sch 6	
paras 55, 56, 61	33
Land Charges Act 1925	221, 224, 244
s 4(1)	227
18(5)	219
Land Charges Act 1972	284, 347
s 1	231
(1), (2)	222
(6)	223, 224, 226, 227, 228, 230, 232, 233, 234, 235, 236, 237, 239, 240, 242, 243, 244, 245, 246
(6A)	230, 246
(a)–(d)	223
(e)	223, 228
2	220
(1)	229

TABLE OF STATUTES

Land Charges Act 1972—contd	PAGE	Land Registration Act 1925—contd	PAGE
s 2(2)(a)	221	s 10	269, 272, 324
(3)	221	11, 12	269
(4)	227, 240	13	255, 262, 263
(i)–(iii)	221	proviso (b)	256, 267
(iv)	222	proviso (c)	267
(5)	230	15(1)	264, 265, 293
(6)	227	(2)	256, 264
3(1)	229	(3)	264
(1A)	222, 229	17	264, 296
4(2), (3)	229	(1)	256, 289, 290
(5)–(8)	229	(2)	290
5	222	18	276
(1)	219, 225, 279, 286, 348	(1)	306
(b)	226	(e)	324
(2), (3)	225	(5)	324
(4)	286	19	270, 306
(4A)	222, 229	20(1)	270, 306, 324
(6)	279	21	276
(7), (8)	226	(1)(d)	324
(10)	223, 226, 244, 245	(2)	306
(11)	223, 226	(5)	324
6	222, 278	22	270, 306
(1)	286	23(1)	270, 306, 324
(a)	220	25	276, 336
(c)	220, 227, 279, 348	(2)(a)	274
(d)	220	26	274, 336
(1A)	220, 227	30(1), (2)	286
(2)	227, 286	34(2)	336, 337
(2A)	222, 229	(3)	260
(4)	227	(4)	260, 336
(5)	228	(5)	336
7	222	41(1)	259
(1)	220, 228	(2)	272
(2)	228	42(1)	260, 279
8	226, 228	(2)	260, 287
10(6)	231	43	260, 279
13(1), (2)	230	48(2)	258
14(1)–(3)	222	49	274, 275
16(2)	226	50	352
17(1)	219, 220, 223, 226, 227, 228, 229	(3)	260
		52	272, 275
18(5)	231	53	263, 296, 297, 302, 303, 304, 305
(6)	278		
Sch 1		(1)	268, 299
para 1	220, 227	(2)	269
2, 4	227	(3)	269, 300, 301
Land Drainage Act 1991		54	274, 313, 314, 317, 318, 334
s 34(2), (3)	221		
Land Registration Act 1925	251, 257	(1)	272, 273
s 2(1)	280	55	263, 270, 314, 315, 317, 318, 320, 321
3(ii)	253		
(viii)	272, 287	(1)	273, 309, 311
(xv)	259, 274	(2)	273, 312
(xvi)	259	56(1)	256, 269, 273, 296, 297
(xviii)	282	(2)	272
4	342	(3)	268, 273
(1)	269	(4)	273, 301, 303
5	269, 270, 272, 352	57	258
6	269, 339, 342	(1), (2)	278
7	269	(3)	256, 278
8(1)	269	(4)	278
9	269, 270, 272	58	258, 272

TABLE OF STATUTES

Land Registration Act 1925—contd	PAGE
s 58(1)	276
(2)	277
(3)	256, 277
(4)	277, 324, 325
(5)	276
59(1), (2)	272
60	287
61	260, 327
(1)	279, 285, 328, 329, 348
(3)	278, 279, 285, 329, 330, 348
(4)	278, 280
(5)	279, 331
(6)	278
(7)	286, 347, 348
62	260
64(1)(c)	276, 308
(2)	264, 294
67(2)	263
68	261
70	312
(1)(a)	309
(g)	259, 285, 313
(l)	287
(3)	270, 306, 308, 309
72	270
75	270, 345
(3)	258
(5)	258, 306
76	258
77	266, 267, 272
(6)	286
78	280
82	258, 331
(1)	256, 270, 283, 337, 342, 343
(a)	260, 281
(b)–(e)	281
(f)	281, 334, 336
(g)	281, 339, 340, 346
(h)	282, 339, 340, 346
(2)	282
(3)	281, 284, 339, 342, 351, 352
(a)–(c)	282
(4)	282
(5)	260, 281, 283, 352
(6)	265, 283, 337, 339, 340, 343
83	231, 258, 347, 349
(1)	280, 351
(a), (b)	285
(2)	280, 285
(3)	286
(4)	285
(5)(a), (b)	287
(c)	283, 287, 289, 332, 333, 351, 352
(6)	287
(7)	256
(8)(a), (b)	288
(9)	288, 348, 350, 352

Land Registration Act 1925—contd	PAGE
s 83(10)(a), (b)	288
(11), (12)	288
84	289
86(3)	277
87(5)	259
89	277
91(1)	277
97	267
99(1)	278
(3)	289
101	274
103(1)	259
(2)	265
106(1), (2)	274
(3)	272
110(4)	286
(6)	264
111(4)	272
(5)	260
112	254, 261
113	261, 286
114	281
123	222
123A	222
(2)	298
(3)	265, 298
126(7)	261
128(1)	264, 265, 294
(2)	264, 289
(3)	264, 295
132(1)	252
(4)	261
133	252
138	318, 319, 325, 334, 335, 344, 345
(1)	253
(2)–(4)	254
139	260, 290
140	267
(1)	255
(a)	32
141, 142	258
143(1)–(3)	254
147(1)	282
Land Registration Act 1936	251
Land Registration Act 1966	251
Land Registration Act 1986	251
Land Registration Act 1988	251
s 1	254, 260, 261
2	260, 261, 286, 328
Schedule	260, 286, 328
Land Registration Act 1997	251
s 1	222, 265, 298
2	231, 258, 280, 283, 285, 286, 287, 288, 289, 332, 333, 348, 349, 350, 352
4(1)	222, 277
Sch 1	
para 3	222
6(1)–(3)	277

TABLE OF STATUTES

	PAGE
Land Registration and Land Charges Act 1971	251
s 1(1)	283, 285
2(1)	258, 283, 287, 289, 290, 332, 348, 349, 350
(2)	287, 289, 332
(3)	289, 290
(5)	256, 283, 289, 348, 349, 351, 352
Land Transfer Act 1875	282
Land Transfer Act 1897	282
Landlord and Tenant Act 1927	
Sch 1	
para 7	221
Landlord and Tenant Act 1987	
s 24	278
(1)	260
(8)	279
28(5)	219, 278
(6)	278
30(6)	220
61(1)	274, 275
Sch 4	
para 1	274, 275
Lands Tribunal Act 1949	
s 3(4)	33
(11)(a)	33
Law of Property Act 1925	
s 44(1)	231
62	306
84(1)	230, 260
88(1), (2)	260
89(1), (2)	260
91(1), (2)	260
149(3)	322, 323
198(1)	231
Law of Property Act 1969	
s 25(1), (2)	231
(4)–(6)	231
(9)–(11)	231
Law of Property (Miscellaneous Provisions) Act 1989	241
s 2	274, 275, 292, 320, 321
Law of Property (Miscellaneous Provisions) Act 1994	
s 15	222, 229
(1), (4)	278
Leasehold Reform, Housing and Urban Development Act 1993	
s 26	278
(1)	219, 220
50	278
(1)	219, 220
187(1)	274, 275
Sch 21	
para 1	274, 275
Limitation Act 1980	287, 345
s 5	288
15	304, 336
17	270
Local Authority Social Services Act 1970	
s 7D	199, 200, 215, 216

	PAGE
Local Government Act 1972	
ss 101, 102	115
111	98, 99
137	98
222	161, 172
Local Government Act 1986	99
Local Government and Housing Act 1989	115
Local Government Finance Act 1982	
s 20(3)	32
Local Land Charges Act 1975	
ss 1, 10	221
Magistrates' Courts Act 1980	
s 111	33, 79
Matrimonial Causes Act 1973	
s 24	219
Matrimonial Homes Act 1983	221
s 1	222, 223
2	222
(8), (9)	273
Medicines Act 1968	84
Mental Health Act 1983	
s 1(2)	139
2	141
(3)	139
3	141, 142
(2)(a)–(c)	139
(3)	139
4(2)–(4)	138
5(2)–(4)	138
11(1), (4)	139
15	140
20	140
(1)	139
26(1)(a)–(h)	140
(5), (6)	140
29	140
35, 36	139
37	139, 142
38	139
41	139, 143, 207
42(3)	142, 143
47–49	139, 143
65	137
66	142
68	141
71(1)	207
72	143
(1)(a), (b)	142
(3)	142
73(2)	143
(7)	143, 206, 207
78(8)	33
99	227
117(2)	100, 205, 206, 207
135(6)	138
136	138
139(2), (4)	141
145(1)	143
Merchant Shipping Act 1988	172
Mines and Quarries Act 1954	
s 150(3), (4)	33
Sch 3	
Pt I	33

	PAGE
National Assistance Act 1948	
s 21	198, 200
National Health Service Act 1977	
s 3(1)	205, 206
(e)	207
National Health Service and Community Care Act 1990	
s 46(2)	198, 200, 215, 216
Norfolk and Suffolk Broads Act 1988	
s 21	221
Sch 6	
para 14	221
Nurses, Midwives and Health Visitors Act 1997	
s 23(1)	33
Sch 4	33
Pensions Appeal Tribunals Act 1943	
s 6(2)	33
Police Act 1996	
s 103(1)	127
Sch 7	
Pt I	
para 1(1)	127
2(1)	127
Police Act 1997	
s 134(1)	127
Sch 9	
para 36	127
Police and Magistrates' Courts Act 1994	
s 43	127
Sch 4	
Pt II	
para 51	127
Prevention of Terrorism (Temporary Provisions) Act 1989	
s 13(8)	278
Sch 4	
para 6	219, 220, 278
Prison Act 1952	136
s 1	131
7(1)	131
8	131
12(1)	133
47(1)	131, 133
Prison Security Act 1992	
s 1(1), (2), (5)	132
Proceedings Against Estates Act 1970	16
Prosecution of Offences Act 1985	
s 22	90
Race Relations Act 1976	161
ss 17, 41, 71	126
Registered Homes Act 1984	
ss 39–45	33
Rent Act 1977	
s 65	33
Sch 10	33
Restrictive Practices Court Act 1976	
s 10(1)	33
Road Traffic Regulation Act 1984	173
School Inspections Act 1996	122
Security Service Act 1989	
s 5(4)	158

	PAGE
Settled Land Act 1925	270, 322
s 24(1)	259
42(1)	323
101, 108, 109	323
Sex Discrimination Act 1975	161
s 22	126
Shops Act 1950	172
Social Security Act 1975	
ss 98, 99	162
Social Security Act 1980	
s 14	153
Social Security Adminstration Act 1992	
ss 17–19	151
20, 22	150
23(1)	150
(9)(a), (b)	152
24	151, 153
33(1)(a), (b)	150
34(1)	150
(4)	152
46(2)	150
48(1)	150
(3)(a), (b)	152
51(1)(b)	152
65(3)(a)	151
(5)(a)–(c)	151
68	154
Social Security Contributions and Benefits Act 1992	150
s 138(1)(a), (b)	151
139	151
140	151, 154
Solicitors Act 1974	
s 81	214, 235, 298, 336, 352
Stamp Act 1891	
s 13(1)	33
Supreme Court Act 1981	92
s 16	181, 182
18(1)(a)	180, 182, 189
(1A)	19, 24, 25
28	79
29	75, 79
(3)	90
31	76, 178, 187, 188
(2)	81
(3)	158, 159
(4)	82
(6)	164, 176, 179
35A	40, 41, 42, 51
51	188, 290
(1)	177, 179
68(1)	5
(a)	17, 37
(b)	17
(2)	5
87	16
Supreme Court of Judicature Act 1873	30
Supreme Court of Judicature Act 1875	30
Taxes Management Act 1970	
s 1	148
20(2)	148
46(2)	145
56	32

	PAGE
Tithe Act 1918	
ss 4, 6	221
Tithe Act 1936	
s 30(1)	221
Tithe Annuities Apportionment Act 1921	
s 1	221
Town and Country Planning Act 1990	319
s 92	321
284	156
288(3)	156
Tribunals and Inquiries Act 1958	
s 11	156
Tribunals and Inquiries Act 1992	
s 10(1), (2), (5)	137
11	32, 129
(1)	33, 137
(3)	156
12(1)	158
(3)	156
13(1)	33
Sch 1	129, 137
paras 8, 13	33
15(a)	32
28, 31	33

	PAGE
Trusts of Land and Appointment of Trustees Act 1996	
ss 6, 8	276
25	272
(1)	220, 227, 259, 274, 275, 278, 280
(2)	277, 287
Sch 3	
para 5(1)	259, 274, 275, 280
(2)	259, 274
(5)	274, 275
(6)	280
(10)	259
12(1)	220, 227, 278
(2)	220, 227
(3)	220, 227, 278
Sch 4	272, 277, 287
Water Act 1989	
s 190(1)	221
Sch 25	
para 52	221

Table of Rules and Regulations

	PAGE
Agricultural Land Tribunals (Rules) Order 1978, SI 1978/259	
r 33	32
Civil Legal Aid (General) Regulations 1989, SI 1989/339	
reg 51(b)(vi)	170
Community Charges (Administration and Enforcement) Regulations 1989, SI 1989/438	
reg 45(5)	274, 275
Council Tax (Admistration and Enforcement) Regulations 1992, SI 1992/613	
reg 51(5)	274, 275
County Court Rules 1981, SI 1981/1687	
Ord 3	
r 1	254
4	225
(2)(b), (c)	246
7	246
(1)	65
Ord 5	
r 3	5
Ord 19	
r 11(a)	35, 65
(b), (c)	35
12	66
13(a)–(e)	35
(g)	67
(i)	35
(h)(i), (ii)	35
Ord 31	227
r 1	290
Ord 44	32
Ord 50	
r 6	246
County Court (Forms) Rules 1982, SI 1982/586	
r 2(4)	246
Crown Court Rules 1982, SI 1982/1109	
r 29	170
Education (Particulars of Independent Schools) Regulations 1997, SI 1997/2918	32
Education (School Government) Regulations 1989, SI 1989/1503	123
reg 4–8	124
12–15	124
19–29	124
Education (School Government) (Amendment) Regulations 1991, SI 1991/2845	
reg 2–8	124
Education (School Government) (Amendment) Regulations 1993, SI 1993/3107	
regs 2, 4–6	124

	PAGE
Education (School Government) (Amendment) Regulations 1996, SI 1996/2050	
regs 5–7	124
Education (Special Educational Needs) Regulations 1994, SI 1994/1047	128
High Court and County Courts Jurisdiction Order 1991/724	
art 2(8)	221, 223, 228, 230, 231, 246
Schedule	221, 223, 228, 230, 231, 246
Housing Act 1996 (Consequential Amendments) Order 1997, SI 1997/74	
art 2	222
Schedule	
para 10(a)	222
Income Tax (Building Societies) Regulations 1986, SI 1986/482	147
Insolvency (Amendment of Subordinate Legislation) Order 1986, SI 1986/2001	222
Insolvency (Amendment) Rules 1987, SI 1987/1919	
r 3	228
Schedule	228
Insolvency (Amendment) Rules 1991, SI 1991/495	228
Insolvency Rules 1986, SI 1986/1925	
r 6.13	226, 279, 348
6.27	226
6.34(1)	228
(2)(a)	228, 279, 348
6.43	226, 279, 348
6.46(1)	228
(2)(a)	228, 279
6.213(1)	226
7.1	225
7.2	224, 225
7.3–7.10	225
Sch 4	
Form 6.14	226
6.26	228
Land Charges (Amendment) Rules 1990, SI 1990/485	222
Land Charges (Amendment) Rules 1995, SI 1995/1355	222
Land Charges Fees Rules 1990, SI 1990/327	
r 4	232
Land Charges Rules 1974, SI 1974/1286	
r 2(2)	232
10	226, 230
11	230
12	232
13	237

Land Charges Rules 1974—contd	PAGE
r 15(1)	231
20(1), (2)	232
22	237
Sch 1	
item 4(iv)	235
Sch 2	
Forms K1–K5	222
K11	226, 230, 232
K12, K13	230
K20	228, 232
Land Registration (Charities) Rules 1993, SI 1993/1704	277
Land Registration (Companies and Insolvency) Rules 1986, SI 1986/2116	280, 327
Land Registration (Conduct of Business) Regulations 1997, SI 1997/713	293, 304
reg 2(b)	252
3	294, 295, 315, 316, 318, 323, 346
(1)	252
4	252, 294, 295, 315, 316, 318, 323, 346
6	252
Schedule	252
Land Registration (District Registries) Order 1998, SI 1998/140	252
Land Registration (Official Searches) Rules 1993, SI 1993/3276	
rr 3–9	286
Land Registration (Open Register) Rules 1991, SI 1991/122	
rr 2, 3	261, 348
8(1)	269
9	286
Land Registration Rules 1925, SR & O 1925/1093	251
r 1(5c)	273
13	284
14	339, 340, 343, 346
(a), (b)	284
15	265
23	267
25	263, 266, 267
27	266
28, 29	267
31, 32	263, 266
34	263
(1)	267
(2)	267, 292
35	263
(1)	267
(2)	267, 294
37	342
40	287, 291, 292, 352
46	258, 324
(1)	267
48	263, 266, 267, 272
56	277
57	272, 277
58	277, 323
59(1)	323

Land Registration Rules 1925—contd	PAGE
rr 59A, 60	277
64	269, 299
67	269, 300
68(1)	269
69	269, 301
78	277
99, 100, 102	277
104, 106A	277
123(1)	277
128	276
131	259, 270, 280
147	260
149	336
157, 158	255
170, 171	277
174	260
(1)	279
175	260, 279
176	260, 279, 331
177	260, 279
178	260
179	260, 327, 328, 329
180	260, 278, 327, 328, 330
181	260, 279, 280, 327, 328, 330
182	260, 280, 327, 328
183–185	260
186	258
(3)	267
195, 196	287
197	270
(1)	306
198	270
211	280
213, 214	277
215(1), (2)	272
(4)	272, 313
217	273
218	263, 270, 310, 311, 315, 317, 318, 320, 321
(1)	273, 309
(2)	273
219	263, 273, 312
220	253
(1)	263, 273, 312
(2)	262, 273, 315, 316
(3)	256, 265, 273, 315, 316
(4)	255, 262, 273, 315, 317, 318, 319, 321
221, 222	273
230(1), (2)	278
231, 232	278
235	276
(2)	277
236	276
236B	325
237	265, 278, 323
(1)	277, 324
(2)	324
238	272
239	274
(1)	275

TABLE OF RULES AND REGULATIONS xxiii

Land Registration Rules 1925—contd
rr 240–243	275
248, 249	280
250	258
(2)(a), (b)	306
251	270, 306
252	270, 307, 308
(1), (2)	306
253	270
(2)	308, 309
254	270, 306
255	306
256, 257	270, 306
258	309
259	277
262	337
264	261
266	270
271	263
275	261
276	267
281	258
284	280
285	258
290	252
298	32, 252, 253, 263, 293, 294
(1)	256, 265, 269, 270, 295, 309
(a)	262
(2)	255, 262, 267, 269, 270, 283, 304, 305, 309, 346
299	256, 296, 297, 316, 343, 344, 345
300	263, 273, 294, 315
301	254, 256
302	259, 281, 352
(1), (2)	260, 283
311	267, 294
312	267
(2)	267
313	267, 269, 300, 307, 310, 330, 340
(2)	308
314	267
315	267, 340
(1)	329, 330
316(4)	265
320	294
321(1), (2)	289
(3)	290
322	267, 270
(1), (2)	265
Sch 1	
Form CT1	269
Sch 2	
Form 9	277, 323
10, 11	277
14	272
15	300
16	269
63, 69	272
71	273
75	276

Land Registration Rules 1995, SI 1995/140
r 4	275

Land Registration Rules 1996,
SI 1996/2975	276, 277, 323

Land Registration Rules 1997,
SI 1997/3037	269, 272, 276, 300

Mental Health Review Tribunal Rules 1983,
SI 1983/942
r 23(1)	142
31(a)	142

Prison Rules 1964, SI 1964/388 . . . . 136, 203, 204
r 1	134
2(3)	135
7(1)	133
8	133
43, 43A, 45	133
46(1), (4)	133
56	132
98A	131

Registered Homes Tribunal Rules 1984,
SI 1984/1346	33

Restrictive Practices Court Rules 1976,
SI 1976/1897
rr 11–18	33

Rules of the Supreme Court 1883
Ord XXXIII
r 1	6

Ord XXXIV
r 1	6, 30
2–8	30

Ord LXV
rr 1, 2	6

Rules of the Supreme Court 1965,
SI 1965/1776	158, 199

Ord 1
r 4(1)	12, 17
9	234, 296, 319, 325, 334, 345, 350
(2)	62, 200

Ord 2
r 1	179

Ord 3
r 5	180

Ord 5
r 2	305
3	224, 254, 257, 278
4	20

Ord 4
r 3	37

Ord 6
r 5	244, 296, 319, 325, 335, 345, 350

Ord 7
r 3(2)	319, 325, 335, 350
5(2)	319, 325, 335, 350

Ord 8
r 3(3)	244, 296
(5)	296, 345
5(3)	345

Ord 13 23
Ord 14 . . . . 20, 21, 22, 23, 24, 53

TABLE OF RULES AND REGULATIONS

Rules of the Supreme Court 1965—*contd*
Ord 14A 6, 7, 21, 51, 52, 53,
54, 55, 56
r 1(1)(a). 20
(b) 19, 24
(2). 19, 24
(3)(a) 22, 23
(b) 22
(4). 20, 23
(5) 20
2 22
Ord 15
r 3(1) 29
5(1), (2) 5
6A 16
Ord 16 . . . . 7, 350
r 1(1)(c). 29
(2) 29
8(1)(c). 28
(3) 28
10(1), (2) 12
Ord 17 56
r 5 7
(1)(a). 27
(b) 27, 57
(2)(a), (b) 26
(c). 6
7 27
Ord 18
r 6(1)(a) 37, 200, 244
11 . . . . 6, 7, 15, 47, 48
13(1), (2) 23
14(3) 23
19 . . . . 15, 20, 22, 23,
24, 54
Ord 22 11
r 1(2), (4) 12
3(1) 12
7, 14 12
Ord 24 . . . . 184, 195
r 2(5)(a) 10
4 . . . . 6, 7
(1), (2) 25
7 56
Ord 26 . . . . 184, 195
r 7 23
Ord 27
r 2 23
3 . . . . 20, 23
Ord 28
r 8 . . . . 93, 187
Ord 32
r 1 22
11(1)(d) 23
14(1)(d) 23
Ord 33
r 1 17
2 . . . . 17, 27, 28
3 . . . . 6, 7, 8, 13, 15, 20, 25,
43, 44, 45, 46
4(2) 7, 8, 12, 20
4A 39
(1)–(3) 12

Rules of the Supreme Court 1965—*contd*
Ord 33—*contd*
r 7 . . . . 10, 18, 24, 25, 41,
42, 48, 49
Ord 36 5
r 1(2) 17
2 17
3(1), (2), (4). 17
4 17
8, 9 6
10 . . . . 10, 37
11(1) 6, 17
(3) 17
Ord 37
r 1 42
(1), (2). 10
2 . . . . 10, 42
4 42
(1)(a)–(d) 10
(3) 10
Ord 38
r 1 . . . . 10, 18
2 . . . . 10, 18
(3) 119, 184, 195
3 . . . . 178, 185
(2) 18
4–7 18
8 . . . . 10, 18
27, 28 13
36 (1) 18
Ord 41
r 1(8) 214, 235
2(1) 297, 336, 352
5 23
(1), (2) 178
Ord 42
r 5 12
5A(1) 12
(2)(A) 12
(3), (4) 12
6 12
Ord 43
r 1 20
Ord 46
r 1 28
2(1) 28
4(1) 28
(3) 7, 28
Ord 49
r 1(1) 27
5 . . . . 6, 7, 27
6(1) 27
(2) 6, 7
Ord 50 227
Ord 53 . . . . 76, 89, 91, 92
r 2 178
3 213
(1) 178
(b) 214
(2) 193
(a) 178, 191, 200, 202,
204, 210

TABLE OF RULES AND REGULATIONS

Rules of the Supreme Court 1965—*contd*
Ord 53—*contd*
r 3(2)(b) 178, 191, 216
  (3) 179, 191
  (4)(a) 180, 191, 192
    (b) 180, 191
  (5) 180, 191, 192
  (6) 179, 192
  (7) 159
  (8) 179, 192
  (9) 179, 184, 192
  (10)(a) 182, 192
    (b) 192
4(1) 164, 178, 191
 (2) 179
5(1) 181, 183
 (2) 181, 192, 195
  (a) 182, 183
  (b) 183
 (3) 182, 183, 193
 (4) 183
 (5) 183, 193
 (6) 182, 193
 (7) 182, 194, 195
6 178
 (2) 185, 193, 194, 195
 (3) 193
 (4) 184, 193
 (5) 193
7(1) 82, 195
 (2) 178, 185
8 . . . . 119, 184
 (1) 186
9(1) 184, 187, 194, 195
 (2) 183
 (4) 195
 (5) 93, 187, 195
Ord 54 140
Ord 55
 r 1(1), (4) 257
 3(1) 254, 257
 (2), (3) 257
 4(1)(b) 257, 296, 345
 (2), (4) 257, 296, 345
 5 . . . . 257, 296, 345
 6(3) 257
 7(2), (3) 257
 25 151
Ord 56 . . . . 30, 32, 138
 rr 5, 6 33
 7–12 . . . . 32, 33
Ord 57
 r 1(1)(c) 257
 2 257
 4(1) 191
 6 195
Ord 58
 r 1 188
Ord 59
 r 1A(3) 19
  (6)(AA) 24
 1B 188
 4(1) 189

Rules of the Supreme Court 1965—*contd*
Ord 59—*contd*
 r 13 189
 14(3) 180, 192
Ord 61
 rr 1, 3 33
Ord 62
 r 2 290
 9 58
  (c) 12
 12 295
 29 289
Ord 64
 r 4 180
Ord 71
 r 9(2) 7, 28
Ord 72
 r 2 17
Ord 73
 r 2(2) 30
Ord 77
 r 7(1) 20
Ord 81
 r 4(2) 29
  (3)(d) 29
  (4) 7, 29
Ord 86 20
Ord 91
 r 1(a) 32, 33
Ord 93
 r 10 . . . . 304, 317, 318, 346
  (1) 257
  (2) 254
  (f) 32, 296, 305, 319, 325,
                   335, 345, 350
  (m) 32
  (3) 257
Ord 94 138
 r 7 32
 9 . . . . 32, 33
 11 33
Ord 98 32
Ord 101 33
Ord 111 33
Appendix A
 Form 8 . . . . 234, 237, 319, 325,
                        335, 350
  13 . . . . 296, 345
  23, 24 12
  48 . . . . 41, 49
  86A 163, 164, 176, 178, 185,
                213, 214, 215, 216
  86B 180
Rules of the Supreme Court (Amendment)
  1996, SI 1996/2092
 r 6 57
 18 . . . . 32, 33
Social Fund (Applications) Regulations 1988,
  SI 1988/524 151
Social Security (Adjudication) Regulations
  1995, SI 1995/1801
 reg 2(1)(a) 153
 3(3), (4), (7) 152

Social Security (Adjudication) Regulations 1995—contd
    reg 5(1), (2) 153
    7(3) 152
    11 153
Social Security Commissioners Procedure Regulations 1987, SI 1987/214
    reg 22(1), (2) 154
Special Educational Needs Tribunal Regulations 1995, SI 1995/3113 .. 129

Supreme Court Fees Order 1980, SI 1980/821
    Schedule
        Fee No 4 178
        5A 195
        8 26
Supreme Court Fees (Amendment) Order 1996, SI 1996/3191
    art 5 .... 26, 178

Table of Cases

	PAGE
ADIDAS SARL's Trade Mark [1983] RPC 262	145
Abbey National Building Society v Cann [1991] 1 AC 56, [1990] 1 All ER 1085, [1990] 2 WLR 832, 60 P & CR 278, [1990] 2 FLR 122, [1990] Fam Law 397, 22 HLR 360, [1990] 17 LS Gaz R 32, [1990] NLJR 477, HL	259, 282, 313
Addis v Crocker [1960] 1 QB 87, [1959] 2 All ER 773, [1959] 3 WLR 527, 103 Sol Jo 636; affd [1961] 1 QB 11, [1960] 2 All ER 629, [1960] 3 WLR 339, 104 Sol Jo 584, CA	13, 15
Adler v Dickson [1955] 1 QB 158, [1954] 3 All ER 397, [1954] 3 WLR 696, [1954] 2 Lloyd's Rep 267, 98 Sol Jo 787, CA	16
Agricultural, Horticultural and Forestry Industry Training Board v Aylesbury Mushrooms Ltd [1972] 1 All ER 280, [1972] 1 WLR 190, 7 ITR 16, 116 Sol Jo 57	102, 103
Airey v Airey [1958] 2 All ER 59, [1958] 1 WLR 729, [1958] 1 Lloyd's Rep 326; affd [1958] 2 QB 300, [1958] 2 All ER 571, [1958] 1 WLR 729, [1958] 2 Lloyd's Rep 8, 102 Sol Jo 489, CA	16
Al-Mehdawi v Secretary of State for the Home Department [1990] 1 AC 876, [1989] 3 All ER 843, [1989] 3 WLR 1294, [1990] Imm AR 140, 134 Sol Jo 50, [1990] 1 LS Gaz R 32, HL	104
Algemene Transport-en Expeditie Onderneming van Gend en Loos NV v Nederlandse Belastingadministratie: 26/62 [1963] ECR 1, [1963] CMLR 105, ECJ	168
Ali v Secretary of State for the Home Department [1984] 1 All ER 1009, sub nom R v Secretary of State for the Home Department, ex p Momin Ali [1984] 1 WLR 663, [1984] Imm AR 23, 128 Sol Jo 332, [1984] LS Gaz R 1051, CA	189
Ali v Tower Hamlets London Borough Council [1993] QB 407, [1992] 3 All ER 512, [1992] 3 WLR 208, 90 LGR 501, [1993] 2 FCR 406, [1993] Fam Law 123, 24 HLR 474, [1992] 20 LS Gaz R 35, 136 Sol Jo LB 113, CA	94, 95
Allen v Gulf Oil Refining Ltd [1980] QB 156, [1979] 3 All ER 1008, [1979] 3 WLR 523, 123 Sol Jo 737, CA; revsd [1981] AC 1001, [1981] 1 All ER 353, [1981] 2 WLR 188, 125 Sol Jo 101, [1981] RVR 70, HL	21
Allsop v North Tyneside Metropolitan Borough Council (1992) 90 LGR 462, [1992] ICR 639, [1992] RVR 104, CA	98
Amministrazione delle Finanze dello Stato v Simmenthal SpA: 106/77 [1978] ECR 629, [1978] 3 CMLR 263, ECJ	169
An Bord Bainne Co-operative Ltd (Irish Dairy Board) v Milk Marketing Board [1984] 2 CMLR 584, 128 Sol Jo 417, [1984] LS Gaz R 2223, CA	93
Anisminic Ltd v Foreign Compensation Commission [1969] 2 AC 147, [1969] 1 All ER 208, [1969] 2 WLR 163, 113 Sol Jo 55, HL	156, 157
Anklagemyndigheden v Hansen & Son I/S: 326/88 [1990] ECR I-2911, [1992] ICR 277, ECJ	173
Ashton, Re. See R v Crown Court Court at Manchester, ex p DPP	
Archer v Catton & Co Ltd [1954] 1 All ER 896, [1954] 1 WLR 775, 98 Sol Jo 337	16
Argyle Building Society v Hammond (1984) 49 P & CR 148, CA	281
Ashburn Anstalt v Arnold [1989] Ch 1, [1988] 2 All ER 147, [1988] 2 WLR 706, 55 P & CR 137, 132 Sol Jo 416, [1987] 2 EGLR 71, [1988] 16 LS Gaz R 43, 284 Estates Gazette 1375, CA	259, 313
Ashmore v Corpn of Lloyd's (No 2) [1992] 2 Lloyd's Rep 620	146
Associated Provincial Picture Houses Ltd v Wednesbury Corpn [1948] 1 KB 223, [1947] 2 All ER 680, 45 LGR 635, 112 JP 55, [1948] LJR 190, 92 Sol Jo 26, 177 LT 641, 63 TLR 623, CA	97, 102, 107, 108
A-G v Crayford UDC [1962] Ch 575, [1962] 2 All ER 147, [1962] 2 WLR 998, 60 LGR 261, [1962] 1 Lloyd's Rep 163, 126 JP 308, 106 Sol Jo 175, CA	99
A-G v Great Eastern Rly Co (1880) 5 App Cas 473, 44 JP 648, 49 LJ Ch 545, 28 WR 769, 42 LT 810, [1874-80] All ER Rep Ext 1459, HL	99
A-G v Nissan [1970] AC 179, [1969] 1 All ER 629, [1969] 2 WLR 926, 113 Sol Jo 207, HL	16
A-G v Smethwick Corpn [1932] 1 Ch 562, 30 LGR 117, 96 JP 105, 101 LJ Ch 137, [1932] All ER Rep 304, 146 LT 480, 48 TLR 227, CA	99
A-G for New South Wales v Quin (1990) 170 CLR 1	109
A-G of Hong Kong v Ng Yuen Shiu [1983] 2 AC 629, [1983] 2 All ER 346, [1983] 2 WLR 735, 127 Sol Jo 188, PC	119

xxvii

TABLE OF CASES

	PAGE
Avon County Council v Buscott [1988] QB 656, [1988] 1 All ER 841, [1988] 2 WLR 788, 86 LGR 569, 20 HLR 385, 132 Sol Jo 567, [1988] 14 LS Gaz R 49, CA	95
Azam v Secretary of State for the Home Department [1974] AC 18, [1973] 2 All ER 765, [1973] 2 WLR 1058, 137 JP 626, [1973] Crim LR 512, 117 Sol Jo 546, 123 NLJ 612, HL	167
Backhouse v Lambeth London Borough Council (1972) 116 Sol Jo 802, (1972) Times, 14 October	111
Balen v IRC [1978] 2 All ER 1033, [1978] STC 420, 52 TC 406, [1978] TR 181, L(TC) 2694, CA	149
Bank of Scotland, Petitioner (1988) Times, 21 November	146
Barclays Bank Ltd v Taylor [1974] Ch 137, [1973] 1 All ER 752, [1973] 2 WLR 293, 23 P & CR 172, 117 Sol Jo 109, 227 Estates Gazette 497, CA	272
Barnard v National Dock Labour Board [1953] 2 QB 18, [1953] 1 All ER 1113, [1953] 2 WLR 995, [1953] 1 Lloyd's Rep 371, 97 Sol Jo 331, CA	114
Bates v Lord Hailsham of St Marylebone [1972] 3 All ER 1019, [1972] 1 WLR 1373, 116 Sol Jo 584	102
Bearmans Ltd v Metropolitan Police District Receiver [1961] 1 All ER 384, [1961] 1 WLR 634, 125 JP 268, 105 Sol Jo 365, CA	13, 17
Bedei v Ealing London Borough (7 November 1997, unreported)	121
Beecham Group plc v Gist-Brocades NV [1986] 1 WLR 51, [1985] FSR 610, [1986] RPC 203, 129 Sol Jo 889, [1986] LS Gaz R 206, HL; refd sub nom Allen & Hanburys Ltd v Generics (UK) Ltd: 434/85 [1988] 2 All ER 454, [1989] 1 WLR 414, [1985] ECR 1245, [1988] 1 CMLR 701, [1988] FSR 312, 133 Sol Jo 628, ECJ; apld [1988] 3 All ER 1057n, [1989] 1 WLR 414, HL	80
Beecham Group plc v IRC [1992] STC 935, 65 TC 219	149
Belcourt v Belcourt [1989] 2 All ER 34, [1989] 1 WLR 195, 133 Sol Jo 323, 17 LS Gaz R 41	256
Birmingham City Council v Equal Opportunities Commission [1989] AC 1155, [1989] 2 WLR 520, 87 LGR 557, [1989] IRLR 173, 133 Sol Jo 322, [1989] 15 LS Gaz R 36, [1989] NLJR 292, sub nom Equal Opportunities Commission v Birmingham City Council [1989] 1 All ER 769, HL	126
Bland v Chief Supplementary Benefit Officer [1983] 1 All ER 537, [1983] 1 WLR 262, 127 Sol Jo 53, CA	152, 154, 167
Boddington v British Transport Police [1998] 2 All ER 203, [1998] 2 WLR 639, 162 JP 455, [1998] NLJR 515, HL	96
Bone v Mental Health Review Tribunal [1985] 3 All ER 330	138, 143, 167
Boobyer v Thornville Properties Ltd (1968) 19 P & CR 768	224, 237, 239, 240
Bottomley v Hurst and Blackett Ltd and Houston (1928) 44 TLR 451, CA	13, 14
Bourgoin SA v Ministry of Agriculture, Fisheries and Food [1986] QB 716, [1985] 3 All ER 585, [1985] 3 WLR 1027, [1986] 1 CMLR 267, 129 Sol Jo 828, [1985] LS Gaz R 3534, CA:	82, 171
Boyle's Claim, Re [1961] 1 All ER 620, [1961] 1 WLR 339, 105 Sol Jo 155	285
Bozson v Altrincham UDC [1903] 1 KB 547, 1 LGR 639, 67 JP 397, 72 LJKB 271, 51 WR 337, 47 Sol Jo 316, 19 TLR 266, CA	18
Bradbury v London Borough of Enfield [1967] 3 All ER 434, [1967] 1 WLR 1311, 66 LGR 115, 132 JP 15, 111 Sol Jo 701, CA	123
Bradford and Bingley Building Society v Darin (15 May 1996, unreported)	265
Breslin v A-G for Northern Ireland [1992] 1 All ER 609, sub nom R v A-G for Northern Ireland, ex p Breslin [1992] 1 WLR 262, 136 Sol Jo LB 82, HL	83
Bridges v Mees [1957] Ch 475, [1957] 2 All ER 577, [1957] 3 WLR 215, 101 Sol Jo 555, 169 Estates Gazette 817	281, 282
British and Argentine Meat Co Ltd v Randall [1939] 4 All ER 293, 83 Sol Jo 943, 162 LT 91, CA	35
British and Commonwealth Holdings plc v Quadrex Holdings Inc [1989] QB 842, [1989] 3 All ER 492, [1989] 3 WLR 723, 133 Sol Jo 694, CA	21
British Oxygen Co Ltd v Minister of Technology [1971] AC 610, [1970] 3 All ER 165, [1970] 3 WLR 488, 49 ATC 154, [1970] TR 143, 114 Sol Jo 682, HL	115
Bromley London Borough Council v Greater London Council [1983] 1 AC 768, [1982] 1 All ER 153, [1982] 2 WLR 62, 80 LGR 1, [1982] RA 47, 126 Sol Jo 16, HL	100, 111
Bruce v Legal Aid Board [1992] 3 All ER 321, [1992] 2 FLR 398, [1993] Fam Law 69, [1992] NLJR 969, sub nom R v Legal Aid Board, ex p Bruce [1992] 1 WLR 694, [1992] 32 LS Gaz R 37, 136 Sol Jo LB 207, HL	83
Brunyate v Inner London Education Authority [1989] 2 All ER 417, 87 LGR 725, 133 Sol Jo 749, [1989] 1 Admin LR 65, sub nom Inner London Education Authority v Brunyate [1989] 1 WLR 542, sub nom R v Inner London Education Authority, ex p Brunyate [1989] COD 435, HL	124

TABLE OF CASES xxix

PAGE

Bugdaycay v Secretary of State for the Home Department [1987] AC 514, [1987] 1 All ER 940, [1987] 2 WLR 606, [1987] Imm AR 250, 131 Sol Jo 297, [1987] LS Gaz R 902, [1987] NLJ Rep 199, HL 112
Bugg v DPP [1993] QB 473, [1993] 2 All ER 815, [1993] 2 WLR 628, [1993] Crim LR 374, sub nom Bugg and Greaves v DPP 157 JP 673 96

CILFIT Srl and Lanificio di Gavardo v Ministry of Health: 283/81 [1982] ECR 3415, [1983] 1 CMLR 472, ECJ 170
Calderbank v Calderbank [1976] Fam 93, [1975] 3 All ER 333, [1975] 3 WLR 586, 119 Sol Jo 490, CA 12
Calgary and Edmonton Land Co Ltd v Discount Bank (Overseas) Ltd [1971] 1 All ER 551, [1971] 1 WLR 81, 22 P & CR 1, 115 Sol Jo 77 260
Calgary and Edmonton Land Co Ltd v Dobinson [1974] Ch 102, [1974] 1 All ER 484, [1974] 2 WLR 143, 26 P & CR 516, 118 Sol Jo 99 . . . . 225, 226, 237, 239, 240, 244, 260
Calveley v Chief Constable of the Merseyside Police [1989] AC 1228, [1989] 1 All ER 1025, [1989] 2 WLR 624, 133 Sol Jo 456, [1989] 15 LS Gaz R 42, [1989] NLJR 469, HL . . . 82, 94
Campbell and Fell v United Kingdom (1982) 5 EHRR 207, ECtHR 135, 136
Campbell and Fell v United Kingdom (1984) 7 EHRR 165, ECtHR 136
Capital and Counties Bank Ltd v Rhodes [1903] 1 Ch 631, 72 LJ Ch 336, 51 WR 470, 47 Sol Jo 335, 88 LT 255, 19 TLR 280, CA 282
Carl Zeiss Stiftung v Herbert Smith & Co, Dehn and Lauderdale [1969] 1 Ch 93, [1968] 2 All ER 1002, [1968] 3 WLR 281, [1969] RPC 329, 112 Sol Jo 441, CA 14, 15, 17
Carltona Ltd v Works Comrs [1943] 2 All ER 560, CA 115
Carter (R G) Ltd v Clarke [1990] 2 All ER 209, [1990] 1 WLR 578, CA 21
Cartlidge v Chief Adjudication Officer [1986] QB 360, [1986] 2 All ER 1, [1986] 2 WLR 558, [1986] ICR 256, [1986] IRLR 182, 130 Sol Jo 185, CA 153
Caswell v Dairy Produce Quota Tribunal for England and Wales [1990] 2 AC 738, [1990] 2 All ER 434, [1990] 2 WLR 1320, [1990] 25 LS Gaz R 36, [1990] NLJR 742, HL . . 80, 83, 164, 179
Champion v Chief Constable of the Gwent Constabulary [1990] 1 All ER 116, [1990] 1 WLR 1, 88 LGR 297, 154 LG Rev 432, 134 Sol Jo 142, [1990] 2 LS Gaz R 36, HL 108
Chesworth v Farrar [1967] 1 QB 407, [1966] 2 All ER 107, [1966] 2 WLR 1073, 110 Sol Jo 307, 198 Estates Gazette 195 . . . . 16, 30
Chief Adjudication Officer v Foster [1992] QB 31, [1991] 3 All ER 846, [1991] 3 WLR 473, CA; affd [1993] AC 754, [1993] 1 All ER 705, [1993] 2 WLR 292, [1993] 14 LS Gaz R 45, [1993] NLJR 296n, 136 Sol Jo LB 37, HL 93, 152
Chief Constable of the North Wales Police v Evans [1982] 3 All ER 141, [1982] 1 WLR 1155, 147 JP 6, 126 Sol Jo 549, [1982] LS Gaz R 1257, HL 80, 105
Chief Supplementary Benefit Officer v Leary [1985] 1 All ER 1061, [1985] 1 WLR 84, 128 Sol Jo 852, CA 154
Chowood Ltd v Lyall (No 2) [1930] 1 Ch 426; affd [1930] 2 Ch 156, 99 LJ Ch 405, [1930] All ER Rep 402, 143 LT 546, CA 281, 282, 284
Chowood's Registered Land, Re [1933] Ch 574, 102 LJ Ch 289, [1933] All ER Rep 946, 149 LT 70, 49 TLR 320 285
Cinema Press Ltd v Pictures and Pleasures Ltd [1945] KB 356, [1945] 1 All ER 440, 114 LJKB 368, 172 LT 295, 61 TLR 282, CA 6
City of London Building Society v Flegg [1988] AC 54, [1987] 3 All ER 435, [1987] 2 WLR 1266, 54 P & CR 337, [1988] 1 FLR 98, [1988] Fam Law 17, 19 HLR 484, 131 Sol Jo 806, [1987] LS Gaz R 1966, [1987] NLJ Rep 475, HL 259, 274
Clark v Chief Land Registrar [1994] Ch 370, [1994] 4 All ER 96, [1994] 3 WLR 593, [1995] 1 FLR 212, [1995] Fam Law 132, [1994] 24 LS Gaz R 47, 138 Sol Jo LB 123, CA 272
Clearbrook Property Holdings Ltd v Verrier [1973] 3 All ER 614, [1974] 1 WLR 243, 27 P & CR 430, 118 Sol Jo 117 . . . . 260, 273
Cocks v Thanet District Council [1983] 2 AC 286, [1982] 3 All ER 1135, [1982] 3 WLR 1121, 81 LGR 81, 6 HLR 15, 126 Sol Jo 820, [1984] RVR 31, HL 94, 121
Coenen v Payne [1974] 2 All ER 1109, [1974] 1 WLR 984, [1974] 2 Lloyd's Rep 270, 118 Sol Jo 499, CA 10
Colegio Oficial de Agentes de la Propiedad Immobiliaria v J L Aguirre Borrell: C-104/91 [1992] ECR I-3003, ECJ 172
Comet BV v Produktschap voor Siergewassen: 45/76 [1976] ECR 2043, [1977] 1 CMLR 533, CMR 8383, ECJ 171
Commission for the New Towns v Cooper (Great Britain) Ltd [1995] Ch 259, [1995] 2 All ER 929, [1995] 2 WLR 677, 72 P & CR 270, [1995] NPC 34, [1995] 2 EGLR 113, [1995] 26 EG 129, 139 Sol Jo LB 87, CA 241, 321

TABLE OF CASES

	PAGE
Congreve v Home Office [1976] QB 629, [1976] 1 All ER 697, [1976] 2 WLR 291, 119 Sol Jo 847, CA	111
Connor v Strathclyde Regional Council 1986 SLT 530	88
Cooper v Wilson [1937] 2 KB 309, [1937] 2 All ER 726, 35 LGR 436, 101 JP 349, 106 LJKB 728, 81 Sol Jo 357, 157 LT 290, 53 TLR 623, CA	165
Cotterell v Secretary of State for the Environment [1991] 2 PLR 20, (1991) Times, 24 January	106
Cottle v Cottle [1939] 2 All ER 535, 83 Sol Jo 501, DC	106
Council of Civil Service Unions v Minister for the Civil Service [1985] AC 374, [1984] 3 All ER 935, [1984] 3 WLR 1174, [1985] ICR 14, 128 Sol Jo 837, [1985] LS Gaz R 437, sub nom R v Secretary of State for Foreign and Commonwealth Affairs, ex p Council of Civil Service Unions [1985] IRLR 28, HL 77, 83, 84, 89, 97, 98, 101, 104, 107, 112, 113	
Covent Garden Community Association Ltd v Greater London Council [1981] JPL 183	162
Cow v Casey [1949] 1 KB 474, [1949] 1 All ER 197, [1949] LJR 565, 93 Sol Jo 102, 65 TLR 84, CA	21
Dalton Main Collieries Ltd v Rossington Main Colliery Co and Amalgamated Denaby Collieries Ltd [1940] 4 All ER 384, 84 Sol Jo 704, 164 LT 225, 57 TLR 126; affd [1941] Ch 268, [1941] 1 All ER 544, 110 LJ Ch 182, 165 LT 289, 57 TLR 456, CA	60
Dances Way, West Town, Hayling Island, Re [1962] Ch 490, [1962] 2 WLR 815, sub nom Re Freehold Land in Dances Way, West Town, Hayling Island, Hants [1962] 2 All ER 42, CA	262, 282
Dartstone Ltd v Cleveland Petroleum Co Ltd [1969] 3 All ER 668, [1969] 1 WLR 1807, 20 P & CR 795, 113 Sol Jo 626, 211 Estates Gazette 285	230
Davis (PBJ) Manufacturing Co Ltd v Fahn (Fahn, claimant) [1967] 2 All ER 1274, [1967] 1 WLR 1059, 111 Sol Jo 479, CA	26
Davy v Spelthorne Borough Council [1984] AC 262, [1983] 3 All ER 278, [1983] 3 WLR 742, 82 LGR 193, 47 P & CR 310, 127 Sol Jo 733, [1984] JPL 269, HL	93
Deadman, Re, Smith v Garland [1971] 2 All ER 101, [1971] 1 WLR 426, 115 Sol Jo 206	187, 278
De Falco v Crawley Borough Council [1980] QB 460, [1980] 1 All ER 913, [1980] 2 WLR 664, [1980] 1 CMLR 437, 78 LGR 180, 124 Sol Jo 82, CA	120
Dennis v Malcolm [1934] Ch 244, 103 LJ Ch 140, [1933] All ER Rep 293, 50 TLR 170, sub nom Re Cheam Common School, Dennis v Malcolm 150 LT 394	256, 309, 342
Deptford High Street (No 139), Re, ex p British Transport Commission [1951] Ch 884, [1951] 1 All ER 950, [1951] 1 TLR 1045	282
DPP v Crown Court at Manchester and Huckfield [1993] 4 All ER 928, 98 Cr App Rep 461, [1993] NLJR 1711, sub nom R v Crown Court at Manchester, ex p DPP [1993] 1 WLR 1524, [1994] 1 CMLR 457, HL	77, 79, 90
Down v Yearley [1874] WN 158	214, 235
Doyle v Northumbria Probation Committee [1991] 4 All ER 294, [1991] 1 WLR 1340, [1992] ICR 121, [1991] NLJR 855	91, 96
Duke v GEC Reliance Ltd (formerly Reliance Systems Ltd) [1988] AC 618, [1988] 1 All ER 626, [1988] 2 WLR 359, [1988] 1 CMLR 719, [1988] ICR 339, [1988] IRLR 118, 132 Sol Jo 226, [1988] 11 LS Gaz R 42, HL	169
Duncan v Lawson (1889) 41 Ch D 394, 53 JP 532, 58 LJ Ch 502, 37 WR 524, 60 LT 732	34
Dyson v A-G [1911] 1 KB 410, 80 LJKB 531, 55 Sol Jo 168, 103 LT 707, 27 TLR 143, CA	94
EC Commission v EC Council: 22/70 [1971] ECR 263, [1971] CMLR 335, ECJ	173
EC Commission v United Kingdom: 31, 53/77R [1977] ECR 921, [1977] 2 CMLR 359, ECJ:	174
EEC Commission v Italy: 7/61 [1961] ECR 317, [1962] CMLR 39, ECJ	173
Ealing London Borough v Race Relations Board [1972] AC 342, [1972] 1 All ER 105, [1972] 2 WLR 71, 116 Sol Jo 60, HL	81
Elias v Mitchell [1972] Ch 652, [1972] 2 All ER 153, [1972] 2 WLR 740, 23 P & CR 159, 116 Sol Jo 15, 222 Estates Gazette 1397	272
Ellis v Dubowski [1921] 3 KB 621, 19 LGR 641, 85 JP 230, 91 LJKB 89, 27 Cox CC 107, [1921] All ER Rep 272, 126 LT 91, 37 TLR 910	114
Ellis v Ministry of Defence [1985] ICR 257, EAT	106
Elliston v Reacher [1908] 2 Ch 665, 78 LJ Ch 87, [1908-10] All ER Rep 612, 99 LT 701, CA:	352
Emma Hotels Ltd v Secretary of State for the Environment (1980) 41 P & CR 255, 258 Estates Gazette 64, [1981] JPL 283	108
Emma Silver Mining Co v Grant (1879) 11 Ch D 918, 40 LT 804	13
Emmott v Minister for Social Welfare and A-G: C-208/90 [1991] ECR I-4269, [1991] 3 CMLR 894, [1993] ICR 8, [1991] IRLR 387, ECJ	171

TABLE OF CASES xxxi

	PAGE
Engall's Agreement, Re [1953] 2 All ER 503, [1953] 1 WLR 977, 97 Sol Jo 506, 161 Estates Gazette 737	224
Ettridge v Morrell (1986) 85 LGR 100, CA	94
European Asian Bank AG v Punjab and Sind Bank (No 2) [1983] 2 All ER 508, [1983] 1 WLR 642, [1983] 1 Lloyd's Rep 611, [1983] Com LR 128, 127 Sol Jo 379, CA	21
Everett v Ribbands [1952] 2 QB 198, [1952] 1 All ER 823, 50 LGR 389, 116 JP 221, 96 Sol Jo 229, [1952] 1 TLR 933, CA	15
Fairmount Investments Ltd v Secretary of State for the Environment [1976] 2 All ER 865, [1976] 1 WLR 1255, 75 LGR 33, 120 Sol Jo 801, HL	105
Fairpo v Humberside County Council [1997] 1 All ER 183, [1997] 3 FCR 181, [1997] 1 FLR 339, [1997] ELR 12	129
Findlay v Railway Executive [1950] 2 All ER 969, 94 Sol Jo 778, 66 (pt 2) TLR 836, CA	12
Finnegan v Clowney Youth Training Programme Ltd [1990] 2 AC 407, [1990] 2 All ER 546, [1990] 2 WLR 1305, [1990] 2 CMLR 859, [1990] ICR 462, [1990] IRLR 299, [1990] 24 LS Gaz R 44, HL	169
Finnigan v New Zealand Rugby Football Union [1985] 2 NZLR 159	87
Fletcher's Application, Re [1970] 2 All ER 527n, CA	79
Foster v British Gas plc: C-188/89 [1991] 1 QB 405, [1990] 3 All ER 897, [1991] 2 WLR 258, [1990] ECR I-3313, [1990] 2 CMLR 833, [1991] ICR 84, [1990] IRLR 353, ECJ; apld [1991] 2 AC 306, [1991] 2 All ER 705, [1991] 2 WLR 1075, [1991] 2 CMLR 217, [1991] ICR 463, [1991] IRLR 268, [1991] 18 LS Gaz R 34, HL	168
Fowler v Lanning [1959] 1 QB 426, [1959] 1 All ER 290, [1959] 2 WLR 241, 103 Sol Jo 157	15, 16
Francovich and Bonifaci v Italy: C 6, 9/90 [1991] ECR I-5357, [1993] 2 CMLR 66, [1995] ICR 722, [1992] IRLR 84, ECJ	171
Fredericks and Pelhams Timber Buildings v Wilkins [1971] 3 All ER 545, [1971] 1 WLR 1197, 115 Sol Jo 349, CA	26
Freeman v Dartford Brewery Co Ltd [1938] 3 All ER 120, 159 LT 62, 54 TLR 672	67
Freer v Unwins Ltd [1976] Ch 288, [1976] 1 All ER 634, [1976] 2 WLR 609, 31 P & CR 335, 120 Sol Jo 267	285
Freight Transport Association Ltd v London Boroughs Transport Committee [1991] 3 All ER 915, sub nom London Boroughs Transport Committee v Freight Transport Association Ltd [1991] 1 WLR 828, [1992] 1 CMLR 5, 156 JP 69, 135 Sol Jo LB 101, HL	77, 173, 182
French (A Martin) v Kingswood Hill Ltd [1961] 1 QB 96, [1960] 2 All ER 251, [1960] 2 WLR 947, 104 Sol Jo 447, CA	12
Friends of the Earth, Re [1988] JPL 93, CA	164, 179
Furniss (Inspector of Taxes) v Dawson [1984] AC 474, [1984] 1 All ER 530, [1984] 2 WLR 226, [1984] STC 153, 55 TC 324, 128 Sol Jo 132, HL	201, 202
GEC Ltd v Price Commission [1975] ICR 1, 119 Sol Jo 166, CA	97
Garden Cottage Foods Ltd v Milk Marketing Board [1984] AC 130, [1983] 2 All ER 770, [1983] 3 WLR 143, [1983] 3 CMLR 43, [1984] FSR 23, [1983] Com LR 198, 127 Sol Jo 460, HL	171
Gilbert's Application, Re [1961] 2 All ER 313, [1961] 1 WLR 822, 105 Sol Jo 322, CA	257, 265, 297
Gillick v West Norfolk and Wisbech Area Health Authority [1986] AC 112, [1985] 3 All ER 402, [1985] 3 WLR 830, [1986] 1 FLR 224, [1986] Crim LR 113, 129 Sol Jo 738, 2 BMLR 11, [1985] LS Gaz R 3551, [1985] NLJ Rep 1055, HL	77, 96
Glasgow Navigation Co v Iron Ore Co [1910] AC 293, 79 LJPC 83, 11 Asp MLC 387, 102 LT 435, HL	16
Gold v Patman and Fotheringham Ltd [1958] 2 All ER 497, [1958] 1 WLR 697, [1958] 1 Lloyd's Rep 587, 102 Sol Jo 470, CA	10, 15, 16
Golder v United Kingdom (1975) 1 EHRR 524, ECtHR	135
Gouriet v Union of Post Office Workers [1978] AC 435, [1977] 3 All ER 70, [1977] 3 WLR 300, 141 JP 552, 121 Sol Jo 543, HL	81
Gowa v A-G [1985] 1 WLR 1003, 129 Sol Jo 541, HL	117
Grand Junction Canal v Dimes (1852) 3 HL Cas 759, 8 State Tr NS 85, 17 Jur 73, 19 LTOS 317	106
Grampian Regional Council v City of Aberdeen District Council (1983) 47 P & CR 633, [1984] FSR 590, [1984] JPL 590, 1984 SLT 197, HL	111
Green Lane (No 462), Ilford, Re, Gooding v Borland [1971] 1 All ER 315, [1971] 1 WLR 138, 22 P & CR 50, 114 Sol Jo 953	278, 305, 346
Gregory v London Borough of Camden (or Camden London Borough Council) [1966] 2 All ER 196, [1966] 1 WLR 899, 64 LGR 215, 18 P & CR 69, 130 JP 244, 110 Sol Jo 213, 197 Estates Gazette 19	160

	PAGE
Guevara v Hounslow London Borough Council (1987) Times, 17 April	93
Gyeabour v Secretary of State for the Home Department [1989] Imm AR 94	119
HK (Infant), Re [1967] 2 QB 617, [1967] 2 WLR 962, 111 Sol Jo 296, sub nom Re K (H) (infant) [1967] 1 All ER 226	119
Haley v London Electricity Board (1965) 109 Sol Jo 295, CA	10
Haley v London Electricity Board [1965] AC 778, [1964] 3 All ER 185, [1964] 3 WLR 479, 63 LGR 1, 129 JP 14, 108 Sol Jo 637, HL	10
Hall & Co Ltd v Shoreham-by-Sea UDC [1964] 1 All ER 1, [1964] 1 WLR 240, 62 LGR 206, 15 P & CR 119, 128 JP 120, 107 Sol Jo 1001, CA	100, 111
Halonen v Westminster City Council (1997) 141 Sol Jo 1080	121
Hannam v Bradford City Council [1970] 2 All ER 690, [1970] 1 WLR 937, 68 LGR 498, 134 JP 588, 114 Sol Jo 414, CA	106
Hardwick, The (1884) 9 PD 32, 53 LJP 32, 5 Asp MLC 199, 32 WR 598, 50 LT 128	18
Harkness v Bell's Asbestos and Engineering Ltd [1967] 2 QB 729, [1966] 3 All ER 843, [1967] 2 WLR 29, 110 Sol Jo 793, CA	179
Haslemere Estates Ltd v Baker [1982] 3 All ER 525, [1982] 1 WLR 1109, 126 Sol Jo 463	225
Hawkins v New Mendip Engineering Ltd [1966] 3 All ER 228, [1966] 1 WLR 1341, 1 KIR 226, 110 Sol Jo 633, CA	10
Hazell v Hammersmith and Fulham London Borough Council [1992] 2 AC 1, [1991] 1 All ER 545, [1991] 2 WLR 372, 89 LGR 271, [1991] RVR 28, HL	98
Healey v A Waddington & Sons [1954] 1 All ER 861n, [1954] 1 WLR 688, 98 Sol Jo 286, CA:	10
Herring v Templeman [1973] 3 All ER 569, 72 LGR 162, 117 Sol Jo 793, CA	79, 87
Hesz v Sotheby & Co [1960] 1 WLR 285, 104 Sol Jo 271	10
Heywood v BDC Properties Ltd [1963] 2 All ER 358, [1963] 1 WLR 634, 107 Sol Jo 437; affd [1963] 2 All ER 1063, [1963] 1 WLR 975, 107 Sol Jo 494, CA	224
Heywood v BDC Properties Ltd (No 2) [1964] 2 All ER 702, [1964] 1 WLR 971, 108 Sol Jo 403, CA	244
Hinde v Power [1913] WN 184	186
Hines v Birkbeck College (No 2) [1992] Ch 33, [1991] 4 All ER 450, [1991] 3 WLR 557, CA:	129
Hodges v Jones [1935] Ch 657, 104 LJ Ch 329, 79 Sol Jo 522, 153 LT 373	282
Hodgson v Marks [1971] Ch 892, [1971] 2 All ER 684, [1971] 2 WLR 1263, 22 P & CR 586, 115 Sol Jo 224, CA	285
Hogg v Vickers Ltd (1921) 14 BWCC 229, CA	6
Hooker v Wyle [1973] 3 All ER 707, [1974] 1 WLR 235, 28 P & CR 27, 117 Sol Jo 545	224, 225
Howard v Macarthur (1935 unreported 1935/H/1139)	46, 50
Howell v Dering [1915] 1 KB 54, 84 LJKB 198, 58 Sol Jo 669, 111 LT 790, CA	6
Hultquist v Universal Pattern and Precision Engineering Co Ltd [1960] 2 QB 467, [1960] 2 All ER 266, [1960] 2 WLR 886, 104 Sol Jo 427, CA	12
Independent Automatic Sales Ltd v Knowles and Foster [1962] 3 All ER 27, [1962] 1 WLR 974, 106 Sol Jo 720	15
IRC v National Federation of Self Employed and Small Businesses [1982] AC 617, [1981] 2 All ER 93, [1981] 2 WLR 722, [1981] STC 260, 55 TC 133, 125 Sol Jo 325, HL	76, 83, 148, 159, 160, 162, 163
Israel Discount Bank of New York v Hadjipateras [1983] 3 All ER 129, [1984] 1 WLR 137, [1983] 2 Lloyd's Rep 490, 127 Sol Jo 822, [1984] LS Gaz R 37, CA	21
J (an infant), Re [1960] 1 All ER 603, [1960] 1 WLR 253, 104 Sol Jo 232	23
Jackson v Chief Adjudication Officer: C-63, 64/91 [1993] QB 367, [1993] 3 All ER 265, [1993] 2 WLR 658, [1992] ECR I-4737, [1992] 3 CMLR 389, [1993] Fam Law 477, [1993] 21 LS Gaz R 46, ECJ	172
Janaway v Salford Area Health Authority [1989] AC 537, [1988] 3 All ER 1079, [1988] 3 WLR 1350, [1989] 1 FLR 155, [1989] Fam Law 191, 3 BMLR 137, [1989] 3 LS Gaz R 42, HL	88
Jeffrey v Evans [1964] 1 All ER 536, [1964] 1 WLR 505, 62 LGR 543, 128 JP 352, 108 Sol Jo 120	33
Johnson v Chief Adjudication Officer: C-31/90 [1993] QB 252, [1992] 2 All ER 705, [1993] 2 WLR 192, [1991] ECR I-3723, [1991] 3 CMLR 917, [1993] ICR 204, ECJ	172
Johnston v Chief Constable of the Royal Ulster Constabulary: 222/84 [1987] QB 129, [1986] 3 All ER 135, [1986] 3 WLR 1038, [1986] ECR 1651, [1986] 3 CMLR 240, [1987] ICR 83, [1986] IRLR 263, 130 Sol Jo 953, [1987] LS Gaz R 188, ECJ	172

TABLE OF CASES

	PAGE
Jones v Secretary of State for Wales (1990) 88 LGR 942, 61 P & CR 238, [1990] 3 PLR 102, [1990] JPL 907, CA	111
Jones v Swansea City Council [1990] 3 All ER 737, [1990] 1 WLR 1453, 89 LGR 90, 134 Sol Jo 1437, HL	82
Keays v Murdoch Magazines (UK) Ltd [1991] 4 All ER 491, [1991] 1 WLR 1184, [1991] NLJR 893, CA	16
Keir and Williams v Hereford and Worcester County Council (1985) 84 LGR 709, [1985] IRLR 505, CA	128
Kemmis v Kemmis (Welland intervening) [1988] 1 WLR 1307, [1988] 2 FLR 223, [1989] 3 LS Gaz R 43, CA	259, 313
Kent v University College London (1991) Times, 24 October; affd (1992) 156 LG Rev 1003, (1992) Times, 18 February, CA	87, 94, 129
Khawaja v Secretary of State for the Home Department [1984] AC 74, [1983] 1 All ER 765, [1983] 2 WLR 321, [1982] Imm AR 139, 127 Sol Jo 137, HL	119
Kincardine and Deeside District Council v Forestry Comrs 1992 SLT 1180, 1991 SCLR 729	171
Kirklees Metropolitan Borough Council v Wickes Building Supplies Ltd [1993] AC 227, [1992] 3 All ER 717, [1992] 3 WLR 170, [1992] 2 CMLR 765, 90 LGR 391, [1992] NLJR 967, HL	172
Knight v Home Office [1990] 3 All ER 237, 4 BMLR 85, [1990] NLJR 210	136
Korso Finance Establishment Anstalt v Wedge (15 February 1994, unreported)	21
Kronstein v Korda [1937] 1 All ER 357, 81 Sol Jo 176, CA	17
Ladd v Marshall [1954] 3 All ER 745, [1954] 1 WLR 1489, 98 Sol Jo 870, CA	189
Laker Airways Ltd v Department of Trade [1977] QB 643, [1977] 2 All ER 182, [1977] 2 WLR 234, 121 Sol Jo 52, CA	81
Lambert v Ealing London Borough Council [1982] 2 All ER 394, [1982] 1 WLR 550, 80 LGR 487, 2 HLR 58, 126 Sol Jo 228, CA	120
Lambourne, ex p (1993) 25 HLR 172	95
Lavender (H) & Son Ltd v Minister of Housing and Local Government [1970] 3 All ER 871, [1970] 1 WLR 1231, 68 LGR 408, 135 JP 186, 114 Sol Jo 636, 214 Estates Gazette 269:	115
Law v National Greyhound Racing Club Ltd [1983] 3 All ER 300, [1983] 1 WLR 1302, 127 Sol Jo 619, 80 LS Gaz R 2367, CA	87
Lee v Barrey [1957] Ch 251, [1957] 1 All ER 191, [1957] 2 WLR 245, 101 Sol Jo 129, CA	280
Lee v Secretary of State for Education and Science (1967) 66 LGR 211, 111 Sol Jo 756	103
Leech v Deputy Governor of Parkhurst Prison [1988] AC 533, [1988] 1 All ER 485, [1988] 2 WLR 290, 132 Sol Jo 191, [1988] 11 LS Gaz R 42, [1988] NLJR 38, HL	132
Leighton's Conveyance, Re [1936] 1 All ER 667; on appeal [1937] Ch 149, [1936] 3 All ER 1033, 106 LJ Ch 161, 81 Sol Jo 56, 156 LT 93, 53 TLR 273, CA	281
Lester v Burgess (1973) 26 P & CR 536, 230 Estates Gazette 107	260, 281
Letang v Cooper [1965] 1 QB 232, [1964] 2 All ER 929, [1964] 3 WLR 573, [1964] 2 Lloyd's Rep 339, 108 Sol Jo 519, CA	16
Lever v Land Securities Co Ltd (1893) 7 R 16, 42 WR 104, 38 Sol Jo 38, 70 LT 323, CA	15
Liverpool, Brazil and River Plate Steam Navigation Co v London and St Katherine Steam Navigation Co [1875] WN 203	10
Lloyd v McMahon [1987] AC 625, [1987] 1 All ER 1118, [1987] 2 WLR 821, 85 LGR 545, 131 Sol Jo 409, [1987] LS Gaz R 1240, [1987] NLJ Rep 265, [1987] RVR 58, HL	102, 105
Lloyds Bank plc v Rosset [1991] 1 AC 107, [1990] 1 All ER 1111, [1990] 2 WLR 867, 60 P & CR 311, [1990] 2 FLR 155, [1990] Fam Law 395, 22 HLR 349, [1990] 16 LS Gaz R 41, [1990] NLJR 478, HL	259, 282, 313
London and Clydeside Estates Ltd v Aberdeen District Council [1979] 3 All ER 876, [1980] 1 WLR 182, 39 P & CR 549, 124 Sol Jo 100, 253 Estates Gazette 1011, 1980 SC (HL) 1, 1980 SLT 81, HL	102
Lonrho plc v Secretary of State for Trade and Industry [1989] 2 All ER 609, sub nom R v Secretary of State for Trade and Industry, ex p Lonrho plc [1989] 1 WLR 525, 5 BCC 633, 133 Sol Jo 724, [1989] 26 LS Gaz R 35, [1989] NLJR 717, HL	145
Lonrho plc v Tebbit [1992] 4 All ER 280, [1993] BCLC 96, [1992] BCC 779, CA	93
Luxembourg v European Parliament: 230/81 [1983] ECR 255, [1983] 2 CMLR 726, ECJ	173
M v Home Office [1992] QB 270, [1992] 4 All ER 97, [1992] 2 WLR 73, CA; affd sub nom M, Re [1994] 1 AC 377, [1993] 3 WLR 433, [1993] 37 LS Gaz R 50, [1993] NLJR 1099, 137 Sol Jo LB 199, sub nom M v Home Office [1993] 3 All ER 537, HL	79, 81, 180, 182

	PAGE
MEPC Ltd v Christian-Edwards [1978] Ch 281, [1978] 3 All ER 795, [1978] 3 WLR 230, 36 P & CR 1, 122 Sol Jo 435, 248 Estates Gazette 867, CA; affd [1981] AC 205, [1979] 3 All ER 752, [1979] 3 WLR 713, 39 P & CR 256, 123 Sol Jo 786, HL	256
McC (a minor), Re [1985] AC 528, [1984] 3 WLR 1227, 81 Cr App Rep 54, 149 JP 225, [1985] Crim LR 152, 128 Sol Jo 837, [1985] LS Gaz R 117, sub nom McC v Mullan [1984] 3 All ER 908, HL	157
McCarthy & Stone (Developments) Ltd v London Borough of Richmond upon Thames [1992] 2 AC 48, [1991] 4 All ER 897, [1991] 3 WLR 941, 90 LGR 1, 63 P & CR 234, [1992] 3 LS Gaz R 33, [1992] JPL 467, 135 Sol Jo LB 206, HL	77, 98, 100
McKay v Essex Area Health Authority [1982] QB 1166, [1982] 2 All ER 771, [1982] 2 WLR 890, 126 Sol Jo 261, CA	24
Malloch v Aberdeen Corpn [1971] 2 All ER 1278, [1971] 1 WLR 1578, 115 Sol Jo 756, 1971 SC (HL) 85, 1971 SLT 245, HL	88
Mandla v Dowell Lee [1983] 2 AC 548, [1983] 1 All ER 1062, [1983] 2 WLR 620, [1983] ICR 385, [1983] IRLR 209, 127 Sol Jo 242, HL	126
Maradana Mosque Board of Trustees v Mahmud [1967] 1 AC 13, [1966] 1 All ER 545, [1966] 2 WLR 921, 110 Sol Jo 310, PC	105
Markowska v Hammersmith (11 April 1997, unreported)	121
Marleasing SA v La Comercial Internacional de Alimentación SA: C-106/89 [1990] ECR I-4135, [1992] 1 CMLR 305, [1993] BCC 421, 135 Sol Jo 15, ECJ	169, 171
Maze, The. See R v Board of Visitors of HM Prison, The Maze, ex p Hone	
Meade v London Borough of Haringey [1979] 2 All ER 1016, [1979] 1 WLR 637, 77 LGR 577, [1979] ICR 494, 123 Sol Jo 216, CA	123
Miller v Wandsworth London Borough Council (1980) Times, 19 March	120
Milne v Wandsworth London Borough Council (1992) 90 LGR 515, [1994] ELR 28, CA	101
Minister of Health v R, ex p Yaffé [1931] AC 494, 100 LJKB 306, [1931] All ER Rep 343, 75 Sol Jo 232, 47 TLR 337, sub nom R v Minister of Health, ex p Yaffé 29 LGR 305, 95 JP 125, 145 LT 98, HL	155
Minister of Labour v Dyas and Fowle Ltd (No 2) [1967] 3 All ER 278, [1967] 1 WLR 1390, 46 ATC 147, [1967] TR 141, 131 JP 518, 111 Sol Jo 742, DC	257
Minister of Labour v Genner Iron and Steel Co (Wollescote) Ltd [1967] 3 All ER 278, [1967] 1 WLR 1386, 46 ATC 147, [1967] TR 141, 131 JP 518, 111 Sol Jo 718	257
Ministry of Housing and Local Government v Sharp [1970] 2 QB 223, [1970] 1 All ER 1009, [1970] 2 WLR 802, 68 LGR 187, 21 P & CR 166, 134 JP 358, 114 Sol Jo 109, 213 Estates Gazette 1145, CA	231
Montgomery v Foy, Morgan & Co [1895] 2 QB 321, 65 LJQB 18, 8 Asp MLC 36, 14 R 575, 43 WR 691, 73 LT 12, 11 TLR 512, CA	6
Morris v Beardmore [1981] AC 446, [1980] 2 All ER 753, [1980] 3 WLR 283, [1980] RTR 321, 71 Cr App Rep 256, 144 JP 331, 124 Sol Jo 512, HL	113
Morris v Sandess (or Sanders) Universal Products [1954] 1 All ER 47, [1954] 1 WLR 67, 98 Sol Jo 10, CA	16
Mulder v EC Council and EC Commission: C-104/89, C-37/90 [1992] ECR I-3061, ECJ	174
Murray v Two Strokes Ltd [1973] 3 All ER 357, [1973] 1 WLR 823, 26 P & CR 1, 117 Sol Jo 447	259
Musisi, Re [1987] AC 514, [1987] 2 WLR 606, [1987] Imm AR 250, 131 Sol Jo 297, [1987] LS Gaz R 902, sub nom Bugdaycay v Secretary of State for the Home Department [1987] 1 All ER 940, [1987] NLJ Rep 199, HL	119
National and Local Government Officers' Association v Secretary of State for the Environment (1992) Times, 2 December, CA	113, 169
National Real Estate and Finance Co Ltd v Hassan [1939] 2 KB 61, [1939] 2 All ER 154, 108 LJKB 380, 83 Sol Jo 238, 160 LT 373, 55 TLR 570, CA	16, 48
Neill v North Antrim Magistrates' Court [1992] 4 All ER 846, [1992] 1 WLR 1220, 97 Cr App Rep 121, 158 JP 197, [1993] Crim LR 945, [1993] 9 LS Gaz R 44, HL	80
Nichol v Gateshead Metropolitan Borough Council (1988) 87 LGR 435, CA	130
Nordsee Deutsche Hochseefischerei GmbH v Reederei Mond Hochseefischerei Nordstern AG & Co KG: 102/81 [1982] ECR 1095, ECJ	170
Norfolk County Council v Secretary of State for the Environment [1973] 3 All ER 673, [1973] 1 WLR 1400, 72 LGR 44, 26 P & CR 273, 137 JP 832, 117 Sol Jo 650	117
Norman v Hardy [1974] 1 All ER 1170, [1974] 1 WLR 1048, 27 P & CR 509, 118 Sol Jo 516	260
Norwich and Peterborough Building Society v Steed (No 2) [1993] Ch 116, [1993] 1 All ER 330, [1992] 3 WLR 669, CA	281

TABLE OF CASES

	PAGE
Nottinghamshire County Council v Secretary of State for the Environment [1986] AC 240, [1986] 1 All ER 199, [1986] 2 WLR 1, 84 LGR 305, 130 Sol Jo 36, [1985] NLJ Rep 1257, HL	112
Ogwr Borough Council v Baker [1989] COD 489	111
O'Reilly v Mackman [1983] 2 AC 237, [1982] 3 All ER 1124, [1982] 3 WLR 1096, 126 Sol Jo 820, HL	83, 88, 89, 91, 92, 94, 184
Osk and Partners Sdn v Tenku Noone Aziz [1983] 1 MLJ 179	144
Ostler v Secretary of State for the Environment [1977] 1 WLR 258, HL	158
Padfield v Minister of Agriculture, Fisheries and Food [1968] AC 997, [1968] 1 All ER 694, [1968] 2 WLR 924, 112 Sol Jo 171, HL	79, 99, 108, 111
Parker v Bournemouth Corpn (1902) 66 JP 440, 86 LT 449, 18 TLR 372	111
Parti Ecologiste Les Verts v European Parliament: 294/83 [1986] ECR 1339, [1987] 2 CMLR 343, ECJ	173
Patel v University of Bradford Senate [1979] 2 All ER 582, [1979] 1 WLR 1066, 123 Sol Jo 436, CA	79
Paul (R & W) Ltd v Wheat Commission [1937] AC 139, [1936] 2 All ER 1243, 105 LJKB 563, 80 Sol Jo 753, 155 LT 305, 52 TLR 702, HL	113
Pearce v University of Aston in Birmingham [1991] 2 All ER 461, CA	129
Pearce v University of Aston in Birmingham (No 2) [1991] 2 All ER 469	129
Pepper (Inspector of Taxes) v Hart [1993] AC 593, [1993] 1 All ER 42, [1992] 3 WLR 1032, [1992] STC 898, 65 TC 421, [1993] ICR 291, [1993] IRLR 33, [1993] NLJR 17, [1993] RVR 127, HL	99, 107, 169
Perez-Adamson v Perez-Rivas [1987] Fam 89, [1987] 3 All ER 20, [1987] 2 WLR 500, 55 P & CR 5, [1987] 2 FLR 472, [1987] Fam Law 416, 131 Sol Jo 939, [1987] LS Gaz R 2273, [1987] NLJ Rep 409, CA	219, 225
Pergamon Press Ltd, Re [1971] Ch 388, [1970] 3 All ER 535, [1970] 3 WLR 792, 114 Sol Jo 569, CA	105, 145
Perry v Phoenix Assurance plc [1988] 3 All ER 60, [1988] 1 WLR 940, 56 P & CR 163, 132 Sol Jo 1147, [1988] 33 LS Gaz R 42	219
Pharmaceutical Society of Great Britain v Dickson [1970] AC 403, [1968] 2 All ER 686, [1968] 3 WLR 286, 112 Sol Jo 601, HL	84
Phillips v Mobil Oil Co Ltd [1989] 3 All ER 97, [1989] 1 WLR 888, 59 P & CR 292, [1989] 2 EGLR 246, CA	222
Pickering v Associated Newspapers Holdings plc [1991] 2 AC 370, [1991] 2 WLR 513, sub nom Pickering v Liverpool Daily Post and Echo Newspapers plc [1991] 1 All ER 622, HL	94
Pickstone v Freemans plc [1989] AC 66, [1988] 2 All ER 803, [1988] 3 WLR 265, [1988] ICR 697, [1988] IRLR 357, 132 Sol Jo 994, [1988] NLJR 193, HL	168
Piercy v Young (1880) 15 Ch D 475, 42 LT 292	7, 13, 14
Pioneer Plastic Containers Ltd v Customs and Excise Comrs [1967] Ch 597, [1967] 1 All ER 1053, [1967] 2 WLR 1085, 111 Sol Jo 235	18
Poh, Re [1983] 1 All ER 287, [1983] 1 WLR 2, 127 Sol Jo 16, HL	180
Polskie Towarzystwo Handlu Zagranicznego Dla Elektrotechniki Elecktrim Spolka Z Ograniczona Odpowiadziolnoscia v Electric Furnace Co Ltd [1956] 2 All ER 306, [1956] 1 WLR 562, 100 Sol Jo 379, CA	8, 10, 13
Portland (Duke of) v Lady Topham. See Topham v Duke of Portland	
Practice Direction [1981] 3 All ER 61, [1981] 1 WLR 1296	17, 186
Practice Direction [1982] 3 All ER 800, [1982] 1 WLR 1375, 126 Sol Jo 746, CA	181
Practice Direction [1984] 1 All ER 720, [1984] 1 WLR 447, 128 Sol Jo 156	62
Practice Direction (Crown Office List: Consent Orders) [1997] 1 WLR 825	187
Practice Note [1932] WN 6	260
Practice Note [1983] 2 All ER 1020, sub nom Practice Direction [1983] 1 WLR 925, 77 Cr App Rep 184	178, 179
Practice Note [1983] 3 All ER 33, sub nom Practice Direction [1983] 1 WLR 922, 77 Cr App Rep 185, 127 Sol Jo 512	178, 235, 297
Practice Note [1987] 1 All ER 368, sub nom Practice Direction [1987] 1 WLR 232, 84 Cr App Rep 268, 131 Sol Jo 192	186
Practice Note [1989] 1 All ER 1024, [1989] 1 WLR 358, 153 JP 363	181, 184
Practice Note [1991] 1 All ER 1055, 155 JP 591, sub nom Practice Direction [1991] 1 WLR 280	179
Practice Note [1994] 4 All ER 671, sub nom Practice Direction [1994] 1 WLR 1551, [1994] 42 LS Gaz R 37, 138 Sol Jo LB 220	178, 187, 195

	PAGE
Practice Note [1995] 2 All ER 511, sub nom Practice Direction [1995] 1 WLR 510, [1995] 16 LS Gaz R 43	178, 235, 297
Practice Note [1997] 1 All ER 128, sub nom Practice Direction (Crown Office list: legislation bundle) [1997] 1 WLR 52	178, 195
Presho v Insurance Officer [1984] AC 310, [1984] 1 All ER 97, [1984] 2 WLR 29, [1984] ICR 463, [1984] IRLR 74, 128 Sol Jo 18, HL	153
Preston, Re [1985] AC 835, [1985] 2 WLR 836, sub nom Preston v IRC [1985] 2 All ER 327, [1985] STC 282, 59 TC 1, 129 Sol Jo 317, [1985] LS Gaz R 1944, [1985] NLJ Rep 463, HL	99, 104, 148, 149, 166
Prince v Gregory [1959] 1 All ER 133, [1959] 1 WLR 177, 103 Sol Jo 130, CA	15
Pritchard v Briggs [1980] Ch 338, [1980] 1 All ER 294, [1979] 3 WLR 868, 40 P & CR 1, 123 Sol Jo 705, CA	222
Proctor v Kidman (1986) 51 P & CR 67, CA	281
Publishers Association v EC Commission (No 2): T-66/89 [1992] 4 All ER 70, [1992] ECR II-1995, [1992] 5 CMLR 120, [1992] ICR 842, CFI	172
Puhlhofer v Hillingdon London Borough Council [1986] AC 484, [1986] 1 All ER 467, [1986] 2 WLR 259, 84 LGR 385, [1986] 2 FLR 5, [1986] Fam Law 218, 18 HLR 158, 130 Sol Jo 143, [1986] LS Gaz R 785, [1986] NLJ Rep 140, HL	108, 120
Pyx Granite Co Ltd v Ministry of Housing and Local Government [1960] AC 260, [1959] 3 All ER 1, [1959] 3 WLR 346, 58 LGR 1, 10 P & CR 319, 123 JP 429, 103 Sol Jo 633, HL	94
Quigly v Chief Land Registrar [1992] 3 All ER 940, [1992] 1 WLR 834; affd [1993] 4 All ER 82, [1993] 1 WLR 1435, CA	256
R v Advertising Standards Authority Ltd, ex p Insurance Service plc (1989) 133 Sol Jo 1545, [1990] COD 42, [1990] 2 Admin LR 77	78, 86
R v Advertising Standards Authority Ltd, ex p Vernons Organisation Ltd [1993] 2 All ER 202, [1992] 1 WLR 1289, [1992] 45 LS Gaz R 27	86, 182
R v Altrincham Justices, ex p Pennington [1975] QB 549, [1975] 2 All ER 78, [1975] 2 WLR 450, 73 LGR 109, 139 JP 434, 119 Sol Jo 64	106
R v Amber Valley District Council, ex p Jackson [1984] 3 All ER 501, [1985] 1 WLR 298, 50 P & CR 136, 128 Sol Jo 853, [1983] JPL 742	106
R v Amersham Justices, ex p Fanthorne [1964] Crim LR 825, 108 Sol Jo 841, DC	188
R v Army Board of the Defence Council, ex p Anderson [1992] QB 169, [1991] 3 All ER 375, [1991] 3 WLR 42, [1991] ICR 537, [1991] IRLR 425, [1991] COD 191, [1991] 23 LS Gaz R 35	83, 105
R v Association of Futures Brokers and Dealers Ltd, ex p Mordens Ltd [1991] COD 40, [1991] 3 Admin LR 254	78, 144, 146, 147, 149
R v Aston University Senate, ex p Roffey [1969] 2 QB 538, [1969] 2 WLR 1418, 113 Sol Jo 308, sub nom R v Senate of University of Aston, ex p Roffey [1969] 2 All ER 964, 133 JP 463	87
R v A-G, ex p ICI plc [1985] 1 CMLR 588, 60 TC 1; on appeal [1987] 1 CMLR 72, 60 TC 1, CA	149, 160
R v Barnet London Borough Council, ex p Johnson (1990) 89 LGR 581, CA	111
R v Barnet London Borough Council, ex p Pardes House School Ltd [1989] EGCS 64	160
R v Barnsley Metropolitan Borough Council, ex p Hook [1976] 3 All ER 452, [1976] 1 WLR 1052, 74 LGR 493, 140 JP 638, 120 Sol Jo 182, CA	105, 113
R v Birmingham City Council, ex p Equal Opportunities Commission (No 2) (1993) 91 LGR 14, [1993] Fam Law 338, CA	126
R v Birmingham City Council, ex p Ferrero Ltd [1993] 1 All ER 530, 89 LGR 977, 155 JP 721, [1991] 26 LS Gaz R 32, CA	167
R v Blundeston Prison Board of Visitors, ex p Fox-Taylor [1982] 1 All ER 646	132
R v Board of Inland Revenue, ex p MFK Underwriting Agencies Ltd [1990] 1 All ER 91, sub nom R v IRC, ex p MFK Underwriting Agents Ltd [1990] 1 WLR 1545, [1989] STC 873, 62 TC 607	104, 148, 199, 200
R v Board of Visitors of Dartmoor Prison, ex p Smith [1987] QB 106, [1986] 2 All ER 651, [1986] 3 WLR 61, 130 Sol Jo 505, CA	78, 131
R v Board of Visitors of Gartree Prison, ex p Mealy (1981) Times, 14 November	132
R v Board of Visitors of HM Prison, The Maze, ex p Hone [1988] AC 379, [1988] 2 WLR 177, 132 Sol Jo 158, [1988] 8 LS Gaz R 35, sub nom Hone v Maze Prison Board of Visitors [1988] 1 All ER 321, HL	132
R v Board of Visitors of Hull Prison, ex p St Germain [1979] QB 425, [1979] 1 All ER 701, [1979] 2 WLR 42, 68 Cr App Rep 212, 122 Sol Jo 697, CA	132

	PAGE
R v Bolton Justices, ex p Scally [1991] 1 QB 537, [1991] 2 All ER 619, [1991] 2 WLR 239, [1991] RTR 84, 155 JP 501, [1991] Crim LR 550	78
R v Boston General Comrs, ex p C D Freehouses & Co Ltd [1990] STC 186	145
R v Bow Street Metropolitan Stipendiary Magistrate, ex p Roberts [1990] 3 All ER 487, [1990] 1 WLR 1317, 92 Cr App Rep 129, 154 JP 634, 134 Sol Jo 1041, [1990] NLJR 782	179, 195
R v Brent London Borough Council, ex p Assegai (1987) Times, 18 June	113
R v Brent London Borough Council, ex p Gladbaum and Woods [1990] 2 Admin LR 634	115
R v Brent London Borough Council, ex p Gunning (1985) 84 LGR 168	102
R v BBC, ex p Lavelle [1983] 1 All ER 241, [1983] 1 WLR 23, [1983] ICR 99, [1982] IRLR 404, 126 Sol Jo 836	78, 88, 93
R v British Coal Corpn, ex p Price (No 2) (1993) Times, 23 February	86
R v Broadcasting Complaints Commission, ex p BBC (1992) Times, 16 October	83
R v Broadcasting Complaints Commission, ex p Owen [1985] QB 1153, [1985] 2 All ER 522, [1985] 2 WLR 1025, 129 Sol Jo 349	79, 83
R v Bromsgrove District Council, ex p Kennedy [1992] COD 129	183
R v Camden London Borough and Hampstead School Governors, ex p H [1996] ELR 360, CA	127
R v Camden London Borough Council, ex p Mohammed (1997) 30 HLR 315, [1997] 35 LS Gaz R 34	121
R v Camden London Borough Council, ex p S (1990) 89 LGR 513, [1991] COD 195	128
R v Cardiff City Council, ex p Barry (1990) 22 HLR 261, [1990] COD 94, CA	81
R v Central Criminal Court, ex p Director of the Serious Fraud Office [1993] 2 All ER 399, [1993] 1 WLR 949, 96 Cr App Rep 248, [1993] Crim LR 134	146, 182
R v Central Criminal Court, ex p Randle and Pottle [1992] 1 All ER 370, [1991] 1 WLR 1087, 92 Cr App Rep 323, [1991] Crim LR 551, 135 Sol Jo 116	91
R v Central Criminal Court, ex p Raymond [1986] 2 All ER 379, [1986] 1 WLR 710, 83 Cr App Rep 94, 130 Sol Jo 430, [1986] LS Gaz R 1553, [1986] NLJ Rep 395	90
R v Central Criminal Court, ex p Spens (1992) Times, 31 December, (1992) Independent, 1 December, [1993] COD 194	90
R v Chantrell (1875) LR 10 QB 587, 39 JP 472, 44 LJMC 94, 23 WR 707, 33 LT 305	32
R v Chief Adjudication Officer, ex p Bland (1985) Times, 6 February	151
R v Chief Constable of Cambridgeshire, ex p M [1991] 2 QB 499, [1991] 2 All ER 777, [1991] 2 WLR 1226, 91 Cr App Rep 325, 154 JP 535, [1991] Crim LR 382, [1990] NLJR 889:	83
R v Chief Constable of Merseyside Police, ex p Calveley [1986] QB 424, [1986] 1 All ER 257, [1986] 2 WLR 144, 130 Sol Jo 53, [1986] LS Gaz R 124, CA	166
R v Chief Constable of the Kent County Constabulary, ex p L (a minor) [1993] 1 All ER 756, 93 Cr App Rep 416, 155 JP 760, [1991] Crim LR 841	83
R v Chief Rabbi of the United Hebrew Congregations of Great Britain and the Commonwealth, ex p Wachmann [1993] 2 All ER 249, [1992] 1 WLR 1036, [1991] 3 Admin LR 721	78, 86
R v Chief Registrar of Friendly Societies, ex p New Cross Building Society [1984] QB 227, [1984] 2 All ER 27, [1984] 2 WLR 370, 128 Sol Jo 173, [1984] LS Gaz R 509, CA	83
R v City of London Corpn, ex p Matson [1997] 1 WLR 765, CA	108
R v City of Westminster, ex p Hilditch [1990] COD 434	164
R v Civil Service Appeal Board, ex p Bruce (A-G intervening) [1989] 2 All ER 907, [1989] ICR 171, CA	166
R v Civil Service Appeal Board, ex p Cunningham [1991] 4 All ER 310, [1992] ICR 816, [1991] IRLR 297, [1991] NLJR 455, CA	108
R v Clerk to Birmingham Justices, ex p Offei (28 November 1985, unreported)	119
R v Cleveland County Council, ex p Commission for Racial Equality (1992) 91 LGR 139, [1993] 1 FCR 597, [1994] ELR 44, CA	126
R v Cobham Hall School, ex p S (1997) Times, 13 December	86
R v Code of Practice Committee of the Association of the British Pharmaceutical Industry, ex p Professional Counselling Aids Ltd (1990) 10 BMLR 21, [1991] 3 Admin LR 697	78, 86
R v Collector of Taxes, ex p Robert Goodall (Builders) Ltd [1989] STC 206, 61 TC 219	145
R v Commission for Racial Equality, ex p Cottrell and Rothon [1980] 3 All ER 265, [1980] 1 WLR 1580, 124 Sol Jo 882, 255 Estates Gazette 783	115
R v Committee of Advertising Practice, ex p Bradford Exchange Ltd [1991] COD 43	179
R v Committee of Lloyd's, ex p Moran (1983) Times, 24 June	146
R v Committee of Lloyds, ex p Postgate (1983) Times, 12 January	87, 146
R v Comptroller-General of Patents, Designs and Trade Marks, ex p Gist-Brocades. See Trade Marks, ex p Gist-Brocades NV	
R v Comr for Local Administration, ex p Croydon London Borough Council [1989] 1 All ER 1033, sub nom R v Local Ombudsman, ex p London Borough of Croydon [1989] Fam Law 187, [1989] COD 226	84, 125, 164

TABLE OF CASES

	PAGE
R v Cornwall County Council, ex p Huntington [1992] 3 All ER 566, [1992] NLJR 348; affd [1994] 1 All ER 694, CA	158, 178
R v Criminal Injuries Compensation Board, ex p Lain [1967] 2 QB 864, [1967] 2 All ER 770, [1967] 3 WLR 348, 111 Sol Jo 331	77, 84
R v Cripps, ex p Muldoon [1984] QB 686, [1984] 2 All ER 705, [1984] 3 WLR 53, 82 LGR 439, 128 Sol Jo 431, [1984] LS Gaz R 1916, CA	83
R v Crocker (19 December 1997, unreported)	115
R v Crown Court at Bristol, ex p Cooper [1990] 2 All ER 193, [1990] 1 WLR 1031, CA	106
R v Crown Court at Cardiff, ex p M (a minor) (1998) Times, 28 April	90
R v Crown Court at Croydon, ex p Smith (1983) 77 Cr App Rep 277	79
R v County Court at Croydon, ex p Watson (1987) Times, 18 March, CA	166
R v Crown Court at Harrow, ex p Perkins (1998) Times, 28 April	91
R v Crown Court at Ipswich, ex p Baldwin [1981] 1 All ER 596, [1981] RTR 298, sub nom R v Felixstowe Justices, ex p Baldwin 72 Cr App Rep 131, [1981] Crim LR 242	119
R v Crown Court at Isleworth, ex p Willington [1993] 2 All ER 390, [1993] 1 WLR 713, [1992] 33 LS Gaz R 39, 136 Sol Jo LB 259	91
R v Crown Court at Knightsbridge, ex p Marcrest Ltd [1983] 1 All ER 1148, [1983] 1 WLR 300, CA	80
R v Crown Court at Leicester, ex p S (a minor) [1992] 2 All ER 659, [1993] 1 WLR 111n, 94 Cr App Rep 153, 155 JP 405, [1991] Crim LR 365	90
R v Crown Court at Lewes, ex p Sinclair [1992] 33 LS Gaz R 35, 136 Sol Jo LB 227	91
R v Crown Court at Maidstone, ex p Gill [1987] 1 All ER 129, [1986] 1 WLR 1405, [1987] RTR 35, 84 Cr App Rep 96, [1986] Crim LR 737, 130 Sol Jo 712, [1986] LS Gaz R 2750, [1986] NLJ Rep 823	90
R v Crown Court at Maidstone, ex p Schulz and Steinkellner (1992) 157 JP 601	90
R v Crown Court at Manchester, ex p DPP [1994] AC 9, [1993] 2 WLR 846, 97 Cr App Rep 203, 157 JP 497, [1993] Crim LR 959, [1993] 24 LS Gaz R 40, [1993] NLJR 687, 137 Sol Jo LB 144, sub nom DPP v Crown Court at Manchester and Ashton [1993] 2 All ER 663, HL	79, 90, 91
R v Crown Court at Norwich, ex p Stiller (1992) 156 JP 624, [1992] 4 Admin LR 709	90
R v Crown Court at Reading, ex p Ecclestone and Jennings (23 September 1986, unreported):	90
R v Crown Court at St Albans, ex p Cinnamond [1981] QB 480, [1981] 1 All ER 802, [1981] 2 WLR 681, [1981] RTR 139, 145 JP 277, [1981] Crim LR 243, 125 Sol Jo 289	111
R v Crown Court at Sheffield, ex p Brownlow [1980] QB 530, [1980] 2 All ER 444, [1980] 2 WLR 892, 71 Cr App Rep 19, 124 Sol Jo 272, CA	90
R v Crown Court at Southwark, ex p Watts [1992] 1 CMLR 446, 156 LG Rev 343, 156 JP 273, [1992] 2 LS Gaz R 33, 135 Sol Jo LB 197, CA	173
R v Crown Court of Inner London, ex p Benjamin (1986) 85 Cr App Rep 267, [1987] Crim LR 417	90
R v Customs and Excise Comrs, ex p Cooke and Stevenson (or ex p Cook) [1970] 1 All ER 1068, [1970] 1 WLR 450, 114 Sol Jo 34, DC	145
R v Dalton [1995] QB 243, [1995] 2 All ER 349, [1995] 2 WLR 377, [1995] 2 Cr App Rep 340, [1994] 41 LS Gaz R 40, 138 Sol Jo LB 216, CA	134
R v Darlington Borough Council, ex p Association of Darlington Taxi Owners (1994) Times, 21 January, [1994] COD 424	162
R v Department of Transport, ex p Presvac Engineering Ltd (1991) Times, 10 July, CA	160
R v Deputy Chief Constable of the North Wales Police, ex p Hughes [1991] 3 All ER 414, [1991] ICR 180, CA	83
R v Deputy Governor of Camphill Prison, ex p King [1985] QB 735, [1984] 3 All ER 897, [1985] 2 WLR 36, 128 Sol Jo 769, [1984] LS Gaz R 3012, CA	132
R v Deputy Governor of Parkhurst Prison, ex p Hague [1992] 1 AC 58, [1991] 3 WLR 340, 135 Sol Jo LB 102, sub nom Hague v Deputy Governor of Parkhurst Prison [1991] 3 All ER 733, HL	82, 94, 131, 133, 136, 204
R v Deputy Industrial Injuries Comr, ex p Jones [1962] 2 QB 677, [1962] 2 All ER 430, [1962] 2 WLR 1215, 106 Sol Jo 311	153
R v Derbyshire County Council, ex p Noble (1990) 154 LG Rev 575, [1990] ICR 808, [1990] IRLR 332, 4 BMLR 103, CA	78, 183
R v Derbyshire County Council, ex p Times Supplements Ltd (1991) 155 LG Rev 123, [1991] COD 129, [1990] NLJR 1421, [1991] 3 Admin LR 241	77, 99, 111, 185
R v Devon County Council, ex p Baker [1995] 1 All ER 73, 91 LGR 479, 11 BMLR 141, CA:	104, 200
R v DPP, ex p Bull [1998] 2 All ER 755	188
R v DPP, ex p First Division Association [1988] NLJR 158	114

TABLE OF CASES xxxix

PAGE

R v Director of Serious Fraud Office, ex p Smith [1993] AC 1, [1992] 3 WLR 66, 95 Cr App
Rep 191, [1992] 27 LS Gaz R 34, [1992] NLJR 895, 136 Sol Jo LB 182, sub nom Smith
v Director of Serious Fraud Office [1992] 3 All ER 456, [1992] BCLC 879, HL 84, 145
R v Disciplinary Committee of the Jockey Club, ex p Aga Khan [1993] 2 All ER 853, [1993] 1
WLR 909, CA 78, 84, 85, 87
R v Disciplinary Committee of the Jockey Club, ex p Massingberd-Mundy [1993] 2 All ER 207,
[1990] COD 260, [1990] 2 Admin LR 260 87
R v Durham City Council, ex p Robinson (1992) Times, 31 January 96
R v Durham County Council, ex p Curtis and Broxson [1995] 1 All ER 73, 91 LGR 479, 11
BMLR 141, CA 200
R v Ealing District Health Authority, ex p Fox [1993] 3 All ER 170, [1993] 1 WLR 373, 11
BMLR 59, 136 Sol Jo LB 220 . . . . 83, 100, 143, 207
R v Ealing London Borough, ex p Richardson (1982) 4 HLR 125, 265 Estates Gazette 691,
[1983] JPL 533, CA 108
R v Ealing London Borough, ex p Times Newspapers Ltd (1986) 85 LGR 316, [1987] IRLR
129, DC 111
R v Ealing London Borough Council, ex p Lewis (1992) 90 LGR 571, 24 HLR 484, CA 100
R v East Berkshire Health Authority, ex p Walsh [1985] QB 152, [1984] 3 All ER 425, [1984] 3
WLR 818, [1984] ICR 743, [1984] IRLR 278, 128 Sol Jo 664, [1984] LS Gaz R 2223,
CA 78, 88, 93
R v Epping and Harlow General Comrs, ex p Goldstraw [1983] 3 All ER 257, [1983] STC 693,
57 TC 536; affd [1983] 3 All ER 257, [1983] STC 693, 57 TC 536, CA 166
R v Essex County Council, ex p C (1993) 92 LGR 46, [1994] 1 FCR 343, [1994] Fam Law 128,
[1994] ELR 54; affd (1993) 93 LGR 10, CA 128
R v Federation of Communication Services Ltd, ex p Kubis CO 1466/97 (9 September 1997,
unreported) 78
R v Felixstowe Justices, ex p Leigh [1987] QB 582, [1987] 1 All ER 551, [1987] 2 WLR 380, 84
Cr App Rep 327, 151 JP 65, [1987] Crim LR 125, 130 Sol Jo 767, [1987] LS Gaz R 901,
[1986] NLJ Rep 988 159
R v Financial Intermediaries, Managers and Brokers Regulatory Association, ex p Cochrane
[1991] BCLC 106, [1990] COD 33 . . . . 78, 146
R v Football Association Ltd, ex p Football League Ltd [1993] 2 All ER 833, [1992] COD 52: 78, 85, 87
R v Football Association of Wales, ex p Flint Town United Football Club [1991] COD 44 . . . 87
R v Forest Betting Licensing Committee, ex p Noquet (1988) Times, 21 June 116
R v Further Education Funding Council, ex p Parkinson [1997] 2 FCR 67 124
R v Gaming Board for Great Britain, ex p Benaim and Khaida [1970] 2 QB 417, [1970] 2 All ER
528, [1970] 2 WLR 1009, 134 JP 513, 114 Sol Jo 266, CA 105
R v General Council of the Bar, ex p Percival [1991] 1 QB 212, [1990] 3 All ER 137, [1990] 3
WLR 323, [1990] 24 LS Gaz R 44 . . . . 79, 85
R v General Medical Council, ex p Colman [1990] 1 All ER 489, 4 BMLR 33, [1990] COD
202, [1989] NLJR 1753, CA 77, 83
R v General Medical Council and the Review Board for Overseas Qualified Practitioners, ex p
Popat [1991] COD 245 80
R v Gough [1993] AC 646, [1992] 4 All ER 481, [1993] 2 WLR 883, 95 Cr App Rep 433, 157
JP 434, [1992] 26 LS Gaz R 30, [1992] NLJR 787, 136 Sol Jo LB 197, CA; affd [1993]
AC 646, [1993] 2 All ER 724, [1993] 2 WLR 883, 97 Cr App Rep 188, 157 JP 612,
[1993] Crim LR 886, [1993] NLJR 775, 137 Sol Jo LB 168, HL 106
R v Governor of Broadmoor, ex p Argles (28 June 1984, unreported) 140
R v Governor of Winchester Prison, ex p Roddie [1991] 2 All ER 931, sub nom R v Crown
Court at Southampton, ex p Roddie [1991] 1 WLR 303, 93 Cr App Rep 190, [1991]
Crim LR 619 90
R v Governors of the Bishop Challoner Roman Catholic Comprehensive Girls' School, ex p
Choudhury [1992] 2 AC 182, [1992] 3 WLR 99, 90 LGR 445, [1992] 2 FCR 507,
[1992] 2 FLR 444, [1993] Fam Law 23, [1992] 27 LS Gaz R 36, sub nom Choudhury v
Governors of Bishop Challoner Roman Catholic Comprehensive School [1992] 3 All ER
277, HL 84, 125
R v Greater London Council, ex p Blackburn [1976] 3 All ER 184, [1976] 1 WLR 550, 74 LGR
464, 120 Sol Jo 421, CA 159
R v Greater Manchester Coroner, ex p Tal [1985] QB 67, [1984] 3 All ER 240, [1984] 3 WLR
643, 128 Sol Jo 500 157
R v Greenwich London Borough Council, ex p Governors of John Ball Primary School [1990]
COD 103, (1989) Times, 16 November; affd (1990) 88 LGR 589, [1990] Fam Law 469,
CA 125, 164, 210

	PAGE
R v Gwent County Council and Secretary of State for Wales, ex p Bryant [1988] COD 19	102, 130
R v Gwynedd County Council, ex p B [1992] 3 All ER 317, [1991] 2 FLR 365, [1991] Fam Law 377, 7 BMLR 120, sub nom Re B [1991] FCR 800, CA	90
R v HM Inspectorate of Pollution, ex p Greenpeace Ltd (No 2) [1994] 4 All ER 329, [1994] 2 CMLR 548	162
R v HM the Queen in Council, ex p Vijayatunga [1990] 2 QB 444, [1989] 3 WLR 13, 133 Sol Jo 818, [1989] 28 LS Gaz R 40, sub nom R v University of London Visitor, ex p Vijayatunga [1989] 2 All ER 843, CA	87, 129
R v HM Treasury, ex p Daily Mail and General Trust plc [1987] 2 CMLR 1, [1987] STC 157; refd sub nom R v HM Treasury, ex p Daily Mail and General Trust plc: 81/87 [1989] QB 446, [1989] 1 All ER 328, [1989] 2 WLR 908, [1988] ECR 5483, [1988] 3 CMLR 713, [1988] STC 787, [1989] BCLC 206, 133 Sol Jo 693, [1989] 25 LS Gaz R 41, ECJ	145
R v HM Treasury, ex p Petch [1990] COD 19	145
R v HM Treasury, ex p Smedley [1985] QB 657, [1985] 1 All ER 589, [1985] 2 WLR 576, [1985] 1 CMLR 665, 129 Sol Jo 48, CA	81, 112, 149, 160
R v Hackney London Borough Council, ex p Evenbray Ltd (1987) 86 LGR 210, 19 HLR 557:	111
R v Hallstrom, ex p W [1986] QB 1090, [1986] 2 WLR 883, 130 Sol Jo 204, [1986] LS Gaz R 786, sub nom R v Hallstrom, ex p W (No 2) [1986] 2 All ER 306	140
R v Hammersmith and Fulham London Borough Council, ex p Beddowes [1987] QB 1050, [1987] 1 All ER 369, [1987] 2 WLR 263, 85 LGR 270, 18 HLR 458, 130 Sol Jo 696, [1986] LS Gaz R 3001, [1987] RVR 189, CA	117
R v Hammersmith and Fulham London Borough Council, ex p People Before Profit Ltd (1981) 80 LGR 322, 45 P & CR 364, [1981] JPL 869	162, 182, 184
R v Hampshire County Council, ex p K [1990] 2 QB 71, [1990] 2 All ER 129, [1990] 2 WLR 649, 88 LGR 618, [1990] FCR 545, [1990] 1 FLR 330, [1990] Fam Law 253	105
R v Harrow London Borough Council, ex p M [1997] 3 FCR 761, [1997] ELR 62	124
R v Hastings Licensing Justices, ex p John Lovibond & Sons Ltd [1968] 2 All ER 270, [1968] 1 WLR 735, 66 LGR 422, 132 JP 332, 112 Sol Jo 313, 206 Estates Gazette 211, DC	188
R v Headmaster of Fernhill Manor School, ex p Brown (1992) Times, 5 June, Independent, 25 June	86, 127
R v Hertfordshire County Council, ex p Cheung (1986) Times, 4 April, CA	129, 179
R v Highbury Corner Magistrates Court, ex p Ewing [1991] 3 All ER 192, sub nom Ex p Ewing [1991] 1 WLR 388, CA	179
R v Hillingdon Health Authority, ex p Goodwin [1984] ICR 800	103
R v Hillingdon London Borough, ex p Governing Body of Queensmead School [1997] ELR 331	124
R v Hillingdon London Borough Council, ex p Royco Homes Ltd [1974] QB 720, [1974] 2 All ER 643, [1974] 2 WLR 805, 72 LGR 516, 28 P & CR 251, 138 JP 505, 118 Sol Jo 389	111, 167
R v Holderness Borough Council, ex p James Robert Developments Ltd (1992) 66 P & CR 46, [1993] 1 PLR 108, [1992] NPC 156, [1993] JPL 659, 5 Admin LR 470, CA	179
R v Horseferry Road Justices, ex p Independent Broadcasting Authority [1987] QB 54, [1986] 2 All ER 666, [1986] 3 WLR 132, 130 Sol Jo 446, [1986] LS Gaz R 1553, [1986] NLJ Rep 139	78
R v Hull Prison Board of Visitors, ex p St Germain (No 2) [1979] 3 All ER 545, [1979] 1 WLR 1401, [1979] Crim LR 726, 123 Sol Jo 768	105, 132
R v Huntingdon District Council, ex p Cowan [1984] 1 All ER 58, [1984] 1 WLR 501, 82 LGR 342, 148 JP 367, 128 Sol Jo 246	167
R v IT Acts Special Purposes Comr, ex p Napier [1988] 3 All ER 166, sub nom R v Special Comr, ex p Napier [1988] STC 573, 61 TC 206, CA	145
R v IT Acts Special Purposes Comr, ex p Stipplechoice Ltd [1985] 2 All ER 465, sub nom R v Special Comr, ex p Stipplechoice Ltd [1985] STC 248, CA	145
R v Immigration Appeal Tribunal, ex p Manshoora Begum [1986] Imm AR 385	111, 112
R v Immigration Appeal Tribunal and Surinder Singh, ex p Secretary of State for the Home Department: C-370/90 [1992] 3 All ER 798, [1992] ECR I-4265, [1992] 3 CMLR 358, [1993] 1 FCR 453, [1993] 1 FLR 798, [1993] Fam Law 272, [1992] Imm AR 565, [1993] 21 LS Gaz R 45, ECJ	173
R v Independent Broadcasting Authority, ex p Whitehouse (1985) Times, 4 April, CA	160
R v Independent Television Commission, ex p TV NI Ltd (1991) Times, 30 December, CA	146, 164, 179
R v Independent Television Commission, ex p Television South West (1992) Times, 7 February, CA; affd sub nom R v Independent Television Commission, ex p TSW Broadcasting Ltd [1996] EMLR 291, HL	83, 104, 146

TABLE OF CASES xli

PAGE

R v Industrial Injuries Comr, ex p Amalgamated Engineering Union (No 2) [1966] 2 QB 31, [1966] 1 All ER 97, [1966] 2 WLR 97, 109 Sol Jo 934, CA 153
R v Inland Revenue Board, ex p Goldberg [1989] QB 267, [1988] 3 All ER 248, [1988] 3 WLR 522, [1988] STC 524, 132 Sol Jo 1035, [1988] 27 LS Gaz R 40, [1988] NLJR 125, sub nom R v IRC, ex p Goldberg 61 TC 403 148
R v IRC, ex p Camacq Corpn [1990] 1 All ER 173, [1990] 1 WLR 191, [1989] STC 785, 62 TC 651, [1990] 5 LS Gaz R 41, CA 148
R v IRC, ex p J Rothschild Holdings plc [1986] STC 410; affd [1987] STC 163, 61 TC 178, CA 147, 185
R v IRC, ex p Kaye [1992] STC 581, 65 TC 82, [1992] 26 LS Gaz R 32 . . . . 147, 202
R v IRC, ex p Mead [1993] 1 All ER 772, [1992] STC 482, 65 TC 1 147
R v IRC, ex p Opman International UK [1986] 1 All ER 328, [1986] 1 WLR 568, [1986] STC 18, 59 TC 352, 130 Sol Jo 373, [1986] LS Gaz R 1803 . . . . 149, 186
R v IRC, ex p Taylor [1989] 1 All ER 906, [1988] STC 832, 62 TC 562, CA 184
R v IRC, ex p Taylor (No 2) [1989] 3 All ER 353, [1989] STC 600, 62 TC 578; affd [1990] 2 All ER 409, [1990] STC 379, 62 TC 578, CA 145
R v Inner London Education Authority, ex p Ali (1990) 154 LGR 852, [1990] COD 317, [1990] 2 Admin LR 822 123
R v Inner London Education Authority, ex p Westminster City Council [1986] 1 All ER 19, [1986] 1 WLR 28, 84 LGR 120, 130 Sol Jo 51, [1986] LS Gaz R 359 . . . . 99, 111
R v Inspector of Taxes, ex p Clarke [1974] QB 220, [1972] 1 All ER 545, [1973] 3 WLR 673, 117 Sol Jo 815, sub nom R v Freshwell General Comrs for Income Tax, ex p Clarke 47 TC 691, 50 ATC 389, L(TC) 2431, CA 102
R v International Stock Exchange of the United Kingdom and the Republic of Ireland Ltd, ex p Else (1982) Ltd [1993] QB 534, [1993] 1 All ER 420, [1993] 2 WLR 70, [1993] 2 CMLR 677, [1993] BCLC 834, [1993] BCC 11, CA 170
R v Jockey Club, ex p RAM Racecourses Ltd [1993] 2 All ER 225, [1990] COD 346, [1991] 5 Admin LR 265 . . . . 87, 104, 199, 200
R v Kensington and Chelsea Royal London Borough Council, ex p Hammell [1989] QB 518, [1989] 1 All ER 1202, [1989] 2 WLR 90, 87 LGR 145, [1989] FCR 323, [1989] 2 FLR 223, [1989] Fam Law 430, 20 HLR 666, 133 Sol Jo 45, [1989] 3 LS Gaz R 43, CA . . . 81, 182
R v Lambeth London Borough, ex p N [1996] ELR 299 123
R v Lambeth London Borough Council, ex p Barnes (1992) 25 HLR 140, [1993] COD 50 . . . 82, 121
R v Lancashire County Council, ex p Huddleston [1986] 2 All ER 941, [1986] NLJ Rep 562, CA 108
R v Lancashire County Council, ex p M (1989) 87 LGR 567, [1989] 2 FLR 279, [1989] Fam Law 395, 133 Sol Jo 484, [1989] 17 LS Gaz R 37, CA 128
R v Law Society, ex p Reigate Projects Ltd [1992] 3 All ER 232, [1993] 1 WLR 1531, [1991] COD 401 85
R v Leeds County Court, ex p Morris [1990] 1 QB 523, [1990] 1 All ER 550, [1990] 2 WLR 175, 154 JP 385, 134 Sol Jo 285, [1990] 4 LS Gaz R 41 90
R v Legal Aid Board, ex p Bateman [1992] 3 All ER 490, [1992] 1 WLR 711, [1992] 16 LS Gaz R 33, [1992] NLJR 347, 136 Sol Jo LB 98 . . . . 83, 84, 159
R v Lewisham London Borough Council, ex p Shell UK Ltd [1988] 1 All ER 938, [1990] PLR 241 111
R v Licensing Authority established under Medicines Act 1968, ex p Smith Kline & French Laboratories Ltd (No 2) [1990] 1 QB 574, [1989] 2 WLR 378, 133 Sol Jo 263, [1989] 11 LS Gaz R 43, sub nom R v Licensing Authority, ex p Smith Kline & French Laboratories Ltd (Generics (UK) Ltd intervening) (No 2) [1989] 2 All ER 113, CA 81
R v Life Assurance Unit Trust Regulatory Organisation Ltd, ex p Ross [1993] QB 17, [1992] 1 All ER 422, [1992] BCLC 34, [1991] COD 503, [1991] NLJR 1001; affd [1993] QB 17, [1993] 1 All ER 545, [1992] 3 WLR 549, [1992] BCLC 509, CA 78, 144, 146, 147, 149
R v Lincoln's Inn Benchers (1825) 4 B & C 855, 7 Dow & Ry KB 351 79
R v Liverpool City Council, ex p Newman [1993] COD 65, 5 Admin LR 699 . . . . 179, 186
R v Liverpool City Justices, ex p Topping [1983] 1 All ER 490, [1983] 1 WLR 119, 76 Cr App Rep 170, 147 JP 154, [1983] Crim LR 181, 127 Sol Jo 51 106
R v Liverpool Corpn, ex p Liverpool Taxi Fleet Operators' Association [1972] 2 QB 299, [1972] 2 WLR 1262, 71 LGR 387, 116 Sol Jo 201, sub nom Re Liverpool Taxi Owners' Association [1972] 2 All ER 589, CA 78
R v Lloyd's of London, ex p Briggs [1993] 1 Lloyd's Rep 176 . . . . 87, 146, 178
R v London Beth Din (Court of Chief Rabbi), ex p Bloom CO 2495/96 (18 November 1997, unreported) 78, 85, 86

	PAGE
R v London Borough of Enfield, ex p T F Unwin (Roydon) Ltd (1989) 153 LG Rev 890, [1989] COD 466, 46 BLR 1	105
R v London Borough of Hammersmith and Fulham, ex p NALGO [1991] IRLR 249, [1991] COD 397	89, 116
R v London Borough of Islington, ex p Building Employers' Confederation [1989] IRLR 382, 45 BLR 45	162
R v London Rent Assessment Panel Committee, ex p Metropolitan Properties Co (FGC) Ltd [1969] 1 QB 577, [1968] 3 WLR 694, 112 Sol Jo 585, [1968] RVR 490, 505, sub nom Metropolitan Properties Co (FGC) Ltd v Lannon [1968] 3 All ER 304, 19 P & CR 856, CA	106
R v Lord Chancellor, ex p Child Poverty Action Group [1998] 2 All ER 755, [1998] NLJR 205	188
R v Lord Chancellor, ex p Maxwell [1996] 4 All ER 751, [1997] 1 WLR 104, [1996] NLJR 986, 140 Sol Jo LB 157	84
R v Lord Chancellor, ex p Stockler [1996] 8 Admin LR 590, Times, 7 May, CA	84
R v Lord Chancellor, ex p Witham [1997] 2 All ER 779, [1998] 2 WLR 849, [1997] NLJR 378, 141 Sol Jo LB 82	99, 108
R v Lord Chancellor's Department, ex p Nangle [1992] 1 All ER 897, [1991] ICR 743, [1991] IRLR 343	89
R v Lord President of the Privy Council, ex p Page [1993] AC 682, [1992] 3 WLR 1112, [1993] ICR 114, [1993] 10 LS Gaz R 33, 137 Sol Jo LB 45, sub nom Page v Hull University Visitor [1993] 1 All ER 97, [1993] NLJR 15, HL	79, 86, 87, 100, 129, 147, 157
R v Managers of South Western Hospital, ex p M [1993] QB 683, [1994] 1 All ER 161, [1993] 3 WLR 376, [1993] 12 LS Gaz R 32	140
R v Manchester City Magistrates' Court, ex p Davies [1989] QB 631, [1989] 1 All ER 90, [1988] 3 WLR 1357, [1989] RA 261, 152 JP 605, [1989] 2 LS Gaz R 36, [1988] NLJR 260, CA:	157
R v Medical Appeal Tribunal, ex p Gilmore [1957] 1 QB 574, [1957] 2 WLR 498, 101 Sol Jo 248, sub nom Re Gilmore's Application [1957] 1 All ER 796, CA	77, 152, 155
R v Mental Health Act Commission, ex p Mark Witham (26 May 1988, unreported)	185
R v Mental Health Review Tribunal, ex p Clatworthy [1985] 3 All ER 699	143
R v Merseyside Mental Health Review Tribunal, ex p K [1990] 1 All ER 694, CA	142
R v Metropolitan Police Comr, ex p Blackburn [1968] 2 QB 118, [1968] 1 All ER 763, [1968] 2 WLR 893, 112 Sol Jo 112, CA	79, 162
R v Metropolitan Police Comr, ex p Blackburn (No 3) [1973] QB 241, [1973] 1 All ER 324, [1973] 2 WLR 43, 137 JP 172, [1973] Crim LR 185, 117 Sol Jo 57, CA	79, 162
R v Mid Glamorgan Family Health Services Authority, ex p Martin [1995] 1 All ER 356, [1995] 1 WLR 110, [1995] 2 FCR 578, [1995] 1 FLR 283, [1994] 5 Med LR 383, 21 BMLR 1, [1994] 38 LS Gaz R 42, 138 Sol Jo LB 195, CA	115
R v Monopolies and Mergers Commission, ex p Argyll Group plc [1986] 2 All ER 257, [1986] 1 WLR 763, 130 Sol Jo 467, [1986] LS Gaz R 1225, CA	145, 149, 163
R v Monopolies and Mergers Commission, ex p Elders IXL Ltd [1987] 1 All ER 451, [1987] 1 WLR 1221, 2 BCC 99, 179, 131 Sol Jo 1120, [1987] LS Gaz R 2764	145
R v Monopolies and Mergers Commission, ex p Matthew Brown plc [1987] 1 All ER 463, [1987] 1 WLR 1235, 4 BCC 171, 131 Sol Jo 1120, [1987] LS Gaz R 2606	105, 145
R v Monopolies and Mergers Commission, ex p National House Building Council [1992] NPC 122, 6 Admin LR 161, Times, 7 October; affd [1994] NPC 3, (1994) Times, 25 January, CA	145
R v Monopolies and Mergers Commission, ex p Stagecoach Holdings plc (1995) Times, 23 July	84
R v Monopolies and Mergers Commission, ex p Visa International Service Association (1991) 10 Tr L 97, [1991] CCLR 13, CA	145
R v Nat Bell Liquors Ltd [1922] 2 AC 128, 91 LJPC 146, 27 Cox CC 253, [1922] All ER Rep 335, 127 LT 437, 38 TLR 541, PC	155
R v National Coal Board, ex p National Union of Mineworkers [1986] ICR 791	85
R v National Insurance Comr, ex p Michael [1977] 2 All ER 420, [1977] 1 WLR 109, [1977] ICR 121, 120 Sol Jo 856, CA	153
R v National Insurance Comr, ex p Secretary of State for Social Services [1981] 2 All ER 738, [1981] 1 WLR 1017, 125 Sol Jo 376, CA	153
R v National Insurance Comr, ex p Stratton [1979] QB 361, [1979] 2 All ER 278, [1979] 1 WLR 389, [1979] ICR 290, 123 Sol Jo 32, CA	153
R v National Joint Council for the Craft of Dental Technicians (Disputes Committee), ex p Neate [1953] 1 QB 704, [1953] 1 All ER 327, [1953] 2 WLR 342, 97 Sol Jo 116	85
R v Newcastle under Lyme Justices, ex p Massey [1995] 1 All ER 120, 158 JP 1037, [1994] NLJR 1444, sub nom R v Stoke-on-Trent Justices, ex p Knight [1994] 1 WLR 1684	188

TABLE OF CASES

xliii

	PAGE
R v North West London Mental Health NHS Trust, ex p Stewart [1997] 4 All ER 871, [1998] 2 WLR 189, CA	143
R v North Western Traffic Comrs, ex p Brake [1995] NPC 167, [1996] COD 248	162
R v Northamptonshire County Council, ex p Tebbutt (26 June 1986, unreported)	179, 210
R v Northavon District Council, ex p Ashman [1992] NPC 65, [1992] COD 451	111
R v O'Kane and Clarke, ex p Northern Bank Ltd [1996] STC 1249, 69 TC 187	113
R v Oldham Metropolitan Borough Council, ex p Garlick [1993] AC 509, [1993] 2 WLR 609, 91 LGR 287, [1993] 2 FCR 133, [1993] 2 FLR 194, 25 HLR 319, [1993] 26 LS Gaz R 38, [1993] NLJR 437, sub nom Garlick v Oldham Metropolitan Borough Council [1993] 2 All ER 65, HL	100
R v Oxford, ex p Levey (1987) 151 LGR 371, CA	179
R v Panel on Take-overs and Mergers, ex p Datafin plc [1987] QB 815, [1987] 1 All ER 564, [1987] 2 WLR 699, [1987] BCLC 104, 3 BCC 10, 131 Sol Jo 23, [1987] LS Gaz R 264, [1986] NLJ Rep 1207, CA	77, 79, 86, 145, 149
R v Panel on Take-overs and Mergers, ex p Guinness plc [1990] 1 QB 146, [1989] 1 All ER 509, [1989] 2 WLR 863, [1989] BCLC 255, 4 BCC 714, 133 Sol Jo 660, [1988] NLJR 244, CA	103, 145, 147
R v Parliamentary Comr for Standards, ex p Al Fayed [1998] 1 All ER 93, [1998] 1 WLR 669, [1997] 42 LS Gaz R 31, CA	79
R v Parole Board, ex p Bradley [1990] 3 All ER 828, [1991] 1 WLR 134, [1990] COD 375	84
R v Parole Board, ex p Wilson [1992] QB 740, [1991] 2 All ER 576, [1992] 2 WLR 707, [1992] 17 LS Gaz R 49, 136 Sol Jo LB 83, CA	134
R v Peak Park Joint Planning Board (1976) 74 LGR 376, DC	80
R v Police Complaints Board, ex p Madden [1983] 2 All ER 353, [1983] 1 WLR 447, [1983] Crim LR 263, 127 Sol Jo 85	109, 115
R v Poole Borough Council, ex p Beebee [1991] 2 PLR 27, [1991] COD 264, [1991] JPL 643:	160
R v Poplar Coroner, ex p Thomas [1993] QB 610, [1993] 2 All ER 381, [1993] 2 WLR 547, CA	89
R v Port of London Authority, ex p Kynoch Ltd [1919] 1 KB 176, 16 LGR 937, 83 JP 41, 88 LJKB 553, 120 LT 177, 35 TLR 103, CA	79
R v Preston Supplementary Benefits Appeal Tribunal, ex p Moore [1975] 2 All ER 807, [1975] 1 WLR 624, 119 Sol Jo 285, CA	152
R v Race Relations Board, ex p Selvarajan. See Selvarajan v Race Relations Board	
R v Registrar General, ex p Smith [1991] 2 QB 393, [1991] 2 All ER 88, [1991] 2 WLR 782, [1991] FCR 403, [1991] 1 FLR 255, 135 Sol Jo 52, CA	84
R v Registrar of Companies, ex p Central Bank of India [1986] QB 1114, [1986] 1 All ER 105, [1986] 2 WLR 177, [1985] BCLC 465, 129 Sol Jo 755, CA	85, 145, 158
R v Registrar of Trade Marks, ex p Adidas Fabrique de Chaussures de Sport (2 March 1983, unreported)	84
R v Rochdale Metropolitan Council, ex p Schemet (1992) 91 LGR 425, [1993] 1 FCR 306, [1993] COD 113	124
R v Royal Life Saving Society, ex p Howe [1990] COD 440	78
R v St Edmundsbury and Ipswich Diocese Chancellor, ex p White [1948] 1 KB 195, [1947] 2 All ER 170, 91 Sol Jo 369, 177 LT 488, 63 TLR 523, CA	77
R v Sandhutton Parish Council, ex p Todd [1992] COD 409	178, 185
R v Secretary of State for Defence, ex p Equal Opportunities Commission [1992] COD 276, Independent, 27 February	81, 161
R v Secretary of State for Defence, ex p Sancto [1993] COD 144, 5 Admin LR 673, (1992) Times, 9 September	160
R v Secretary of State for Education, ex p J [1993] COD 146	184
R v Secretary of State for Education and Science, ex p Avon County Council (1990) 88 LGR 716	130
R v Secretary of State for Education and Science, ex p Avon County Council (No 2) (1990) 88 LGR 737n, CA	130
R v Secretary of State for Education and Science, ex p Birmingham District Council (1984) 83 LGR 79	80
R v Secretary of State for Education and Science, ex p Davis [1989] 2 FLR 190, [1989] Fam Law 319	128
R v Secretary of State for Education and Science, ex p E [1993] 2 FCR 753, [1992] 1 FLR 377, [1992] Fam Law 189, CA	128
R v Secretary of State for Education and Science, ex p Inner London Education Authority (1990) Times, 17 May, CA	130

	PAGE
R v Secretary of State for Education and Science, ex p Newham London Borough Council [1991] COD 279	130
R v Secretary of State for Education and Science, ex p P (1992) Times, 13 March	128
R v Secretary of State for Education and Science, ex p Talmud Torah Machzikei Haddass School Trust (1985) Times, 12 April	123
R v Secretary of State for Education and Science, ex p Threapleton [1988] COD 102, (1988) Times, 2 June	130, 179, 210
R v Secretary of State for Employment, ex p Equal Opportunities Commission [1993] 1 All ER 1022, [1993] 1 WLR 872, [1993] 1 CMLR 915, [1993] ICR 251, [1993] IRLR 10, [1993] NLJR 332n, CA; on appeal [1995] 1 AC 1, [1994] 2 WLR 409, [1995] 1 CMLR 391, 92 LGR 360, [1994] IRLR 176, [1994] 18 LS Gaz R 43, [1994] NLJR 358, sub nom Equal Opportunities Commission v Secretary of State for Employment [1994] 1 All ER 910, [1994] ICR 317, HL	81, 161, 162, 171
R v Secretary of State for Foreign Affairs, ex p World Development Movement Ltd [1995] 1 All ER 611, [1995] 1 WLR 386, [1995] NLJR 51	162
R v Secretary of State for Foreign and Commonwealth Affairs, ex p Everett [1989] QB 811, [1989] 1 All ER 655, [1989] 2 WLR 224, [1989] Imm AR 155, 133 Sol Jo 151, [1989] 8 LS Gaz R 43, CA	84, 119
R v Secretary of State for Health, ex p United States Tobacco International Inc [1992] QB 353, [1992] 1 All ER 212, [1991] 3 WLR 529	104, 113, 198, 200
R v Secretary of State for Social Services, ex p Association of Metropolitan Authorities [1986] 1 All ER 164, [1986] 1 WLR 1, 83 LGR 796, 130 Sol Jo 35	80, 102, 103
R v Secretary of State for Social Services, ex p Child Poverty Action Group [1990] 2 QB 540, [1989] 1 All ER 1047, [1989] 3 WLR 1116, CA	151, 161, 162
R v Secretary of State for Social Services, ex p Connolly [1986] 1 All ER 998, [1986] 1 WLR 421, 130 Sol Jo 205, [1986] LS Gaz R 786, CA	154, 166
R v Secretary of State for Social Services, ex p Stitt [1991] COD 68, [1991] 3 Admin LR 169, CA	154
R v Secretary of State for Trade, ex p Perestrello [1981] QB 19, [1980] 3 All ER 28, [1980] 3 WLR 1, 124 Sol Jo 63	106, 145
R v Secretary of State for Trade and Industry, ex p Vardy [1993] ICR 720, sub nom R v British Coal Corpn and Secretary of State for Trade and Industry, ex p Vardy [1993] IRLR 104	86
R v Secretary of State for Transport, ex p APH Road Safety Ltd [1993] COD 150	184
R v Secretary of State for Transport, ex p Factortame Ltd (No 2) [1991] 1 AC 603, [1990] 3 WLR 818, [1990] 3 CMLR 375, [1990] 2 Lloyd's Rep 365n, [1991] 1 Lloyd's Rep 10, 134 Sol Jo 1189, [1990] 41 LS Gaz R 36, [1990] NLJR 1457, sub nom Factortame Ltd v Secretary of State for Transport (No 2) [1991] 1 All ER 70, HL	21, 171
R v Secretary of State for Transport, ex p Factortame Ltd (No 3): C-221/89 [1992] QB 680, [1991] 3 All ER 769, [1992] 3 WLR 288, [1991] ECR I-3905, [1991] 3 CMLR 589, [1991] 2 Lloyd's Rep 648, [1991] NLJR 1107, ECJ	172
R v Secretary of State for Transport, ex p Greater London Council [1986] QB 556, [1985] 3 All ER 300, [1985] 3 WLR 574, 129 Sol Jo 590	112
R v Secretary of State for Transport, ex p Pegasus Holdings (London) Ltd [1989] 2 All ER 481, [1988] 1 WLR 990, 132 Sol Jo 1182, [1988] 36 LS Gaz R 41, 1 S & B AvR II/1	113
R v Secretary of State for the Environment, ex p Brent London Borough Council [1982] QB 593, [1983] 3 All ER 321, [1982] 2 WLR 693, 80 LGR 357, 126 Sol Jo 118, [1981] RVR 279	79, 116
R v Secretary of State for the Environment, ex p British Telecommunications plc [1991] RA 307, [1991] NPC 93	99
R v Secretary of State for the Environment, ex p Doncaster Borough Council [1990] COD 441	184
R v Secretary of State for the Environment, ex p Hackney London Borough Council [1983] 3 All ER 358, [1983] 1 WLR 524, 81 LGR 688, 127 Sol Jo 224; affd [1984] 1 All ER 956, [1984] 1 WLR 592, 128 Sol Jo 280, CA	188
R v Secretary of State for the Environment, ex p Hammersmith and Fulham London Borough Council [1991] 1 AC 521, [1990] 3 WLR 898, 89 LGR 129, [1990] NLJR 1422, [1990] RVR 188, sub nom Hammersmith and Fulham London Borough Council v Secretary of State for the Environment [1990] 3 All ER 589, 134 Sol Jo 1226, HL	112, 187
R v Secretary of State for the Environment, ex p Islington London Borough Council [1992] COD 67, [1991] NPC 90, CA	184
R v Secretary of State for the Environment, ex p Kirkstall Valley Campaign Ltd [1996] 3 All ER 304, [1996] NLJR 478	106
R v Secretary of State for the Environment, ex p Lancashire County Council [1994] 4 All ER 165, 93 LGR 29, [1994] 9 LS Gaz R 40, 138 Sol Jo LB 53	115

TABLE OF CASES

PAGE

R v Secretary of State for the Environment, ex p Rose Theatre Trust Co [1990] 1 QB 504, [1990] 1 All ER 754, [1990] 2 WLR 186, 59 P & CR 257, 134 Sol Jo 425, [1990] JPL 360	85, 159, 160, 162
R v Secretary of State for the Environment, ex p Tower Hamlets London Borough Council [1993] QB 632, [1993] 3 All ER 439, [1993] 3 WLR 32, 25 HLR 524, [1993] Imm AR 495, CA	81, 120
R v Secretary of State for the Environment, ex p Ward [1984] 2 All ER 556, [1984] 1 WLR 834, 82 LGR 628, 48 P & CR 212, 128 Sol Jo 415, [1984] LS Gaz R 2148, [1984] JPL 90	160
R v Secretary of State for the Home Department, ex p Al-Nafeesi [1990] COD 106	183
R v Secretary of State for the Home Department, ex p Angur Begum [1989] COD 398, [1989] CLY 3011, CA	183
R v Secretary of State for the Home Department, ex p Benson [1989] COD 329, (1988) Times, 8 November	135
R v Secretary of State for the Home Department, ex p Brind [1991] 1 AC 696, [1991] 2 WLR 588, 135 Sol Jo 250, sub nom Brind v Secretary of State for the Home Department [1991] 1 All ER 720, HL	112, 113
R v Secretary of State for the Home Department, ex p Brown (1984) Times, 6 February	186
R v Secretary of State for the Home Department, ex p Capti-Mehmet [1997] COD 61	166
R v Secretary of State for the Home Department, ex p Causabon-Vincent (1996) Times, 19 July	134
R v Secretary of State for the Home Department, ex p Chahal [1995] 1 All ER 658, [1995] 1 WLR 526, [1994] Imm AR 107, [1992] COD 214, [1993] 46 LS Gaz R 38, 137 Sol Jo LB 255, CA	113, 119
R v Secretary of State for the Home Department, ex p Cheblak [1991] 2 All ER 319, [1991] 1 WLR 890, CA	104, 105
R v Secretary of State for the Home Department, ex p Cox [1992] COD 72, (1991) Times, 10 September	112, 113
R v Secretary of State for the Home Department, ex p Creamer [1993] COD 162, (1992) Independent, 23 October	134
R v Secretary of State for the Home Department, ex p D (1996) Times, 10 May, CA	143
R v Secretary of State for the Home Department, ex p Darendranath Doorga [1990] COD 109	183
R v Secretary of State for the Home Department, ex p Doody [1993] QB 157, [1993] 1 All ER 151, [1992] 3 WLR 956, CA; affd [1994] 1 AC 531, [1993] 3 WLR 154, [1993] NLJR 991, sub nom Doody v Secretary of State for the Home Department [1993] 3 All ER 92, HL	115, 131
R v Secretary of State for the Home Department, ex p Fayed [1997] 1 All ER 228, [1998] 1 WLR 763, CA	108
R v Secretary of State for the Home Department, ex p Handscomb (1987) 86 Cr App Rep 59, 131 Sol Jo 326, [1987] LS Gaz R 1328	135
R v Secretary of State for the Home Department, ex p Herbage (No 2) [1987] QB 1077, [1987] 1 All ER 324, [1987] 2 WLR 226, 131 Sol Jo 134, [1986] LS Gaz R 3836, CA	136
R v Secretary of State for the Home Department, ex p Hosenball [1977] 3 All ER 452, [1977] 1 WLR 766, 141 JP 626, 121 Sol Jo 255, CA	104
R v Secretary of State for the Home Department, ex p K [1991] 1 QB 270, [1990] 3 All ER 562, [1990] 3 WLR 755, 134 Sol Jo 1106, CA	142, 143
R v Secretary of State for the Home Department, ex p Leech [1994] QB 198, [1993] 4 All ER 539, CA	133
R v Secretary of State for the Home Department, ex p McAvoy [1984] 3 All ER 417, [1984] 1 WLR 1408, 128 Sol Jo 646	133
R v Secretary of State for the Home Department, ex p McAvoy [1998] 1 WLR 790, [1998] 01 LS Gaz R 23, 142 Sol Jo LB 39, CA	105
R v Secretary of State for the Home Department, ex p Mughal [1974] QB 313, [1973] 3 All ER 796, [1973] 3 WLR 647, 137 JP 846, 117 Sol Jo 680, CA	105
R v Secretary of State for the Home Department, ex p Nwanurue [1992] Imm AR 39	110
R v Secretary of State for the Home Department, ex p Oladehinde [1991] 1 AC 254, [1990] 3 WLR 797, 134 Sol Jo 1264, [1990] 41 LS Gaz R 36, [1990] NLJR 1498, sub nom Oladehinde v Secretary of State for the Home Department [1990] 3 All ER 393, HL	115
R v Secretary of State for the Home Department, ex p P [1992] COD 295	119
R v Secretary of State for the Home Department, ex p Phansopkar [1976] QB 606, [1975] 3 All ER 497, [1975] 3 WLR 322, 119 Sol Jo 507; on appeal [1976] QB 606, [1975] 3 All ER 497, [1975] 3 WLR 322, 139 JP 813, 119 Sol Jo 507, CA	79

TABLE OF CASES

	PAGE
R v Secretary of State for the Home Department, ex p Prem Singh [1993] COD 501, (1993) Times, 27 April, Independent, 11 July	134
R v Secretary of State for the Home Department, ex p Ruddock [1987] 2 All ER 518, [1987] 1 WLR 1482, 131 Sol Jo 1551, [1987] LS Gaz R 3335	104, 164
R v Secretary of State for the Home Department, ex p Rukshanda Begum [1990] Imm AR 1, [1990] COD 107, CA	179
R v Secretary of State for the Home Department, ex p Sinclair [1992] Imm AR 293	108
R v Secretary of State for the Home Department, ex p Sivakumaran [1988] AC 958, [1988] 1 All ER 193, [1988] 2 WLR 92, [1988] Imm AR 147, 132 Sol Jo 22, [1988] 6 LS Gaz R 37, [1987] NLJ Rep 1206, HL	179
R v Secretary of State for the Home Department, ex p Swati [1986] 1 All ER 717, [1986] 1 WLR 477, [1986] Imm AR 88, 130 Sol Jo 186, [1986] LS Gaz R 780, [1986] NLJ Rep 189, CA	119, 166
R v Secretary of State for the Home Department, ex p Tarrant [1985] QB 251, [1984] 1 All ER 799, [1984] 2 WLR 613, 128 Sol Jo 223, [1984] LS Gaz R 1045	132, 204
R v Secretary of State for the Home Department, ex p Thompson [1997] 3 All ER 97, [1997] 3 WLR 23, [1997] 34 LS Gaz R 27, [1997] NLJR 955, HL	134
R v Secretary of State for the Home Department, ex p Turkoglu [1988] QB 398, [1987] 2 All ER 823, [1987] 3 WLR 992, [1987] Imm AR 484, 131 Sol Jo 1186, [1987] LS Gaz R 2692, CA	119, 182
R v Secretary of State for the Home Department, ex p Uzoenyi [1992] COD 217	119, 213
R v Secretary of State for the Home Department, ex p Venables [1997] 3 All ER 97, [1997] 3 WLR 23, [1997] 34 LS Gaz R 27, [1997] NLJR 955, HL	134
R v Secretary of State for the Home Department, ex p Wynne [1992] QB 406, [1992] 2 All ER 301, [1992] 2 WLR 564, CA; affd sub nom Wynne v Secretary of State for the Home Department [1993] 1 All ER 574, sub nom R v Secretary of State for the Home Department, ex p Wynne [1993] 1 WLR 115, [1993] 11 LS Gaz R 43, 137 Sol Jo LB 38, HL	133
R v Secretary of State for the Home Office, ex p Attiror (1987) Independent, 23 October, CA:	166
R v Secretary of State for Wales, ex p Rozhon (1993) 91 LGR 667, CA	179
R v Sevenoaks General Comrs and IRC, ex p Thorne [1989] STC 560, 62 TC 341, [1989] 25 LS Gaz R 44	149
R v Sheffield City Council, ex p Chadwick (1985) 84 LGR 563	108
R v Showmen's Guild of Great Britain, ex p Print CO 2014/96 (31 July 1997, unreported)	78, 85
R v Social Fund Inspector, ex p Ali [1993] COD 263, (1992) Times, 25 November	154
R v Social Fund Inspector and Secretary of State for Social Services, ex p Healey, Stitt (No 2), Ellison [1992] COD 335, [1992] 4 Admin LR 713, CA	154
R v Social Security Comr, ex p Akbar [1991] COD 245, [1992] 4 LS Gaz R 34, 135 Sol Jo LB 214	154
R v Social Security Comr, ex p Pattni [1993] Fam Law 214, CA	154
R v Solicitor General, ex p Taylor and Taylor [1996] 1 FCR 206, [1996] COD 61	77
R v Somerset County Council and ARC Southern Ltd, ex p Dixon (1997) 75 P & CR 175, [1997] COD 323, [1997] NPC 61	160
R v Special Educational Needs Tribunal, ex p Fairpo [1996] ELR 213, [1996] COD 180	166
R v Statutory Committee of the Pharmaceutical Society, ex p Lewis and Jeffreys Ltd (20 December 1982, unreported)	84
R v Stratford-on-Avon District Council, ex p Jackson [1985] 3 All ER 769, [1985] 1 WLR 1319, 84 LGR 287, 51 P & CR 76, 129 Sol Jo 854, [1985] LS Gaz R 3533, CA	164
R v Supreme Court Taxing Office, ex p John Singh & Co (1995) Times, 3 May, [1995] 7 Admin LR 849	86
R v Sussex Justices, ex p McCarthy [1924] 1 KB 256, 22 LGR 46, 88 JP 3, 93 LJKB 129, [1923] All ER Rep 233, 68 Sol Jo 253, sub nom R v Hurst, ex p McCarthy 27 Cox CC 590, 130 LT 510, 40 TLR 80	106
R v Swale Borough Council, ex p Royal Society for the Protection of Birds [1991] 1 PLR 6, [1991] JPL 39	179
R v Tameside Metropolitan Borough Council, ex p Governors of Audenshaw High School (1990) Times, 27 June	130
R v Test Valley Borough Council, ex p Goodman [1992] COD 101	179
R v Thames Magistrates' Court, ex p Polemis [1974] 2 All ER 1219, [1974] 1 WLR 1371, [1974] 2 Lloyd's Rep 16, 138 JP 672, 118 Sol Jo 734, DC	105
R v Torbay Borough Council, ex p Cleasby [1991] COD 142, CA	104
R v Tower Hamlets, ex p Tower Hamlets Combined Traders Association [1994] COD 325	162
R v Tower Hamlets London Borough Council, ex p Ali (1993) 25 HLR 218	179

TABLE OF CASES xlvii

PAGE

R v Tower Hamlets London Borough Council, ex p Ferdous Begum [1993] AC 509, [1993] 2 WLR 609, 91 LGR 287, [1993] 2 FCR 133, 25 HLR 319, [1993] 26 LS Gaz R 38, [1993] NLJR 437, sub nom Garlick v Oldham Metropolitan Borough Council [1993] 2 All ER 65, HL 94
R v Tower Hamlets London Borough Council, ex p Thrasyvalou (1990) 23 HLR 38, [1991] COD 123 160
R v Trafford Borough Council, ex p Colonel Foods Ltd [1990] COD 351 188
R v Trent Regional Health Authority, ex p Jones (1986) Times, 19 June 88
R v University of Liverpool, ex p Caesar-Gordon [1991] 1 QB 124, [1990] 3 All ER 821, [1990] 3 WLR 667 .... 84, 87, 130
R v Vaccine Damage Tribunal, ex p Loveday (1984) Times, 10 November; affd [1985] 2 Lancet 1137, CA 77
R v Visitors to the Inns of Court, ex p Calder [1994] QB 1, [1993] 2 All ER 876, [1993] 3 WLR 287, CA 79, 85, 100
R v Waltham Forest London Borough Council, ex p Baxter [1988] QB 419, [1987] 3 All ER 671, [1988] 2 WLR 257, 86 LGR 254, 132 Sol Jo 227, [1988] LS Gaz R 36, [1987] NLJ Rep 947, [1988] RVR 6, CA 185
R v Warwickshire County Council, ex p Dill-Russell (1990) 89 LGR 640, [1991] 3 Admin LR 1; affd (1990) 89 LGR 640, CA 124
R v Wessex Mental Health Review Tribunal, ex p Wiltshire County Council (1989) 4 BMLR 145, CA 142
R v West Norfolk Valuation Panel, ex p H Prins Ltd (1975) 73 LGR 206, [1975] RA 101, 285 Estates Gazette 375 79
R v Westminster City Council, ex p Augustin [1993] 1 WLR 730, 91 LGR 89, CA 81
R v Westminster City Council, ex p Residents Association of Mayfair [1991] COD 182 .... 179, 184
R v Wolverhampton Coroner, ex p McCurbin [1990] 2 All ER 759, [1990] 1 WLR 719, 155 JP 33, CA 89
R v Wycombe District Council, ex p Bruce [1990] COD 353 184
R v Yorkshire Purchasing Organisation, ex p British Educational Suppliers Ltd [1998] ELR 195, CA 99
Racal Communications Ltd, Re [1981] AC 374, [1980] 2 All ER 634, [1980] 3 WLR 181, 124 Sol Jo 495, HL 157, 158
Racz v Home Office (1992) Times, 17 December, CA; revsd [1994] 2 AC 45, [1994] 1 All ER 97, [1994] 2 WLR 23, [1994] NLJR 89, 138 Sol Jo LB 12, HL 136
Radstock Co-operative and Industrial Society v Norton-Radstock UDC [1967] Ch 1094, [1967] 2 All ER 812, [1967] 3 WLR 588, 65 LGR 518, 131 JP 387, 111 Sol Jo 398, 202 Estates Gazette 1017; affd [1968] Ch 605, [1968] 2 All ER 59, [1968] 2 WLR 1214, 66 LGR 457, 132 JP 238, 112 Sol Jo 135, 205 Estates Gazette 991, CA 13, 16, 48
Ramage v Womack [1900] 1 QB 116, 69 LJQB 40, 81 LT 526, 16 TLR 63 15
Rask and Christensen v ISS Kantineservice A/S: C-209/91 [1992] ECR I-5755, [1993] IRLR 133, ECJ 172
Rawlplug Co Ltd v Kamvale Properties Ltd (1968) 20 P & CR 32, 112 Sol Jo 723, 208 Estates Gazette 147 260
Raymond v Honey [1983] 1 AC 1, [1982] 1 All ER 756, [1982] 2 WLR 465, 75 Cr App Rep 16, 126 Sol Jo 188, HL 113, 131, 133
Receiving Order (in Bankruptcy), Re [1947] Ch 498, [1947] 1 All ER 843, [1948] LJR 38, 91 Sol Jo 338, 177 LT 397 226
Regan & Blackburn Ltd v Rogers [1985] 2 All ER 180, [1985] 1 WLR 870, 50 P & CR 58, 129 Sol Jo 449, [1985] LS Gaz R 2740 225
Reid, Hewitt & Co v Joseph [1918] AC 717, 88 LJKB 1, 62 Sol Jo 715, 119 LT 688, HL 6
Richards v Naum [1967] 1 QB 620, [1966] 3 All ER 812, [1966] 3 WLR 1113, 110 Sol Jo 794, CA 16, 24
Ridge v Baldwin [1964] AC 40, [1963] 2 All ER 66, [1963] 2 WLR 935, 61 LGR 369, 127 JP 295, 107 Sol Jo 313, HL 88, 165
Rignall Developments Ltd v Halil [1988] Ch 190, [1987] 3 All ER 170, [1987] 3 WLR 394, 54 P & CR 245, 20 HLR 7, 131 Sol Jo 1039, [1987] 1 EGLR 193, [1987] LS Gaz R 2273, 282 Estates Gazette 1414 231
Roberts v Hopwood [1925] AC 578, 23 LGR 337, 89 JP 105, 94 LJKB 542, [1925] All ER Rep 24, 69 Sol Jo 475, 133 LT 289, 41 TLR 436, HL 99, 111
Rooke's Case (1598) 5 Co Rep 99b 111
Rossage v Rossage [1960] 1 All ER 600, [1960] 1 WLR 249, 104 Sol Jo 231, CA 23
Roy v Kensington and Chelsea and Westminster Family Practitioner Committee [1992] 1 AC 624, [1992] 1 All ER 705, [1992] 2 WLR 239, [1992] IRLR 233, 8 BMLR 9, [1992] 17 LS Gaz R 48, 136 Sol Jo LB 62, HL 84, 89, 94

TABLE OF CASES

PAGE

Royal College of Nursing of the United Kingdom v Department of Health and Social Security [1981] AC 800, [1981] 1 All ER 545, [1981] 2 WLR 279, 125 Sol Jo 149, 1 BMLR 40, HL 162
Royster v Cavey [1947] KB 204, [1946] 2 All ER 642, [1947] LJR 149, 90 Sol Jo 584, 176 LT 16, 62 TLR 709, CA 21
Russian Commercial and Industrial Bank v British Bank for Foreign Trade Ltd [1921] 2 AC 438, 90 LJKB 1089, [1921] All ER Rep 329, 65 Sol Jo 733, 126 LT 35, 37 TLR 919, HL . . 81
Rye (Dennis) Pension Fund Trustees v Sheffield City Council [1997] 4 All ER 747, [1998] 1 WLR 840, CA 93

Sagnata Investments Ltd v Norwich Corpn [1971] 2 QB 614, [1971] 2 All ER 1441, [1971] 3 WLR 133, 69 LGR 471, 115 Sol Jo 406, CA 109
Sampson v Crown Court at Croydon [1987] 1 All ER 609, 84 Cr App Rep 376, 131 Sol Jo 225, [1987] LS Gaz R 825, [1987] NLJ Rep 169, sub nom Re Sampson [1987] 1 WLR 194, HL 90
Schmidt v Secretary of State for Home Affairs [1969] 2 Ch 149, [1969] 1 All ER 904, [1969] 2 WLR 337, 133 JP 274, 113 Sol Jo 16, CA 104
Schooley v Nye [1950] 1 KB 335, [1949] 2 All ER 950, 93 Sol Jo 791, 66 (pt 1) TLR 3, CA . . 35
Scottish Old People's Welfare Council ("Age Concern"), Petitioners 1987 SLT 179 162
Sea View Gardens, Re, Claridge v Tingey [1966] 3 All ER 935, [1967] 1 WLR 134, 110 Sol Jo 567 282
Secretary of State for Education and Science v Tameside Metropolitan Borough Council [1977] AC 1014, [1976] 3 All ER 665, [1976] 3 WLR 641, 75 LGR 190, 120 Sol Jo 735, HL 100, 111
Secretary of State for Employment v Globe Elastic Thread Co Ltd [1980] AC 506, [1979] 2 All ER 1077, [1979] 3 WLR 143, [1979] ICR 706, [1979] IRLR 327, 123 Sol Jo 504, HL 117
Secretary of State for the Environment v Essex, Goodman & Suggitt [1986] 2 All ER 69, [1986] 1 WLR 1432, 4 Con LR 104, 130 Sol Jo 574, [1985] 2 EGLR 168, [1986] LS Gaz R 2755, 32 BLR 140, 276 Estates Gazette 308, 1 Const LJ 302 14
Secretary of State for the Home Department v Hastrup [1996] Imm AR 616, CA 115
Secretary of State for the Home Department v Mental Health Review Tribunal for Mersey Regional Health Authority [1986] 3 All ER 233, [1986] 1 WLR 1170, 130 Sol Jo 697, [1986] LS Gaz R 3001 143
Secretary of State for the Home Department v Mental Health Review Tribunal for Wales [1986] 3 All ER 233, [1986] 1 WLR 1170, 130 Sol Jo 697, [1986] LS Gaz R 3001 143
Seldon v Davidson [1968] 2 All ER 755, [1968] 1 WLR 1083, 112 Sol Jo 463, CA 17
Selim Ltd v Bickenhall Engineering Ltd [1981] 3 All ER 210, [1981] 1 WLR 1318, 43 P & CR 186, 259 Estates Gazette 1073 225
Selvarajan v Race Relations Board [1976] 1 All ER 12, sub nom R v Race Relations Board, ex p Selvarajan [1975] 1 WLR 1686, [1975] IRLR 281, 119 Sol Jo 644, CA 115
Shah v Barnet London Borough Council [1983] 2 AC 309, [1983] 1 All ER 226, [1983] 2 WLR 16, 81 LGR 305, 127 Sol Jo 36, HL 129
Short v Tower Hamlets London Borough Council (1985) 18 HLR 171, CA 102, 103
Silver v United Kingdom (1983) 5 EHRR 347 135
Silvestri v Crawley Borough Council [1980] QB 460, [1980] 1 All ER 913, [1980] 2 WLR 664, [1980] 1 CMLR 437, 78 LGR 180, 124 Sol Jo 82, CA 120
Smalley, Re [1985] AC 622, [1985] 2 WLR 538, 80 Cr App Rep 205, 149 JP 319, [1985] Crim LR 371, 129 Sol Jo 172, [1985] LS Gaz R 1638, [1985] NLJ Rep 229, sub nom Smalley v Crown Court at Warwick [1985] 1 All ER 769, HL 79, 90
Smith v Cardiff Corpn (No 2) [1955] Ch 159, [1955] 1 All ER 113, [1955] 2 WLR 126, 53 LGR 176, 119 JP 128, 99 Sol Jo 76 111
Smith v Croft (No 2) [1988] Ch 114, [1987] 3 All ER 909, [1987] 3 WLR 405, [1987] BCLC 206, 355, 3 BCC 218, 131 Sol Jo 1038, [1987] LS Gaz R 2449 . . . . 15, 24
Smith v East Elloe RDC [1956] AC 736, [1956] 1 All ER 855, [1956] 2 WLR 888, 54 LGR 233, 6 P & CR 102, 120 JP 263, 100 Sol Jo 282, HL 156
Smith v Hargrove (1885) 16 QBD 183, 34 WR 294 10
Smith Kline & French Laboratories Ltd, Re [1990] 1 AC 64, [1989] 2 WLR 397, [1989] 17 LS Gaz R 42, sub nom Smith Kline & French Laboratories Ltd v Licensing Authority (Generics (UK) Ltd intervening) [1989] 1 All ER 578, 133 Sol Jo 263, HL 84
Société Cooperative Sidmetal v Titan International Ltd [1966] 1 QB 828, [1965] 3 All ER 494, [1965] 3 WLR 847, [1965] 2 Lloyd's Rep 313, 109 Sol Jo 777 28

TABLE OF CASES xlix

	PAGE
Solihull Metropolitan Borough Council v Maxfern Ltd [1977] 2 All ER 177, [1977] 1 WLR 127, 75 LGR 327, 141 JP 309, 120 Sol Jo 802	161
South East Asia Fire Bricks Sdn Bhd v Non-Metallic Mineral Products Manufacturing Employees Union [1981] AC 363, [1980] 2 All ER 689, [1980] 3 WLR 318, 124 Sol Jo 496, PC	157
South Oxfordshire District Council v Secretary of State for the Environment [1981] 1 All ER 954, [1981] 1 WLR 1092, 125 Sol Jo 444	109
South Yorkshire Transport Ltd v Monopolies and Mergers Commission [1993] 1 All ER 289, [1993] NLJR 128, sub nom R v Monopolies and Mergers Commission, ex p South Yorkshire Transport Ltd [1993] 1 WLR 23, [1993] BCC 111, HL	77, 84
Sowerby v Sowerby (1982) 44 P & CR 192	225
Standard Property Investment plc v British Plastics Federation (1985) 53 P & CR 25	229
State Bank of India v Murjani Marketing Group Ltd (27 March 1991, unreported)	21
Stevens v Chown [1901] 1 Ch 894, 65 JP 470, 70 LJ Ch 571, 49 WR 460, 84 LT 796, 17 TLR 313	17
Stevens v William Nash Ltd [1966] 3 All ER 156, [1966] 1 WLR 1550, 110 Sol Jo 710, CA	10
Stichting (Dr Sophie Redmond) v Bartol: C-29/91 [1992] ECR I-3189, [1992] IRLR 366, ECJ	172
Stockler v Fourways Estates Ltd [1983] 3 All ER 501, [1984] 1 WLR 25, 127 Sol Jo 823, [1984] LS Gaz R 359	220, 227
Stoke-on-Trent City Council v B & Q plc: C-169/91 [1993] AC 900, [1993] 1 All ER 481, [1993] 2 WLR 730, [1992] ECR I-6635, [1993] 1 CMLR 426, 91 LGR 237, ECJ; affd sub nom Stoke-on-Trent City Council v B & Q plc [1993] AC 900, [1993] 2 All ER 297n, [1993] 2 WLR 730, [1993] 2 CMLR 509, 91 LGR 237, 137 Sol Jo LB 120, HL	172
Strand Securities Ltd v Caswell [1965] Ch 958, [1965] 1 All ER 820, [1965] 2 WLR 958, 109 Sol Jo 131, 193 Estates Gazette 633, CA	258
Strathblaine Estates Ltd, Re [1948] Ch 228, [1948] 1 All ER 162, [1948] LJR 905, 92 Sol Jo 54, 64 TLR 178	259
Sullivan v West Yorkshire Passenger Transport Executive [1985] 2 All ER 134, CA	18
Sumner v William Henderson & Sons Ltd [1963] 2 All ER 712n, [1963] 1 WLR 823, [1963] 1 Lloyd's Rep 537, 107 Sol Jo 436, CA	16, 21
Tanks and Drums Ltd v Transport and General Workers' Union [1992] ICR 1, [1991] IRLR 372, 135 Sol Jo LB 68, CA	115
Tarn, Re, ex p Tarn [1893] 2 Ch 280, 57 JP 789, 9 TLR 489, CA	26
Taylor v Brighton and Hove County Council (18 August 1997, unreported)	121
Taylor v Taylor [1968] 1 All ER 843, [1968] 1 WLR 378, 19 P & CR 193, 112 Sol Jo 111, CA:	226
Teh Cheng Poh (alias Char Meh) v Public Prosecutor, Malaysia [1980] AC 458, [1979] 2 WLR 623, [1979] Crim LR 180, 125 Sol Jo 16, PC	79
Tehrani v Rostron [1972] 1 QB 182, [1971] 3 All ER 790, [1971] 3 WLR 612, 136 JP 40, 115 Sol Jo 641, CA	155
Thomas v Chief Adjudication Officer [1991] 2 QB 164, [1991] 3 All ER 315, [1991] 2 WLR 886, sub nom Thomas v Adjudication Officer and Secretary of State for Social Security [1990] 3 CMLR 611, [1990] IRLR 436, CA; on appeal sub nom Thomas v Chief Adjudication Officer: C-328/91 [1993] QB 747, [1993] 3 WLR 581, [1993] ECR I-1247, [1993] ICR 673, sub nom Secretary of State for Social Security v Thomas [1993] 4 All ER 556, [1993] IRLR 292, ECJ	169
Thomas v Rose [1968] 3 All ER 765, [1968] 1 WLR 1797, 20 P & CR 13, 112 Sol Jo 907	224
Thomas v University of Bradford (No 2) [1992] 1 All ER 964	129
Thorne v Sevenoaks General Comrs and IRC [1989] STC 560, 62 TC 341, [1989] 25 LS Gaz R 44	145
Thornton v Kirklees Metropolitan Borough Council [1979] QB 626, [1979] 2 All ER 349, [1979] 3 WLR 1, 77 LGR 417, 144 JP 15, 123 Sol Jo 285, CA	94
Thynne, Wilson and Gunnell v United Kingdom (1990) 13 EHRR 666, ECtHR	134
Tilling v Whiteman [1980] AC 1, [1979] 1 All ER 737, [1979] 2 WLR 401, 38 P & CR 341, 123 Sol Jo 202, 250 Estates Gazette 51, HL	24
Tiverton Estates Ltd v Wearwell Ltd [1975] Ch 146, [1974] 1 All ER 209, [1974] 2 WLR 176, 27 P & CR 24, 117 Sol Jo 913, 228 Estates Gazette 1213, CA	260
Topham v Duke of Portland (1863) 1 De GJ & Sm 517, 32 LJ Ch 257, 1 New Rep 496, 11 WR 507, 8 LT 180; on appeal sub nom Portland (Duke of) v Lady Topham (1864) 11 HL Cas 32, 34 LJ Ch 113, 10 Jur NS 501, 12 WR 697, [1861-73] All ER Rep 980, 10 LT 355	34, 62
Tower Hamlets London Borough Council v Abdi (1992) 91 LGR 300, 25 HLR 80, [1993] 1 EGLR 68, [1993] 06 EG 102, CA	95
Trent Bridge Buildings, Re, Hallam v Burrows (1948, unreported 1948/H/2020)	236

TABLE OF CASES

	PAGE
Tucker v British Museum Trustees (1967) Times, 22 April; affd (1967) 112 Sol Jo 70, CA	16
Tyldesley v Tyldesley (1940, unreported 1940/T/1606)	51
United Bank of Kuwait plc v Sahib [1995] 2 All ER 973, [1995] 2 WLR 94, [1996] 1 FLR 379, [1996] Fam Law 87; affd [1997] Ch 107, [1996] 3 All ER 215, [1996] 3 WLR 372, 73 P & CR 177, [1996] 2 FLR 666, [1997] Fam Law 17, [1996] NPC 12, CA 275, 292	
Van Duyn v Home Office: 41/74 [1975] Ch 358, [1975] 3 All ER 190, [1975] 2 WLR 760, [1974] ECR 1337, [1975] 1 CMLR 1, 119 Sol Jo 302, ECJ	169
Vilvarajah v United Kingdom (1991) 14 EHRR 248, ECtHR	119
Vine v National Dock Labour Board [1957] AC 488, [1956] 3 All ER 939, [1957] 2 WLR 106, [1956] 2 Lloyd's Rep 567, 101 Sol Jo 86, HL 88, 115	
Von Colson and Kamann v Land Nordrhein-Westfalen: 14/83 [1984] ECR 1891, [1986] 2 CMLR 430, 134 NLJ 473, ECJ	168
W (an infant), Re [1971] AC 682, [1971] 2 All ER 49, [1971] 2 WLR 1011, 135 JP 259, 115 Sol Jo 286, HL	107
Wagman v Vare Motors Ltd [1959] 3 All ER 326, [1959] 1 WLR 853, 103 Sol Jo 600, CA . . .	12
Waldron, ex p [1986] QB 824, [1985] 3 WLR 1090, 129 Sol Jo 892, [1986] LS Gaz R 199, sub nom R v Hallstrom, ex p W [1985] 3 All ER 775, CA 140, 167	
Wallasey Local Board v Gracey (1887) 36 Ch D 593, 51 JP 740, 56 LJ Ch 739, 35 WR 694, 57 LT 51	161
Walsall Overseers of the Poor v London and North Western Rly Co (1878) 4 App Cas 30, 43 JP 108, 48 LJMC 65, 27 WR 189, 39 LT 453, [1874-80] All ER Rep Ext 1602, HL 30, 32	
Wandsworth London Borough Council v Orakpo (1986) 19 HLR 57, CA	166
Wandsworth London Borough Council v Winder [1985] AC 461, [1984] 3 All ER 976, [1984] 3 WLR 1254, 83 LGR 143, 17 HLR 196, 128 Sol Jo 838, [1985] LS Gaz R 201, [1985] NLJ Rep 381, HL 95, 96	
Waters v Sunday Pictorial Newspapers Ltd [1961] 2 All ER 758, [1961] 1 WLR 967, 105 Sol Jo 492, CA	15
Watt v Kesteven County Council [1955] 1 QB 408, [1955] 1 All ER 473, [1955] 2 WLR 499, 53 LGR 254, 119 JP 220, 99 Sol Jo 149, CA	123
Watts v Waller [1973] QB 153, [1972] 3 All ER 257, [1972] 3 WLR 365, 24 P & CR 39, 116 Sol Jo 599, CA 222, 254, 281	
Waverley Borough Council v Hilden [1988] 1 All ER 807, [1988] 1 WLR 246, 86 LGR 271, 132 Sol Jo 192, [1988] 8 LS Gaz R 36, [1988] JPL 175	95
Webb v O'Doherty (1991) Times, 11 February, [1991] 3 Admin LR 731	99
Webster v Southwark London Borough Council [1983] QB 698, [1983] 2 WLR 217, 81 LGR 357, 127 Sol Jo 53	81
Weight v MacKay [1984] 2 All ER 673, [1984] 1 WLR 980, 79 Cr App Rep 324, 148 JP 673, 128 Sol Jo 515, [1984] LS Gaz R 2769, 134 NLJ 746, HL	77
Wells v Minister of Housing and Local Government [1967] 2 All ER 1041, [1967] 1 WLR 1000, 65 LGR 408, 18 P & CR 401, 131 JP 431, 111 Sol Jo 519, 202 Estates Gazette 1123, CA	117
West Glamorgan County Council v Rafferty [1987] 1 All ER 1005, [1987] 1 WLR 457, 85 LGR 793, 57 P & CR 261, 18 HLR 375, 131 Sol Jo 472, [1987] LS Gaz R 1493, [1988] JPL 169, CA	109
Western Fish Products Ltd v Penwith District Council [1981] 2 All ER 204, 77 LGR 185, 38 P & CR 7, 122 Sol Jo 471, [1978] JPL 623, CA	117
Whall v Bulman [1953] 2 QB 198, [1953] 2 All ER 306, [1953] 3 WLR 116, 97 Sol Jo 437, CA	21
Wheeler v Leicester City Council [1985] AC 1054, [1985] 2 All ER 151, 83 LGR 725, 129 Sol Jo 332, [1985] LS Gaz R 1710, [1985] NLJ Rep 413, CA; revsd [1985] AC 1054, [1985] 2 All ER 1106, [1985] 3 WLR 335, 83 LGR 725, 129 Sol Jo 558, [1985] LS Gaz R 3175, [1985] NLJ Rep 781, HL 99, 100, 111	
White v Brunton [1984] QB 570, [1984] 2 All ER 606, [1984] 3 WLR 105, 128 Sol Jo 434, CA	19
White v Chief Adjudication Officer [1986] 2 All ER 905, 130 Sol Jo 448, [1984] LS Gaz R 1319, CA	152
White Rose Cottage, Re [1964] Ch 483, [1964] 1 All ER 169, [1964] 2 WLR 396, 108 Sol Jo 156, 189 Estates Gazette 19; revsd [1965] Ch 940, [1965] 1 All ER 11, [1965] 2 WLR 337, 108 Sol Jo 917, CA	272
Whittingham v Whittingham [1979] Fam 9, [1978] 3 All ER 805, [1978] 2 WLR 936, 36 P & CR 164, 8 Fam Law 171, 122 Sol Jo 247, CA	225
Williams v Giddy [1911] AC 381, 80 LJPC 102, 104 LT 513, 27 TLR 443	111

TABLE OF CASES li

	PAGE
Williams & Humbert Ltd v W & H Trade Marks (Jersey) Ltd [1986] AC 368, [1986] 1 All ER 129, [1986] 2 WLR 24, 130 Sol Jo 37, [1986] LS Gaz R 37, [1986] NLJ Rep 15, HL	15, 24
Williams and Glyn's Bank Ltd v Boland [1981] AC 487, [1980] 2 All ER 408, [1980] 3 WLR 138, 40 P & CR 451, 124 Sol Jo 443, [1980] RVR 204, HL	259, 274, 313
Willies-Williams v National Trust for Places of Historic Interest or Natural Beauty (1993) 65 P & CR 359, CA	225
Winch v Jones [1986] QB 296, [1985] 3 All ER 97, [1985] 3 WLR 729, 129 Sol Jo 669, CA	141
Windsor Refrigerator Co Ltd v Branch Nominees Ltd [1961] Ch 375, [1961] 1 All ER 277, [1961] 2 WLR 196, 105 Sol Jo 205, CA	16
Wither v Cowie 1991 SLT 401	170
Wood v Ealing London Borough Council [1967] Ch 364, [1966] 3 All ER 514, [1966] 3 WLR 1209, 65 LGR 282, 131 JP 22, 110 Sol Jo 944	123
Woolf Project Management Ltd v Woodtrek Ltd (1987) 56 P & CR 134, [1988] 1 EGLR 179, [1988] 12 EG 111	272
Woolfall v Knowsley Borough Council (1992) Times, 26 June, CA	117
Woolwich Building Society v Dickman [1996] 3 All ER 204, 72 P & CR 470, 28 HLR 661, CA	313
Woolwich Equitable Building Society v IRC [1993] AC 70, [1992] 3 WLR 366, [1992] STC 657, 65 TC 265, [1992] 32 LS Gaz R 38, 136 Sol Jo LB 230, sub nom Woolwich Building Society v IRC (No 2) [1992] 3 All ER 737, HL	147, 149
Wynne v Secretary of State for the Home Department. See R v Secretary of State for the Home Department, ex p Wynne	
Yeoman Credit Ltd v Latter [1961] 2 All ER 294, [1961] 1 WLR 828, 105 Sol Jo 300, CA	8, 16, 35

Decisions of the European Court of Justice are listed below numerically. These decisions are also included in the preceding alphabetical list.

7/61: EEC Commission v Italy [1961] ECR 317, [1962] CMLR 39, ECJ	173
26/62: Algemene Transport-en Expeditie Onderneming van Gend en Loos NV v Nederlandse Belastingadministratie [1963] ECR 1, [1963] CMLR 105, ECJ	168
22/70: EC Commission v EC Council [1971] ECR 263, [1971] CMLR 335, ECJ	173
41/74: Van Duyn v Home Office [1975] Ch 358, [1975] 3 All ER 190, [1975] 2 WLR 760, [1974] ECR 1337, [1975] 1 CMLR 1, 119 Sol Jo 302, ECJ	169
45/76: Comet BV v Produktschap voor Siergewassen [1976] ECR 2043, [1977] 1 CMLR 533, CMR 8383, ECJ	171
31, 53/77R: EC Commission v United Kingdom [1977] ECR 921, [1977] 2 CMLR 359, ECJ	174
106/77: Amministrazione delle Finanze dello Stato v Simmenthal SpA [1978] ECR 629, [1978] 3 CMLR 263, ECJ	169
102/81: Nordsee Deutsche Hochseefischerei GmbH v Reederei Mond Hochseefischerei Nordstern AG & Co KG [1982] ECR 1095, ECJ	170
230/81: Luxembourg v European Parliament [1983] ECR 255, [1983] 2 CMLR 726, ECJ	173
283/81: CILFIT Srl and Lanificio di Gavardo v Ministry of Health [1982] ECR 3415, [1983] 1 CMLR 472, ECJ	170
14/83: Von Colson and Kamann v Land Nordrhein-Westfalen [1984] ECR 1891, [1986] 2 CMLR 430, 134 NLJ 473, ECJ	168
294/83: Parti Ecologiste Les Verts v European Parliament [1986] ECR 1339, [1987] 2 CMLR 343, ECJ	173
222/84: Johnston v Chief Constable of the Royal Ulster Constabulary [1987] QB 129, [1986] 3 All ER 135, [1986] 3 WLR 1038, [1986] ECR 1651, [1986] 3 CMLR 240, [1987] ICR 83, [1986] IRLR 263, 130 Sol Jo 953, [1987] LS Gaz R 188, ECJ	172
326/88: Anklagemyndigheden v Hansen & Son I/S [1990] ECR I-2911, [1992] ICR 277, ECJ	173
C-106/89: Marleasing SA v La Comercial Internacional de Alimentación SA [1990] ECR I-4135, [1992] 1 CMLR 305, [1993] BCC 421, 135 Sol Jo 15, ECJ	171
C-188/89: Foster v British Gas plc [1991] 1 QB 405, [1990] 3 All ER 897, [1991] 2 WLR 258, [1990] ECR I-3313, [1990] 2 CMLR 833, [1991] ICR 84, [1990] IRLR 353, ECJ; apld [1991] 2 AC 306, [1991] 2 All ER 705, [1991] 2 WLR 1075, [1991] 2 CMLR 217, [1991] ICR 463, [1991] IRLR 268, [1991] 18 LS Gaz R 34, HL	168
C-213/89: R v Secretary of State for Transport, ex p Factortame Ltd (No 2) [1991] 1 AC 603, [1990] 3 WLR 818, [1990] ECR I-2433, [1990] 3 CMLR 1, [1990] 2 Lloyd's Rep 351, [1990] 41 LS Gaz R 33, sub nom Factortame Ltd v Secretary of State for Transport (No 2) [1991] 1 All ER 70, [1990] NLJR 927, ECJ	171
C-6, 9/90: Francovich and Bonifaci v Italy [1991] ECR I-5357, [1993] 2 CMLR 66, [1995] ICR 722, [1992] IRLR 84, ECJ	171

	PAGE
C-31/90: Johnson v Chief Adjudication Officer [1993] QB 252, [1992] 2 All ER 705, [1993] 2 WLR 192, [1991] ECR I-3723, [1991] 3 CMLR 917, [1993] ICR 204, ECJ	172
C-208/90: Emmott v Minister for Social Welfare and A-G [1991] ECR I-4269, [1991] 3 CMLR 894, [1993] ICR 8, [1991] IRLR 387, ECJ	171
C-370/90: R v Immigration Appeal Tribunal and Surinder Singh, ex p Secretary of State for the Home Department [1992] 3 All ER 798, [1992] ECR I-4265, [1992] 3 CMLR 358, [1993] 1 FCR 453, [1993] 1 FLR 798, [1993] Fam Law 272, [1992] Imm AR 565, [1993] 21 LS Gaz R 45, ECJ	173
C-29/91: Dr Sophie Redmond Stichting v Bartol [1992] ECR I-3189, [1992] IRLR 366, ECJ:	172
C-63, 64/91: Jackson v Chief Adjudication Officer [1993] QB 367, [1993] 3 All ER 265, [1993] 2 WLR 658, [1992] ECR I-4737, [1992] 3 CMLR 389, [1993] Fam Law 477, [1993] 21 LS Gaz R 46, ECJ	172
C-169/91: Stoke-on-Trent City Council v B & Q plc [1993] AC 900, [1993] 1 All ER 481, [1993] 2 WLR 730, [1992] ECR I-6635, [1993] 1 CMLR 426, 91 LGR 237, ECJ; affd sub nom Stoke-on-Trent City Council v B & Q plc [1993] AC 900, [1993] 2 All ER 297n, [1993] 2 WLR 730, [1993] 2 CMLR 509, 91 LGR 237, 137 Sol Jo LB 120, HL:	172
T-66/89: Publishers Association v EC Commission (No 2) [1992] 4 All ER 70, [1992] ECR II-1995, [1992] 5 CMLR 120, [1992] ICR 842, CFI	172

ISSUES

Practice

A: GENERAL

1.	Scope of title	5
2.	Terminology	5
3.	Separate trials of separate issues	6
4.	Separation of issues of liability and damages	8
5.	Written offer on liability	10
6.	Preliminary questions or issues	12
7.	Preliminary point of law	14
8.	Directions for trial of preliminary issue or question or point of law	16
9.	Evidence on trial of preliminary question or issue	18
10.	Determination of action after decision of preliminary issue	18

B: DISPOSAL OF CASE ON POINT OF LAW OR CONSTRUCTION

11.	Scope of Rules of the Supreme Court 1965 Order 14A	19
12.	Suitable question of law or construction	20
13.	Hearing or consent of parties	21
14.	Mode of application	22
15.	Supporting evidence	23
16.	Finality of determination of a point of law	24
17.	Appeal	24

C: SPECIFIC QUESTIONS AND ISSUES

18.	Question or issue for discovery of documents	25
19.	Question or issue in interpleader proceedings	25
20.	Question in garnishee proceedings	27
21.	Issue or question on application for execution	28
22.	Issue on application to set aside registration of a foreign judgment	28
23.	Question or issue between defendant and another party	28
24.	Question or issue between defendant and non-party	29
25.	Question as to liability of partner of firm	29
26.	Special case and case stated	29
27.	Special case	30
28.	Case stated	31
29.	Case for opinion of Scottish or Commonwealth court	33
30.	Questions and issues in the county court	34

Forms

A: HIGH COURT

1.	*Summons for order for separate trial of issue of liability before issue of damages*	37
2.	*Order for separate trial of issue of liability before issue of damages*	38
3.	*Written offer on liability by defendant*	39
4.	*Notice of acceptance of offer on liability*	39
5.	*Summons for interlocutory judgment for agreed proportion of liability*	40
6.	*Judgment for defendant after separate trial of issue of liability only*	41

7.	*Judgment for plaintiff after separate trial of issue of liability* . .	41
8.	*Summons for directions for assessment of damages* . . .	42
9.	*Summons for trial of preliminary issue on the pleadings* . .	43
10.	*Order for trial of preliminary issue on the pleadings* . . .	44
11.	*Summons for trial of preliminary issues or questions* . . .	44
12.	*Order for trial of preliminary issue*	45
13.	*Order directing trial of partnership issue*	46
14.	*Summons for trial of preliminary point of law* . . .	47
15.	*Order for trial of preliminary point of law*	47
16.	*Order dismissing action after determination of preliminary issue* .	48
17.	*Judgment after trial of preliminary question or issue* . . .	49
18.	*Order after trial of preliminary issue treated as trial of action* .	49
19.	*Order on hearing of preliminary point of law disposing of whole action* .	50
20.	*Summons by plaintiff for judgment upon the determination of point of law*	51
21.	*Summons by plaintiff for judgment upon the construction of a document* .	52
22.	*Summons by the plaintiff for judgment on a point of law under Order 14A or alternatively for summary judgment under Order 14 of the Rules of the Supreme Court 1965*	52
23.	*Summons by the defendant for the dismissal of action on point of law under Order 14A of the Rules of the Supreme Court 1965* . .	53
24.	*Summons by the defendant for the dismissal of action on a point of law under Order 14A or alternatively under Order 18 Rule 19 of the Rules of the Supreme Court 1965 or the inherent jurisdiction of the court* .	54
25.	*Judgment for the plaintiff upon the determination of a point of law* .	55
26.	*Judgment for the defendant upon the determination of a question of law* .	55
27.	*Judgment for the plaintiff (defendant) upon an oral application for the determination of a point of law*	56
28.	*Judgment on trial of question or issue in interpleader proceedings* .	56
29.	*Order directing trial of issue on application to set aside registration of a foreign judgment*	57
30.	*Summons for leave to formulate special case*	58
31.	*Order giving leave to formulate special case*	59
32.	*Special case*	59
33.	*Order on special case: Chancery Division*	60
34.	*Order on special case: Queen's Bench Division* . . .	61
35.	*Notice of motion for case to be settled for opinion of Scottish court* .	61
36.	*Case stated for opinion of Scottish court*	62
37.	*Memorandum identifying case stated for opinion of Scottish court* .	63
38.	*Notice of motion to apply opinion*	64

B: COUNTY COURT

39.	*Notice of application in county court for order referring question to district judge or referee*	65
40.	*Order in county court referring question to district judge or referee* .	66
41.	*Report of district judge or referee*	66

For actions generally	. .	*see title* ACTIONS Vol 1 (1992 Issue)
accounts	. . .	ACCOUNTS Vol 1 (1992 Issue)
appeals	. . .	APPEALS Vol 5 (1997 Issue)
arbitrations	. . .	ARBITRATION Vol 6 (1994 Issue)
case stated under statutes	.	*see titles referred to in footnotes in* Paragraph 28 *post*
chancery chambers proceedings	.	ACCOUNTS Vol 1 (1992 Issue); ADMINISTRATION OF ESTATES Vol 2 (1994 Issue); JUDGMENTS AND ORDERS *post*

county court proceedings generally	COUNTY COURTS Vol 13 (1992 Issue)
inquiries . . .	REFERENCES AND INQUIRIES BY THE COURT Vol 33 (1997 Issue); TRIBUNALS AND INQUIRIES Vol 40 (1996 Issue)
interlocutory proceedings .	INTERLOCUTORY PROCEEDINGS Vol 22 (1) (1996 Issue)
interpleader . . .	INTERPLEADER Vol 22 (1) (1996 Issue)
judgments and orders . .	JUDGMENTS AND ORDERS post
official referees . .	REFERENCES AND INQUIRIES BY THE COURT Vol 33 (1997 Issue)
inquiries . . .	REFERENCES AND INQUIRIES BY THE COURT Vol 33 (1997 Issue)
registration of foreign judgments	EXECUTION AND ENFORCEMENT OF JUDGMENTS AND ORDERS Vol 19 (1) (1996 Issue)
special referees . .	REFERENCES AND INQUIRIES BY THE COURT Vol 33 (1997 Issue)
stay of proceedings . .	STAY OF PROCEEDINGS Vol 37 (1995 Issue)
transfer . . .	TRANSFER AND CONSOLIDATION Vol 39 (1995 Issue)
trial . . .	TRIAL AND JURIES Vol 40 (1996 Issue)
tribunals, proceedings before .	TRIBUNALS AND INQUIRIES Vol 40 (1996 Issue)

For rules of court, see The Supreme Court Practice 1997; The County Court Practice 1998

Practice

A: GENERAL

1. Scope of title. This title deals with the practice relating to the trial of separate or specific or particular questions or issues arising in proceedings, and also with the practice of disposing of proceedings upon the determination of suitable questions of law or construction without a full trial of the action. It is concerned with the trial of only a part of the proceedings, such part having been isolated from the whole and made the subject of a separate, self-contained trial by an order of the court, but it is also concerned to avoid the need for the full trial of the action by making a determination of any suitable question of law or construction arising in the proceedings.

The title does not deal with the practice relating to separate trials arising from the joinder of causes of action or of parties, which might embarrass or delay the trial or be otherwise inconvenient[1], or arising from the making of a counterclaim which it appears ought to be disposed of by a separate action[2].

Nor does the title deal with trials before and inquiries and references conducted by official referees i.e. circuit judges nominated by the Lord Chancellor to deal with official referees' business or special referees or by masters, district judges or other officers of the court[3].

On the other hand, the title does deal very generally with questions and issues arising in interpleader or garnishee proceedings or in the course of an execution and with questions and issues arising between a defendant and another party or a non-party, or as to the liability of a partner or firm. The title also considers the nature of a special case and a case stated and the distinction between them, and deals with the practice relating to them.

1 RSC Ord 15 r 5 (1); CCR Ord 5 r 3. See Vol 13 (1992 Issue) title COUNTY COURTS Paragraph 73; Vol 30 (1994 Issue) title PARTIES TO ACTIONS Paragraph 7 and Vol 32 (1996 Issue) title PLEADINGS Paragraph 57.
2 RSC Ord 15 r 5 (2).
3 Supreme Court Act 1981 s 68 (1)(as amended and as further amended by the Civil Procedure Act 1997 s 10, Sch 2 para 1 (1), (3)(not yet in force)), (2)(as amended by the Civil Procedure Act 1997 s 10, Sch 2 para 1 (1), (3)(not yet in force)). These amendments, once in force, will substantially amend the Supreme Court Act 1981 s 68 (1) (11 Halsbury's Statutes (4th Edn) COURTS AND LEGAL SERVICES); and see RSC Ord 36 and Vol 33 (1997 Issue) title REFERENCES AND INQUIRIES BY THE COURT.

2. Terminology. There is a certain amount of confusion that arises over the terminology relating to questions, issues and points of law. At common law, issues were divided into issues of fact and issues of law, and the division was important, since an issue of fact was decided by the jury and an issue of law, which would usually be raised by a demurrer, was decided by the court[1]. With the abolition of the demurrer in 1875, issues came to be differently distinguished, so that an issue may be of fact or law or mixed fact and law. Sometimes, however, a distinction is drawn between "issues of fact" and "questions of law"[2], but this does not disclose the real distinction between the words "issue" and "question".

The current Rules of the Supreme Court 1965 employ these terms without defining them. The general formula used is "question or issue"[3], although occasionally the formula is limited to "question or issue of fact"[4]. Elsewhere one finds "issue or question"[5], or "question at issue"[6], or "point of law"[7]. It may be said, however, that the term "question" has a wider meaning than the term "issue", since a "question" may be resolved or determined by a choice being made from several solutions or answers and is not necessarily limited to a dispute involving a proposition made by one party and disputed by another[8], whereas an "issue" does involve a dispute between opposite parties, so that the issue can only be determined by accepting one party's proposition or rejecting that of the other[9]. For this reason, the common practice is to use the phrases "issue of fact" and "questions of law", though it must be emphasised that both an issue and a question may be of fact or of law or of mixed fact and law. The term "point of law", which does not admit any mixing of facts, forms the basis of a new procedure for the disposal of actions without a full trial of the action[10].

1 Under the common law system of pleading the parties were said to be "at issue" when one party by his pleading affirmed and the other party by his pleading denied a material proposition of law or fact. RSC 1883 Ord XXXIII r 1 (revoked) enabled the court, where it appeared that the issues of fact were not sufficiently defined, to prepare issues, and if the parties differed, the issues would be settled by the court.
2 RSC 1883 Ord XXXIV r 1 (revoked); RSC 1883 Ord LXV r 2 (revoked).
3 For example, RSC Ord 33 r 3. The rule adds "whether of fact or law or partly of fact and partly of law".
4 RSC Ord 36 rr 8, 9, 11 (1).
5 RSC Ord 24 r 4.
6 RSC Ord 17 r 5 (2)(c) ("Where ... the question at issue ... is a question of law and the facts are not in dispute, the court may summarily determine the question at issue"); RSC Ord 49 rr 5, 6 (2).
7 RSC Ord 18 r 11. This term has now been given a high profile as the title of a new order, see RSC Ord 14A, "Disposal of Case on Point of Law" and Paragraph 11 post.
8 *Hogg v Vickers Ltd* (1921) 14 BWCC 229 at 233, CA, per LORD STERNDALE MR; *Montgomery v Foy, Morgan & Co* [1895] 2 QB 321 at 324, CA, per LORD ESHER MR.
9 The importance of the meaning of the word "issue" is not as great as it was when the practice existed, until 1929, under RSC 1883 Ord LXV rr 1, 2, of awarding separate costs on the separate issues: for example, *Howell v Dering* [1915] 1 KB 54 at 62, CA, per BUCKLEY LJ; *Reid, Hewitt & Co v Joseph* [1918] AC 717, HL, per LORD FINLAY LC; *Cinema Press Ltd v Pictures and Pleasures Ltd* [1945] KB 356, [1945] 1 All ER 440, CA (costs of the "issue" of damages).
10 See RSC Ord 14A and Paragraph 11 post.

3. Separate trials of separate issues. The general power[1] of the court to order the separate trial of separate issues or questions is conferred by rules of court[2] or may be exercised under the inherent jurisdiction of the court[3].

Thus, the court may order any question or issue arising in a cause or matter, whether of fact or law or partly of fact and partly of law, and whether raised by the pleadings or otherwise, to be tried before, at or after the trial of the cause or matter, and may give directions as to the manner in which the question or issue is to be stated[4].

Again, in any action begun by writ, different questions may be ordered to be tried at different places or by different modes of trial, and one or more questions or issues may be ordered to be tried before the others[5].

The separate trial of separate issues is a departure from the general policy of the law that all the disputes in the same proceedings should be tried together[6]. It must be remembered that separate trials of separate issues are often as expensive as separate actions and should only be granted on special grounds[7].

On the other hand, the objects of these rules are to avoid the trial of unnecessary questions or issues, to avoid any undue expense or delay being occasioned by the preparation for trial of questions or issues which may not ultimately arise for decision or determination, and to speed the process and lessen the cost of litigation by the determination or decision of a crucial question or issue. Whenever any of these objects can be achieved, the court may in its discretion[8] order the separate trial of a separate question or issue. The court's task is to strike a proper balance between the interest of the parties that the litigation should be determined finally and entirely[9] and that the solution of one question or issue or point of law may end the litigation more quickly, conveniently and cheaply.

An order for the separate trial of a separate question or issue may be made:
1. at any stage of the proceedings;
2. in any cause or matter, whether the proceedings are begun by writ or originating summons or otherwise;
3. whether the question or issue is one of fact or of law or partly of fact and partly of law;
4. whether the question or issue is raised by the pleadings or otherwise; and
5. whether the separate trial is to be before, at or after the main trial[10].

The more frequent types of order are:
1. for separate trials of the issues of liability and damages[11];
2. for the trial of preliminary questions or issues[12]; and
3. for the trial of preliminary points of law[13].

---

1   Specific power to order the separate trial of separate issues or questions is conferred by RSC Ord 16 (questions or issues between a defendant and another party or a third party and subsequent parties); RSC Ord 17 r 5 (issues in interpleader proceedings); RSC Ord 24 r 4 (issue or question in relation to the discovery of documents); RSC Ord 49 rr 5, 6 (2) (issues in garnishee proceedings); RSC Ord 46 r 4 (3) (questions or issues in execution proceedings); RSC Ord 71 r 9 (2) (issue on application to set aside registration of foreign judgment); and RSC Ord 81 r 4 (4) (questions as to the liability of a partner or firm).
2   RSC Ord 33 rr 3, 4 (2).
3   Under this power the court, including the county court, may decide a preliminary issue of law without the need for a specific order to this effect, or may try the issue of liability without proceeding to deal with the issue of damages.
4   RSC Ord 33 r 3. This rule should be read with RSC Ord 18 r 11 (raising a point of law on the pleadings) and RSC Ord 14A (disposal on a point of law).
5   RSC Ord 33 r 4 (2).
6   *Piercy v Young* (1880) 15 Ch D 475 at 479, per SIR GEORGE JESSEL MR.
7   *Piercy v Young* (1880) 15 Ch D 475.

8 *Polskie etc v Electric Furnace Co Ltd* [1956] 2 All ER 306, [1956] 1 WLR 562, CA.
9 *Yeoman Credit Ltd v Latter* [1961] 2 All ER 294 at 299, [1961] 1 WLR 828 at 835, CA, per HARMAN LJ.
10 RSC Ord 33 r 3. It will be seen that RSC Ord 33 r 3 is wider in its terms and effect than RSC Ord 33 r 4 (2) but this latter rule, which deals only with an action begun by writ and only on an application made on the summons for directions or later, empowers the court to order the trial of different questions or issues "at different places or by different modes of trial".
11 See Paragraph 4 post.
12 See Paragraph 6 post.
13 See Paragraph 7 post.

4. Separation of issues of liability and damages. One of the more common instances in which the court may order the separate trial of the questions or issues in an action occurs where the issue of liability is ordered to be tried before the issue of damages[1].

Although such an order[2] may be made at any stage of the action, it is only in very exceptional circumstances that it will be made before the close of pleadings, though it is quite often made by the judge at the trial itself, either at the beginning of the hearing or even during the course of the trial. On the other hand, the usual occasion for the making of such an order is after the close of pleadings and before the trial, generally on or under the summons for directions or under a separate summons[3]. The application is made to the master or district judge, who may give directions relating to the trial of the issue of liability, and although the master or district judge can, at this stage, also give directions as to the place and mode of trial of the issue of damages, this is generally left over to be dealt with by the trial judge or until after the issue of liability has been determined in favour of the party claiming damages[4].

While the court will exercise, with care and circumspection, its power to decide that separate issues of liability and damages should be tried separately, where the question as to the amount of damages is of such a nature that it will be more convenient to refer it to an official referee[5] or a master or district judge[6] or the Admiralty registrar[7] the court may order the question of liability to be heard separately and the question of damages to be postponed until afterwards[8]. Indeed, although the normal practice of trying the issues of liability and damages together should still be adhered to, the court should be ready to order separate trials of the issues of liability and damages whenever it is just and convenient to do so[9].

In such event the court will usually order that the discovery and inspection of documents be limited to the issue of liability only[10].

Instances in which the separation of issues of liability and damages may be ordered may arise in actions for breach of contract or for negligence or breach of statutory duty, and perhaps other torts where there is a clear line of demarcation between the two issues. An order for the separate trial of the issues of liability and damages will not be made where the two issues, although separate, interact upon each other, for example, where the liability for particular classes of damage depends upon the nature and extent of the determination of the issue of liability[11]; nor will such an order be made where it might cause undue prejudice to a party, for example, by depriving him of the opportunity of cross-examination on the issue of damages where this may throw light on the issue of liability.

In actions for damages for personal injuries the court has power, before or at the trial, to order the separation of the issues of liability and damages, for example, where there is an element of uncertainty about the plaintiff's future[12], or where no firm prognosis is possible until some years after the accident[13].

Again, if several plaintiffs bring separate actions for damages for personal injuries arising out of the same accident, the court may order that all the actions be consolidated up to the determination of liability, with liberty to each plaintiff to have the quantum of damages separately assessed[14].

Where the issues of liability and damages have been ordered to be tried separately or have in fact been so tried, and the issue of liability has been determined in favour of the defendant, the court has power to enter judgment for the defendant[15]. If, however, the issue of liability has been determined in favour of the plaintiff, the court may give interlocutory judgment for the plaintiff for damages to be assessed[16], and the plaintiff may then, in accordance with any directions given before or at the trial, proceed to the assessment of the damages[17].

If no provision is made by the judgment as to how the damages or provisional damages are to be assessed, the damages or provisional damages will be assessed by the master or district judge[18]. For this purpose it is necessary to obtain an appointment from the master or district judge for the assessment of damages or provisional damages, and, at least seven days before the appointment, to serve notice of the appointment on the defendant[19]. Alternatively, the court may direct, by so providing in the order for the separate trial of the issue of liability, in the judgment, or on application made after judgment, that the assessment of damages or provisional damages be referred to an official referee or a special referee[20] or a master or district judge[21], or in the case of an Admiralty order the Admiralty registrar[22], or should be tried by a judge with or without a jury[23].

If the court should order that the action should proceed to trial, it may proceed to give directions as on a summons for directions[24].

In the proceedings for the assessment of damages it is sometimes necessary or desirable for directions to be given. Application for such directions may be made to the master or district judge by summons[25], and the master or district judge may give any necessary directions, for example, for service of particulars of special damages claimed, discovery and inspection of documents, and even interrogatories. The hearing of the assessment of damages is a continuation of the trial, and on that basis proceeds on the evidence of witnesses, who are examined orally and in open court[26], although the court has power to admit evidence by affidavit[27].

When the assessment of the damages or provisional damages has taken place, judgment will be entered for the amount so found[28]. In the Chancery Division the certificate of the master or district judge is drawn up in Chancery chambers and filed there[29]; in the Queen's Bench Division it is filed by the party entering judgment[30]; in a district registry, it is filed in the registry in which the action was proceeding[31].

1 Such a process is sometimes referred to as "the split trial" or as "bifurcating" the issues. In very rare cases, in which there is no dispute between two or more defendants that the plaintiff is entitled to succeed, but the question is either which of the defendants is liable to the plaintiff or in what proportions all the defendants are liable, the court may order the trial of the issue of damages before the issue of liability.
2 See Form 2 post.
3 See Form 1 post.
4 It should be noted that the separation of the trial of the issues of liability and damages can be ordered not only on a claim but also on a counterclaim.

5   RSC Ord 37 r 4 (1)(a). A reference to a special referee under RSC Ord 36 r 10 is very rare and may be regarded as obsolete. For the position of Official Referees see Vol 33 (1997 Issue) title REFERENCES AND INQUIRIES BY THE COURT Paragraph 15.
6   RSC Ord 37 r 4 (1)(b).
7   RSC Ord 37 r 4 (1)(c).
8   *Smith v Hargrove* (1885) 16 QBD 183. See also *Liverpool, Brazil and River Plate Steam Navigation Co v London and St Katherine Steam Navigation Co* [1875] WN 203. In *Gold v Patman and Fotheringham Ltd* [1958] 2 All ER 497, [1958] 1 WLR 697, CA, the parties had agreed that the trial judge should try all the issues except damages.
9   *Coenen v Payne* [1974] 2 All ER 1109, [1974] 1 WLR 984, CA. See the Report of the Committee on Personal Injuries Litigation 1968 (Cmnd 3691) Paragraph 494 (c) and Appendix 21.
10 RSC Ord 24 r 2 (5)(a); and see Form 2 post.
11 *Polskie etc v Electric Furnace Co Ltd* [1956] 2 All ER 306, [1956] 1 WLR 562, CA.
12 *Stevens v William Nash Ltd* [1966] 3 All ER 156 at 160, [1966] 1 WLR 1550 at 1554, CA, per WINN LJ.
13 *Hawkins v New Mendip Engineering Ltd* [1966] 3 All ER 228, [1966] 1 WLR 1341, CA.
14 *Healey v A Waddington & Sons Ltd* [1954] 1 All ER 861n, [1954] 1 WLR 688, CA. For a summons in such a case see Vol 39 (1995 Issue) title TRANSFER AND CONSOLIDATION Form 52.
15 RSC Ord 33 r 7. For a judgment see Form 6 post. Where the trial judge determines the issue of liability in favour of the defendant but he has also heard the evidence relating to the issue of damages, it is generally more convenient that he should also assess the damages, so that, in the event of his decision on liability being reversed, judgment can be entered for the amount so assessed, duplication of proceedings being thus avoided: for example, *Haley v London Electricity Board* [1965] AC 778, [1964] 3 All ER 185, HL (as to liability), (1965) 109 Sol Jo 295, CA (as to damages).
16 RSC Ord 33 r 7; see Form 7 post. Such a judgment has the effect of being final as to liability but interlocutory as to damages.
17 RSC Ord 37.
18 RSC Ord 37 r 1 (1).
19 RSC Ord 37 r 1 (1), (2).
20 RSC Ord 37 r 4 (1)(a).
21 RSC Ord 37 r 4 (1)(b).
22 RSC Ord 37 r 4 (1)(c).
23 RSC Ord 37 r 4 (1)(d).
24 RSC Ord 37 r 4 (3).
25 See Form 8 post.
26 RSC Ord 38 rr 1, 8; *Hesz v Sotheby & Co* [1960] 1 WLR 285.
27 RSC Ord 38 r 2.
28 If the damages are assessed by a master or district judge, he must certify the amount of the damages, and judgment will be entered upon his certificate: RSC Ord 37 r 2.
29 RSC Ord 37 r 2.
30 RSC Ord 37 r 2. See the Supreme Court Practice 1997 para 37/2/2.
31 RSC Ord 37 r 2.

5. Written offer on liability. Where, in an action begun by writ, an order is made for the issue of liability to be tried before any issue or question concerning the amount of damages if liability is established[1], the party against whom a finding of liability is sought may, without prejudice to his defence, make an offer to accept liability up to a specified proportion[2]. Any such offer may be brought to the attention of the judge after the issue of liability has been decided but not before[3].

A written offer on liability may not be made unless and until an order is made for the separate trial of the issue of liability before the issue of damages[4]. It may be made in any description of action in which damages are claimed, but of course it is primarily intended for actions for personal injuries[5].

Unlike the machinery of Rules of the Supreme Court 1965 Order 22[6] relating to payment of money into and out of court, this rule does not provide a prescribed form for making a written offer on liability[7], nor does it make any provision for the time within which such an offer may be accepted nor provide a prescribed form for such acceptance[8]. In the absence of such express provisions or forms, it becomes all the more necessary to exercise greater care in the operation of this rule.

Thus, the written offer on liability by the defendant should be clear and unambiguous. If there is more than one cause of action in which a claim for damages is made, the written offer must specify the cause of action in respect of which it is made[9]. It would be more advisable to serve such a written offer in the form of a notice rather than by way of an informal letter[10]. Equally, if the plaintiff accepts the offer, he should do so promptly[11] and by way of a formal notice rather than by an informal letter[12].

The acceptance by the plaintiff of the defendant's offer of liability may be regarded as constituting an agreement between the parties as to the terms on which the issue of liability has been disposed of or settled between them[13]. Accordingly, the plaintiff will presumably be entitled to apply by summons for an interlocutory judgment to be entered for damages and interest thereon to be assessed, and for judgment for the amount representing the proportion of liability that the defendant has offered to accept. Such a summons could be expressed as being "by consent" and endorsed by the solicitors of both parties, and in such event such an interlocutory judgment may be entered in an appropriate case administratively without the summons being considered by a judge[14].

If, however, the plaintiff should decide to refuse to accept the written offer on liability, it would be helpful if he were to communicate this fact to the defendant, though of course there is no obligation to do so. This would resolve the element of uncertainty as to whether the offer will or will not be accepted, though if the acceptance is delayed and the defendant incurs costs during such period of delay, the court may award him costs on the issue of liability from the expiry of a reasonable time after the date of the written offer.

After having tried and decided the issue of liability, the court must of course proceed to deal with the costs of the issue. In exercising its discretion as to costs in such a case the court must take into account any written offer on liability made by the defendant[15]. In such event, the court will be likely to proceed to deal with the question of costs on the issue of liability by analogy with the operation of Rules of the Supreme Court 1965 Order 22 as to the payment of money into court[16]. Accordingly, if the court should find that the proportion of liability offered by the defendant is less or lower than the recovery by the plaintiff, the plaintiff will be entitled to judgment for the whole or the proportion of the liability found in his favour with costs on the issue of liability; and conversely if the court should find that the proportion of liability offered is more or greater than the proportion found for the plaintiff the defendant will be entitled to the costs on the issue of liability from the date of his written offer[17].

In third party proceedings, where a written offer of contribution has been made by the third party to the defendant or by a defendant to a co-defendant, the offer must not ordinarily be brought to the attention of the judge until all questions of liability and amount of debt or damages have been decided[18]. On the other hand, if the issue of liability has been tried and an issue or question concerning the amount of the debt or damages remains to be tried separately and the question of the costs of the issue of liability falls to be decided, any party may bring to the attention of the court the fact that a payment into court has or has not been made, and the date (but not the amount) of such payment or of the first payment if more than one[19].

1   That is, under RSC Ord 33 r 4 (2). See Form 2 post.
2   RSC Ord 33 r 4A (1), (2). For a form see Form 3 post.
3   RSC Ord 33 r 4A (3). This is the comparable position with a payment of money into court in satisfaction under RSC Ord 22 r 1; see RSC Ord 22 r 7. As to the position in third party proceedings see text and notes 18, 19 below.
4   RSC Ord 33 r 4A (1), (2).
5   See the Supreme Court Practice 1997 para 33/4A/1. As to "an action for personal injuries" see RSC Ord 1 r 4 (1).
6   RSC Ord 22.
7   See RSC Ord 22 r 1 (2) and RSC Appendix A Form No 23. See also RSC Ord 22 r 14 and *Calderbank v Calderbank* [1976] Fam 93, [1975] 3 All ER 333, CA.
8   See RSC Ord 22 r 3 (1) and RSC Appendix A Form No 24.
9   As is required in RSC Ord 22 r 1 (4).
10 For form of notice see Form 3 post.
11 On the analogy of the operation of RSC Ord 22, the notice of acceptance should be served within 21 days of the written offer (see RSC Ord 22 r 3 (1)); otherwise the plaintiff may be at risk as to the scope of the order for costs on the issue of liability that may be made.
12 For form of notice of acceptance, see Form 4 post.
13 A payment into court under RSC Ord 22 is itself "simply an offer to dispose of the claim on terms": *A Martin French v Kingswood Hill Ltd* [1961] 1 QB 96 at 103, [1960] 2 All ER 251 at 252, CA, per DEVLIN LJ.
14 For a form of summons see Form 5 post. Such an interlocutory judgment may be entered administratively in the Queen's Bench Division, other than in the Admiralty and Commercial Courts and the Official Referees' Court or where one of the parties is a litigant in person or under a disability, where the summons is marked "By Consent" and is endorsed by the solicitors of both parties (see RSC Ord 42 r 5A (1), (2)(a), (3), (4)); but in other proceedings, in the absence of the prerequisite conditions, such a judgment may be entered only pursuant to an order of the court (see RSC Ord 42 r 5 (Queen's Bench Division) and RSC Ord 42 r 6 (Chancery Division)).
15 RSC Ord 62 r 9 (c).
16 *Hultquist v Universal Pattern and Precision Engineering Co Ltd* [1960] 2 QB 467, [1960] 2 All ER 266, CA; *Findlay v Railway Executive* [1950] 2 All ER 969, CA; *Wagman v Vare Motors Ltd* [1959] 3 All ER 326, [1959] 1 WLR 853, CA.
17 See the Supreme Court Practice 1997 para 33/4A/1.
18 RSC Ord 16 r 10 (1); see Vol 37 (1995 Issue) title THIRD PARTY PROCEDURE Paragraph 24.
19 RSC Ord 16 r 10 (2).

6. Preliminary questions or issues. The court has power at any stage of the proceedings to order that a question or issue, whether of fact or of law or partly of fact and partly of law, and whether raised in the pleadings or otherwise, should be tried as a preliminary question or issue[1].

The circumstances in which such an order should be made cannot be precisely defined, and no firm rule for the making of such an order can or ought to be laid down. Nevertheless, speaking generally, the kind of case in which an order of this sort can usefully be made is one in which the matter directed to be tried first will, when decided one way or the other, really be likely to dispose of the case[2]. In other words, an order directing the trial of a preliminary issue will be made where there is a real probability or serious reason to believe that the determination of such issue might put an end to the action[3]. The application of the rule should therefore be limited to extraordinary and exceptional cases and will only be granted on special grounds[4].

An issue which involves dealing with the whole subject matter of the action without any evidence is not a "preliminary" issue and should not be ordered to be tried as such[5].

Instances in which orders have been or may be made for the trial of the following preliminary questions or issues are:

1. whether the plaintiff was a legitimate child and so entitled to an account from trustees[6];
2. whether the plaintiff was an heir-at-law[7];
3. whether the plaintiff was entitled to bring a representative action[8];
4. whether two defendants were promoters of the company[9];
5. whether the proceedings before the Disciplinary Committee of the Law Society are judicial in character, so as to confer absolute privilege in respect of the publication of its findings and order[10];
6. whether specified documents are admissible at the trial[11];
7. whether the writ of summons was duly served on the defendant[12];
8. whether a binding contract was concluded between the parties;
9. whether an action should be stayed or dismissed on the ground that a binding contract of compromise or settlement has been arrived at between the parties[13];
10. whether the defendant solicitors would be accountable to the plaintiffs for fees, costs and disbursements received by them as solicitors for parties against whom the plaintiffs have brought an action if the plaintiffs establish their claim against those parties[14]; or
11. whether the cause of action has become barred by the operation of the Limitation Acts[15].

Instances in which the trial of the following preliminary question or issue has been refused are:

1. whether the plaintiff in a partnership action had agreed to sell to the defendant his interest in the partnership at a stated price[16]; and
2. whether the plaintiff in an action for libel had given the defendants an undertaking to indemnify them against any action for libel[17].

1 RSC Ord 33 r 3. For the procedure see Paragraph 8 post. For summonses see Forms 9, 11 post and for orders see Forms 10, 12, 13 post.
2 *Polskie etc v Electric Furnace Co Ltd* [1956] 2 All ER 306 at 308, [1956] 1 WLR 562 at 566, CA, per JENKINS LJ.
3 *Emma Silver Mining Co v Grant* (1879) 11 Ch D 918 at 927, per SIR GEORGE JESSEL MR; but see also Paragraph 7 note 9 post.
4 *Piercy v Young* (1880) 15 Ch D 475 at 480, per SIR GEORGE JESSEL MR; *Bottomley v Hurst and Blackett Ltd and Houston* (1928) 44 TLR 451 at 452, CA, per SCRUTTON LJ.
5 *Radstock Co-operative and Industrial Society v Norton-Radstock UDC* [1968] Ch 605, [1968] 2 All ER 59, CA.
6 As cited by SIR GEORGE JESSEL MR in *Emma Silver Mining Co v Grant* (1879) 11 Ch D 918 as illustrations of the cases in which he had been concerned.
7 As cited by SIR GEORGE JESSEL MR in *Emma Silver Mining Co v Grant* (1879) 11 Ch D 918 as illustrations of the cases in which he had been concerned.
8 As cited by SIR GEORGE JESSEL MR in *Emma Silver Mining Co v Grant* (1879) 11 Ch D 918 as illustrations of the cases in which he had been concerned.
9 *Emma Silver Mining Co v Grant* (1879) 11 Ch D 918. The order was made subject to the plaintiffs undertaking not to seek relief against the defendants in respect of any cause of action other than that covered by the issue so ordered to be tried, and the discontinuance of such portion of the action.
10 *Addis v Crocker* [1960] 1 QB 87, [1959] 2 All ER 773; affd on appeal [1961] 1 QB 11, [1960] 2 All ER 629, CA.
11 *Bearmans Ltd v Metropolitan Police District Receiver* [1961] 1 All ER 384, [1961] 1 WLR 634, CA (decided under the Evidence Act 1938: see now the Civil Evidence Act 1995 (17 Halsbury's Statutes (4th Edn) EVIDENCE) and RSC Ord 38 rr 27, 28)).

12 Such an order may be made on an application by the defendant to set aside the service of the writ, or, more usually, on an application to set aside a default judgment on the ground that the writ was not properly served. On such an issue the burden of proof that the writ was duly served lies on the plaintiff, and he should accordingly be made the plaintiff on the issue.
13 See Vol 12 (1) (1996 Issue) title COMPROMISE AND SETTLEMENT Paragraph 5. For an order see Vol 12 (1) (1996 Issue) title COMPROMISE AND SETTLEMENT Form 56.
14 *Carl Zeiss Stiftung v Herbert Smith & Co* [1969] 1 Ch 93, [1968] 2 All ER 1002, CA.
15 *Secretary of State for the Environment v Essex Goodman & Suggitt* [1986] 2 All ER 69, [1986] 1 WLR 1432.
16 *Piercy v Young* (1880) 15 Ch D 475.
17 *Bottomley v Hurst and Blackett Ltd and Houston* (1928) 44 TLR 451, CA.

7. Preliminary point of law. A preliminary point of law is a particular form of a preliminary question or issue in which the only question for the decision of the court is a point of law.

The trial of a preliminary point of law must be distinguished from the determination of a point of law otherwise than by trial, for example, a determination that the pleading does not disclose a reasonable cause of action or ground of defence[1]. The distinction is:

1. the trial of a preliminary point of law takes place in open court, whereas the determination of a point of law by the normal interlocutory process takes place in chambers; and
2. the jurisdiction to determine a point of law in the interlocutory process can only be exercised in plain and obvious cases, whereas on the trial of a preliminary point of law the court can decide the question in the ordinary way according to its view of what is the law[2].

A party may by his pleading raise any point of law[3], and of course amendments of the pleading may be allowed so as to raise a point of law[4]. Indeed, where there is a substantial point of law which may dispose of the whole action, it is not only convenient that it should be pleaded[5] but it is also desirable that it should be raised as a preliminary issue, for otherwise, if the issues of fact should occupy a substantial part of the trial, the successful party may be deprived of part of his costs[6].

Nevertheless, a point of law may be raised at the trial even though it is not pleaded[7]; and in a proper case the court may allow it to be raised and argued without any pleading[8].

Not every point of law that arises in proceedings will be ordered to be tried as a preliminary point; otherwise, of course, a case may be fragmented into numerous separate trials. It is only where it is really probable that the determination of the point of law will put an end to the action that it will be allowed to be tried as a preliminary issue[9]. It is, however, not necessary that the decision on the point of law should dispose of the action whatever way it is decided[10]; it is enough if the decision one way or the other will have the effect of disposing of the action[11].

An order for the trial of a preliminary point of law[12] will not be made or allowed where the point is abstract[13], or hypothetical[14], or where the facts are disputed[15] or ought to be ascertained before the question of law[16]. Nor will an order be made for the trial of a preliminary point of law, where the whole action can be dealt with without any evidence, for example, where the facts are admitted or deemed to be admitted[17].

Indeed, the courts have warned against the lack of wisdom, save in very exceptional cases, of adopting this procedure of preliminary points of law, on the grounds that the shortest cut so attempted inevitably turns out to be the longest way round, and that it is highly undesirable that the court should be constrained to tie itself in so many knots[18].

Instances in which a preliminary point of law has been ordered to be tried, generally where the point has been raised in the pleadings, are where the following questions are raised:

1. whether the exemption clauses in a contract with a limited company operated to exempt the servants of the company from liability for their personal negligence[19];
2. whether in an action for trespass to the person it is necessary for the plaintiff to allege either that the trespass was intentional or that it was caused by the negligence of the defendant[20]; or
3. whether an action is barred by the operation of the Limitation Acts[21].

Another instance in which it might be desirable to try a preliminary point of law is where a question is raised as to the construction of an agreement[22], but not where there is likely to be a dispute as to the "factual matters" affecting the point of construction.

In a defamation action the court may order the trial of a preliminary issue of whether the words complained of are capable of bearing the alleged defamatory meaning[23].

Where a preliminary point of law is ordered to be tried, it is necessary that the order should contain a clear and precise definition of what is the point of law raised[24].

1 See also *Prince v Gregory* [1959] 1 All ER 133, [1959] 1 WLR 177, CA (striking out statement of claim on the ground that it did not disclose a reasonable cause of action, where from the facts alleged the defendant could not reasonably have been expected to apprehend danger to children), and *Fowler v Lanning* [1959] 1 QB 426, [1959] 1 All ER 290 (striking out statement of claim on a preliminary point of law in an action of trespass where there was no allegation that the trespass was intentional or negligent). In *Addis v Crocker* [1960] 1 QB 87, [1959] 2 All ER 773, the master or district judge ordered the statement of claim to be struck out on an interlocutory application on the ground that it disclosed no reasonable cause of action, but on the direction of the judge this question was tried as a preliminary issue with the same result. See Paragraph 11 post.
2 As to whether the court should exercise its jurisdiction to strike out an action under RSC Ord 18 r 19 or under its inherent jurisdiction or order the trial of a preliminary issue on a point of law under RSC Ord 33 r 3 see *Williams & Humbert Ltd v W & H Trade Marks (Jersey) Ltd* [1986] AC 368, [1986] 1 All ER 129, HL, and *Smith v Croft (No 2)* [1988] Ch 114, [1987] 3 All ER 909.
3 RSC Ord 18 r 11.
4 *Lever v Land Securities Co Ltd* (1893) 70 LT 323, CA.
5 *Independent Automatic Sales Ltd v Knowles and Foster* [1962] 3 All ER 27, [1962] 1 WLR 974.
6 *Gold v Patman and Fotheringham Ltd* [1958] 2 All ER 497, [1958] 1 WLR 697, CA. See Paragraph 11 post.
7 *Independent Automatic Sales Ltd v Knowles and Foster* [1962] 3 All ER 27, [1962] 1 WLR 974.
8 *Ramage v Womack* [1900] 1 QB 116. As to trial without pleadings see RSC Ord 18 r 21.
9 *Everett v Ribbands* [1952] 2 QB 198 at 206, [1952] 1 All ER 823 at 827, CA, per ROMER LJ; *Gold v Patman and Fotheringham Ltd* [1958] 2 All ER 497, [1958] 1 WLR 697, CA; *Waters v Sunday Pictorial Newspapers Ltd* [1961] 2 All ER 758 at 763, [1961] 1 WLR 967 at 974, CA, per DANCKWERTS LJ. But see also *Carl Zeiss Stiftung v Herbert Smith & Co* [1969] 1 Ch 93, [1968] 2 All ER 1002 at 1004, CA, where LORD DENNING MR said that if the matter was "a sword suspended over their heads" then "the defendants have received in good faith moneys for the defence of this action. They ought to know whether they can safely go on receiving them. If the issue of law is decided in their favour it will dispose of the claim against them, *irrespective of the main action*. I would order a preliminary issue to be tried".

10 The view to this effect of HARMAN LJ in *Yeoman Credit Ltd v Latter* [1961] 2 All ER 294 at 299, [1961] 1 WLR 828 at 835, CA, would place too great a restriction on the beneficial use of the procedural device of allowing the trial of preliminary points of law and was expressly disapproved in *Carl Zeiss Stiftung v Herbert Smith & Co* [1969] 1 Ch 93, [1968] 2 All ER 1002, CA.
11 *Carl Zeiss Stiftung v Herbert Smith & Co* [1969] 1 Ch 93, [1968] 2 All ER 1002, CA. See also note 9 above.
12 For a summons and order see Forms 14, 15 post.
13 *Glasgow Navigation Co v Iron Ore Co* [1910] AC 293, HL.
14 *Sumner v William Henderson & Sons Ltd* [1963] 2 All ER 712n, [1963] 1 WLR 823, CA.
15 *Windsor Refrigerator Co Ltd v Branch Nominees Ltd* [1961] Ch 375, [1961] 1 All ER 277, CA. In this case both CROSS J and the Court of Appeal remonstrated about deciding the preliminary point of law where the facts were not really agreed, but nevertheless proceeded to do so. See also *A-G v Nissan* [1970] AC 179, [1969] 1 All ER 629, HL, per LORD WILBERFORCE and LORD PEARSON, both stressing the disadvantages of ordering the trial of a preliminary point of law on assumed facts.
16 *Richards v Naum* [1967] 1 QB 620, [1966] 3 All ER 812, CA.
17 *Radstock Co-operative and Industrial Society Ltd v Norton-Radstock UDC* [1968] Ch 605, [1968] 2 All ER 59, CA.
18 See *Richards v Naum* [1967] 1 QB 620, [1966] 3 All ER 812, CA, citing with approval *Sumner v William Henderson & Sons Ltd* [1963] 2 All ER 712n, [1963] 1 WLR 823, CA.
19 *Adler v Dickson* [1955] 1 QB 158, [1954] 3 All ER 397, CA.
20 *Fowler v Lanning* [1959] 1 QB 426, [1959] 1 All ER 290, approved in *Letang v Cooper* [1965] 1 QB 232, [1964] 2 All ER 929, CA.
21 *Airey v Airey* [1958] 2 All ER 59, [1958] 1 WLR 72; affd [1958] 2 QB 300, [1958] 2 All ER 571, CA (whether an action is barred against the personal representatives of a deceased tortfeasor); see RSC Ord 15 r 6A, made under the Supreme Court Act 1981 s 87 (as amended by the Civil Procedure Act 1997 s 10, Sch 2 para 1 (1), (6)(not yet in force)) (11 Halsbury's Statutes (4th Edn) COURTS AND LEGAL SERVICES) and replacing the Proceedings Against Estates Act 1970; *Archer v Catton & Co Ltd* [1954] 1 All ER 896, [1954] 1 WLR 775; *Chesworth v Farrar* [1967] 1 QB 407, [1966] 2 All ER 107.
22 *Gold v Patman and Fotheringham Ltd* [1958] 2 All ER 497, [1958] 1 WLR 697, CA; *Tucker v British Museum Trustees* (1967) Times, 22 April. See also Form 19 post.
23 *Keays v Murdoch Magazines (UK) Limited* [1991] 4 All ER 491, [1991] 1 WLR 1184, CA, doubting *Morris v Sandess Universal Products* [1954] 1 All ER 47, [1954] 1 WLR 67, CA.
24 *National Real Estate and Finance Co Ltd v Hassan* [1939] 2 KB 61, [1939] 2 All ER 154, CA.

8. Directions for trial of preliminary issue or question or point of law.

Application for the determination of a preliminary question or issue or point of law is made by summons[1] to a master or district judge or on the summons for directions[2]. Application subsequent to the summons for directions is made by notice under the summons on two clear days' notice to the other side[3]. A point of law decisive of the action should be disposed of at the close of pleadings or shortly afterwards[4].

If at the hearing of the application the master or district judge makes an order[5] for the trial of a preliminary question or issue or a preliminary point of law, he will proceed to give any necessary directions, for example, as to the service of pleadings and the discovery and inspection of documents. One of the more important directions will be as to which party should be the plaintiff and which the defendant on the issue. The guiding principle is that the plaintiff on the issue should be that party on whom lies the burden of proof or who asserts the affirmative on the question or issue ordered to be tried[6]. The master or district judge will also give directions as to the place and mode of trial.

The place of trial of any preliminary question or issue or point of law arising in a cause or matter must be determined by the court, and will be either the Royal Courts of Justice or a place where sittings of the High Court are held[7]. The mode of trial of any preliminary question or issue or point of law is almost invariably by judge alone[8].

In the Chancery Division the practice is for the preliminary question or issue or point of law to be set down in the Judges Listing Office, Chancery, and if it is anticipated that evidence will not be adduced at the hearing it will take its place in the Non-Witness List[9].

In the Queen's Bench Division the practice is for the master or district judge to direct that the preliminary question or issue or point of law should be set down for hearing by a judge alone in the Non-Jury List, and an application may be made to the Clerk of the Lists to fix a date for its trial[10].

In the Commercial Court the preliminary question or issue or point of law will be set down for hearing by the judge in charge of the Commercial List[11].

An official referee[12] has, for the purposes of disposing of any cause or matter, including any interlocutory application, the same jurisdiction, powers and duties as a judge[13], whether the proceedings have been commenced[14] or have been transferred to be dealt with[15] as official referee's business. Accordingly, an official referee may make an order for the trial before himself of a preliminary question or issue or point of law arising in the proceedings, and he will then give such further direction for such trial as he thinks desirable.

With the consent of all the parties, and pursuant to an order of the court, the master or district judge may try a preliminary question of fact or of mixed fact and law[16], and such case on appeal lies directly from the master or district judge to the Court of Appeal[17].

1 See Forms 9, 11, 14 post.
2 Vol 1 (1992 Issue) title ACTIONS Form 110; see Forms 9, 11, 14 post.
3 Vol 1 (1992 Issue) title ACTIONS Form 111.
4 *Carl Zeiss Stiftung v Herbert Smith & Co* [1969] 1 Ch 93, [1968] 2 All ER 1002, CA.
5 See Forms 10, 12, 13, 15 post.
6 *Stevens v Chown* [1901] 1 Ch 894; and see RSC Ord 35 r 7 and *Seldon v Davidson* [1968] 2 All ER 755, [1968] 1 WLR 1083, CA.
7 RSC Ord 33 r 1.
8 As to the mode of trial see RSC Ord 33 r 2.
9 See Form 15 post.
10 Practice Direction [1981] 3 All ER 61, [1981] 1 WLR 1296, para 6 (a), (c); see Forms 2, 10, 12 post.
11 RSC Ord 72 r 2.
12 An official referee is a circuit judge, deputy circuit judge or recorder nominated by the Lord Chancellor to deal with official referee's business: Supreme Court Act 1981 s 68 (1)(a)(as amended) (11 Halsbury's Statutes (4th Edn) COURTS AND LEGAL SERVICES); RSC Ord 1 r 4 (1). For official referee's business see RSC Ord 36 r 1 (2). Provision is made for a "special referee" as an alternative to an "official referee" see: Supreme Court Act 1981 s 68 (1)(b) but such provision has fallen into complete disuse and there is no likelihood of it being resurrected. In *Kronstein v Korda* [1937] 1 All ER 357, CA where with the consent of the parties a master was trying an issue as a preliminary point of law, he was described as acting as "a special referee" which he was not, though he may have been acting as arbitrator.
13 RSC Ord 36 r 4. This includes the powers of committee and discretion as to costs.
14 RSC Ord 36 r 2.
15 RSC Ord 36 r 3 (1), (2), (4).
16 RSC Ord 36 r 11 (1), (3) applying RSC Ord 36 r 4 to a master or district judge as it applies to an official referee.
17 See *Bearmans Ltd v Metropolitan Police District Receiver* [1961] 1 All ER 384, [1961] 1 WLR 634, CA.

9. Evidence on trial of preliminary question or issue. The general rules of evidence which apply to the trial of actions[1] apply equally to the trial of preliminary issues or questions of fact or points of law[2].

There is, however, an extremely important exception to this general rule, namely that the provisions for the exchange of witnesses' statements do not apply to the trial of issues or questions of fact or law[3] on such a trial, therefore any fact required to be proved by the evidence of witnesses should in general be proved by the examination of the witnesses orally in open court[4], although the court may permit affidavit evidence[5], and may order that evidence of any particular fact be given in such manner as may be specified, for example, by statement on oath of information or belief, by the production of documents or entries in books, or copies of them, or even, in appropriate cases, by the production of specified newspapers[6]. The leave of the court or the agreement of all parties may be necessary to adduce expert evidence[7], and the evidence of expert witnesses may be limited by order and provision may be made by order for the use of plans, photographs and models[8].

On the other hand, if the facts are agreed, or are admitted on the pleadings, leaving only the question of law to be decided, no evidence, not even affidavit evidence, can be admitted at the trial of the preliminary issue or point of law[9].

1 That is, RSC Ord 38 rr 1–7 for which see Vol 18 (1996 Issue) title EVIDENCE Paragraph 2, where the rules are briefly summarised.
2 RSC Ord 38 r 8.
3 RSC Ord 38 r 8.
4 RSC Ord 38 rr 1, 8.
5 RSC Ord 38 r 2.
6 RSC Ord 38 r 3 (2).
7 See RSC Ord 38 r 36 (1) and *Sullivan v West Yorkshire Passenger Transport Executive* [1985] 2 All ER 134, CA.
8 RSC Ord 38 rr 4, 5.
9 *Pioneer Plastic Containers Ltd v Customs and Excise Comrs* [1967] Ch 597, [1967] 1 All ER 1053. The practice may be different in salvage cases: see *The Hardwick* (1884) 9 PD 32.

10. Determination of action after decision of preliminary issue. If it appears to the court that the decision of any question or issue arising in a cause or matter and tried separately from the cause or matter substantially disposes of the cause or matter or renders the trial of the cause or matter unnecessary, it may dismiss the cause or matter[1] or make such other order or give such judgment in it as may be just[2], including an order for the costs of the issue, and indeed of the whole action.

If the order dismissing the action or giving judgment has the effect of finally disposing of the rights of the parties, the order is a final order for the purposes of an appeal[3].

Indeed, the decision in an issue ordered to be tried as a preliminary issue is not a decision preliminary to a final order but it is to be treated itself as a final order[4].

1 See Form 16 post.
2 RSC Ord 33 r 7. See Forms 17, 19 post.
3 *Bozson v Altrincham UDC* [1903] 1 KB 547, CA.

4 *White v Brunton* [1984] QB 570, [1984] 2 All ER 606, CA. Accordingly, leave to appeal under the Supreme Court Act 1981 s 18 (1A) (11 Halsbury's Statutes (4th Edn) COURTS AND LEGAL SERVICES) is not required. See the Supreme Court Practice 1997 para 33/3/1. See also however RSC Ord 59 r 1A (3) which provides that such an order or judgment is not final unless it would have finally determined the whole case whichever way the court had decided the issues beforehand.

B: DISPOSAL OF CASE ON POINT OF LAW OR CONSTRUCTION

11. Scope of Rules of the Supreme Court 1965 Order 14A[1]. Where it appears to the court at any stage of the proceedings that any question of law or construction of any document arises which is:

1. suitable for determination without a full trial of the action[2]; and
2. such determination will finally determine the entire cause or matter or any claim or issue therein[3];

the court may make such determination and may thereupon dismiss the action or make such order or judgment as it thinks just[4]. RSC Order 14A is expressed in very wide terms. It applies throughout the High Court[5]. It may be invoked by the plaintiff or the defendant and even by the court itself acting of its own motion[6]. It applies to all actions however begun, whether by writ or originating summons, and whether in respect of the claim, the defence or counterclaim and at any pre-trial stage of the proceedings[7]. Further, the jurisdiction under RSC Order 14A may be exercised by a master or district judge[8].

Moreover, it is expressly provided that nothing in RSC Order 14A shall limit the powers of the court whether under Rules of the Supreme Court 1965 Order 18 Rule 19 or under any other provision of the Supreme Court[9]. This means that all the other provisions of the rules which empower the court to make a final judicial decision at the pre-trial stage remain in place and will continue to operate as they did before RSC Order 14A was introduced[10]. It may therefore be said that RSC Order 14A has the effect of enlarging the powers of the court to terminate proceedings by a process of summary adjudication i.e. giving a final judgment or making a final order before and without a full trial[11].

Further RSC Order 14A enables the court to make a final determination of any question without the need for a prior order[12] for the determination of a preliminary question of law, whether raised by the pleadings or otherwise[13].

RSC Order 14A provides an alternative procedure to that provided by way of an originating summons for the construction of a document or some other question of law[14].

RSC Order 14A does not apply to any proceedings by or against the Crown[15].

1 RSC Ord 14A.
2 RSC Ord 14A r 1 (1)(a).
3 RSC Ord 14A r 1 (1)(b) subject only to any possible appeal.
4 RSC Ord 14A r 1 (2).

5 That is, the Chancery and Queen's Bench Divisions, including of course the Patents Court, the Admiralty Court, the Commercial Court and the Official Referees' Court. It is, however, hardly suitable in the Family Division. See the Supreme Court Practice 1997 para 14A/1–2/1.
6 See RSC Ord 14A r 1 (1).
7 See RSC Ord 14A r 1 (1). See the Supreme Court Practice 1997 para 14A/1–2/1.
8 RSC Ord 14A r 1 (4).
9 See RSC Ord 14A r 1 (5) and RSC Ord 18 r 19.
10 These provisions include RSC Ord 14 (summary judgment); RSC Ord 18 r 19 (striking out pleadings and endorsements); RSC Ord 27 r 3 (admissions); RSC Ord 33 r 3 (time of trial of questions or issues); RSC Ord 33 r 4 (determining the place and mode of trial); RSC Ord 43 r 1 (summary order for account); RSC Ord 86 (summary judgments in actions for specific performance). This will also include the powers of the court derived from its inherent jurisdiction.
11 See RSC Ord 14A r 1 (1)(a).
12 That is, under RSC Ord 33 rr 3, 4 (2).
13 See the Supreme Court Practice 1997 para 14A/1–2/1.
14 That is, under RSC Ord 5 r 4. See the Supreme Court Practice 1997 para 14A/1–2/1.
15 For such proceedings see RSC Ord 77 r 7 (1).

12. Suitable question of law or construction. When considering the ambit of Rules of the Supreme Court 1965 Order 14A the Court of Appeal laid down the following principles[1]:
   1. an issue is "a disputed point of fact or law relied on by way of claim or defence";
   2. a question of construction is well capable of constituting an issue;
   3. if a question of construction will finally determine whether an important issue is suitable for determination under RSC Order 14A and where it is a dominant feature of the case a court ought to proceed to so determine such issue; and
   4. respondents to an application under RSC Order 14A are not entitled to contend they should be allowed to hunt around for evidence or something that might turn up on discovery which could be relied upon to explain or modify the meaning of the relevant document. If there were material circumstances of which the court should take account in construing the document, they must be taken to have been known, and could only be such as were known, to the parties when the agreement was made. In the absence of such evidence the court should not refrain from dealing with the application.

The point of law for determination under RSC Order 14A should be formulated with great care and stated with clarity and precision, leaving no difficulty or ambiguity about its meaning or effect[2], and this is all the more necessary since its determination will be final. Moreover, the point must not be based on, or include hypothetical or future facts[3] still less fictitious facts even though they are admitted in the pleading[4], for otherwise the determination will be null and void.

A point of law may be suitable for determination under RSC Order 14A even though it may be difficult and complex and may require an extended hearing; what may be called a "full hearing" is not the same thing as a "full trial".

Thus, if on an application for summary judgment under Rules of the Supreme Court 1965 Order 14[5], the court is satisfied that the point of law raised by the defendant is really unarguable[6] or that there are no issues of fact between the parties, it would be pointless to give leave to defend on the basis that there is a triable issue of law[7]. On the other hand, if the determination of the question of law is not decisive of all the issues between the parties or if the issue is of such a character as would not justify its being determined as a preliminary issue or if the answer to the question is dependent on undecided issues of fact, the court will give leave to defend[8]. But when the determination of the point of law would require the prolonged examination over a number of days of a vast quantity of documents or other evidence, it would seem that the court is nevertheless empowered to proceed to determine the question under RSC Order 14A or it may prefer that it should be determined at a full trial, though there may not be much difference between these two courses except for the timing and the listing of the case for hearing, and of course, who hears the case, namely the master or district judge[9].

When the issues of fact are interwoven with the legal issues raised, it will not be desirable for the court to split the legal and factual determinations, for to do so will in effect give legal rulings in vacuo or on a hypothetical basis which the court will not do[10].

If on a contested application for an interim injunction, it appears that the only question at issue between the parties is one of law, the court may proceed directly to decide that issue[11].

1 RSC Ord 14A. See the Supreme Court Practice 1997 para 14A/1–2/4 and *Korso Finance Establishment Anstalt v John Wedge* (15 February 1994, unreported).
2 *Allen v Gulf Oil Refining Ltd* [1980] QB 156, [1979] 3 All ER 1008, CA; rvsd on another point [1981] AC 1001, [1981] 1 All ER 353, HL.
3 See *Sumner v William Henderson & Sons* [1963] 2 All ER 712n, [1963] 1 WLR 823, CA.
4 See *Royster v Cavey* [1947] KB 204, [1946] 2 All ER 642, CA. See also *Whall v Bulman* [1953] 2 QB 198, [1953] 2 All ER 306, CA, in which LORD DENNING said, "The parties cannot agree on a false hypothesis and ask the court to adjudicate upon it".
5 RSC Ord 14.
6 See *Cow v Casey* [1949] 1 KB 474 at 481, CA, per LORD GREENE MR; *European Asian Bank AG v Punjab and Sind Bank (No 2)* [1983] 2 All ER 508, [1983] 1 WLR 642, CA; *Israel Discount Bank of New York v Hadjipateras* [1983] 3 All ER 129 at 135, [1984] 1 WLR 137 at 145, CA. See the Supreme Court Practice 1997 para 14/3–4/11.
7 *RG Carter Ltd v Clarke* [1990] 2 All ER 209, [1990] 1 WLR 578, CA.
8 *RG Carter Ltd v Clarke* [1990] 2 All ER 209, [1990] 1 WLR 578, CA and see the Supreme Court Practice 1997 para 14/3–4/11.
9 See *British and Commonwealth Holdings plc v Quadrex Holdings Inc* [1989] QB 842, [1989] 3 All ER 492, CA, per SIR NICOLAS BROWNE-WILKINSON VC.
10 See *State Bank of India v Murjani Marketing Group Ltd* (27 March 1991, unreported).
11 *R v Secretary of State for Transport, ex p Factortame Ltd (No 2)* [1991] 1 AC 603, sub nom *Factortame Ltd v Secretary of State for Transport (No 2)* [1991] 1 All ER 70, HL, per LORD JAUNCEY.

13. Hearing or consent of parties. One of two conditions is required to be fulfilled before the court determines any question under Rules of the Supreme Court 1965 Order 14A[1], namely:
1. that the parties have had an opportunity of being heard on the question[2]; or
2. that the parties have consented to an order or judgment on such determination[3].

As regards the first condition, that the parties have had the opportunity to be heard, if a party does not attend this hearing, it will be necessary to prove, by affidavit of service or otherwise (e.g. a letter acknowledging service of the summons), that he was given due notice of the date, time and place of the hearing of the summons[4].

As regards the second condition, that the parties had consented to an order or judgment on the determination of the question of law or construction, it may be helpful if such consent is stated in writing[5].

Whichever condition has been fulfilled, it is desirable that it be read into the order made or judgment given following the determination by the court of the question of law or construction raised before it.

1   RSC Ord 14A.
2   RSC Ord 14A r 1 (3)(a). See also the Supreme Court Practice 1997 paras 14A/1–2/6, 14A/12/7.
3   RSC Ord 14A r 1 (3)(b).
4   As a precautionary step and to avoid the need for an affidavit of service of the summons, the party served should be asked to acknowledge service of the summons.
5   If there may be any doubt about this, perhaps the applicant party should specifically request such consent in writing, to produce to the court.

14. Mode of application. An application under Rules of the Supreme Court 1965 Order 14A Rule 1[1] may be made by summons or motion and it may even be made orally in the course of any interlocutory application to the court[2]. It may be made at any time after the defendant has given notice of intention to defend[3]. It may be included in a summons for some other interlocutory relief, e.g. in a summons by the plaintiff for summary judgment under Rules of the Supreme Court 1965 Order 14 or in a summons by the defendant to strike out the statement of claim as disclosing no reasonable cause of action under Rules of the Supreme Court 1965 Order 18 Rule 19 or under the inherent jurisdiction of the court, and of course it may be made by a separate summons to come on at the same time as some other appropriate application[4].

The application should ordinarily be made by summons to the master or district judge who is invested with the jurisdiction of the court under Rules of the Supreme Court 1965 Order 14A[5]. If, however, the application includes a claim for an injunction, which, in the absence of consent, the master or district judge has no jurisdiction to deal with[6], the application should be made by motion[7] or by summons which should be made returnable before the judge[8].

The summons should state in plain and precise terms what is the question of law or construction which the court is required to determine.

The summons should also specify as clearly as can be, what judgment or order is being claimed upon the determination of the question of law or construction.

1   RSC Ord 14A r 1.
2   RSC Ord 14A r 2. The entitlement to make an oral application is given notwithstanding the requirement of RSC Ord 32 r 1 that every application in chambers not made ex parte must be made by summons. It should be stressed that an oral application can only be made in the course of hearing another application, as a kind of unexpected interruption of that hearing. To prevent surprise or an adjournment, if any party thinks that such an oral application is likely to be made, he should give the other party notice of such a possible development. No particular form is required for making an oral application, but the point of law must be very carefully stated and identified, and if necessary, the court may wish to hear the parties on that point before making its final determination. See Forms 20–24 post.

3 This is not expressly stated in RSC Ord 14A, but is implicitly required as the defendant must have had an opportunity to be heard, see RSC Ord 14A r 1 (3)(a) and of course if there is default in giving such notice, the plaintiff may enter a judgment in default under RSC Ord 13.
4 RSC Ord 14; RSC Ord 18 r 19. However, where the application under RSC Ord 14A is conjoined with some other application, it will be for the court to determine in what sequence the different applications should be dealt with.
5 RSC Ord 14A. See RSC Ord 14A r 1 (4).
6 See for Queen's Bench Division RSC Ord 32 r 11 (1)(d) and for Chancery Division see RSC Ord 32 r 14 (1)(d).
7 This may be the better course in the Chancery Division.
8 In the Queen's Bench Division the application will initially be entered in the General List and as it will be likely to last more than ten minutes it will immediately and automatically be transferred to the Special Appointments List. In the Chancery Division the summons will be made returnable before the motions judge and it should be issued in the Listing Office.

15. Supporting evidence. The summons or motion must be supported by affidavit evidence deposing to all the material facts relating to the question of law or construction to be determined by the court. For the purposes of affidavit evidence, proceedings under Rules of the Supreme Court 1965 Order 14A[1] are not interlocutory proceedings, since by its nature, the application will decide the right of the parties and will terminate the action or otherwise finally dispose of it[2].

Accordingly, it may not contain statements of information or belief with the sources and grounds thereof, and must contain only such facts as the defendant is able of his own knowledge to prove[3].

In addition to the material facts proved by the evidence of the parties, the court will take into account all those facts which have been duly admitted, whether by the pleadings or otherwise[4] including those arising by the operation of the crucial rules of pleading that any allegation of fact made in a pleading is deemed to be admitted by the opposite party unless it is traversed by that party in his pleading or a joinder of issue operates as a denial of it[5]. Accordingly there may be circumstances where either evidence in support is required or, the parties being content with this, the affidavits contain statements of information or belief.

1 RSC Ord 14A.
2 See Supreme Court Practice 1997 para 41/5/2 and see *Rossage v Rossage* [1960] 1 All ER 600, [1960] 1 WLR 249, CA; *Re J (An infant)* [1960] 1 All ER 603, [1960] 1 WLR 253.
3 RSC Ord 41 r 5.
4 See RSC Ord 27 r 3, for example, in response to a notice to admit under RSC Ord 27 r 2. It may be that answers to interrogatories containing admissions may not be used on an application under RSC Order 14A, since they can only be put in evidence at the trial of an action: see RSC Ord 26 r 7.
5 See RSC Ord 18 r 13 (1). A traverse may be made either by a denial or by a statement of non-admission, and either expressly or by necessary implication: RSC Ord 18 r 13 (2). A joinder of issue operates as a denial of every material allegation of fact made in the pleading on which there is an implied or express joinder of issue: RSC Ord 18 r 14 (4), but there can be no joinder of issue on a statement of claim or counterclaim: RSC Ord 18 r 14 (3).

16. Finality of determination of a point of law. A necessary quality of a point of law or construction for determination under Rules of the Supreme Court 1965 Order 14A[1] is that such determination will finally determine the entire cause or matter or any claim or issue thereon[2]. This requirement emphasises the overall objective of RSC Order 14A which is to provide a new procedure for the disposal of actions by judicial determination without a full trial. It meets the criticism levelled against the practice to allow preliminary points of law to be tried before all the facts have first been found[3].

Upon making its determination, the court will proceed to dismiss the action or give judgment for the plaintiff or may make such order or judgment as it thinks just[4].

For this purpose, the powers of the court to give finality to its determination, in the sense of terminating the whole or part of the litigation, have been greatly strengthened. Thus, where it appears that an application to strike out pleadings, whether the statement of claim or defence under Rules of the Supreme Court 1965 Order 18 Rule 19[5] or under the inherent jurisdiction of the court is likely to involve a serious and prolonged argument, the court is enabled to proceed under RSC Order 14A and after a full hearing, to strike out the offending pleading and give judgment or make such other order as may be just[6].

1 RSC Ord 14A.
2 RSC Ord 14A r 1 (1)(b), though of course such determination will be subject to any possible appeal.
3 See *Tilling v Whiteman* [1980] AC 1, [1979] 1 All ER 737, HL, as per LORD WILBERFORCE and LORD SCARMAN; and see also *Richards v Naum* [1967] 1 QB 620, [1966] 3 All ER 812, CA.
4 RSC Ord 14A r 1 (2); and see RSC Ord 33 r 7. See Forms 25–27 post.
5 RSC Ord 18 r 19.
6 See *Williams & Humbert Ltd v W & H Trade Marks (Jersey) Ltd* [1986] AC 368, [1986] 1 All ER 129, HL; *McKay v Essex Area Health Authority* [1982] QB 1166, [1982] 2 All ER 771, CA; *Smith v Croft (No 2)* [1988] Ch 114, [1987] 3 All ER 909.

17. Appeal. An appeal against a judgment given or a final order made by a master or a district judge pursuant to Rules of the Supreme Court 1965 Order 14A[1] lies in the ordinary way to a judge.

An appeal against the judgment or order given or made by the judge in chambers under RSC Order 14A must be treated as interlocutory for the purposes of an appeal to the Court of Appeal[2], thus equating it with an appeal against a judgment or order under Rules of the Supreme Court 1965 Order 14[3], except for the refusal of unconditional leave to defend[4].

Accordingly, leave to appeal to the Court of Appeal against a judgment or order under RSC Order 14A must first be obtained from the Judge in Chambers or the Court of Appeal[5]. In this respect, the judgment or order under RSC Order 14A differs from a judgment or order of the court after the full trial of the action or after the trial of a preliminary issue under the order of the court[6].

1 RSC Ord 14A.
2 RSC Ord 59 r 1A (6)(aa).
3 RSC Ord 14.
4 RSC Ord 59 r 1A (6)(aa). A defendant who has been refused unconditional leave to defend is entitled as of right to appeal to the Court of Appeal: Supreme Court Act 1981 s 18 (1A) (11 Halsbury's Statutes (4th Edn) COURTS AND LEGAL SERVICES).

5 See Supreme Court Act 1981 s 18 (1A).
6 See RSC Ord 33 rr 3, 7.

C: SPECIFIC QUESTIONS AND ISSUES

18. Question or issue for discovery of documents. Where an application is made for the discovery of documents, and it appears to the court that any issue or question in the cause or matter should be determined before any discovery of documents is made by the parties, the court may order that that issue or question should be first determined[1]; and the court may give directions for the determination of such issue or question[2]. This facility is seldom employed.

1 RSC Ord 24 r 4 (1).
2 RSC Ord 24 r 4 (2).

19. Question or issue in interpleader proceedings. There are two ways in which an issue between claimants in interpleader proceedings[1] may be dealt with or disposed of: it may be determined summarily or it may be ordered to be stated and tried. These will be considered separately.

Summary determination of interpleader issue. Where the applicant on an interpleader summons is a sheriff[2], or all the claimants consent or any of them so requests[3], or the question at issue between the claimants is a question of law and the facts are not in dispute[4], the court may summarily determine the question at issue between the claimants and make an order accordingly on such terms as may be just[5].

This method of determining the issue between claimants summarily is the one most commonly employed, as in most cases the issue is plain and capable of summary disposal. The summary determination of an issue is the reverse of the trial of an issue, and does not involve the stating or directing of an issue, but nevertheless the issue must be determined on its merits[6]. Summary disposal however should be adopted only in straightforward cases where expedition is desirable, e.g. sheriff's charges are mounting up, or the goods deteriorating, or the issues are simple and readily disposed of. If the goods are of considerable value and if difficult questions of law are likely to arise, or the issues are complicated and there is considerable conflict of evidence, summary disposal is inappropriate even if the parties have consented[7]. For this purpose the master or district judge may adjourn the summons for summary determination in his private room, in the Queen's Bench Division[8], and, and if so requested, must[9] hear oral evidence or may allow or direct the deponent of any affidavit filed by or on behalf of a claimant to be further examined or cross-examined. No order need be drawn up until after the master or district judge has made his determination unless there is a failure to carry out any directions given[10]; the master or district judge, in the Queen's Bench Division, will endorse his determination on the summons, and the order will then require to be drawn up. In the Chancery Division the Orders and Accounts section will draft the order.

Interpleader issue ordered to be stated and tried. Where on the hearing of an interpleader summons all the persons by whom adverse claims are made[11] to the subject matter in dispute appear[12] the court may order that an issue[13] between the claimants be stated and tried and may direct which of the claimants is to be plaintiff and which defendant[14].

If the application for interpleader relief is not made in a pending action it must be made by originating summons, which must be entitled "In the matter of Order 17 of the Rules of the Supreme Court 1965" and must name each of the claimants[15]. It is the practice for each claimant to file an affidavit stating the grounds of his claim, and on the basis of such evidence the master or district judge will direct which of them will be plaintiff and which defendant. The guiding principle is that the plaintiff should be the claimant, on whom lies the burden of establishing his title against the other, or who is seeking to disturb the present possession of the goods or funds in question.

Although the rule suggests that an issue be stated, it is not the present practice to make such a direction, for the issue or question to be tried can and will usually be stated or set out in the order itself.

Where the grounds of the claimants' claims are likely to be complex the master or district judge may order pleadings to be served between them, otherwise pleadings will be dispensed with, but it is usual for directions to be given as to discovery and inspection of documents and as to the mode of trial. If the parties consent, or one of them so requests, as they usually do, the issue will be directed to be tried by a master or district judge; otherwise it will be ordered to be tried by a judge[16].

If interpleader relief is sought in a pending action the issue will become an issue in the action. The application, which is usually made by the defendant, must be made by summons to a master or district judge, directed to the plaintiff in the action and to the claimant. It must be supported by the usual affidavit claiming interpleader relief. The court may order that any claimant be made a defendant in the action with respect to the subject matter in dispute in substitution for or in addition to the defendant who is applying for interpleader relief[17], and, if in substitution, the court may order all further proceedings against that defendant in the action to be stayed[18].

1 See generally Vol 22 (1) (1996 Issue) title INTERPLEADER.
2 RSC Ord 17 r 5 (2)(a).
3 RSC Ord 17 r 5 (2)(b).
4 RSC Ord 17 r 5 (2)(c).
5 RSC Ord 17 r 5 (2).
6 *PBJ Davis Manufacturing Co Ltd v Fahn* [1967] 2 All ER 1274, [1967] 1 WLR 1059, CA. See also *Re Tarn* [1893] 2 Ch 280 at 283, CA.
7 *Fredericks and Pelhams Timber Buildings v Wilkins (Read Claimant)* [1971] 3 All ER 545, [1971] 1 WLR 1197, CA.
8 Such an adjourned hearing is treated as a reference, and the appropriate fee will be charged: see the Supreme Court Fees Order 1980, SI 1980/821, Schedule Fee No 8 (a)(as amended and as further amended by SI 1996/3191, art 5), presently £30.
9 See note 6 above.
10 Queen's Bench Masters' Practice Directions No 30 (as reissued as from 20 April 1993): Supreme Court Practice 1997 para 743.
11 The words "are made" appear to have been accidentally omitted from the rule, which reads more clearly with them.
12 "Appear" here is used in the sense of "attend and participate" rather than "an acknowledgment of service".

13 The rule uses the word "issue" only, but it is submitted that in this context it includes questions of law and/or issues of fact.
14 RSC Ord 17 r 5 (1)(b).
15 For the heading see Form 28 post.
16 For a judgment on the trial of the issue see Form 28 post.
17 RSC Ord 17 r 5 (1)(a).
18 RSC Ord 17 r 7.

20. Question in garnishee proceedings. In garnishee proceedings[1] questions may arise for determination or trial in two different circumstances, namely, where the garnishee disputes his liability and where there are claims made by third persons.

Question where garnishee disputes liability. Where on the further consideration of garnishee proceedings[2] the garnishee disputes liability to pay the debt due or claimed to be due from him to the judgment debtor, the court may summarily determine the question at issue or order that any question necessary for determining the liability of the garnishee be tried in any manner in which any question or issue in an action may be tried[3], without, if it orders trial before a master or district judge, the need for any consent by the parties[4].

In this event the question will arise as between the judgment creditor and the garnishee.

Question on claim by third person. Where a person, other than the judgment debtor, who is or claims to be entitled to the debt sought to be attached or who has or claims to have a charge or lien upon it, attends before the court in compliance with an order requiring him to attend and to state the nature of his claim with particulars of it[5], the court may summarily determine the question at issue between the claimants or make such other order as it thinks just, including an order that any question or issue necessary for determining the validity of the claim of that other person be tried in any manner in which any question or issue in an action may be tried, without, if it orders trial before a master or district judge, the need for any consent by the parties[6].

In this event the question or issue will arise as between the judgment creditor and the added claimant. In effect, on the analogy of interpleader, the garnishee will have no interest in the dispute between the judgment creditor and the added claimant and he will thus be eliminated from the proceedings relating to that dispute.

As in the case of interpleader proceedings, questions in garnishee proceedings, whether between the judgment creditor and the garnishee or between the judgment creditor and an added claimant, may be dealt with or disposed of in two ways, either summarily or ordered to be tried; and the practice stated above in relation to interpleader proceedings[7] will apply mutatis mutandis to garnishee proceedings.

1 See also Paragraph 22 post.
2 RSC Ord 49 r 1 (1); and Vol 19 (1) (1996 Issue) title EXECUTION AND ENFORCEMENT OF JUDGMENTS AND ORDERS Paragraphs 29-32.
3 RSC Ord 33 r 2.
4 RSC Ord 49 r 5.
5 RSC Ord 49 r 6 (1).
6 RSC Ord 49 r 6 (2).
7 See Paragraph 19 ante.

21. Issue or question on application for execution. Upon an application for leave to issue a writ of execution to enforce a judgment or order[1] the court may, instead of granting leave, order that any issue or question or decision on which it is necessary to determine the rights of the parties be tried in any manner in which any question of fact or law arising in an action may be tried[2], and may impose such terms as to costs or otherwise as it thinks just[3].

An application for leave to issue a writ of execution in the cases in which leave is required is normally made and granted ex parte[4], but if the master or district judge should think that an issue or question requires to be tried (though this happens very rarely) he will direct that the application be made by summons[5], which must be served on the parties whose rights are to be determined, even if they are not parties in the action. On the hearing of the summons the master or district judge will give such directions as may be necessary, including directions as to the service of pleadings and discovery and inspection of documents for the trial of the issue or question, and he will also direct which party should be plaintiff and which defendant.

1 For the cases where leave to issue the writ is necessary see RSC Ord 46 r 2 (1) and Vol 19 (1) (1996 Issue) title EXECUTION AND ENFORCEMENT OF JUDGMENTS AND ORDERS. "Writ of execution" includes writs of fieri facias, possession, delivery, sequestration, and any further writ in aid of any of those writs: RSC Ord 46 r 1.
2 RSC Ord 33 r 2.
3 RSC Ord 46 r 4 (3).
4 RSC Ord 46 r 4 (1).
5 RSC Ord 46 r 4 (1).

22. Issue on application to set aside registration of a foreign judgment. On the hearing of an application to set aside the registration of a foreign judgment, the court may order any issue between the judgment creditor and the judgment debtor to be tried in any manner in which an issue in an action may be ordered to be tried[1].

1 RSC Ord 71 r 9 (2); *Société Cooperative Sidmetal v Titan International Ltd* [1966] 1 QB 828, [1965] 3 All ER 494; see Form 29 post.

23. Question or issue between defendant and another party. Where in any action a defendant who has given notice of intention to defend requires that any question or issue relating to or connected with the original subject matter of the action should be determined not only as between the plaintiff and himself but also as between either or both of them and some other person who is already a party to the action, the defendant may, without leave, issue and serve on that person a notice[1] stating the question or issue required to be determined[2]. The procedure then follows similar lines to the procedure on a third party notice[3].

1 Vol 37 (1995 Issue) title THIRD PARTY PROCEDURE Form 38.
2 RSC Ord 16 r 8 (1)(c).
3 See RSC Ord 16 r 8 (3) and Vol 37 (1995 Issue) title THIRD PARTY PROCEDURE Paragraph 22.

SPECIFIC QUESTIONS AND ISSUES

24. Question or issue between defendant and non-party. Where in any action a defendant who has given notice of intention to defend requires that any question or issue relating to or connected with the original subject matter of the action should be determined not only as between the plaintiff and the defendant but also as between either or both of them and a person not already a party to the action, the defendant may issue a third party notice[1] stating the question or issue required to be determined[2]. Unless the action was begun by writ and the defendant issues the notice before he serves his defence on the plaintiff, leave to issue the notice is required[3]. Details of third party procedure are given elsewhere in this work[4].

1 Vol 37 (1995 Issue) title THIRD PARTY PROCEDURE Form 2.
2 RSC Ord 16 r 1 (1)(c). In some cases, it may be more appropriate to join the additional person as a defendant to the counter-claim: RSC Ord 15 r 3 (1).
3 RSC Ord 16 r 1 (2).
4 Vol 37 (1995 Issue) title THIRD PARTY PROCEDURE Table 1.

25. Question as to liability of partner of firm. Where a person served with a writ as a partner acknowledges service of the writ under protest, stating in his acknowledgment of service that he denies that he was a partner in the defendant firm at any material time[1], the court may, at any stage of the proceedings, on the application of the plaintiff or of the defendant, order that any question as to the liability of the defendant or as to the liability of the defendant firm be tried in such manner and at such time as the court directs[2].

Such an order is usually made on the hearing of a summons by the defendant to set aside service of the writ on him on the ground that he was not a partner or was not liable as such[3]. On the other hand, such a question will be ordered to be tried as a preliminary issue after the close of proceedings either on the summons for directions or on a summons issued for the specific purpose of obtaining such an order[4].

1 RSC Ord 81 r 4 (2); Vol 30 (1995 Issue) title PARTNERSHIPS AND FIRMS Paragraph 7 and Form 7.
2 RSC Ord 81 r 4 (4).
3 RSC Ord 81 r 4 (3)(b).
4 For a summons and an order see Vol 30 (1995 Issue) title PARTNERSHIPS AND FIRMS Forms 8, 11.

26. Special case and case stated[1]. No general definition of the terms "special case" and "case stated" is to be found in the statutes or rules. Sometimes these terms are used indiscriminately to describe a written statement of facts upon which the court is asked to determine the question at issue between the parties according to law. Indeed, the terms are so interchangeable that sometimes they slide into each other, as, for example, "a special case stated"[2].

A distinction may, however, be drawn between a "special case" and a "case stated" according to the form in which the case is presented to the court.

A special case is one where the facts of the case are stated for the opinion of the court as to the law and/or for the decision of the court[3].

A case stated is one where the facts of the case are stated but a decision as to the law has already been arrived at, or a question of law on the facts is referred to the court upon the answer to which a decision will be arrived at.

Whether in any particular circumstances or proceedings a special case or a case stated is the proper form to be used depends upon the relevant statute, rule or order of the court. Care must therefore be taken when formulating the case to ensure that the requirements of the particular statute, rule or order are complied with.

1 See Paragraphs 27, 28 post.
2 RSC Ord 73 r 2 (2). See also Supreme Court Practice 1997 para 73/2/1.
3 "All courts have from time to time had powers given to them to answer questions put to them upon special cases": see *Walsall Overseers of the Poor v London and North Western Rly Co* (1878) 4 App Cas 30 at 41, HL, per LORD CAIRNS LC.

27. Special case. The practice of the old Court of Chancery enabled the parties to concur in stating a question in the form of a special case for the opinion of the court[1], although in the common law courts a special case could be stated only under an order of the court. After the Judicature Acts 1873–1875[2] the parties to any High Court proceedings could concur in stating a special case, or the court could order that a special case be stated, for the opinion of the court[3]. Under the modern Rules of the Supreme Court 1965, however, a case can no longer be stated by agreement between the parties; it can be stated only by order or direction of the court and, indeed, the court's power so to order or direct is not expressly stated[4].

Nevertheless, the court can, where it thinks it desirable or convenient, and either on the application of the parties[5] or of its own motion, order or direct that a question or issue should be stated in the form of a special case, and the court can give directions as to the manner in which the question or issue should be stated[6].

In this event the court will direct which party should prepare the draft case and deliver it to the other party for approval subject to any modification, addition or omission he may desire to make. If necessary the order will provide that if the parties differ, the form of the case must be settled by the master or district judge[7].

The case should be instituted in the court and in the action in which the question or issue arises, together with the names of the parties, and it should set out the agreed facts in numbered paragraphs[8]. It should conclude with a formulation of the question or issue to be determined by the court, and should be signed by counsel, if settled by him, or by the solicitors or by a party if acting in person.

If the decision on the case determines the result of the whole proceedings judgment will be ordered to be entered accordingly[9].

1 Court of Chancery Act 1850 s 1 (13 & 14 Vict c 35) (repealed).
2 Supreme Court of Judicature Act 1873 (36 & 37 Vict c 66) (repealed); Supreme Court of Judicature Act 1875 (38 & 39 Vict c 77) (repealed).
3 RSC 1883 Ord XXXIV rr 1–8 (revoked).
4 RSC Ord 56; see Paragraph 3 ante.
5 For a summons see Form 30 post.
6 For an example see *Chesworth v Farrar* [1967] 1 QB 407, [1966] 2 All ER 107. Although the case set out in the judgment in that case is there described as a "statement of agreed facts", it is in fact in the form of a special case, for it formulates the question to be determined by the court.

7   For an order see Form 31 post.
8   See Form 32 post.
9   See Forms 33, 34 post.

28. Case stated. A case stated may either be a form of appeal, whereby an aggrieved party applies to the High Court[1] to reverse the decision arrived at by an inferior court or tribunal on the facts stated, or it may take the form of referring a question of law on the facts stated for the opinion or determination of the High Court[2] so that the inferior court or tribunal may then itself make the decision in accordance with the answers given[3].

There is a multitude of examples of statutes and rules under which a case stated may arise. Amongst them are the following:

Agricultural arbitrator: statement of special case arising in arbitration concerning agricultural holding for opinion of county court[4];

Agricultural land tribunal: question of law referred for decision of Queen's Bench Divisional Court[5];

Bankruptcy proceedings: case stated by county court for opinion of and determination by Chancery judge[6];

Building society: case stated by Chief Registrar of Friendly Societies, arbitrator, Central Office of the Registry of Friendly Societies or county court for opinion of a Chancery judge[7];

District audit: case stated by Secretary of State for the Environment for opinion of Queen's Bench Divisional Court[8];

Friendly society: case stated by Chief Registrar of Friendly Societies, arbitrator or county court for opinion of a Chancery judge[9];

Income tax: case stated by General or Special Commissioners or Board of Referees for opinion of a Chancery judge[10];

Independent schools: case stated by Independent Schools Tribunal for determination by Queen's Bench Divisional Court[11];

Industrial and provident societies: case stated by Chief Registrar of Friendly Societies for opinion of county court or Chancery judge[12];

Land registration: case stated or question referred by Chief Land Registrar for opinion of a Chancery judge[13];

Lands Tribunal: case stated by Lands Tribunal for decision of Court of Appeal[14];

Licensing justices: case stated by licensing justices for opinion of Queen's Bench Divisional Court[15];

Loss of office: case stated or question of law referred by referees as to compensation for loss of office, for determination by Queen's Bench Divisional Court[16];

Magistrates: case stated by magistrates for opinion of Queen's Bench Divisional Court or single judge of Queen's Bench Division[17];

Mental health: case stated by Mental Health Review Tribunal for determination by a single judge of the Queen's Bench Division[18];

Mining: case stated by tribunal cancelling or suspending certificate of competency relating to mining, for opinion of Queen's Bench Divisional Court[19];

Pensions Appeal Tribunal: case stated by Pensions Appeal Tribunal for decision of nominated Queen's Bench judge[20];

Residential care homes: case stated on appeal from Registered Homes Tribunal for opinion of Queen's Bench Divisional Court[21];

Rent assessment committee: case stated by rent assessment committee for opinion of Queen's Bench Divisional Court[22];

Rent tribunal: case stated by rent tribunal for opinion of Queen's Bench Divisional Court[23];

Restrictive trade practices: case stated by Restrictive Practices Court for determination by Court of Appeal[24];

Social security: case referred by Secretary of State for Social Services for decision by a Queen's Bench judge[25];

Stamp duty: case stated by Inland Revenue Commissioners for opinion of a Chancery judge[26];

Trade effluent: case stated by Secretary of State for the Environment for decision of Queen's Bench Divisional Court[27];

Tribunals and inquiries: case stated by tribunal for opinion of Queen's Bench Divisional Court[28].

1 In three of the examples listed below the case is stated to the Court of Appeal, in one example to a county court, but in all the others to the High Court.
2 RSC Ord 56.
3 For a historical review of the development of the case stated see *R v Chantrell* (1875) LR 10 QB 587, per FIELD J and *Walsall Overseers of the Poor v London and North Western Rly Co* (1878) 4 App Cas 30 at 41, HL, per LORD CAIRNS LC. For the form of case stated, see the form as settled by LORD GODDARD CJ.
4 Agricultural Holdings Act 1986 Sch 11 paras 26, 30 (1 Halsbury's Statutes (4th Edn) AGRICULTURE); CCR Ord 44; Vol 4 (1995 Issue) title AGRICULTURAL LAND Paragraph 50, Table 1 steps 27–31, Forms 41, 42.
5 Agriculture (Miscellaneous Provisions) Act 1954 s 6 (1), (2) (1 Halsbury's Statutes (4th Edn) AGRICULTURE); Agricultural Land Tribunals (Rules) Order 1978, SI 1978/259, r 33; RSC Ord 94 r 7; Vol 4 (1995 Issue) title AGRICULTURAL LAND.
6 Insolvency Act 1986 s 375 (2) (4 Halsbury's Statutes (4th Edn) BANKRUPTCY AND INSOLVENCY); in addition to appeals being heard by a single judge of the High Court, appeals may also be heard by a circuit judge who exercises the powers of a judge in the Chancery division, in the areas outside London where such a circuit judge sits: Practice Note [1995] 4 All ER 129; Vol 7 (1997 Issue) title BANKRUPTCY AND INSOLVENCY.
7 Building Societies Act 1986 s 84 (5)(as amended by the Building Societies Act 1997 ss 43, 46 (2), Sch 7 para 36, Sch 9) (5 Halsbury's Statutes (4th Edn) BUILDING SOCIETIES); Vol 36 (1997 Issue) title SOCIETIES AND CLUBS.
8 Local Government Finance Act 1982 s 20 (3) (25 Halsbury's Statutes (4th Edn) LOCAL GOVERNMENT); RSC Ord 98; Vol 25 (1994 Issue) title LOCAL GOVERNMENT.
9 Friendly Societies Act 1974 s 83 (7) (19 Halsbury's Statutes (4th Edn) FRIENDLY SOCIETIES); Vol 36 (1997 Issue) title SOCIETIES AND CLUBS.
10 Taxes Management Act 1970 s 56 (as amended) (42 Halsbury's Statutes (4th Edn) TAXATION); RSC Ord 91 r 1 (a); Vol 34 (1) (1994 Issue) title REVENUE.
11 Education Act 1996 ss 470, 472, 476 (1), Sch 34 (15 Halsbury's Statutes (4th Edn) EDUCATION); Tribunals and Inquiries Act 1992 s 11 (as amended and as further amended by the Education Act 1996 s 582 (1), Sch 37 Pt I para 118 (1), (2); the Employment Rights Act 1996 s 240, Sch 1 para 57; the Industrial Tribunals Act 1996 s 43, Sch 1 para 9 (1), (2)), Sch 1 para 15 (a)(as amended by the Education Act 1996 s 582 (1), Sch 37 Pt I para 118 (1), (3)) (10 Halsbury's Statutes (4th Edn) CONSTITUTIONAL LAW); RSC Ord 56 rr 7–12; RSC Ord 94 r 9 (as amended by SI 1996/2892, r 18). See also The Education (Particulars of Independent Schools) Regulations 1997, SI 1997/2918.
12 Industrial and Provident Societies Act 1965 s 60 (9)(as substituted by the Arbitration Act 1996 s 107, Sch 3 para 20, Sch 4) (21 Halsbury's Statutes (4th Edn) INDUSTRIAL AND PROVIDENT SOCIETIES); RSC Ord 93 r 10 (2)(m); Vol 36 (1997 Issue) title SOCIETIES AND CLUBS.
13 Land Registration Act 1925 s 140 (1)(a) (37 Halsbury's Statutes (4th Edn) REAL PROPERTY); Land Registration Rules 1925, SR & O 1925/1093, r 298 (16 Halsbury's Statutory Instruments (1994 Issue) REAL PROPERTY); RSC Ord 93 r 10 (2)(f); title LAND REGISTRATION post.

14 Lands Tribunal Act 1949 s 3 (4) proviso, (11)(a) (9 Halsbury's Statutes (4th Edn) COMPULSORY ACQUISITION); RSC Ord 61 rr 1, 3; Vol 24 (2) (1995 Issue) title LANDS TRIBUNAL.
15 Magistrates' Courts Act 1980 s 111 (27 Halsbury's Statutes (4th Edn) MAGISTRATES); *Jeffrey v Evans* [1964] 1 All ER 536, [1964] 1 WLR 505; title INTOXICATING LIQUOR ante.
16 Tribunals and Inquiries Act 1992 s 11 (as so amended); RSC Ord 56 rr 7–12; RSC Ord 94 r 9 (as amended by SI 1996/2892, r 18).
17 Magistrates' Courts Act 1980 s 111; RSC Ord 56 rr 5, 6; Vol 5 (1997 Issue) title APPEALS.
18 Mental Health Act 1983 s 78 (8) (28 Halsbury's Statutes (4th Edn) MENTAL HEALTH); RSC Ord 56 rr 7–12; RSC Ord 94 r 11; Vol 26 (1996 Issue) title MENTAL HEALTH.
19 Mines and Quarries Act 1954 s 150 (3)(as amended), (4), Sch 3 Part I (as amended and as further amended by the Judicial Pensions and Retirement Act 1993 s 26 (10), Sch 6 para 61) (29 Halsbury's Statutes (4th Edn) MINES, MINERALS AND QUARRIES); Tribunals and Inquiries Act 1992 s 11 (as so amended), Sch 1 para 31; RSC Ord 56 rr 7–12; RSC Ord 94 r 9 (as amended by SI 1996/2892, r 18).
20 Pensions Appeal Tribunals Act 1943 s 6 (2) (33 Halsbury's Statutes (4th Edn) PENSIONS AND SUPERANNUATION); RSC Ord 101; Vol 36 (1997 Issue) title SOCIAL SECURITY AND PENSIONS.
21 Registered Homes Act 1984 ss 39 (as amended), 40 (as amended by the Judicial Pensions and Retirement Act 1993 s 26 (10), Sch 6 para 55), 41, 42 (as amended by the Nurses, Midwives and Health Visitors Act 1997 s 23 (1), Sch 4), 43 (as amended by the Arbitration Act 1996 s 107 (1), Sch 3 para 41), 44, 45 (35 Halsbury's Statutes (4th Edn) PUBLIC HEALTH AND ENVIRONMENTAL PROTECTION); Tribunals and Inquiries Act 1992 s 13 (1), Sch 1 para 8; Registered Homes Tribunal Rules 1984, SI 1984/1346 (16 Halsbury's Statutory Instruments (1994 Issue) PUBLIC HEALTH); RSC Ord 56 rr 7–12; RSC Ord 94 r 9 (as amended by SI 1996/2892, r 18).
22 Rent Act 1977 s 65, Sch 10 (as amended and as further amended by the Judicial Pensions and Retirement Act 1993 s 26 (10), Sch 6 para 56; the Housing Act 1996 ss 222, 227, Sch 18 Pt IV para 22 (1)(a), (2), Sch 19 Pt XIII) (23 Halsbury's Statutes (4th Edn) LANDLORD AND TENANT); Tribunals and Inquiries Act 1992 s 11 (as so amended), Sch 1 paras 13, 28; RSC Ord 56 rr 7–12; RSC Ord 94 r 9 (as amended by SI 1996/2892, r 18). See Vol 24 (1), (2)(1995 Issue) title LANDLORD AND TENANT.
23 Tribunals and Inquiries Act 1992 s 11 (as so amended), Sch 1 para 28; RSC Ord 56 rr 7–12; RSC Ord 94 r 9 (as amended by SI 1996/2892, r 18).
24 Restrictive Practices Court Act 1976 s 10 (1) (47 Halsbury's Statutes (4th Edn) TRADE AND INDUSTRY); Restrictive Practices Court Rules 1976, SI 1976/1897, rr 11–18 (20 Halsbury's Statutory Instruments (1997 Issue) TRADE AND INDUSTRY); RSC Ord 60.
25 RSC Ord 111; Vol 36 (1997 Issue) title SOCIAL SECURITY AND PENSIONS.
26 Stamp Act 1891 s 13 (1) (41 Halsbury's Statutes (4th Edn) STAMP DUTIES); RSC Ord 91 r 1 (a); Vol 34 (1) (1994 Issue) title REVENUE.
27 RSC Ord 56 rr 7–12; Vol 32 (1996 Issue) title PUBLIC HEALTH.
28 Tribunals and Inquiries Act 1992 s 11 (1)(as amended and as further amended by the Education Act 1996 s 582 (1), Sch 37 Pt I para 118 (1), (2)); RSC Ord 56 rr 7–12; RSC Ord 94 r 9 (as amended by SI 1996/2892, r 18); Vol 40 (1996 Issue) title TRIBUNALS AND INQUIRIES.

29. Case for opinion of Scottish or Commonwealth court. In English courts the law and judicial procedure of other countries, including Scotland and countries within the Commonwealth, must be proved as a matter of fact, except in the House of Lords or Privy Council on appeals from the courts of those countries. The usual practice is to call as a witness a lawyer from the appropriate country, who may refer to works of authority. However, the system is not always satisfactory because expert witnesses may disagree. A century ago two Acts were passed, one dealing with British dominions[1] and one with foreign countries[2], to provide reciprocal machinery for stating cases for the opinion of the courts of another country, but, because the necessary conventions with regard to foreign countries were never concluded, only the Act dealing with British dominions is effective[3].

If in any action pending in any court within Her Majesty's dominions it is the opinion of any such court that it is necessary or expedient for the proper disposal of the action to ascertain the law in any other part of the dominions, the court may direct a case to be prepared setting forth the facts as found or agreed, or settled in case the parties do not agree, with the questions of law arising on which the other court's opinion is desired, and may remit the case to the superior court of the other country[4]. Application for the case is by summons or motion[5].

Any party may petition the other court to hear parties or their counsel, or to pronounce its opinion without hearing parties or counsel[6]. It is usual to send the case, identified by a memorandum signed by the senior master[7], to a practitioner in the other court for him to arrange the petition and hearing and in due course to return the case with the opinion. A copy of the opinion, when pronounced, is given to each party[8], and any party may lodge it with the home court with a notice of motion stating that he will move the court to apply the opinion[9].

On appeal the House of Lords or Privy Council may review and adopt or reject the opinion[10].

1 British Law Ascertainment Act 1859 (17 Halsbury's Statutes (4th Edn) EVIDENCE).
2 Foreign Law Ascertainment Act 1861 (24 & 25 Vict c 11) (repealed).
3 See however the European Convention on Information on Foreign Law (Treaty Series No 117 (1969) Cmnd 4229) which was ratified by the United Kingdom on 16 September 1969 and came into force on 17 December 1969. The convention provides machinery for the contracting states, originally member states of the Council of Europe, to supply each other through "receiving" and "transmitting" agencies, with information on their law and procedure in civil and commercial fields as well as their judicial organisation. No rules of court are required to be made under the convention and no particular forms are prescribed or necessary. It is thought that the convention is not much used so far as the United Kingdom is concerned.
4 British Law Ascertainment Act 1859 s 1. For examples see *Topham v Duke of Portland* (1863) 32 LJ Ch 257 at 261, 275 and *Duncan v Lawson* (1889) 41 Ch D 394.
5 See Form 35 post.
6 British Law Ascertainment Act 1859 s 1.
7 See Forms 36, 37 post.
8 British Law Ascertainment Act 1859 s 2.
9 British Law Ascertainment Act 1859 s 3; Form 38 post.
10 British Law Ascertainment Act 1859 s 4.

30. Questions and issues in the county court. The nature of county court proceedings generally avoids the necessity for the separate trial of questions of law or issues of fact[1].

The judge may, however, refer to the district judge or a referee for inquiry and report any question[2] arising in the proceedings[3], directing how the reference is to be conducted[4].

The order[5] may be made on an application by any party before the hearing on notice[6], on an application by any party at the hearing[7], or at any stage by the judge of his own motion[8]. After conducting the inquiry[9] in the same manner, as nearly as circumstances will permit, as if it were the hearing of an action[10], the district judge or referee submits a written report[11], which is filed in the court office, the district judge giving notice of filing to each party[12].

SPECIFIC QUESTIONS AND ISSUES

If the further consideration of the proceedings was not adjourned to a day named, the district judge must fix a day and give not less than 10 days' notice to the parties[13]. On the day named or fixed any party may apply to the judge to adopt the report or, on giving not less than 5 days' notice of his intention, may apply to the judge to vary the report[14] or remit it for further inquiry and report[15]. The judge may also adopt, set aside or disregard the report[16]. On considering the report the judge may give such judgment or make such order in the proceedings as may be just[17].

1 With its extended jurisdiction however, seperate trials are now more likely to arise. For an instance of the hearing of a preliminary point of law in the county court see *Yeoman Credit Ltd v Latter* [1961] 2 All ER 294, [1961] 1 WLR 828, CA.
2 The context, which reserves "any right to have particular cases tried with a jury", suggests that "question" here means issue of fact.
3 County Courts Act 1984 s 65 (1)(d) (11 Halsbury's Statutes (4th Edn) COUNTY COURTS). See further Vol 33 (1997 Issue) title REFERENCES AND INQUIRIES BY THE COURT Paragraphs 34-36.
4 County Courts Act 1984 s 65 (3).
5 See Form 40 post.
6 CCR Ord 19 r 11 (a); and see Form 39 post.
7 CCR Ord 19 r 11 (b).
8 CCR Ord 19 r 11 (c).
9 CCR Ord 19 r 13 (a)–(e). The district judge or referee may submit any question (that is, presumably, any question of law) arising in the inquiry for the judge's decision: CCR Ord 19 r 13 (f).
10 CCR Ord 19 r 13 (d).
11 See Form 41 post.
12 CCR Ord 19 r 13 (g)(i).
13 CCR Ord 19 r 13 (h)(i).
14 It should be noted that neither party is obliged to apply to adopt the report, and difficulties can occasionally arise if neither party accepts its conclusions.
15 CCR Ord 19 r 13 (h)(ii). The notice must specify the variation or remission sought.
16 *British and Argentine Meat Co Ltd v Randall* [1939] 4 All ER 293, CA; *Schooley v Nye* [1950] 1 KB 335, [1949] 2 All ER 950, CA.
17 County Courts Act 1984 s 65 (3).

ISSUES

Forms

A: HIGH COURT

1
SUMMONS for order for separate trial of issue of liability before issue of damages[1]

IN THE HIGH COURT OF JUSTICE [Ch] 19... B. No. ...[2]
[Chancery *or* Queen's Bench] Division[3]
    [......... District Registry][4]
Between   A. B.   ...   Plaintiff
             and
             C. D.   ...   Defendant

LET ALL PARTIES concerned attend before [[*in the Queen's Bench Division* Master *or* District Judge ....] *or in the Chancery Division* Master .... *or* District Judge ....], [Room No. ...in Chambers *or* Room No. ..., Central Office], Royal Courts of Justice, Strand, London WC2A 2LL, on .... 19... at...am/pm, on the hearing of an application by the [Plaintiff] for an Order that the question or issue of the liability of the Defendant to the Plaintiff in this action be tried as a preliminary issue before the question or issue of damages, if any, and that, subject to the determination of the issue of liability in favour of the Plaintiff, the issue of damages [be tried subsequently in such manner as may be directed by the trial Judge or by further Order *or* be referred for trial to [an Official Referee[5] *or* a Master *or* District Judge]], [and that such further or other directions may be given for the trial of the issue of liability as may be necessary].

And that the costs of and occasioned by this application be costs in the [cause *or* action].

DATED .... 19...

This Summons was taken out by E. F. & Co of (*address*), [Agents for (*name*) of (*address*),] Solicitors for the [Plaintiff].

To the [Defendant] and to G. H. & Co of (*address*), his Solicitors.

1 See Paragraph 4 ante. For an order see Form 2 post.
2 The reference number must be included in every pleading: RSC Ord 18 r 6 (1)(a).
3 A cause or matter may, at any stage of the proceedings, be transferred from one division of the High Court to another by order of the court made in the division in which the cause or matter is proceeding: RSC Ord 4 r 3.
4 Add this if the proceeding is in the district registry.
5 That is, a (deputy) circuit judge or a recorder nominated by the Lord Chancellor to deal with Official Referees' business under the Supreme Court Act 1981 s 68 (1)(a)(as amended) (11 Halsbury's Statutes (4th Edn) COURTS AND LEGAL SERVICES). See RSC Ord 36 r 10. See Vol 33 (1997 Issue) title REFERENCES AND INQUIRIES BY THE COURT Paragraph 13.

2
ORDER for separate trial of issue of liability before issue of damages[1]

IN THE HIGH COURT OF JUSTICE [Ch] 19... B. No. ...[2]
   [Chancery *or* Queen's Bench] Division[3]
    [......... District Registry][4]
      [Master .... *or* District Judge.........]
Between   A. B.   ...   Plaintiff
               and
                C. D.   ...   Defendant

UPON HEARING [Counsel *or* the Solicitors] for the Plaintiff and for the Defendant

AND UPON READING [the Affidavit of .... filed on .... 19...]

IT IS ORDERED that the question or issue of the liability of the Defendant to the Plaintiff in this action be tried as a preliminary issue before the question or issue of damages if any and that subject to the determination of the issue of liability in favour of the Plaintiff the issue of damages [be tried subsequently in such manner as may be directed by the trial Judge or by further Order *or* be referred for trial to [an Official Referee[5] *or* a Master *or* a District Judge]]

AND that the Plaintiff and the Defendant respectively do by .... 19... [serve upon each other *or* exchange] a list of documents stating what documents are or have been in [his *or* their] possession custody or power limited to the issue of liability in this action[6] [and that they do within the like period file an affidavit verifying such list] and that there be inspection of such documents by .... 19... [service of such lists *or* filing of such affidavits]

AND that the question or issue be tried in [London] by a Judge alone and be set down by .... 19... in the [Non-Jury General[7]] List Category [A *or* B *or* C[8]] the estimated length being ... [hours *or* days]

AND that the costs of this application be costs [in the issue *or* in the cause *or* in the action *or* reserved]

DATED .... 19...

1 See Paragraph 4 ante. For a summons see Form 1 ante.
2 See Form 1 note 2 ante.
3 See Form 1 note 3 ante.
4 See Form 1 note 4 ante.
5 See Form 1 note 5 ante.
6 See Paragraph 4 ante.
7 See Queen's Bench Practice Directions No 28: Supreme Court Practice 1997 para 975/10 for the practice relating to the setting down of actions in the Non-Jury List in the Queen's Bench Division.
8 Supreme Court Practice 1997 para 25/3/7.

3
WRITTEN OFFER ON LIABILITY by defendant[1]

IN THE HIGH COURT OF JUSTICE   19... B. No. ...[2]
   Queen's Bench Division
     [......... District Registry][3]
   Between   A. B.   ...   Plaintiff
                        and
                        C. D.   ...   Defendant

TAKE NOTICE that, following upon the Order of [the Master *or* District Judge ....] dated .... 19..., that the issue of liability be tried before any issue or question concerning the amount of damages, the Defendant (pursuant to Order 33 Rule 4A of the Rules of the Supreme Court 1965[4]) offers to accept liability up to [fifty per cent *or* two-thirds *or as the case may be, specifying the proportion of liability being accepted*].

This offer is made without prejudice to the defence of the Defendant who intends to bring this offer to the attention of the trial Judge after the issue of liability is decided.

[AND FURTHER TAKE NOTICE that unless this offer is accepted within [42] days from its receipt by you, it can only be accepted by the Plaintiff on condition that he pays the costs incurred by the Defendant after the date of such receipt.]

The receipt of this offer is required to be acknowledged within [10] days of this date.

DATED .... 19...

                        (*Signature*)
                        Solicitors for the Defendant

To E. F. & Co of (*address*), Solicitors for the Plaintiff.

---

1   See Paragraph 5 ante. For notice of acceptance see Form 4 post; for summons for interlocutory judgment see Form 5 post.
2   See Form 1 note 2 ante.
3   See Form 1 note 4 ante.
4   RSC Ord 33 r 4A.

4
NOTICE OF ACCEPTANCE of offer on liability[1]

IN THE HIGH COURT OF JUSTICE   19... B. No. ...[2]
   Queen's Bench Division
     [......... District Registry][3]
   Between   A. B.   ...   Plaintiff
                        and
                        C. D.   ...   Defendant

TAKE NOTICE that the Plaintiff accepts the written offer on liability made by the Defendant by Notice dated .... 19...

[AND FURTHER TAKE NOTICE that following upon such acceptance the Plaintiff intends to apply to the Court for interlocutory judgment to be entered for damages and interest under Section 35A of the Supreme Court Act 1981[4] to be assessed, and for payment of such amount as represents the agreed proportion of liability with costs to be taxed.]

DATED .... 19...

(*Signature*)
Solicitors for the Plaintiff

To G. H. & Co of (*address*), Solicitors for the Defendant.

1 See Paragraph 5 ante. For a written offer see Form 3 ante; for a summons for interlocutory judgment see Form 5 post.
2 See Form 1 note 2 ante.
3 See Form 1 note 4 ante.
4 Supreme Court Act 1981 s 35A (as inserted) (11 Halsbury's Statutes (4th Edn) COURTS AND LEGAL SERVICES).

5
SUMMONS for interlocutory judgment for agreed proportion of liability[1]

IN THE HIGH COURT OF JUSTICE   19... B. No. ...[2]
   Queen's Bench Division
      [......... District Registry][3]
Between   A. B.   ...   Plaintiff
                        and
                        C. D.   ...   Defendant

LET ALL PARTIES concerned attend before [[*in the Queen's Bench Division* Master .... *or* District Judge ....] *or in the Chancery Division* Master .... *or* District Judge ....], [Room No. ... in Chambers *or* Room No. ..., Central Office], Royal Courts of Justice, Strand, London WC2A 2LL, on .... 19... at ... am/pm, on the hearing of an application by the Plaintiff for an Order that judgment be entered for the Plaintiff for damages and interest pursuant to Section 35A of the Supreme Court Act 1981[4] to be assessed, the Plaintiff having by Notice[5] dated .... 19... accepted the offer on liability made by the Defendant by Notice[6] dated .... 19..., and for payment by the Defendant to the Plaintiff of such amount as represents the agreed proportion of liability, namely [fifty per cent *or as the case may be*] with costs to be taxed.

DATED .... 19...

(*Signature*)
Solicitors for the Plaintiff

To G. H. & Co of (*address*), Solicitors for the Defendant.

1 See Paragraph 5 ante.
2 See Form 1 note 2 ante.
3 Supreme Court Act 1981 s 35A (as inserted) (11 Halsbury's Statutes (4th Edn) COURTS AND LEGAL SERVICES).
4 See Form 1 note 4 ante.
5 See Form 4 ante.
6 See Form 3 ante.

6
JUDGMENT for defendant after separate trial of issue of liability only[1]

IN THE HIGH COURT OF JUSTICE   19... B. No. ...[2]
    Queen's Bench Division
       [......... District Registry][3]
Between   A. B.   ...   Plaintiff
                     and
                     C. D.   ...   Defendant

DATED AND ENTERED .... 19...

The [issue *or* question] of liability in this action by the Order dated .... 19... ordered to be tried before the [issue *or* question] of damages, if any, having on .... 19... been tried before the Honourable Mr Justice .... without a jury in [London]

AND Mr Justice .... on .... 19... having found for the Defendant and directed that judgment be entered for the Defendant with costs

IT IS ADJUDGED that [the Plaintiff do pay to the Defendant his costs to be taxed *or as the case may be*]

---

1   Adapted from RSC Appendix A Form No 48. See RSC Ord 33 r 7 and Paragraph 4 ante.
2   See Form 1 note 2 ante.
3   See Form 1 note 4 ante.

7
JUDGMENT for plaintiff after separate trial of issue of liability[1]

IN THE HIGH COURT OF JUSTICE   19... B. No. ...[2]
    Queen's Bench Division
       [......... District Registry][3]
Between   A. B.   ...   Plaintiff
                     and
                     C. D.   ...   Defendant

DATED AND ENTERED .... 19...

The [issue *or* question] of liability in this action by the Order dated .... 19... ordered to be tried before the [issue *or* question] of damages, if any, having on .... 19... been tried before the Honourable Mr Justice .... without a jury in [London]

AND Mr Justice .... on .... 19... having found for the Plaintiff on the issue of liability and directed that interlocutory judgment for damages and interest to be assessed be entered for the Plaintiff with costs

[AND further directing that the assessment of damages and interest be [tried by a Judge alone *or* referred to [an Official Referee[4] *or* a Master *or* District Judge] [of the Queen's Bench Division]]

IT IS THIS DAY ADJUDGED that the Defendant do pay to the Plaintiff damages and interest under Section 35A of the Supreme Court Act 1981[5] to be assessed

The amount found due to the Plaintiff under this Judgment having been [assessed by [the Honourable Mr Justice .... or His Honour Judge ....], at £...... or certified[6] at £...... as appears by the Master's Certificate filed on .... 19...]

IT IS ADJUDGED that the Defendant do pay to the Plaintiff £...... and costs to be taxed

The above costs have been taxed and allowed at £...... as appears by a Taxing Master's Certificate dated .... 19...

1   RSC Ords 33 r 7, 37 rr 1, 4. See Paragraph 4 ante.
2   See Form 1 note 2 ante.
3   See Form 1 note 4 ante.
4   See Form 1 note 5 ante.
5   Supreme Court Act 1981 s 35A (as inserted) (11 Halsbury's Statutes (4th Edn) COURTS AND LEGAL SERVICES).
6   RSC Ord 37 r 2. See Paragraph 4 ante.

8
SUMMONS for directions for assessment of damages[1]

IN THE HIGH COURT OF JUSTICE   [Ch] 19... B. No. ...[2]
  [Chancery or Queen's Bench] Division[3]
  [......... District Registry][4]
Between   A. B.   ...   Plaintiff
                                 and
                                C. D.   ...   Defendant

LET ALL PARTIES concerned attend before [[*in the Queen's Bench Division* Master .... *or* District Judge ....] *or in the Chancery Division* Master ....*or* District Judge ....], [Room No. ... in Chambers *or* Room No. ..., Central Office], Royal Courts of Justice, Strand, London WC2A 2LL, on .... 19... at ... am/pm, on the hearing of an application on the part of the Defendant for an Order that the assessment of damages and interest pursuant to the Judgment dated .... 19... be [tried by a Judge [alone *or* with a jury] *or* referred for trial to [an Official[5] *or* a Special[6]] Referee]

And that the Plaintiff do serve upon the Defendant within [14] days full particulars [of the injuries alleged to have been suffered by him and] of all special damages claimed by him

And that the Plaintiff do serve upon the Defendant within [28] days of today a list of documents stating what documents are or have been in his possession custody or power relating to the question or issue of damages claimed by him in this action [and that he do within the like period file an affidavit verifying such list] and that there be inspection of such documents within [14] days of the [service of such lists *or* filing of such affidavits]

And that the costs of this application be costs in [the issue of damages *or* the cause *or* the action].

DATED .... 19...

This Summons was taken out by G. H. & Co of (*address*), [Agents for (*name*) of (*address*),] Solicitors for the Defendant.

To the Plaintiff and to E. F. & Co of (*address*), his Solicitors.

1 See Paragraph 4 ante.
2 See Form 1 note 2 ante.
3 See Form 1 note 3 ante.
4 See Form 1 note 4 ante.
5 See Form 1 note 5 ante.
6 It has been many years since a special referee has been appointed: Supreme Court Practice 1997 para 36/10/1.

9
SUMMONS for trial of preliminary issue on the pleadings[1]

IN THE HIGH COURT OF JUSTICE [Ch] 19... B. No. ...[2]
[Chancery *or* Queen's Bench] Division[3]
[......... District Registry][4]

Between   A. B.   ...   Plaintiff
and
    C. D.   ...   Defendant

LET ALL PARTIES concerned attend before [[*in the Queen's Bench Division* Master .... *or* District Judge ....] *or in the Chancery Division* Master .... *or* District Judge ....], [Room No. ... in Chambers *or* Room No. ..., Central Office], Royal Courts of Justice, Strand, London WC2A 2LL, on .... 19... at ... am/pm, on the hearing of an application by the Plaintiff for an Order that the following question or issue raised by the pleadings in this action be tried as a preliminary issue before the trial of the other questions or issues in this action and that until the determination of the preliminary issue all further proceedings in this action be stayed [and that such further directions be given for the trial of the preliminary issue as may be necessary]

And that the costs of and occasioned by this application be costs in [the cause *or* the action].

The above-mentioned question or issue is the following:

WHETHER (*recite the question or issue to be determined*).

DATED .... 19...

This Summons was taken out by E. F. & Co of (*address*), [Agents for (*name*) of (*address*),] Solicitors for the [Plaintiff].

To the [Defendant] and to G. H. & Co of (*address*), his Solicitors.

1 RSC Ord 33 r 3. See Paragraphs 6, 8 ante. For an order see Form 10 post.
2 See Form 1 note 2 ante.
3 See Form 1 note 3 ante.
4 See Form 1 note 4 ante.

10

ORDER for trial of preliminary issue on the pleadings[1]

IN THE HIGH COURT OF JUSTICE [Ch] 19... B. No. ...[2]
   [Chancery *or* Queen's Bench] Division[3]
      [......... District Registry][4]
         [Master .... *or* District Judge ....]
Between   A. B.   ...   Plaintiff
                and
                C. D.   ...   Defendant

UPON HEARING [Counsel *or* the Solicitors] for the Plaintiff and for the Defendant

AND UPON READING [the Affidavit of .... filed on .... 19...]

IT IS ORDERED:

1. that the following question or issue raised by the pleadings in this action be tried as a preliminary issue before the trial of the [other questions *or* issues] in this action namely:

WHETHER *(recite the question or issue to be determined)*;

2. that until the determination of the preliminary issue all further proceedings in this action be stayed;

3. that the Defendant in the action be Plaintiff in the preliminary issue [and that the Plaintiff in the action be Defendant in the preliminary issue];

4. that the preliminary issue be tried in [London] by a Judge alone and be set down by .... 19... in the [Non-Jury General[5]] List Category [A *or* B *or* C[6]] the estimated length being ... days;

5. that there be a Certificate for the speedy trial of the preliminary issue;

6. that the costs of and occasioned by this application be costs in the preliminary issue.

[Certificate for Counsel]

DATED .... 19...

1   RSC Ord 33 r 3. See Paragraphs 6, 8 ante. For a summons see Form 9 ante.
2   See Form 1 note 2 ante.
3   See Form 1 note 3 ante.
4   See Form 1 note 4 ante.
5   See Form 2 note 7 ante and Paragraph 8 ante.
6   See Form 2 note 8 ante.

11

SUMMONS for trial of preliminary issues or questions[1]

IN THE HIGH COURT OF JUSTICE [Ch] 19... B. No. ...[2]
   [Chancery *or* Queen's Bench] Division[3]
      [......... District Registry][4]
Between   A. B.   ...   Plaintiff
                and
                C. D.   ...   Defendant

LET ALL PARTIES concerned attend before [[*in the Queen's Bench Division* Master .... *or* District Judge ....] *or in the Chancery Division* Master .... *or* District Judge ....], [Room No. ... in Chambers *or* Room

No. ..., Central Office], Royal Courts of Justice, Strand, London WC2A 2LL, on .... 19... at ... am/pm, on the hearing of an application on the part of the Defendant for an Order that the following questions or issues of [fact *or* law *or* mixed fact and law] be tried as a preliminary issue in this action before the trial of the action and that until the determination of the preliminary issue all further proceedings in the action be stayed

And that the costs of and occasioned by this application be costs in [the cause *or* the action].

The above-mentioned questions or issues are the following:

WHETHER a binding contract of compromise or settlement of this matter has been concluded between the parties;

WHETHER the Defendant is an accounting party and liable to account to the Plaintiff in respect of his dealings on the Stock Exchange between .... 19... and .... 19...

DATED .... 19...

This Summons was taken out by G. H. & Co of (*address*), [Agents for (*name*) of (*address*),] Solicitors for the Defendant.

To the Plaintiff and to E. F. & Co of (*address*), his Solicitors.

---

1   RSC Ord 33 r 3. See Paragraphs 6, 8 ante. For an order see Form 12 post.
2   See Form 1 note 2 ante.
3   See Form 1 note 3 ante.
4   See Form 1 note 4 ante.

12
ORDER for trial of preliminary issue[1]

IN THE HIGH COURT OF JUSTICE [Ch] 19... B. No. ...[2]
[Chancery *or* Queen's Bench] Division[3]
[......... District Registry][4]
[Master .... *or* District Judge ....]

Between   A. B.   ...   Plaintiff
                    and
                   C. D.   ...   Defendant

UPON HEARING [Counsel *or* the Solicitors] for the Plaintiff and for the Defendant

AND UPON READING [the Affidavit of .... filed on .... 19...]

IT IS ORDERED:

1. that the following questions or issues be tried as a preliminary issue in this action before the trial of the action, namely:

WHETHER a binding contract of compromise or settlement of this matter has been concluded between the parties;

WHETHER the Defendant is an accounting party and liable to account to the Plaintiff in respect of his dealings on the Stock Exchange between .... 19... and .... 19...;

2. that until the determination of the preliminary issue all further proceedings in this action be stayed;

3. that the Defendant in the action be Plaintiff in the preliminary issue [and that the Plaintiff in the action be Defendant in the preliminary issue];

4. that the preliminary issue be tried in [London] by Judge alone and be set down by .... 19... in the [Non-Jury General[5]] List Category [A *or* B *or* C[6]] the estimated length being ... days;

5. that there be a Certificate for the speedy trial of the preliminary issue;

6. that the costs of and occasioned by this application be costs in the preliminary issue.

[Certificate for Counsel]

DATED .... 19...

1 RSC Ord 33 r 3. See Paragraphs 6, 8 ante. For a summons see Form 11 ante.
2 See Form 1 note 2 ante.
3 See Form 1 note 3 ante.
4 See Form 1 note 4 ante.
5 See Form 2 note 7 ante and Paragraph 8 ante.
6 See Form 2 note 8 ante.

13
ORDER directing trial of partnership issue[1]

IN THE HIGH COURT OF JUSTICE   Ch 19... B. No. ...[2]
   Chancery Division
     [......... District Registry][3]
     Mr Justice ....
     .... 19...

Between   A. B.   ...   Plaintiff
   and
   C. D.   ...   Defendant

UPON MOTION made by Counsel for the [Defendant]

AND UPON HEARING Counsel for the [Plaintiff]

AND UPON READING the documents on the Court File recorded as having been read

[AND the Plaintiff by his Counsel undertaking that he will on or before .... 19... set the issue down for trial]

IT IS ORDERED that the following issue be tried before this Court that is to say:

WHETHER or not [the partnership in the pleadings mentioned is a partnership at will *or as the case may be*]

AND IT IS ORDERED that the issue be set down within [14] days of today for trial by a Judge alone in London in the [Witness List Part 2[4]], Category [B[5]] the estimated length being ... days and that the costs of this application be [costs in the issue].

1 Adapted from the order made in the Chancery Division in *Howard v Macarthur* (unreported, 1935/H/1139). See Paragraphs 6, 8 ante. For judgment after the trial of this issue see Form 18 post. For partnership generally see Vol 30 (1994 Issue) title PARTNERSHIPS AND FIRMS.
2 See Form 1 note 2 ante.
3 See Form 1 note 4 ante.
4 Chancery Division Practice Directions No 12A: Supreme Court Practice 1997 para 844.
5 See Form 2 note 7 ante.

14
SUMMONS for trial of preliminary point of law[1]

IN THE HIGH COURT OF JUSTICE [Ch] 19... B. No. ...[2]
  [Chancery or Queen's Bench] Division[3]
    [......... District Registry][4]
  Between   A. B.   ...   Plaintiff
                   and
                   C. D.   ...   Defendant

LET ALL PARTIES concerned attend before [[in the Queen's Bench Division Master .... or District Judge ....] or in the Chancery Division Master .... or District Judge ....], [Room No. ... in Chambers or Room No. ..., Central Office], Royal Courts of Justice, Strand, London WC2A 2LL, on .... 19... at ... am/pm, on the hearing of an application by the Defendant for an Order that the following point of law be tried as a preliminary point of law before the trial of this action and that until the point of law has been determined all further proceedings in this action [except for the determination of the point of law] be stayed

And that the costs of and incidental to this application be costs in the action.
The above-mentioned point of law is the following:
WHETHER (set out the precise point of law).

DATED .... 19...

This Summons was taken out by G. H. & Co of (address), [Agents for (name) of (address),] Solicitors for the Defendant.
To the Plaintiff and to E. F. & Co of (address), his Solicitors.

---

1 RSC Ord 18 r 11. See the Supreme Court Practice 1997 para 18/11/2 and Paragraphs 7, 8 ante. The application is often made on the summons for directions. For an order see Form 15 post.
2 See Form 1 note 2 ante.
3 See Form 1 note 3 ante.
4 See Form 1 note 4 ante.

15
ORDER for trial of preliminary point of law[1]

IN THE HIGH COURT OF JUSTICE [Ch] 19... B. No. ...[2]
  [Chancery or Queen's Bench] Division[3]
    [......... District Registry][4]
    Mr Justice ....
    .... 19...
  Between   A. B.   ...   Plaintiff
                   and
                   C. D.   ...   Defendant

[In the Queen's Bench Division UPON THE APPLICATION of the [Defendant] by Summons dated .... 19...

AND] UPON HEARING Counsel for the Plaintiff and for the Defendant
AND UPON READING [the documents on the Court File recorded as having been read (Chancery Division) or the Affidavit of .... filed on .... 19... and the exhibits in the said Affidavit referred to (Queen's Bench Division)]

IT IS ORDERED that the following point of law raised by the [Defence of the Defendant] in this action, that is to say, WHETHER (*set out the precise point of law*[5]) be set down within [28] days of today for hearing [by a Judge alone in [London]] in the [Non-Witness List *or as the case may be*[6]] Category [A *or* B *or* C[7]] for hearing before the trial of this action, the estimated length being ... days.

AND IT IS FURTHER ORDERED that until the point of law shall have been determined all further proceedings in this action except for the determination of the point of law be stayed.

The costs of and incidental to this application are to be [costs in the action *or as the case may be*].

[Certificate for Counsel]

1 RSC Ord 18 r 11. See the Supreme Court Practice 1997 para 18/11/2 and Paragraphs 7, 8 ante. For a summons see Form 14 ante.
2 See Form 1 note 2 ante.
3 See Form 1 note 3 ante.
4 See Form 1 note 4 ante.
5 The point must be clearly defined in the order: *National Real Estate and Finance Co Ltd v Hassan* [1939] 2 KB 61, [1939] 2 All ER 154, CA.
6 See Paragraph 8 ante. In the Queen's Bench Division the directions for trial and setting down would be as in Form 2 ante.
7 See Form 2 note 8 ante.

16

ORDER dismissing action after determination of preliminary issue[1]

IN THE HIGH COURT OF JUSTICE   Ch 19... B. No. [2]
    Chancery Division
        [......... District Registry][3]
        Mr Justice ....
        .... 19...
Between   A. B.   ...   Plaintiff
    and
         C. D.   ...   Defendant

UPON THE TRIAL of the preliminary issue directed by the Order dated .... 19...

AND UPON HEARING Counsel for the Plaintiff and for the Defendant

AND UPON READING the documents on the Court File recorded as having been read

THE COURT in answer to the question DECLARES that [the Plaintiff is not in point of law entitled to damages or an injunction as claimed in his Statement of Claim *or as the case may be*]

AND IT IS ORDERED pursuant to Order 33 Rule 7 of the Rules of the Supreme Court 1965[4] that this action do stand dismissed out of this Court with costs to be taxed if not agreed and paid by the Plaintiff to the Defendant.

1 Adapted from the order made on 9 March 1967 in *Radstock Co-operative and Industrial Society Ltd v Norton-Radstock UDC* [1967] Ch 1094, [1967] 2 All ER 812; affd [1968] Ch 605, [1968] 2 All ER 59, CA; RSC Ord 33 r 7. See Paragraph 10 ante.

2   See Form 1 note 2 ante.
3   See Form 1 note 4 ante.
4   RSC Ord 33 r 7.

17
JUDGMENT after trial of preliminary question or issue[1]

IN THE HIGH COURT OF JUSTICE   19... B. No. ...[2]
  Queen's Bench Division
        [......... District Registry][3]
  Between   A. B.   ...   Plaintiff
                              and
                             C. D.   ...   Defendant

DATED AND ENTERED .... 19...

The [question *or* issue] arising in this action by the Order[4] dated ....
19... ordered to be tried before [Master .... *or* District Judge ....]
having on .... 19... been tried before [Master *or* District Judge] and
[Master .... *or* District Judge ....] having [ordered that judgment as
provided be entered for the [Plaintiff] *or* dismissed the action]

IT IS ADJUDGED that [the Defendant do pay to the Plaintiff £...... and
his costs of this action to be taxed *or* the Plaintiff do pay to the Defendant his
costs of defence to be taxed *or as the case may be*].

1   Adapted from RSC Appendix A Form No 48; RSC Ord 33 r 7. See Paragraph 10 ante.
2   See Form 1 note 2 ante.
3   See Form 1 note 4 ante.
4   See Forms 10, 12, 13, 15 ante.

18
ORDER after trial of preliminary issue treated as trial of action[1]

IN THE HIGH COURT OF JUSTICE   Ch 19... B. No. ...[2]
  Chancery Division
        [......... District Registry][3]
            Mr Justice ....
                  .... 19...
  Between   A. B.   ...   Plaintiff
                              and
                             C. D.   ...   Defendant

UPON THE TRIAL of the preliminary issue directed by the Order dated
.... 19...

AND UPON HEARING Counsel for the Plaintiff and for the Defendant

AND UPON READING the documents on the Court File recorded as having
been read

AND the Plaintiff and Defendant by their Counsel consenting that the
trial of the issue should be treated as the trial of this action and the Plaintiff
by his Counsel undertaking not to make any application for the appointment
of any other person as receiver of the partnership between the Plaintiff and
the Defendant in the pleadings mentioned so long as there is no ground for
complaint as to the conduct of the Defendant as receiver

IT IS DECLARED that the partnership ought to stand dissolved as from .... 19... AND IT IS ORDERED accordingly

AND IT IS ORDERED that the following account and inquiry be taken and made, that is to say:

1. an account of all dealings and transactions between the Plaintiff and Defendant as co-partners from .... 19...

2. an inquiry of what the credits property and effects now belonging to the partnership consist

but this Order is to be without prejudice to the question whether the Defendant is entitled to take over the partnership assets or any part at a valuation

The further consideration of this action is adjourned and the parties are to be at liberty to apply as to the question

---

1 Adapted from the order made in *Howard v Macarthur* (unreported, 1935/H/1139). For an order directing the trial of the issue, see Form 13 ante.
2 See Form 1 note 2 ante.
3 See Form 1 note 4 ante.

19

ORDER on hearing of preliminary point of law disposing of whole action[1]

IN THE HIGH COURT OF JUSTICE   Ch 19... B. No. ...[2]
    Chancery Division
        [......... District Registry][3]
          Mr Justice ....
          .... 19...

Between   A. B.   ...   Plaintiff
                and
                C. D.   ...   Defendant

THE POINT OF LAW as to [the construction of the settlement dated .... 19... referred to in the Statement of Claim] and by the Order dated .... 19... directed to be set down for argument before this Court coming on this day to be argued before this Court in the presence of Counsel for the Plaintiff and for the Defendant

AND UPON READING the documents on the Court File recorded as having been read

IT IS DECLARED [upon true construction of the settlement dated .... 19... and made between the Plaintiff of the one part and the Defendant of the other part that the provision contained for .... does not extend to .... *or as the case may be*]

AND IT APPEARING that the foregoing Declaration gives to the Plaintiff all the relief claimed by him in this action

IT IS ORDERED that it be referred to a Taxing Master to tax [on an indemnity basis] the costs of the Plaintiff and of the Defendant of the action

AND IT IS ORDERED that such costs when taxed be raised retained and paid out of the Plaintiff's fund subject to the trusts of the [settlement]

1 Adapted from the order made in *Tyldesley v Tyldesley* (unreported, 1940/T/1606). See Paragraph 10 ante.
2 See Form 1 note 2 ante.
3 See Form 1 note 4 ante.

20
SUMMONS by plaintiff for judgment upon the determination of point of law[1]

IN THE HIGH COURT OF JUSTICE [Ch] 19... B. No. ...[2]
    [Chancery *or* Queen's Bench] Division[3]
    [......... District Registry][4]
Between   A. B.   ...   Plaintiff
            and
            C. D.   ...   Defendant

LET ALL PARTIES concerned attend before [[*in the Queen's Bench Division* Master ....*or* District Judge ....] *or in the Chancery Division* Master .... *or* District Judge ....], [Room No. ... in Chambers *or* Room No. ..., Central Office], Royal Courts of Justice, Strand, London WC2A 2LL, on .... 19... at ... am/pm, on the hearing of an application by the Plaintiff for:

1. the determination by the Court pursuant to Order 14A of the Rules of the Supreme Court 1965[5] of the following [question *or* point] of law, namely:

(*state with precision and clarity what is the question or point of law to be determined by the court*) and;

2. final judgment in this action against the Defendant for the amount claimed in the [Writ *or* Statement of Claim] with interest under Section 35A of the Supreme Court Act 1981[6] with costs to be taxed and paid by the Defendant (*or otherwise as the case may be specifying the full and precise terms of the remedies or relief claimed in the action*)

[AND FURTHER TAKE NOTICE that it is the intention of the Plaintiff to attend this application by Counsel.]

DATED .... 19...

This Summons was taken out by E. F. & Co of (*address*), Solicitors for the Plaintiff.

To the Defendant and to G. H. & Co of (*address*), his Solicitors.

1 See Paragraphs 11, 14 ante.
2 See Form 1 note 2 ante.
3 See Form 1 note 3 ante.
4 See Form 1 note 4 ante.
5 RSC Ord 14A.
6 Supreme Court Act 1981 s 35A (as inserted) (11 Halsbury's Statutes (4th Edn) COURTS AND LEGAL SERVICES).

21

SUMMONS by plaintiff for judgment upon the construction of a document[1]

IN THE HIGH COURT OF JUSTICE [Ch] 19... B. No. ...[2]
   [Chancery *or* Queen's Bench] Division[3]
    [......... District Registry][4]
Between   A. B.   ...   Plaintiff
                  and
                  C. D.   ...   Defendant

LET ALL PARTIES concerned attend before [[*in the Queen's Bench Division* Master .... *or* District Judge ....] *or in the Chancery Division* Master .... *or* District Judge ....], [Room No. ... in Chambers *or* Room No. ..., Central Office], Royal Courts of Justice, Strand, London WC2A 2LL, on .... 19... at ... am/pm, on the hearing of an application on the part of the Plaintiff for the determination of the law pursuant to Order 14A of the Rules of the Supreme Court 1965[5] of the true construction of the following document, namely (*specify with precision the document in question, for example, its nature, its date, the parties to it and so forth*) and therefore for judgment against the Defendant in this action for (*specify the terms of the judgment sought*) with costs of this action to be taxed and paid by the Defendant.

DATED .... 19...

This Summons was taken out by E. F. & Co of (*address*), [Agents for (*name*) of (*address*),] Solicitors for the [Plaintiff].

To the [Defendant] and to G. H. & Co of (*address*), his Solicitors.

1   See Paragraphs 11, 14 ante.
2   See Form 1 note 2 ante.
3   See Form 1 note 3 ante.
4   See Form 1 note 4 ante.
5   RSC Ord 14A.

22

SUMMONS by the plaintiff for judgment on a point of law under Order 14A or alternatively for summary judgment under Order 14 of the Rules of the Supreme Court 1965[1]

IN THE HIGH COURT OF JUSTICE [Ch] 19... B. No. ...[2]
   [Chancery *or* Queen's Bench] Division[3]
    [......... District Registry][4]
Between   A. B.   ...   Plaintiff
                  and
                  C. D.   ...   Defendant

LET ALL PARTIES concerned attend before [[*in the Queen's Bench Division* Master .... *or* District Judge ....] *or in the Chancery Division* Master .... *or* District Judge ....], [Room No. ... in Chambers *or* Room No. ..., Central Office], Royal Courts of Justice, Strand, London WC2A 2LL, on .... 19... at ... am/pm, on the hearing of an application by the Plaintiff for:

[Either:
1. the determination by the Court pursuant to Order 14A of the Rules of the Supreme Court 1965 of the following [question *or* point] of law, namely (*state with clarity and precision what is the question or point of law to be determined by the court*) and [for final judgment in this action against the Defendant for the amount claimed in the Statement of Claim with interest *or as the case may be, stating the terms of the judgment sought*] and costs to be taxed.
Or:
2. final judgment against the Defendant in this action under Order 14 of the Rules of the Supreme Court 1965 for £...... and interest (*outline the interest*) and the costs of this action to be taxed and paid by the Defendant.]

DATED .... 19...

This Summons was taken out by E. F. & Co of (*address*), [Agents for (*name*) of (*address*),] Solicitors for the [Plaintiff].

To the [Defendant] and to G. H. & Co of (*address*), his Solicitors.

1 RSC Ords 14, 14A. See Paragraph 14 ante.
2 See Form 1 note 2 ante.
3 See Form 1 note 3 ante.
4 See Form 1 note 4 ante.

23

SUMMONS by the defendant for the dismissal of action on point of law under Order 14A of the Rules of the Supreme Court 1965[1]

IN THE HIGH COURT OF JUSTICE   [Ch] 19... B. No. ...[2]
  [Chancery *or* Queen's Bench] Division[3]
    [......... District Registry][4]
  Between   A. B.   ...   Plaintiff
                                and
                               C. D.   ...   Defendant

LET ALL PARTIES concerned attend before [[*in the Queen's Bench Division* Master .... *or* District Judge ....] *or in the Chancery Division* Master .... *or* District Judge ....], [Room No. ... in Chambers *or* Room No. ..., Central Office], Royal Courts of Justice, Strand, London WC2A 2LL, on .... 19... at ... am/pm, on the hearing of an application by the Defendant for the determination by the Court pursuant to Order 14A of the Rules of the Supreme Court 1965 of the following [question *or* point] of law, namely, (*state with precision and clarity what is the question or point of law to be determined by the court*)

And for this action to be dismissed with costs to be taxed and paid by the Plaintiff to the Defendant.

DATED .... 19...

This Summons was taken out by G. H. & Co of (*address*), [Agents for (*name*) of (*address*),] Solicitors for the [Defendant].

To the [Plaintiff] and to E. F. & Co of (*address*), his Solicitors.

1 RSC Ord 14A. See Paragraph 14 ante.

2   See Form 1 note 2 ante.
3   See Form 1 note 3 ante.
4   See Form 1 note 4 ante.

24

SUMMONS by the defendant for the dismissal of action on a point of law under Order 14A or alternatively under Order 18 Rule 19 of the Rules of the Supreme Court 1965 or the inherent jurisdiction of the court[1]

IN THE HIGH COURT OF JUSTICE [Ch] 19... B. No. ...[2]
[Chancery or Queen's Bench] Division[3]
   [......... District Registry][4]
Between   A. B.   ...   Plaintiff
                            and
                           C. D.   ...   Defendant

LET ALL PARTIES concerned attend before [[*in the Queen's Bench Division* Master .... *or* District Judge ....] *or in the Chancery Division* Master .... *or* District Judge ....], [Room No. ... in Chambers *or* Room No. ..., Central Office], Royal Courts of Justice, Strand, London WC2A 2LL, on .... 19... at .... am/pm, on the hearing of an application by the Defendant for:

1. the determination by the Court pursuant to Order 14A of the Rules of the Supreme Court 1965 of the following [question *or* point] of law, namely (*state with clarity and precision what is the question of law determined by the court*) and consequent that this action be dismissed with costs to be taxed and paid by the Plaintiff to the Defendant;

2. alternatively, the Statement of Claim to be struck out and the action be dismissed under Order 18 Rule 19 of the Rules of the Supreme Court 1965 or under the inherent jurisdiction of the Court on the grounds that:
   2.1. it discloses no reasonable cause of action;
   2.2. it is frivolous and vexatious; and
   2.3. it is an abuse of the Court
and consequent that this action be dismissed with costs to be taxed and paid by the Plaintiff to the Defendant.

DATED .... 19...

This Summons was taken out by G. H. & Co of (*address*), [Agents for (*name*) of (*address*),] Solicitors for the [Defendant].

To the [Plaintiff] and to E. F. & Co of (*address*), his Solicitors.

1   RSC Ords 14A, 18 r 19. See Paragraph 14 ante.
2   See Form 1 note 2 ante.
3   See Form 1 note 3 ante.
4   See Form 1 note 4 ante.

25
JUDGMENT for the plaintiff upon the determination of a point of law[1]

IN THE HIGH COURT OF JUSTICE   19... B. No. ...[2]
   Queen's Bench Division
      [........ District Registry][3]
Between   A. B.   ...   Plaintiff
                       and
                       C. D.   ...   Defendant

DATED AND ENTERED .... 19...

The Plaintiff by Summons dated .... 19... having made an application for [the final disposal of this action on a point of law pursuant to Order 14A of the Rules of the Supreme Court 1965]

[AND the Plaintiff and the Defendant by their Counsel consenting to a judgment or Order being given or made on the determination of the point of law] and the Court having found for the Plaintiff and having directed that judgment be entered for the Plaintiff as appears

IT IS THIS DAY ADJUDGED that the Defendant do pay to the Plaintiff the sum of £... with interest at the rate of ... % from .... 19... and the costs of this action to be taxed.

[The above costs have been taxed and allowed at £... as appears by a Taxing Officer's Certificate dated .... 19...]

1   See Paragraph 16 ante.
2   See Form 1 note 2 ante.
3   See Form 1 note 4 ante.

26
JUDGMENT for the defendant upon the determination of a question of law[1]

IN THE HIGH COURT OF JUSTICE   19... B. No. ...[2]
   Queen's Bench Division
      [........ District Registry][3]
Between   A. B.   ...   Plaintiff
                       and
                       C. D.   ...   Defendant

DATED AND ENTERED .... 19...

The Defendant by Summons dated .... 19... having made an application for [the dismissal of this action on a point of law]

AND the Court having found for the Defendant on such point of law and decided that this action be dismissed

IT IS THIS DAY ADJUDGED that this action be dismissed with costs to be taxed and paid by the Plaintiff to the Defendant.

1   See Paragraph 16 ante.
2   See Form 1 note 2 ante.
3   See Form 1 note 4 ante.

27

JUDGMENT for the plaintiff (defendant) upon an oral application for the determination of a point of law[1]

IN THE HIGH COURT OF JUSTICE 19... B. No. ...[2]
   Queen's Bench Division
      [......... District Registry][3]
   Between   A. B.   ...   Plaintiff
                 and
                 C. D.   ...   Defendant

DATED AND ENTERED .... 19...

The [Plaintiff *or* Defendant] having during the course of the hearing of a Summons for an Order for discovery of particular documents under Order 24 Rule 7 of the Rules of the Supreme Court 1965[4] [*or as the case may be, stating the nature of the interlocutory application*] made an oral application for the final disposal of this action on a point of law [pursuant to Order 14A of the Rules of the Supreme Court 1965[5]]

[AND the Plaintiff and the Defendant by their Counsel consenting to a judgment or Order being given or made on the determination of the point of law]

AND the Court having found for the [Plaintiff *or* Defendant] and directed that judgment be entered for the [Plaintiff *or* Defendant] as appears

IT IS THIS DAY ADJUDGED that:
[Either:
1. the Defendant do pay to the Plaintiff the sum of £...... with interest at the rate of ... % from the ....19... and the costs of this action to be taxed.
Or:
2. this action be dismissed with costs to be taxed and paid by the Plaintiff to the Defendant.]

1 See Paragraph 16 ante.
2 See Form 1 note 2 ante.
3 See Form 1 note 4 ante.
4 RSC Ord 24 r 7.
5 RSC Ord 14A.

28

JUDGMENT on trial of question or issue in interpleader proceedings[1]

IN THE HIGH COURT OF JUSTICE 19... B. No. [2]
   Queen's Bench Division
      [......... District Registry][3]
[Either (*if the interpleader proceedings are in an action*):
   Between   A. B.   ...   Plaintiff
                 and
                 C. D.   ...   Defendant
                 and
                 J. K.   ...   Claimant
Or (*if the interpleader proceedings do not arise in an action*):
In the Matter of the Rules of the Supreme Court 1965 Order 17[4]]

And in the Matter of an issue ordered to be tried
Between   A. B.   ...   Plaintiff in the issue[5]
and
C. D.   ...   Defendant in the issue[6]

DATED AND ENTERED .... 19...

The above issue by the Order of [Master .... *or* District Judge ....] dated .... 19... ordered to be tried and the [Master *or* District Judge] having tried the issue and having found that at the time of the seizure by the Sheriff part of the goods seized, namely (*describe them*), were the property of the Plaintiff in the issue as against the Defendant in the issue

IT IS ADJUDGED that judgment be entered for the Plaintiff in the issue and that the costs of the issue be taxed and paid by the Defendant in the issue to the Plaintiff in the issue.

1   RSC Ord 17 r 5 (1)(b). See Paragraph 19 ante. For an order directing the trial of an interpleader issue see Queen's Bench Masters' Practice Forms No PF 31: Supreme Court Practice 1997 para 228.
2   See Form 1 note 2 ante.
3   See Form 1 note 4 ante.
4   RSC Ord 17 (as amended by SI 1996/2892, r 6).
5   That is, the claimant.
6   That is, the judgment creditor.

29

ORDER directing trial of issue on application to set aside registration of a foreign judgment[1]

IN THE HIGH COURT OF JUSTICE   19... B. No. ...[2]
    Queen's Bench Division
       [......... District Registry][3]
         [Master .... *or* District Judge.........[in Chambers]]

In the Matter of the registration in the Court of the Judgment of the .... Court, in the [Republic of Austria]

And in the Matter of the Foreign Judgments (Reciprocal Enforcement) Act 1933[4]

Between   A. B.   ...   Judgment Creditor
and
C. D.   ...   Judgment Debtor

UPON HEARING [Counsel *or* the Solicitors] for the Plaintiff and for the Defendant

AND UPON READING the Affidavit of A. B. filed on .... 19... and the Affidavit of C. D. filed on .... 19...

IT IS ORDERED that an issue be tried as to whether the [Austrian] Judgment dated .... 19... registered in the Court pursuant to the Foreign Judgments (Reciprocal Enforcement) Act 1933 should be set aside on the ground that [the Austrian Court had no jurisdiction in the circumstances of the case]

AND that the Judgment Debtor be the Plaintiff and the Judgment Creditor be the Defendant in the issue

AND the costs of, and incidental to, the Order and the issue be [costs in the issue *or as the case may be*]

1   RSC Ord 71 r 9. See Paragraph 22 ante.
2   See Form 1 note 2 ante.
3   See Form 1 note 4 ante.
4   Foreign Judgments (Reciprocal Enforcement) Act 1933 (22 Halsbury's Statutes (4th Edn) JUDGMENTS AND EXECUTION).

30
SUMMONS for leave to formulate special case[1]

IN THE HIGH COURT OF JUSTICE [Ch] 19... B. No. ...[2]
   [Chancery *or* Queen's Bench] Division[3]
      [......... District Registry][4]
   Between   A. B.   ...   Plaintiff
                      and
                      C. D.   ...   Defendant

LET ALL PARTIES concerned attend before [[*in the Queen's Bench Division* Master `......... *or* District Judge ....] *or in the Chancery Division* Master .... *or* District Judge ....], [Room No. ... in Chambers *or* Room No. ..., Central Office], Royal Courts of Justice, Strand, London WC2A 2LL, on .... 19... at ... am/pm, on the hearing of an application by the [Plaintiff] for an Order:

1. that the parties be at liberty to state in the form of a special case for the opinion of the Court the question arising in this action, namely (*specify briefly the question of law*), such case to be agreed by the parties or in case they cannot agree to be settled by a Barrister nominated by the parties or by a [Master *or* District Judge in Chambers];

2. that in the meantime all proceedings in this action other than those necessary for formulating and determining the special case be stayed;

3. that the costs of and occasioned by this application be costs in the cause.

DATED .... 19...

This Summons was taken out by E. F. & Co of (*address*), [Agents for (*name*) of (*address*),] Solicitors for the [Plaintiff].

To the [Defendant] and to G. H. & Co of (*address*), his Solicitors.

1   See Paragraph 27 ante. For an order and a special case see Forms 31, 32 post.
2   See Form 1 note 2 ante.
3   See Form 1 note 3 ante.
4   See Form 1 note 4 ante.

31
ORDER giving leave to formulate special case[1]

IN THE HIGH COURT OF JUSTICE   [Ch] 19... B. No. ...[2]
   [Chancery *or* Queen's Bench] Division[3]
      [......... District Registry][4]
         [Master .... *or* District Judge ....]
Between   A. B.   ...   Plaintiff
               and
               C. D.   ...   Defendant

UPON HEARING Counsel for the Plaintiff and for the Defendant
AND UPON READING the Affidavit of .... filed on .... 19...

IT IS ORDERED [by consent] that the question of law arising in this action namely (*specify the question of law*) be stated for the opinion of the Court in the form of a special case to be agreed by the parties or in the case of their disagreeing to be settled by a Barrister nominated by the parties or by a [Master *or* District Judge] in Chambers and that upon the judgment of the Court being in the affirmative on the question of law raised by the special case the sum of £...... or a sum ascertained in such manner as the Court may direct shall be paid by the Defendant to the Plaintiff together with the costs of the action to be agreed or taxed or that upon such judgment being in the negative judgment be entered for the Defendant with the costs of the action to be agreed or taxed

AND IT IS ORDERED that in the meantime all proceedings in this action other than those necessary for the stating and determination of such special case be stayed and that the costs of and occasioned by this application be costs in the action

1   See Paragraph 27 ante. For a summons see Form 30 ante; for a special case see Form 32 post.
2   See Form 1 note 2 ante.
3   See Form 1 note 3 ante.
4   See Form 1 note 4 ante.

32
SPECIAL CASE[1]

IN THE HIGH COURT OF JUSTICE   [Ch] 19... B. No. ...[2]
   [Chancery *or* Queen's Bench] Division[3]
      [......... District Registry][4]
Between   A. B.   ...   Plaintiff
               and
               C. D.   ...   Defendant

SPECIAL CASE formulated for the opinion of the Court pursuant to the Order of [Master .... *or* District Judge ....] dated .... 19...

This is an action brought by the Plaintiff A. B. against the Defendant C. D. for (*state the action shortly but clearly*).

(*State in numbered paragraphs all the facts as agreed by the parties*).

The question for the opinion of the Court is WHETHER the Plaintiff's cause of action (if any) lies in trespass.

If the Court shall be of opinion in the positive, judgment is to be given for the Plaintiff for the sum of £... (or a sum to be ascertained in such manner as the Court may direct) to be paid by the Defendant to the Plaintiff together with the costs of the action to be agreed or taxed.

If the Court shall be of opinion in the negative, judgment is to be given for the Defendant with the costs of the action to be taxed or agreed.

DATED .... 19...

(*Signature*)

[of Counsel *or* Solicitors for each party]

1 See Paragraph 28 ante. For an order giving leave to formulate the case see Form 31 ante.
2 See Form 1 note 2 ante.
3 See Form 1 note 3 ante.
4 See Form 1 note 4 ante.

33
ORDER on special case: Chancery Division[1]

IN THE HIGH COURT OF JUSTICE Ch 19... B. No. ...[2]
Chancery Division
 [......... District Registry][3]
  Mr Justice ....
   .... 19...

Between A. B. ... Plaintiff
 and
 C. D. ... Defendant

This SPECIAL CASE stated for the opinion of this Court and filed .... 19... coming on on .... 19... and this day to be heard before this Court in the presence of Counsel for the Plaintiff and for the Defendant

AND UPON HEARING what was alleged by Counsel for the Plaintiff and for the Defendant

THIS COURT BEING OF THE OPINION that:

1. [upon the true construction of the .... mentioned and defined in the special case and in the events stated in the special case the .... are as between the Defendant and the Plaintiff to be deemed to be .... *or as the case may be*] and;

2. that the costs of this special case and of this action ought to be paid by the Plaintiff

IT IS DECLARED AND ORDERED accordingly

AND IT IS ORDERED that it be referred to the Taxing Master to tax the costs of the Defendant of the special case

1 Adapted from the order made in *Dalton Main Collieries Ltd v Rossington Main Colliery Co Ltd* [1940] 4 All ER 384; affd [1941] CH 268, [1941] 1 All ER 544, CA. See Paragraph 27 ante.

2   See Form 1 note 2 ante.
3   See Form 1 note 4 ante.

34
ORDER on special case: Queen's Bench Division[1]

IN THE HIGH COURT OF JUSTICE   19... B. No. ...[2]
 Queen's Bench Division
  [......... District Registry][3]
   Mr Justice ....
Between   A. B.   ... Plaintiff
        and
        C. D.   ... Defendant

UPON READING the special case stated dated .... 19...

AND UPON HEARING Counsel for the Plaintiff and for the Defendant

THIS COURT ANSWERS the question submitted by the special case in the [affirmative or negative]

AND IT IS THEREUPON ORDERED that judgment be entered for the [Plaintiff for the sum of £...... and or Defendant with] costs [including the costs of this hearing to be taxed on the [standard or indemnity] basis]

1   See Paragraph 27 ante.
2   See Form 1 note 2 ante.
3   See Form 1 note 4 ante.

35
NOTICE OF MOTION for case to be settled for opinion of Scottish court[1]

(Royal Arms)[2]

IN THE HIGH COURT OF JUSTICE   Ch 19... B. No. ...[3]
 Chancery Division
  [......... District Registry][4]

In the Matter of a settlement dated .... 19... and made between P. Q. of the first part and R. S. of the second part and A. B. and J. K. of the third part

Between   (1) A. B.
       (2) C. D.   ... Plaintiffs
      and
      (1) C. D.
      (2) D. D.
      (3) E. D.   ... Defendants

TAKE NOTICE that the Court will be moved on .... 19... at ... am/pm or as soon as Counsel can be heard by Counsel for the above-named Plaintiffs A. B. and J. K. for an Order that a case may be prepared setting forth the facts and that such case and the questions of Scottish law arising out of the same may be settled by the Court for the purpose of ascertaining whether by the law of Scotland the purported appointment of a sum of

£...... contained in a deed of appointment dated .... 19... under hand and seal of F. D. is a valid and effective exercise of the power of appointment conferred on him by the above-mentioned settlement being a settlement in Scottish form relating to property in Scotland or whether the sum passes on the death of F. D. intestate under the trusts of the settlement in default of appointment and that such case and questions when so approved and settled may be remitted to the Court of Session in Scotland and that the Court may be requested to pronounce its opinion on such questions upon the law administered by the Court as applicable to the facts to be set forth in such case and that the costs of the application be costs in the matter.

DATED .... 19...

(*Signature*)

of (*address*), [Agents for (*name*) of (*address*),] Solicitors for the Plaintiffs

To the Defendants and to G. H. & Co of (*address*), their Solicitors.

1 British Law Ascertainment Act 1859 s 1 (17 Halsbury's Statutes (4th Edn) EVIDENCE). See Paragraph 29 ante. For a case see Form 36 post. For an order as to the validity of an appointment by Scottish law see *Topham v Duke of Portland* (1863) 1 De GJ & Sm 517 at 578–580. Nowadays such an application should be made by summons to the master; it should only be by motion if there is a sufficient degree of urgency or other good reason: Practice Direction [1984] 1 All ER 720, [1984] 1 WLR 447, para 2.
2 A replica of the Royal Arms must be printed or embossed at the first page of every originating process: RSC Ord 1 r 9 (2).
3 See Form 1 note 2 ante.
4 See Form 1 note 4 ante.

36
CASE STATED for opinion of Scottish court[1]

IN THE HIGH COURT OF JUSTICE Ch 19... B. No. ...[2]
Chancery Division
[......... District Registry][3]

In the Matter of a settlement dated .... 19... and made between P. Q. of the first part and R. S. of the second part and A. B. and J. K. of the third part

Between
(1) A. B.
(2) C. D. ... Plaintiffs
and
(1) C. D.
(2) D. D.
(3) E. D. ... Defendants

CASE under the British Law Ascertainment Act 1859 for the opinion of the Court of Session

1. By a settlement in Scottish form dated .... 19... and made between P. Q. of the first part, R. S. of the second part, and A. B. and J. K. of the third part, P. Q., who was a domiciled Scotsman, settled certain property in Scotland upon trust for R. S. for her life and after her death

upon trust to raise and pay the sum of £...... to such persons and on such trusts as F. D. should by document under seal during his life or by testamentary disposition appoint and in default of such appointment as mentioned.

2. By a deed of appointment in English form under the hand and seal of F. D. and dated .... 19... F. D. purported to appoint the sum of £...... to C. D. the son of G. D. of (*address*) absolutely on attaining the age of 21 years.

3. R. S. died on .... 19...

4. F. D. died intestate on .... 19...

5. The Plaintiffs are the present trustees of the settlement and are domiciled in England.

6. The Defendant C. D., who has attained 21 years of age, is the same person as C. D. mentioned in the deed of appointment.

7. The Defendants D. D. and E. D. are the persons entitled under the trusts of the settlement in default of appointment by F. D.

The opinion of the Court of Session is requested with reference to the Scottish law as administered by that Court and so far as the same is applicable to the facts set forth in the above case in terms of the British Law Ascertainment Act 1859 upon the following, namely:

QUESTION

WHETHER by the law of Scotland the purported appointment of a sum of £... contained in a deed of appointment dated .... 19... under hand and seal of F. D. is a valid and effective exercise of the power of appointment conferred on him by the above-mentioned settlement being a settlement in Scottish form relating to property in Scotland or whether the sum passes on the death of F. D. intestate under the trusts of the settlement in default of appointment.

DATED .... 19...

(*Signature*)
of (*address*), [Agents for (*name*) of (*address*),] Solicitors for the Plaintiffs

To the Defendants and to G. H. & Co of (*address*), their Solicitors.

1 British Law Ascertainment Act 1859 s 1 (17 Halsbury's Statutes (4th Edn) EVIDENCE). See Paragraph 29 ante. For a notice of motion see Form 35 ante.
2 See Form 1 note 2 ante.
3 See Form 1 note 4 ante.

37

MEMORANDUM identifying case stated for opinion of Scottish court[1]

IN THE HIGH COURT OF JUSTICE Ch 19... B. No. ...[2]
    Chancery Division
        [......... District Registry][3]

In the Matter of a settlement dated .... 19... and made between P. Q. of the first part and R. S. of the second part and A. B. and J. K. of the third part

Between (1) A. B.
(2) C. D. ... Plaintiffs
and
(1) C. D.
(2) D. D.
(3) E. D. ... Defendants

This case and the question of law arising out of the same above-stated have been settled and approved by Mr Justice .... as the case and questions to be remitted for the opinion of the Court of Session in Scotland pursuant to the Order in this matter dated .... 19...

DATED .... 19...

(*Signature*)

Senior Master of the Supreme Court

1 See Paragraph 29 ante.
2 See Form 1 note 2 ante.
3 See Form 1 note 4 ante.

38

NOTICE OF MOTION to apply opinion[1]

(*Royal Arms*)[2]

IN THE HIGH COURT OF JUSTICE   Ch 19... B. No. ...[3]
Chancery Division
[......... District Registry][4]

In the Matter of a settlement dated .... 19... and made between P. Q. of the first part and R. S. of the second part and A. B. and J. K. of the third part

Between (1) A. B.
(2) C. D. ... Plaintiffs
and
(1) C. D.
(2) D. D.
(3) E. D. ... Defendants

TAKE NOTICE that the Court will be moved on .... 19... at ... am/pm or so soon as Counsel can be heard by Counsel for the above-named Plaintiffs for an Order that the opinion of the Court of Session in Scotland upon the case and questions remitted to that Court pursuant to the Order in this matter dated .... 19... and which opinion has been filed in the Central Office of the Supreme Court of Judicature may be applied to the facts set forth in such case.

DATED .... 19...

(*Signature*)

of (*address*), [Agents for (*name*) of (*address*),] Solicitors for the Plaintiffs

To the Defendants and to G. H. & Co of (*address*), their Solicitors.

1 British Law Ascertainment Act 1859 s 3 (17 Halsbury's Statutes (4th Edn) EVIDENCE). See Paragraph 29 ante.
2 See Form 35 note 2 ante.
3 See Form 1 note 2 ante.
4 See Form 1 note 4 ante.

B: COUNTY COURT

39

NOTICE OF APPLICATION in county court for order referring question to district judge or referee[1]

IN THE ……… COUNTY COURT   Case No. …[2]
Between   A. B.   …   Plaintiff
                            and
                           C. D.   …   Defendant

The above named [Defendant] wishes to apply for an Order that the following question arising in these proceedings, namely (*state the question*) may be referred to [the District Judge of this Court or Mr J. K. of (*address*)] for inquiry and report pursuant to Section 65 of the County Courts Act 1984 and that the costs of and incidental to this application may be costs in the action.

DATED ……… 19…

(*Signature*)
Solicitors for the [Defendant]

THIS SECTION TO BE COMPLETED BY THE COURT

TO THE [PLAINTIFF]
TAKE NOTICE that this application will be heard by the Judge at (*address*) on ……… 19… at … am/pm.

IF YOU DO NOT ATTEND, THE COURT WILL MAKE SUCH ORDER AS IT THINKS FIT

1 County Courts Act 1984 s 65 (1)(d) (11 Halsbury's Statutes (4th Edn) COUNTY COURTS); CCR Ord 19 r 11 (a). See Paragraph 30 ante. For an order see Form 40 post.
2 Every document filed, served or issued must bear the title of the action or matter and the distinguishing number allotted to it by the court. CCR Ord 3 r 7 (1)

40

ORDER in county court referring question to district judge or referee[1]

IN THE .... COUNTY COURT   Case No. ...[2]
Between   A. B.   ...   Plaintiff
                                     and
                                     C. D.   ...   Defendant

TO ALL PARTIES

IT IS ORDERED that these proceedings and [all questions arising *or* the following questions arising in these proceedings namely (*state the questions*)] be referred to [the District Judge of this Court *or* Mr J. K. of (*address*)] for inquiry and report, pursuant to Section 65 of the County Courts Act 1984 (*add directions, if any, as to how the reference is to be conducted*)

AND IT IS ORDERED that these proceedings stand adjourned for the consideration of the report [until .... 19... at...am/pm].

DATED .... 19...

(*Signature*)

Judge

1 Adapted from County Court Form N280. See the County Courts Act 1984 s 65 (11 Halsbury's Statutes (4th Edn) COUNTY COURTS); CCR Ord 19 r 12 and Paragraph 30 ante. For notice of application see Form 39 ante.
2 See Form 39 ante.

41

REPORT of district judge or referee[1]

IN THE .... COUNTY COURT   Case No. ...[2]
Between   A. B.   ...   Plaintiff
                                     and
                                     C. D.   ...   Defendant

REPORT

WHEREAS, by the Order[3] in this action dated .... 19... the following question was referred to me for inquiry and report, namely (*state the question*)

Now I hereby report that I have been attended by [Counsel *or* the Solicitors] for the Plaintiff and the Defendant, and have taken the evidence on oath of the following witnesses (*list them*)

The documents set forth in the Schedule have been put in and proved where necessary

And I further report: (*set out in numbered paragraphs the findings of fact, referring in each case to the evidence supporting the finding and stating the inferences drawn from those findings, with the conclusions of law arrived at*[4]).

DATED .... 19...

(*Signature*)

[District Judge *or* Referee]

1 County Courts Act 1984 s 65 (1) (11 Halsbury's Statutes (4th Edn) COUNTY COURTS); CCR Ord 19 r 13 (g). See Paragraph 30 ante.
2 See Form 39 note 2 ante.
3 See Form 40 ante.
4 For a consideration of what the report should contain, having regard to the purpose of the procedure, see *Freeman v Dartford Brewery Co Ltd* [1938] 3 All ER 120.

JUDICIAL REVIEW

Practice

A: INTRODUCTION AND SCOPE OF THE TITLE

1. Introduction 75
2. Historical development 75
3. The Law Commission's reforms 75
4. Scope of the title 76

B: THE NATURE OF JUDICIAL REVIEW AND ITS REMEDIES

1: REMEDIES

5. Remedies 76
6. Certiorari 77
7. Prohibition 78
8. Mandamus 78
9. Discretion 79
10. Declaration 80
11. Injunction and stay 81
12. Damages 81

2: AMENABILITY TO REVIEW

13. Introduction 82
14. Who or what constitutes a public law body? . . 83
15. Source of the power 83
16. Powers deriving from the prerogative or creation of an organisation by Royal Charter 84
17. Contract as the source of the proposed respondent's powers . 85
18. The "Nature of the Power" or "Functions" test . . 85
19. Examples of bodies held to be amenable to review pursuant to the application of a "functions" test . . 86
20. "Domestic" bodies and informal tribunals . . 87
21. The special field of Crown or public employment . 87
22. Civil servants' employment 88
23. Statutory duties and employment law . . . 89
24. Inferior courts and tribunals 89
25. The Crown Court 90

3: EXCLUSIVITY OF PROCEDURE: THE PUBLIC/PRIVATE LAW DIVIDED

26. Exclusivity of public and private law procedural routes of challenge 91
27. Current trends in the public/private divide . . 91
28. The history of the procedural divide . . . 91
29. The exceptions to the "rule" 92
30. Transfer of proceedings 93
31. Collateral public law issues 93
32. Dual public and private elements within single statutory provisions 93
33. Matters of law 94
34. Collateral defences 94

35. Use of the "Winder" doctrine by public law defendants . . 95
36. Criminal Proceedings 96
37. Consent 96

C: GENERAL GROUNDS FOR OBTAINING JUDICIAL REVIEW

1: INTRODUCTION

38. Introduction 97

2: ILLEGALITY

39. The nature of "illegality" 97
40. Statutory construction 98
41. Improper purposes 99
42. Matters of law 100
43. Procedural ultra vires 101
44. Illegality by other miscellaneous means 101

3: PROCEDURAL IMPROPRIETY

45. Introduction 101
46. Statutory procedures 102
47. Duty to consult 102
48. Natural justice and fairness 103
49. Legitimate expectation 103
50. Exclusions 104
51. The content of natural justice 104
52. Bias 105

4: IRRATIONALITY, UNREASONABLENESS AND PROPORTIONALITY

53. Introduction 106
54. Irrationality vs. unreasonableness 107
55. Meaning of "unreasonableness" 107
56. Application 107
57. Examination of reasoning by the courts 108
58. "No evidence" cases of irrationality 109
59. Examples of irrationality 109
60. Qualifications to the doctrine 111
61. Proportionality 112
62. The future 113

5: UNLAWFUL DELEGATION, RIGIDITY AND ESTOPPEL

63. Introduction 114
64. Unlawful delegation 114
65. Fettering discretion 115
66. Legitimate expectation 116
67. Estoppel 116

D: SPECIFIC CASES

1: IMMIGRATION CASES

68. Immigration cases 118

2: HOMELESS PERSONS

69. Homeless persons 120
70. Rehousing duty 120
71. Applicants have an absolute right to require the local housing authority to review its decision 120

72. Applications for judicial review 121
73. Reasons 121
74. Damages 121

3: EDUCATION AND JUDICIAL REVIEW

75. Introduction 122
76. Reform 122
77. General duties of local education authorities . . . 123
78. General duties of school governors 123
79. Scope for judicial review 124
80. Admissions 125
81. Appeals arrangements 125
82. Complaints mechanisms 125
83. Discrimination in education 126
84. Exclusions 127
85. Special educational needs and provision 127
86. Assessment of special educational needs 127
87. Appeal 128
88. Other uses of review in the field of education . . . 129

4: PRISONERS' RIGHTS AND JUDICIAL REVIEW

89. Introduction 130
90. Amenability to review: governors and visitors . . . 131
91. Disciplinary hearings 132
92. "Managerial" decisions 132
93. Parole decisions etc 133
94. Unreasonableness 134
95. International aspects 135
96. Reform 135
97. Private law claims 135
98. Breach of statutory duty 136

5: MENTAL HEALTH CASES

99. Introduction 137
100. Authorised detention 138
101. Remedies 140
102. Discharges by bodies other than Mental Health Review Tribunals 141
103. Discharge by tribunals 141
104. Procedural provisions 143

6: TAXATION AND COMMERCIAL MATTERS

105. Introduction 144
106. Amenability to review 144
107. Grounds for review 146
108. Restrictions on review 148
109. Breach of statutory duty as an alternative to an application for review 149

7: SOCIAL SECURITY DECISIONS

110. Introduction 150
111. The decision makers 150
112. Judicial review or other remedies 151
113. Tribunals 151
114. Commissioners 153
115. Social Fund 154

E: PRE-REQUISITES AND OBSTACLES

1: OUSTER AND FINALITY CLAUSES

116. Introduction	155
117. Finality clauses	155
118. Ouster clauses before Anisminic	155
119. The effect of the Anisminic Case	156

2: LOCUS STANDI

120. Introduction	158
121. The type of interest that will suffice	159
122. Statutory locus standi	161
123. Inadequate locus standi	161
124. Locus standi of associations or groups of individuals	161
125. The relevance of the strength of the case	162
126. Locus standi – a two stage test?	162
127. The future of locus standi	163

3: TIME LIMITS

128. Time limits	163

4: THE NEED FOR PRIOR EXHAUSTION OF OTHER REMEDIES

129. Introduction	165
130. The exhaustion rule	165
131. When exhaustion is not required	166
132. Summary	167

F: EUROPE

1: EUROPEAN COMMUNITY LAW

133. Introduction	167
134. General relevance to proceedings in domestic courts	168
135. Legal analysis	169
136. Remedies	170
137. Special relevance of EC law for judicial review	171
138. Review of community institutions before the European Court of Justice	173
139. European Court actions against member states	174

2: THE EUROPEAN CONVENTION ON HUMAN RIGHTS

140. General	174

G: JUDICIAL REVIEW PROCEDURE

1: APPLICATIONS AND LEAVE

141. Applications and leave	175
142. Renewing leave applications	180
143. Substantive hearings	180
144. Special directions on leave applications	181
145. Service of the proceedings after the grant of leave	182
146. Entering a motion for hearing	182
147. Time and other procedural provisions	183

2: POST-LEAVE PROCEDURE

148. Challenging leave	183
149. Conditional grants of leave: security for costs	183
150. Appealing setting aside decisions	184
151. Respondent's evidence in reply	184
152. Discovery	184
153. Orders for cross-examination	185
154. Further evidence from applicants	185
155. Amendment of Form 86A	185
156. Settlement and compromise	185
157. Listing, dates for hearing	186
158. Discontinuance and standing out of lists	186
159. Preparation of documents	186
160. Uncontested applications	187
161. Procedure at the hearing	187
162 Precedent and issue estoppel	187
163. Costs	188
164. Appeals	188

Procedural Table

Applications for judicial review	191

Forms

1	*Notice of application for leave to apply for a range of remedies, including interim relief*	197
2	*Notice of application for leave to apply for a range of remedies based on legitimate expectation and unreasonableness*	200
3	*Notice of application for leave to apply for a range of remedies based on failure to take account of a relevant consideration [and or] procedural impropriety (prisoners' rights)*	202
4	*Notice of application for leave to apply for a range of remedies based on illegality and unreasonableness (mental health law)*	205
5	*Notice of application for leave to apply for a range of remedies based on unreasonableness, failure to take account of a relevant consideration, fettering of discretion by rigid adherence to a policy [and or] procedural impropriety; giving reasons for delay (education law)*	208
6	*Notice of application for leave to apply for a range of remedies based on failure to take relevant matters into account, taking irrelevant matters into account, error of law and unreasonableness (immigration law)*	211
7	*Affidavit of applicant in support of application for leave*	213
8	*Affidavit of respondent*	214

For affidavits	. see title	AFFIDAVITS Vol 3 (1994 Issue)
appeals		APPEALS Vol 5 (1997 Issue)
coroners		CORONERS Vol 13 (1992 Issue)
costs		COSTS Vol 13 (1992 Issue)
declaration, action for		DECLARATORY JUDGMENTS Vol 14 (1996 Issue)
evidence		EVIDENCE Vol 18 (1996 Issue)

injunctions . . .	INJUNCTIONS Vol 22 (1) (1996 Issue)
interim orders . .	INTERIM ORDERS Vol 22 (1) (1996 Issue)
interlocutory proceedings .	INTERLOCUTORY PROCEEDINGS Vol 22 (1) (1996 Issue)
tribunals and inquiries .	TRIBUNALS AND INQUIRIES Vol 40 (1996 Issue)

For the substantive law, see 1 (1) Halsbury's Laws (4th Edn) title ADMINISTRATIVE LAW paras 1–193

For the rules, see The Supreme Court Practice 1997

For cases, see 1 Digest (1992 Re-issue) title ADMINISTRATIVE LAW paras 838–2035

Practice

A: INTRODUCTION AND SCOPE OF THE TITLE

1. Introduction. "In recent years judicial review has become one of the most socially important and legally fertile areas of the law[1]." Judicial review is one of the principal means by which the courts seek to ensure the legality of the actions of the state and public bodies. In a development typical of English law, ancient doctrines developed in a very different economic, political and legal era were adapted and updated to help the courts come to terms with a society unimaginably larger and more complex than when the courts first began to control administrative action.

1 Lord Browne-Wilkinson in his foreword to Supperstone and Goudie *Judicial Review* (2nd edn, 1997).

2. Historical development. Judicial review has its roots in the early prerogative writs, in particular mandamus, prohibition and certiorari. These were originally granted at the suit of the Crown and were available only to the Crown to ensure that public authorities and inferior bodies carried out their duties and did not exceed their jurisdiction. By the end of the sixteenth century they were available to ordinary litigants, who could take such proceedings in the Crown's name without having to seek authority. Before 1933 there were two stages to the procedure. The applicant had to obtain an order of the court (a "rule") calling upon the respondent to show cause why the prerogative writ should not be issued, and this would be decided at a further hearing[1]. In 1933 a new system was introduced which required an applicant to obtain leave from the High Court to apply for the remedy, and this would be done on an ex parte motion[2]. In 1938 the three writs referred to above became prerogative orders and the formalities were simplified[3].

1 A similar procedure still exists for habeas corpus applications. See Vol 31 (1998 Issue) title PERSONAL RIGHTS Paragraph 28.
2 Administration of Justice (Miscellaneous Provisions) Act 1933 s 5 (repealed).
3 Administration of Justice (Miscellaneous Provisions) Act 1938 s 7, replaced by Supreme Court Act 1981 s 29 (11 Halsbury's Statutes (4th Edn) COURTS AND LEGAL SERVICES).

3. The Law Commission's reforms. In a report in 1967[1] the Law Commission referred to "procedural complexities and anomalies", the suggestion that "the law of judicial control ... is at present at the mercy of a formulary system of remedies" and the view that "we still lack a sufficiently developed and coherent body of legal principles in this field". In a later report it detailed all the anomalies and uncertainties[2] and in its final report on the subject it recommended a unified judicial review procedure with all remedies available in one action. This formed the basis in 1977 of a new Order 53 of the Rules of the Supreme Court 1965[3] and was given statutory force by Section 31 of the Supreme Court Act 1981[4].

1   Law Commission Working Paper 13.
2   Law Commission Working Paper 40 in 1971.
3   *Remedies in Administrative Law* Law Com no 73 Cmnd 6407.
4   Supreme Court Act 1981 s 31 (11 Halsbury's Statutes (4th Edn) COURTS AND LEGAL SERVICES).

4. Scope of the title. This title is concerned with the operation of the judicial review procedure introduced by the 1977-1981 reforms. An applicant may now make a single application to apply for any of the prerogative orders or other appropriate remedy or relief without having to select in advance any particular one to the exclusion of others. The title examines the remedies and reliefs and what they can achieve, identifies the issues that are justiciable and the bodies against which proceedings can be brought, establishes the grounds on which judicial review may be sought, looks at examples of the use of the procedure in relation to a range of different administrative decisions, and highlights some of the procedural barriers and difficulties. Explanations are offered of how to follow the procedure and make the application, and the appropriate specimen forms and precedents are provided.

B: THE NATURE OF JUDICIAL REVIEW AND ITS REMEDIES

1: REMEDIES

5. Remedies. Six remedies may be sought in proceedings for judicial review. They are: certiorari, prohibition, mandamus, declaration, injunction and damages. The first three have their origins in public law, the last three in private law. Each is dealt with below. The case law as to reviewability and grounds for review is to a large extent to be regarded as interchangeable. Before the reforms of 1977 each prerogative remedy had its own rules, particularly as to standing; but since 1977, unified rules for standing have been developed by the courts[1]. It is common practice, as is shown below, to apply for more than one remedy in the same application.

1   See *IRC v National Federation for Self-Employed and Small Businesses* [1982] AC 617, [1981] 2 All ER 93, HL.

6. Certiorari. Certiorari is employed to quash decisions (that is, those which have already been taken; not intended or prospective decisions) of a variety of public bodies. It is a discretionary remedy[1]. Historically, certiorari lay to control the judicial functions of inferior courts and tribunals. The remedy may not be directed by the High Court to any tribunal which is a branch of the High Court, or to an ecclesiastical court (although prohibition may lie against such a court[2]).

An order of certiorari will lie to quash:

1. the decisions of the Crown Court not relating to trial on indictment[3], and all inferior courts, both civil and criminal, and all statutory tribunals in England and Wales[4];
2. the administrative determinations of statutory bodies, for example local authorities[5];
3. the decisions of non-statutory bodies and those which derive their authority from prerogative power[6];
4. guidance circulars and codes issued for advisory purposes without statutory authority[7];
5. the decisions of public and quasi-public bodies such as: the Panel on Takeovers and Mergers[8], the Advertising Standards Authority[9], the Code of Practice Committee of the British Pharmaceutical Industry[10], the Life Assurance and Unit Trust Regulatory Organisation[11], the Association of Futures Brokers and Dealers[12], and the Financial Intermediaries Managers and Brokers Regulatory Association[13]; but not the activities of domestic or private tribunals such as those set up by trade unions, business associations, clubs, students bodies; nor decisions taken in the context of private employment[14].

Certiorari may be ordered to quash a decision for excess or lack of jurisdiction, error of law on the face of the record, unfairness and breach of the rules of natural justice, or decisions made in bad faith or procured by fraud or perjury[15].

1 See Paragraph 9 post.
2 *R v St Edmundsbury and Ipswich Diocese Chancellor, ex p White* [1948] 1 KB 195, [1947] 2 All ER 170, CA.
3 For the principles governing the grant of an order, see *Weight v McKay* [1984] 2 All ER 673, [1984] 1 WLR 980, HL, and *DPP v Crown Court at Manchester and Huckfield* [1993] 4 All ER 928, sub nom *R v Manchester Crown Court, ex p DPP* [1993] 1 WLR 1524, HL.
4 For example, medical appeal tribunals, as in *R v Medical Appeal Tribunal, ex p Gilmore* [1957] 1 QB 574, sub nom *Re Gilmore's Application* [1957] 1 All ER 796, CA; vaccine damage tribunals, as in *R v Vaccine Damage Tribunal, ex p Loveday* (1984) Times, 10 November; *Freight Transport Association Ltd v London Boroughs Transport Committee* [1991] 3 All ER 916, [1991] 1 WLR 828, HL.
5 See *R v Derbyshire County Council, ex p Times Supplements Ltd* [1991] 3 Admin LR 241 (local authority whose decision not to place advertisements in the Times Educational Supplement was made in bad faith and motivated by vindictiveness); *McCarthy & Stone (Developments) Ltd v London Borough of Richmond upon Thames* [1992] 2 AC 48, [1991] 4 All ER 897, HL.
6 *R v Criminal Injuries Compensation Board, ex p Lain* [1967] 2 QB 864, [1967] 2 All ER 770; *Council of Civil Service Unions v Minister for the Civil Service* [1985] AC 374, [1984] 3 All ER 935, HL and see *R v Solicitor General, ex p Taylor and Taylor* [1996] 1 FCR 206, [1996] COD 61.
7 *Gillick v West Norfolk and Wisbech Health Authority* [1986] AC 112, [1985] 3 All ER 533, HL; *R v General Medical Council, ex p Colman* [1990] 1 All ER 489, [1990] COD 202.
8 *R v Panel on Take-overs and Mergers, ex p Datafin plc* [1987] QB 815, [1987] 1 All ER 564, CA; *South Yorks Transport Ltd v Monopolies and Mergers Commission* [1993] 1 All ER 289, [1993] 1 WLR 23, HL.

9   R v Advertising Standards Authority Ltd, ex p Insurance Service plc (1989) 133 Sol Jo 1545.
10 R v Code of Practice Committee of the British Pharmaceutical Industry, ex p Professional Counselling Aids Ltd [1991] 3 Admin LR 697.
11 R v Life Assurance and Unit Trust Regulatory Organisation, ex p Ross [1993] QB 17, [1992] 1 All ER 422, CA.
12 R v Association of Futures Brokers and Dealers, ex p Mordens Ltd [1991] 3 Admin LR 254.
13 R v Financial Intermediaries Managers and Brokers Regulatory Association, ex p Cochrane [1991] BCLC 106.
14 R v BBC, ex p Lavelle [1983] 1 All ER 241, [1983] 1 WLR 23. The fact that employment is by a public body does not mean necessarily that certiorari will lie: R v East Berkshire Health Authority, ex p Walsh [1985] QB 152, [1984] 3 All ER 425, CA; R v Derbyshire County Council, ex p Noble [1990] ICR 808, CA; R v Royal Life Saving Society, ex p Howe (Heather Rose Mary) [1990] COD 440; R v Chief Rabbi of the United Hebrew Congregations of Great Britain and the Commonwealth, ex p Wachman [1993] 2 All ER 249, [1992] 1 WLR 1036; R v Football Association Ltd, ex p Football League Ltd [1993] 2 All ER 833, [1992] COD 52; R v Disciplinary Committee of the Jockey Club, ex p Aga Khan [1993] 2 All ER 853, [1993] 1 WLR 909; R v Showman's Guild of Great Britain, ex p Print CO 2014/96, 31 July 1997; R v Federation of Communication Services Ltd, ex p Kubis CO 1466/97, 3 September 1997; R v London Beth Din (Court of the Chief Rabbi), ex p Bloom CO 2495/96, 18 November 1997.
15 R v Bolton Justices, ex p Scally [1991] 1 QB 537, [1991] 2 All ER 619.

7. Prohibition. Prohibition will issue to prohibit the future decisions and determinations of the same public and quasi-public bodies which may be challenged by way of certiorari. It may issue conditionally, and in interim form[1]; nevertheless, where interim relief is required, an applicant should consider seeking an injunction[2].

Prohibition has issued to prevent magistrates from exceeding their jurisdiction[3], and to prevent a prison board of visitors from hearing a charge they were not entitled to hear[4].

1   R v Liverpool Corp, ex p Liverpool Taxi Fleet Operators' Association [1972] 2 QB 299, sub nom Re Liverpool Taxi Owners' Association [1972] 2 All ER 589, CA.
2   See Paragraph 11 post.
3   R v Horseferry Road Justices, ex p Independent Broadcasting Authority [1987] QB 54, [1986] 2 All ER 666.
4   R v Board of Visitors of Dartmoor Prison, ex p Smith [1987] QB 106, [1986] 2 All ER 651, CA.

8. Mandamus. Mandamus will issue to compel the performance of a public duty, in all cases where there is a legal right but no specific legal remedy for enforcing the right. An applicant will often seek orders of certiorari and mandamus together, for example, certiorari to quash an unlawful decision, with mandamus to compel the public body to re-take that decision in accordance with law, as clarified by the court[1].

The court will not order mandamus against the Crown, but may do so against Ministers[2]. The order will not issue against any superior court other than the Crown Court; nor against the Benchers of the Inns of Court to require them to admit a person to membership or call a person to the Bar[3]; but it will issue to compel the visitor to a university to act and determine a matter in a judicial manner[4].

The applicant seeking to enforce a statutory right must show that the public body is under a statutory duty whose performance is not a matter of discretion. However, mandamus will issue to enforce the performance of a duty to exercise a discretion, or to exercise a genuine discretion, or to exercise a discretion based on the appropriate legal principles[5].

Statutory and non-statutory (but not domestic) tribunals may be ordered by mandamus to "hear and determine according to law". Such a tribunal may have refused outright to hear the case[6], or may have acted in a manner amounting to a refusal.

Mandamus will not issue to the Crown Court in relation to its jurisdiction in trials on indictment[7], but an order of mandamus will lie to require the Crown Court to grant an applicant leave to appeal out of time against conviction[8], or where the Crown Court has refused to state a case for appeal to the High Court[9]. The same power exists in respect of magistrates[10].

Mandamus may lie to compel a chief officer of police to enforce the law[11], but will not issue to compel the Parliamentary Commissioner for Administration to investigate a complaint, in view of his full discretionary power[12]. A court might (but in the case in point did not) order the General Council of the Bar to hear a disciplinary matter[13].

1 See *R v Panel on Take-overs and Mergers, ex p Datafin plc* [1987] QB 815, [1987] 1 All ER 564, CA.
2 *Teh Cheng Poh v Public Prosecutor, Malaysia* [1980] AC 458, [1979] 2 WLR 623, PC; *Re M* [1994] 1 AC 377, sub nom *M v Home Office* [1993] 3 All ER 537, HL; *Padfield v Minister of Agriculture, Fisheries and Food* [1968] AC 997, [1968] 1 All ER 694, HL; *R v Secretary of State for the Home Department, ex p Phansopkar* [1976] QB 606, [1975] 3 All ER 497.
3 *R v Lincoln's Inn Benchers* (1825) 4 B & C 855.
4 That is, not to impeach on questions of either fact or law but to review an act outside jurisdiction, or abuse of power or breach of natural justice: *Patel v University of Bradford Senate* [1979] 2 All ER 582, [1979] 1 WLR 1066, CA; *Herring v Templeman* [1973] 3 All ER 569, CA; and see *R v Lord President of the Privy Council, ex p Page* [1993] AC 682, sub nom *Page v Visitor of the University of Hull* [1993] 1 All ER 97, HL; *R v Visitors of the Inns of Court, ex p Calder* [1994] QB 1, CA.
5 See *R v Port of London Authority, ex p Kynoch Ltd* [1919] 1 KB 176, CA; *Padfield v Minister of Agriculture, Fisheries and Food* [1968] AC 997, [1968] 1 All ER 694, HL; *R v Secretary of State for the Environment, ex p Brent LBC* [1982] QB 593, [1983] 3 All ER 321.
6 *R v West Norfolk Valuation Panel, ex p H Prins Ltd* (1975) 73 LGR 206.
7 *Re Smalley* [1985] AC 622, [1985] 1 All ER 769, HL; *R v Manchester Crown Court, ex p DPP* [1993] 1 WLR 1524, HL; *R v Crown Court at Manchester, ex p DPP* [1994] AC 9, HL.
8 *R v Crown Court at Croydon, ex p Smith* (1983) 77 Cr App Rep 277.
9 Supreme Court Act 1981 ss 28 (as amended), 29 (11 Halsbury's Statutes (4th Edn) COURTS AND LEGAL SERVICES).
10 Magistrates Courts Act 1980 s 111 (6) (27 Halsbury's Statutes (4th Edn) MAGISTRATES).
11 *R v Metropolitan Police Com, ex p Blackburn* [1968] 2 QB 118, [1968] 1 All ER 763, CA; *R v Metropolitan Police Com, ex p Blackburn (No 3)* [1973] QB 241, [1973] 1 All ER 324, CA.
12 *Re Fletcher's Application* [1970] 2 All ER 527n, CA; also applying a similar principle, *R v Broadcasting Complaints Commission, ex p Owen* [1985] QB 1153, [1985] 2 All ER 522; *R v Parliamentary Com for Standards, ex p Al Fayed* [1998] 1 All ER 93, [1998] 1 WLR 669, CA.
13 *R v General Council of the Bar, ex p Percival* [1991] 1 QB 212, [1990] 3 All ER 137.

9. Discretion. The granting of relief[1] is discretionary. The court will in all cases consider whether the conduct of the applicant is such as to disentitle him from relief. This may be undue delay[2], unreasonable or unmeritorious conduct[3], acquiescence in the conduct complained of[4], or waiver of the right to complain.

The court will not make an order which is unnecessary or futile[5].

The court may refuse mandamus where practical problems would arise from making the order[6], or where the form of the order would require detailed supervision by the court[7], or where the applicant has already obtained that which he sought to obtain by way of judicial review.

1   *Chief Constable of the North Wales Police, v Evans* [1982] 3 All ER 141, [1982] 1 WLR 1155, HL; *Neill v North Antrim Magistrates' Court* [1992] 4 All ER 846, [1992] 1 WLR 1220, HL; *R v Secretary of State for Social Services, ex p Association of Metropolitan Authorities* [1986] 1 All ER 164, [1986] 1 WLR 1.
2   *Caswell v Dairy Produce Quota for England and Wales* [1990] 2 AC 738, [1990] 2 All ER 434, HL.
3   *R v Crown Court at Knightsbridge, ex p Marcrest Ltd* [1983] 1 All ER 1148, [1983] 1 WLR 300, CA; *R v Secretary of State for Education and Science, ex p Birmingham District Council* (1984) 83 LGR 79.
4   See *R v Secretary of State for Education and Science, ex p Birmingham District Council* (1984) 83 LGR 79.
5   *R v General Medical Council and the Review Body for Overseas Qualified Practitioners, ex p Popat* [1991] COD 245; *R v Comptroller – General of Patents, Designs and Trade Marks, ex p Gist-Brocades* [1986] 1 WLR 51, [1985] FSR 610, HL.
6   *Chief Constable of the North Wales Police, v Evans* [1982] 3 All ER 141, [1982] 1 WLR 1155, HL.
7   *R v Peak Park Joint Planning Board* (1976) 74 LGR 376.

10. Declaration. A declaration states the rights of the parties without any reference to the enforcement of those rights, and, although binding, cannot as such be enforced. It has become the usual remedy in respect of statutory instruments and local byelaws. The court will grant a declaration only where the applicant has a real interest in raising a question of law, and where there is another party who has a true interest in opposing the declaration sought[1].

The court will not determine questions posed in the abstract[2]; but the Secretary of State's considered conclusion stated in a letter may amount to a decision susceptible of review, as would an expression of his "views", although a declaration must be intended to have practical consequences and must not merely be of academic interest[3].

In deciding whether to make a declaration or grant an injunction the court must have regard to:
  1. the nature of the matters in respect of which relief may be granted by order of mandamus, prohibition and certiorari;
  2. the nature of the persons and bodies against whom relief may be granted by such orders; and
  3. all the circumstances of the case.

It must consider that it would be just and convenient to make a declaration or grant an injunction[4].

It was held to be appropriate to apply for a declaration where the applicant knew of a draft Order in Council, prior to its being laid before Parliament[5]; or where the Race Relations Board had formed the opinion that the council were guilty of unlawful discrimination, but had not yet taken proceedings[6]; or where a Minister gave guidance requiring the Civil Aviation Authority to revoke an airline's licence[7]; or where a non-binding Code of Guidance issued under statutory authority incorrectly stated the law[8].

The court will expect a public body to abide by a declaration, even though it is not an order; a local authority which defied a declaration that it must make a hall available for an election meeting faced contempt proceedings[9].

1 *Russian Commercial and Industrial Bank v British Bank for Foreign Trade* [1921] 2 AC 438, HL; and see per LORD DIPLOCK in *Gouriet v Union of Post Office Workers* [1978] AC 435, [1977] 3 All ER 70, HL. See also *R v Somerset CC and Arc Southern Ltd, ex p Dixon* [1997] COD 323.
2 *R v Secretary of State for Defence, ex p Equal Opportunities Commission* [1992] COD 276, (1992) Independent, 27 February; it will be contrary to principle for the court to give what amounts to an advisory opinion, or to adjudicate upon an issue when no useful purpose would be served.
3 *R v Secretary of State for Employment, ex p Equal Opportunities Commission* [1992] 1 All ER 545, [1992] 1 WLR 872, CA.
4 Supreme Court Act 1981 s 31 (2) (11 Halsbury's Statutes (4th Edn) COURTS AND LEGAL SERVICES).
5 *R v HM Treasury, ex p Smedley* [1985] QB 657, [1985] 1 All ER 589, CA.
6 *Ealing Borough Council v Race Relations Board* [1972] AC 342, [1972] 1 All ER 105, HL.
7 *Laker Airways Ltd v Department of Trade* [1977] QB 643, [1977] 2 All ER 182, CA.
8 See *R v Secretary of State for the Environment, ex p Tower Hamlets London Borough Council* [1993] QB 632, CA where the Court of Appeal held that two sentences in a paragraph of the Homelessness Code of Guidance were unlawful.
9 *Webster v Southwark London Borough Council* [1983] QB 698, [1983] 2 WLR 217.

11. Injunction and stay. An injunction is a judicial remedy by which a person is ordered to refrain from doing (restrictive injunction) or to do (mandatory injunction) a particular act or thing. The court has power, in the circumstances set out above, to grant an interim injunction or an interim stay[1]. An injunction has the benefit of enforceable sanctions. An injunction may be ordered against the Crown[2].

Where leave to apply for judicial review is granted[3], then the court may grant an injunction in order to "hold the ring"[4]. It is proper where an injunction is to be sought that the applicant should put the proposed respondent on notice, despite the ex parte nature of the application for leave[5]. Where leave to apply for judicial review has been refused and the applicant renews the application to the Court of Appeal, he must show a strong prima facie case that the renewal will succeed in order to obtain an interim injunction pending the determination by the Court of Appeal.

1 See the Supreme Court Act 1981 s 31 (2) (11 Halsbury's Statutes (4th Edn) COURTS AND LEGAL SERVICES).
2 *Re M* [1994] 1 AC 377, sub nom *M v Home Office* [1993] 3 All ER 537, HL. See also *R v Licensing Authority established under the Medicines Act 1968, ex p Smith Kline & French Laboratories Ltd (No 2)* [1990] 1 QB 574, [1989] 2 WLR 378, HL.
3 *R v Cardiff City Council, ex p Barry* (1990) 22 HLR 261, CA.
4 *R v Kensington and Chelsea Royal London Borough Council, ex p Hammell* [1989] QB 518, [1989] 1 All ER 1202, CA.
5 See *R v Westminster City Council, ex p Augustin* [1993] 1 WLR 730, CA, where *R v Kensington and Chelsea Royal London Borough Council, ex p Hammell* [1989] QB 518, [1989] 1 All ER 1202, CA was distinguished.

12. Damages. The court may award damages if the applicant has joined a claim for damages to his application and the court is satisfied that if the claim had been made in private law proceedings, the applicant would have been awarded damages[1]. It follows that unlawful actions or decisions, or instances of maladministration, do not in themselves give rise to an award of damages. The applicant must show, for example, a breach of contract or negligence on the part of the public body. It has been held that a conspicuous failure by a respondent, over a long period, to answer letters, may amount to negligence sounding in damages[2]. Applicants should remember the existence of the tort of misfeasance in public office. However, this is available only against public officials who have exceeded their powers in bad faith or without reasonable cause, and who have been actuated by malice against the applicant[3].

1 Supreme Court Act 1981 s 31 (4) (11 Halsbury's Statutes (4th Edn) COURTS AND LEGAL SERVICES); RSC Ord 53 r 7 (1). See *R v Deputy Governor of Parkhurst Prison, ex p Hague* [1992] 1 AC 58, sub nom *Hague v Deputy Governor of Parkhurst Prison* [1991] 3 All ER 733, HL.
2 *R v London Borough of Lambeth, ex p Barnes (Olive)* (1992) 25 HLR 140 (the applicant also recovered damages to be assessed for breach of the statutory duty to rehouse her).
3 See *Bourgoin SA v Ministry of Agriculture, Fisheries and Food* [1986] QB 716, [1985] 3 All ER 545, CA; *Calveley v Chief Constable of the Merseyside Police* [1989] AC 1228, [1989] 1 All ER 1025, HL; *Jones v Swansea City Council* [1990] 3 All ER 737, [1990] 1 WLR 1453, CA.

2: AMENABILITY TO REVIEW

13. Introduction[1]. Before an action or a decision may be challenged by way of an application for judicial review[2] it must be established that:
1. the decision-maker is a "public law" body;
2. the decision was made under "public law" powers and not merely by agreement between private parties; and
3. the decision will, if validly made, lead to administrative action or abstention from action, by an authority endowed by law with executive powers, which alters the rights or obligations of a person which are enforceable in private law, or which deprive that person of some benefit or advantage which either he has enjoyed and which he could legitimately expect to be permitted to continue, until rational grounds for withdrawal of it have been communicated to him on which he has been given the opportunity to comment, or which he has been assured will not be withdrawn without an opportunity for him to make representations[3].

1 With regard to articles on the public/private law divide, practitioners may find the following useful: Peter Cane "Private Rights and Public Procedures" [1992] PL 192; Helen Power "The Exclusivity Principle" (1992) 142 NLJ 749; David Pannick "Who is subject to judicial review and in respect of what" [1992] PL 1; Jowell and Oliver; *New Directions in Judicial Review* (1988) p 23; Borrie "The Regulation of Public and Private Power" [1989] PL 552; Fredman and Morris "Judicial Review and Civil Servants: contracts of employment declared to exist" [1991] PL 485 (follows on from another article by the same authors in (1991) LQR 107); Arrowsmith "Government Liability in Quebec and the Public Private Law Distinction" [1990] PL 481; Gordon and Barlow "When is a defence not a defence?" (1992) 142 NLJ 1765; Supperstone and Goudie *Judicial Review* (2nd edn, 1997) 2.2. See also Paragraphs 26-33 post.

2　By virtue of the decision in *O'Reilly v Mackman* [1983] 2 AC 237, [1982] 3 All ER 1124, HL, the remedies of injunction and declaration may no longer be claimed in ordinary writ proceedings so as to achieve the same effect as a prerogative remedy in public law proceedings.

3　*Council of Civil Service Unions v Minister for the Civil Service* [1985] AC 374, [1984] 3 All ER 935, HL.

14. Who or what constitutes a public law body[1]**?** In the absence of a written constitution setting out the dividing line between the public and the private sphere, there can be no certainty as to the identity of bodies which will be found amenable to the court's supervisory jurisdiction. The test used by the court as an indication of a sufficient public law element no longer emphasises the "source of the power"; the approach has developed through an examination of the "nature of the power" or of the "functions" concerned, towards a consideration of whether there is a "potential governmental interest" in the domain in question.

1　David Pannick "Who is subject to judicial review and in respect of what?" [1992] PL 1.

15. Source of the power. Any individual or organisation exercising a statutory power or acting under subordinate legislation was traditionally thought to have been public in its origins. So far as public law status is concerned, this doctrine still holds good, but the body thus found to be public will not necessarily be held to be amenable to review, unless the challenged function is also properly seen as a public law function[1]. Where a body is alleged to be in breach of statutory duty, a private law action may be more appropriate than judicial review but that consideration is a different stage of the requisite analysis and does not mean the body itself is a private law body[2].

1　Examples of reviewable bodies are: the Army Board of the Defence Council (*R v Army Board of the Defence Council, ex p Anderson* [1992] QB 169, [1991] 3 All ER 375); Her Majesty's Attorney-General for Northern Ireland (*Breslin v A-G for Northern Ireland* [1992] 1 All ER 609, [1992] 1 WLR 262, HL); the Broadcasting Complaints Commission (*R v Broadcasting Complaints Commission, ex p Owen* [1985] QB 1153, [1985] 2 All ER 522 and *R v Broadcasting Complaints Commission, ex p BBC* (1992) Times, 16 October); Chief Constables (*R v Chief Constable of Cambridgeshire, ex p M* [1991] 2 QB 499, [1991] 2 All ER 777; *R v Chief Constable of Kent, ex p L* [1993] 1 All ER 756; *R v Deputy Chief Constable of North Wales Police, ex p Hughes* [1991] 3 All ER 414, CA); the Dairy Produce Quota Tribunal (*Caswell v Dairy Produce Quota Tribunal* [1990] 2 AC 738, [1990] 2 All ER 434, HL); an Election Court (*R v Cripps, ex p Muldoon* [1984] QB 686, [1984] 2 All ER 705, CA); the Chief Registrar of Friendly Societies (*R v Chief Registrar of Friendly Societies, ex p New Cross Building Society* [1984] QB 227, [1984] 2 All ER 27, CA); the General Medical Council (*R v General Medical Council, ex p Coleman* [1990] 1 All ER 489, CA), health authorities (*R v Ealing DHA, ex p Fox* [1993] 1 WLR 373); the Independent Television Commission (*R v Independent Television, ex p TSW Broadcasting Ltd* [1996 EMLR 291 HL); the Inland Revenue Commissioners (*IRC v National Federation of Self Employed and Small Businesses* [1982] AC 617, HL); the Legal Aid Board (*Bruce v Legal Aid Board* [1992] 3 All ER 321, [1992] 1 WLR 694, HL and *R v Legal Aid Board, ex p*

Bateman [1992] 3 All ER 490, [1992] 1 WLR 711); the Licensing Authority under the Medicines Act 1968 (28 Halsbury's Statutes (4th Edn) MEDICINE AND PHARMACY) (*Re Smith Kline & French Laboratories Ltd* [1990] 1 AC 64, [1989] 1 All ER 578, HL); the Lord Chancellor (*R v Lord Chancellor, ex p Maxwell* [1996] 4 All ER 751, [1997] 1 WLR 104; *R v Lord Chancellor, ex p Stockler* (1996) Times, 7 May, [1996] 8 Admin LR 590, CA); the Monopolies and Mergers Commission (*South Yorkshire Transport Ltd v Monopolies and Mergers Commission* [1993] 1 All ER 289, [1993] 1 WLR 23, HL; *R v Monopolies and Mergers Commission, ex p Stagecoach Holdings plc* CO/1570/95; (1996) Times, 23 July); the Local Ombudsman (*R v Comr for Local Administration, ex p Croydon LBC* [1989] 1 All ER 1033); the Parole Board (*R v Parole Board, ex p Bradley* [1990] 3 All ER 828, [1991] 1 WLR 134); the Statutory Committee of the Pharmaceutical Society (*R v Statutory Committee of the Pharmaceutical Society, ex p Lewis and Jeffreys Ltd* (20 December 1982, unreported) CO/563/82); the Registrar General (*R v Registrar General, ex p Smith* [1991] 2 QB 393, [1991] 2 All ER 88, CA); school governors (*R v Governors of Bishop Challoner Roman Catholic Comprehensive School, ex p Choudhury* [1992] 2 AC 182, [1992] 3 All ER 277, HL); the Director of the Serious Fraud Office (*R v Director of Serious Fraud Office, ex p Smith* [1993] AC 1, [1992] 3 All ER 456, HL); the Registrar of Trade Marks (*R v Registrar of Trade Marks, ex p Adidas Fabrique de Chaussures de Sport* (2 March 1983, unreported) CO/734/85); and universities (*R v Liverpool University, ex p Caesar-Gordon* [1991] 1 QB 124, [1990] 3 All ER 821 in relation to functions under the Education (No 2) Act 1986 s 43 (as amended) (15 Halsbury's Statutes (4th Edn) EDUCATION)).

2   *Roy v Kensington and Chelsea FPC* [1992] 1 AC 624, [1992] 1 All ER 705, HL.

16. Powers deriving from the prerogative or creation of an organisation by Royal Charter. Many functions of government are performed under the Royal Prerogative and several non-departmental bodies have been set up under the prerogative. Most such bodies are amenable in principle to judicial review[1]. In the GCHQ case[2] the House of Lords made it clear that the exercise of prerogative powers could in principle be judicially reviewed, but that particular aspects of the prerogative were unsuitable for resolution by adversarial process[3]. It used to be thought that a chartered body was not bound by principles of vires to the same extent as was a corporation created by statute[4]. The existence of a Royal Charter has been regarded merely as evidence of royal favour towards horse-racing[5]. However, administrative law has reached the stage where non-amenability to review is usually based on precedent[6], the concept of justiciability[7], the existence of ouster or "conclusive evidence"[8] clauses in statute or the creation of powers and duties in respect of which no-one has the locus standi to bring a challenge[9].

1   For example, *R v Criminal Injuries Compensation Board, ex p Lain* [1967] 2 QB 864, [1967] 2 All ER 770.
2   *Council of Civil Service Unions v Minister for the Civil Service* [1985] AC 374, [1984] 3 All ER 935, HL.
3   Some non-justiciable aspects of prerogative powers might be treaty making, defence of the realm, the prerogative of mercy, the granting of honours, the dissolving of Parliament and the appointment of ministers. However, prerogative powers under which a passport may be refused have been held amenable to review: *R v Secretary of State for Foreign and Commonwealth Affairs, ex p Everett* [1989] QB 811, [1989] 1 All ER 655, CA.
4   In *Pharmaceutical Society of Great Britain v Dickson* [1970] AC 403, [1968] 2 All ER 686, HL, LORD UPJOHN stated that such a body could lawfully extend its activities outside its charter, but its members could seek to restrain such action in order to prevent forfeiture by the Crown.
5   *R v Disciplinary Committee of the Jockey Club, ex p the Aga Khan* [1993] 2 All ER 853, [1993] 1 WLR 909, CA, (for commentary and report see (1993) 143 NLJ pp 158-9, 163).

6   As seen in the "sporting body" cases, Paragraph 20 post.
7   Most often seen in challenges to welfare provision, where the "duties" are characterised as mere "target" duties, subject to resources.
8   As seen in *R v Registrar of Companies, ex p Central Bank of India* [1986] QB 1114, [1986] 1 All ER 105, CA and see Paragraphs 116-119 post.
9   As in *R v Secretary of State for the Environment, ex p Rose Theatre Trust Co* [1990] 1 QB 504, [1990] 1 All ER 754 and see Paragraphs 120-127 post.

17. Contract as the source of the proposed respondent's powers. Contractual relations may indicate that the private law sphere is paramount between the parties, if contract is the sole source of the power[1]. This aspect of the test has been used to restrict the court's jurisdiction to supervise the functions of many sporting and professional associations. "Consent" in the sense of non-contractual but voluntary submission to a body's jurisdiction in order to participate in the field regulated by the body, may be regarded as distinct from contract and does not always[2] preclude judicial review.

1   An arbitrator's decisions, although judicial, derive from agreement: *R v National Joint Council for the Craft of Dental Technicians, ex p Neate* [1953] 1 QB 704, [1953] 1 All ER 327. Non-contractual arrangements, such as those pertaining between the General Medical Council and doctors, the Bar Council and barristers and the Law Society and solicitors (*R v General Council of the Bar, ex p Percival* [1991] 1 QB 212, [1990] 3 All ER 137; *R v Law Society, ex p Reigate Projects Ltd* [1992] 3 All ER 232), are amenable to review even though submission to these bodies' jurisdictions could be said to be consensual in a broad sense. Only exceptionally will review run against the Visitors to the Inns of Court: *R v Visitors to the Inns of Court, ex p Calder* [1993] 2 All ER 876, [1994] QB 1, CA.
2   But see *R v Disciplinary Committee of the Jockey Club, ex p the Aga Khan* [1993] 2 All ER 853, [1993] 1 WLR 909; *R v Football Association Ltd, ex p Football League Ltd* [1993] 2 All ER 833, [1992] COD 52; *R v Showmen's Guild of Great Britain, ex p Print* (CO 2014/96, 31 July 1997); *R v London Beth Din, ex p Bloom* (CO 2495/96, 18 November 1997).

18. The "Nature of the Power" or "Functions" test. The traditional analysis of functions performed by public bodies was that they were either judicial, quasi-judicial, administrative, "managerial" or "executive" in nature. The first three types of functions generally attracted judicial review, but the content of natural justice or the duty to act fairly would differ according to the judicial extent of the function concerned. The latter two types of function were rarely amenable to review[1]. Nowadays the nature of the function concerned is being used to determine the amenability of the proposed respondent to review and whether the precise conduct challenged is a "public law" action or decision[2]. However, the "functions" test is an additional step in the procedure, before an application for judicial review may be issued; it is not sufficient on its own. The body must still constitute a "public law" body; even recognised disciplinary functions exercised by a body found to be essentially domestic or private may not be made the subject of a judicial review, only of an action based on breach of implied terms[3].

1   See *National Coal Board, ex p National Union of Mineworkers* [1986] ICR 791, in which MACPHERSON J characterised the decision to close a colliery as executive - a business decision, so not amenable to review. This case was criticised as "probably wrongly decided" in the pit closure challenges brought against the President of the Board of

Trade and British Coal: *R v Secretary of State for Trade and Industry, ex p Vardy* [1993] ICR 720 and *R v British Coal Corp, ex p Price (No 2)* (1993) Times, 23 February, seeking to amend the declaration granted in *Vardy*. The court found that the respondents were under a statutory duty to consult under the Coal Industry Nationalisation Act 1946 (29 Halsbury's Statutes (4th Edn) MINES, MINERALS AND QUARRIES).

2   Examples of this approach may be seen in respect of non-statutory and non-contractual bodies, such as the Panel for Take-overs and Mergers, the self-regulatory organisations assumed to exist by the Financial Services Act 1986, Lloyds and various bodies regulating ethical or professional standards in the professions and commerce. The leading "functions" case is *R v Panel on Take-overs and Mergers, ex p Datafin plc* [1987] QB 815, [1987] 1 All ER 564, CA. Despite lacking prerogative, statutory or contractual powers the Panel's monopolistic powers and the implied devolution of responsibility for take-over regulation by the government were sufficient to attract review.

3   In *R v Fernhill Manor School, ex p Brown* (1992) Times, 5 June, neither the uncertainty of a private law action brought by a pupil's parents, nor the fact that pupils schooled in state schools might have grounds for judicial review against their local education authorities would entitle a private school pupil to use the public procedure. See, however, *R v Cobham Hall School, ex p S* (CO 3691/97, (1997) Times, 13 December) in which it was held that decisions of independent schools participating in the assisted places scheme were susceptible to judicial review. A private law challenge might be to the form or content of a procedure, or to a failure to apply it to an individual. In the latter case, the existence of a suspension or dismissal procedure within a contract of employment or education might lead to the grant of an injunction or a declaration within a writ action. In the former case, the form and content would be construed by the court, but not made to comply with administrative law standards, if it is merely a domestic procedure. In the case of universities, the court will not even seek to construe its domestic legislation, because the jurisdiction of a Visitor extends to the construction of matters of internal law: *R v Lord President of the Privy Council, ex p Page* [1993] 1 All ER 97, [1993] AC 682, HL.

19. Examples of bodies held to be amenable to review pursuant to the application of a "functions" test.

Decisions of the Advertising Standards Authority[1] and the Code of Practice Committee of the British Pharmaceutical Industry[2] have been found to attract the court's supervisory jurisdiction, but review was not available to challenge the decisions of the Chief Rabbi of the United Hebrew Congregations of Great Britain and the Commonwealth[3] nor those of Lloyds of London[4] nor those of most sporting bodies despite their monopolistic powers in areas of great concern to large numbers of the public[5].

1   See *R v Advertising Standards Authority Ltd, ex p Insurance Service plc* [1990] COD 42; *R v Advertising Standards Authority Ltd, ex p Vernons Organisation Ltd* [1993] 2 All ER 202, [1992] 1 WLR 1289. See also *R v Code of Practice Committee of the British Pharmaceutical Industry, ex p Professional Counselling Aids Ltd* [1991] 3 Admin LR 697. In the first ASA case, GLIDEWELL J in the DC used the "governmental interest" approach, holding that but for the ASA its functions would be exercised by the Director General of Fair Trading. David Pannick has suggested that there are similarities between this test and that adopted by the European Court of Justice concerning whether a respondent is a state body in respect of which a Directive should have direct effect, see [1992] PL 1 p 5. See *R v Supreme Court Taxing Master, ex p John Singh & Co* [1995] 7 Admin LR 849, (1995) Times, 3 May, in which the question of jurisdiction has to be resolved by looking at the function being performed by the person or body whose decision is being challenged and not the office held by the person or the general description of the body.

2   See *R v Code of Practice Committee of the British Pharmaceutical Industry, ex p Professional Counselling Aids Ltd* [1991] 3 Admin LR 697.

3   *R v Chief Rabbi of the United Hebrew Congregations of Great Britain and the Commonwealth, ex p Wachmann* [1993] 2 All ER 249, [1992] 1 WLR 1036 (his powers being essentially spiritual and religious and not of governmental concern); *R v London Beth Din, ex p Bloom* (CO 2495/96, 18 November 1997).

4 See *R v Lloyd's of London, ex p Briggs* [1993] 1 Lloyd's Rep 176, at least with regard to matters arising from contracts with members. See also *R v Committee of Lloyds, ex p Postgate* (1983) Times, 12 January concerning the exercise of statutory functions.
5 See Paragraph 20 post.

20. "Domestic" bodies and informal tribunals. Sporting bodies and informal tribunals that may be said to be dispensing domestic justice rather than the law of the land may not be judicially reviewable. The courts have tended to hold that whilst the public is very interested in sport, the regulation of sporting interests is not a matter of the public interest[1]. It has been assumed that university senate committees could be made amenable to review[2], but it was suggested in a later case that a disciplinary decision of a university is made pursuant to a contract[3]. Certain university visitors now appear to have exclusive jurisdiction as to the meaning of university statutes by virtue of their status as eleemosynary charitable bodies. This means that they may not be judicially reviewed on the grounds of error of law, but are still susceptible to review for breaches of procedural fairness, or charges of bad faith or irrationality[4].

1 See *Law v National Greyhound Racing Club Ltd* [1983] 3 All ER 300, [1983] 1 WLR 1302, CA; *R v Disciplinary Committee of the Jockey Club, ex p Massingberd-Mundy* [1993] 2 All ER 207, despite its near monopolistic powers in an area in which many earn a livelihood; *R v Jockey Club, ex p RAM Racecourses Ltd* [1993] 2 All ER 225; and *R v Disciplinary Committee of the Jockey Club, ex p Aga Khan* [1993] 2 All ER 853, [1993] 1 WLR 909, CA (for commentary and report see (1993) 143 NLJ pp 158-9, 163); *R v Football Association Ltd, ex p Football League Ltd* [1993] 2 All ER 833, [1992] COD 52; *R v Football Association of Wales, ex p Flint Town UFC* [1991] COD 44. Compare the law in New Zealand, where *Finnigan v New Zealand Rugby Football Union Inc* [1985] 2 NZLR 159 established that tenuous contractual linking of the regulatory body and the aggrieved members of clubs around the country did not detract from the public law element in the case.
2 *R v Aston University Senate, ex p Roffey* [1969] 2 QB 538, [1969] 2 All ER 964; *R v University of Liverpool, ex p Caesar-Gordon* [1991] 1 QB 124, [1990] 3 All ER 821.
3 *Herring v Templeman* [1973] 3 All ER 569 at 585; *Kent v University College London* (1992) Times, 18 February, (1992) 156 LG Rev 1003, CA.
4 *R v HM the Queen in Council, ex p Vijayatunga* [1990] 2 QB 444; *r v Lord President of the Privy Council, ex p Page* [1993] AC 682, [1993] 1 All ER 97, HL: this involved construction of the University of Hull's statutes, which allowed for dismissal of lecturers for good cause but not for redundancy. The Court of Appeal held the Visitor's refusal to overturn a dismissal was amenable to review but also that he had not misconstrued the statute. The House of Lords held by a majority that where the Visitor had power to enter into the adjudication, errors of law or fact within that adjudication were not amenable to review.

21. The special field of Crown or public employment. Claims for breach of contract are based on private law rights, and employment contracts are no different, even though the employer may be a public authority. It is not enough that the public has an interest in the performance of a public employee's duties, if his or her challenge merely concerns the infringement of contractual rights[1]. There has to be a statutory provision directly bearing on the right of the public authority to dismiss or suspend before sufficient "statutory underpinning" will be established to attract review of treatment meted out to public employees[2]. Where a challenge amounts to a personal claim against the employer, or relates to the factual circumstances of dismissal, no more than an ordinary master and servant situation is concerned and the proper procedure to use is the ordinary law or that of unfair dismissal before an industrial tribunal. Office holders may be better off if they have been appointed by those acting under a prerogative or statutory power. Where the challenge involves an allegation of a breach of a disciplinary code imposed on the employer by statute or the prerogative, or is to a code applied by a body set up under statute or the prerogative, then a necessary public element will be established and review will be available.

A better remedy before an ordinary civil court or industrial tribunal may exist for certain sorts of civil servant[3]. The vital distinction is between those who are subject to a code by virtue of appointment, and those who are subject to it by virtue of incorporation through a contract; the former may generally bring review proceedings, whilst the latter are obliged to use ordinary proceedings, unless their complaint is that the code has not been duly incorporated as required by statute.

1   In the case of *R v BBC, ex p Lavelle* [1983] 1 All ER 241, [1983] 1 WLR 23 an employee of the BBC was sacked and brought judicial review proceedings. She was criticised for her choice of procedure for what was seen as a private law employment matter between master and servant. In *R v East Berkshire HA, ex p Walsh* [1985] QB 152, [1983] 3 All ER 425, CA, an NHS nursing officer applied for review of an authority's decision to dismiss him, saying that the procedural code had been breached. The disciplinary procedure was approved by the Secretary of State in regulations but it had also been incorporated into his contract of employment. This made it an essentially private law problem. See also *R v Trent RHA, ex p Jones* 1986 Times, 19 June (consultant surgeon); *Connor v Strathclyde Regional Council* (1986) SLT 530 (teacher) and contrast with *Janaway v Salford Area Health Authority* [1989] AC 537, [1988] 3 All ER 1079, HL (secretary's dismissal by health authority amenable to judicial review).
2   See, for example, *Ridge v Baldwin* [1964] AC 40, [1963] 2 All ER 66, HL; *Vine v National Dock Labour Board* [1957] AC 488, [1956] 3 All ER 939, HL; *Malloch v Aberdeen Corp* [1971] 2 All ER 1278, [1971] 1 WLR 1578, HL (all pre-*O'Reilly v Mackman* [1983] 2 AC 237, [1982] 3 All ER 1124, HL, see Paragraph 26 post).
3   For example, contractual terms can only be varied by consent. See Fredman and Morris "Judicial Review and Civil Servants: contracts of employment declared to exist" [1991] PL 485 following on from (1991) 107 LQR and see also B Walsh "Judicial Review of Dismissal from Employment: Coherence or Confusion?" [1989] PL 131.

22. Civil servants' employment. The function of employment by bodies operating in the public field has been the commonest example of a non-reviewable function. In particular, civil servants have been in an ambiguous position, the traditional doctrine being that they were not employed under contract. Review has been seen as an attractive remedy because certiorari would wipe out the dismissal leaving the individual in possession of his job. In private law only damages would have been available, and the employment protection legislation rarely gives rise to reinstatement. In *R v Lord Chancellor's Department, ex p Nangle*[1] it was decided that the requisite intention to create legal relations does exist, so they do all enjoy a contractual position. This closed the door to judicial review of most aspects of civil servants' employment. One way in which an employee of the Crown or a public body is better off, however, is that a general policy decision of their employer may be challenged on grounds for judicial review[2].

1   *R v Lord Chancellor's Department, ex p Nangle* [1992] 1 All ER 897. Nangle was an officer in the Lord Chancellor's Department. He pursued alternative remedies for his having been disciplined for sexual harassment, and finally claimed judicial review on the grounds of breach of natural justice in one of the internal hearings he had been given. A comparison was made with cases in which the Civil Service Appeal Board had been judicially reviewed. Whilst the CSAB was set up under the prerogative, the proceedings here resulted directly from the decisions of the employer and ended up with a decision from that employer, not a tribunal. Note that although it was held that he had a contract of employment and could have used an industrial tribunal for redress, it was more generally held that the absence of a private law remedy would not mean that an individual could automatically use public law.
2   For example, the GCHQ case: *Council of Civil Service Unions v Minister for the Civil Service* [1985] AC 374, [1984] 3 All ER 935, HL and *R v London Borough of Hammersmith and Fulham, ex p NALGO* [1991] IRLR 249.

23. Statutory duties and employment law. In *Roy v Kensington and Chelsea FPC*[1], a Family Practitioner Committee acting under statutory powers withheld a proportion of a doctor's basic pay, alleging that he had given insufficient hours to his work. The full rate was payable only if the Committee was satisfied with the hours put in. He issued a writ contending he had done enough hours. The Committee said he should have proceeded by way of judicial review. The House of Lords disagreed. Lord Lowry called Lord Diplock's exclusivity rule "a procedural minefield". He refused to say whether the doctor's rights were actually contractual, since he was satisfied they were private in any event. He said that if Dr Roy's complaint against the Committee succeeded, he would be entitled to the payment of the money withheld, and a person should not be required to use Order 53 of the Rules of the Supreme Court 1965 to claim a non-discretionary remedy. The Lords' view of the *O'Reilly*[2] doctrine was that it meant that one had to use judicial review only if no private law rights were invoked.

1   *Roy v Kensington and Chelsea and Westminster Family Practitioner Committee* [1992] 1 AC 624, [1992] 1 All ER 705, HL.
2   *O'Reilly v Mackman* [1983] 2 AC 237, [1982] 3 All ER 1124, HL. See Paragraphs 26–37 post.

24. Inferior courts and tribunals. No relief may be granted in judicial review proceedings against any Superior Court, ie the House of Lords, the Court of Appeal and the High Court. Most other inferior bodies are required by Parliament to apply the law correctly; in so far as they make errors of law, they are amenable to review. Inferior courts[1] such as magistrates' courts, coroners' courts[2] and county courts[3] are not allowed to make errors of law either and certiorari is available against them too. However, Parliament can, if it wishes, confine a decision on a question of law to a particular inferior court and provide that it shall be final, and if it does so, then the supervisory jurisdiction of the High Court is ousted.

1   The Courts Martial Appeal Court is a superior court by virtue of the Courts-Martial (Appeals) Act 1968 s 1 (2) (3 Halsbury's Statutes (4th Edn) ARMED FORCES).
2   *R v Wolverhampton Coroner, ex p McCurbin* [1990] 2 All ER 759, [1990] 1 WLR 719, CA; *R v Poplar Coroner, ex p Thomas* [1993] QB 610, [1993] 2 All ER 381, CA.

3 For example, *R v Leeds County Council, ex p Morris* [1990] 1 QB 523, [1990] 1 All ER 550; *R v Gwynedd County Council, ex p B* [1992] 3 All ER 317, CA.

25. The Crown Court. Although the Crown Court is part of the Supreme Court, the High Court possesses all such jurisdiction as it possesses in relation to inferior courts, in relation to all Crown Court decisions other than those relating to trial on indictment, under the Supreme Court Act 1981[1]. The test in that section is whether the impugned decision was an integral part of the trial process: if so, review is not available[2]. If the decision is truly collateral, judicial review may lie. The following decisions have been held to be amenable to review:

1. forfeiture of the recognisance of a surety[3];
2. forfeiture of property belonging to a person not a defendant in the criminal proceedings[4];
3. a bind-over of an acquitted defendant[5];
4. a decision to make an order under Section 39 of the Children and Young Persons Act 1933 prohibiting publication of proceedings calculated to lead to the identification of a child[6];
5. extension of custody limits under Section 22 of the Prosecution of Offences Act 1985[7];

but examples of matters held to relate to trial on indictment are as follows:

1. order by a trial judge that proceedings be held in camera[8];
2. an order that counts of an indictment should lie on the file[9];
3. jury vetting before trial[10];
4. an order that an acquitted defendant pay a contribution to his legal aid costs[11] or that his costs not be paid out of public funds[12];
5. warrant of imprisonment ordering a sentence to run consecutively rather than concurrently with another[13];
6. a decision to reverse an order discharging a legal aid certificate[14];
7. a decision whether or not to stay the trial of an indictment on the ground of abuse of process[15];
8. a decision to make no order as to costs after no evidence was offered[16].

1 Supreme Court Act 1981 s 29 (3) (11 Halsbury's Statutes (4th Edn) COURTS AND LEGAL SERVICES).
2 *Re Smalley* [1985] AC 622, HL; *Re Ashton* [1993] 2 All ER 663, [1994] AC 9, HL; *R v Manchester Crown Court, ex p DPP* [1993] 1 WLR 1524, 94 Cr App Rep 461, HL.
3 *Re Smalley* [1985] AC 622, [1985] 1 All ER 769, HL.
4 *R v Crown Court at Maidstone, ex p Gill* [1987] 1 All ER 129, [1986] 1 WLR 1405.
5 *R v Crown Court at Inner London, ex p Benjamin* (1986) 85 Cr App Rep 267.
6 Children and Young Persons Act 1933 s 39 (as amended) (6 Halsbury's Statutes (4th Edn) CHILDREN). *R v Crown Court at Leicester, ex p S (a minor)* [1992] 2 All ER 659, [1993] 1 WLR 111n; *R v Cardiff Crown Court, ex p M (a minor)* (1998) Times, 28 April.
7 Prosecution of Offences Act 1985 s 22 (as amended). *R v Maidstone Crown Court, ex p Schulz* (1992) 157 JP 601; *R v Governor of Winchester Prison, ex p Roddie* [1991] 2 All ER 931, [1991] 1 WLR 303; *R v Norwich Crown Court, ex p Stiller* [1992] 4 Admin LR 709, 156 JP 624.
8 *R v Reading Crown Court, ex p Ecclestone and Jennings* (23 September 1986, unreported, CO/1034/86).
9 *R v Central Criminal Court, ex p Raymond* [1986] 2 All ER 379, [1986] 1 WLR 710.
10 *R v Crown Court at Sheffield, ex p Brownlow* [1980] QB 530, [1980] 2 All ER 444, CA.
11 *Sampson v Crown Court at Croydon* [1987] 1 All ER 609, HL.
12 *R v Central Criminal Court, ex p Spens* (1992) Independent, 1 December, [1993] COD 194.

13 *R v Crown Court at Lewes, ex p Sinclair* (1992) 136 Sol Jo LB 227.
14 *R v Crown Court at Isleworth, ex p Willington* [1993] 2 All ER 390, [1993] 1 WLR 713.
15 *R v Crown Court at Manchester, ex p DPP* [1994] AC 9 [1993] 2 All ER 663, [1993] 2 WLR 846, HL, overturning *R v Central Criminal Court, ex p Randle and Pottle* [1992] 1 All ER 370, [1992] 1 WLR 1087 on this point.
16 *R v Harrow Crown Court, ex p Perkins* (1998) Times, 28 April.

3: EXCLUSIVITY OF PROCEDURE: THE PUBLIC/PRIVATE LAW DIVIDED

26. Exclusivity of public and private law procedural routes of challenge. The general rule since 1983 has been that it is an abuse of the process of the court to use an ordinary action to challenge a public law decision of a public authority; this is because a plaintiff would be able to evade the special provisions of RSC Order 53[1], said to have been introduced for the protection of public authorities[2].

1 RSC Ord 53.
2 "As a general rule it would be contrary to public policy, and as such an abuse of the process of the Court, to permit a person seeking to establish that a decision of a public authority infringed rights to which he was entitled under public law, to proceed by way of ordinary action, and by this means to evade the provisions of RSC Order 53 for the protection of such authorities" per LORD DIPLOCK *O'Reilly v Mackman* [1983] 2 AC 237, [1982] 3 All ER 1124, HL.

27. Current trends in the public/private divide. Due to sustained professional and academic criticism, there has been a marked tendency for the courts to withdraw from a formalistic approach to the public/private divide and to move instead towards a pragmatic constructive analysis of the problem[1].

1 *Doyle v Northumbria Probation Committee* [1991] 4 All ER 294, [1991] 1 WLR 1340, per HENRY J "... there have been eight reported cases on this topic cited ... five of those eight went to the House of Lords; all eight went to the Court of Appeal. In four cases the Plaintiffs were allowed to proceed with their chosen method of action and in four they were not. The principles that LORD DIPLOCK expected would emerge from the decision in *O'Reilly v Mackman* [1983] 2 AC 237, [1982] 3 All ER 1124, HL, have clearly not yet fully been worked out, and the reason for this seems to me to be clear, namely that the circumstances in which there may be such a mixture of private and public law claims are infinitely various and can arise in very disparate situations. But the wealth of authority on this point and the potential for expensive appeals on it leads one to conclude that until the principles are worked out, there is potentially a formidable extra hurdle for plaintiffs in litigation where public law and private law mix. It seems to me that this is at present an area of the law where the forms of action abolished by the Common Law Procedure Act 1854 in the 19th Century appear to be in danger of returning to rule us from their graves".

28. The history of the procedural divide. During the 1970s, before judicial review began to flourish, litigants were free to use the familiar remedies of injunction and declaration in a writ action, to achieve the equivalent of judicial review of the legality of official action or decision-making[1]. In the late 1970s the Law Commission considered judicial review in great detail, but its job was only to consider procedural change. It advised an overhaul of the judicial review procedure to get rid of some of the procedural drawbacks and make the system more flexible and responsive to litigants' needs. The Commission drafted a Bill which was not taken forward. The Rules Committee of the Supreme Court tried to achieve the Commission's aims for reform without the need for legislation. Its reforms were repeated practically verbatim by the legislature in the Supreme Court Act 1981[2]. However, the reforms created two separate methods for seeking an injunction or declaration against a public official, namely the ordinary writ action and the newly reformed judicial review procedure[3]. In *O'Reilly v Mackman* the judges found on public interest grounds that the reforms had been made not merely with the litigant in mind - another purpose must have been to protect the state from unmeritorious claims[4]. Therefore, if one sued the state, one had to take the new procedural route, and if one pursued a writ action it would be struck out as an abuse of the process of the court.

In 1994, the Law Commission supported the trend towards limiting insistence on the use of RSC Order 53[5] to claims raising issues solely of public law whilst recognizing that uncertainty and potential for litigation over procedural issues remained. The Commission recommended that the rules of court be amended to enable an action commenced by writ to be transferred into Order 53 and to continue as an application for judicial review provided the plaintiff satisfied the criteria for the granting of leave[6].

1 There were procedural advantages in so doing, instead of embarking on a proper application for judicial review under as yet unreformed procedural rules: longer time limits, no leave application, the use of pleadings, interim relief, live witnesses and cross-examination, clearer rules as to locus standi and the availability of damages.
2 Supreme Court Act 1981 (11 Halsbury's Statutes (4th Edn) COURTS AND LEGAL SERVICES).
3 The Law Commission had decided that this was unimportant and that the choice should be left to the litigant (see Law Comm No 73, Cmnd 6407, para 34), but the judges did not agree. To some it seemed unfair for litigants to take the benefit of the more generous procedural rules in ordinary proceedings if they were suing the state, whilst those who chose the new procedure still had to surmount extra hurdles.
4 *O'Reilly v Mackman* [1983] 2 AC 237, [1982] 3 All ER 1124, HL.
5 RSC Ord 53.
6 Administrative Law: Judicial review and Statutory Appeals (1994 Law Com no. 226).

29. The exceptions to the "rule". In *O'Reilly v Mackman*[1] Lord Diplock mentioned possible exceptions to the general rule precluding the use of a writ action in challenging a public law decision or action:
    1. where the invalidity of the decision arises as a collateral issue in a claim for infringement of a right of a plaintiff arising under private law ie where the validity of a decision is a live and relevant issue with regard to the maintenance or defence of a pre-existing private right;
    2. where none of the parties objects;
    3. other exceptions which might arise on a case by case basis.

1 *O'Reilly v Mackman* [1983] 2 AC 237, [1982] 3 All ER 1124, HL.

30. Transfer of proceedings. There is power to turn judicial review proceedings into an ordinary action proceeding by way of writ[1] but there is no power to turn an ordinary action into a public law application[2]. In the former case, consequential directions may be given[3]. The Court of Appeal has however given guidance as to procedure which may be followed in the latter case[4].

1   See RSC Ord 53 r 9 (5) with regard to applications in which a declaration, injunction or damages have been claimed. In *R v BBC, ex p Lavelle* [1983] 1 All ER 241, [1983] 1 WLR 23, the applicant was allowed to turn her proceedings into private law ones, but in *R v East Berkshire Health Authority, ex p Walsh* [1985] QB 152, [1983] 3 All ER 425, CA, he was refused leave so to do.
2   Woolf LJ maintains that the absence of express power need not prevent a judge from doing it; see his article on the division between private and public law: [1986] PL 220 at 232. In *Chief Adjudication Officer v Foster* [1992] 1 QB 31, [1991] 3 All ER 846, CA, the Master of the Rolls himself purported to do it. He turned an application made in the course of a statutory appeal into a judicial review application. In 1993 the Law Commission gave consideration to the question whether an express power to order transfer into RSC Ord 53 would be helpful to the rational development of the law.
3   See RSC Ord 28 r 8.
4   See *Dennis Rye Pension Fund Trustees v Sheffield City Council* [1997] 4 All ER 747, [1998] 1 WLR 840, CA.

31. Collateral public law issues. Where an action claims alternative remedies, only some of which involve a challenge to a public law decision, the court may sever the issues and require separate public law proceedings to be taken in respect of those issues. For example, in an action for negligent advice, claiming damages resulting from reliance on it, it may also be contended that the defendant has committed some public law wrong. If a declaration were granted or an injunction granted to prevent implementation of such a decision, the plaintiff's need for damages would disappear. Such claims are truly alternative, and the public law issue is not "collateral" to the private law remedy[1]. Yet in certain situations it may be possible to assert that an official has actually been negligent in acting ultra vires, and further, if malice is alleged, that misfeasance in public office is made out. Such a claim concerning ultra vires is more properly characterised as collateral and may be permitted to proceed by way of private law[2].

1   *Davy v Spelthorne Borough Council* [1984] AC 262, [1983] 3 All ER 278, HL.
2   See *Lonrho plc v Tebbit* [1992] 4 All ER 280, CA but see also *Guevara v Hounslow London Borough Council* (1987) Times, 17 April where a failure to make proper provision for a child in local authority care was said to raise a substantial public law issue even though negligence was claimed by the plaintiff. In *An Bord Bainne Co-operative v Milk Marketing Board* [1984] 2 CMLR 584, CA a plaintiff combined a claim for damages with an injunction to restrain breaches of obligations under European law, raising issues of public law: it was held that the issues were inextricably linked, and so the claims were allowed to proceed together.

32. Dual public and private elements within single statutory provisions. Certain decisions in the last decade have suggested that public authorities might sometimes act under statute in such a way as to give rise to both public and private law rights[1]. The courts have drawn a distinction between an authority's decision-making functions, and its executive or managerial functions in actually implementing a decision made. If a successful claim for damages depends on a valid public law decision in favour of the claimant, the claim is probably best brought by way of action. If the claim depends on invalidating a public law decision, then it is better to use public law procedure.

1 See *Cocks v Thanet District Council* [1983] 2 AC 286, [1982] 3 All ER 1135, HL; *Thornton v Kirklees Metropolitan Borough Council* [1979] QB 626, [1979] 2 All ER 349, CA, both concerning primary legislation. But see also *Pickering v Associated Newspapers Holdings plc* [1991] 2 AC 370, [1991] 1 All ER 622, HL; *R v Deputy Governor of Parkhurst Prison, ex p Hague* [1992] 1 AC 58, [1990] 3 All ER 687, HL; and *Calveley v Chief Constable of Merseyside* [1989] AC 1228, [1989] 1 All ER 1025, HL, where no private law action was thought possible for breach of statutory duty arising under subordinate legislation.

33. Matters of law. It is as yet unclear whether an action (as opposed to an application) for a declaration may be brought to vindicate the challenger's interpretation of statutory terms as matters of law, or whether such a claim must still be made by way of judicial review[1].

1 See *Dyson v A-G* [1911] 1 KB 410, CA. More recently, in *R v Tower Hamlets London Borough Council, ex p Ferdous Begum* [1993] AC 509 [1993] 2 All ER 65, HL, the House held that the meaning of the word "applicant" was for the local authority concerned with the housing of the person in question, and not the court. See Gordon and Barlow (1992) 142 NLJ 1765 for a discussion of the case of *Ali v Tower Hamlets London Borough Council* [1993] QB 407, [1992] 3 All ER 512, CA, concerning the meaning of "suitability" of accommodation under the Housing Act 1985 (21 Halsbury's Statutes (4th Edn) HOUSING). The case of *Ettridge v Morrell* (1986) 85 LGR 100, CA, also suggested that a statutory duty to provide an election candidate with a room for a meeting was enforceable in private law. In *O'Reilly v Mackman* [1983] 2 AC 237, [1982] 3 All ER 1124, HL, LORD DIPLOCK referred to the case of *Pyx Granite Ltd v Ministry of Housing and Local Government* [1960] AC 260, [1959] 3 All ER 1, HL as an example of approval by the House of Lords of the practice of suing for a declaration in matters of legal right, where no decision of a public official need be involved. In *Kent v University College London* (1992) Times, 18 February, (1992) 156 LG Rev 1003, CA, a college argued that it was entitled to require a student to pay overseas students' fees. National regulations provided a statutory criterion by which to decide whether or not a student was "overseas" or "domestic". The student issued ordinary proceedings for a declaration that he was domestic. The Court of Appeal said that the choice of proceedings was obviously wrong and that it was "not concerned with the private rights of Mr Kent at all". See also *Roy v Kensington and Chelsea Family Practitioner Committee* [1992] 1 AC 624, [1992] 1 All ER 705, HL. However, the parties had agreed that the matter should go ahead in this form. The Court of Appeal said that although consent to the procedure was irrelevant to the proper forum for the dispute, the first instance judge had been entitled to decide as a question of fact that the student was a domestic student.

34. "Collateral" defences. Another acknowledged exception to the exclusivity rule is in the defence of civil or criminal proceedings, if the defence depends on a public law challenge. In such circumstances the defendant is not obliged to bring judicial review proceedings but may have the matter resolved within the proceedings concerned[1]. The House of Lords in *Wandsworth London Borough Council v Winder* regarded this argument as distinct from Lord Diplock's "collateral issue" exception but later limitations to the right of defendants generally to raise public law points have placed this case into a sub-category of that exception. The courts have held since that if the defendant's public law point would not actually provide a defence in law to the claim being asserted, all the defendant can do is apply for an adjournment of the proceedings or a stay of any exercise of the plaintiff public body's executive powers in order that the defendant may apply for leave for judicial review of the public law decision. Whether the trial judge will grant such relief will depend on his or her assessment of the merits of the public law point[2]. This exception to the exclusivity rule was departed from in connection with duties imposed by the Housing Act 1985[3].

1   This approach has been subject to the criticism that it negates one of the advantages flowing from the rule: that judicial review issues are only decided by High Court judges experienced in the field. In *Wandsworth London Borough Council v Winder* [1985] AC 461, [1984] 3 All ER 976, HL, a council tenant was sued in ordinary proceedings in the county court for arrears of rent. His defence alleged that the rent increases were unlawful and invalid, since they were not "reasonably" required pursuant to the Housing Act. If he was right in his contention, the rent "arrears" would not have arisen and he would not have committed any private law wrong: his public law argument gave him a defence to the private law claim against him. The House of Lords held that it was acceptable to raise a public law defence in an ordinary action without having to comply with the procedural restrictions applicable to judicial review. Note that Mr Winder had tried and failed to get leave for judicial review of the rent increases at the time when they were made. Woolf LJ has expressed extra-judicial criticism of this decision: see (1986) PL 220. Compare *Wandsworth London Borough Council v Winder* [1985] AC 461, [1984] 3 All ER 976, HL, with *Avon County Council v Buscott* [1988] QB 656, [1988] 1 All ER 841, CA: travellers raised a public law defence to an action for possession of land on which they were squatting: they said that the council was acting unlawfully through not having housed them pursuant to their statutory duty. They were not allowed to raise the issue in their defence; instead they were granted an adjournment and advised to issue judicial review proceedings at the same time as conducting their defence in the ordinary court. Even if they proved that the council was acting ultra vires, it would not have given them a private law defence to squatting.
2   See for instance *Waverley Borough Council v Hilden* [1988] 1 All ER 807, [1988] 1 WLR 246 where the judge refused a stay based on the merits.
3   Housing Act 1985 (21 Halsbury's Statutes (4th Edn) HOUSING). See *Ex p Lambourne* (1993) 25 HLR 172 and *Tower Hamlets London Borough Council v Abdi* (1993) 25 HLR 80, CA where defendants were not allowed to raise the defence of unsuitability of alternative accommodation offered in private law possession proceedings. See Gordon and Barlow (1992) 142 NLJ 1765 for criticism of these cases. The analysis of these cases must surely depend on how "the private law right" of a council tenant is characterised: if it amounts to a right to stay in accommodation until "suitable" accommodation is offered, then even if "suitability" is for the council to assess (as decided in *Ali v Tower Hamlets London Borough Council* [1993] QB 407, [1992] 3 All ER 512, CA) the public law point impinges crucially on the private law right. But if it is merely to stay in the accommodation until contractual notice is given, and the existence thereafter of a merely statutorily protected status until possession proceedings have been brought is not seen as such a right, the question of suitability cannot provide a contractual or "private law" defence. In both of these cases it is important to note that the tenant was non-secure, by reason of occupation of property let to the authority for temporary accommodation, which might provide a ground for distinction. In certain claims for possession against secure tenants, on certain grounds only, the county court judge must him or herself be satisfied as to suitability of alternative accommodation, so it is suggested that in such a situation the above cases would not determine the procedural issue.

35. Use of the "Winder" doctrine by public law defendants. The *Wandsworth LBC v Winder*[1] analysis may not be used defensively to force a plaintiff down the public law route. A defendant may not rely on a public law defence to contend that the plaintiff should have raised the issue in public law proceedings rather than pursue a claim in contract, if an action in contract was equally sustainable by that plaintiff[2].

1   *Wandsworth London Borough Council v Winder* [1985] AC 461, [1984] 3 All ER 976, HL.
2   In *Doyle v Northumbria Probation Committee* [1991] 4 All ER 294, [1991] 1 WLR 1340 the defendants tried to use the illegality of their own earlier conduct as a defence to contractual proceedings, to argue that the plaintiff should have brought public law proceedings against them many years sooner. Doyle was employed under a contract of employment by the committee; according to regulations, he was entitled to a mileage allowance which, under a decision of the committee in 1975, included journeys between office and home. When the committee discontinued the allowance to save money, the plaintiff issued a writ. The committee claimed its own decision about the office-to-home entitlement had been ultra vires the regulations for conditions of service, and that the action raised issues of public law. But the court said that since the documents were clear, Doyle did not need to refer to public law or establish any public law wrong in order to make out his private law claim in contract.

36. Criminal proceedings. In the absence of a clear parliamentary intention to the contrary, a defendant is entitled to raise as a defence to a criminal charge the contention that subordinate legislation under which the prosecution is made or an administrative decision made thereunder was ultra vires and unlawful. For the purpose of the challenge, no distinction was to be drawn between subordinate legislation or an administrative decision bad on its face and that which was bad for procedural irregularity. In every case it is necessary to examine the particular statutory context to determine whether a court had jurisdiction to rule on a defence based upon arguments of invalidity of subordinate legislation or an administrative act under it[1].

1   *Boddington v British Transport Police* [1998] 2 All ER 203, [1998] 2 WLR 639, HL, overruling *Bugg v DPP* [1993] QB 473, [1993] 2 All ER 815.

37. Consent. *Gillick v West Norfolk and Wisbech Area Health Authority*[1] illustrated two of the express exceptions to the exclusivity rule. Some members of the House of Lords thought the claim raised essentially private law matters, so that the public law element was merely collateral, whilst others deemed the public authority to have waived its procedural privileges by not raising the procedural point. More recently the court has tended to discount consent as sufficient to avoid the rule, using the argument that its supervisory jurisdiction cannot be based on the parties' own views[2].

1   *Gillick v West Norfolk and Wisbech Area Health Authority* [1986] AC 112, [1985] 3 All ER 402, HL. It concerned the DHSS's decision to issue advice to NHS GPs that it was acceptable and lawful to give contraceptive advice to girls under 16 without their parents' knowledge or consent. A mother applied in ordinary proceedings for a declaration that it was unlawful and an infringement of her parental rights. The DHSS did not complain that she ought to have brought judicial review proceedings within three months of the issue of the advice. LORDS FRASER and SCARMAN saw the case as essentially a private law issue, because an internal examination of a child without the effective consent of an adult would raise the private law tort of assault on the child. LORDS BRIDGE and TEMPLEMAN saw the claim as a public law challenge to the power of the DHSS to issue advice but the court said that the case was so important that it should go ahead regardless of the procedure used.
2   See *R v Durham City Council, ex p Robinson* (1992) Times, 31 January.

C: GENERAL GROUNDS FOR OBTAINING JUDICIAL REVIEW

1: INTRODUCTION

38. Introduction. The basis on which judicial review or its predecessor procedures can provide a remedy has been expressed in various ways[1]. The contemporary starting point is provided by Lord Diplock[2]: "Judicial review has I think developed to a stage today when ... one can conveniently classify under three heads the grounds on which administrative action is subject to judicial review. The first ground I would call "illegality" the second "irrationality" and the third "procedural impropriety". That is not to say that further development on a case by case basis may not in course of time add further grounds ... By "illegality" as a ground for judicial review I mean that the decision maker must understand correctly the law that regulates his decision making power and must give effect to it. Whether he has or not is par excellence a justiciable question to be decided, in the event of dispute, by those persons, the judges, by whom the judicial power of the state is exercisable. By "irrationality" I mean what can by now be succinctly referred to as "Wednesbury unreasonableness"[3]. It applies to a decision which is so outrageous in its defiance of logic or accepted moral standards that no sensible person who had applied his mind to the question to be decided could have arrived at it. Whether a decision falls within this category is a question that judges by their training and experience should be well equipped to answer, or else there would be something badly wrong with our judicial system ... I have described the third head as "procedural impropriety" rather than failure to observe basic rules of natural justice or failure to act with procedural fairness towards the person who will be affected by the decision. This is because susceptibility to judicial review under this head also covers failure by an administrative tribunal to observe procedural rules that are expressly laid down ... even where such failure does not involve any denial of natural justice".

1 For an earlier comprehensive statement see LORD DENNING MR in *GEC Ltd v Price Commission* [1975] ICR 1, CA.
2 *Council of Civil Service Unions v Minister for the Civil Service* [1985] AC 374, [1984] 3 All ER 935, HL.
3 *Associated Provincial Picture Houses Ltd v Wednesbury Corp* [1948] 1 KB 223, [1947] 2 All ER 680, CA.

2: ILLEGALITY

39. The nature of "illegality"[1]. Illegality is a primary ground for judicial review of administrative actions or decisions. It is constituted by a public body consciously or unconsciously exceeding its express or implied statutory or de facto powers, or misconstruing the extent of its duties[2].

Evidence of dishonest conduct, bad faith, or merely innocent misconstruction of matters of law, procedural irregularities contravening mandatory provisions, or unreasonableness which thwarts the policy behind legislation, have all been described as illegality in various cases, although they can also be brought within other categories of grounds for review; the precise classification of the alleged wrong is no longer important[3]. Allegations of illegality are particularly common in cases where the extent of statutory discretion is in issue. The court cannot determine the "right" way to exercise a discretionary power; it can only indicate the parameters of such powers.

1 See Michael Fordham *Judicial Review Handbook* (2nd edn, 1997) ch 48.
2 In *Council of Civil Service Unions v Minister for the Civil Service* [1985] AC 374, [1984] 3 All ER 935, HL, LORD DIPLOCK described illegality as occurring when a decision maker fails to understand correctly the law that regulates his decision making power, or fails to give effect to it. Examples of illegal conduct turning upon the Local Government Act 1972 s 111 (25 Halsbury's Statutes (4th Edn) LOCAL GOVERNMENT) in recent years have been the local authority 'swaps' case, *Hazell v Hammersmith and Fulham London Borough Council* [1992] 2 AC 1, [1991] 1 All ER 545, HL (debt-management not a function of the local authority and swaps not conducive nor incidental to any other function) and *McCarthy & Stone (Developments) Ltd v London Borough of Richmond upon Thames* [1992] 2 AC 48, [1991] 4 All ER 897, HL (charging for pre-planning application advice given over the telephone was not conducive to nor incidental to the discharge of its statutory functions). See also *Allsop v North Tyneside Metropolitan Borough Council* [1992] ICR 639, CA (illegality of enhanced redundancy payments to local authority staff). Note that the Local Government Act 1972 s 137 (as amended) gives a right to a local authority to spend a limited amount of money each year on anything which, in its opinion, is in the interests of, and will bring direct benefit to the whole or any part of its area or to some or all of the inhabitants of that area. The courts have treated the interpretation of what is capable of coming within those qualifying conditions as a matter of law for the court, not the local authority, whereas the question of whether such things do actually amount to benefit for the area is for the authority, subject to further tests laid down in the legislation.
3 See Paragraphs 53-62 post which deal with unreasonableness.

40. Statutory construction. Whether or not conduct exceeds its lawful scope depends primarily on construction of the statute or code delimiting the powers concerned[1] (or existing case law, where the power claimed arises from the Royal Prerogative). Conduct can be expressly or impliedly unlawful, or substantively or procedurally unlawful. Statutes containing words such as "shall" and "may" invite a decision as to the true nature of the authority given by the provisions concerned. They may be imperative or permissive, and disputes involving this issue are said to raise questions of illegality[2]. Despite permissive language, it may indeed be held that there is a duty to act in a certain way whenever the promotion of the policy of the statute so requires in the absence of a good reason for not so acting, although this is rare. Despite seemingly absolute language, the courts may be prepared to read a large measure of operational discretion into certain statutory functions. In other circumstances the court may hold that an apparently unfettered discretion is limited by general legal obligations imposed on the body concerned. Other instances of illegality turning upon statutory construction usually involve a mistake by the public body about the relevance[3] of considerations that it has either taken into account or failed to take into account, or, alternatively, actions which negate the assumed purpose of the legislation in question. Reference may be had to Hansard in respect of statements of promoters of Bills so as to assist the court with regard to the policy behind legislation[4].

1   See *R v Secretary of State for the Environment, ex p British Telecommunications plc* [1991] RA 307, [1991] NPC 93; *R v Lord Chancellor, ex p Witham* [1997] 2 All ER 779, [1998] 2 WLR 849.
2   For examples of the varying degrees of discretion that have been found to arise under ostensible discretionary or mandatory powers, see Supperstone and Goudie *Judicial Review* (2nd edn, 1997) ch 5.
3   Relevance is also described in Paragraph 59 post as an aspect of unreasonableness or irrationality, an alternative ground for review. For cases illustrating the courts' approach to relevance, see Supperstone and Goudie *Judicial Review* (2nd edn, 1997) ch 5.
4   *Pepper v Hart* [1993] AC 593, [1993] 1 All ER 42, HL.

41. Improper purposes. Officials may act for motives unrelated in a legal sense to the real purpose of their statutory powers[1]. This may not be clear to the official concerned until after the court has opined on the implied purpose behind the provision in question or the extent of the powers incidental to or consequential upon[2] that which is expressly authorised[3]. It is not unusual for the courts to use principles of constitutional law or administrative morality as principles of statutory interpretation governing the determination of the legality of conduct[4].

1   For example, in *Padfield v Minister of Agriculture, Fisheries and Food* [1968] AC 997, [1968] 1 All ER 694, HL, the Minister refused to refer a complaint to a statutory committee because he might be politically embarrassed by a favourable finding, despite the fact that he had a statutory role to play in the referral of complaints. In *R v Derbyshire County Council, ex p The Times Supplements Ltd* [1991] 3 Admin LR 241, [1990] NLJR 1421, the decision to ban the Times Education Supplement from authority libraries was found to be vindictive and an abuse of power. For other examples of improper motive see *Re Preston* [1985] AC 835, sub nom *Preston v IRC*, [1985] 2 All ER 327, HL and *Wheeler v Leicester City Council* [1985] AC 1054.
2   See Local Government Act 1972 s 111 (25 Halsbury's Statutes (4th Edn) LOCAL GOVERNMENT) for codification of this principle: a local authority shall have power to do anything "... calculated to facilitate, or conducive or incidental to the discharge of any of their functions.". See also cases cited at Paragraph 39 note 2 ante for authority on the meaning of the section. Non-profit making ancillary works were considered to be lawful with regard to the function of publishing agenda, minutes and reports and re-binding damaged books: *A-G v Smethwick Corpn* [1932] 1 Ch 562, CA; compare *A-G v Crayford UDC* [1962] Ch 575, [1962] 2 All ER 147, CA, where it was held to be intra vires to offer insurance cover to local authority tenants notwithstanding the fact that the scheme resulted in the authority obtaining a commission from insurers.
3   See, for example, *Roberts v Hopwood* [1925] AC 578, HL, where the court implied that the council was promoting socialist philanthropy and feminist ambition in awarding its staff standard and equal salaries. Also in *R v ILEA, ex p Westminster City Council* [1986] 1 All ER 19, [1986] 1 WLR 28, decided before the Local Government Act 1986 (25 Halsbury's Statutes (4th Edn) LOCAL GOVERNMENT) introduced restrictions on political advertising, a local authority believed it was entitled to use advertising campaigns to persuade the public against education budget cuts, but its publicity powers were construed by the court to extend only to informing the public. In *Webb v O'Doherty* [1991] 3 Admin LR 731, a private law case, it was held that it was ultra vires for an educational charity to conduct a political campaign against the Gulf War. See further *A-G v Great Eastern Rly Co* (1880) 5 App Cas 473, HL, LORD SELBORNE'S speech, for elaboration of the "reasonably incidental" rule of construction. The modern approach can be found in *R v Yorkshire Purchasing Organisation, ex p British Educational Suppliers Ltd* [1998] ELR 195, CA.

4   For example, a judge might hold that the principle that there should be no taxation without statutory authority informed his conclusions about what Parliament intended when authorising all conduct incidental to the statutory duties of a public body: see *McCarthy & Stone (Developments) Ltd v London Borough of Richmond upon Thames* [1992] 2 AC 48, [1991] 4 All ER 897, HL. Alternatively, the principle that citizens ought not to be punished by the exercise of public power in relation to conduct which is not criminal might inform the court's construction of the extent of a council's power to deprive individuals of access to council premises: see *Wheeler v Leicester City Council* [1985] AC 1054, [1985] 2 All ER 1106, HL. Alternatively, the principle that a man's property shall not be taken from him without clear statutory authority may be used to strike down the requisitioning of property without compensation in the guise of planning conditions: see *Hall & Co Ltd v Shoreham-by-Sea UDC* [1964] 1 All ER 1, [1964] 1 WLR 240, CA.

42. Matters of law. Sometimes the jurisdiction of public officials to embark upon or fulfil the decision-making part of their function will depend upon the construction of words of apparent ambiguity and their application to an individual or a situation. In such circumstances it must be decided whether the construction question is one which Parliament intended to be left to the decision-making body, subject to an irrational conclusion being reached, or whether it is a matter of law for the court[1]. There is a general presumption that Parliament did not intend inferior tribunals or magistrates' courts to be their own judges of matters affecting their jurisdiction, but there have been identified recently certain bodies that do enjoy this power[2]. However, it is still safe to assume that the county court and coroners' courts will be given more leeway in their findings as to matters going to their jurisdiction. Cases which raise issues such as these may be seen as instances of illegality but are dealt with in the section concerning ouster clauses[3], because they raise the fundamental question of the meaning of jurisdiction.

1   For instance, in the Fare's Fair case, *Bromley LBC v GLC* [1983] 1 AC 768, [1982] 1 All ER 153, HL, the fares structure suggested by the GLC was unlawful largely because of the meaning of the word "economic" as defined by the House of Lords. In *Secretary of State for Education and Science v Tameside MBC* [1977] AC 1014, [1976] 3 All ER 665, HL, the Secretary of State's default powers were triggered by his perception of unreasonable conduct by local authorities, but the court construed "unreasonable" as meaning the same as Wednesbury unreasonableness (see Paragraph 54 post), not merely policies and conduct with which the Secretary of State disagreed. But in *R v Oldham MBC, ex p Garlick* [1993] AC 509, sub nom *Garlick v Oldham MBC* [1993] 2 All ER 65, HL, the House of Lords (LORD SLYNN dissenting) held that the meaning of the word "applicant" under the Housing Act 1985 (21 Halsbury's Statutes (4th Edn) HOUSING) was a matter of fact for the authority, subject only to review for irrationality. In *R v Ealing District Health Authority, ex p Colin Fox* [1993] 1 WLR 373, the Mental Health Act 1983 s 117 (2)(as amended) (28 Halsbury's Statutes (4th Edn) MENTAL HEALTH) providing that "it shall be the duty of the District Health Authority and of the local social services authority to provide, in co-operation with relevant voluntary agencies, after-care services for any person ..." was relied upon by OTTON J in holding that this was a mandatory duty and not one where the doctors could substitute their own reasonable opinions of what was appropriate. The Court of Appeal in *R v Ealing LBC, ex p Lewis* (1992) 90 LGR 571, CA, held that the identification of items of expenditure capable of coming within the words "management of houses and other property" was a matter of law for the court, and not the local authority.
2   For example, University Visitors and Superior Court judges, sitting as Visitors to the Inns of Court. This immunity from review extends only so far as matters of law are concerned, and does not prevent review on grounds of irrationality or procedural impropriety. See *R v Lord President of the Privy Council, ex p Page* [1993] AC 682, sub nom *Page v Hull University Visitor* [1993] 1 All ER 97, [1994] QB 1, HL and *R v Visitors to the Inns of Court, ex p Calder* [1993] 2 All ER 876, CA.
3   See Paragraph 116 et seq post.

43. Procedural ultra vires. If statute lays down a prescribed procedure for the fulfilment of a statutory duty or exercise of a power, failure to comply with it may render the action which follows ultra vires. Procedural obligations may be mandatory or directory, or both, in the sense that they may be mandatory but capable of substantial as opposed to absolute compliance[1]. If a procedure is mandatory, the court will, subject to other discretionary principles[2], generally grant relief. If it is directory only, the court will not need to consider the discretionary granting of relief because the default will not have been ultra vires.

1   In *Milne v London Borough of Wandsworth* (1992) 90 LGR 515, CA, it was held that the validity of objections against the cessation of maintenance of a county school depended on ten local government electors making an objection and that as a matter of law, two objections, neither signed by ten electors, but together signed by fourteen separate electors, could not be taken together to constitute a valid objection under the Education Act 1980 s 12 (3), (5)(repealed by Education Act 1996 s 582 (2), Sch 38 Pt I and replaced by the Education Act 1996 ss 36 (1), (2), (4), 37 (1), (3), 168 (1), (2), (4), 169 (1), (3)) (15 Halsbury's Statutes (4th Edn) EDUCATION). It did not however clarify whether a local authority could ever make an incorrect but reasonable decision as to validity or whether the court would always treat validity as a matter of fact and law for the court.
2   See Paragraph 9 ante.

44. Illegality by other miscellaneous means. The fettering of discretion of a public body by over-rigid adherence to a policy or familiar convention may be regarded as unlawful if the body leaves no scope for reconsideration in an exceptional case[1]. The other side of this problem is that it may be unfair in a general sense for a public body not to adhere to a policy which it has made public or abided by in the past, if an individual can identify what is known as a "legitimate expectation"[2]. Finally, estoppel may occasionally be used in public law to oblige a public body to adhere to a representation made within the express or implied scope of the representor's powers, so long as what is represented is not contrary to a statutory duty[3].

1   See Paragraph 65 post.
2   See Paragraph 66 post.
3   See Paragraph 67 post.

3: PROCEDURAL IMPROPRIETY

45. Introduction. A public body will be open to challenge where it has acted unfairly towards the applicant, by failing to observe basic rules of natural justice, or by failing to act with procedural fairness. Even where the applicant has not been denied natural justice, there may be a good challenge where the public body has failed to observe procedural rules expressly laid down by statute or delegated legislation[1].

The overall considerations are that public administration should be orderly, open, carried out in good time, and fair.

1   *Council of Civil Service Unions v Minister for the Civil Service* [1985] AC 374, [1984] 3 All ER 945, HL.

46. Statutory procedures. When considering statutory requirements, the courts will be less concerned with distinctions such as that between "mandatory" and "directory" requirements, and more with the desirability of achieving justice in a particular case[1]. Where the likelihood of prejudice is low, the court may treat an apparently strict requirement as merely directory[2]; but where private rights are at issue, provisions may be treated as mandatory even where there has been no prejudice.

The court may not only require that the procedure prescribed by statute be followed, but may also imply additional procedural safeguards so as to ensure the attainment of fairness[3].

1 *London and Clydesdale Estates Ltd v Aberdeen District Council* [1979] 3 All ER 876, [1980] 1 WLR 182, HL.
2 *R v Inspector of Taxes, ex p Clarke* [1974] QB 220, [1972] 1 All ER 545, CA.
3 *Lloyd v McMahon* [1987] AC 625, [1987] 1 All ER 1118, HL.

47. Duty to consult. Failure to perform a duty to consult, or failure to satisfy a legitimate expectation of consultation, are popular grounds for application, particularly in cases concerning groups of citizens aggrieved by the actions of public bodies, for example, parents threatened by school closure[1].

A distinction must be drawn between a duty of fair consultation arising from statute, and a duty to satisfy a legitimate expectation. The applicant should always look for the former. Failure to perform a statutory duty will amount to a procedural impropriety which, subject to the court's discretion will entitle an applicant to judicial review. In the latter case, even if the decision-maker fails in the duty, a later decision-making process may rectify the earlier unfairness[2].

Where statute expressly defines those entitled to be consulted, it is unlikely that others will be able to claim the right[3]. Where statute provides for a power to consult such bodies as appear representative, then the discretion as to who is to be consulted is reviewable on *Wednesbury* grounds[4].

Fair consultation means:
1. consultation when the proposals are still at a formative stage[5];
2. adequate information to which to respond[6];
3. adequate time in which to respond[7]; and
4. conscientious consideration by an authority of the response to consultation[8].

A decision may be treated as invalid merely in relation to the party not consulted[9]; and the court may in its discretion refuse to quash regulations made in the absence of mandatory consultation, where great inconvenience would result[10].

1 *R v London Borough of Brent, ex p Gunning* (1985) 84 LGR 168.
2 *R v Gwent County Council and the Secretary of State for Wales, ex p Bryant* [1988] COD 19, per HODGSON J.
3 *Bates v Lord Hailsham* [1972] 3 All ER 1019, [1972] 1 WLR 1373.
4 *Agricultural, Horticultural and Forestry Industry Training Board v Aylesbury Mushrooms* [1972] 1 All ER 280, [1972] 1 WLR 190; *Associated Provincial Picture Houses Ltd v Wednesbury Corpn* [1948] 1 KB 223, [1947] 2 All ER 680, CA.
5 *Short v Tower Hamlets London Borough Council* (1985) 18 HLR 171, CA, where the council did not start consultation until it had determined in principle to sell a housing estate; but a challenge on the ground that this was too late failed.
6 *R v Secretary of State for Social Services, ex p AMA* [1986] 1 All ER 164, [1986] 1 WLR 1.

7 *Lee v Secretary of State for Education and Science* (1967) 111 Sol Jo 756 where four days were considered too short.
8 In *R v Hillingdon Health Authority, ex p Goodwin* [1984] ICR 800, WOOLF J held that it is proper for a consultor to decide what course he wishes to adopt if unpersuaded by the representations; see *Short v Tower Hamlets London Borough Council* (1985) 18 HLR 171, CA: the consultor may well already have formulated the proposal.
9 See *Agricultural, Horticultural and Forestry Industry Training Board v Aylesbury Mushrooms Ltd* [1972] 1 All ER 280, [1972] 1 WLR 190.
10 *R v Secretary of State for Social Services, ex p AMA* [1986] 1 All ER 164, [1986] 1 WLR 1.

48. Natural justice and fairness. The rules of natural justice are the minimum standards of fair decision making imposed by common law[1]. The common law recognises two rules: *audi alteram partem* (hear the other side) and *nemo judex in causa sua* (no-one may be judge in their own cause).

An applicant will be wise to rely on a fairness or natural justice ground. Whereas the court will in other respects permit a decision maker a wide range of reasonable decisions, not substituting its own decision for that of the decision maker, questions of fairness are for the court to decide[2].

Where individuals are adversely affected by a decision, there will be a strong presumption that the principles of natural justice will apply.

1 See Supperstone and Goudie *Judicial Review* (2nd edn, 1997) ch 8.
2 *R v Panel on Take-overs and Mergers, ex p Guinness plc* [1990] 1 QB 146, [1989] 1 All ER 509, CA.

49. Legitimate expectation. Lord Denning was the first to distinguish legitimate expectation from a right or interest; an expectation of which it would be unfair to deprive an applicant without hearing what he had to say[1]. The applicant should always turn first to the words of Lord Diplock in the GCHQ case[2] in which he held that the decision in question must affect a person either:
1. by altering rights or obligations of that person enforceable by or against him in private law; or
2. by depriving him of some benefit or advantage which either
    2.1. he had been permitted by the decision maker to enjoy and which he could legitimately expect to be permitted to continue to enjoy unless there had been communicated to him some rational grounds for withdrawing it on which he had been given an opportunity to comment; or
    2.2. he had received assurance from the decision maker that they would not be withdrawn without giving him first an opportunity of advancing reasons for contending that they should not be withdrawn.

In more recent cases the courts have insisted that there are five conditions which must be satisfied before an application based on legitimate expectation can be successful:
1. there must be a clear and unambiguous representation by the public body;
2. the applicant must be within the class of persons entitled to rely on the representation;
3. the applicant must have relied on it;
4. this reliance must have been to his detriment; and

5. there must be no overriding public interest entitling the public body to change its policy to the detriment of the applicant[3].

The court will therefore proceed from the principle of administrative fairness; but the right to legitimate expectation is increasingly seen as similar in extent and application to the private law principle of estoppel. Moreover, as the cases cited show, this is a fast-developing area of law; the practitioner must look at the latest decisions[4].

1 *Schmidt v Secretary of State for Home Affairs* [1969] 2 Ch 149, [1969] 1 All ER 904, CA (whether an alien, a scientology student, should have been deported without making representations).
2 *Council of Civil Service Unions v Minister for the Civil Service* [1985] AC 374, [1984] 3 All ER 935, HL.
3 See *Re Preston* [1985] AC 835, sub nom *Preston v IRC*, [1985] 2 All ER 327, HL (revenue would be guilty of unfairness amounting to abuse of power if they resiled from representations in a way which would give rise to an action for breach of contract or estoppel in private law); *R v Board of Inland Revenue, ex p MFK Underwriting Agencies Ltd* [1990] 1 All ER 91, [1990] 1 WLR 1545 (revenue might be bound by an assurance, providing it was clear and unambiguous, and the taxpayer had made full disclosure); *R v Independent Television Commission, ex p Television South West* (1992) Times, 7 February, CA (legitimate expectation is not a "magic password"); *R v Jockey Club, ex p RAM Racecourses Ltd* [1993] 2 All ER 225 (the five principles explained); *R v Torbay Borough Council, ex p Cleasby* [1991] COD 142, CA (in default of private rights, all that can be legitimately expected, is that the policy for the time being will be fairly carried out); *R v Secretary of State for Health, ex p United States Tobacco International Inc* [1992] QB 353, [1992] 1 All ER 212 (change of policy: applicants failed on legitimate expectation, succeeded on fairness); *R v Devon County Council, ex p Baker* [1995] 1 All ER 73, (1993) 91 LGR 479, CA.
4 See also Paragraph 66 post.

50. Exclusions. National security considerations will permit the government to fail to consult or to give a hearing where otherwise such failure would be challengeable[1]. Principles of fairness may also, very exceptionally, be relaxed by reason of emergency. It should also be borne in mind that the rules of natural justice are concerned with the propriety of the decision-maker; an applicant cannot complain if he had no hearing through the fault of his legal advisers[2].

1 See *Council of Civil Service Unions v Minister for the Civil Service* [1985] AC 374, [1984] 3 All ER 935; *R v Secretary of State for the Home Department, ex p Ruddock* [1987] 2 All ER 518, [1987] 1 WLR 1482; *R v Secretary of State for the Home Department, ex p Hosenball* [1977] 3 All ER 452, [1977] 1 WLR 766, CA; *R v Secretary of State for the Home Department, ex p Cheblak* [1991] 2 All ER 319, [1991] 1 WLR 890, CA.
2 *Al-Mehdawi v Secretary of State for the Home Department* [1990] 1 AC 876, [1989] 3 All ER 843, HL.

51. The content of natural justice. The individual must be told in detail of the case he must meet[1]. He must have a fair opportunity to correct or contradict that case[2], and sufficient time to prepare an answer[3]. The decision makers should not rely on points not argued before them, must disclose reports or other evidence upon which they propose to rely, and should not rely on their own private investigations[4]. In some circumstances, all relevant evidence must be disclosed, save that which is protected by public policy[5];

but the courts have also permitted public bodies to disclose the substance rather than the detail of a case[6]. The individual may, depending on the circumstances, be entitled to put his own case orally or in writing[7]; may have a right to examine witnesses[8]; and may have a right to legal representation[9].

The right to the protection of the rules of natural justice can arise in many different circumstances. Questions of the revocation of a licence frequently give rise to challenge; there are now many activities subject to the granting of a licence, for example by a local authority[10]; similarly whereas a licence is for a fixed term, the licence-holder may well have a legitimate expectation that the licence will be reissued unless there is good reason not to do so. Further it was held that a potential applicant for a gaming licence was entitled to an indication of the matters considered relevant to the question of fitness, and to the opportunity to comment on impressions formed, but not the sources of information[11].

1   *Chief Constable of the North Wales Police v Evans* [1982] 3 All ER 141, [1982] 1 WLR 1155, HL (police officer required to resign not told of allegations about private life); *R v Hampshire County Council, ex p K* [1990] 2 QB 71, [1990] 2 All ER 129 (council refused to disclose medical evidence of sexual abuse to parents); *R v Enfield London Borough Council, ex p T F Unwin (Roydon) Ltd* (1989) 46 BLR 1, [1989] COD 466 (contractors not told of accusations before removal from approved list).
2   See *Maradana Mosque Board of Trustees v Mahmud* [1967] 1 AC 13, [1966] 1 All ER 545, PC.
3   *R v Thames Magistrates' Court, ex p Polemis* [1974] 2 All ER 1219, [1974] 1 WLR 1371 where an adjournment was refused.
4   *Fairmount Investments Ltd v Secretary of State for the Environment* [1976] 2 All ER 865, [1976] 1 WLR 1255, HL.
5   *R v Army Board of the Defence Council, ex p Anderson* [1992] 1 QB 169, [1991] 3 All ER 375.
6   *R v Secretary of State for the Home Department, ex p Mughal* [1974] QB 313, [1973] 3 All ER 796, CA; *R v MMC, ex p Matthew Brown plc* [1987] 1 All ER 463, [1987] 1 WLR 1235; *Re Pergamon Press Ltd* [1971] Ch 388, [1970] 3 All ER 535, CA; *R v Secretary of State for the Home Department, ex p McAvoy* [1998] 1 WLR 790, CA (a prisoner is entitled only to the gist of reports considered when the decision as to release on licence is made).
7   *Lloyd v McMahon* [1987] AC 625, [1987] 1 All ER 1118, HL (the auditor acted fairly in inviting written representations; no-one had sought an oral hearing); *R v Army Board of the Defence Council, ex p Anderson* [1992] QB 169, [1991] 3 All ER 375 (decision making bodies other than courts can arrange their own procedure, providing they achieve the degree of fairness appropriate to their task).
8   *R v Hull Prison Visitors, ex p St Germain (No 2)* [1979] 3 All ER 545, [1979] 1 WLR 1401.
9   Even where there is an oral hearing, there is not necessarily a right to legal representation: *R v Secretary of State for the Home Department, ex p Cheblak* [1991] 2 All ER 319, [1991] 1 WLR 890, CA.
10 *R v Barnsley Metropolitan Borough Council, ex p Hook* [1976] 3 All ER 452, [1976] 1 WLR 1052, CA.
11 *R v Gaming Board for Great Britain, ex p Benaim and Khaida* [1970] 2 QB 417, [1970] 2 All ER 528, CA.

52. Bias. The second rule of natural justice is that the decision maker must have no material interest, whether by way of gain or detriment, in the outcome of proceedings, unless such interest has been disclosed and no objection made or objection waived.

Where the decision maker has a direct pecuniary interest, bias will be conclusively presumed[1]. Where there is a non-pecuniary interest, the court has in part been concerned to uphold the principle that justice should not only be done, but should manifestly and undoubtedly be seen to be done[2]. The test was, broadly speaking, one of "reasonable suspicion"[3]. The House of Lords has now narrowed this down to whether there is a "real likelihood of bias"[4].

Non-pecuniary interest may take the form of family connection[5]; personal friendship[6]; active interest in an organisation[7]; previous involvement in the case[8]; contact during an adjournment[9]; or preconceived views[10].

The situation may be different with administrative (as opposed to judicial) decision making. Where Board of Trade officers were acting in a policing role, the principle did not apply; although they were still obliged not to exceed or abuse their powers[11]. See also the role of local planning authorities[12].

1   *Grand Junction Canal v Dimes* (1852) 3 HL Cas 759 (Lord Chancellor affirmed Vice-Chancellor's order; but he had a large shareholding in the company). See note 3 below.
2   *R v Sussex Justices, ex p McCarthy* [1924] 1 KB 256 (clerk to justices hearing dangerous driving case was a member of the firm acting for other party, and abstained from taking part in the hearing).
3   *R v London Rent Assessment Panel Committee, ex p Metropolitan Properties Co (FGC) Ltd* [1969] 1 QB 577, [1968] 3 All ER 304, CA; *Hannam v Bradford City Council* [1970] 2 All ER 690, [1970] 1 WLR 937, CA; *R v Liverpool Justices, ex p Topping* [1983] 1 All ER 490, [1983] 1 WLR 119 - the test is whether there is the appearance of bias, rather than whether there is actual bias, that is, would a reasonable and fair-minded person sitting in court and knowing all the relevant facts have a reasonable suspicion that a fair trial for the applicant was not possible?
4   *R v Gough* [1993] AC 646, CA and HL.
5   *R v London Rent Assessment Panel Committee, ex p Metropolitan Properties Co (FGC) Ltd* [1969] 1 QB 577, [1968] 3 All ER 304, CA.
6   *Cottle v Cottle* [1939] 2 All ER 535.
7   *R v Altrincham Justices, ex p Pennington* [1975] QB 549, [1975] 2 All ER 78.
8   *R v Crown Court at Bristol, ex p Cooper* [1990] 2 All ER 193, [1990] 1 WLR 1031, CA.
9   *Cotterell v Secretary of State for the Environment* [1991] 2 PLR 20.
10 *Ellis v Ministry of Defence* [1985] I CR 257.
11 *R v Secretary of State for Trade, ex p Perestrello* [1981] QB 19, [1980] 3 All ER 28.
12 *R v Amber Valley District Council, ex p Jackson* [1984] 3 All ER 501, [1985] 1 WLR 298 and *R v Secretary of State for the Environment, ex p Kirkstall Valley Campaign Ltd* [1996] 3 All ER 304, [1996] COD 337.

4: IRRATIONALITY, UNREASONABLENESS AND PROPORTIONALITY

53. Introduction[1]. "Irrationality" is the ground used in judicial review proceedings for challenging the quality of a decision by reference to the reasoning behind it. In the case which gave its name to the concept, *Associated Provincial Picture Houses Ltd v Wednesbury Corp*[2] the council had power to grant licences for Sunday entertainment subject to such conditions as it thought fit; it licensed a cinema subject to the condition that no child under 15 be admitted. It was held that this exercise of the discretion was not such that no other reasonable authority would have done the same.

1   Practitioners may find the following references helpful: HWR Wade and Forsyth *Administrative Law* (7th edn, 1994) pp 399-436; Supperstone and Goudie *Judicial Review* (2nd edn, 1997) ch 6; Jones "Mistake of Fact in Administrative Law" [1990] PL 507; Jowell and Oliver "Proportionality: neither novel nor dangerous", *New Directions in Judicial Review* (1988) p 51; Laws J "Is the High Court the Guardian of Fundamental Constitutional Rights?" [1993] PL 59.

2 *Associated Provincial Picture Houses Ltd v Wednesbury Corpn* [1948] 1 KB 223, [1947] 2 All ER 680, CA.

54. Irrationality vs. unreasonableness. The concept of *Wednesbury*[1] unreasonableness was reconsidered by the House of Lords in the GCHQ case[2] where it was re-named "irrationality". Lord Diplock described irrationality as applying "to a decision which is so outrageous in its defiance of logic or of accepted moral standards that no sensible person who had applied his mind to the question to be decided could have arrived at it".

1 *Associated Provincial Picture Houses Ltd v Wednesbury Corpn* [1948] 1 KB 223, [1947] 2 All ER 680, CA.
2 *Council of Civil Service Unions v Minister for the Civil Service* [1985] AC 374, [1984] 3 All ER 935, HL.

55. Meaning of "unreasonableness". As was pointed out in *Re W*[1] in the House of Lords, two reasonable men can perfectly well come to opposite conclusions about something without either forfeiting a claim to reasonableness. But "unreasonableness" in the administrative law sense has been taken to mean that which no other ordinary individual or body would do. It is not enough for a judge to conclude that there exists a more reasonable way of acting in the circumstances. The judiciary maintains that it has merely upheld the will of Parliament in its elucidation of "unreasonableness" but it is arguable that decisions about what is a relevant consideration to have considered, or what was a lawful purpose to have pursued in the circumstances, are inevitably based on social or political value judgments[2]. It is therefore sensible for a practitioner to situate the facts of his or her particular case in the context of the political atmosphere of the day.

1 *Re W* [1971] AC 682, [1971] 2 All ER 49, HL.
2 It remains to be seen to what extent *Pepper v Hart* [1993] AC 593, [1993] 1 All ER 42, HL, will enable the judiciary to assess Parliament's intention at the time of the passing of the legislation more accurately.

56. Application. Two meanings of reviewable unreasonableness emerged from Lord Greene MR's judgment[1]: it is a synonym for a range of other more specific criticisms (such as acting for no reason, or legally irrelevant reasons or acting in bad faith), and secondly, it can be a description of a decision so extreme or absurd that it is "substantively" unreasonable. The second meaning suggests a long-stop role for the concept of "pure" unreasonableness, if none of the other more formal criticisms seems to apply to the facts. So it is conventional to regard the concept as giving rise to two main types of challenge: irrelevancy and unreasonableness in the sense of absurdity[2]. To some extent, all illegality could be characterised as taking irrelevant considerations into account (or at least those which the judges think ought not to have been taken into account). But Lord Greene MR's concept of unreasonableness went further than that: true irrationality can occur even within a decision-making process which is otherwise unexceptionable.

1   *Associated Provincial Picture Houses Ltd v Wednesbury Corpn* [1948] 1 KB 223, [1947] 2 All ER 680, CA.
2   Variously described as "irrational partiality or inequality of operation", "manifest injustice", "capriciousness", "arbitrariness", "oppression", "gratuitousness", "acting perversely" or "verging on absurdity": *Puhlhofer v Hillingdon London BoroughCouncil* [1986] AC 484, [1986] 1 All ER 467, HL and "totally unreasonable": *Champion v Chief Constable of the Gwent Constabulary* [1990] 1 All ER 116, [1990] 1 WLR 1, HL.

57. Examination of reasoning by the courts. The legal relevancy of matters considered by decision making bodies must be extracted from the express provisions in the enabling statute, any overriding statutory provisions from other statutes, the general common law, EC law and the European Convention on Human Rights, in cases of ambiguity. To the extent that a statute requires an official to be satisfied of something before he proceeds to act, the court will investigate the existence of the underlying facts, tending to leave the evaluation of them for the decision maker unless the evidence suggests that the weight given to the aspects of the evaluation was itself unreasonable. The absence of reasons for a decision will not of itself support a contention of irrationality, since there is no general duty to give reasons in administrative law[1]. However, inferences may be drawn from their absence[2]. The mere existence of admissible reasons in favour of a respondent's decision is not enough to stop a finding of irrationality, because the court will still consider their rationality nevertheless. The court will intervene where the facts taken as a whole could not logically warrant the conclusion of the decision maker; for instance if the evidence is overwhelmingly in favour of the opposite conclusion[3]. The court will normally examine both the rationality of the findings of fact on which the impugned decision is based, and that of the decision maker's evaluation of those facts, in concluding as he or she did. The court will grant relief where there was some evidence pointing to the finding, but no reasonable tribunal could have regarded it as sufficient to warrant such a finding[4]. Giving undue weight[5] even to a legitimate consideration, might turn it into an irrelevance[6].

1   But see the observations of LORD DONALDSON MR in *R v Lancashire County Council, ex p Huddleston* [1986] 2 All ER 941, CA, that generally speaking public bodies should be ready at least to assist the court, with a full explanation of why they have acted or decided in a particular way. Express relief from a duty to give reasons did not implicitly relieve a Minister from a duty of disclosure during the process of reaching his decision: *R v Secretary of State for the Home Department, ex p Fayed* [1997] 1 All ER 228, [1998], CA. See also *R v City of London Corpn, ex p Matson* [1997] 1 WLR 765, [1996] COD 161, CA: a duty to give reasons may by implied in appropriate circumstances, which include the nature of the adjudicating process; the decision not to confirm the applicant as an Alderman was one which should be explained.
2   See, for example, *Padfield v Minister of Agriculture, Fisheries and Food* [1968] AC 997, [1968] 1 All ER 694, HL; *R v Secretary of State for the Home Department, ex p Sinclair* [1992] Imm AR 293; *R v Civil Service Appeal Board, ex p Cunningham* [1991] 4 All ER 310, CA. Note that LAWS J suggests that *Padfield v Minister for Agriculture, Fisheries and Food* [1968] AC 997, [1968] 1 All ER 694, HL, could be extended so as to give rise to a presumption that a statute's purpose cannot include or permit any interference with fundamental rights, unless there is only one possible interpretation of the statute: [1993] PL 59 at 76 and see *R v Lord Chancellor, ex p Witham* [1997] 2 All ER 779, [1998] 2 WLR 849.
3   See, for example, *Emma Hotels Ltd v Secretary of the State for the Environment* (1980) 41 P & CR 255; *R v Sheffield City Council, ex p Chadwick* (1985) 84 LGR 563.
4   See, for example, *R v Ealing London Borough, ex p Richardson* (1982) 4 HLR 125, CA.

5   *West Glamorgan County Council v Rafferty* [1987] 1 All ER 1005, [1987] 1 WLR 457, CA.
6   For instance, over-reliance on fairness: *R v Police Complaints Board, ex p Madden* [1983] 2 All ER 353, [1983] 1 WLR 447; *South Oxfordshire District Council v Secretary of State for the Environment* [1981] 1 All ER 954, [1981] 1 WLR 1092: over-reliance on a long expired planning permission as vitally material to the decision.

58. "No evidence" cases of irrationality. Sometimes the court will be persuaded that there was no evidence at all to support a finding of fact made by a decision maker[1]. It could be said in relation to "no evidence" cases that quashing a decision when no weight has been given to a consideration necessarily forming part of the statutory purpose, is simply quashing for illegality. Alternatively, it can be argued that if a decision is made and there was simply no evidence to support it, then it has been made irrationally. It is asserted by the judiciary that this sort of intervention is not merely righting mistakes of fact made by decision makers. In theory the court will not countenance acting as an appellate court. It is maintained that the court is merely ensuring that decisions are not made for which there is no rational basis, without interfering with the decision maker's function of resolving disputed matters of fact within his jurisdiction[2].

1   *Sagnata Investments Ltd v Norwich Corpn* [1971] 2 QB 614, [1971] 2 All ER 1441, CA, where the lack of evidence for an opinion about the effects of amusement arcades within a community was held to have vitiated a policy.
2   For a discussion of *A-G for New South Wales v Quin* (1990) 170 CLR 1 in this regard see Craig (1992) 108 LQR 79.

59. Examples of irrationality. *Irrelevancies.* It is not unlawful to regard the displeasure of the party whip as a consideration in voting at local authority debates, nor is it wrong to bear in mind promises made to electors before the election. But it can be wrong to give them too much weight, because a councillor is a representative not merely a delegate of those who voted for him or her[1].

In *Roberts v Hopwood*[2] it was held that irrelevant philanthropic concerns had entered into the council's exercise of the statutory duty of setting a wage for its workers, and that fiduciary duties and consideration of the costs of living and comparability with other authorities had been ignored. A boycott of a company's products was unlawful because the council's concerns about apartheid and race relations were legally irrelevant to its contracting power, and it was held unreasonable to seek to spread the boycott to other boroughs[3]. In *R v Derbyshire County Council, ex p Times Supplements Ltd*[4] it was held that political reasons and personal spite had impinged on the decision to remove education advertising from The Times in the wake of a separate libel action between the parties. In *R v Northavon District Council, ex p Ashman*[5] an environmental health officer relied on certain documentation in choosing the higher of two estimates for an item of work on a house that was unfit for human habitation. The court held that the documents did not support the conclusion and went on to identify the real reason behind the decision was that it affected the prospects of a particular witness being called to give evidence in proceedings; the court held this to be an irrelevant consideration.

Mixed grounds for review. There are many instances in the cases where the court has coupled a finding of unreasonableness with one of illegality, based upon either irrelevancy or mistake of law. The practitioner may be assured that the precise classification of the conduct does not matter, since these "causes of action" overlap in public law. Party political considerations at central government level are frowned upon and regarded as legally extraneous and such as by which no reasonable politician could be swayed[6]. In *Congreve v Home Office*[7] the threat of TV licence revocation was used as a means of deterring people from saving money by buying a new licence before the old one expired. This was characterised as an attempt to extract money which the executive was not empowered to demand; at once unlawful and unreasonable in the Wednesbury sense. *Wheeler v Leicester City Council*[8] was a case which combined irrelevancy and unreasonableness: the council attempted to coerce members of a rugby team to support its views about apartheid by threatening to terminate the club's rights to use a pitch which it administered under statute unless its members cancelled their trip to South Africa. Since local authorities can only operate within a statutory context, charges of unreasonableness against them are more usually determined on the basis of illegality or irrelevancy, rather than "pure" irrationality. A local authority is not entitled to take into account considerations not fairly and reasonably relating to the subject matter of the statutory power in question: for example, a non-planning purpose, such as furtherance of a housing policy, when applied to a planning application, will be illegal[9].

Pure unreasonableness. In *Rooke's Case*[10] a court struck down a charge levied by commissioners of sewers against the claimant. The charge was held to have been levied outside the width of discretion allowed to the commissioners: Rooke had been charged for the whole cost of repair, even though others had benefited too[11]. In *R v London Borough of Hackney, ex p Evenbray Ltd*[12] proprietors of a hotel catering partly for the homeless of the borough succeeded in obtaining a finding of unreasonableness when Hackney directed that no-one could occupy the premises for want of adequate kitchen facilities. No local authority having chosen to accommodate its homeless on the site could reasonably invoke the statutory powers used. In *Ogwr Borough Council v Baker*[13] justices had dismissed information that Baker plied for hire an unlicensed vehicle. The court held that to suggest that the proximity of a hot-dog stand could give the man an excuse for parking his vehicle in a line of waiting cabs was absurd, and it quashed the dismissal. In *R v St Albans Crown Court, ex p Cinnamond*[14] a disqualification of 18 months for careless driving was held to be irrational. In *Backhouse v Lambeth Borough Council*[15] a rent increase on a vacant derelict property from £7 per week to £18,000 was held to be wholly unreasonable (it had been done to evade statutory provisions). In *Williams v Giddy*[16] giving a retiring civil servant a gratuity of one penny per year of service was unreasonable. In *Hall v Shoreham on Sea UDC*[17] a planning condition required construction of a road at a site owner's expense, when he would have got compensation for giving up the land, had alternative procedures been followed, and the condition was held to be unreasonable[18]. It has been held unreasonable to make decisions reserving arbitrary power to the authority for the future. The use of byelaws to oblige persons to contract with the council has been outlawed too[19]. It has been held unreasonable to require that which cannot lawfully be done eg requiring an individual to do something amounting to a trespass. However, in the planning field, conditions have been imposed to the effect that something outside the power of the applicant be done and these have sometimes survived scrutiny as not necessarily unreasonable[20]. Manifest injustice was said to arise from immigration rules providing for dependent parents to be admitted to the UK on compassionate circumstances only if the immigrant's standard of living was substantially below the norm of his or her own country. It was held that there was no possible basis in sense or justice for a requirement that would automatically disqualify all those from the poorer countries of the world[21].

1 *Bromley LBC v GLC* [1983] 1 AC 768, [1982] 1 All ER 129, HL. See also *Secretary of State for Education and Science v Tameside MBC* [1977] AC 1014, [1976] 3 All ER 665, HL.
2 *Roberts v Hopwood* [1925] AC 578, HL.
3 *R v Lewisham LBC, ex p Shell UK Ltd* [1988] 1 All ER 938.
4 *R v Derbyshire County Council, ex p Times Supplements Ltd* [1991] 3 Admin LR 241.
5 *R v Northavon District Council, ex p Ashman* [1992] COD 451.
6 *Padfield v Minister of Agriculture, Fisheries and Food* [1968] AC 997, [1968] 1 All ER 694, HL.
7 *Congreve v Home Office* [1976] QB 629, [1976] 1 All ER 697, CA.
8 *Wheeler v Leicester City Council* [1985] AC 1054, [1985] 2 All ER 1106, HL.
9 *R v Hillingdon LBC, ex p Royco Homes Ltd* [1974] QB 720, [1974] 2 All ER 643: a condition requiring letting of properties to those on council's waiting list and the grant of ten years, security of tenure, was held unlawful. Further, a library authority cannot ban publications as leverage in an industrial dispute. *R v Ealing LBC, ex p Times Newspapers Ltd* (1987) 85 LGR 316, CA. See also *R v ILEA, ex p Westminster City Council* [1986] 1 All ER 19, [1986] 1 WLR 28: the council's motive in spending money on an advertising campaign was to persuade the public to accept the undesirability of education cuts; to do so with informing the public in mind would have been legitimate but the improper motive dominated its reasoning. In *R v Barnet LBC, ex p Johnson* (1990) 89 LGR 581 the High Court had found the byelaw conditions relating to activities of political groups in its parks were open to such a variety of possible meanings as to be meaningless and unreasonable. The Court of Appeal found that "party-political activities" was a comprehensible term but that illegality was made out in that the council had purported to inhibit the manner in which the public used the park, rather than regulate public enjoyment of it.
10 *Rooke's Case* (1598) 5 Co Rep 99b.
11 For examples of decisions based on similar reasoning in the 17th and 18th centuries see Craig (1992) 108 LQR 79.
12 *R v London Borough of Hackney, ex p Evenbray Ltd* (1987) 86 LGR 210.
13 *Ogwr Borough Council v Baker* [1989] COD 489.
14 *R v St Albans Crown Court, ex p Cinnamond* [1981] QB 480, [1981] 1 All ER 802.
15 *Backhouse v Lambeth London Borough Council* (1972) 116 Sol Jo 802. Yet see *Smith v Cardiff Corpn (No 2)* [1955] Ch 159, [1955] 1 All ER 113 where rents were held not to be reviewable even though they subsidised tenants at the ratepayers' expense.
16 *Williams v Giddy* [1911] AC 381.
17 *Hall & Co Ltd v Shoreham-on-Sea UDC* [1964] 1 All ER 1, [1964] 1 WLR 240, CA.
18 But note that statutory powers may in fact overcome this judicial presumption of "no sequestration without compensation"; it is a matter of construction as to whether or not they do.
19 *Parker v Bournemouth Corpn* (1902) 66 JP 440.
20 See *Grampian Regional Council v City of Aberdeen District Council* (1983) 47 P & CR 633, HL, but see also *Jones v Secretary of State for Wales* (1990) 61 P & CR 238, CA.
21 *R v Immigration Appeal Tribunal, ex p Manshoora Begum* [1986] Imm AR 385.

60. Qualifications to the doctrine. There are several qualifications to the applicability of irrationality as a ground for review. Certain activities, where the prerogative is the only source of power for the conduct or decision, would generally involve government policy[1] and might be held to be non-justiciable[2]. With regard to ministerial proposals considered or approved by Parliament, in *Nottinghamshire County Council v Secretary of State for the Environment*[3] the House of Lords began a retreat from reviewing this field. It held that only in exceptional circumstances would it be appropriate to intervene in such decisions or policies. Lord Scarman identified bad faith, improper motives or extreme unreasonableness as such circumstances, suggesting that he was merely excluding review based on irrelevancies having been taken into account in the formulation of the decision. Lord Bridge in *R v Secretary of State for the Environment, ex p Hammersmith and Fulham LBC*[4] clarified the doctrine and held that Parliament's approval precludes examination of the rationality of an exercise of statutory power short of the extremes of bad faith, improper motive or manifest absurdity. Mere irrelevancy is not enough because such a finding would be a usurpation of the minister's right and duty to decide the appropriate factors and weight to be given to them. It is possible that there are areas of administration which will be given particularly intense scrutiny: where for instance, the decision imperils life or liberty[5]. But where the allocation of financial resources are concerned in the exercise of powers or duties, the concept of justiciability may again be used to explain judicial restraint. In other words, the limits of review are dependent upon the subject matter and nature of the decision.

1 It has been suggested that the court will review the rationality of the implementation of policy decisions where it arises in the exercise of statutory powers. Examples given are *R v Secretary of State for Transport, ex p GLC* [1986] QB 556, [1985] 3 All ER 300; *R v Immigration Appeal Tribunal, ex p Manshoora Begum* [1986] Imm AR 385; *R v HM Treasury, ex p Smedley* [1985] QB 657, [1985] 1 All ER 589, CA. See Supperstone and Goudie *Judicial Review* (2nd edn, 1997) ch 6.
2 But even actions done on the basis of national security can be reviewed, in theory, on grounds of reasonableness: see LORD DIPLOCK in *Council of Civil Service Unions v Minister for the Civil Service* [1985] AC 374, [1984] 3 All ER 935, HL.
3 *Nottinghamshire County Council v Secretary of State for the Environment* [1986] AC 240, [1986] 1 All ER 199, HL.
4 *R v Secretary of State for the Environment, ex p Hammersmith and Fulham London Borough Council* [1991] 1 AC 521, [1990] 3 All ER 589, HL.
5 The court should ask whether the decision maker could reasonably have concluded there was a competing interest sufficiently strong to warrant that interference with human rights: *R v Secretary of State for the Home Department, ex p Brind* [1991] 1 AC 696, [1991] 1 All ER 720, HL, and applied by POPPLEWELL J in *R v Secretary of State for the Home Department, ex p Cox* [1992] COD 72; and see LORD BRIDGE'S speech in *Re Musisi* [1987] AC 514, sub nom *Bugdaycay v Secretary of State for the Home Department*, [1987] AC 514, [1987] 1 All ER 940, HL.

61. Proportionality. Since the UK joined the wider European arena, practitioners and academics have explored the relevance of the community law doctrine of proportionality[1] to review of decision making in the national courts. Proportionality is recognised in the administrative law of several members of the EEC. It originated from the legal systems of civil law countries such as Germany. It requires an appropriate balance between the adverse effects which an authority's decision may have on the rights, liberties or interests of the person concerned and the purpose which the authority is seeking to pursue[2]. A conceptual difficulty which probably explained judicial reluctance to develop the doctrine is that the community concept involves judges weighing finely in the balance the propriety of measures adopted by the state to achieve social policies, on the one hand, against the effect on individuals' acknowledged "rights" on the other.

1   English cases in which the doctrine has been used without being identified as such were: *R v Barnsley MBC, ex p Hook* [1976] 3 All ER 452, [1976] 1 WLR 1052, CA, and *R v Brent LBC, ex p Assegai* (1987) Times, 18 June. LORD DIPLOCK referred to proportionality as a possible fourth ground for judicial review in *Council of Civil Service Unions v Minister for the Civil Service* [1985] AC 374, [1984] 3 All ER 945, HL, although he recognised that it was not yet part of UK administrative law.
2   Committee of Ministers of the Council of Europe in 1980: Rec No R(80)2 11 March 1980.

62. The future. The House of Lords in *R v Secretary of State for the Home Department, ex p Brind*[1] characterised proportionality not as an independent head of review but merely as an aspect of irrationality[2]. But the speeches of Lords Bridge, Roskill and Templeman demonstrate that recognition of proportionality as a test for identifying abuse of power may still be a possibility. The Court of Appeal has already begun to develop the law based on those speeches[3]. Furthermore, Laws J has expressed the view extra-judicially[4] that a domestic concept of proportionality may indeed have to be used in cases involving decisions affecting fundamental human rights[5]. The likely incorporation of the European Convention and its principles within community law, which is in turn already binding on the UK, will widen the relevance of the principle[6].

1   *R v Secretary of State for the Home Department, ex p Brind* [1991] 1 AC 696, [1991] 1 All ER 720, HL.
2   See also *R v Secretary of State for Transport, ex p Pegasus Holdings (London) Ltd* [1989] 2 All ER 481, [1988] 1 WLR 990 and *R v Secretary of State for Health, ex p United States Tobacco Inc* [1992] QB 353, [1992] 1 All ER 212 for similar treatment.
3   See *National and Local Government Officers' Association v Secretary of State for the Environment*, (1992) Times, 2 December, CA, in which NEILL LJ appeared to consider that there might be greater scope for proportionality in review cases against public bodies and local authorities as opposed to cases against central government.
4   At a meeting of the Administrative Law Bar Association in June 1992 and in an article at [1993] PL 59 at 69, 74.
5   See also Lord Browne-Wilkinson "The Infiltration of a Bill of Rights" [1992] PL 397 citing inter alia *Paul (R & W) Ltd v Wheat Commission* [1937] AC 139, [1936] 2 All ER 1243, HL; *Morris v Beardmore* [1981] AC 446, [1980] 2 All ER 753, HL; and *Raymond v Honey* [1983] 1 AC 1, [1982] 1 All ER 756, HL, in support of his contention that the judiciary is already constitutionally capable of applying the European Convention of Human Rights without express incorporation, at least in areas affected by European Community legislation. See also *R v Secretary of State for the Home Department, ex p Chahal* [1995] 1 All ER 658, [1995] 1 WLR 526, CA; *R v Secretary of State for the Home Department, ex p Cox; R v O'Kane and Clarke, ex p Northern Bank Ltd* [1996] STC 1249.
6   See Koopmans [1991] PL 53; Grief [1991] PL 555, on the existence of a European Public Law and the domestic impact of the Convention as mediated through community law.

5: UNLAWFUL DELEGATION, RIGIDITY AND ESTOPPEL

63. Introduction. A person aggrieved by the decision of a public body will often be able to establish simply by reference to the governing statute, that in taking the decision the public body has acted beyond its powers - ultra vires. In addition, it should be noted that some clear principles have been established as to the manner in which a statutory power or duty must be performed.

64. Unlawful delegation[1]. There is a presumption, strongest in the case of judicial and similar powers, that the person or corporation required by statute to exercise a power or perform a duty must do so personally or corporately - *delegatus not potest delegare* (the delegate is not permitted to delegate)[2]. The exercise of a decision making power may be regarded as unlawful if it is delegated further than the enabling statute envisaged or authorised[3]. A decision making body may properly delegate executive and administrative functions (for example, the gathering of evidence), providing it retains the final decision[4].

Unlawful delegation must also be distinguished from lawful delegation where constitutional convention[5], or subordinate legislation[6], permits delegation to certain categories of other persons. The courts have held that powers which have been expressly entrusted to government ministers may be exercised by their officials[7]. It is likely that decisions which involve a judicial or quasi-judicial exercise of evaluation and discretion will be confined strictly to those designated for the job, whereas functions of a more administrative nature may be permitted by the courts to be done by the most efficient and convenient level of officials[8].

A complainant may, in addition (or, conceivably, as a sole ground of challenge), be able to show that the public body entrusted with the decision has in fact agreed in advance to abide by the decision of another body[9].

Local authorities have very wide powers of delegation to committees, sub-committees and officers[10]; but the hierarchy of delegation must always be preserved so far as appointments to committees are concerned[11].

Acting in accordance with or subject to the wishes or instructions of a third party[12] is also a form of "delegation" in that it involves an unlawful involvement of a party not intended to participate in the decision making.

1 See generally Supperstone and Goudie *Judicial Review* (2nd edn, 1997) ch 5.
2 The classic case is *Barnard v National Dock Labour Board* [1953] 2 QB 18, [1953] 1 All ER 1113, CA, where a joint committee of employers and employees was entitled by statute to exercise disciplinary powers; they acted unlawfully when they delegated these to the port manager. See also *Ellis v Dubowski* [1921] 3 KB 621 where the local authority's condition that no film should be screened which had not been approved by the British Board of Film Censors was unlawful.
3 This principle arises primarily because of the rule of statutory interpretation that a delegate is not permitted to delegate. See *R v DPP, ex p First Division Association* [1988] NLJR 158 in which the CPS practice of letting non-legally qualified staff make the decision whether to prosecute on the basis of the files before them was declared unlawful.

4   See *R v Race Relations Board, ex p Selvarajan* [1975] 1 WLR 1686, CA; *R v Commission for Racial Equality, ex p Cottrell and Rothon* [1980] 3 All ER 265, [1980] 1 WLR 1580. In *Tanks and Drums Ltd v Transport and General Workers Union* [1992] ICR 1, CA, where the General Secretary lawfully gave authority to call a strike to a regional officer; the operative decision was that a strike should be called if necessary.

5   It is accepted practice for a Minister's operational functions to be performed in his name by his officials. This is because the department is regarded as the alter ego of the Minister: *Carltona Ltd v Works Comrs* [1943] 2 All ER 560, CA. See also *R v Secretary of State for the Home Department, ex p Doody* [1993] QB 157, [1993] 1 All ER 151, CA, where it was held acceptable for junior ministers and not the Secretary of State personally to decide what the tariff sentence should be for life prisoners so long as they were accountable to Parliament, even though the freedom of the individual was at stake.

6   For example, the precise rules under the Education (School Government) Regulations 1989, SI 1989/1503 providing for delegation by governors to the head and to subcommittees.

7   In *R v Secretary of State for the Home Department, ex p Oladehinde* [1991] 1 AC 254 the House of Lords upheld delegation by the Home Secretary to Immigration Inspectors of the important power to order deportation.

8   See *Vine v National Dock Labour Board* [1957] AC 488, [1956] 3 All ER 939, HL. As to "colourable" authority see *R v Crocker* CACD 19 December 1997.

9   In *H Lavender & Son Ltd v Minister of Housing and Local Government* [1970] 3 All ER 871, [1970] 1 WLR 1231 the Minister refused planning permission pursuant to his policy of refusing unless the Minister of Agriculture was not opposed. In *R v Police Complaints Board, ex p Madden* [1983] 2 All ER 353, [1983] 1 WLR 447 the PCB unlawfully adopted a policy that it would not institute disciplinary proceedings where the DPP had decided not to prosecute on the same facts.

10   Local Government Act 1972 ss 101 (as amended), 102 (as amended) (25 Halsbury's Statutes (4th Edn) LOCAL GOVERNMENT).

11   *R v Brent London Borough Council, ex p Gladbaum and Woods* [1990] 2 Admin LR 634; but note that the decision was to some extent superseded by the "party political proportionality" provisions of the Local Government and Housing Act 1989.

12   Even if this was not intended by the third party: *R v Police Complaints Board, ex p Madden* [1983] 2 All ER 353, [1983] 1 WLR 447.

65. Fettering discretion. A public body will be perfectly entitled (and often well-advised) to adopt a policy for dealing with large numbers of similar applications, and such a policy may lawfully amount to a rule. But it must not in consequence refuse to listen to an application at all[1]; there must be a willingness to consider each case on its merits. An express refusal to hear representations from an affected body before exercising a discretionary power in accordance with an announced policy has been held to be unlawful[2].

When faced with a policy the practitioner must ask first of all whether the policy adopted is a lawful policy[3], not otherwise void for unreasonableness etc, and if so, then nevertheless has it been applied too rigidly? It is possible that the greater the element of procedural fairness or natural justice involved in a decision making process, the more likely will be the court's willingness to interfere with policies about procedural aspects such as refusal of legal representation.

1   The leading case is *British Oxygen Co Ltd v Ministry of Technology* [1971] AC 610, [1970] 3 All ER 165, HL, where there was a policy not to make grants for individual items of equipment worth less than £25, pursuant to which grants were declined for items purchased for £20 each. See also *Secretary of State for the Home Department, v Hastrup* [1996] Imm AR 616, CA - a minister of the Crown would fetter his discretion unlawfully if he laid down a policy which had to be applied rigidly in particular cases. See further *R v Mid Glamorgan Family Health Services, ex p Martin* [1995] 1 All ER 356, [1995] 1 WLR 110; *R v Secretary of State for the Environment, ex p Lancashire County Council* [1994] 4 All ER 165, 93 LGR 29.

2   *R v Secretary of State for the Environment, ex p Brent London Borough Council* [1982] QB 593, [1983] 3 All ER 321. See also Supperstone & Goudie *Judicial Review* (2nd edn,1997) 5.24.
3   In *R v Forest Betting Licensing Committee, ex p Noquet* (1988) Times, 21 June, a licensing policy was found to be unlawful because the statutory provisions in question did not justify a policy that an applicant for a betting shop licence had to have a legal interest in the premises. A policy which would only offend against sex discrimination laws depending on its method of implementation was upheld as lawful in *R v London Borough of Hammersmith & Fulham, ex p NALGO* [1991] IRLR 249.

66. Legitimate expectation[1]**.** The other side of the "fettering" problem is that it may be unfair in a general sense for a public body not to adhere to a policy which it has made public and abided by in the past, because the public may have relied on it in accepting or rejecting private law rights and duties. However, it will not be in the public interest for public law bodies charged with statutory powers and duties to be able to enlarge their jurisdictions merely by assertion to the public. Nor can it be right that particular individuals should be better off than others in dealings with authority simply because of a mistake by an official which misled the individual.

1   See also the section on procedural fairness or propriety in particular Paragraphs 45-52 ante.

67. Estoppel. A contract by which a public body agrees not to exercise a statutory function will be unlawful, although an express term restricting the future exercise of that function may not be[1]. Similarly, a public body may not create or enlarge its powers by contract or estoppel, nor can a tribunal in this way enlarge its jurisdiction[2].

The estoppel of public bodies by way of binding[3] contract may be seen as an aspect of illegality in the sense that arrangements with third parties can be said to fetter the discretion of public authorities. The issue is whether entering into a contract having irrevocable consequences is an unlawful fetter of a present duty or power to exercise a discretion.

Estoppel by representation (as distinct from proprietary estoppel and issue estoppel) may be seen as an aspect of legitimate expectation, but it is generally agreed that it may, in respect of statutory bodies, amount to a lawful substantive fetter of the exercise of discretion, which operates as a rule of evidence rather than as a source of legal right. Where a representation is made by or on behalf of a public body, and an estoppel would arise in private law if the parties were in a pre-existing contractual relationship (since detrimental reliance follows the making of the representation), it is arguable that an analogous result should obtain in public law.

If the representation was itself ultra vires the public body concerned, an estoppel would, however, have the effect of legitimising unlawful conduct, which would not be in the public interest. The courts have tried to balance these competing principles on a case by case basis and it may be said that the issue turns upon the discrete questions, first, whether or not actual or implied authority existed for the maker of the representation to say what he said, and secondly whether or not mandatory or merely directory procedural technicalities are involved. In the latter case, authority establishes that a public body can in certain circumstances waive a technicality so as to invalidate that which would otherwise be valid[4].

In the case of the former, however, there can be no enlargement of a public power, even if detriment has been suffered. Statutory preconditions to the acquisition of a right or status cannot be overridden[5], but the courts will in certain situations construe apparently mandatory provisions as directory, and go on to infer implied authority for individuals to make representations, even where proper delegation procedures have not been completed.

Where a public body has resolved not to grant a permission, and by mistake the applicant is informed that permission has been granted, but the mistake is put right within a short time, the body will not be bound by the error, even where the applicant has suffered detriment[6]. However, where a function has been delegated to an officer, the officer gives an assurance or makes a decision, this is relied upon by the applicant to his detriment, and it is reasonable for the applicant to believe that the officer had delegated authority, the public body may be estopped from acting in breach of the assurance or decision[7].

1 In *R v Hammersmith and Fulham London Borough Council, ex p Beddowes* [1987] QB 1050, [1987] 1 All ER 369, CA, the council sold a block of flats subject to covenants as to future lettings of other flats retained by the council; this was lawful.
2 *Secretary of State for Employment v Globe Elastic Thread Ltd* [1980] AC 506, [1979] 2 All ER 1077, HL.
3 A statement of present policy regarding an individual does not necessarily amount to an offer or acceptance taking effect as a contract. In *Woolfall v Knowsley Borough Council* (1992) Times, 26 June, CA, a council had written letters to taxi cab operators appearing to guarantee licences to those coming within a certain category, subject to compliance with conditions precedent. Despite fulfilment of those conditions, the applicants were denied licences because the council changed its policy before their application was heard. It was held that none of the parties had been thinking in terms of contract or even estoppel at the time of earlier correspondence and that the lack of intention to create legal intentions prevented the statement of policy from having contractual force.
4 *Wells v Minister of Housing and Local Government* [1967] 2 All ER 1041, [1967] 1 WLR 1000, CA.
5 But see *Gowa v A-G* [1985] 1 WLR 1003, HL, in which the House of Lords, whilst doubtful, left open the Court of Appeal's holding that the Crown was bound by an assurance that the applicants were citizens of the United Kingdom.
6 *Norfolk County Council v Secretary of State for the Environment* [1973] 3 All ER 673, [1973] 1 WLR 1400.
7 *Western Fish Products Ltd v Penwith District Council* [1981] 2 All ER 204, CA. This is the leading case on estoppel, showing that in most cases public bodies will not be inhibited from exercising a statutory discretion by virtue of an estoppel.

D: SPECIFIC CASES

1: IMMIGRATION CASES

68. Immigration cases. Immigration applications form the largest category of applications for judicial review. Most immigration decisions are susceptible to judicial review, for example, decisions of an entry clearance officer, an immigration officer, an adjudicator, a tribunal, or a criminal court carrying out immigration functions[1] (subject to the question whether case stated or judicial review is more appropriate[2]). Decisions of the Secretary of State, such as the exercise of the prerogative power to grant or refuse a passport, may also be reviewed[3], subject to express statutory provision to the contrary[4].

However, the applicant must, except in exceptional cases, have exhausted any appeal which lies to one of the immigration appellate authorities[5]. For example, the fact that a visitor had to appeal from abroad was not such a disadvantage as to make the appeal useless, and therefore to give rise to such exceptional circumstances[6].

In illegal entry cases it is the High Court's duty, in view of the necessity of safeguarding the liberty of the subject, to inquire whether there has been sufficient evidence to justify the immigration officer's belief that the entry was illegal[7]. That is a "precedent fact" which must be established by the executive. The court will not review the merits of a decision, with potentially serious consequences in asylum cases; nevertheless, the European Court of Human Rights has held that the powers of the High Court in judicial review proceedings provide an effective degree of control over the decisions of administrative authorities in asylum cases[8].

A common ground for challenge in immigration cases is *Wednesbury* unreasonableness, for example, failing to take into account relevant circumstances[9]. Where the Secretary of State considered evidence submitted on an applicant's behalf, but did not explain whether he accepted it, or whether he simply regarded it as irrelevant, his reasoning was held to be inadequate[10].

The Asylum and Immigration Appeals Act 1993 and the Asylum and Immigration Act 1996 provide, inter alia, a fast track appeals procedure for asylum claims. An accelerated procedure exists for cases where the claim for asylum has been certified by the Secretary of State as "without foundation" and provides for appeal to a special adjudicator. A claim is without foundation if it does not raise any issue as to the UK's obligations under the United Nations Convention Relating to the Status of Refugees 1951 or is otherwise frivolous and vexatious[11]. Appeal lies from the decision of the Secretary of State[12] to a special adjudicator on the ground that any one of the conditions set out in the Asylum and Immigration Act 1996[13] was not fulfilled when the certificate was issued or has ceased to be fulfilled. Only if the certificate is set aside may the applicant appeal to the Immigration Appeal Tribunal[14], or to a special adjudicator on convention grounds[15].

SPECIFIC CASES 119

Appeal from substantive decisions of the Tribunal lies, with leave, on a point of law to the Court of Appeal Civil Division[16]. An applicant may rely on procedural impropriety; as deportation has serious consequences, the High Court has held that in all their dealings with immigrants, immigration officers must act honestly and fairly[17]. A legitimate expectation may arise as a result of a private promise or assurance or as the result of a general policy; while a policy may be changed in accordance with statutory powers, it may be unfair to do so without giving notice or an opportunity to explain[18]. However, the applicability and extent of the doctrine in the immigration context have been held to be uncertain, and a legitimate expectation will not arise where an applicant has obtained leave to enter by fraud[19].

In an appropriate case, such as an illegal entry case, the applicant may apply to cross-examine, for example, an immigration officer[20].

The High Court has jurisdiction to grant bail either on application for leave to apply for judicial review or as a substantive application[21]. Where bail is refused, an appeal lies to the Court of Appeal.

1 *R v Clerk to Birmingham Justices, ex p Offei* (28 November 1985, unreported).
2 *R v Crown Court at Ipswich, ex p Baldwin* [1981] 1 All ER 596.
3 *R v Secretary of State for Foreign and Commonwealth Affairs, ex p Everett* [1989] QB 811, [1989] 1 All ER 655, CA.
4 See, for example, the British Nationality Act 1981 s 44 (2) (31 Halsbury's Statutes (4th Edn) NATIONALITY AND IMMIGRATION); the British Nationality (Hong Kong) Act 1990 s 1 (5) (31 Halsbury's Statutes (4th Edn) NATIONALITY AND IMMIGRATION).
5 That is the adjudicator or the immigration appeals tribunal.
6 *R v Secretary of State for the Home Department, ex p Swati* [1986] 1 All ER 717, [1986] 1 WLR 477, CA.
7 *Khawaja v Secretary of State for the Home Department* [1984] AC 74, [1983] 1 All ER 765, HL.
8 *Vilvarajah v United Kingdom* (1992) 14 EHRR 248, ECtHR.
9 See *Re Musisi* [1987] AC 514, sub nom *Bugdaycay v Secretary of State for the Home Department,* [1987] 1 All ER 940, HL; *R v Secretary of State for the Home Department, ex p Uzoenyi* [1992] COD 217; *R v Secretary of State for the Home Department, ex p P* [1992] COD 295.
10 *R v Secretary of State for the Home Department, ex p Chahal* [1995] 1 All ER 658, CA.
11 Asylum and Immigration Appeals Act 1993; Asylum and Immigration Act 1996 (31 Halsbury's Statutes (4th Edn) NATIONALITY AND IMMIGRATION). As to the cases to which the accelerated procedure applies see Asylum and Immigration Act 1996 Sch 2 paras 2, 4. United Nations Convention Relating to the Status of Refugees 1951.
12 Asylum and Immigration Act 1996 s 3.
13 Asylum and Immigration Act 1996 s 2 (2).
14 Asylum and Immigration Act 1996 s 3 (1)(b)(i).
15 Asylum and Immigration Act 1996 s 3 (1)(b)(ii). Appeal from the decision of a special adjudicator on appeal under the Asylum and Immigration Appeals Act 1993 s 8 lies, with leave of the Tribunal to the Immigration Appeal Tribunal.
16 Asylum and Immigration Appeals Act 1993; Asylum and Immigration Act 1996.
17 *Re HK (Infant)* [1967] 2 QB 617, [1967] 1 All ER 226.
18 *A-G of Hong Kong v Ng Yuen Shiu* [1983] 2 AC 629, [1983] 2 All ER 346, PC; *Gyeabour v Secretary of State for the Home Department* [1989] Imm AR 94.
19 See *R v Secretary of State for Home Department, ex p Nwanurue* [1992] Imm AR 39.
20 Application should be made under RSC Ord 53 r 8 for an order under RSC Ord 38 r 2 (3).
21 *R v Secretary of State for the Home Department, ex p Turkoglu* [1988] QB 398, [1987] 2 All ER 823, CA.

2: HOMELESS PERSONS

69. Homeless persons. Prior to the introduction of the internal review procedure and appeal to the county court[1], applications from homeless persons formed the second largest category of applicants for judicial review (after immigrants and refugees). The House of Lords sought to discourage applicants in such cases save where there has been abuse of power (such as bad faith), a mistake in construing the limits of a power, a procedural irregularity, or *Wednesbury* unreasonableness[2].

1   Housing Act 1996 ss 202-204 (21 Halsbury's Statutes (4th Edn) HOUSING).
2   *Puhlhofer v Hillingdon London Borough Council* [1986] AC 484, [1986] 1 All ER 467, HL.

70. Rehousing duty. Local housing authorities are under an obligation to house applicants who are homeless[1], eligible for assistance, in priority need[2], and who they are satisfied have not become homeless intentionally[3]. Local housing authorities must have regard to the Code of Guidance published by the Department of the Environment[4], failure to do so may give rise to challenge, although local housing authorities may depart from the Code, providing they have first had regard to it[5]. It is possible for a local housing authority to challenge the provisions of the Code; for example, as regards the local housing authority's liability to illegal immigrants[6].

1   Housing Act 1996 s 188 (21 Halsbury's Statutes (4th Edn) HOUSING).
2   Housing Act 1996 s 189.
3   Housing Act 1996 s 193, the duty to house such persons is to house for a minimum period of two years. A person found to be intentionally homeless and in priority need will be housed for such period as the authority considers will give him a reasonable opportunity of finding housing: Housing Act 1996 s 190 (2)(a).
4   Housing Act 1996 s 182.
5   See *De Falco and Silvestri v Crawley Borough Council* [1980] QB 460, [1980] 1 All ER 913, CA; *Miller v Wandsworth London Borough Council* (1980) Times, 19 March; *Lambert v London Borough of Ealing* [1982] 2 All ER 394, [1981] 1 WLR 550, CA.
6   See *R v Secretary of State for the Environment, ex p London Borough of Tower Hamlets* [1993] QB 632, [1993] 3 All ER 439, CA.

71. Applicants have an absolute right to require the local housing authority to review its decision[1]. Appeal lies to the county court on a point of law arising from the decision on review or, on the failure to notify the applicant within 56 days[2] of the outcome of the review, the original decision[3]. On appeal the county court has power to make such an order confirming, quashing or varying the decision as it thinks fit[4]. The local housing authority may house the applicant pending the decisions on the initial application[5], the review[6] and the appeal to the county court (or further appeal)[7].

1 Housing Act 1996 s 202 (21 Halsbury's Statutes (4th Edn) HOUSING).
2 The Allocation of Housing and Homelessness (Review Procedures and Amendment) Regulations 1996, SI 1996/3122, reg 4.
3 Housing Act 1996 s 204 (1).
4 Housing Act 1996 s 204 (3).
5 Housing Act 1996 s 188 (1).
6 Housing Act 1996 s 188.
7 Housing Act 1996 s 204 (4).

72. Applications for judicial review. Recourse to the High Court has been much reduced by the provisions of the Housing Act 1996[1]. It appears that it may nonetheless be appropriate to seek judicial review to obtain an order for interim housing under Section 188 of the Act[2]. The county court may have the jurisdiction to order interim housing where an appeal has been lodged under the Housing Act 1996 Section 204[3].

1 Housing Act 1996 (21 Halsbury's Statutes (4th Edn) HOUSING).
2 *R v Camden London Borough Council, ex p Mohammed* (1997) 30 HLR 315. The authority's policy of exercising its discretion to provide interim housing on the basis of exceptional circumstances was lawful. The unfettered right to request a review meant that Housing Act 1996 did not envisage that the discretionary power would be exercised as a matter of course in an applicant's favour.
3 Housing Act 1996 s 204. See *Markowska v Hammersmith* (11 April 1997, unreported); *Halonen v Westminster City Council* (1997) 141 Sol Jo 1080; *Taylor v Brighton and Hove City Council* (18 August 1997, unreported); *Bedei v London Borough of Ealing* (7 November 1997, unreported); (1998) 142 SJ 104.

73. Reasons. The local housing authority must inform the applicant of their decision and, so far as any issue is decided against his interests, the reasons for their decision[1].

1 Housing Act 1996 s 184 (3) (21 Halsbury's Statutes (4th Edn) HOUSING).

74. Damages. An applicant could recover damages for breach of statutory duty by a local housing authority, for example in failing to provide him with suitable accommodation[1] and in a proper case, for example where a local housing authority has for a period of eight months failed to answer correspondence, it may be possible to establish negligence giving rise to damages[2].

1 Housing Act 1996 s 193 (21 Halsbury's Statutes (4th Edn) HOUSING); *Cocks v Thanet District Council* [1983] 2 AC 286, per LORD BRIDGE.
2 *R v Lambeth London Borough Council, ex p Barnes (Olive)* [1993] COD 50.

3: EDUCATION AND JUDICIAL REVIEW

75. Introduction. The Education Reform Act 1988 made sweeping changes to the public sector of education, to the curriculum, complaints mechanisms and school admissions procedures; it also introduced local management of schools and grant-maintained status for schools which opt out of local authority control. The Further and Higher Education Act 1992 removed further education and sixth form colleges from local authority control and placed them under a funding council, exercising statutory duties[1]. Part II of the Further and Higher Education Act 1992 abolished the division between polytechnics and universities in higher education and established single Funding Councils for England and Wales[2]. The Schools Inspection Act 1996 provides for arrangements for the inspection of schools and the inspectorate which operates under a Chief Inspector[3].

1 Education Reform Act 1988; Education Reform Act 1996 s 409 (15 Halsbury's Statutes (4th Edn) EDUCATION); Further and Higher Education Act 1992 ss 54 (as amended), 55, 56 (as amended), 57 (as amended), 58, 59 (1)–(4)(repealed by Education Act 1996 s 582 (2), Sch 38 Pt I and replaced by ss 175 (1), (2), 35 (6), 41 (8), 167 (5), 173 (4)), 60, 61 (15 Halsbury's Statutes (4th Edn) EDUCATION) include provision for the Secretary of State to intervene to assure quality, but there is no ouster of the courts' jurisdiction over what is bound to be regarded as a public law body exercising public functions.
2 Further and Higher Education Act 1992 Pt II. See Further and Higher Education Act 1992 s 62 (as amended); Further and Higher Education Act 1992 s 81 obliges compliance by the Council with directions from the Secretary of State but that does not remove the courts' jurisdiction at the suit of, for example, a student, parent or institution with locus standi (see Paragraphs 120-127 post) to challenge a Council decision.
3 See generally the School Inspections Act 1996 (15 Halsbury's Statutes (4th Edn) EDUCATION).

76. Reform. The reform of the opting out procedure, special educational provision and parental rights in that field and further financial delegation from local education authorities to governing bodies was consolidated in the Education Act 1996[1]. Grant-maintained schools and maintained schools co-operate on admissions information and procedures. The Education Assets Board was given powers under the Further and Higher Education Act 1992 to resolve disputes between local education authorities and providers of further education, and has enhanced powers to do the same as between local education authorities and schools[2].

Both schools and local education authorities will have the right of appeal to the Secretary of State. Responsibility for education is divided between local education authorities and the Funding Agency for Schools. Any dispute as to whether a function is exercisable by the funding agency or a local authority is determined by the Secretary of State[3].

1 Education Act 1996 (15 Halsbury's Statutes (4th Edn) EDUCATION).
2 Further and Higher Education Act 1992 s 36 (15 Halsbury's Statutes (4th Edn) EDUCATION).
3 Education Act 1996 s 28.

77. General duties of local education authorities. Local education authorities must contribute towards the development of the community by securing that efficient education throughout the stages of primary, secondary and further education shall be available to meet the needs[1] of the population in their area, and to ensure that sufficient schools are available for primary and secondary education. Whilst judicial review and indeed private law have provided little help to parents in respect of these general duties[2], authorities have been made amenable to review in relation to admissions policies and procedures, duties of consultation and assessment and provision of special education[3].

1   Education is suitable if it equips children for a place in the community in which they live, rather than anywhere, so long as it leaves them with the means to adopt some other way of life should they so choose in future: *Secretary of State for Education and Science, ex p Talmud Torah Machzikei Haddass School Trust* (1985) Times, 12 April.
2   For example, in *R v Inner London Education Authority, ex p Ali* [1990] 2 Admin LR 822 it was held that teacher shortages in inner London would be a good defence to a claim of breach of duty under the Education Act 1944 s 8 (repealed by Education Act 1996 s 582 (2), Sch 38 Pt I and replaced by Education Act 1996 ss 2 (1), (2), 14 (1)–(3), (5)–(7)). There could be no claim for damages because the section was not meant to give rise to a civil cause of action. See further *Meade v Haringey LBC* [1979] 2 All ER 1016, [1979] 1 WLR 637, CA, where default powers under the Education Act 1944 s 99 (repealed by Education Act 1996 s 582 (2), Sch 38 Pt I and replaced by Education Act 1996 ss 71, 497, 498) did not exclude private law remedies if what had been done amounted to a breach of statutory duty by a positive ultra vires act; no breach was made out on the facts, which involved the temporary closure of a school for reasons connected with an industrial relations dispute. In *Wood v Ealing LBC* [1967] Ch 364, [1966] 3 All ER 514 the duty to provide sufficient schools was construed as relating only to curriculum, as opposed to conditions of entry; in *Watt v Kesteven City Council* [1955] 1 QB 408, [1955] 1 All ER 473, CA the relevance of the wishes of parents in the context of the Minister's default powers under the Education Act 1944 s 99 was discussed. See *R v Lambeth London Borough Council, ex p N* [1996] ELR 299 where a local education authority proposing to close a maintained special school was obliged to take reasonable steps to ensure parents were informed of the proposal and invited to make oral or written representations specifically regarding closure which could include the proposed timetable and the effect of closure on their children and themselves.
3   See, for example, Education Act 1996 ss 35 (5), 37 (5), 41 (7), 43 (2), 167 (3), 169 (5) (15 Halsbury's Statutes (4th Edn) EDUCATION) imposing a duty of consultation on local education authorities before any significant changes of various sorts can be made at a school eligible for grant-maintained status. In *Bradbury v Enfield London Borough Council* [1967] 3 All ER 434, [1967] 1 WLR 1311, CA, failure to submit plans and obtain approval before establishing new schools was dealt with by private law proceedings.

78. General duties of school governors. School governors are now largely in charge of the day to day management and financing of schools. The role of local education authorities is now generally confined to a mere partnership with the governors. The Education (School Government) Regulations 1989[1] provide for government of all county, voluntary and maintained special schools, and cover matters such as disqualification as a governor[2], meetings[3] (with very specific aspects of procedural fairness set out), delegation of duties[4] (a very detailed framework is provided) and selection panels[5]. The governors of schools get their powers from the Education Act 1996[6]. It is highly unlikely that judicial review would be available in respect of the contracting and procurement, employment or property management roles of school governors, but in relation to balloting, the provision of statutorily required information, disciplinary and discretionary powers, they will be amenable to review.

1 Education (School Government) Regulations 1989, SI 1989/1503.
2 Education (School Government) Regulations 1989 regs 4, 5 (as substituted by SI 1991/2845, reg 2 and as amended by SI 1993/3107, reg 2), 6 (as amended by SI 1991/2845, reg 3), 7, 8 (as amended by SI 1991/ 2845, reg 4), 15.
3 Education (School Government) Regulations 1989 regs 12, 13 (as amended by SI 1991/2845, reg 5, SI 1993/3107, reg 4, SI 1996/2050, reg 5), 14 (as amended by SI 1993/3107, reg 5, SI 1996/2050, reg 6), 19 (as amended by SI 1993/3107, reg 6), 20 (as amended by SI 1991/2845, reg 6), 21, 22, 23 (as amended by SI 1996/2050, reg 7), 24.
4 Education (School Government) Regulations 1989 regs 25 (as amended by SI 1991/2845, reg 7), 26 (as amended by SI 1991/2845, reg 8), 27.
5 Education (School Government) Regulations 1989 regs 28, 29.
6 Education Act 1996 s 218 (4), Sch 22 (15 Halsbury's Statutes (4th Edn) EDUCATION).

79. Scope for judicial review. One of the features of education law is the enormous number of statutory instruments in force, potentially giving rise to challenges to their validity. Further, this is a field in which furtherance of government policy is controlled by the issuing of circulars[1] and recommendations; although these do not have legal force, the Secretary of State is given a pivotal role by virtue of various appellate decision making functions, thereby enhancing the executive's implementation of national policy. The extent of ambiguous statutory powers and duties in this field gives rise to potential for applications based on illegality (misconstruction of the duties or frustration of the legislation's purpose), procedural impropriety and irrationality[2]. The legal framework provides much scope for review but at the same time the practitioner must be aware of the risk of the courts holding that alternative remedies provided by the legislation itself[3], restrict the courts' supervisory jurisdiction, or at least attract the discretionary withholding of relief[4].

1 See, for example, Circulars Nos 2/94 on Local Management of Schools and 10/88 and 21/89 on grant-maintained schools.
2 For an example of an unlawful policy see *R v Rochdale MBC, ex p Schemet* (1992) 91 LGR 425: a policy decision to cease paying the travelling expenses of a child educated at a school not maintained by the authority was unlawful. The parents of children at schools outside the district for whom the authority had provided free passes had a legitimate expectation (see Paragraph 67 ante) that such passes would continue to be provided until some rational grounds had been communicated to them for withdrawing the passes and they had had a chance to comment. See also *Brunyate v Inner London Education Authority* [1989] 2 All ER 417, [1989] 1 WLR 542, HL: the removal of particular governors for political reasons was unlawful, but compare *R v Warwickshire CC, ex p Dill-Russell* (1990) 89 LGR 640: when an election altered the local balance of power it was held lawful to remove all nominated governors of a particular persuasion from the authority's schools; as to duties in relation to the provision of special education see *R v Harrow LBC, ex p M* [1997] 3 FCR 761; *R v Further Education Funding Council and Bradford MDC, ex p Parkinson* [1997] 2 FCR 67; *R v Hillingdon LBC, ex p Governing Body of Queensmead School* [1997] ELR 331.
3 See Paragraph 81 post.
4 See Paragraph 82 post.

80. Admissions. Governors and local education authorities have duties relating to information for parents covering admissions policies and parental preference and appeals against rejections. Subject to conditions in Section 411 of the Education Act 1996[1], such preference must be complied with. Choice may be denied if compliance prejudices efficient education or use of resources[2].

1 Education Act 1996 s 411 (as amended) (15 Halsbury's Statutes (4th Edn) EDUCATION).
2 See *R v Greenwich LBC, ex p Governors of John Ball Primary School* (1989) 88 LGR 589: an admissions policy favouring the borough's pupils was found to be unlawful for it positively damaged educational efficiency; sibling and proximity policies were reasonable and not in conflict with any other duty. Further, in *R v Governors of the Bishop Challoner Catholic Comprehensive Girls' School, ex p Choudhury* [1992] 2 AC 182, [1992] 3 All ER 277, HL, the House of Lords held that the refusal of admission to Hindu and Muslim applicants fulfilling admissions criteria in order that the character of the school be preserved was not unlawful under similar provisions in the Education Act 1980 s 6 (3)(a)(repealed by Education Act 1996 s 582 (2), Sch 38 Pt I and replaced by the Education Act 1996 s 411 (3)(as amended)).

81. Appeals arrangements. Section 423 of the Education Act 1996[1] requires the existence of appeal mechanisms for the resolution of admission disputes by committees. The appellant must give written notice of appeal stating the grounds and may be represented or accompanied by a friend. Appeal decisions bind the local education authority and governors of a school. Grant-maintained schools have a similar regime under model articles of government[2]. Furthermore they must not be rigidly applied, or else judicial review will be available to free the authority concerned of this unlawful fetter on its discretion[3].

1 Education Act 1996 s 423 (as amended) (15 Halsbury's Statutes (4th Edn) EDUCATION). See *R v Com for Local Administration, ex p Croydon London Borough Council* [1989] 1 All ER 1033, which established that all admissions appeals relating to one entrance date should be dealt with at one session by the appeal committee.
2 Education Act 1996 s 429, Sch 23 para 6 (as amended).
3 See Form 5 post for an application based on such circumstances.

82. Complaints mechanisms. Sections 496[1] and 497[2] of the Education Act 1996 provide routes to the exercise of default powers by the Minister but these are rarely used. A statutory duty is imposed on all local education authorities to set up complaints machinery[3] to deal with complaints arising out of the curriculum and religious education in maintained schools[4]. Guidance as to procedure to be followed may be found in Circular 1/89[5]. Two types of machinery exist: statutory complaints procedures, and those established merely at the discretion of local authorities and schools. Access to local councillors or the local ombudsman exists alongside these procedures.

1 Education Act 1996 s 496 (15 Halsbury's Statutes (4th Edn) EDUCATION) in respect of unreasonable conduct in relation to any duty imposed on a local education authority or governing body.
2 Education Act 1996 s 497 in respect of failure to fulfil statutory duties.
3 Education Act 1996 s 409.

4   Education Act 1996 s 367 provides redress in respect of directions that the national curriculum should not apply to a child.
5   Published by the Department of Education and Science on 9 January 1989.

83. Discrimination in education. The Sex Discrimination Act 1975[1] and the Race Relations Act 1976[2] forbid discrimination[3] on the grounds of sex or race in education if committed by an education authority[4], governors or proprietors of independent schools with regard to the admission of pupils to schools or to the benefits, facilities and services provided by, and any exclusion from, a school[5]. Further, all local education authorities must carry out their functions without discrimination and positively ensure that facilities provided by them are provided without discrimination[6].

1   Sex Discrimination Act 1975 s 22 (as amended and as further amended by the Further and Higher Education Act 1992 s 93 (1), Sch 8 paras 75, 76) (6 Halsbury's Statutes (4th Edn) CIVIL RIGHTS AND LIBERTIES).
2   Race Relations Act 1976 s 17 (as amended and as further amended by the Further and Higher Education Act 1992 s 93 (1), Sch 8 paras 84, 85) (6 Halsbury's Statutes (4th Edn) CIVIL RIGHTS AND LIBERTIES).
3   The choice of remedies depends upon whether the institution concerned is in the public or private sector. In the former, remedies may be obtained either by judicial review or from the county court after notice to the Secretary of State, who has two months to consider what he might do. The Equal Opportunities Commission and the Commission for Racial Equality have been granted locus standi to bring public law proceedings (though see the cases at Paragraph 128 note 1 post for some reconsideration of this point) and can also assist private litigants, investigate, recommend and report. See generally Vol 31 (1998 Issue) title PERSONAL RIGHTS Paragraphs 133, 139 et seq.
4   See *Mandla v Dowell-Lee* [1983] 2 AC 548, [1983] 1 All ER 1062, HL, which related to a requirement that Sikhs should not wear turbans in a uniformed school where it was held unlawful; and see also *Birmingham City Council v Equal Opportunities Commission* [1989] AC 1155, [1989] 1 All ER 769, HL, in which the number of single-sex school places in an area meant that girls had to get higher marks to get into schools of their choice and this was held unlawful. Following this, in the second case between the parties, *R v Birmingham City Council, ex p Equal Opportunities Commission (No 2)* (1992) 91 LGR 14, CA, the council tried to comply with their duties by closing a boys' school, but when it opted out, the council argued that it could ignore that school in determining the number of available places. It was held that the duty under the Education Act 1944 s 8 (repealed by Education Act 1996 s 582 (2), Sch 38 Pt I and replaced by Education Act 1996 ss 2 (1), (2), 14 (1)–(3), (5)–(7)) was not a duty to provide schools, but a duty to secure sufficient schools and that the relevant pool was the pool of free places in single-sex schools providing a grammar school education; consequently the boys' places at the grant-maintained school still had to be counted for the purpose of achieving equality.
5   Timetabling, subject choices, sports allocation, punishment etc may be covered. Separate facilities are not prohibited so long as they are equal. Single-sex schooling is not discriminatory, but the closure of a single-sex school together with continued maintenance of many such schools for the other sex in the area would be unlawful. A large number of the available places in an area resulting in a requirement of relatively higher entrance exam marks for one sex would be unlawful. See note 4 above.
6   *R v Cleveland County Council, ex p Commission for Racial Equality* (1992) 91 LGR 139, CA, held that a local education authority was neither permitted nor obliged by the Race Relations Act 1976 to refuse to act on a parent's request to move a child from one school to another even though it considered the parent's motives to be racist. Even if giving effect to the duty under the Education Act 1980 s 6 (repealed by Education Act 1996 s 582 (2), Sch 38 Pt I and replaced by Education Act 1996 ss 411 (1), (2)(as amended), (3)(as amended), (4), (5), 413) was a "function" for the purposes of the Act, it was protected by the Race Relations Act 1976 s 41, since it was done in pursuance of a statute. See also Race Relations Act 1976 s 71 (as amended and as further amended by

Police and Magistrates' Courts Act 1994 s 43, Sch 4 Pt II para 51; Police Act 1996 s 103 (1), Sch 7 Pt I paras 1 (1), 2 (1); Police Act 1997 s 134 (1), Sch 9 para 36; Police Act 1997 s 134 (1), Sch 9 para 36).

84. Exclusions. Governing bodies of maintained[1] schools are in charge of discipline but generally delegate their functions to head teachers. Head teachers have a statutory power to exclude pupils from schools, under a strict framework in the Education Act 1996[2], and are obliged to inform the parents of the duration of the exclusion, the reasons for it and the right to make representations about it to the governors and local education authority[3]. The Education Act 1996 provides appeal mechanisms in respect of both exclusions and permanent exclusions from maintained and grant-maintained schools respectively[4].

1   In *R v Fernhill Manor School, ex p Brown* (1992) Independent, 25 June, [1993] 1 FLR 620, it was held that where independent schools were concerned, the relationship between the parent and the school was purely contractual, such that judicial review was not available to challenge any exclusion. Regulation of private schools by some statutory provisions did not make them amenable to public law.
2   Education Act 1996 s 156 (as amended) (15 Halsbury's Statutes (4th Edn) EDUCATION).
3   Education Act 1996 s 157 (1), (2). See also *R v Camden London Borough Council ex p H (a minor)* (1996) Times, 15 August, [1996] ELR 360, CA — in considering whether to reinstate two pupils permanently excluded from school by their head teacher for their involvement in the shooting of another pupil with a pellet gun, the school governors and local education authority representative acted unlawfully in failing properly to investigate inculpatory accounts of the incident and in failing properly to investigate the effect on the victim of the excluded pupils' return.
4   Education Act 1996 ss 159, 307A and Schs 16 (as amended), 25A (as inserted).

85. Special educational needs and provision. The Education Act 1996[1] imposes duties on local education authorities to identify children with special educational needs, and to provide special education for them if it is necessary to do so. Such needs exist if the child has a significantly greater difficulty in learning than the majority of children of the age of the child, or a disability preventing or making it difficult for the child to use facilities generally provided in schools. "Special educational provision" is that which is additional to or otherwise different from the provision made generally for children of the age in the area concerned[2]. The Act aims to ensure that so far as possible, such needs are catered for in ordinary schools. The local education authority must arrange this, subject to the provision of efficient education for the other children in such schools and the efficient use of resources.

1   Education Act 1996 Pt IV (15 Halsbury's Statutes (4th Edn) EDUCATION).
2   Education Act 1996 s 312 (4).

86. Assessment of special educational needs. The legislation provides for a general monitoring responsibility imposed on local education authorities and governing bodies such that children who may have special educational needs are identified. Those with serious difficulties will be assessed by the local education authority and those with more minor problems will be given remedial teaching in their existing schools. The assessment procedure provides for parental consultation and representations, expert educational and psychological advice and sight of draft statements before completion of the process. At this stage the authority has a discretion if it is of the opinion that it should determine the special provision that should be made for the child, to make a statement of his special needs. This will usually be done where assessment suggests that special schooling is needed. The extent to which knowledge on the part of the experts about the available resources may be taken into account in the determination of what is appropriate provision for a child assessed to have special educational needs is still unclear. The Education (Special Educational Needs) Regulations 1994[1] cover the form and content of such statements and the extent of detail required for the part setting out the provision. The local education authority is then under a mandatory duty to provide that which is specified as needed, unless the parent chooses to arrange the provision instead. At various stages of the procedure there is provision for reconsideration, appeal to a local authority committee[2], review, redrafting and eventually an appeal to a Tribunal[3], with regard to the identification of needs, or the amount or nature of the provision specified[4].

1 Education (Special Educational Needs) Regulations 1994, SI 1994/1047 (6 Halsbury's Statutory Instruments (1997 Issue) EDUCATION).
2 See *R v Camden London Borough Council, ex p S* (1990) 89 LGR 513 (appeal committee considering special educational needs was not properly constituted if one of the panel dropped out and was replaced by another before the decision was made, despite the scope for a majority decision).
3 See Paragraph 87 below.
4 See *Keir v Hereford and Worcester County Council* (1985) 84 LGR 709, CA (a statement goes beyond a mere record: it is mandatory that what is specified is provided. The statement of needs and provision is analogous to a medical diagnosis and prescription); *R v Secretary of State for Education and Science, ex p E* [1992] 1 FLR 377; *R v Lancashire County Council, ex p Moore* [1989] 2 FLR 279, CA (speech therapy can constitute special educational provision even though speech therapists are employed by the district health authority, not the education service); *R v Secretary of State for Education and Science, ex p Davis* [1989] 2 FLR 190 (no retrospective rights to recover independent school fees accrue by virtue of the legislation); *R v Secretary of State for Education and Science, ex p P* (1992) Times, 13 March (the provision of non-stressful transport for certain pupils was an absolute duty under s 55 (1) of the Education Act 1944 (repealed by Education Act 1996 s 582 (2), Sch 38 Pt I and replaced by Education Act 1996 s 509 (1), (2))). But compare *R v Essex County Council, ex p C* (1993) 92 LGR 46 in which it was held that a local authority could lawfully elect to discharge its obligations to provide free transport to schools over three miles away from pupils' homes, by choosing the nearest of several schools, even if parents wanted their child to attend one further away.

87. Appeal. An appeal lies to the Special Educational Needs Tribunal[1] for parents[2] against a decision not to make a special educational needs statement. The Tribunal may dismiss the appeal, order the making of a statement, or remit the case to reconsider whether it is necessary for the local education authority to determine the special educational provision after all. Section 326 of the Education Act 1996[3] provides that the parent of a statemented child may appeal on the making of a statement, or on amendment of the description in the statement of the authority's assessment of the special educational needs or on amendment of the special educational provision, or on a decision not to amend the statement, to the Tribunal, against the description in the statement of the child's educational needs, the special educational provision specified in the statement or the failure to name a school in the statement. On an appeal the Tribunal may dismiss the appeal, order the local education authority to amend the statement or order the authority to maintain the statement[4]. Automatic reviews of statements are provided for once every 12 months starting with the date of the making of the statement or the first review of an existing one[5].

1 Education Act 1996 s 325 (15 Halsbury's Statutes (4th Edn) EDUCATION). The Tribunal has a president, a panel of persons serving as chairs of local tribunals and a panel of lay persons serving as the other two members on each Tribunal. Special Educational Needs Tribunal Regulations 1995, SI 1995/3113 govern the procedure, time limits and forms for appeals, enabling chairs to decide preliminary matters, as to representation, discovery such as might be granted by the county court, the power to call witnesses and for disclosure of documents, the administering of oaths and affirmations, the award of costs and expenses. The Council on Tribunals has jurisdiction over the Tribunal. Appeal lies to the High Court from the Tribunal in relation to points of law, by any party to the proceedings: Tribunals and Inquiries Act 1992 s 11 (as amended and as further amended by the Education Act 1966 s 582 (1), Sch 37 Pt I para 118 (1), (2); Employment Rights Act 1996 s 240, Sch 1 para 57; Industrial Tribunals Act 1996 s 43, Sch 1 para 9 (1), (2)), Sch 1 (as amended) (10 Halsbury's Statutes (4th Edn) CONSTITUTIONAL LAW).
2 A local authority foster parent came within the definition of "parent" for the purposes of making an appeal in relation to a child in her care for whom the local authority had declined to make a statement of special educational needs: *Fairpo v Humberside County Council* [1997] 1 All ER 183.
3 Education Act 1996 s 326.
4 Education Act 1996 s 326 (3).
5 Education Act 1996 s 328 (5).

88. Other uses of review in the field of education. Judicial review has been used by employees of universities[1], students challenging the determination of their grants[2], speakers at higher education establishments[3], parents trying to prevent closure of their children's schools[4] and by local education authorities trying to evade the consequences of parents choosing grant-maintained status[5].

1 For example, *R v HM the Queen in Council, ex p Vijayatunga* [1990] 2 QB 444, [1989] 2 All ER 843, CA, involving a complaint that an examiner was unqualified in a student's subject: questions of academic judgment not justiciable; *R v Lord President of the Privy Council, ex p Page* [1993] AC 682, [1993] 1 All ER 97, HL (visitor not amenable to review in respect of alleged errors of law arising out of his construction of internal rules. But more often such issues are litigated by way of writ action in contract). See *Pearce v University of Aston in Birmingham* [1991] 2 All ER 461, CA; *Pearce v University of Aston in Birmingham (No 2)* [1991] 2 All ER 469; *Hines v Birkbeck College (No 2)* [1992] Ch 33, [1991] 4 All ER 450, CA (the Education Reform Act 1988 s 206 (15 Halsbury's Statutes (4th Edn) EDUCATION) conferred on the court jurisdiction in matters which had previously been within the exclusive jurisdiction of the visitor, subject to referral by either party); *Thomas v University of Bradford (No 2)* [1992] 1 All ER 964 (fundamental procedural irregularities existed but the applicant had acquiesced and was taken to have waived her right to insist on the correct procedure).
2 For example, *Shah v Barnet London Borough Council* [1983] 2 AC 309, [1983] 1 All ER 226, HL and *R v Hertfordshire County Council, ex p Cheung* (1986) Times, 4 April, CA, on grants; but see also use of private law procedure for a declaration as to domestic or foreign status for fees purposes: *Kent v University College London* (1992) Times, 18 February, although the Court of Appeal disapproved of the choice of procedure.

3   See *R v University of Liverpool, ex p Caesar-Gordon* [1991] 1 QB 124, [1991] 3 All ER 821 in relation to the statutory duty to ensure freedom of speech in universities.
4   On the meaning of "a report" for the purposes of the Education Acts, it has been said that such requires a review of the options, with arguments for and against a proposal, a statement of the conclusions and an indication of the reasons for the conclusion: *R v Secretary of State for Education and Science, ex p Threapleton* [1988] COD 102; further, *R v Gwent County Council, ex p Bryant* [1988] COD 19: the definition of "consultation" in the context of proposed closure of a primary school involves consultation at a formative stage of the proposals, adequate information, adequate time in which to respond and conscientious consideration of the responses. Where failure to consult was mere breach of a legitimate expectation, later consideration of the matter by the Minister could cure it; per HODGSON J in *Nichol v Gateshead Metropolitan Borough Council* (1988) 87 LGR 435, CA: although it was acceptable to bring review proceedings within three months of a minister's decision, the fact that that hearing had arisen out of a fatally flawed decision two years earlier, meant it would probably be detrimental to good administration to grant relief in such circumstances.
5   See *R v Secretary of State for Education and Science, ex p Avon County Council* (1990) 88 LGR 716 and *R v Secretary of State for Education and Science, ex p Avon County Council (No 2)* (1990) 88 LGR 737n, CA: in giving approval to an application for grant-maintained status the Minister failed to consider the disruption, delay and uncertainty involved for the rest of the area. However, in the second case, once those considerations were taken into account, the diametrically opposed but reasonable viewpoints of the Minister and the local education authority could not and should not be litigated by way of judicial review proceedings. Parliament had given the decision to the Minister. See further *R v Secretary of State for Education and Science, ex p Newham London Borough Council* [1991] COD 279 where a lack of evidence that the quality or range of teaching would improve as a result of opting out was held to be irrelevant to the Minister's decision, so his approval could not be challenged. In *R v Tameside Metropolitan Borough Council, ex p Audenshaw Governors* (1991) Times, 27 June, land and buildings were sold to a company controlled by the local education authority and paid for with council money in order to make opting out less attractive; held, not unlawful per se, but the lack of any consultation with the governors vitiated the process. In *R v Secretary of State for Education and Science, ex p Inner London Education Authority* (1990) Times, 17 May, CA, the Minister refused to require a school to repay sums spent by the local education authority on improvements, on the basis that the same pupils would still benefit once it was turned into a City Technological College, and his refusal was upheld.

4: PRISONERS' RIGHTS AND JUDICIAL REVIEW

89. Introduction[1]. Judicial review[2] has proved particularly useful for prisoners, making up for a perception in English law until the last decade that prisoners enjoyed less than a full complement of private law rights by virtue of their incarceration. Further, the officials who deal with prisoners are public servants (even if they are employed by private companies) and are therefore generally amenable to judicial review. Judicial review has been used across a wide range of circumstances relating to prisoners, in order to challenge, for instance, decisions concerning transfer and segregation whilst in prison, the legal[3] and procedural aspects of disciplinary decisions taken by both governors and Boards of Visitors, and also decisions taken by the Parole Board and Home Secretary about parole, release on licence and the tariff period for discretionary and mandatory life prisoners. In addition, prisoners' cases have provided scope for development of the law relating to damages claims within public law proceedings, by virtue of the fact that private law claims for false imprisonment within prison, misfeasance in public office and personal injury can easily arise out of alleged ultra vires conduct towards prisoners.

1 Practitioners may find the following references helpful: Genevra Richardson "The House of Lords and Prison Discipline" [1988] PL 183-7; Tim Owen "Judicial Review and Prisoners" Jan 1990 LAG 14 and "Prisoners' Rights" [1991] NLJ 1328; Richard Gordon "Prisoners' Rights and Judicial Review" [1988] Law Soc Gazette 22; Alec Samuels "Legal Representation before Boards of Visitors" [1989] Crim Law Rev 701-8; Graham Zellick "Reforms in Prison Discipline" (1989) 139 NLJ 1295; Genevra Richardson "Prisoners and the Law: Beyond Rights" in McCrudden and Chambers (eds.) *Individual Rights and the Law in Britain* (1994); V Teggin "New prison rules and offences" May 1992 LAG 13. See also *R v Secretary of State for the Home Department, ex p Doody* [1994] 1 AC 531, [1993] 3 All ER 92.
2 See further Vol 31 (1998 Issue) title PERSONAL RIGHTS.
3 *R v Board of Visitors of Dartmoor, ex p Smith* [1987] QB 106, [1987] 2 All ER 651, CA (misconstruction of the Prison Rules).

90. Amenability to review: governors and visitors. Prison governors have power delegated by the Home Secretary[1] to control the prison service under the Prison Act 1952 and the Prison Rules 1964[2]. The legislation permits the Secretary of State to make rules for the regulation and management of prisons and for the classification, treatment, employment, discipline and control of persons detained there[3]. In addition, circulars and standing orders issued to governors relating to letters, visits and petitions contribute to the framework for management but their legal status is unclear because there is no express power to issue them provided by the legislation[4]. The governor[5] is appointed by the Secretary of State; deputy governors are frequently employed in large prisons. Prison officers have all the powers, authority, protection and privileges of a constable[6]. Prison custody officers are charged with responsibility for transferring prisoners between prisons and to court[7]. At one time it was thought that prison governors could not be reviewed, because all of their functions were characterised as "managerial"[8] and could not be compared to those judicial functions of the old Boards of Visitors[9]. The case of *Leech v Deputy Governor of Parkhurst Prison*[10] established that the disciplinary decisions of governors were amenable to review after all[11].

1 Prison Act 1952 s 1 (34 Halsbury's Statutes (4th Edn) PRISONS) gives the Home Secretary all power in relation to prisons and prisoners.
2 Prison Rules 1964, SI 1964/388 (15 Halsbury's Statutory Instruments (1996 Issue) PRISONS).
3 Prison Act 1952 s 47 (1)(as amended).
4 But LORD WILBERFORCE expressed approval of the practice in *Raymond v Honey* [1983] 1 AC 1, [1982] 1 All ER 756, HL. An example is the administrative practice known as the "ghost train" by prisoners arising under CI 10/1974, considered in *R v Deputy Governor of Parkhurst Prison, ex p Hague, Weldon v Home Office* [1992] 1 AC 58 sub nom *Hague v Deputy Governor of Parkhurst Prison* [1991] 3 All ER 733, HL, and held by the Court of Appeal to be unlawful. It was consequently amended by the Home Office incorporating improved safeguards for prisoners.
5 Prison Act 1952 s 7 (1). In remand prisons where the management has been contracted out under the Criminal Justice Act 1991 s 84 (as substituted) (34 Halsbury's Statutes (4th Edn) PRISONS) there is a director and a controller fulfilling the functions of governor: Criminal Justice Act 1991 s 85 (1)(as substituted). Only the controller is permitted to exercise disciplinary functions: Criminal Justice Act 1991 s 85 (3)(a); Prison Rules 1964 r 98A (as inserted).
6 Prison Act 1952 s 8. However, Prison Act 1952 s 8 does not apply to prisons which have contracted out under Criminal Justice Act 1991 s 84: Criminal Justice Act 1991 s 97 (1), (3)(as substituted).

7   Criminal Justice Act 1991 s 80 (1)(as substituted).
8   *R v Deputy Governor of Camphill Prison, ex p King* [1985] QB 735, [1984] 3 All ER 897, CA.
9   *R v Board of Visitors of Hull Prison, ex p St Germain* [1979] QB 425, [1979] 1 All ER 701, CA, established that Boards were amenable to review, so far as their disciplinary functions were concerned.
10 *Leech v Deputy Governor of Parkhurst Prison* [1988] AC 533, [1988] 1 All ER 485, HL.
11 *Leech v Deputy Governor of Parkhurst Prison* [1988] AC 533, [1988] 1 All ER 485, HL, per LORD OLIVER: "The susceptibility of a decision ... must depend ... upon the nature and consequences of the decision and not upon the personality or individual circumstances of the person called upon to make the decision".

91. Disciplinary hearings. The Prison Rules 1964[1] set out an internal disciplinary code which creates various offences and governs the procedure to be followed in respect of charges under this code. Offences which amount to breaches of the ordinary criminal law may be dealt with by the Crown Prosecution Service in the ordinary way. The Prison Security Act 1992[2] introduced a new criminal offence of prison mutiny[3]. Mere disciplinary charges are heard by the governor who has a range of punishment powers ranging from denial of remission and forfeiture of privileges to confinement in the cells. A prisoner may petition the Secretary of State who may quash any disciplinary finding of guilt and vary any disciplinary punishment awarded[4]. The procedure to be followed at such hearings which is set forth in the Prison Rules 1964 has been supplemented by judicial pronouncements, in applications for review, about minimum standards of natural justice concerning notice of the charge, the facilities for hearing witnesses etc and legal representation[5].

1   Prison Rules 1964, SI 1964/388 (15 Halsbury's Statutory Instruments (1996 Issue) PRISONS).
2   Prison Security Act 1992 (34 Halsbury's Statutes (4th Edn) PRISONS).
3   Punishable on indictment by ten years in prison or a fine or both: Prison Security Act 1992 s 1 (1). "Mutiny" is defined as "conduct which is intended to further a common purpose of overthrowing lawful authority in that prison": Prison Security Act 1992 s 1 (2). The consent of the Director of Public Prosecutions is necessary for prosecutions: Prison Security Act 1992 s 1 (5).
4   Prison Rules 1964 r 56 (as amended).
5   See, for instance, *R v Board of Visitors of Hull Prison, ex p St Germain (No 2)* [1979] 3 All ER 545, [1979] 1 WLR 1401 which dealt with the refusal to arrange for the attendance of witnesses for reasons of administrative inconvenience; *R v Secretary of State for the Home Department, ex p Tarrant* [1985] QB 251, [1984] 1 All ER 799 (considerations guiding the grant or denial of representation and standard of proof to be applied); *R v Board of Visitors of HM Prison, The Maze, ex p Hone* [1988] AC 379, [1988] 1 All ER 321, HL (absence of a right to any legal representation even where serious offences involved); *R v Blundeston Prison Board of Visitors, ex p Fox-Taylor* [1982] 1 All ER 646 (investigating officer failed to inform Board of witness unknown to prisoner); *R v Board of Visitors of Gartree Prison, ex p Mealy* (1981) Times, 14 November (visitors refused a prisoner permission to question a witness and comment on the evidence).

92. "Managerial" decisions. The Prison Rules 1964 deal with aspects of non-disciplinary organisation such as the power to segregate prisoners in the interests of good order[1], confinement[2] and restraint[3]. The governor has power to order the restraint of a prisoner if necessary to prevent injury to himself or others, property damage or disturbance[4]. Prisoners may be lawfully confined in any prison[5] and so can be moved around at the discretion of the governor[6]. The Rules require that prisoners be classified by age, temperament and record. Further provisions exist as to food, clothing, exercise, letters[7], educational facilities, work and rates of pay. There is a code on privileges in every prison and these may be lost as part of the disciplinary system. Prisoners' requests and complaints are governed by the Rules[8] and are dealt with first by the prison and then the area manager, unless the Rules require certain issues be raised directly with the latter. Boards of Visitors also visit prisons and hear complaints while there. If dissatisfied with a response to a complaint the prisoner may petition the Secretary of State[9] and, inter alia, the Parliamentary Commissioner for Administration. The question arises to what extent judicial review is available to challenge decision-making in respect of these non-disciplinary measures. In the case of *Hague v Deputy Governor of Parkhurst Prison*[10], the prisoner claimed that review was available in respect of transfer and segregation. The House of Lords approved of the government's decision not to challenge the finding of the court below that Rule 43[11] was justiciable and that the government's administrative Circular 10/1974 was unlawful as not being within the terms of the Rule.

1   Prison Rules 1964, SI 1964/388, rr 43 (as amended), 43A (as inserted by SI 1998/23, r 2) (15 Halsbury's Statutory Instruments (1996 Issue) PRISONS).
2   Prison Rules 1964 r 45.
3   Prison Rules 1964 r 46 (as amended).
4   Prison Rules 1964 r 46 (1). The Rules go on to provide for confirmation by the medical officer of the prison and the time limits for such restraint. The Secretary of State's or the Board of Visitors' approval is required for restraint beyond 24 hours: Prison Rules 1964 r 46 (4)(as amended).
5   Prison Act 1952 s 12 (1) (34 Halsbury's Statutes (4th Edn) PRISONS).
6   See *R v Secretary of State for the Home Department, ex p McAvoy* [1984] 3 All ER 417, [1984] 1 WLR 1408 on the relevance of various considerations (for example, access to legal advisors and family) when determining whether to transfer, and the courts' approach to considerations of security.
7   More generous provisions exist for the regulation of correspondence with solicitors, because the courts have held such to be related to access to the courts and consequently inviolable, unless Parliament should provide otherwise. See *Raymond v Honey* [1983] 1 AC 1, [1982] 1 All ER 756, HL, and *R v Secretary of State for the Home Department, ex p Leech (No 2)* [1994] QB 198, [1993] 4 All ER 539 in which it was held that provisions in the Prison Rules 1964 authorising the stopping of letters to solicitors for prolixity or objectionability of contents were ultra vires the Prison Act 1952 s 47 (1). As to the production of prisoners for civil court proceedings and the payment of the costs of production see *R v Secretary of State for the Home Department, ex p Wynne* [1992] QB 406, [1992] 2 All ER 301, CA; affd sub nom *Wynne v Secretary of State for the Home Department* [1993] 1 All ER 574, HL.
8   Prison Rules 1964 r 8 (as amended).
9   Prison Department Standing Order 5C, recognised by Prison Rules 1964 r 7 (1) (as amended).
10 *R v Deputy Governor of Parkhurst Prison, ex p Hague* [1992] 1 AC 58, sub nom *Hague v Deputy Governor of Parkhurst Prison* [1991] 3 All ER 733, HL.
11 Prison Rules 1964 r 43 (as amended).

93. Parole decisions etc. The regime for parole, remission and early release is governed by the Criminal Justice Act 1991[1]. The role of the Parole Board is to advise the Secretary of State on all matters related to release on licence and recall of short and long-term prisoners[2]. Mandatory lifers are still dependent on the Secretary of State's unfettered discretion to release such prisoners if recommended by the Board to do so, but judicial review has impinged on the procedural aspect of this discretion[3]. A prisoner is now entitled to appear before a Parole Board and have legal representation and legal aid. The Secretary of State is obliged to supply the Board and the prisoner with information concerning him, and any reports made by psychiatrists etc. The prisoner is entitled to see all the reports in most cases and to commission his own reports[4]. Withholding of reports is allowed with the agreement of the Board if it would adversely affect the health or welfare of the prisoner but in such a case the barrister, solicitor or medical practitioner may see the documents[5]. Hearings after the expiry of the tariff period will be held in accordance with the Parole Board Rules and it is noteworthy that they can never be held in public[6]. The chair of the panel can regulate the procedure of the hearing subject to the rules of natural justice[7].

1   Criminal Justice Act 1991 (34 Halsbury's Statutes (4th Edn) PRISONS). See John Wadham [1992] September LAG 11 for a commentary.
2   *Thynne, Wilson and Gunnell v United Kingdom* Series A Vol 190, (1990) 13 EHRR 666 which held that the previous purely discretionary executive-based procedure was a breach of the European Convention on Human Rights art 5 (4). The Act was drafted in response to this decision and it provides an independent procedure for decision making related to release and recall to prison of discretionary lifers. See, further, the Parole Board Rules made under the Criminal Justice Act 1991 s 32 (5).
3   The tariff period is fixed in open court and the sentence and the tariff are subject to appeal to the Court of Appeal Criminal Division: *R v Dalton* [1995] QB 243, [1995] 2 All ER 349, CA. See, for example, *R v Secretary of State for the Home Department, ex p Causabon-Vincent* (1996) Times, 19 July; *R v Secretary of State for the Home Department, ex p Venables and Thompson* [1997] 3 All ER 97, [1997] 3 WLR 23, HL.
4   *R v Parole Board, ex p Wilson* [1992] QB 740, [1991] 2 All ER 576, CA. Note that *R v Secretary of State for Home Department, ex p Creamer* [1993] COD 162, (1992) Independent, 23 October maintains that mandatory life sentence servers are still not entitled to see the information held on them by the Parole Board. But *R v Secretary of State for the Home Department, ex p Prem Singh* [1993] COD 501, (1993) Independent, 11 June held that a young offender is covered by the rules pertaining to discretionary lifers, on achieving adulthood.
5   However, the case of *R v Parole Board, ex p Wilson* [1992] 1 QB 740, [1991] 2 All ER 576, CA, may mean that the Rules are not effective to reinstate the right to withhold reports previously enjoyed by the Secretary of State; see John Wadham's commentary [1992] September LAG 11.
6   John Wadham suggests that this may be a breach of the European Convention on Human Rights art 6 (1).
7   See further Paragraph 48 ante.

94. Unreasonableness. The Prison Rules 1964 set forth that the purpose of training and treatment of convicted prisoners is to encourage and assist them to lead a good and useful life[1]. Prisoners must be treated in such a way as to maintain and enhance their self-respect and sense of personal responsibility[2]. Those guiding principles could theoretically be used in a review application if a public official acts contrary to them to mount a claim of unreasonableness or failure to take into account relevant considerations. It is unlikely that challenges based on unreasonableness will succeed in this area because government policy relating to prisoners and prisons is easily characterised as non-justiciable[3].

1   Prison Rules 1964, SI 1964/388, r 1 (15 Halsbury's Statutory Instruments (1996 Issue) PRISONS).

2 Prison Rules 1964 r 2 (3).
3 But see *R v Secretary of State for the Home Department, ex p Handscomb* (1987) 131 Sol Jo 326 where a plea of irrationality succeeded concerning the practice of waiting an arbitrary 34 years to seek the trial judge's views before setting a date for the first review of a life prisoner's sentence; and further, *R v Secretary of State for the Home Department, ex p Benson* [1989] COD 329, (1988) Independent, 16 November regarding irrelevant considerations taken into account in rejection of the Board's recommendations for release on licence.

95. International aspects. Prisoners may submit applications to the European Human Rights Commission in respect of violations of the Convention[1] such as the meting out of inhuman or degrading treatment or breach of the right to aspects of family life and integrity of correspondence[2]. A number of such cases led to changes in the system for prison management[3]. The United Nations has drawn up and approved both the Standard Minimum Rules for the Treatment of Prisoners and the Body of Principles for the Protection of all Persons under any Form of Detention or Imprisonment. Neither instrument is legally binding or enforceable, but reference may be made to the standards there set out.

1 See Vol 17 (1997 Issue) title EUROPEAN COURTS and the European Convention arts 3, 5, 6, 8.
2 The impact of the Convention in relation to prisoners was fully analysed some years ago by Douglas and Jones in *The Effect on English Domestic Law of Membership of the European Communities and of Ratification of the European Convention on Human Rights* (1983); Genevra Richardson "Prisoners and the Law: Beyond Rights" in McCrudden and Chambers (eds.) *Individual Rights and the Law in Britain* (1994).
3 See *Campbell and Fell v United Kingdom* (1982) 5 EHRR 207 (Commission's report), (1984) 7 EHRR 165 (Court's judgment); *Golder v United Kingdom* (1975) 1 EHRR 524 and *Silver v United Kingdom* (1983) 5 EHRR 347 relating to the reading of prisoners' correspondence.

96. Reform. Lord Justice Woolf recommended the abolition of the disciplinary role for Boards of Visitors so that their watchdog role would not be compromised[1]. Accordingly, offences of a substantial nature were removed from the disciplinary system and have been dealt with by the courts since 1 April 1992. Guidelines have been issued to governors suggesting which offences ought to be referred to the police, and that the wishes of the prisoner victim should be taken into account. If the Crown Prosecution Service decides not to prosecute, then the matter is referred back to the governor. There is still an appeal from the governor to the area manager, which is primarily a review of procedure and sentence. However, the area manager has power to mitigate or remit a sentence, so some examination of the merits must be envisaged[2].

1 See *Prison Disturbances* (Cmnd 1456) (1990).
2 Prison Service Guidelines January 1992, dealing with assault, escape, possession of unauthorised weapons or drugs, criminal damage, arson, robbery and mass disobedience.

97. Private law claims. Disciplinary decisions in which, for instance, forfeiture of remission is awarded, do not infringe any private rights of the prisoner concerned. Remission is a matter of indulgence, not of right[1]. All the plaintiff has is a legitimate expectation based on practice that he will get remission if he behaves well. This will be sufficient to constitute locus standi[2] but will not constitute a ground in itself for judicial review or for claiming any private law right. The duty of care in private law which is owed to prisoners is to take reasonable care for their health and safety[3]. Claims for tortious damages have been brought against officers and fellow prisoners, and in the latter case the prison authorities have sometimes been primarily liable as well, because of negligent supervision. Fellow prisoners may be sued for false imprisonment if they detain one another because they have no authority to do so. Individual prison officers may also render themselves liable if they deliberately subject a prisoner to an unlawful restraint. There is no reason why a negligence action should not be commenced in respect of physical or mental deterioration arising out of intolerable conditions, if the evidence will sustain it[4]. In most cases the Home Office will be vicariously liable for its servants and agents, but not for misfeasance in public office[5], because it involves proof of malice; the individual prison officer must be joined as a defendant.

1   For public law purposes and European human rights law, it does not matter whether a right or a privilege is asserted. See *Campbell and Fell v United Kingdom* (1982) 5 EHRR 207 (Commission's report), (1984) 7 EHRR 165 (Court's judgment).
2   See Paragraph 120 et seq post.
3   For a case in the context of the duty owed to prisoners known to have suicidal tendencies, see *Knight v Home Office* [1990] 3 All ER 237.
4   See the use to which the English Bill of Rights was put in *R v Secretary of State for the Home Department, ex p Herbage (No 2)* [1987] QB 1077, [1987] 1 All ER 324, CA (reference to freedom from cruel and unusual punishment as a fundamental right was enough to justify the grant of leave for an application for judicial review).
5   *Racz v Home Office* (1992) Times, 17 December, CA.

98. Breach of statutory duty. The Prison Act 1952[1] and the Prison Rules 1964[2] also set out requirements for the size, lighting, heating, ventilation and fittings of prison cells, and provide for their inspection. It has been held, however, that the Prison Rules are regulatory and not intended to give rise to civil causes of action for breach of statutory duty. It has also been decided that even if conditions of imprisonment fall below that set out in the Rules, otherwise lawful imprisonment does not become the tort of false imprisonment[3].

1   Prison Act 1952 (34 Halsbury's Statutes (4th Edn) PRISONS).
2   Prison Rules 1964, SI 1964/388 (15 Halsbury's Statutory Instruments (1996 Issue) PRISONS).
3   *R v Deputy Governor of Parkhurst Prison, ex p Hague* [1992] 1 AC 58, sub nom *Hague v Deputy Governor of Parkhurst Prison* [1991] 3 All ER 733, HL; a prisoner's claims are restricted here to assault (if force was used), negligence, or misfeasance in public office, if malice or conscious abuse of power is established.

SPECIFIC CASES

5: MENTAL HEALTH CASES

99. Introduction[1]. Mental Health Review Tribunals ('MHRTs') are subject to the supervision of the Council on Tribunals and they appear in Schedule 1 of the Tribunals and Inquiries Act 1992[2] which imposes certain procedural rules on tribunals[3]. They operate within a statutory framework[4] giving them a wide range of powers and duties dependent on the existence of certain conditions precedent or upon their being satisfied as to certain facts. As a consequence they are both amenable to review and likely to come under rigorous scrutiny, considering the fundamental importance to the individual of their regulatory role. However, by virtue of the Tribunals and Inquiries Act 1992, there is a statutory right of appeal to the High Court on a point of law[5], so that the dissatisfied individual may have a choice of remedies, and the judicial review court may insist as an aspect of its discretion that the other remedy be tried in preference to clogging up the judicial review lists[6]. Legal aid is available for representation in proceedings before MHRT[7]. Lay persons may also represent detainees before tribunals.

1 See R M Jones *Mental Health Act Manual* (1996); B Hoggett *Mental Health Law* (3rd edn, 1991); L Gostin *Mental Health: Tribunal Procedure* (2nd edn); articles by Stephen Roberts "Detention under the Mental Health Act 1983: Advising on Validity" [1991] May LAG 15 and "Advising on Routes of Discharge" [1991] June LAG 19; see also Audrey Sander "Preparing for a Mental Health Review Tribunal" [1989] July LAG 11. Note that MIND (telephone no 0181 519 2122) can supply names of independent psychiatrists. The Law Society also has a Mental Health Sub-Committee (telephone no 0171 320 5695). The Mental Health Act Commission (telephone no 0115 943 7100) may be approached for advice about other bodies who may be of assistance to detainees.
2 Tribunals and Inquiries Act 1992 Sch 1 (10 Halsbury's Statutes (4th Edn) CONSTITUTIONAL LAW).
3 Tribunals and Inquiries Act 1992 s 10 (1) provides that scheduled tribunals shall be under a duty to furnish a statement, either written or oral, of the reasons for the decision, if requested, on or before the giving or notification of the decision, to state the reasons. A statement may be refused or restricted on grounds of national security: Tribunals and Inquiries Act 1992 s 10 (2). All such statements constitute part of the record of the decision: Tribunals and Inquiries Act 1992 s 10 (5).
4 Tribunals are constituted under the Mental Health Act 1983 s 65 (as amended) (28 Halsbury's Statutes (4th Edn) MENTAL HEALTH). See 30 Halsbury's Laws (4th Edn) title MENTAL HEALTH paras 1351–1385.
5 Tribunals and Inquiries Act 1992 s 11 (1)(as amended and as further amended by the Education Act 1996 s 582 (1), Sch 37 Pt I para 118 (1), (2)).
6 In fact it is much more common for those aggrieved by a tribunal decision to apply for judicial review than use the case stated procedure. Judicial review provides a broader basis for consideration of the issues and a more comprehensive range of relief. The powers of the High Court on hearing a stated case are limited to giving any direction which the tribunal ought to have given under the Act, and there will be cases where no

direction would have been appropriate. In *Bone v Mental Health Review Tribunal* [1985] 3 All ER 330 NOLAN J decided a point in favour of an applicant, but a direction in his favour would have been a discharge, which might have posed a risk to the public. He suggested that the matter be reheard before a different tribunal but could have ordered that to occur had the application been by way of judicial review. In case stated procedure, the point of law must have been raised at the tribunal hearing. See RSC Ords 56, 94 for procedural steps in applying for a case to be stated.

7   It was introduced after the 31st Annual Report (1980–81) of the Council on Tribunals identified Mental Health Review Tribunals as tribunals for which an extension of legal aid was urgent. It is not available for the patient, if the nearest relative has made the application to the tribunal.

100. Authorised detention. The provisions in the Mental Health Act 1983 which authorise detention relate to emergency admission[1], longer term assessment[2] or treatment[3] and admission from a criminal court or prison[4]. "Mental disorder"[5] is a pre-requisite for detention under the Act. In considering the validity of admission and detention, administrative law principles apply, so that for instance the purpose of the statute must not be frustrated, the decision-maker must direct him or herself properly as to the law, and procedural fairness must be observed. A distinction must be borne in mind between those criteria in the Act which appear to be objective, and those which depend on a subjective evaluation of the circumstances[6]. There is a further distinction between defects which invalidate an application for admission and detention[7] and those which can be amended under Section 15 of the Act within 14 days of the date of admission[8].

Unreasonable use[9] of the provisions might be found if a diagnosis was made in bad faith, or for the purpose of ensuring that an individual continues to take medication etc[10]. Illegal use of the sections would be made out if a prisoner were transferred to hospital after his release date or if a magistrates' court made a hospital order in respect of a non-imprisonable offence.

1   Mental Health Act 1983 s 4 (28 Halsbury's Statutes (4th Edn) MENTAL HEALTH) permits emergency admissions "in case of urgent necessity" for a period of not more than 72 hours: Mental Health Act 1983 s 4 (4). It is often used as a preliminary stage of admitting for longer term treatment but where the procedural requirements for such would cause undesirable delay. Application may be made either by an approved social worker or the nearest relative of the person being admitted: Mental Health Act 1983 s 4 (2). One medical recommendation is required: Mental Health Act 1983 s 4 (3). Mental Health Act 1983 s 5 (2), (4) deal with detention of those already in hospital on a voluntary basis or where immediate restraint is necessary for the health and safety of an individual or for the protection of others and it is not practicable to secure the attendance of a practitioner for the purpose of a section 2 detention. In the former case detention for 72 hours is the maximum permitted: Mental Health Act 1983 s 5 (2); in the latter, a period of up to six hours is allowed: Mental Health Act 1983 s 5 (4). Registered medical practitioners either already in charge of the patient or else nominated by the responsible medical officer may apply under the former provision: Mental Health Act 1983 s 5 (2), (3), and a nurse of the prescribed class may make the latter application: Mental Health Act 1983 s 5 (4). Mental Health Act 1983 s 135 permits a justice of the peace to issue warrants authorising entry to premises and removal of individuals to be detained for up to 72 hours in a place of safety. Application is made by an approved social worker. Constables are given power under s 136 of the Mental Health Act 1983 to remove persons from public places appearing to be suffering from disorder and in immediate need of care or control, for detention in a place of safety for up to 72 hours. "Place of safety" can be a hospital or any other suitable place including an ordinary home: Mental Health Act s 135 (6)(as amended).

2   Mental Health Act 1983 s 2 permits detention for up to 28 days on grounds that a person is suffering from mental disorder of a nature or degree which warrants the detention of the patient in a hospital for assessment for at least a limited period and he ought to be so detained in the interests of his own health or safety or with a view to the protection of other persons. Application may be made either by the nearest relative or approved social worker: Mental Health Act 1983 s 11 (1), and must be supported by written recommendation of two medical practitioners both evidencing their opinions that the grounds are made out: Mental Health Act 1983 s 2 (3).

3   Mental Health Act 1983 ss 3, 20 (1) authorise detention for treatment for up to six months on grounds that an individual is suffering from mental illness, severe mental impairment, psychopathic disorder or mental impairment and his disorder is of a nature or degree which makes it appropriate for him to receive medical treatment in a hospital: Mental Health Act 1983 s 3 (2)(a). In the case of psychopathic disorder or impairment, such treatment must be likely to alleviate or prevent a deterioration of his condition: Mental Health Act 1983 s 3 (2)(b). In any event it must be necessary for the health and safety of the patient or for the protection of other persons that he should receive such treatment and it cannot be provided unless he is detained: Mental Health Act 1983 s 3 (2)(c). Application is made by the nearest relative or approved social worker but the latter must consult with the nearest relative before admission unless this is not reasonably practicable or would involve unreasonable delay: Mental Health Act 1983 s 11 (4). The relative may object and their so doing precludes an application under this section. The medical opinions required under this section must contain a statement that the grounds are made out, particulars of the grounds for that opinion and a statement of reasons why it is necessary that treatment should be given and cannot be provided unless the individual is detained: Mental Health Act 1983 s 3 (3). This section gives rise to renewable periods of detention after expiration of the initial detention.

4   Mental Health Act 1983 ss 35–37 (as amended by the Crime (Sentences) Act 1997, ss 55, 56 (2), Sch 4 para 12 (1), (3), Sch 6), 38 (as amended by the Crime (Sentences) Act 1997 s 49 (1)), 41 (as amended by the Crime (Sentences) Act 1997 s 49 (1), (2)), 47 (as amended by the Crime (Sentences) Act 1997 ss 49 (1), (3), 56 (2), Sch 6), 48, 49 relate to detention in hospital via the criminal courts depending on whether the disorder was at the time of the offence, the trial, the sentence or once custody has commenced. The Crown Court and magistrates are given powers on satisfaction of statutory criteria to authorise detention in specified hospitals. Interim orders for assessment may be made in cases of doubt and prisoners may be remanded to hospital instead of back to prison. Further powers exist to restrict discharge, if necessary to protect the public from serious harm. In the case of restriction orders, Mental Health Review Tribunals have discharge powers, but the nearest relative cannot discharge such a detainee and the hospital managers and responsible medical officer can only do so with the consent of the Home Secretary; with regard to detainees subject to restriction directions, a Mental Health Review Tribunal can only discharge them with the Home Secretary's consent.

5   Defined by Mental Health Act 1983 s 1 (2) as mental illness, arrested or incomplete development of mind, psychopathic disorder, and any other disorder or disability of mind. "Mental illness" is not defined further. By Mental Health Act 1983 s 1 (3), mere promiscuity, immoral conduct, sexual deviancy, drug or alcohol dependence are insufficient to amount to mental disorder. Psychopathic disorder is a persistent disorder or disability of mind which results in abnormally aggressive or seriously irresponsible conduct: Mental Health Act 1983 s 1 (2).

6   Access to Health Records Act 1990 (6 Halsbury's Statutes (4th Edn) CIVIL RIGHTS AND LIBERTIES) provides for access to the section papers from the hospital concerned unless the holder considers that disclosure would be likely to cause serious harm to the physical or mental health of the patient or other individual: Access to Health Records Act 1990 ss 3 (as amended by the Children (Scotland) Act 1995 s 105 (4), Sch 4 para 50 (1), (2)), 4 (as amended by the Children (Scotland) Act 1995 s 105 (4), Sch 4 para 50 (1), (3)), 5 (as amended by the Children (Scotland) Act 1995 s 105 (4), Sch 4 para 50 (1), (4)). An application may be made to the High Court or county court (under Access to Health Records Act 1990 s 8) for an order in such a case.

7   And cannot be rectified; examples are the absence of a signature on the medical recommendation or signature by someone not empowered to sign, a gap of more than five days between the two medical practitioners' examinations, no common

identification of mental disorder in the recommendations, or expiry of more than 14 days since the applicant last saw the detained person. "Nearest relative" is defined as a husband or wife (including a person who is living with a detained person as that person's husband or wife and has been doing so for not less than six months), son or daughter, father or mother, brother or sister, grandparent, grandchild, uncle or aunt, nephew or niece: Mental Health Act 1983 s 26 (1)(a)–(h), (6). Relatives of the full blood take precedence over those of the half blood and the elder takes precedence over the younger. Various statutory exclusions to this code are set out in Mental Health Act 1983 s 26 (5) (as amended). Application may be made to replace the nearest relative if the real one unreasonably objects to making an application for admission for treatment or is likely to exercise their power of discharge: Mental Health Act 1983 s 29.

8   Mental Health Act 1983 s 15. Examples are a medical recommendation insufficient to warrant detention, blanks which should have been completed, omission to make deletions where necessary. Minor defects in the spelling of the detainee's name will not normally defeat the application.

9   See the Code of Practice laid before Parliament in December 1989 and revised in 1993. Published by the Department of Health and the Welsh Office (appended to the Mental Health Act 1983 for guidance). Factors which should be taken into account include the patient's wishes and view of his or her own needs, their social circumstances, information from other friends and relatives, the patient's family's need etc. The Secretary of State also issues circulars such as 15/86 for guidance of the professionals in the field, but circulars are not statements of the law as such, merely an expression of opinion.

10 In *R v Hallstrom, ex p W* [1986] QB 1090, [1986] 2 All ER 306 the court held that detention under the Mental Health Act 1983 s 3 could not be used as a means of attaching conditions to a person being an out-patient, and that Mental Health Act 1983 s 20 could only be used to renew the authority to detain a patient whose mental condition was believed to require his continued detention as an in-patient.

101. Remedies. Habeas corpus[1] is the most expeditious form of proceeding to take against unlawful detention[2]. An action is commenced in the High Court against those detaining the detainee and involves an ex parte application and an affidavit as to the circumstances of detention. On the grant of the order, the hospital managers are obliged to produce the detainee in court on a specified day. Habeas corpus is most appropriate for a challenge to the validity of the detention on the face of the record of recommendations and the admission[3]. Judicial review proceedings are available against courts, hospitals or doctors fulfilling their statutory functions; an application may be brought on very quickly and expedited after the grant of leave. The availability of other forms of remedy may be used by the leave court to encourage applicants to follow other routes before using judicial review[4]. Damages for false imprisonment may be claimed in a private law action[5] or joined in a public law application. Hospital orders made by magistrates may be appealed to the Crown Court and those made by a Crown Court are appealed to the Court of Appeal.

1   Governed by RSC Ord 54.
2   See generally Vol 31 (1998 Issue) title PERSONAL RIGHTS Paragraphs 25-34.
3   See *R v Governor of Broadmoor, ex p Argles* (28 June 1984, unreported) where MELFORD STEVENSON J held that the detention was lawful because the documents were properly completed, "even though there may be a terrible hinterland which demonstrates that it should not have been done"; likewise in *R v Managers of South Western Hospital, ex p M* [1993] QB 683, [1994] 1 All ER 161.
4   In *Ex p Waldron* [1986] QB 824, [1985] 3 All ER 775, CA, ACKNER LJ suggested that the Mental Health Review Tribunal should not be regarded as an appropriate alternative forum for the applicant if the underlying validity of the admission is being challenged, because the tribunal's role is meant to be review of the need for continued detention, not its original legality.

5 Save that the Mental Health Act 1983 s 139 (28 Halsbury's Statutes (4th Edn) MENTAL HEALTH) provides that no person shall be liable whether on the ground of want of jurisdiction or on any other ground to any civil or criminal proceedings to which he would have been liable apart from this section in respect of any act purporting to be done in pursuance of this Act or any regulations or rules made under this Act unless the act was done in bad faith or without reasonable care. Mental Health Act 1983 s 139 (2) requires that the leave of the High Court be sought for civil proceedings, but the section is wholly inapplicable to proceedings against the Secretary of State, a health authority, or an NHS trust: Mental Health Act 1983 s 139 (4)(as amended). It could be relevant to actions against local authorities based on the conduct of social workers. Where it does apply, leave under the section is generally given if the plaintiff can show that the case requires fuller investigation of the kind that could only occur if the action was allowed to proceed: *Winch v Jones* [1986] QB 296, [1985] 3 All ER 97, CA. The whole section is inapplicable to judicial review because applications for review do not constitute "civil proceedings".

102. Discharges by bodies other than Mental Health Review Tribunals.
Discharge by the responsible medical officer, the nearest relative[1] and the hospital managers[2] is provided for in the legislation. All such methods are applicable to those admitted under Sections 2 and 3 of the Mental Health Act 1983[3].

1 Subject to a barring order by the responsible medical officer certifying that in his or her opinion the detained person would be likely to act in a manner dangerous to other persons or to him or herself; discharge by the nearest relative is then barred for another six months, but they may apply to a Mental Health Review Tribunal in respect of admissions under the Mental Health Act 1983 s 3 (28 Halsbury's Statutes (4th Edn) MENTAL HEALTH). This could be advantageous because the "dangerous" test is much narrower than "treatment in hospital necessary" test applicable to applications by the detainee, and the tribunal must discharge unless satisfied of such danger existing. Mental Health Act 1983 s 2 detainees faced with a barring order can only challenge its validity on grounds of unreasonableness via review or habeas corpus.
2 That is, persons appointed by the health authority to discharge functions related to detained patients, who have power to confirm detention or discharge. Procedures for discharge by the managers differ from hospital to hospital, some involving hearings with representation and cross-examination, others simply a review of the written reports. Managers have a discretion as to how frequently detainees may be given reviews. Green Form advice and assistance is available, but not ABWOR. See Vol 25 (1998 Issue) title LEGAL AID. Managers must refer to a tribunal those patients who have been detained for three years without making any application to a tribunal and those admitted for treatment who do not apply within the first six months: Mental Health Act 1983 s 68 (as amended).
3 Mental Health Act 1983 ss 2, 3.

103. Discharge by tribunals.
A detainee under the Mental Health Act 1983 Section 2 must apply for discharge within 14 days of admission to hospital[1]. A Section 3 detainee is not obliged to apply within any particular period. Those detained under hospital orders are not permitted to apply during the first six months of the order being made. One of the tribunal members will be a consultant psychiatrist who has the right to examine the detainee before the hearing[2]. The hearing will be attended by the responsible medical officer and the social worker. The detainee usually gives evidence and will be questioned by the tribunal members; then he may call his own lay witnesses if he chooses to do so. After this the responsible medical officer and any independent psychiatrist will be called and the evidence will finish with the social workers. Occasionally the medical evidence is heard earlier

on in the hearing, depending on the type of admission and state of the evidence. The proceedings are not conventionally adversarial[3]. The tribunal will consider not only whether the person is fit to be discharged but also where they will go next. Its powers are limited. It must discharge in some cases[4] and may do so in others[5]. It has a general discretion to discharge all patients other than those subject to restriction orders. So far as they are concerned, the tribunal must assess the person against statutory criteria and either make an absolute discharge[6] order or a conditional order[7]. It can defer discharge of certain persons until it is satisfied that certain conditions will be fulfilled[8]. Patients subject to a restriction direction may not be discharged by a Mental Health Review Tribunal because they are still subject to the sentence[9]. A report from a social worker defining the extent of care available for the individual will be important. Other witnesses may be called. The decision[10] must be notified to the applicant within seven days of the hearing. The wording of Section 72 of the Mental Health Act 1983 obliges the detainee to satisfy the tribunal that the grounds for continued detention do not apply[11].

1 Mental Health Act 1983 s 66 (as amended) (28 Halsbury's Statutes (4th Edn) MENTAL HEALTH). The hearing must be held within seven days of receipt by the tribunal office: Mental Health Review Tribunal Rules 1983, SI 1983/942, r 31 (a) (13 Halsbury's Statutory Instruments (1994 Issue) MENTAL HEALTH).
2 Research by J Peay has shown that the visit by the medical member and its results are taken into account and given much weight by tribunals: *Tribunals on Trial* (1989).
3 They are held in private unless the client requests a public hearing and the tribunal is satisfied that it would not be contrary to the client's interests.
4 The tribunal must discharge a detainee under the Mental Health Act 1983 s 2 if satisfied that the applicant is not suffering from mental disorder of a nature or degree which warrants detention in hospital for assessment for at least a limited period, or that detention is not justified in the interests of the detainee's health or safety or with a view to the protection of others: Mental Health Act 1983 s 72 (1)(a). Detainees under Mental Health Act 1983 ss 3, 37 must be discharged if the tribunal is satisfied that they are not then suffering from a mental illness, severe mental impairment, psychopathic disorder or mental impairment or from any of those forms of disorder of a nature or degree making detention in hospital for treatment appropriate, or if it is not necessary for the health or safety of the patient or for the protection of other persons that the detainee should receive such treatment: Mental Health Act 1983 s 72 (1)(b).
5 There is power under Mental Health Act 1983 s 72 (3) to discharge on a future date, and the date must be specified and cannot be changed. It is presumed that any delay would have to be reasonable and related to a valid objective such as the availability of aftercare, although if the arrangements cannot be implemented, the order must take effect in any event. In *R v Wessex Mental Health Review Tribunal, ex p Wiltshire County Council* (1989) 4 BMLR 145, CA, the tribunal delayed discharge to allow the authorities time to consider making an application under Mental Health Act 1983 s 3, and on judicial review, counsel conceded that this was ultra vires. Note that this power must be distinguished from a deferred conditional discharge of a restricted patient; see note 7 below.
6 In *R v Merseyside Mental Health Review Tribunal, ex p K* [1990] 1 All ER 694, CA, K had been conditionally discharged in 1985; he then committed a number of offences and received a prison sentence. He applied for absolute discharge, fearing recall to hospital at the end of his term. The Court of Appeal held that the Mental Health Act 1983 empowered tribunals to impose conditional discharges on persons not then suffering from mental disorder. Restricted patients may not be discharged unless the tribunal is satisfied that it is not appropriate for the prisoner to remain liable to recall. After his sentence expired he was recalled by warrant under Mental Health Act 1983 s 42 (3). He sought review of this recall but was unsuccessful: *R v Secretary of State for the Home Department, ex*

p K [1991] 1 QB 270, [1990] 3 All ER 562, CA. There is power under Mental Health Act 1983 s 3 to detain a restricted patient who had been conditionally discharged: *R v North West London Mental Health NHS Trust, ex p Stewart* [1997] 4 All ER 871, CA. A warrant of recall issued under Mental Health Act 1983 s 42 (3) authorised not only a patient's compulsory readmission and detention in hospital but also reinstatement of the stringent regime of control provided by Mental Health Act 1983 s 41: *R v Secretary of State for the Home Department, ex p D* (1996) Times, 10 May, CA.

7   To be ordered when the tribunal is not satisfied about freedom from liability to recall: Mental Health Act 1983 s 73 (2). Either the tribunal or Home Secretary may impose conditions. Psychiatric or social supervision are common conditions. In *Secretary of State for the Home Department v Mental Health Review Tribunal for Wales* [1986] 3 All ER 233, [1986] 1 WLR 1170 a tribunal directed conditional discharge but on condition that the detainee continue to reside in hospital where he had been for many years. This was held to be inconsistent with the direction for discharge and unlawful. The patient in fact needed supervision and training amounting to medical treatment within Mental Health Act 1983 s 145 (1), so was not ready for discharge according to the Act.

8   Mental Health Act 1983 s 73 (7). The effect of such an order is that the discharge direction's coming into effect is postponed until the arrangements specified are made. It is settled that such an order is a final decision which cannot be re-opened by the tribunal. In *Secretary of State for the Home Department v Mental Health Review Tribunal, for the Mersey Regional Health Authority* [1986] 3 All ER 233, [1986] 1 WLR 1170, it was held that the tribunal may not defer discharge until admission, for the best of motives, to another hospital, albeit a less secure one, can be arranged. The decision may take effect without further hearing. If the arrangements cannot be implemented, then it is the duty of the authorities to refer the matter to the Secretary of State so that he may consider referral back to the Mental Health Review Tribunal: *R v Ealing District Health Authority, ex p Fox* [1993] 1 WLR 373. The tribunal is not empowered to set a fixed date for the implementation of the arrangements. See Form 4 post for an example of an application for review based on the facts of this case.

9   Tribunals may also order the discharge of those transferred to hospital from prison under Mental Health Act 1983 ss 47 (as amended by the Crime (Sentences) Act 1997 ss 49 (1), (3), 56 (2), Sch 6) or 48 even before the first six months has elapsed. Anyone covered by a restriction order under Mental Health Act 1983 s 49 may get a finding that had they not been, they would have been entitled to a conditional or absolute discharge. It is then up to the Home Secretary to decide whether they may be released or transferred back to a prison.

10 Taken by a majority vote, the president having a second vote where necessary: Mental Health Review Tribunal Rules 1983 r 23 (1).

11 Mental Health Act 1983 s 72. Whereas a review by hospital managers is not based upon such criteria, so a more favourable approach to the burden of proof may occur at such reviews.

104. Procedural provisions. A detailed framework of procedural provisions covering matters of representation, disclosure of information and the giving of a reasoned decision[1] is set out in the Mental Health Review Tribunal Rules 1983[2].

1   The Rules specifically provide for the giving of substantive reasons for its decision, not mere rehearsal of the statutory criteria. In *Bone v Mental Health Review Tribunal* [1985] 3 All ER 330 it was held that reasons must be genuine, adequate and intelligible and deal with the substantial points that have been raised. Reasons must make it clear why contentions of an RMO or psychiatrist have not been accepted: *R v Mental Health Review Tribunal, ex p Clatworthy* [1985] 3 All ER 699.

2   See Mental Health Review Tribunal Rules 1983, SI 1983/942 (13 Halsbury's Statutory Instruments (1994 Issue) MENTAL HEALTH).

6: TAXATION AND COMMERCIAL MATTERS

105. Introduction. In the last fifteen years judicial review has been used more frequently to challenge the decisions of the Inland Revenue and other taxation authorities. It is suggested that this is probably due to the general broadening in the scope of review[1] and the developments in the principle of legitimate expectation[2] as part of procedural, and sometimes substantive, fairness. Further, with regard to commercial matters, judicial review has become a more feasible form of challenge because of the proliferation of regulatory bodies[3], underpinned by statute in some way, governing most aspects of modern finance and also because of privatisation of the nationalised industries[4]. The amounts at stake in modern takeovers and mergers have made any form of judicial remedy worth considering.

1   See Paragraph 13 ante. In Malaysia it has been held that the stock exchange is amenable to the court's jurisdiction because it is "vouched for" by statute: *OSK and Partners Sdn v Tengku Noone Aziz* [1983] 1 MLJ 179 Fed Ct, per ABDOOLCADER J, and for commentary thereon see G Peiris "Legal Control of Semi-Governmental Bodies: English and South Asian Trends Compared" [1988] ICLQ 844. For a discussion of the extension of review to non-statutory, non-contractual bodies see J Jowell "The Takeover Panel: Autonomy, Flexibility and Legality" [1991] PL 149.
2   See Paragraph 49 ante.
3   See M Beloff QC "Judicial Review and the City Regulators" [1989] MLR 640 and Andrew Lidbetter "Financial Services and Judicial Review" [1991] PL 10 (regarding the Commissioner's refusal to order discovery in *R v Association of Futures Brokers and Dealers Ltd, ex p Mordens Ltd* [1991] COD 40) and "The Right to make Representations" [1992] PL 533 (concerning *R v Life Assurance and Unit Trust Regulatory Organisation Ltd, ex p Ross* [1992] 1 All ER 422; affd sub nom *R v Life Assurance and Unit Trust Regulatory Organisation Ltd, ex p Ross* [1993] QB 17, [1993] 1 All ER 545, CA).
4   See Aileen McHarg "Competition and Service Utilities Act 1992: Utility Regulation and the Charter" [1992] PL 385. A possibility of judicial review of the adequacy of consultation by the new regulators prior to issuing regulations for the industries arises under the Competition and Service (Utilities) Act 1992. Note too that there is no appeal from disputed billing or supply decisions by the regulatory directors and arbitrators, so judicial review will be the only remedy. However the director is under a duty to give reasons and is supervised by the Council on Tribunals.

106. Amenability to review. The Inland Revenue[1] is amenable to judicial review by virtue of the public nature of its status and functions. Review is not available against Special or General Commissioners in relation to the merits of tax cases[2]. Commissioners of Customs and Excise are likewise potential respondents to challenge in VAT cases or customs decisions[3]. The Department of Trade and Industry[4], the Treasury[5], the Monopolies and Mergers Commission[6], the Registrars of Companies[7] and of Trade Marks[8] and the Panel for Takeovers and Mergers[9] have all been judicially reviewed[10]. Most of the new self-regulatory bodies[11] have been challenged, with respect to regulatory or disciplinary decisions and it has never been seriously contended that they were purely private bodies, in spite of their contractual relationship with their members and their subsidiary role as professional bodies or trade associations[12]. Lloyd's of London is the only commercial body which has established that some areas of its operation are beyond the reach of the court's supervisory jurisdiction[13].

1   Generally sued as the Inland Revenue Commissioners, for example, *R v IRC, ex p Taylor (No 2)* [1989] 3 All ER 353; affd [1990] 2 All ER 409, CA (regarding a demand that a solicitor should disclose documents regarding his tax position which included details of clients' affairs) or "Collector of Taxes", for example, *R v Collector of Taxes, ex p Robert Goodall (Builders) Ltd* [1989] STC 206 (whether a collector's refusal to make a direction exonerating a contractor from liability for failing to make a sub-contractor's deduction was reasonable under the Finance (No 2) Act 1975 ss 69, 70 (now repealed)) or "General" or "Special Commissioners for …" depending on the particular statutory powers or duties under challenge; for further examples, see *R v IT Acts Special Purposes Comr, ex p Napier* [1988] 3 All ER 166, CA, regarding the question whether a taxpayer could complain that a stated case failed to state certain matters in dispute and whether the issues were determinable on appeal by case stated or by judicial review; *R v IT Acts Special Purposes Comr, ex p Stipplechoice Ltd* [1985] 2 All ER 465, CA; *R v Boston General Comrs, ex p CD Freehouses & Co Ltd* [1990] STC 186 on an appeal against an estimated assessment, the taxpayer had not been allowed to present its full case and the Commissioners failed to advise the taxpayer of its right of appeal. Further, in *Thorne v Sevenoaks General Comrs and IRC* [1989] STC 560 the court dealt with the fairness of a refusal of an adjournment in the context of neglect to recover tax losses and the taxpayer's illness.
2   Taxes Management Act 1970 s 46 (2)(as amended) (42 Halsbury's Statutes (4th Edn) TAXATION) precludes any other remedy outside an appeal against an assessment, by way of case stated on a point of law.
3   For example, *R v Customs and Excise Comrs, ex p Cook and Stevenson* [1970] 1 All ER 1068, [1970] 1 WLR 450 concerning the amount of interest needed to apply for mandamus to force the Commissioners to abide by law as opposed to policy.
4   For example, *R v Secretary of State for Trade, ex p Perestrello* [1981] QB 19, [1980] 3 All ER 28 concerning the clash of roles for investigators of company affairs produced by the Companies Act 1967 (19 Halsbury's Statutes (4th Edn) FRIENDLY SOCIETIES) making them both prosecutor and judge; *Re Pergamon Press Ltd* [1971] Ch 388, [1970] 3 All ER 535, CA, concerned the extent of procedural fairness in terms of notice within an investigatory context, and *R v Director of Serious Fraud Office, ex p Smith* [1993] AC 1, [1992] 3 All ER 456, HL, is the most recent authority in this context. See also *Lonrho plc v Secretary of State for Trade and Industry* [1989] 2 All ER 609, [1989] 1 WLR 525, HL, a case in which it was reiterated that the mere absence of reasons where there is no duty to give any will not of itself provide support for a contention that the decision is irrational.
5   *R v HM Treasury, ex p Daily Mail and General Trust plc* [1987] STC 157, [1987] 2 CMLR 1 involving a reference to the European Court; *R v HM Treasury, ex p Petch* [1990] COD 19.
6   *R v Monopolies and Mergers Commission, ex p Visa International Service Association* [1991] CCLR 13, CA; *R v Monopolies and Mergers Commission, ex p Elders IXL Ltd* [1987] 1 All ER 451, [1987] 1 WLR 1221; *R v Monopolies and Mergers Commission, ex p Matthew Brown plc* [1987] 1 All ER 463, [1987] 1 WLR 1235 (both partly concerning the extent of detail which must be given by the Commission in executing its investigatory role); *R v Monopolies and Mergers Commission, ex p National House Building Council* [1992] NPC 122, (1992) Times, 7 October; *R v Monopolies and Mergers Commission, ex p Argyll Group plc* [1986] 2 All ER 257, [1986] 1 WLR 763, CA
7   *R v Registrar of Companies, ex p Central Bank of India Ltd* [1986] QB 1114, [1986] 1 All ER 105, CA.
8   *Adidas SARL's Trade Mark* [1983] RPC 262.
9   *R v Panel of Take-overs and Mergers, ex p Datafin Ltd* [1987] QB 815, [1987] 1 All ER 564, CA; *R v Panel on Take-overs and Mergers, ex p Guinness plc* [1990] 1 QB 146, [1989] 1 All ER 509, CA.

10 The Director of the Serious Fraud Office has also been an applicant in relation to a decision to dismiss certain criminal charges against alleged financial fraudsters: *R v Central Criminal Court, ex p Director of Serious Fraud Office* [1993] 2 All ER 399, [1993] 1 WLR 949. Other commercial applicants such as companies involved in the competition for TV franchises have used the review procedure: *R v Independent Television Commission, ex p TSW Broadcasting Ltd* [1996] EMLR 291, HL, (where the requirements for a legitimate expectation were developed); *R v Independent Television Commission, ex p TV NI Ltd* (1991) Times, 30 December. See also Tim Jones "Judicial Review of the Independent Television Commission" [1992] PL 372.

11 For example, *R v Association of Futures Brokers and Dealers Ltd, ex p Mordens Ltd* [1991] COD 40; *Bank of Scotland, Petitioner* (1988) Times, 21 November; *R v Life Assurance and Unit Trust Regulatory Organisation Ltd, ex p Ross* [1993] QB 17, [1993] 1 All ER 545, CA; *R v Financial Intermediaries, Managers and Brokers Regulatory Associaation, ex p Cochrane* [1991] BCLC 106.

12 Contract is not the sole source of these bodies' powers: the Financial Services Act 1986 (30 Halsbury's Statutes (4th Edn) MONEY) created the Securities and Investments Board to ensure that the various self-regulatory bodies assumed by the legislative scheme to exist would be properly responsible for regulation of individuals and companies carrying on commercial business. It is a requirement under the legislation that the Board should not authorise an SRO unless its rules comply with Financial Services Act 1986 s 114 (as amended), Sch 2. Thus these bodies are "underpinned by" references in statutes to their existence and operations.

13 Compare *R v Committee of Lloyd's, ex p Moran* (1983) Times, 24 June and *R v Committee of Lloyd's, ex p Postgate* (1983) Times, 12 January with *R v Lloyd's of London, ex p Briggs* [1993] 1 Lloyd's Rep 176. It is interesting to note that several statutes refer to Lloyd's role, yet despite this it happens to operate solely by contract with its members, obliging obedience to the decisions and directions of its Council. It is not liable in tort for breach of statutory duty: *Ashmore v Corp of Lloyd's (No 2)* [1992] 2 Lloyd's Rep 620, (1992) Times, 17 July.

107. Grounds for review. Generally, the factual situations in the commercial arena in which the courts will intervene are more narrowly defined than in applications against purely governmental bodies. However, the grounds of challenge may still be brought within the familiar three-fold formulation:

1. *Illegality.* Such an allegation may feasibly be made where the body in question has purported to exercise statutory powers or powers conferred by delegated legislation[1], or, by analogy to challenges against government circulars, misconstrued rules drawn up by itself[2]. There may be instances of disputes over jurisdictional facts and if this be the case the court may be prepared to grant applications for cross-examination on the affidavits[3].

2. *Procedural impropriety.* Challenges to procedure will be arguable where the body in question has either failed to abide by its own rules or applied rules or exercised a discretion in a way which may not be fair in the circumstances[4]. In the latter case it may be that if the element of contract or consent to the body's jurisdiction by members is strong, the courts will decline to intervene on the basis that the matter would best be dealt with by way of private law. With regard to natural justice in the tax context, the content of the duty to act fairly is probably lower than in some other fields, because the role of taxation authorities has been characterised as more administrative than judicial. To establish that tax collection procedures or prosecutions should not have been initiated, a taxpayer would have to show that there was no evidence which could have led the Revenue to take action; nothing

upon which a reasonable opinion of another could have been based. There is no principle of absolute equality of treatment between payers of the same class[5].

3. *Unreasonableness.* There has been some discussion of the merits of approaching unreasonableness in the commercial world on a different footing than is usual in review proceedings, but it does not seem to have achieved widespread acceptance[6]. One might think that the identification of certain taxation bodies with government interests would make it impossible to challenge policy or assert that the statutory duty to collect tax should not be executed with regard to an individual[7]. However, this duty has been interpreted to mean as much tax as it is sensible to try to collect, so the Revenue does have a limited managerial discretion[8], and it has developed policies to inform the exercise of that discretion, which it publishes in the form of extra-statutory concessions. Rigid adherence to or sudden departure from such policies may be characterised as fettering of discretion or denial of a legitimate expectation[9]. The Revenue has statutory discretionary power to give assurances, but there is a stringent set of criteria which must be proved before an "estoppel" can be raised. The taxpayer's only legitimate expectation has been described as being taxed according to statute, and not to concession or opinions about the law[10]. But the exercise of the Revenue's powers and duties is amenable to judicial review if for instance its conduct is equivalent to a breach of contract or breach of representation[11]; formally published statements fulfilling the "MFK" criteria[12] are binding in any case falling within its terms.

---

1 See *Woolwich Equitable Building Society v IRC* [1993] AC 70, [1992] 3 All ER 737, HL, where the House of Lords held a cause of action arose immediately on payment in pursuance of a void authority. Here parts of the Income Tax (Building Societies) Regulations 1986, SI 1986/482 had been held to be ultra vires. See further P Birks "When money is paid in pursuance of a void authority: a duty to repay?" [1992] PL 580 where it is pointed out that a claim for restitution, although private in nature may not be added to an application for review as if it were "damages". Quaere whether a declaration that one was entitled to the repayment would suffice.
2 It may be that the analysis in *R v Lord President of the Privy Council, ex p Page* [1993] AC 682, sub nom *Page v Hull University Visitor* [1993] 1 All ER 97, HL, that certain bodies are empowered to make errors of law and remain immune from review, because the law which they are construing is domestic law, not subject to the general law of the land, could be extended to self-regulatory organisations in cases such as this.
3 See *R v IRC, ex p J Rothschild Holdings plc* [1986] STC 410; affd [1987] STC 163, CA, where officials were questioned as to departmental practices to assist the court to make findings of fact upon which power was dependent.
4 For example, *R v Association of Futures Brokers and Dealers Ltd, ex p Mordens Ltd* [1991] COD 40 and *R v Life Assurance and Unit Trust Regulatory Organisation Ltd, ex p Ross* [1993] QB 17, [1993] 1 All ER 545, CA, where it was held, however, that LAUTRO could suspend a non-member's right to deal without giving him a chance to make representations before service of a notice. LAUTRO's rules have since been amended to provide for an appeal for non-members after dealing has been suspended.
5 See *R v IRC, ex p Cook and Mead* [1993] 1 All ER 772; *R v IRC, ex p Kaye* [1992] STC 581.
6 See LORD DONALDSON's judgment in *R v Panel on Take-overs and Mergers, ex p Guinness plc* [1990] 1 QB 146, [1989] 1 All ER 509, CA: the court should approach its task by asking whether something had gone wrong of a nature and degree which required the intervention of the court.
7 See Inland Revenue Regulation Act 1890 s 13 (42 Halsbury's Statutes (4th Edn) TAXATION).

8 Taxes Management Act 1970 s 1 (as amended) (42 Halsbury's Statutes (4th Edn) TAXATION). See *IRC v National Federation of Self Employed and Small Businesses* [1982] AC 617, [1981] 2 All ER 93, HL, where this discretion was said to be subject to the avoidance of discrimination between one group of taxpayers and another, so that there are no favourites nor sacrificial victims.
9 Which might be seen more as procedural unfairness rather than unreasonableness; see Paragraph 67 ante.
10 See *Re Preston* [1985] AC 835, sub nom *Preston v IRC* [1985] 2 All ER 327, HL, where the applicant sought review of the Commissioners' decision to exercise certain powers under the Income and Corporation Taxes Act 1970 Pt XVII.
11 See *Re Preston* [1985] AC 835, sub nom *Preston v IRC* [1985] 2 All ER 327, HL, per LORD TEMPLEMAN, although inconsistency itself would not be enough. Detrimental reliance would be required.
12 *R v Board of Inland Revenue, ex p MFK Underwriting Agencies Ltd* [1990] 1 All ER 91, [1991] 1 WLR 1545 established that if the taxpayer gives full details of transactions on which he is seeking a ruling, and makes it plain that a considered ruling is sought, and obtains a clear, unambiguous ruling, unqualified in any relevant way, he may rely on it and if he suffers positive harm he can bring a challenge against a change of mind on the Revenue's part. For an illustration of such harm see *R v IRC, ex p Camacq Corpn* [1990] 1 All ER 173, [1990] 1 WLR 191, CA, regarding the question whether the Revenue was entitled to withdraw authorisation for direct payment of tax credit upon realising the implications of a company's scheme.

108. Restrictions on review. Alternative remedies existing within the statutory framework in which the particular body operates may restrict the role of review[1]. For instance, there is a tax appeal procedure under the Taxes Management Act 1970 involving an appeal by way of case stated even where the conduct of the Appeal Commissioners is in question[2]. Most of the reported cases in the tax field take this form. Another example is the rights of appeal from various decisions of self-regulating organisations, apparently required by the Financial Services Act 1986 before such bodies may gain approval under the Act. Another special consideration that has deterred a proliferation of applications has been the perceived need to preserve speed and certainty in the City's operations for the good of the reputation of the London markets[3]. This perception has caused the judges to restrict review of interlocutory decisions of commercial regulators[4], to introduce the concept of prospective overruling[5], to enhance the procedures for expedition of hearings in such cases[6] and to be firm with applicants as to costs[7]. In the circumstances it is considered less likely that business concerns will use review as a stalling or wrecking tactic since they will have little to gain personally from challenging the illegality. Another means by which the courts could restrict review would be by elaboration of particularly tight rules of locus standi[8]; if on analysis of the statutory powers and duties in question there is nobody intended by Parliament to be able to bring a challenge, then judicial review remedies may not be obtained[9].

1 Note that the absence of an alternative remedy will operate in favour of an application for review: an example is *R v Inland Revenue Board, ex p Goldberg* [1989] QB 267, [1988] 2 All ER 248 in respect of a notice served under the Taxes Management Act 1970 s 20 (2) (42 Halsbury's Statutes (4th Edn) TAXATION), on the ground that it demanded disclosure of privileged documents, where no appeal was available.

2　Some cases have gone by way of case stated, while others have been by way of judicial review: *R v Sevenoaks General Comrs and IRC, ex p Thorne* [1989] STC 560. In *Re Preston* [1985] AC 835, sub nom *Preston v IRC* [1985] 2 All ER 327, HL, the circumstances when it would be appropriate to seek review rather than appeal were considered and a distinction was drawn between situations in which it would be unfair to the payer to initiate proceedings under that Part at all and where something had gone wrong in the course of the procedure itself.
3　Financial Services Act 1986 (42 Halsbury's Statutes (4th Edn) TAXATION). Counsel in *R v Panel of Take-overs and Mergers, ex p Datafin Ltd* [1987] QB 815, [1987] 1 All ER 564, CA argued that the consequences of amenability to review would be disastrous.
4　*R v Association of Futures Brokers and Dealers Ltd, ex p Mordens Ltd* [1991] COD 40.
5　Whereby ultra vires decisions are nevertheless upheld in the discretion of the court: *R v Monopolies and Mergers Commission, ex p Argyll Group plc* [1986] 2 All ER 257, [1986] 1 WLR 763, CA. The content of the judgment would be of use in the future, but the actual decision taken would not be quashed in cases where large numbers might have acted to their detriment in reliance on it. Whilst there is no compensation for unlawful action in administrative law, this leaves the individual applicant much dissatisfied. The Financial Services Act 1986 s 187 (30 Halsbury's Statutes (4th Edn) MONEY) expressly prohibits a claim for damages arising out of conduct of self-regulatory bodies.
6　*R v Panel of Take-overs and Mergers, ex p Datafin Ltd* [1987] QB 815, [1987] 1 All ER 564, CA, took only 11 days from the date of the application for leave, to the end of the substantive hearing and judgment in the Court of Appeal.
7　In *R v IRC, ex p Opman International UK* [1986] 1 All ER 328, [1986] 1 WLR 568 the applicant was refused his costs after the respondent had conceded its claim because the applicant could have given notice of his intention to take legal action which would probably have avoided the need for legal action altogether.
8　*R v A-G, ex p ICI plc* [1986] 60 TC 1 where the court discussed locus standi and the inappropriateness of retrospective relief in such cases; the applicant was granted standing to challenge the basis on which petroleum revenue tax was based on ethane used by competitors, but this was said to be exceptional and turned upon the impact on this particular applicant. See further *R v HM Treasury, ex p Smedley* [1985] QB 657, [1985] 1 All ER 589, CA, where a taxpayer was given locus standi to challenge a determination by the Chancellor of the Exchequer that an undertaking could be regarded as a Community Treaty for the purposes of the European Communities Act 1972 s 1 (2)(as amended) (10 Halsbury's Statutes (4th Edn) CONSTITUTIONAL LAW).
9　But see *R v Life Assurance and Unit Trust Regulatory Organisation Ltd, ex p Ross* [1993] QB 17, [1993] 1 All ER 545, CA, where locus standi was accorded to a non-member of LAUTRO to challenge the lack of procedural protection in matters affecting the livelihoods of non-members such as himself.

109. Breach of statutory duty as an alternative to an application for review. In the alternative it is sometimes acceptable to seek a declaration by way of writ or originating summons where the propriety of a Revenue attempt to unwind tax avoidance transactions is concerned[1]. Where restitution of payments made pursuant to unlawful demand is concerned, there is also authority supporting the bringing of an ordinary writ action[2].

1　*Balen v IRC* [1978] 2 All ER 1033, CA; *Beecham Group plc v IRC* [1992] STC 935.
2　*Woolwich Equitable Building Society v IRC* [1993] AC 70, [1992] 3 All ER 737, HL, per LORD SLYNN. The disadvantage of review proceedings in such a case is that the procedural right to join a claim for damages to the application does not seem to cover a restitutionary claim. However, a declaration that one was entitled to repayment would appear to produce an appropriate result.

7: SOCIAL SECURITY DECISIONS

110. Introduction[1]. The provision of, and the conditions for obtaining, most social security benefits are governed by the Social Security Contributions and Benefits Act 1992[2]. The Social Security Administration Act 1992 provides for the administration of these benefits and for rights of appeal against various decisions made on entitlement to benefit[3]. Both of these Acts contain wide ranging powers to make subordinate legislation and many statutory instruments and regulations have been made under this and predecessor legislation[4].

1 For a more in depth coverage of this area of the law see Vol 36 (1997 Issue) title SOCIAL SECURITY.
2 Social Security Contributions and Benefits Act 1992 (40 Halsbury's Statutes (4th Edn) SOCIAL SECURITY).
3 Social Security Administration Act 1992 (40 Halsbury's Statutes (4th Edn) SOCIAL SECURITY).
4 These are consolidating statutes. Tables of derivations and destinations can be found, together with relevant parts of both statutes, the regulations and commentaries, in a series of commercial publications which are updated annually and distributed to the various Tribunals by the Independent Tribunal Service.

111. The decision makers. Most decisions on benefits are taken by an adjudication officer[1] with a right of appeal to one of the tribunals established by the legislation: the Social Security Appeal Tribunal[2], the Disability Appeal Tribunal[3] or the Medical Appeal Tribunal[4]. There is a further right of appeal on a point of law to a Social Security Commissioner[5].

The legislation reserves some decisions to the Secretary of State, and in such cases there is no right of appeal to a tribunal, but there are powers of review and reference by the Secretary of State to the High Court on a question of law and a right of appeal to the High Court on a question of law by any person aggrieved[6]. Appeals from a commissioner on a question of law lie to the Court of Appeal[7].

Payments from the social fund, with the exception of funeral and maternity payments[8] and severe weather payments[9] are governed by a different procedure, in which decisions are made by a Social Fund Officer[10]. The Social Security Contributions and Benefits Act 1992 contains principles of determination for the decisions of Social Fund Officers in accordance with which the Secretary of State has issued Social Fund Directions[11], and decisions are subject to review by Social Fund Inspectors, who are appointed, trained and monitored by a Social Fund Commissioner[12]. There is no right of appeal from this procedure to an independent tribunal.

1 Social Security Administration Act 1992 s 20 (as amended) (40 Halsbury's Statutes (4th Edn) SOCIAL SECURITY).
2 Social Security Administration Act 1992 ss 22, 33 (1)(b).
3 Social Security Administration Act 1992 s 33 (1)(a).
4 Social Security Administration Act 1992 s 46 (2).
5 Social Security Administration Act 1992 ss 23 (1), 34 (1), 48 (1). Selected decisions are reported by the Commissioners and published by HMSO.

6 Social Security Administration Act 1992 ss 17-19. For procedure see RSC Ord 55. Decisions of the Secretary of State are not published.
7 Social Security Administration Act 1992 s 24. For procedure see RSC Ord 55 r 25.
8 Social Security Contributions and Benefits Act 1992 s 138 (1)(a) (40 Halsbury's Statutes (4th Edn) SOCIAL SECURITY).
9 Social Security Contributions and Benefits Act 1992 s 138 (2).
10 Social Security Contributions and Benefits Act 1992 ss 138 (1)(b), 139.
11 Social Security Contributions and Benefits Act 1992 s 140. See also the Social Fund (Applications) Regulations 1988, SI 1988/524.
12 Social Security Administration Act 1992 s 65 (3)(a), (5)(a)–(c). The first reported decision of a Social Fund Inspector can be found at [1993] Journal of Social Welfare and Family Law 210-213.

112. Judicial review or other remedies. There is no doubt that social security decisions at all of these levels are in principle subject to judicial review. The Court of Appeal has held that adjudication officers, although acting administratively and not exercising a judicial function (because at this stage there are no conflicting parties between whom to adjudicate), are under an obligation to carry out their adjudicating role fairly[1]. In the same case the court was prepared, in judicial review proceedings, to consider the duty of the Secretary of State to submit a claim "forthwith to an adjudication officer for determination", although in the event relief was refused[2].

However, the courts have been reluctant to interfere with the assumed technical expertise of these decision makers and more recently a greater obstacle to judicial review is likely to be the requirement that alternative remedies first be exhausted and that statutory rights of appeal be exercised[3].

As there is always a right of appeal against the decision of an adjudication officer to a tribunal, and against that of the Secretary of State to the High Court, it is almost certain that judicial review would be refused in cases where these remedies had not been followed. Adjudication officers act under guidance but the divisional court has refused judicial review of the guidance in a case of widespread importance concerning striking miners, leaving the applicant to appeal to the tribunal[4].

1 *R v Secretary of State for Social Services, ex p Child Poverty Action Group* [1990] 2 QB 540, [1989] 1 All ER 1047, CA.
2 *R v Secretary of State for Social Services, ex p Child Poverty Action Group* [1990] 2 QB 540, [1989] 1 All ER 1047, CA. The Court of Appeal held that the duty was to submit the claim as soon as reasonably possible once the Department was satisfied that it was in possession of the basic information required to enable the claim to be determined. Until that information was received the duty did not arise.
3 See Paragraph 130 post regarding "prior exhaustion".
4 *R v Chief Adjudication Officer, ex p Bland* (1985) Times, 6 February.

113. Tribunals. It has been clear for many years that the tribunals are subject to judicial review[1] but there was the reluctance to interfere with the assumed technical expertise of the tribunal[2]. As tribunal decisions are subject to appeal to the Social Security Commissioners, the courts are likely to take the view that this course should be followed in preference to judicial review proceedings. This is perhaps all the more likely to be the approach since the House of Lords has confirmed that both tribunals and commissioners have the right to decide whether regulations are ultra vires[3].

There are some decisions taken in tribunal proceedings that do not carry a right of appeal to the commissioners and where judicial review might be the only method of challenging the decision. An appeal to a commissioner from a tribunal lies only with the leave of a tribunal chairman or of a commissioner[4]. There is no right of appeal as such against a chairman's refusal of leave, but it is unlikely that judicial review will lie, since the application for leave may be reinstated before the commissioner. There are time limits on appealing to a tribunal, usually three months from the written decision being given to the appellant[5]. The time limit may be extended by a tribunal chairman for special reasons[6]. There is no right of appeal against a chairman's decision on this, and judicial review would be the only method of challenging the decision[7]. Similar considerations would apply to a decision of a chairman to strike out proceedings for want of prosecution[8] or to give directions for the disposal of any purported appeal where he is satisfied that the tribunal does not have jurisdiction to entertain the appeal[9]. However, there are other decisions which do not carry a right of appeal but where there would be a tribunal decision which would carry a right of appeal, and in such cases the court would almost certainly refuse to consider judicial review of the initial decision. These would include the refusal of the chairman to postpone the hearing[10] and decisions in exercise of the chairman's power to determine the procedure at the tribunal[11].

The tribunal itself has certain procedural powers which do not carry a right of appeal, including the power to grant or refuse an adjournment, and the power to set aside a tribunal decision on certain grounds[12] and the exercise of these powers are in principle subject to challenge on judicial review.

1   In a series of cases commencing with the leading case of *R v Medical Appeal Tribunal, ex p Gilmore* [1957] 1 QB 574, sub nom *Re Gilmore's Application* [1957] 1 All ER 796, CA.
2   For example, *R v Preston SBAT, ex p Moore* [1975] 2 All ER 807, [1975] 1 WLR 624, CA.
3   *Chief Adjudication Officer v Foster* [1993] AC 754, [1993] 1 All ER 705, HL. Had this decision gone the other way then judicial review proceedings would have provided the only method of challenging the vires of a regulation.
4   Social Security Administration Act 1992 ss 23 (9)(a), (b), 34 (4), 48 (3)(a), (b) (40 Halsbury's Statutes (4th Edn) SOCIAL SECURITY).
5   Social Security (Adjudication) Regulations 1995, SI 1995/1801, reg 3 (as amended), Sch 2 (as amended) (18 Halsbury's Statutory Instruments (1997 Issue) SOCIAL SECURITY).
6   Social Security (Adjudication) Regulations 1995 reg 3 (3)(as substituted). An application for an extension of time which has been refused may not be renewed: Social Security (Adjudication) Regulations 1995 reg 3 (4). In practice such decisions are taken by the full–time chairmen appointed under the Social Security Administration Act 1992 s 51 (1)(b).
7   *White v Chief Adjudication Officer* [1986] 2 All ER 905, CA: the Court of Appeal held that there was no right of appeal against the decision of a commissioner to refuse an extension of time to appeal, but that such a decision could be challenged on judicial review if the commissioner failed to take into account some relevant consideration or had taken into account an irrelevant consideration or had made a perverse decision. See also *Bland v Chief Supplementary Benefit Officer* [1983] 1 All ER 537, [1983] 1 WLR 262, CA.
8   Social Security (Adjudication) Regulations 1995 reg 7 (as amended). On application by the party concerned the chairman may give leave to reinstate an appeal that has been struck out: Social Security (Adjudication) Regulations 1995 reg 7 (3)(as amended). It may be that the court would require such an application to have been made and refused before granting judicial review. For details of the national procedure for listing and striking out Social Security Appeal Tribunal appeals see Mesher *Income Related Benefits* (1992 Supp) p 11.
9   Social Security (Adjudication) Regulations 1995 reg 3 (7).

10 Social Security (Adjudication) Regulations 1995 reg 5 (1)(as substituted).
11 Social Security (Adjudication) Regulations 1995 reg 2 (1)(a).
12 Social Security (Adjudication) Regulations 1995 regs 5 (2)(as amended), 11.

114. Commissioners. As in the case of tribunals, so it is clear that in principle the decisions of the commissioners are subject to judicial review[1]. Similarly the courts were wary of questioning the expertise of the commissioners[2]. In 1980 a right of appeal from the commissioners to the Court of Appeal was established[3] and this further reduced the role of the divisional court[4].

The existence of a statutory right of appeal to the Court of Appeal against a decision of the commissioner means that such a course must usually be followed in preference to judicial review proceedings[5]. However, commissioners make procedural decisions, in a similar fashion to some of the decisions made by tribunal chairmen as discussed above. The Court of Appeal has held that a decision by a commissioner to refuse leave to appeal to a commissioner from the decision of a tribunal did not carry a right of appeal to the Court of Appeal and that the correct remedy in such a case was judicial review[6].

Commissioners are not required to give reasons for refusing to give leave to appeal to them[7], although they are free to do so. The Court of Appeal has declined to lay down a general principle that they should do so and held that refusal to do so is not in breach of the requirements of natural justice[8]. The onus is on an applicant for judicial review of a refusal of leave to show that the reasons were improper or insufficient or that there were no good grounds on which leave could be refused. If good grounds existed on which leave could have been refused, the court will assume that the decision was made on those grounds[9]. However, in an appropriate case judicial review will be granted to overturn a refusal of leave[10].

The effect of judicial review of a social security decision on other past decisions is unclear[11].

1 See, for example, *R v Deputy Industrial Injuries Comr, ex p Jones* [1962] 2 QB 677, [1962] 2 All ER 430; *R v National Insurance Comr, ex p Secretary of State for Social Services* [1981] 2 All ER 738, [1981] 1 WLR 1017, CA
2 *R v Industrial Injuries Comr, ex p AEU (No 2)* [1966] 2 QB 31, [1966] 1 All ER 97, CA; *R v National Insurance Comr, ex p Michael* [1977] 2 All ER 420, [1977] 1 WLR 109, CA. In *R v National Insurance Comr, ex p Stratton* [1979] QB 361, [1979] 2 All ER 278, CA, LORD DENNING MR took the view that the court should treat as binding the decision of a commissioner that has remained undisturbed for a long time, not amended by regulation, nor challenged by certiorari, and has been acted on by all concerned, and should only interfere in exceptional circumstances, such as where commissioners have made conflicting decisions. This approach has been approved by the House of Lords in *Presho v Insurance Officer* [1984] AC 310, [1984] 1 All ER 97 and by the Court of Appeal in *Cartlidge v Chief Adjudication Officer* [1986] QB 360, [1986] 2 All ER 1.
3 Social Security Act 1980 s 14 (repealed), Social Security Administration Act 1992 s 24 (40 Halsbury's Statutes (4th Edn) SOCIAL SECURITY).
4 In *R (SB) 52/83* a Tribunal of Commissioners stated obiter that divisional court rulings on applications for judicial review from the old Supplementary Benefit Appeal Tribunals (SBAT) are of persuasive authority only for the Commissioner since the Commissioners' jurisdiction in supplementary benefit cases replaced and is co-ordinate with that of the

divisional court. In *Chief Supplementary Benefit Officer v Leary* [1985] 1 All ER 1061, [1985] 1 WLR 84, CA, the Court of Appeal indorsed this view in relation to the brief period from 1978 to 1980 when there was a right of appeal from the SBAT to a single High Court judge but said that the commissioners were bound by the High Court when it was exercising its supervisory jurisdiction.
5   See Paragraph 130 post regarding "prior exhaustion".
6   *Bland v Chief Supplementary Benefit Officer* [1983] 1 All ER 537, [1983] 1 WLR 262, CA.
7   Social Security Commissioners Procedure Regulations 1987, SI 1987/214, reg 22 (1) (18 Halsbury's Statutory Instruments (1997 Issue) SOCIAL SECURITY). See, in contrast, the wording of Social Security Commissioners Procedure Regulations 1987 reg 22 (2).
8   *R v Secretary of State for Social Services, ex p Connolly* [1986] 1 All ER 998, [1986] 1 WLR 421, CA.
9   *R v Secretary of State for Social Services, ex p Connolly* [1986] 1 All ER 998, [1986] 1 WLR 421, CA. There is a general onus on an applicant for judicial review to disclose an arguable ground for relief, and if a judge grants leave to apply in the absence of such a ground, the leave should be set aside: *R v Social Security Comr, ex p Pattni* [1993] Fam Law 214, CA.
10 *R v Social Security Comr, ex p Akbar* [1991] COD 245.
11 Social Security Administration Act 1992 s 68. See discussion of this provision in Rowland *Medical and Disability Appeals Tribunals* (1993).

115. Social Fund. There have been a number of judicial review applications concerning the discretionary payments introduced in April 1988 which are payable out of the social fund. This was to be expected as there is no statutory appeal procedure, the fund is cash limited, and decisions are made in accordance with directions and guidance given by the Secretary of State[1] The Court of Appeal has come to the view, with some reluctance, that the Secretary of State's power in this respect is very wide and has declined to declare any of the directions to be ultra vires[2]. The Court of Appeal has also accepted that the Secretary of State has power to define the needs that are covered, that not all needs are covered, and that there is, therefore, power to exclude from provision certain categories of need[3]. There has been some discussion in the cases of the distinction between guidance and direction[4] and the court has stated that if there is any inconsistency between the two, the guidance would not necessarily be followed[5]. In the cases, the court has been prepared to consider the granting of judicial review remedies on the normal grounds but has also been influenced by the consideration that the social fund inspectors are an independent body of experts.

1   Social Security Contributions and Benefits Act 1992 s 140 (40 Halsbury's Statutes (4th Edn) SOCIAL SECURITY).
2   *R v Secretary of State for Social Security, ex p Stitt* [1991] COD 68, [1991] 3 Admin LR 169.
3   *R v Social Fund Inspector and Secretary of State for Social Security, ex p Healey, Stitt (No 2), Ellison* [1992] COD 335, CA.
4   See Buck [1993] Journal of Social Welfare and Family Law 162–3.
5   *R v Social Fund Inspector, ex p Ali* [1993] COD 263, (1992) Times, 25 November.

E: PRE-REQUISITES AND OBSTACLES

1: OUSTER AND FINALITY CLAUSES

116. Introduction. The old writ of certiorari was used historically to control the statutory powers of administrative bodies, especially local justices of the peace, and especially from the early 18th century. The courts often exercised the power to issue certiorari pedantically, being very ready to find fault with the procedure or the formalities of local administrative bodies. This was often politically and administratively inconvenient for the government, and the practice developed of inserting into legislation various kinds of finality or no-certiorari clauses to protect administrative decision making from the close scrutiny of the courts.

Traditionally, a distinction had been drawn between two types of error that could be made by an official body. The first was where a body made a decision that it simply never had the right to make, one that was outside its jurisdiction or ultra vires. This was sometimes referred to as a jurisdictional error and was often said to be void ab initio. The second type of error was where a body had the general power to make such a decision but made an error in a particular case and its decision was subject to reversal. This was sometimes referred to as an error within jurisdiction and was treated as voidable, but valid until it had been reversed.

The no-certiorari clauses referred to above were held by the courts not to apply to ultra vires decisions, when the ability of the court to issue certiorari was unaffected, but they did apply to errors within jurisdiction, where the power of the court to issue certiorari was effectively removed[1].

1   For a summary of these developments see Wade and Forsyth *Administrative Law* (7th edn, 1994) especially pages 726–742. See also *R v Nat Bell Liquors Ltd* [1922] 2 AC 128, PC.

117. Finality clauses. Various forms of words other than no-certiorari clauses were used to try to exclude the courts from interfering with administrative decisions. The courts dealt with some of these as they arose. It was held that a provision that "a decision shall be final" merely means that there is no appeal on the facts and does not exclude what would now be referred to as judicial review[1]. An order which was to operate "as if enacted by parliament" could still be reviewed for conformity to the parent Act[2].

1   *R v Medical Appeal Tribunal, ex p Gilmore* [1957] 1 QB 574, sub nom Re Gilmore's Aplication [1957] 1 All ER 796; *Tehrani v Rostron* [1972] 1 QB 182, [1971] 3 All ER 790, CA.
2   *Minister of Health v R, ex p Yaffé* [1931] AC 494, HL.

118. Ouster clauses before Anisminic[1]. A majority decision of the House of Lords on a no-certiorari clause, however, did provoke concern and led to legislation. In *Smith v East Elloe RDC*[2] there was a provision that a compulsory purchase order could be challenged by a person aggrieved on grounds of ultra vires or procedural irregularity within six weeks but otherwise "shall not ... be questioned in any legal proceedings whatsoever". This was held to exclude review after the six week period even where the challenge was based on bad faith or fraud. There are many such provisions in planning legislation[3] and their effectiveness to exclude review was raised again in subsequent cases.

However, Section 11 of the Tribunals and Inquiries Act 1958[4] was passed, which is now in effect re-enacted as Section 12 of the Tribunals and Inquiries Act 1992[5] and provides that:
1. any provision in an Act passed before 1 August 1958 that any order or determination shall not be called into question in any court; or
2. any provision in such an Act which by similar words excludes any of the powers of the High Court;

shall not have effect so as to prevent the removal of the proceedings into the High Court by order of certiorari or to prejudice the powers of the High Court to make orders of mandamus.

That dealt with the problem of ouster clauses up to that point, but there have been many such clauses enacted since 1958 which have been discussed in the courts, and the 1958 Act created a specific exception from the operation of Section 11 for the Foreign Compensation Commission[6].

1 *Anisminic Ltd v Foreign Compensation Commission* [1969] 2 AC 147, [1969] 1 All ER 208, HL.
2 *Smith v East Elloe RDC* [1956] AC 736, [1956] 1 All ER 855, HL.
3 For example, the Town and Country Planning Act 1990 ss 284, 288 (3) (46 Halsbury's Statutes (4th Edn) TOWN AND COUNTRY PLANNING).
4 Tribunals and Inquiries Act 1958 s 11 (repealed).
5 Tribunals and Inquiries Act 1992 s 12 (10 Halsbury's Statutes (4th Edn) CONSTITUTIONAL LAW).
6 Established by the Foreign Compensation Act 1950 (10 Halsbury's Statutes (4th Edn) CONSTITUTIONAL LAW). The exception was created in the Tribunals and Inquiries Act 1958 s 11 (3)(repealed). The current exceptions are now contained in the Tribunals and Inquiries Act 1992 s 12 (3).

119. The effect of the Anisminic Case[1]. The Foreign Compensation Act 1950 provided that any determination by the Commission "shall not be called into question in any court of law"[2]. The plaintiffs had applied unsuccessfully for compensation and argued that the Commission had misconstrued the law by wrongly interpreting the meaning of "successor in title". The House of Lords held[3] that the Commission had made an error of law and that therefore there was no "determination" and therefore the ouster clause did not operate to exclude review[4]. It was not clear what kind of error operated to prevent a purported determination being a valid determination. It clearly applied when there was an error of law, and Lord Reid also applied the doctrine to breach of the rules of natural justice, taking into account irrelevant considerations, and the presence of bad faith by the decision maker. It was not clear that all of their Lordships went that far, but these are issues that remain to be tested in the courts. Without defining what he meant by an error of law, in a subsequent House of Lords case[5] Lord Diplock said that the *Anisminic* decision meant that, "... as respects administrative tribunal and authorities, the old distinction between errors of law that went to jurisdiction and errors of law that did not was for practical purposes abolished. Any error of law that could be shown to have been made by them in the course of reaching their decision on matters of fact or of administrative policy would result in their having asked themselves the wrong question with the result that the decision they reached would be a nullity".

It is clear that this approach does not apply to decisions of a High Court or county court judge[6]. However, it is not always clear what is included as an administrative tribunal or authority. It does seem to include magistrates' courts[7] as well as coroners' courts[8]. However, by a three to two majority the House of Lords has decided that judicial review will not lie against a university visitor unless the visitor acts outside jurisdiction or in breach of the rules of natural justice; there is no jurisdiction to review the visitor's construction of the university's statutes[9]. Although this case did not involve a statutory ouster clause the distinction between an error of law and a jurisdictional error made by the majority of their Lordships seems to fly in the face of the *Anisminic* and *Racal* decisions[10].

In a case which is consistent with those decisions, the Court of Appeal has distinguished between a true ouster clause and a provision excluding challenge to an item of evidence[11].

The effectiveness of time-limit ouster clauses has also been upheld[12] and, to the extent that there is any conflict on this point between the *East Elloe* and the *Anisminic* cases, the former prevails except that the possibility of precluding the operation of a time-limit ouster clause where there is bad faith has been left open[13].

Parliament has continued to create ouster clauses[14] but, apart from the Foreign Compensation Act 1969[15] has not used the formulation "purported" or "apparent" decision which, as one commentator has said, "would be likely to exclude the court's jurisdiction save at the price of a departure from all our accepted canons of statutory construction"[16].

1 *Anisminic Ltd v Foreign Compensation Commission* [1969] 2 AC 147, [1969] 1 All ER 208, HL.
2 Foreign Compensation Act 1950 s 4 (4)(repealed).
3 *Anisminic Ltd v Foreign Compensation Commission* [1969] 2 AC 147, [1969] 1 All ER 208, HL.
4 The Foreign Compensation Act 1969 (10 Halsbury's Statutes (4th Edn) CONSTITUTIONAL LAW) attempts to restore the original policy of the 1950 Act by providing in the Foreign Compensation Act 1969 s 3 (3) that "determination" includes a provisional determination and anything which purports to be a determination. This formulation has not been tested in the courts.
5 *Re Racal Communications Ltd* [1981] AC 374 at 380, [1980] 2 All ER 634 at 638, 639, HL. LORD KEITH agreed with LORD DIPLOCK. The rest of their Lordships did not deal with this point. The Privy Council case of *South East Asia Fire Bricks Sdn Bhd v Non-Metallic Mineral Products Manufacturing Employees Union* [1981] AC 363, [1980] 2 All ER 689, PC, was decided nine days earlier and can be seen as contradicting this approach but most commentators have supported LORD DIPLOCK'S approach. For a fuller discussion see Supperstone and Goudie *Judicial Review* 2nd edn, (1997) ch 4.
6 That was the issue in *Re Racal Communications Ltd* [1981] AC 374, [1980] 2 All ER 634, HL.
7 *Re McC (a minor)* [1985] AC 528, sub nom *McC v Mullan* [1984] 3 All ER 908, HL; *R v Manchester City Magistrates' Court, ex p Davies* [1989] QB 631, [1989] 1 All ER 90, CA.
8 *R v Greater Manchester Coroner, ex p Tal* [1985] QB 67, [1984] 3 All ER 240.
9 *R v Lord President of the Privy Council, ex p Page* [1993] AC 682 [1993] 1 All ER 97, HL.
10 LORD MUSTILL and LORD SLYNN dissenting would have held that judicial review does lie against the visitor for error of law within jurisdiction. It might be possible to reconcile the majority decision with *Anisminic Ltd v Foreign Compensation Commission* [1969] 2 AC 147, [1969] 1 All ER 208, HL and *Re Racal Communications Ltd* [1981] AC 374, [1980]

2 All ER 634, HL by arguing that the visitor is a judge rather than an administrative authority. In this case the visitor was HM The Queen on whose behalf the Lord President dealt with the matter after taking advice from LORD JAUNCEY OF TULLICHETTLE, a Lord of Appeal in Ordinary. LORD GRIFFITHS delivering his opinion said that "I do not regard a judge who makes what an appellate court later regards as a mistake of law as abusing his powers ... he is exercising them to the best of his ability albeit some other court thinks he was mistaken" (at 100). It is not clear why the same argument should not apply to members of the judiciary sitting in inferior tribunals although LORD GRIFFITHS did point out that the visitor is either a person holding a high judicial office or is advised by such a person.

11 *R v Registrar of Companies, ex p Esal (Commodities) Ltd* [1986] QB 1114, [1986] 1 All ER 105. The Companies Act 1948 s 92 (2) had provided that "the certificate of registering a charge shall be conclusive evidence that the requirements ... as to registration have been complied with".

12 Tribunals and Inquiries Act 1992 s 12 (1) (10 Halsbury's Statutes (4th Edn) CONSTITUTIONAL LAW) also excludes time limited application provisions from the repeal of pre-August 1958 ouster clauses.

13 *Ostler v Secretary of State for the Environment* [1977] 1 WLR 258, HL; *R v Cornwall County Council, ex p Huntingdon* [1992] 3 All ER 566. In the latter the Divisional Court rejected the argument that there were degrees of invalidity or different grounds of jurisdictional error and that only non-fundamental errors were immune from review.

14 For example, British Nationality Act 1981 s 44 (2) (31 Halsbury's Statutes (4th Edn) NATIONALITY AND IMMIGRATION); Interception of Communications Act 1985 s 7 (8) (34 Halsbury's Statutes (4th Edn) POST OFFICE); Security Service Act 1989 s 5 (4) (10 Halsbury's Statutes (4th Edn) SOCIAL SECURITY).

15 See note 4 above.

16 See Supperstone and Goudie *Judicial Review* 2nd edn, (1997) ch 4.

2: LOCUS STANDI

120. Introduction. Applicants for judicial review must have a "sufficient interest"[1] in the matter to which the application relates in order to get leave to apply, and before they may be granted final relief[2]. An applicant's connection with a public law decision might range from his being directly addressed and affected by it to his being merely intellectually interested in it as a nice point of administrative law theory. The issue of standing is a question of mixed fact and law[3], and probably judicial discretion as well. The requirement is not defined further either by the Rules of the Supreme Court 1965 or Section 31 (3) of the Supreme Court Act 1981, but it is generally considered that the pre-1977 case law concerning this issue is of less relevance now that the Rules refer to a single requirement of interest, regardless of the remedy being sought[4]. The future development of the law of standing will depend upon judicial views about the nature of administrative law and the role of the courts.

1 In private law actions, an element of locus standi is generally one of the constituents which the plaintiff must prove in order to recover damages, for example, in contract, the rules of privity prevent persons from bringing proceedings on contracts to which they were not parties and in tort, the plaintiff must be found to come within the scope of the duty of care owed by the defendant. In public law there is more judicial discretion at work in the development of the law relating to locus standi and the question goes to the jurisdiction of the court, rather than merely to the prospects of success of the claim. See generally, Schiemann J "Locus Standi" [1990] PL 342 and P Cane: "Statutes, Standing and Representation" [1990] PL 307.

2   The court shall not grant leave unless it considers the applicant has sufficient interest in the matter to which the application relates: RSC Ord 53 r 3 (7). No application for judicial review shall be made unless the leave of the High Court has been obtained in accordance with the rules of court, and the court shall not grant leave to make such an application unless it considers that the applicant has a sufficient interest in the matter to which the application relates: Supreme Court Act 1981 s 31 (3) (11 Halsbury's Statutes (4th Edn) COURTS AND LEGAL SERVICES).

3   Per LORD WILBERFORCE in *IRC v National Federation of Self Employed and Small Businesses* [1982] AC 617, [1981] 2 All ER 93, HL.

4   See Wade and Forsyth *Administrative Law* (7th edn, 1994) pp 696-718. In *IRC v National Federation of Self Employed and Small Businesses* [1982] AC 617, [1981] 2 All ER 93, HL, LORDS DIPLOCK, SCARMAN and ROSKILL thought, obiter, that this was the case post-1977. LORD FRASER was less sure: "I do not think it can have had the effect of throwing over all the older law and of leaving the grant of judicial review in the uncontrolled discretion of the court". In *R v Felixstowe Justices, ex p Leigh* [1987] QB 582, [1987] 1 All ER 551 a journalist established locus for a declaration against the magistrates' policy of non-disclosure of the names of the presiding JPs but was said to lack locus for mandamus. However, his purposes were served by the declaration and he had no need to know the names of the justices of the peace in the specific case. It had been suggested that since mandamus requires public bodies to perform positive actions, often involving expenditure, the court will inevitably look for a stronger interest on the part of the applicant in such cases. Pre-1977 cases establishing locus based on particular facts will still be helpful by analogy to practitioners in support of their contentions.

121. The type of interest that will suffice. Under the old law, the prerogative remedies were granted more freely, in terms of locus standi, than the traditionally private law remedies of injunction and declaration. Within the prerogative group, the test was stricter for mandamus than for certiorari and prohibition. Moral[1], proprietary and more and less direct financial interests have all been considered with regard to the "sufficient interest" test[2]. In the latter part of the 1980s and early 1990s judges tended to construe the statute concerned, if any, to see if persons such as the applicant were apprehended by the scope of the duty, in much the same way as is done when the issue arises as to whether breach of a statutory duty gives rise to a civil right of action[3]. If so, then locus standi will be accorded. Sometimes, however, the court will conclude that the wording of the duty in question was not intended to give individuals or even groups of persons a right to challenge its existence or performance by way of review (or indeed, by private law action)[4]. Commentators have split the cases up into those involving taxpayers[5], ratepayers, etc but since the determination of standing still depends to some extent on the merits and statutory context of the case, the utility of such classification is limited.

1   See, for example, *R v Greater London Council, ex p Blackburn* [1976] 3 All ER 184, [1976] 1 WLR 550, CA (a pre-reform case) where Mr Blackburn's interest merely as a parent and a citizen attracted standing, per LORD DENNING MR, and Mrs Blackburn's interest as a ratepayer satisfied STEPHENSON LJ.

2   For example, *R v Legal Aid Board, ex p Bateman* [1992] 3 All ER 490, [1992] 1 WLR 711 where it was held that a client's moral interest in seeing her solicitors properly remunerated by the Legal Aid Board for having successfully represented her was insufficient to give her locus to apply for review of the board's determination of fees payable to the solicitors. In this case the court was plainly concerned that the more obvious applicant, the firm itself, was hiding behind the client's application, which was itself legally aided. Although this did not make the client a "busybody", she stood to gain nothing but satisfaction from her application. SCHIEMANN J in *R v Secretary of State for the Environment, ex p Rose Theatre Trust Co* [1990] 1 QB 504, [1990] 1 All ER 754 laid down

that it was not necessary to have a direct financial interest in a decision. In *R v Department of Transport, ex p Presvac Engineering Ltd* (1991) Times, 10 July, CA, the court considered the business interests of trade competitors with respect to the issue of locus of one to challenge the procedure followed for another company's product testing by a public body. It held that locus in such a case could rarely be denied. In *R v Barnet LBC, ex p Pardes House School Ltd* [1989] EGCS 64 a tenderer was given locus to challenge a decision to remove it from the list of tenderers for a local authority contract. Yet in *R v Tower Hamlets LBC, ex p Thrasyvalou* (1990) 23 HLR 38 the financial interest of an hotelier in remaining on a list of hostels used by a local authority for placement of the homeless was held to be insufficient for the establishment of locus standi. In *R v Independent Broadcasting Authority, ex p Whitehouse* (1985) Times, 4 April, CA, a TV licence holder had locus to challenge the IBA's passing of certain programmes even though the BBC were the recipients of the licence revenue. In *R v HM Treasury, ex p Smedley* [1985] QB 657, [1985] 1 All ER 589, CA, a taxpayer acquired locus to challenge the legality of government expenditure; in *R v A-G, ex p ICI* (1987) 60 TC 1, CA, a taxpayer was granted locus to challenge the Revenue's method of valuing its rival's profits. In *R v Poole Borough Council, ex p Beebee* [1991] JPL 643 a wildlife society was granted locus on the basis that it had expended money over a long period on the site in which it was concerned, and also that the local authority had specifically referred to consultation with the society as a condition of the grant of planning permission. These two facts gave rise to locus to challenge the authority's decision not to conduct an environmental impact assessment.

3   It might be contended that if it is merely the existence or application of a statutory duty to a given situation that is in dispute, (and not the manner of the exercise of a discretion under an admitted duty to exercise it) there is no reason why an individual should not simply bring a private law action for a declaration as to their rights, regardless of the procedural divide between public and private law. In *R v Secretary of State for Defence, ex p Sancto* [1993] COD 144, (1992) Times, 9 September the court emphasised that public law proceedings could only be brought in respect of private law rights or legitimate expectations, and since the applicants could not point to any recognised private "right to know" in the UK, they were not entitled to challenge the Department's refusal to let them have sight of a report into their son's death, even though that decision was substantively "outrageous", according to the judge.

4   See *R v Secretary of State for the Environment, ex p Rose Theatre Trust Co* [1990] 1 QB 504, [1990] 1 All ER 754. Consider the extent to which this test is appropriate: it could be argued that it merely goes to the amenability of review of certain decisions or actions. In *Gregory v Camden LBC* [1966] 2 All ER 196, [1966] 1 WLR 899, PAULL J reasoned directly by analogy with private law for the determination of standing to challenge a grant of planning permission, and found there was no legal right to do so on the part of a neighbour. Cane argues that it is a non-sequitur to infer from the standing arguments pertaining to private law actions for public nuisance that the same test should be used for access to public law proceedings: "The Function of Standing Rules in Administrative Law" [1980] PL 303. In *R v Secretary of State for the Environment, ex p Ward* [1984] 2 All ER 556, [1984] 1 WLR 834, WOOLF LJ determined that a gypsy deserved locus standi to challenge a failure to direct local authorities to provide caravan sites, on the basis that the authorities suggesting that no duties were owed under the legislation to gypsies as a class or individually were derived from private law, and were thus irrelevant. See also Supperstone and Goudie *Judicial Review* 2nd edn, (1997) Chs 15, 16.

5   As a matter of general principle one taxpayer does not have sufficient interest to complain of the way in which another's affairs are treated, but in exceptional cases a public spirited citizen would not be shut out: *IRC v National Federation of Self Employed and Small Businesses* [1982] AC 617, [1981] 2 All ER 93, HL, by a majority. See also *R v A-G, ex p ICI plc* (1987) 60 TC 1, CA, regarding sufficiency of interest to challenge the Revenue's treatment of business rivals;and *R v HM Treasury, ex p Smedley* [1985] QB 657, [1985] 1 All ER 589, CA, where even though the applicant could not claim a personal interest, there was no-one else who could have asserted a better claim, in respect of a serious issue raised by his application, thereby justifying the grant of locus. See *R v Somerset County Council and ARC Southern Ltd, ex p Dixon* [1997] COD 323, [1997] NPC 61 for a consideration of the authorities on standing and sufficient interest.

122. Statutory locus standi. Certain bodies enjoy locus standi under statutory provisions informing their general powers to bring legal proceedings[1]. The courts have tended to construe specific statutory provisions restrictively[2].

1 For example, local authorities have power to bring proceedings which they consider to be expedient for the promotion or protection of the interests of the inhabitants of their area: Local Government Act 1972 s 222 (25 Halsbury's Statutes (4th Edn) LOCAL GOVERNMENT). This provision has been liberally interpreted: *Solihull Metropolitan Borough Council v Maxfern Ltd* [1977] 2 All ER 177, [1977] 1 WLR 127. The Equal Opportunities Commission and the Commission for Racial Equality have a statutory right to bring proceedings under the Sex Discrimination Act 1975 and the Race Relations Act 1976 (6 Halsbury's Statutes (4th Edn) CIVIL RIGHTS AND LIBERTIES) respectively but see *R v Secretary of State for Defence, ex p Equal Opportunities Commission* [1992] COD 276 (1992) Independent, 27 February where it was held that no locus existed to challenge the validity of an RAF internal order on the grounds it was contrary to EEC law, because the proper channel for such a point was a claim by someone actually affected by the order, where the European Court of Justice could determine the question if necessary on a reference. *R v Secretary of State for Employment, ex p Equal Opportunities Commission* [1993] 1 All ER 1022, [1993] 1 WLR 872, CA, explored inconclusively the question whether the Equal Opportunities Commission does possess standing in judicial review cases (compare the approaches of DILLON LJ and KENNEDY LJ), but also decided that the procedure was inappropriate to challenge the minister's view that he was not in breach of any community law obligation relating to part-time workers. For the Divisional Court's judgment see [1992] 1 All ER 545.
2 *Wallesey Local Board v Gracey* (1887) 36 Ch D 593.

123. Inadequate locus standi. A corporate body cannot acquire standing simply by way of including a power to pursue a particular object in its memorandum of association. Parties cannot agree between themselves that the locus test is met, because the question of locus goes to the jurisdiction of the court[1].

1 Per WOOLF LJ in *R v Secretary of State for Social Services, ex p Child Poverty Action Group* [1990] 2 QB 540, [1989] 1 All ER 1047, CA.

124. Locus standi of associations or groups of individuals[1]. Whilst it is presently clear that a number of persons, none of whom would qualify as having locus standi individually, cannot simply band together and claim locus by force of numbers[2], charities or bodies in the public eye for other reasons, have acquired locus standi before the courts[3].

1 The Law Commission considers that group actions can be seen in one of three ways: groups whose members are personally affected by the impugned decision; groups which exist for the benefit of persons not able or inclined to bring test cases, but whose members are not personally affected by the decision, and groups to whom statute lends locus standi for specific purposes. The commission recommended that unincorporated associations should be permitted to make an application through a member in a representative capacity where the court is satisfied that the members of the association have been or would be adversely affected or are raising an issue of public interest warranting judicial review and the members of the association are appropriate persons to bring the challenge: *Administrative Law: Judicial Review and Statutory Appeals* (Law Com no 226) (1994).

2   See *R v Secretary of State for the Environment, ex p Rose Theatre Trust Co* [1990] 1 QB 504, [1990] 1 All ER 754.
3   In *R v Secretary of State for Social Services, ex p Child Poverty Action Group* [1990] 2 QB 540, [1989] 1 All ER 1047, CA, the CPAG was accorded locus to challenge the minister under the Social Security Act 1975 ss 98, 99 (repealed) for failure to appoint sufficient adjudication officers and to refer cases to them. The case was lost on the substantive point but the Court of Appeal emphasised that the locus point was not merely academic and that in this case the CPAG would have been granted locus had it been an issue. The Royal College of Nursing was able to challenge the legality of a circular concerning abortion in *Royal College of Nursing of the United Kingdom v Department of Health and Social Security* [1981] AC 800, [1981] 1 All ER 545, HL. See also *Covent Garden Community Association Ltd v GLC* [1981] JPL 183; *R v Hammersmith and Fulham LBC, ex p People Before Profit Ltd* (1981) 80 LGR 322; *R v HM Inspectorate of Pollution, ex p Greenpeace Ltd (No 2)* [1994] 4 All ER 329, [1994] 2 CMLR 548; *R v Secretary of State for Foreign Affairs, ex p World Development Movement* [1995] 1 All ER 611, [1995] 1 WLR 386; *R v Secretary of State for Employment, ex p Equal Opportunities Commission* [1995] 1 AC 1, [1994] 1 All ER 910. The Building Employers' Federation was given locus to challenge draft clauses in local authority contracts in *R v Islington LBC, ex p Building Employers' Confederation* (1989) 45 BLR 45 but compare with *Scottish Old People's Welfare Council ("Age Concern"), Petitioners* 1987 SLT 179. The court has not approached the standing of unincorporated associations uniformly: compare *R v Darlington Borough Council, ex p Association of Darlington Taxi Owners* [1994] COD 424; *R v London Borough of Tower Hamlets, ex p Tower Hamlets Combined Traders Association* [1994] COD 325 and *R v North Western Traffic Comrs, ex p Brake* [1996] COD 248.

125. The relevance of the strength of the case. Where there is a serious issue to be tried, the courts will inevitably be less concerned with precedent on the issue of locus standi[1]. In the *IRC v National Federation of Self Employed and Small Businesses* case[2], the House of Lords confirmed the relevance of locus standi even at the substantive inter partes hearing, and said that a prima facie conclusion as to the applicant's locus may alter in the light of further evidence that may be revealed to the court at the full hearing. The court also said that at the full hearing it was undesirable for the issue of locus to be considered as a preliminary issue, so the strength of the substantive points must be of some continued relevance to the final decision as to locus. It may be that the ground chosen for the application for review may bear upon the extent of locus required[3].

1   For example, in *R v Metropolitan Police Comr, ex p Blackburn* [1968] 2 QB 118, [1968] 1 All ER 763, CA, and *R v Metropolitan Police Comr, ex p Blackburn (No 3)* [1973] QB 241, [1973] 1 All ER 324, CA, it was not denied that an individual might have locus to challenge a police policy as to the types of crime to be pursued by a force.
2   *IRC v National Federation of Self Employed and Small Businesses* [1982] AC 617, [1981] 2 All ER 93, HL.
3   For instance, if procedural impropriety is the main ground for review in a particular case, the court may not accord locus to anyone other than the party who suffered the effects of the defect, but if illegality is raised, perhaps as to a tribunal's analysis of a jurisdictional question that might affect other people in the future, then a weaker connection than actually having been affected by a tribunal decision might suffice for locus standi.

126. Locus standi – a two stage test? Locus has traditionally been seen as a threshold test at the leave stage, when the court only has the applicant's contentions before it[1] but the *IRC* case[2] made it clear that it would also be considered at the inter partes hearing at the point of the granting of relief to a successful applicant. At this point, consideration of locus is best seen as an aspect of the discretionary nature of the remedies[3] in public law, and should not be dealt with by way of a preliminary point at that stage. However it has been stated that locus is not merely a question of judicial discretion[4] and it will rarely be used as the sole basis for a denial of a remedy at the substantive hearing, if the applicant has made out his substantive ground for review.

1 As to the circumstances in which it might be prudent to invite the respondent to the leave hearing, see Paragraph 141 post.
2 IRC v National Federation of Self Employed and Small Businesses [1982] AC 617, [1981] 2 All ER 93, HL.
3 In R v Monopolies and Mergers Commission, ex p Argyll Group plc [1986] 2 All ER 257, [1986] 1 WLR 763, CA, DONALDSON MR thought that the strength of the applicant's interest was a factor to be weighed in the exercise of the discretion to grant a remedy, in the light of the purpose of the administrative process in question in the case.
4 By SIR THOMAS BINGHAM in "Should Public Law Remedies be Discretionary?" [1991] PL 64.

127. The future of locus standi. On the one hand commentators have identified the introduction of a generous and public-interest oriented doctrine of standing since the *IRC* case[1] (an "open" system), but on the other, it has been asserted that the statutory wording of the locus test would be deprived of any meaning if every member of the public could complain of every breach of duty by every decision maker, and that public law in this country is still fundamentally about the vindication and remedying of private law concerns (a "closed" system). The Law Commission has recommended reform of locus standi[2].

1 IRC v National Federation of Self Employed and Small Businesses [1982] AC 617, [1981] 2 All ER 93, HL.
2 Administrative Law: Judicial Review and Statutory Appeals (Law Com no 226) (1994).

3: TIME LIMITS

128. Time limits. The applicant must always bear in mind the requirement of the Rules of the Supreme Court 1965 that an application for judicial review must be made promptly, and in any event within three months from the date when the grounds for the application first arose[1]. Therefore, even when a challenge is made within the three month period, the court may hold that it is out of time[2]. This is particularly so where third parties may have committed themselves to expenditure on the strength of the decision[3].

Further, where the court considers that there has been undue delay in making the application for judicial review (meaning the application for leave), the court may refuse to grant leave for making the application, or any relief sought on the application, if it considers that the granting of the relief sought would cause substantial hardship to, or substantially prejudice the rights of, any person or would be detrimental to good administration[4].

The applicant must include any reasons for delay in the appropriate section of RSC Appendix A Form No 86A. However, not all delays must be explained in the RSC Appendix A Form No 86A; it is a question of degree. Nevertheless, there will be some cases within the three month limit in which the applicant should set out the reasons why delay has occurred; for example, where time is of the essence in relation to the implementation of the decision sought to be challenged[5].

The court has power to grant leave to apply despite the fact that the application is late. It will do so by extending the period for applying[6]. The judge will rarely have the necessary materials to consider the issues of hardship, prejudice or detriment on an ex parte application for leave and even on an inter partes application will probably confine considerations of delay to questions of good reasons for extending the period[7]. Therefore, even where the judge on the application for leave has been persuaded to extend the period and grant leave, the court at the substantive hearing can consider issues of hardship, prejudice and detriment to good administration. Providing no prejudice has been caused, the court will not wish to apply the time limit provisions in a technical manner[8]. For example, the period was extended where the applicant had had problems with legal aid[9].

Where the relief sought is directed at restraining the future implementation of an allegedly unlawful policy, the court may extend the time for making application, even though the policy has been in place for as long as three years[10]. If the policy is unlawful, prima facie it ought to be discontinued, and arguments by a respondent based on delay will not be well received. If there has been delay, and the court would not otherwise be minded to grant leave, nevertheless if the matters raised are of general public importance, it would be a wrong exercise of discretion to reject the application on grounds of delay, leaving the substantive issues unresolved[11].

Where the applicant wishes to apply for mandamus to require a public body to perform a duty, then it will be possible to start time running by a letter seeking performance within a stated time; failure to perform within that time will be treated as a refusal, giving rise to grounds for judicial review (and marking the start of the three month period for application).

1   RSC Ord 53 r 4 (1).
2   *Re Friends of the Earth Ltd* [1988] JPL 93, CA, application one day within the period.
3   *R v Independent Television Commission, ex p TV NI Ltd* (1991) Times, 30 December, CA.
4   Supreme Court Act 1981 s 31 (6) (11 Halsbury's Statutes (4th Edn) COURTS AND LEGAL SERVICES).
5   RSC Appendix A Form No 86A; *R v Greenwich London Borough Council, ex p Governors of John Ball Primary School* [1990] COD 103; affd [1990] Fam Law 469, CA.
6   *R v Stratford-on-Avon District Council, ex p Jackson* [1985] 3 All ER 769, [1985] 1 WLR 1319, CA; *Caswell v Dairy Produce Quota Tribunal* [1990] 2 AC 738, [1990] 2 All ER 434, HL.
7   *Caswell v Dairy Produce Quota Tribunal* [1990] 2 AC 738, [1990] 2 All ER 434, HL, per LORD GOFF.
8   *R v Comr for Local Administration, ex p Croydon London Borough Council* [1989] 1 All ER 1033.
9   *R v Stratford-on-Avon District Council, ex p Jackson* [1985] 3 All ER 769, [1985] 1 WLR 1319, CA.
10 *R v City of Westminster, ex p Hilditch* [1990] COD 434.
11 *R v Secretary of State for the Home Department, ex p Ruddock* [1987] 2 All ER 518, [1987] 1 WLR 1482.

4: THE NEED FOR PRIOR EXHAUSTION OF OTHER REMEDIES

129. Introduction. The discretionary nature of the grant of relief on application for judicial review is well established[1]. One basis for the discretionary refusal of relief is that there is an alternative remedy available to the applicant which has not been exhausted[2]. It is, however, clear that the mere existence of an alternative remedy does not preclude relief, and the exercise of any rights under an alternative procedure does not imply a waiver of any right to seek judicial review[3]. On the other hand, a failure to exercise a statutory right of appeal will not inevitably deprive an applicant of such a right[4].

1 On discretion in connection with this topic see Supperstone and Goudie *Judicial Review* 2nd edn, (1997) pp 15-26.
2 There is a similar although more rigidly applied rule imposed before a remedy can be obtained under the European Convention on Human Rights art 26 of the convention. For procedure see Vol 17 (1997 Issue) title EUROPEAN COURTS.
3 *Ridge v Baldwin* [1964] AC 40, [1963] 2 All ER 66, HL, reversing the Court of Appeal on this point.
4 See, for example, *Cooper v Wilson* [1937] 2 KB 309, [1937] 2 All ER 726, CA.

130. The exhaustion rule. The normal rule is that an applicant for judicial review should first exhaust whatever other rights he has by way of appeal[1]. Lord Scarman has said, "... a remedy by way of judicial review is not to be made available where an alternative remedy exists. This is a proposition of great importance. Where Parliament has provided by statute appeal procedures ... it will only be very rarely that the courts will allow the collateral process of judicial review to be used to attack an appealable decision"[2].

This approach can work harshly. For example, in immigration cases the statutory appeals procedure must be used before making an application for judicial review, in the absence of exceptional circumstances, even when the applicant must leave the country in order to appeal[3].

The absence of damages as a remedy in appeal proceedings is not in itself a ground for allowing an application for judicial review to be made[4].

In one case judicial review was refused where the applicant had invoked an alternative appeal procedure but had, on legal advice, abandoned it[5]. Judicial review has also been refused where an applicant who wanted to challenge a decision on the basis of a judge's misconduct was entitled to appeal to the divisional court of the Chancery Division[6] and where a dismissed civil servant could obtain redress in Industrial Tribunal proceedings[7].

May LJ provided one of the reasons for the usual approach of the courts to this issue in a case concerning the appeals procedure from the Attendance Allowance Board, when he said, "In my view, when Parliament has provided for an appellate structure, the High Court should be very slow to intervene before the statutory machinery for appeals has been exhausted, it should do so, if at all, only for the purpose of ensuring that in an appropriate case this procedure is followed in accordance with the law. If the High Court were to make an order quashing a decision reached at an intermediate level in this appellate structure, it would almost inevitably be interfering with the statutory machinery"[8].

1   R v Chief Constable of the Merseyside Police, ex p Calveley [1986] QB 424 at 431, [1986] 1 All ER 257 at 263, CA, per MAY LJ.
2   Re Preston [1985] AC 835, sub nom Preston v IRC [1985] 2 All ER 327 at 330, HL. See also R v Epping and Harlow General Comrs, ex p Goldstraw [1983] 3 All ER 257; R v Special Educational Needs Tribunal, ex p Fairpo [1996] COD 180, [1996] ELR 213; and R v Secretary of State for the Home Department, ex p Capti-Mehmet [1997] COD 61.
3   R v Secretary of State for the Home Department, ex p Swati [1986] 1 All ER 717, [1986] 1 WLR 477, CA.
4   Wandsworth London Borough Council v Orakpo (1986) 19 HLR 57, CA.
5   R v Secretary of State for the Home Office, ex p Attiror (1987) Independent, 23 October, CA.
6   R v Croydon County Court, ex p Watson (1987) Times, 18 March, CA.
7   R v Civil Service Appeal Board, ex p Bruce [1989] 2 All ER 907, [1989] ICR 171, CA.
8   R v Secretary of State for Social Services, ex p Connolly [1986] 1 All ER 998, [1986] 1 WLR 421, CA.

131. When exhaustion is not required. In practice, the rule is not imposed quite as rigorously as the above might suggest. Even if the High Court should be "very slow to intervene", it does seem that where a decision is liable to be upset as a matter of law because it is "clearly made without jurisdiction or in consequence of an error of law" then this would be a proper case to go for certiorari (and presumably for judicial review in general) even in a planning case in which there is a statutory appeal to the Secretary of State and a further right of appeal to the High Court on a question of law[1]. Similar views have been expressed in cases involving habeas corpus and immigration appeals[2].

Where the Social Security Commissioner refused leave to appeal against a tribunal decision, and refused leave to appeal against the refusal of leave, the Court of Appeal confirmed that the refusal of leave was not itself an appealable decision, but having sympathy with the view that the tribunal had made an error of law, held that the proper remedy was to seek judicial review and that it was inappropriate for the Court of Appeal to seek to define the limits of the review jurisdiction of the Divisional Court[3].

Glidewell J supplied a useful test for the way in which the discretion of the court is to be exercised in such a case:

"Where there is an alternative remedy available but judicial review is sought, then in my judgment the court should always ask itself whether the remedy that is sought in the court, or the alternative remedy which is available to the applicant by way of appeal, is the most effective and convenient, in other words, which of them will prove to be the most effective and convenient in all the circumstances, not merely for the applicant, but in the public interest"[4].

In that case, concerning the refusal of an entertainments licence, he granted certiorari, taking into account the facts that the decision affected the conduct by local authorities throughout the country of their functions under the legislation and that there was a point of law involved which had not been previously decided.

Similarly, in a case concerning the reasoning of a Mental Health Review Tribunal, Nolan J said that consideration should be given to whether an application for judicial review should be made as an alternative to a special case stated, since the judicial review procedure allows a broader consideration of the issues and offers a much more comprehensive range of reliefs[5].

1   R v Hillingdon London Borough Council, ex p Royco Homes Ltd [1974] QB 720, [1974] 2 All ER 643.
2   Azam v Secretary of State for the Home Department [1974] AC 18, [1973] 2 All ER 765 HL.
3   Bland v Chief Supplementary Benefits Officer [1983] 1 All ER 537, [1983] 1 WLR 262, CA.
4   R v Huntingdon District Council, ex p Cowan [1984] 1 All ER 58, [1984] 1 WLR 501 and see Ex p Waldron [1986] 1 QB 824.
5   Bone v Mental Health Review Tribunal [1985] 3 All ER 330 but compare R v Birmingham City Council, ex p Ferrero Ltd [1993] 1 All ER 530, CA.

132. Summary. The position has been well summarised as follows: "In general, however, the approach of the courts to this area has not been a consistent one. There are dicta of high authority that alternative remedies must usually be exhausted before judicial review will be granted: but in practice the courts are often more generous in granting judicial review than those dicta might suggest"[1].

1   Supperstone and Goudie *Judicial Review* 2nd edn, (1997) p 15.25.

F: EUROPE

1: EUROPEAN COMMUNITY LAW

133. Introduction[1]**.** The European Union is a legal order with legislative powers, capable of binding member states and their nationals[2] to varying extents[3], dependent upon whether the nature of the measure in question brings it within the categories of measure described in Article 189 of the Treaty[4]. Section 2 (1) of the European Communities Act 1972[5], which incorporated the contents of the Treaty into UK law, provides that all rights and remedies emanating from the Treaties themselves shall be recognised and available in law in the UK's courts. Article 5 of the EC Treaty[6] requires member states to take all appropriate measures to ensure fulfilment of the obligations arising out of the Treaty or from action taken by the Community institutions.

1   European community legislation is made up of primary legislation (that is, treaties) and secondary legislation such as directives and decisions. All proposed and adopted legislation is published in the Official Journal of the Communities. The Bulletin of the European Communities reports on activities and issues supplements on specific areas. The European Court Reports (ECR) is the official series for cases in the European Court and Court of First Instance, and the Common Market Law Reports (CMLR) deal with national member states' decisions which contain an element of EC law. LEXIS covers the above and some unreported decisions and opinions of the Advocates General. The

Commission Information Office (telephone no 0171 973 1992) and the European Parliament Information Office (telephone no 0171 227 4300) will provide information about the institutions and publications of the European Community. See 51, 52 Halsbury's Laws (4th Edn) title EUROPEAN COMMUNITIES. The main journals for practitioners are the CMLRev, EBLR, ECLR and ELR. For a straightforward guide to the law, see Penelope Kent *European Community Law* (1992) from which this digest of further sources in this field is adapted. For a discussion in the context of administrative law, see Supperstone and Goudie *Judicial Review* 2nd Edn, (1997) ch 12.

2 *Algemene Transport–en Expeditie Ondernemeing van Gend en Loos NV v Nederlandse administratie der belasting*: 26/62 [1963] ECR 1, ECJ.
3 Specifically depending on the nature of particular directives. See Vol 17 (1997 Issue) title EUROPEAN COURTS and 51, 52 Halsbury's Laws (4th Edn) title EUROPEAN COMMUNITIES.
4 EC Treaty art 189 (as substituted by the Treaty on European Union art G (60)) (50 Halsbury's Statutes (4th Edn) TREATIES OF THE EUROPEAN ECONOMIC COMMUNITIES). Note that the Council and Commission have operated by way of acts falling outside the five-fold categorisation of measures in the article, with the effect that the European Court has been hampered in reviewing the resulting measures. The Treaty of Rome is a term commonly used to refer to the European Economic Treaty (the "EEC Treaty") signed at Rome in 1957. This treaty was amended in name and in substance by the Treaty on European Union (the "TEU") signed at Maastricht in 1992 which came into force on 1 November 1993. Throughout this title reference will be made to the EC Treaty (as amended) and not to the EEC Treaty.
5 European Communities Act 1972 s 2 (1) (17 Halsbury's Statutes (4th Edn) EUROPEAN COMMUNITIES).
6 EC Treaty art 5.

134. General relevance to proceedings in domestic courts. Some of the treaty provisions give rise to obligations or commitments between member states[1]; these are relevant as guidance to the interpretation of national legislation[2]. Some lesser provisions are clear, immediate and unconditional[3] and these have direct effect and may be implemented by national courts in proceedings brought by individuals and legal persons. There are some general principles of European law (some of which originated from UK law) of relevance in cases against emanations of the state. Equality, proportionality[4], legal certainty, legitimate expectation[5], procedural fairness[6] and solidarity[7] are among them. Section 2 (4) of the 1972 Act[8] attempts to resolve any conflict between UK and European legislation by providing that "... any enactment passed or to be passed ... shall be construed and have effect subject to the foregoing ..." that is, the foregoing incorporation of European community law into the UK system[9]. In a case of apparent conflict, it now seems clear that the offending national provision must not be given effect or must be declared inapplicable, unless Parliament had clearly intended to withdraw from the community by passing conflicting legislation[10].

1 As to what constitutes a member state, the ECJ has held that it is any body whatever its legal form which has been made responsible pursuant to a measure adopted by the state for providing a public service under the control of the state and has for that purpose special powers beyond those which result from the normal rules applicable in relations between individuals. See *Foster v British Gas plc*: C – 188/89 [1991] 1 QB 405, [1990] 3 All ER 897, ECJ.
2 See *Von Colson and Kamann v Land Nordrhein-Westfalen*: 14/83 [1984] ECR 1891, ECJ. In interpreting statutes, the courts have always tried to avoid putting the government in breach of international obligations by resolving ambiguities in favour of a consistent interpretation. National provisions designed to implement European law are construed in the light of those obligations: see *Pickstone v Freemans plc* [1988] AC 66, [1988] 2 All ER 803, HL, where the court was prepared to look at Hansard to see what Parliament intended in this regard.

3   See, for instance, *Van Duyn v Home Office (No 2)*: 41/74 [1974] ECR 1337 (Directive). Examples of direct effect of treaty provisions have been found in the areas of equal pay, competition and free movement of goods and persons.
4   Meaning that the methods used to attain an end should be no more than is appropriate and necessary for attaining it. UK courts will apply this concept in the context of community law; see, for example, *Thomas v Chief Adjudication Officer* [1991] 2 QB 164, [1991] 3 All ER 315, CA (C – 328/91 [1993] IRLR 292 for ECJ ruling) and *National and Local Government Officers' Association v Secretary of State for the Environment* (1992) Times, 2 December, CA, where NEILL LJ suggested it might be more appropriate for use in review proceedings against inferior bodies as opposed to central government.
5   In the absence of any overriding public interest.
6   Arising from the national laws of member states and from the Convention for the Protection of Human Rights and Fundamental Freedoms (Cmd 8969) commonly referred to as the European Convention on Human Rights.
7   Member states must develop trade between each other on more favourable conditions than with external countries.
8   European Communities Act 1972 s 2 (4) (17 Halsbury's Statutes (4th Edn) EUROPEAN COMMUNITIES).
9   In *Amministrazione delle Finanze dello Stato v Simmenthal SpA*: 106/77 [1978] ECR 629 at 644 it was held that a national court must set aside any provision of national law which may conflict with it, whether prior or subsequent to the community rule.
10 The case of *Pepper v Hart* [1993] 1 All ER 42, [1993] 1 All ER 42, HL, has confirmed that the courts will in certain circumstances look at Hansard to discern Parliament's intention, even in cases which do not give rise to EC issues. The cases of *Duke v GEC Reliance Systems Ltd* [1988] AC 618, [1988] 1 All ER 626, HL and *Finnegan v Clowney Youth Training Programme Ltd* [1990] 2 AC 407, [1990] 2 All ER 546 held that subsequent national legislation must be interpreted consistently with directives, but *Marleasing SA v La Comercial Internacional de Alimentacion SA*: C 106/89 [1990] ECR I-4135, ECJ (see Paragraph 136 note 6 post), appears to demand consistent interpretation in cases of both earlier and later national legislation.

135. Legal analysis. In legal proceedings a question as to the meaning or effect of any of the treaties or as to the validity or meaning of community legislation is to be treated as a question of law. Judicial notice must be taken of judgments and opinions of the court and judgments of the Court of First Instance[1]. Courts or tribunals authorised to give binding decisions of a judicial nature (and professional bodies acting under a degree of governmental supervision operating appeal procedures affecting EC rights[2]) may[3] request the European Court to give a ruling on any question as to the interpretation of the treaties or the validity of acts of community institutions[4]. Before the court may do so, there needs to be a necessity for an answer to enable the court to give judgment in the case[5]. In cases devoid of ambiguity there is no obligation to request a ruling. Article 177[6] provides that a court against whose decisions there is no judicial remedy under national law must refer to the court a question for preliminary ruling where any such question is raised in a case pending before it[7]. This wording still means that even the House of Lords can assert that no ruling is "necessary", if the point can be characterised as free from doubt and unaffected by any EC law. On receipt of a ruling, the member state's court determines issues of fact and applies the ruling to the case. Legal aid automatically extends to proceedings on a reference if it has been granted for UK proceedings[8]. In cases of tribunal decisions where no legal aid is available, the European Court can itself grant assistance[9].

1   European Communities Act 1972 s 3 (1)(as amended), (2)(as amended) (17 Halsbury's Statutes (4th Edn) EUROPEAN COMMUNITIES).

2   Not arbitrators: *Nordsee Deutsche Hochseefisherei GmbH v Reederei Mond Hochseefischerei Nordstern AG & Co KG*: 102/81 [1982] ECR 1095, ECJ.
3   For guidance as to when a reference is not necessary, see *CILFIT Srl v Ministry of Health*: 283/81 [1982] ECR 3415, ECJ. *Wither v Cowie* 1991 SLT 401 established that the High Court of Scotland's justiciary had jurisdiction to entertain appeals against a sheriff's decision to seek a ruling from the ECJ in respect of prosecution for breach of a fishing licence, where the conditions were alleged to be ultra vires EC law. It held that it would intervene only if the decision was plainly wrong, and it was not in this case. Compare *R v International Stock Exchange of the United Kingdom and the Republic of Ireland, ex p Else (1982) Ltd* [1993] QB 534, [1993] 1 All ER 420, CA, exploring whether a reference was necessary with regard to the co-ordination of conditions for official stock exchange listing: the shareholder applicants claimed that they were entitled to notice of proposed suspension of a listed company under art 15 of Directive 79/279. It was held that the directive conferred no enforceable rights on investors and there was no doubt as to the effect of art 15; it was thus unnecessary to ask for a ruling and the first instance judge's request was overturned.
4   EC Treaty art 177 (as substituted by the TEU art G (56)) (50 Halsbury's Statutes (4th Edn) TREATIES OF THE EUROPEAN COMMUNITIES). See Paragraph 133 note 4 ante.
5   See RSC Ord 114 for procedure in the High Court and Court of Appeal; the Crown Court Rules 1982, SI 1982/1109 r 29 (5 Halsbury's Statutory Instruments (1994 Issue) COURTS) governing criminal proceedings and CCR Ord 19 r 11 for the county court procedure.
6   See note 4 above.
7   Inferior courts against whom there is no remedy regarding certain decisions, must also refer for rulings under this article.
8   Civil Legal Aid (General) Regulations 1989, SI 1989/339, reg 51 (b)(vi) (11 Halsbury's Statutory Instruments (1995 Issue) LEGAL AID). A reference is a step in the national proceedings and not a separate action. See Legal Aid Handbook 1996/7 paras 20, 21.
9   See Rules of Procedure of the Court of Justice, art 76 (Vol 17 (1997 Issue) title EUROPEAN COURTS Appendix 3).

136. Remedies. Member states are free to decide what remedies shall exist to secure enforcement of EC law[1]. They must be effective remedies, and a member state must not make it impossible in practice to exercise the community rights in question. A breach of a directly effective provision will be a breach of statutory duty so may obviously give rise to judicial review[2]. Damages may be claimed for breach of European laws which are directly effective[3]; individuals may be awarded damages for breach of those provisions which are designed to protect private rights[4]. But in another case it was held that damages are not available against the Crown for an injury caused to a plaintiff by an administrative ultra vires act done in good faith[5]. With regard to non-directly effective community laws in the national courts, the Court of Justice of the European Communities ("ECJ") has held that it is necessary to construe national legislation in accordance with such directives[6]. Where a directive has as its object the protection of financial interests community law may render the state liable in damages for failure to implement directives[7]. Where an individual suffers loss as a consequence of breach of a European law obligation, the commission or another member state may take action on their behalf against the state in question[8]. If successful[9] it may be held necessary that the member state pays damages for losses flowing from the breach, or even pass retrospective legislation. Interim relief is now clearly available to protect the status quo where a claim here is based on community provisions but a delay is necessitated pending the determination of the ECJ of the meaning of the law in question. The national court need only give interim relief if it is of the view that the factual and legal preconditions for the grant of it under UK principles are met, although the court does not have to be satisfied on a prima facie basis that the national law is invalid. So national procedural rules obstructing such discretion are void too[10]. Judicial review is not a suitable procedure by which to complain about failure of the executive to legislate according to EC law[11].

1 In the absence of any relevant community provision, designation of competent courts and creation of procedural rules is left to member states, subject to the requirement that they be no less favourable than those governing the same type of action in a non-European matter. See *Comet BV v Productschap voor Siergewassen*: 45/76 [1976] ECR 2043, ECJ.
2 But see the cases noted at Paragraph 32 note 1 ante relating to the need for damage within the confines of personal injury, economic loss or damage to property before a civil action may arise from a breach of statutory duty.
3 See *Kincardine and Deeside District Council v Forestry Comrs* 1992 SLT 1180 on the direct effect of Directive 85/337 regarding environmental impact assessment. The council sought review of the commissioners on the ground that they had failed to consider whether an assessment was appropriate in respect of moorland on which certain birds lived. It was held that a directive could have direct effect even if it did not confer any specific rights on a party where a state had failed to implement it or incorrectly implemented it; however, this directive was not sufficiently clear, precise or unconditional to have direct effect.
4 *Garden Cottage Foods Ltd v Milk Marketing Board* [1984] AC 130, [1983] 2 All ER 770, HL.
5 *Bourgoin SA v Minister of Agriculture Fisheries and Food* [1986] QB 716, [1985] 3 All ER 585, CA.
6 *Marleasing SA v La Comercial Internacional de Alimentacion SA*: C – 106/89 [1990] ECR I-4135, [1992] 1 CMLR 305, ECJ.
7 *Francovich and Bonifaci v Italy*: C-9/90 [1995] ICR 722, [1992] IRLR 84, ECJ, held this to be so where the result to be achieved by the directive would result in the creation of individual rights, and there is a causal link between the failure to implement and the damage suffered. See also *Emmott v Minister for Social Welfare and A-G*: C-208/90 [1993] ICR 8, ECJ, concerning the issue whether a state emanation could rely on a time limit when the state concerned was in default in failing to implement a directive (79/7), in a claim for damages for derogation from equal treatment regarding invalidity benefits. The implications of *Francovich* are discussed in C Lewis and S Moore "Duties, Directives and Damages in European Community Law" [1993] PL 151.
8 EC Treaty art 169, 170 (50 Halsbury's Statutes (4th Edn) TREATIES OF THE EUROPEAN COMMUNITIES). See Paragraph 133 note 4 ante.
9 A member state may not plead provisions, practices or circumstances existing in its internal legal system in order to justify failures to comply with obligations and time-limits imposed by directives.
10 *R v Secretary of State for Transport, ex p Factortame (No 2)* [1991] 1 AC 603, sub nom *Factortame Ltd v Secretary of State for Transport (No 2)* [1991] 1 All ER 70, HL.
11 See *R v Secretary of State for Employment, ex p Equal Opportunities Commission* [1993] 1 All ER 1022, [1993] 1 WLR 872, CA, in which it was held that the cause of action most appropriate for breach of article 119 was by the individual against the employer for damages, not against the minister by way of judicial review. But *Francovich* was not taken into consideration in any depth. See C Lewis and S Moore "Duties, Directives and Damages in European Community Law" [1993] PL 151 at 169.

137. Special relevance of EC law for judicial review. Since the objects of the community are the elimination of restrictions on the movement of goods, persons, services and capital, common transport, economic and agricultural policies, they permeate many areas of executive and legislative activity. Further, since some types of European law require implementation by way of order[1], the validity of delegated legislation or its adequacy to implement European policy may be relevant in domestic proceedings for review. It has been suggested that in cases where the exercise of discretionary power affects fundamental rights of citizens, then UK courts can and should develop the concept of irrationality or unreasonableness, so that proportionality would become more important[2]. Community law is effective to negate the effect of ouster clauses barring challenges to decisions made, and of "conclusive evidence" certificates having the same result[3]. Some areas of overlap with European law are as follows: employment of public officers[4], transport, planning and environmental law, competition policy[5], trading quotas[6], import restrictions and immigration rules, social security[7], compulsory competitive tendering[8], and company law, professional regulation[9], Sunday trading[10], safety policy[11], information policy, street trading[12] and immigration[13].

1 See European Communities Act 1972 s 2 (2) (17 Halsbury's Statutes (4th Edn) EUROPEAN COMMUNITIES).
2 See Hon Sir John Laws "Is the High Court the Guardian of Fundamental Constitutional Rights?" [1993] PL 59 and LORD BROWNE-WILKINSON "The Infiltration of a Bill of Rights" [1992] PL 397.
3 See *Johnston v Chief Constable Royal Ulster Constabulary*: 222/84 [1987] QB 129, [1986] 3 All ER 135, ECJ.
4 See S Fredman and G Morris *The State as Employer: Labour Law in the Public Services* (1989).
5 See *Publishers Association v EC Commission (No 2)*: T-66/89 [1992] 4 All ER 70, CFI, relating to the net book agreement, held by a national court to be in the public interest but by the commission said to be infringing rules on competition, so justifying refusal of an exemption for the agreement.
6 See *R v Secretary of State for Transport, ex p Factortame Ltd (No 3)*: C-221/89 [1992] QB 680, [1991] 3 All ER 769, ECJ, in which the ECJ held that the Merchant Shipping Act 1988 was in breach of art 52 of the treaty and the minister's discretionary power to dispense with the nationality requirements thereunder was not an answer to the allegation.
7 See *Jackson v Chief Adjudication Officer* C-63, 64/91 [1993] QB 367, [1993] 3 All ER 265, ECJ, regarding single parents undertaking part-time employment and having to pay child-minding expenses to do so, concerning Directives 76/297 and 79/7; *Johnson v Chief Adjudication Officer*: C-31/90 [1993] QB 252, [1992] 2 All ER 705, ECJ, concerning Directive 79/7 and upbringing of children.
8 See S Arrowsmith *Government Procurement and Judicial Review* (Toronto 1988) and C Turpin *Government Procurement and Contracts* (1989). Recent cases involving the transfer of undertakings in the light of EC law are *Dr Sophie Redmond Stichting v Bartol*: C-29/91 [1992] ECRI-3189, ECJ and *Rask and Christensen v ISS Kantineservice A/S Case*: C 209/91 [1992] ECRI-5755, ECJ. It is likely that courts and tribunals will hold the overwhelming majority of competitive tender contracts to be caught by the 1977 Business Transfers Directive (77/187).
9 See *Colegio Oficial de Agentes de la Propiedad Immobiliaria v JL Aguirre Borrell* [1992] ECRI-3003, ECJ, holding that a decision refusing a national of a member state recognition of a diploma or qualification must be capable of being examined in judicial proceedings in which its legality under EC law can be reviewed and the person can be given reasons for the decision.
10 See *Kirklees Metropolitan Borough Council v Wickes Building Supplies Ltd* [1992] AC 227, [1992] 3 All ER 717, HL, involving proceedings under Local Government Act 1972 s 222 for an injunction restraining trading in breach of the Shops Act 1950. It was alleged to be contrary to art 30 of the EC Treaty. It was held that from the point of view of EC law there was no obligation to impose a cross-undertaking in damages because either EC law required national law to provide compensation, not the local authority, or if it did not, the traders would be unfairly advantaged by the undertaking. This meant that the principles on which interim injunctions were granted were purely a matter of domestic law; further, see *Stoke-on-Trent City Council v B & Q plc*: C – 169/91 [1993] 1 All ER 481, [1993] 2 WLR 730, ECJ and [1993] AC 900, [1993] 2 All ER 297n, HL: art 30 is not applicable to national legislation prohibiting retailers from opening their premises on Sundays.

11 See *Anklagemyndigheden v Hansen & Son I/S*: 326/88 [1990] ECR I-2911, [1992] ICR 277, ECJ, raising the question whether a council regulation precluded imposition of strict liability for breach of maximum daily driving and rest periods for road hauliers provided for by the member state's implementing regulations. And further, *Freight Transport Association Ltd v London Boroughs Transport Committee* [1991] 3 All ER 915, [1991] 1 WLR 828, HL: under the Road Traffic Regulation Act 1984 the GLC prohibited driving of goods vehicles over a certain weight in certain streets during prescribed hours without a permit. One of the conditions attached to a permit was challenged as contrary to Directives 71/320 or 70/156, but it was held that it was not in conflict with them and was consistent with community policy generally.
12 See *R v Crown Court at Southwark, ex p Watts* [1992] 1 CMLR 446, CA, on the relevance of art 52 to the contention that a street trader may lawfully operate by proxy under a licence in one member state, whilst living in another.
13 See *R v Immigration Appeal Tribunal, ex p Secretary of State for the Home Department*: C-370/90 [1992] 3 All ER 798, [1992] ECRI-4265, ECJ, in which an Indian national and his British wife worked in Germany, returned to England and divorced; it was held that art 52 of the Treaty and Council Directive 73/148 required member states to grant leave to enter to the spouse of a national of that state who has gone with that spouse to another member state and returns as envisaged by art 52.

138. Review of community institutions before the European Court of Justice. Community institutions may themselves be sued in courts and tribunals in the member states unless the Court of Justice of the European Communities has been given exclusive jurisdiction over the issue in question. An example of such jurisdiction is the power to annul measures adopted by the community bodies found in Articles 173 and 175[1] of the EC Treaty. The practitioner must consider which acts may be challenged, whether his or her client has locus standi whether the time limits have expired[2], whether the limited grounds for challenge may be made out, and whether the effects of annulment will suit the client. This form of administrative law is based on the French method of supervising state bodies[3]. Community institutions, that is, the parliament, the council and the commission may be sued by member states, the council or the commission without locus standi, and individuals or legal persons (where the decision is addressed to him or is of direct and individual concern to him)[4]. Grounds for annulment are lack of competence, infringement of an essential procedural requirement or infringement of the treaty or rules of law relating to its application, and misuse of powers[5].

1 EC Treaty arts 173, 175 (as substituted by the TEU arts G (53), G (54)) (50 Halsbury's Statutes (4th Edn) TREATIES OF THE EUROPEAN COMMUNITIES). See Paragraph 133 note 4 ante. These articles provide for review of the legality of acts other than recommendations or opinions of the council or commission and acts of the European Parliament intended to produce legal effects vis-à-vis third parties. This has been interpreted to mean all acts which are capable of having a legal effect, and is not confined to regulations, directives or decisions. It has included discussions of guidelines before the signing of the ERTA: *EC Commission v EC Council (Re ERTA)*: Case 22/70 [1971] ECR 263, ECJ; a communication by way of registered letter from the commission informing a company it was no longer immune from fines: *Re Noordwijk's Cement Accord*: 8-11/66 [1967] CMLR 77, ECJ; further, a regulation may be a disguised decision: *NV International Fruit Company v Commission*: 41–44/70 [1971] ECR 411; however, it excluded review of a reasoned opinion under art 169: *EEC Commission v Italy*: 7/61 [1961] ECR 317, ECJ. The parliament's acts may also be challenged; for example, *Luxembourg v European Parliament*: 230/81 [1983] ECR 255, ECJ and *Partie Ecologiste Les Verts v European Parliament*: 294/83 [1986] ECR 1339, [1987] 2 CMLR 343, ECJ.
2 See EC Treaty art 173 (as so amended), providing for limits of two months from the occurrence of various events.

3   The French grounds are known as incompetence, vice de forme, violation de la loi and detournement de pouvoir. They equate roughly to illegality, procedural irregularity and abuse of power in UK law.
4   EC Treaty art 173 (as so amended).
5   See *Mulder v EC Council and Commission* c-104/89, C-37/90 [1992] ECRI-3061, ECJ, involving a claim for compensation by dairy producers arising out of the application of Community regulations within the dairy sector. Legitimate expectation was seen as a superior rule of law for the protection of the individual.

139. European Court actions against member states[1]. Article 169 provides the main means of enforcement of community law against member states by the commission. Article 170[2] provides for such proceedings to be brought by member states. Challenges to derogations from the treaties may be made expeditiously and in private[3]. Challenges to reliance on national provisions despite harmonisation measures adopted by a qualified majority may also be processed quickly[4]. State aids may be questioned under Article 93 (2) of the Treaty[5] and determinations by the commission that the state must repay aid paid are provisionally valid pending judicial decision by the court[6]. Practitioners are referred to specialist works since these aspects of community law are outside the scope of this topic.

1   See Supperstone and Goudie *Judicial Review* 2nd edn, (1997) p 12.18 et seq for actions brought by the Commission.
2   EC Treaty arts 169, 170 (50 Halsbury's Statutes (4th Edn) TREATIES OF THE EUROPEAN COMMUNITIES). See Paragraph 133 note 4 ante.
3   EC Treaty art 225.
4   EC Treaty art 100A (4)(as inserted).
5   EC Treaty art 93 (2).
6   *EC Commission v United Kingdom*: 31, 53/77R [1977] ECR 921, ECJ.

2: THE EUROPEAN CONVENTION ON HUMAN RIGHTS

140. General. The European Convention for the Protection of Human Rights and Fundamental Freedoms[1] has been ratified by the United Kingdom and is likely to be incorporated into English law in 1998. The English courts will have power to grant a declaration that the convention has been breached.

1   The Convention for the Protection of Human Rights and Fundamental Freedoms (Cmd 8969) commonly referred to as the European Convention on Human Rights. See Brownlie *Basic Documents on Human Rights* (3rd edn, 1992) p 326.

G: JUDICIAL REVIEW PROCEDURE

1: APPLICATIONS AND LEAVE

141. Applications and leave.
   The leave stage. Judicial review is a two-stage procedure[1]. Leave to apply must first be obtained[2]. The rationale for the leave stage is that it is an important safeguard against groundless or unmeritorious claims that a decision is a nullity. Application is made ex parte to a judge on the Crown Office List[3]. In practice many applications for review are finally determined by the outcome of the leave application.
   Venue. Applications must be commenced in the Crown Office, Royal Courts of Justice, London save in cases of extreme urgency[4]. District registries of the High Court do not have a judicial review jurisdiction. The county courts have no jurisdiction to make an order of mandamus, certiorari or prohibition[5]. The Crown Office should be consulted by telephone in cases of urgency[6].
   The paperwork (form and contents of application and affidavit). The applicant must file in the Crown Office a notice[7] of application for leave, containing a statement of their name and description, the order, decision or proceeding in respect of which relief is sought, the relief (including interim relief or a request for special directions such as expedition) sought[8], and the grounds upon which it is sought[9], the factual basis for claiming locus standi to apply, any reasons for delay in making the application, and the name and address of their solicitors and the applicant's address for service. It is necessary to deal with issues such as the existence of alternative remedies for the applicant or why they have not been pursued, if this is the case, the existence of any relevant ouster[10], or conclusive evidence clause (time limited or otherwise), or why in certain situations it is contended that the issues give rise to public law considerations. Full and frank disclosure[11] is of the utmost importance lest the respondent apply to set aside the grant of leave and ask for indemnity costs or wasted costs against the applicant and his advisors. The Crown Office is open to telephone enquiries as to procedural matters[12]. If the application raises specialist matters familiar to Commercial Court, Family or Chancery Division judges, it is prudent to include a request in the application that if leave is granted the matter be assigned to such a judge.
   Accompanying this application must be an affidavit by an appropriate deponent[13] verifying the facts relied upon[14], and an index to the documents[15]. The affidavit should exhibit a copy of any order or decision in respect of which certiorari is sought because one must be produced before the full hearing, and its absence might militate against the grant of leave. The applicant must lodge the documents in a paginated bundle, with a list of essential reading, identifying the items which are considered to be essential pre-reading for the court[16]. The applicant's solicitors must also lodge a paginated bundle of relevant statutory material[17].
   Time limits for leave[18]. The application for leave must be made promptly and in any event within three months from the date when grounds for the application first arose unless the court considers that there is good reason for

extending the period within which the application shall be made[19]. If there is any uncertainty about whether there is a risk of a finding of delay, the application must set out the reasons for it[20]. The time limit runs from the date of the making of any judgment, order, conviction or other proceeding, if certiorari is sought in the application[21] but the rules make no specific provision in relation to claims for other forms of relief. It has been held that where a challenge is made to the lawfulness of a policy or its application to an individual, the time limit runs from that application, and not from the inception of the policy itself[22]. In applications for mandamus to enforce the performance of an alleged duty the time limit might run from the date when the duty was first owed[23] or from the date when refusal to perform it was first made known to the applicant. The fact that an application is made within three months does not necessarily mean that it has been made promptly[24]. There is undue delay for the purposes of the Supreme Court Act 1981 Section 31 (6) whenever the application is not made within three months, and even if the court considers there is good reason for extending the period it may refuse relief on the basis of inter alia detriment to good administration[25]. The fact that the applicant has survived the leave stage after an argument as to promptitude does not prevent the court from refusing relief at the full hearing on the grounds of undue delay[26].

Time limits in cases involving internal appeal or review. Where leave is sought to apply to quash any judgment or proceedings which are subject to appeal, and there is a time limit for the bringing of such an appeal, the judge or court may adjourn the leave application until the appeal is determined or the time for appealing has expired[27]. The court is likely to take the view that the time limit should not be seen to have expired for review of the first decision until three months after the second decision, if it was reasonable to pursue the appeal[28].

Paper applications. Leave may be granted by a single judge on consideration of the papers alone unless the applicant requests an oral hearing on RSC Appendix A Form No 86A[29]. The Crown Office will inform the applicant by notice served on his address for service of the order which the judge has made. Where leave is refused on the papers, it is customary for the judge to set out his or her reasons for refusal.

Oral applications. If an applicant chooses an oral hearing from the outset, or an applicant is refused leave on the basis of the papers alone, or if the judge wishes to hear further submissions, an oral hearing may be arranged before a single judge in open court. In the last instance the court may invite the respondent to attend to make representations. If then taking account of brief argument on both sides the judge is satisfied that there is a case fit for further consideration, then he will grant leave[30].

Time estimates for leave applications. Applicants are presumed to be capable of putting their case for leave forward in 20 minutes. Any respondent attending is expected to need no more than ten minutes. So if more than half an hour is considered to be necessary to develop the application, a written time estimate should be given to the Crown Office to fix a special appointment[31].

Choosing between a paper and an oral application for leave. It would normally be sensible to make a paper application first because there is nothing to lose by so doing. It also saves costs. In any case involving urgency or the need for expedition, special directions etc an oral hearing will be arranged more quickly than a paper application will be considered in the normal course of events. In any case where an interim injunction or stay is to be sought it would also be prudent to ask for an oral hearing, so that the respondent may be invited to attend with representation[32].

Service of the respondent with the leave application. The applicant has a choice as to whether to serve the respondent with the proceedings so that an ex parte hearing may turn into an ex parte hearing on notice. Arranging for the respondent to attend may save protracted correspondence about expedition, abridgment of time for service of the respondent's affidavit, or any other special directions sought by the applicant. In certain cases the court itself will invite the respondent to attend. In either situation, the court will not normally award costs to a respondent who successfully defeats the leave application. If the respondent is misled into appearing by an applicant's informing him that an injunction is to be sought when the court decides to refuse leave, then costs may be awarded[33].

The test for leave. On an application for leave the single judge or the court may either allow amendment of the statement[34], adjourn, grant leave, grant interim relief or refuse leave. The threshold test is whether or not there is a point for further investigation on a full inter partes basis with all such evidence as is necessary on the facts and all such argument as is necessary on the law[35]. Leave should only be refused on the other hand if there is no prima facie arguable case at all[36]. Adjournment would be appropriate if the judge or court considers it impossible on the papers and submissions to decide whether there is an arguable case. The respondent may be invited to make representations at the resumed hearing[37]. Other aspects relevant to the granting of leave are locus standi, delay, the existence of alternative remedies, questions of justiciability and the existence of ouster clauses[38].

Limited or conditional leave. Leave may be granted on such terms as to costs and as to giving security as the court or judge thinks fit[39]. If leave is granted specifically with regard to one of several grounds, there is no need to renew the application on any of the other grounds, but the applicant should give notice to the respondent within 21 days of the grant of leave of his intention to rely on any of the other grounds[40].

Costs on leave applications. An application for leave constitutes "proceedings" within the meaning of the Supreme Court Act 1981 Section 51 (1)[41] so that an order for costs can be made in favour of applicants for leave, even where the proposed respondents alter their decision before the leave application is heard. If the application is made ex parte, no provision as to costs is made at the time. The applicant's costs of a successful oral application for leave may be awarded at the full hearing. If the respondent has appeared to oppose the leave application, and leave is granted, costs are generally reserved to the substantive hearing or an order is made that costs should follow the outcome of the full application[42]. If the respondent attends at the applicant's invitation, because a claim for interim relief has been included in the papers, and leave is refused, the applicant can expect to have to pay the respondent's costs[43]. If leave is granted and then the respondent concedes the point in respect of which the challenge has been brought, the applicant may obtain the costs of the application by applying to the court on two clear days' notice of motion supported by affidavit[44]. Guidance as to the costs implications of discontinuance before the full hearing may be found in the cases: the guiding principle would appear to be that costs should be awarded against whichever party has acknowledged likely failure at trial. In the absence of such acknowledgment the court will be extremely reluctant to consider the substantive contentions in the case, merely so as to decide the issue of costs[45].

1 Governed by RSC Ord 53 and the Supreme Court Act 1981 s 31 (11 Halsbury's Statutes (4th Edn) COURTS AND LEGAL SERVICES).
2 RSC Ord 53 r 3 (1). See the Supreme Court Fees Order 1980, SI 1980/821, Fee No 4 (as amended by SI 1996/3191, art 5).
3 RSC Ord 53 r 3 (2).
4 See Practice Note [1983] 2 All ER 1020, sub nom Practice Direction [1983] 1 WLR 925.
5 County Courts Act 1984 s 38 (3)(a)(as substituted) (11 Halsbury's Statutes (4th Edn) COUNTY COURTS).
6 Telephone numbers of Crown Office rooms are set out in note 12 below.
7 RSC Ord 53 r 3 (2)(a); RSC Appendix A Form No 86A may be used in its standard form. See Forms 1–7 post, for varied examples of completed applications.
8 The remedies claimed must be identified alternatively or cumulatively: RSC Ord 53 r 2. If a required remedy is omitted, amendment is possible under RSC Ord 53 r 6. If damages are claimed the applicant must plead them as fully as if the matter were proceeding by way of statement of claim: RSC Ord 53 r 7 (2). See also the Supreme Court Practice 1997 paras 18/12/6, 18/12/16 regarding particulars of damage.
9 The facts upon which the application is based, together with any contentions of law relied upon should be stated in the application, including any authorities in support of the outline propositions of law. The facts and contentions should at least raise a question of breach of duty or abuse of discretion in public law. Some applicants choose to set out the application very baldly and supplement it with the affidavit; others provide a full application and a bare verifying affidavit. Both methods are acceptable to the Crown Office.
10 See *R v Cornwall County Council, ex p Huntington* [1992] 3 All ER 566.
11 The materiality of facts and circumstances known to the applicant is for the judge to decide and not for the assessment of the applicant or his legal advisors. See *R v Lloyd's of London, ex p Briggs* [1993] 1 Lloyd's Rep 176 for the consequences of failure in this regard.
12 Tel no 0171 936 6205 for general inquiries and the lodging of applications; tel no 0171 936 6013 or 0171 936 7366 with regard to listing matters. Any queries relating to the renewal of applications to the Court of Appeal in civil cases or to appeals against substantive review decisions must be made to the Civil Appeals Office, where notices of appeals and applications to the Court of Appeal must also be lodged: tel nos 0171 936 6409/6916 (General Office) and 0171 936 6195/6917 (appeals and applications to full court and applications to a single Lord Justice) and 0171 936 6917 (appeals to Registrar).
13 Whether the solicitor or the applicant swears the affidavit may depend on the nature of the case; it must be borne in mind that the affidavit will form the basis of the case at the full hearing, so in a case turning upon matters close to the applicant, it would be prudent to make him or her the deponent.
14 RSC Ord 53 r 3 (2)(b). The affidavit may contain statements of information and belief so long as their sources and grounds are identified, because the application for leave is interlocutory: RSC Ord 41 r 5 (2). This is not the case once the affidavit is served, with the notice of motion, upon the grant of leave, and will be used for the full hearing: RSC Ord 41 r 5 (1) requires that an affidavit must only contain such facts as the deponent is able of his own knowledge to state. *R v Sandhutton Parish Council, ex p Todd* [1992] COD 409, per SCHIEMANN J, encouraged advisors to consider carefully the drafting of affidavits in review proceedings where fundamental disputes as to fact were likely to arise. A party wishing to have an affidavit containing hearsay considered at the full hearing should ask the court for an order under RSC Ord 38 r 3. Alternatively an opponent should apply to cross-examine the deponent concerned.
15 All documents and the index should conform with Practice Note [1983] 3 All ER 33, sub nom Practice Direction [1983] 1 WLR 922 (as amended by Practice Note [1995] 2 All ER 511, sub nom Practice Direction [1995] 1 WLR 510). The original and two copies of any documents should be provided unless a three judge divisional court is expected to hear the application, in which case three copies should be supplied.
16 Practice Note [1994] 4 All ER 671, sub nom Practice Direction [1994] 1 WLR 1551.
17 Practice Note [1997] 1 All ER 128, sub nom Practice Direction [1997] 1 WLR 52.
18 The time limits have been applied more strictly in recent years.
19 RSC Ord 53 r 4 (1); although the period may be extended if the applicant shows good reason. See further Paragraph 128 ante for a discussion as to the exercise of the discretion to

refuse relief where there has been undue delay and where the grant of relief would be likely to cause substantial hardship to or prejudice the rights of any person or would be detrimental to good administration in accordance with the Supreme Court Act 1981 s 31 (6).

20 If the proposed respondent has acquiesced to delay, evidence should be submitted with the application: Practice Note [1983] 2 All ER 1020, sub nom Practice Direction [1983] 1 WLR 925.
21 RSC Ord 53 r 4 (2).
22 *R v Tower Hamlets London Borough Council, ex p Ali* (1993) 25 HLR 218.
23 *R v Hertfordshire County Council, ex p Cheung* (1986) Times, 4 April, CA and commentary thereon by C Lewis in [1987] PL 21.
24 Examples of this problem may be found in *Re Friends of the Earth* [1988] JPL 93 and *R v Independent Television Commission, ex p TV NI Ltd* (1991) Times, 30 December, CA where prejudice to third parties was considered relevant.
25 *Caswell v Dairy Produce Quotas Tribunal* [1990] 2 AC 738, [1990] 2 All ER 434, HL.
26 *R v Swale Borough Council, ex p Royal Society for Protection of Birds* [1991] 1 PLR 6.
27 RSC Ord 53 r 3 (8).
28 *R v Secretary of State for Education and Science and Bedfordshire County Council, ex p Threapleton* [1988] COD 102 referring to *R v Northamptonshire County Council, ex p Tebbutt* (26 June 1986, unreported, CO/322/86).
29 RSC Ord 53 r 3 (3).
30 See guidelines in *R v Secretary of State for the Home Department, ex p Begum* [1990] COD 107, per LORD DONALDSON MR on this step in the proceedings.
31 Practice Note [1991] 1 All ER 1055, sub nom Practice Direction [1991] 1 WLR 280.
32 Although it is not mandatory to do so.
33 *R v Committee of Advertising Practice, ex p Bradford Exchange Ltd* [1991] COD 43.
34 On such terms, if any, as it thinks fit: RSC Ord 53 r 3 (6).
35 *R v Secretary of State for the Home Department, ex p Begum* [1990] COD 107.
36 For an illustration of the difference between arguability and merits, see *R v Secretary of State for the Home Department, ex p Sivakumaran* [1988] AC 958, [1988] 1 All ER 193, HL.
37 Other factors inclining the court to the respondent's presence are where the applicant is in person and the application is difficult to evaluate, or where the matter is urgent, or there is a likelihood of the respondent remedying the grievance without further order: *R v Oxford, ex p Levey* (1986) 151 LGR 371, CA, and *R v Secretary of State for the Home Department, ex p Begum* [1990] COD 107 per LORD DONALDSON MR.
38 See Paragraphs 116–132 ante.
39 RSC Ord 53 r 3 (9). In *R v Westminster County Court, ex p Residents Association of Mayfair* [1991] COD 182 the court made an order for security for costs when granting leave under this provision and under the Companies Act 1985 s 726 (1) (8 Halsbury's Statutes (4th Edn) COMPANIES). The fact that an applicant is legally aided would be taken into consideration by the court in assessing the amount to be ordered for security, but it is not a bar to the making of the order itself.
40 *R v Bow Street Stipendiary Magistrate, ex p Roberts* [1990] 3 All ER 487, [1990] 1 WLR 1317.
41 Supreme Court Act 1981 s 51 (1)(as substituted). *R v Test Valley Borough Council, ex p Goodman* [1992] COD 101 to the contrary has been doubted by the Court of Appeal in *Rozhon v Secretary of State for Wales* (1993) 91 LGR 667, [1994] COD 111; an ex parte application made on affidavit has constituted "proceedings" within RSC Ord 2 r 1: *Harkness v Bell's Asbestos and Engineering Ltd* [1967] 2 QB 729, [1966] 3 All ER 843, CA; and in *R v Highbury Corner Magistrates' Court, ex p Ewing* [1991] 3 All ER 192, sub nom *Ex p Ewing* [1991] 1 WLR 388, CA, the Court of Appeal held that an application for judicial review constituted the institution of "proceedings" for the purposes of the regime pertaining to vexatious litigants.
42 Although the court may impose such terms as to costs and as to giving security as it thinks fit: RSC Ord 53 r 3 (9).
43 If the respondent attends at the court's invitation, an unsuccessful applicant is less likely to be ordered to pay his costs.
44 See Supreme Court Practice 1997 paras 53/1–14/53.
45 See *R v Holderness Borough Council, ex p James Robert Developments Ltd* (1992) 66 P & CR 46, [1993] 1 PLR 108 and *R v Liverpool City Council, ex p Newman* [1993] COD 65, 5 Admin LR 669.

142. Renewing leave applications. In a civil matter, if leave is refused on consideration of the papers, the applicant is entitled to an oral renewal of the application before a single judge. Notice of intention to renew on RSC Appendix A Form No 86B must be filed in the Crown Office within ten days of service of notice of the judge's decision[1]. The court has power to direct that the hearing should be heard by a divisional Court but otherwise the hearing will take place before a single judge in open court[2].

If leave is refused at an oral hearing requested at the outset, or granted on terms by a judge at such a hearing, the applicant in a civil cause must renew the application before the Court of Appeal[3]. Current practice is that renewed applications for leave are determined by a single Lord Justice rather than a full Court of Appeal. Once leave has been refused by the Court of Appeal no further application can be made, unless new circumstances arise putting the case into an exceptional category[4]. There is no possibility of an appeal to the House of Lords[5].

In a criminal cause, whether after an unsuccessful oral hearing requested at the outset, or after a paper application, a renewed application may be made before a divisional Court[6]. In vacation, proceedings which require an urgent hearing may be brought before a single judge[7]. There is no prospect of renewal to the Court of Appeal or appeal against the refusal to that court[8] or the House of Lords[9].

In both types of cause, if an applicant fails to renew his application within the prescribed time, he may apply for an extension by filing reasons with the notice of renewal or of ex parte application, together with an affidavit in support, even if the time for renewal has expired[10].

1   RSC Ord 53 r 3 (5).
2   RSC Ord 53 r 3 (4)(b).
3   RSC Ord 59 r 14 (3) (application to be made by notice of ex parte application within seven days of the refusal).
4   See *M v Home Office* [1992] QB 270, [1992] 4 All ER 97, CA.
5   *Re Poh* [1983] 1 All ER 287, [1983] 1 WLR 2, HL.
6   RSC Ord 53 r 3 (4)(a).
7   RSC Ord 64 r 4.
8   Supreme Court Act 1981 s 18 (1)(a) (11 Halsbury's Statutes (4th Edn) COURTS AND LEGAL SERVICES).
9   See note 5 above where the point turns upon whether a refusal to grant leave is a "decision" of a divisional Court: Administration of Justice Act 1960 s 1 (12 Halsbury's Statutes (4th Edn) CRIMINAL LAW). *Re Poh* [1983] 1 All ER 287, [1983] 1 WLR 2, HL, decided that it was not an "order" or a "judgment" in a non-criminal context, and that analysis is likely to hold good for criminal causes.
10 RSC Ord 3 r 5.

143. Substantive hearings. If a paper application for leave succeeds in a civil matter the substantive hearing will be before a single judge or a divisional court[1]. If an oral application succeeds either before the judge or the divisional court or the Court of Appeal, the substantive hearing will be normally listed before a single judge unless the court directs it to be heard by a divisional court[2]. It is also possible for the Court of Appeal to reserve the substantive hearing to itself in cases where it has granted leave on a renewed application or where it thinks an appeal is inevitable because the High Court is bound by pre-existing authority or for any other reason[3]. Criminal causes or matters are listed before a divisional court[4].

1 The parties are expected to consider whether a three judge court would be desirable, given issues of particular public importance or complexity, and if so, to make a request at an early stage of preparation.
2 See Practice Direction (Judicial Review: Appeals) [1982] 3 All ER 800, [1982] 1 WLR 1375.
3 See Practice Direction (Judicial Review: Appeals) [1982] 3 All ER 800, [1982] 1 WLR 1375.
4 RSC Ord 53 r 5 (1), (2).

144. Special directions on leave applications.
Expedition. Expedition is arranged by inclusion of the case in Part D of the Crown Office List, on the order of the court giving leave. In expediting a case the court will normally abridge time for service of the respondent's affidavit and/or abridge the normal minimum ten days between leave and the full hearing, if so required. Truly urgent cases may be heard within hours. If the need for expedition arises after the grant of leave, application should be made to the Master of the Crown Office on summons supported by affidavit. If he or she declines to expedite, further application may be made to a nominated judge or divisional court by motion[1].

Bail. Bail may be granted in applications concerning criminal matters in which the relief sought includes certiorari of criminal proceedings in the Crown Court or a magistrates' court[2]. There is no appeal against the divisional court's refusal of bail in a criminal cause or matter[3]. In respect of non-criminal causes, the court may grant bail under its inherent jurisdiction if there is an application pending for leave to apply for judicial review or a substantive application for the same[4]. An appeal does lie against refusal in these circumstances to the Court of Appeal under the Supreme Court Act 1981 Section 16[5].

Injunctions and stays. If an applicant has included a claim for prohibition or certiorari in his applications, a stay of the proceedings to which the application relates until the determination of the application for review, or further order is made, may be directed by the court[6], but only if leave is granted, and not if the application is to be adjourned for some reason. Injunctions may be obtained on an interim basis to enforce public duties[7], or to prevent a body from acting unlawfully. Interim relief, including interim injunction, may be granted against the Crown[8]. The test for an interim injunction will be the balance of convenience, provided there is a serious issue to be tried[9]. Preservation of the status quo may provide justification in a case where the applicant will lose something of value[10], but evidence of irrevocable damage has been required in other cases[11]. If the injunction sought is mandatory in nature, a strong prima facie case will normally have to be shown. The public interest will have to be weighed in the balance, unlike in ordinary civil cases[12]. It is usual for the court to require notice of an application for an injunction to the respondent in all but the most urgent cases. There is little authority about whether ordinary rules concerning undertakings in damages in return for injunctive relief should be applied to applicants in review proceedings[13].

Special directions as to service. The applicant should seek the court's view on the leave application with regard to service of persons possibly affected by the proceedings[14], or as to manner of service in cases of difficulty[15].

1 See Practice Note (Judicial Review: Affidavit in Reply) [1989] 1 WLR 358.

2   See Criminal Justice Act 1948 s 37 (1)(b)(ii), (1)(d)(as amended) (12 Halsbury's Statutes (4th Edn) CRIMINAL LAW) and RSC Ord 79.
3   Supreme Court Act 1981 s 18 (1)(a) (11 Halsbury's Statutes (4th Edn) COURTS AND LEGAL SERVICES).
4   See *R v Secretary of State for the Home Department, ex p Turkoglu* [1988] QB 398, [1987] 2 All ER 823, CA. LORD DONALDSON held that the Court of Appeal may entertain a direct appeal in relation to any refusal of bail by the High Court in whatever proceedings it has been made, and on a renewed application for leave to apply for judicial review. The High Court may grant bail pending appeal after a substantive application for review has failed.
5   Supreme Court Act 1981 s 16.
6   RSC Ord 53 r 3 (10)(a).
7   For example, under the Housing Act 1985 (21 Halsbury's Statutes (4th Edn) HOUSING): *R v Kensington and Chelsea LBC, ex p Hammell* [1989] QB 518, [1989] 1 All ER 1202, CA.
8   *Re M* [1994] 1 AC 377, sub nom *M v Home Office* [1993] 3 All ER 537.
9   The mere fact of the grant of leave is not enough to satisfy that test: *Freight Transport Association v London Boroughs Transport Committee* [1991] 3 All ER 915, [1991] 1 WLR 828, HL.
10 For example, rented accommodation.
11 *R v Advertising Standards Authority, ex p Vernons Organisation Ltd* [1993] 2 All ER 202, [1992] 1 WLR 1289, per LAWS J concerning publication of a decision unfavourable to the applicant.
12 See *R v Kensington and Chelsea LBC, ex p Hammell* [1989] QB 518, [1989] 1 All ER 1202, CA, per PARKER LJ.
13 In *R v Hammersmith and Fulham LBC, ex p People Before Profit Ltd* (1981) 80 LGR 322, COMYN J indicated that he would not have extracted an undertaking if he had decided to grant leave, but would have ordered security for costs.
14 RSC Ord 53 r 5 (3).
15 RSC Ord 53 r 5 (7).

145. Service of the proceedings after the grant of leave. Service of the originating notice of motion (or originating summons, if so ordered[1]), a copy of the affidavit in support and a copy of the notice of application should be executed within 14 days of leave being granted, upon all persons directly affected[2]. This includes the clerk or registrar of an inferior court, where the application is directed against a court in relation to proceedings before it. It also includes any judge against whose conduct a challenge is directed. Any application against court proceedings should include as a respondent any other party to those proceedings[3]. An affidavit must be prepared for filing before a motion (or summons) is entered for hearing, although the two may be filed together. The affidavit of service must contain the names and addresses of all who have been served with the motion or summons, the places and dates of such service, whether anyone who was to be served has not been served, and if so, the reason for their non-service[4].

1   See RSC Ord 53 r 5 (2)(a).
2   RSC Ord 53 r 5 (3); Supreme Court Practice 1997 paras 53/1–14/2.
3   As in *R v Central Criminal Court, ex p Director of the Serious Fraud Office* [1993] 2 All ER 399, [1993] 1 WLR 949.
4   RSC Ord 53 r 5 (6).

146. Entering a motion for hearing. Within 14 days of the grant of leave, a motion for hearing must be entered for hearing[1] in the Crown Office[2]. An originating motion to a divisional court will be necessary in a criminal cause or matter[3], and in the majority of civil cases the application must also be made by motion but to a judge sitting in open court, unless the court has directed it to be made to a divisional court or by summons to a judge in chambers[4]. In the latter case, the judge may direct or adjourn the summons for hearing in open court if he wishes[5].

1 Therefore it must have already been served within that time.
2 RSC Ord 53 r 5 (5); RSC Ord 53 r 5 (3), (2).
3 RSC Ord 53 r 5 (1).
4 RSC Ord 53 r 5 (2)(a), (b).
5 RSC Ord 53 r 5 (2).

147. Time and other procedural provisions. There must be at least ten days between service on a respondent and the full hearing[1], and a copy of any instrument in respect of which certiorari is sought must be lodged in the Crown Office, together with a verifying affidavit before the hearing, if it has not already been supplied[2].

1 RSC Ord 53 r 5 (4).
2 RSC Ord 53 r 9 (2).

2: POST-LEAVE PROCEDURE

148. Challenging leave. The respondent may apply to set aside leave which has been granted, ex parte, but must not delay in making such an application[1], which should be made only:
1. where there has been a material non-disclosure by the applicant;
2. where the case is absolutely unarguable, because the judge was not in possession of sufficient information to appreciate the true nature of the case[2].

Applications to set aside leave should only be made in exceptional circumstances, and should not be seen by respondents as an easy way of having their case heard early[3].

1 *R v Derbyshire County Council, ex p Noble* [1990] ICR 808, CA.
2 *R v Secretary of State for the Home Department, ex p Khalid Al-Nafeesi* [1990] COD 106; *R v Secretary of State for the Home Department, ex p Angur Begum* [1989] COD 398, CA; *R v Secretary of State for the Home Department, ex p Darendranath Doorga* [1990] COD 109.
3 *R v Bromsgrove District Council, ex p Kennedy* [1992] COD 129, per POPPLEWELL J.

149. Conditional grants of leave: security for costs. If the court grants leave, it may impose such terms as to costs as it thinks fit[1]. The court therefore has a greater discretion than in an ordinary action. Nevertheless, it is unlikely that the discretion will be exercised so as to shut out an application which is in the public interest. The discretion has been exercised where, in the view of the court, the application is made in a representative capacity on behalf of others who have funds[2].

1   RSC Ord 53 r 3 (9).
2   See *R v Westminster City Council, ex p Residents Association of Mayfair* [1991] COD 182; *R v Hammersmith and Fulham London Borough Council, ex p People Before Profit Ltd* (1981) 80 LGR 322.

150. Appealing setting aside decisions. The applicant whose leave has been set aside should renew his application, as of right, to the Court of Appeal (ie as if his application had been refused in the first place)[1].

1   Supreme Court Practice 1997 paras 53/1–14/34.

151. Respondent's evidence in reply. The respondent's affidavit must be served within 56 days after service on him of the notice of motion[1]. Application for extension of time may be made to the Crown Office Master, with appeal to the judge, but will not be received sympathetically, in view of the lengthy period already allowed[2]. The court may, at the substantive hearing, permit any person to be heard in opposition to the application to be heard[3]. Although there is no express provision in the Rules of the Supreme Court 1965, the court has also permitted another party to be heard in support of the application.

1   RSC Ord 53 r 6 (4).
2   See Practice Note [1989] 1 All ER 1024, [1989] 1 WLR 358, and *R v Wycombe District Council, ex p Bruce* [1990] COD 353 where, in a wholly exceptional case, a respondent was given four months.
3   RSC Ord 53 r 9 (1).

152. Discovery. Application may be made to a judge for the usual interlocutory orders; for example, discovery pursuant to the Rules of the Supreme Court 1965 Order 24, interrogatories pursuant to the Rules of the Supreme Court 1965 Order 26 and the range of orders relating to evidence pursuant to the Rules of the Supreme Court 1965 Order 38[1]. Such orders may be made (and frequently are made) on an inter partes application for leave (for example, where the applicant seeks an injunction).

Discovery is obtainable upon application whenever and to the extent that the justice of the case requires[2]. The court may, however, decline to allow an applicant to have discovery of internal working documents where it should be possible, on consideration of the decisions themselves, to test whether a decision maker's decision was perverse[3]; and it has been said that an applicant may not have discovery to go behind an affidavit from the respondent unless there is some basis for saying that the affidavit is inaccurate or incomplete[4].

1   RSC Ord 53 r 8, applying RSC Ord 24, RSC Ord 26, RSC Ord 38 r 2 (3).
2   *O'Reilly v Mackman* [1983] 2 AC 237, [1982] 3 All ER 1124, HL, per LORD DIPLOCK. More recent cases on discovery in judicial review include: *R v Secretary of State for Education, ex p J* [1993] COD 146 (discovery should not be ordered on a contingency basis); *R v Secretary of State for Transport, ex p APH Road Safety Ltd* [1993] COD 150 (scope of discovery and inspection on judicial review).
3   *R v Secretary of State for the Environment, ex p Doncaster Borough Council* [1990] COD 441.
4   *R v Secretary of State for the Environment, ex p Islington London Borough Council* [1992] COD 67, [1991] NPC 90, CA; *R v IRC, ex p Taylor* [1989] 1 All ER 906, CA.

153. Orders for cross-examination. Application may also be made, in an appropriate case (for example, some immigration cases[1]), for an order for the attendance of deponents for cross-examination. Cross-examination has also been ordered where there was an issue whether or not a particular form of treatment fell within a statutory definition[2]; where the question arose whether councillors' discretion had been fettered by a Labour Group decision[3]; where there was a question whether Labour councillors were really, as they insisted, influenced by educational considerations in deciding no longer to place advertisements in a particular newspaper[4]; and where the court was obliged to exercise a first instance fact finding jurisdiction[5].

1 As to immigration applications, see Paragraph 68 ante.
2 *R v Mental Health Act Commission, ex p Mark Witham* (26 May 1988, unreported).
3 *R v Waltham Forest London Borough Council, ex p Baxter* [1988] QB 419, [1987] 3 All ER 671, CA.
4 *R v Derbyshire County Council, ex p Times Supplements Ltd* [1991] 3 Admin LR 241.
5 *R v IRC, ex p J Rothschild Holdings plc* [1987] STC 163, CA.

154. Further evidence from applicants. An applicant may often wish to file evidence in reply to the respondent's affidavit, but should remember that the court will be most reluctant to investigate issues of fact. Leave to file additional affidavits should always be sought, either when before the court (for example, on an inter partes application) or on application to the Crown Office Master, on notice to all other parties[1]. The respondent may file further evidence by following the same procedure.

1 See *R v Sandhutton Parish Council, ex p Todd* [1992] COD 409: if a party wishes to prove facts in dispute on the basis of an affidavit containing statements of information and belief, he must seek leave under RSC Ord 38 r 3.

155. Amendment of Form 86A. The Rules of the Supreme Court 1965 Appendix A Form No 86A may be amended in terms of the grounds on which relief is sought and the type of relief, with the leave of the court, and on notice to the other parties, following the same procedure as that for filing further evidence[1]. If an applicant seeks to claim damages by such amendment, then the normal rules of pleading apply, so that as much notice as possible should be given[2].

1 RSC Ord 53 r 6 (2).
2 RSC Ord 53 r 7 (2).

156. Settlement and compromise. Where a respondent acts, between the grant of leave and the substantive hearing, so that the applicant receives that which was sought in the application, for example, for an order of mandamus, then the court can in its discretion order costs[1]. Where the parties have reached agreement, including agreement as to costs, then letters recording such agreement may be sent or faxed to the Crown Office, so that the case may be taken out of the lists[2].

1   See *R v Liverpool City Council, ex p Newman* [1993] COD 65, where the relevant considerations are discussed; but costs may also be refused: *R v IRC, ex p Opman International UK* [1986] 1 All ER 328, [1986] 1 WLR 568, CA.
2   See Paragraph 160 post.

157. Listing, dates for hearing. All judicial review cases are placed in the Crown Office List, which is divided[1] into five parts:
   Part A: cases not yet ready to be heard;
   Part B: cases ready to be heard;
   Part C: cases stood out;
   Part D: expedited cases;
   Part E: cases with hearing dates.

Counsel must provide a time estimate for cases in Part B or Part D.

1   Practice Note [1987] 1 All ER 368, sub nom Practice Direction [1987] 1 WLR 232. See the Supreme Court Practice 1997 paras 53/1–14/45.

158. Discontinuance and standing out of lists. Even where an applicant has obtained leave, the merits of the application should be carefully reconsidered upon receipt of the respondent's affidavit. If the applicant decides to withdraw the application, both parties should apply to the Crown Office Master for an order that the application be withdrawn by consent[1]. Where an applicant simply abandons an application, for example by failing to attend, the respondent may seek costs, having first given notice if possible[2]. Where there is a possibility that a case may settle, but no formal agreement has been reached, but the case has reached the top of List B, the applicant may apply by summons to have the case stood out into Part C[3].

1   RSC Ord 53 r 8 (1); *R v Secretary of State for the Home Department, ex p Brown* (1984) Times, 6 February.
2   *Hinde v Power* [1913] WN 184.
3   Practice Note [1981] 3 All ER 61, [1981] 1 WLR 1296.

159. Preparation of documents. Where a case has entered Part B of the list, the applicant's solicitors will receive a letter informing them of the likelihood of the case being listed. They will be informed when the case is listed and will also be directed that they must lodge a skeleton argument at least five working days before the date fixed for hearing. A skeleton argument should contain:
   1. a time estimate for the length of the hearing, including delivery of the judgment;
   2. a list of issues;
   3. a list of propositions of law to be advanced, together with the authorities relied on, with page references to the passages relied on;
   4. a chronology of events with reference to a properly paginated and indexed bundle of documents;
   5 a list of the documents the court will need to pre-read; and
   6. a list of dramatis personae, where the number of people who feature in the documents warrants it.

A list of authorities must be furnished to the court usher before the morning of the hearing day.

Counsel for the respondent must lodge a skeleton argument no later than three working days before the hearing[1].

1   Practice Note (Crown Office List: Preparation for hearings) [1994] 4 All ER 671, sub nom Practice Direction [1994] 1 WLR 1551; see Supreme Court Practice 1997 para 53/114/48.

160. Uncontested applications. Where the parties have agreed terms for settlement, but need an order of the court to put those terms into effect, they may hand into the Crown Office a document setting out the terms of the proposed agreed order, and a short statement of the matters relied on as justifying the making of the order sought, including reference to authorities or statute, signed by both parties. The judge may then, if satisfied that the order is correct, cause the application to be listed for hearing, and the order pronounced in open court, without the parties' attendance. If he is not satisfied, the application will be listed for an ordinary hearing[1].

1   Practice Direction [1997] 1 WLR 825.

161. Procedure at the hearing. The applicant may appear by counsel or in person; there is no need for a party to appear simply because it has been served, but the court has a wide discretion to hear any person who wishes to be heard and who appears to be a proper person to be heard[1]. The applicant's case is heard first, followed by the respondent's, with a reply by the applicant.

Where it appears to the court that the application has been inappropriately brought under the Rules of the Supreme Court 1965 Order 53, and the relief sought is a declaration, an injunction, or damages, and if the court concludes that such relief might have been granted if it had been sought in an action begun by writ by the applicant at the time of making his application, it may order that the proceedings continue as if they had been begun by writ[2].

1   RSC Ord 53 r 9 (1); see *R v Secretary of State for the Environment, ex p Hammersmith and Fulham London Borough Council* [1991] 1 AC 521, [1990] 3 All ER 589, HL.
2   RSC Ord 53 r 9 (5) and see also RSC Ord 28 r 8 which shall apply as if, in the case of an application made by motion, it had been made by summons and *Re Deadman, Smith v Garland* [1971] 2 All ER 101, [1971] 1 WLR 426.

162. Precedent and issue estoppel. When exercising its jurisdiction under Section 31 of the Supreme Court Act 1981[1] the court will follow the principle of stare decisis, and will follow a court of equal jurisdiction unless the decision appears to be clearly wrong.

The principle of issue estoppel does not apply in judicial review applications. This is because, in the absence of formal pleadings, it would be difficult if not impossible to identify any particular issue as having been decided in an earlier application[2]. Also, there is no lawsuit either between the Crown, in whose name the case is brought, and the respondent, or between the respondent and the ex parte applicant.

1 Supreme Court Act 1981 s 31 (11 Halsbury's Statutes (4th Edn) COURTS AND LEGAL SERVICES).
2 *R v Secretary of State for the Environment, ex p Hackney London Borough Council* [1983] 3 All ER 358, [1983] 1 WLR 524.

163. Costs. The costs of and incidental to any proceedings are in the discretion of the court[1]. The principles employed are the same as in ordinary proceedings in the High Court. The applicant may be refused costs even though the decision challenged was held to be procedurally flawed, if the court used its discretion to decline relief[2]. The court is highly unlikely to make an order for costs against a party which has not appeared or contested the order; but a respondent which delays in performing the act for which the order is sought may face an order for costs[3]. Nevertheless, when justices, having been served with a notice of motion, do not appear at the hearing or resist the application, costs will not normally be awarded against them[4]. The court will be slow to order pre-emptive costs[5].

1 Supreme Court Act 1981 s 51 (1)(as substituted) (11 Halsbury's Statutes (4th Edn) COURTS AND LEGAL SERVICES).
2 *R v Trafford Borough Council, ex p Colonel Foods Ltd* [1990] COD 351.
3 *R v Hastings Licensing Justices, ex p John Lovibond & Sons Ltd* [1968] 2 All ER 270, [1968] 1 WLR 735.
4 *R v Amersham Justices, ex p Fanthorne* (1964) 108 Sol Jo 841, [1964] Crim LR 825; *R v Newcastle under Lyme Justices, ex p Massey* [1995] 1 All ER 120, [1994] 1 WLR 1684.
5 *R v Lord Chancellor, ex p Child Poverty Action Group; R v DPP, ex p Bull* [1998] 2 All ER 755.

164. Appeals. Appeals from the Crown Office Master on an interlocutory application, lie, as a matter of right, to the court[1]; and from a judge, with leave, to the Court of Appeal[2].

Following the substantive hearing, an appeal in a criminal cause or matter lies only to the House of Lords[3]; a certificate that the case involves a point of law of general public importance must be granted by the divisional court and leave must be obtained from the divisional court or from the House of Lords[4]. In non-criminal applications, appeal lies to the Court of Appeal; the time limit for appealing is four weeks from the date of judgment[5]. The Court of Appeal will consider the evidence put before the High Court; but the Court of Appeal has a wider discretion to admit fresh evidence on appeal in public law cases than in ordinary civil litigation[6]. If the evidence has come into being since the date of the substantive hearing, "special grounds" under *Ladd v Marshall*[7] need not be shown.

The court may grant a stay of execution pending an appeal[8]. Costs are within the discretion of the Court of Appeal.

1 RSC Ord 58 r 1.
2 See RSC Ord 59 r 1B.
3 Supreme Court Act 1981 s 18 (1)(a) (11 Halsbury's Statutes (4th Edn) COURTS AND LEGAL SERVICES). Administration of Justice Act 1960 s 1 (1)(a) (12 Halsbury's Statutes (4th Edn) CRIMINAL LAW).
4 Administration of Justice Act 1960 s 1 (2).
5 RSC Ord 59 r 4 (1).
6 *Ali v Secretary of State for the Home Department* [1984] 1 All ER 1009, [1984] 1 WLR 663, CA.
7 *Ladd v Marshall* [1954] 3 All ER 745, [1954] 1 WLR 1489, CA.
8 RSC Ord 59 r 13.

Procedural Table

Applications for judicial review

Steps to be Taken	Form No	RSC
1. Applicant prepares: 　(1) notice of application containing statement of the name and description of the applicant, the relief sought and grounds, the name and address of his solicitors (if any), and his address for service; and 　(2) affidavit in support verifying facts relied upon in the application[1].	1 8	**53,** 3 (2)(a) **53,** 3 (2)(b)
2. Applicant attends with notice of application at Fees and Forms Room (Room E01), Royal Courts of Justice. 　*Fee*[2]:		
3. Applicant attends Crown Office (Room C314) and: 　(1) files notice of application and affidavit; 　(2) lodges 2 copies of each (in a non-criminal cause or matter, 1 copy will suffice); 　(3) completes form of request if an oral hearing of the application is required[3]. 　Applicant will be informed in due course of hearing date. Where the documents exceed 10 pages they must be paginated and indexed and be accompanied by a list of essential pre-reading[4]. Copies of relevant statutory material must be provided[5]. 　*Time*: Promptly, and in any event within 3 months from the date when the grounds for the application first arose.		**57,** 4 (1) **53,** 3 (3) **53,** 4 (1)
4. *If no hearing date is requested*, a judge may determine the application without a hearing. 　*If a hearing is requested*, counsel or the applicant may make the application ex parte to a judge in open court.		**53,** 3 (3)
5. Crown Office serves 1 copy of the judge's order on the applicant.		**53,** 3 (3)
6. *If leave to apply is refused or granted on terms without hearing applicant may*: within 10 days of being served with notice of the judge's order lodge notice of intention to renew the application: 　(1) *in a criminal cause or matter* renewing the application to a divisional court; 　(2) *in any other case* renewing the application to a single judge in open court; *or, if the court so directs*, to a divisional court. Applicant files notice of renewal in the Crown Office.		**53,** 3 (5) **53,** 3 (4)(a) **53,** 3 (4)(b)

191

Steps to be Taken	Form No	RSC
7. *If leave to apply is refused after a hearing*: (1) *in a criminal cause or matter* applicant may: within 10 days of being served with notice of the judge's order lodge notice of intention to renew the application, renewing the application to a divisional court. Applicant lodges in the Crown Office: (i) notice of renewal; (ii) 2 copies thereof; (2) *in any other case* applicant may renew the application within 7 days of the decision to the Court of Appeal, Civil Division, ex parte.		**53**, 3 (5) **53**, 3 (4)(a) **59**, 14 (3) **59**, 14 (3)
8. Judge or court may: (i) adjourn application for notice to be given to respondent(s), (ii) refuse leave, in particular where there has been undue delay in making the application, (iii) allow applicant to amend his statement as to grounds or relief or otherwise, (iv) where an order of certiorari is sought in respect of any judgment, conviction, etc., which is subject to appeal within a time limit, adjourn the application pending the determination of the appeal or until the expiry of the time for appealing, (v) when granting leave to apply: (a) impose terms as to costs and giving security, (b) *if an order of certiorari or prohibition is sought*, direct the stay of the proceedings to which the application relates, (c) *if any other relief is sought*, grant such interim relief as could be granted in an action begun by writ, (vi) *if satisfied that the respondent does not dispute that relief ought to be given*, grant peremptory relief. Notice of motion, if not already lodged in anticipation, is lodged as a matter of formality after the order.		**53**, 3 (6) **53**, 3 (8) **53**, 3 (9) **53**, 3 (10)(a) **53**, 3 (10)(b)
9. The judge or court may direct that in a *non-criminal* cause or matter the application be made: (1) by originating summons to a judge in chambers; *or* (2) by originating motion to a divisional court.		**53**, 5 (2)
10. Order is made by the judge or court and copy thereof is sent to the applicant.		
11. *If the application for leave to apply is granted*, applicant: (i) prepares notice of motion (or, if so directed, originating summons)[6]; and (ii) serves copies of the notice of motion (or summons), and notice of application for leave to apply on:		**53**, 5 (2)

APPLICATIONS FOR JUDICIAL REVIEW

Steps to be Taken	Form No	RSC
(a) all persons directly affected; and (b) where the application relates to proceedings in or before a court and the object is to compel the court or a court officer to do any act in relation to the proceedings or to quash them or any order made in them, on the clerk or registrar of the court and, where any objection to the judge's conduct is made, on the judge; (iii) swears affidavit of service; (iv) attends Fees and Forms Room (Room E01) with notice of motion; Fee[7]: (v) enters the motion for hearing by filing in the Crown Office: (a) notice of motion, (b) affidavit of service and (c) 2 copies of each (unless the hearing is to be before a judge when 1 copy of each will suffice). *Time:* Within 14 days of the grant of leave.		**53**, 5 (3) **53**, 5 (3) **53**, 5 (6) **53**, 5 (5) **53**, 5 (5)
12. Where applicant intends to ask to amend his statement or use further affidavits: Applicant gives notice to every other party of that intention and any proposed amendments.		**53**, 6 (3)
13. *If leave is granted only on a specified ground(s) and applicant wishes to pursue other grounds set out in his Form 86A,* Applicant notifies respondent, and Crown Office, of intention to rely on other grounds[8]. *Time:* Within 21 days of grant of leave.		**53**, 3 (2)
14. *Where respondent intends to use affidavit at hearing* he files it in Crown Office as soon as practicable and in any event within 56 days service of the notice of motion.		**53**, 6 (4)
15. *Where applicant wishes to amend his statement or use further affidavits*: he gives notice to every other party of his intention and of any proposed amendment. Further affidavits dealing with new matters arising out of affidavits filed by any other party may be admitted by the judge or court.		**53**, 6 (3) **53**, 6 (2)
16. Copies of affidavits must be supplied by each party to every other party on demand and on payment of proper charges.		**53**, 6 (5)
17. Before the hearing of the application a party may make interlocutory application to a judge or the Master of the Crown Office[9] for eg: (1) discovery[10]; (2) interrogatories[11]; (3) order requiring deponent to attend for cross-examination[12];		

Steps to be Taken	Form No	RSC
(4) order dismissing the proceedings by consent of the parties; (5) expedition; (6) the case to be stood out from Part B or D of the Crown Office List into Part C. Appeal lies from the Master of the Crown Office to a judge. Fee[13]:		
18. At the expiry of the time for filing of affidavits by the Respondent(s) the matter enters Part B of the Crown Office List and the Crown Office sends "warned list" letter to the applicant who forwards copy letter to: (1) his counsel; (2) all respondents, who in turn notify their counsel. Counsel send to Crown Office written estimates of length of hearing of whole case, including judgment.		
19. As case approaches top of Part B of Crown Office List, Crown Office may send a "short warned letter" informing the applicant that the case is likely to be listed from a specified date, usually two weeks ahead. The applicant must send a copy of that letter to his counsel and to all respondents[14].		
20. At least 5 working days before the date fixed for hearing applicant lodges in Crown Office for use of judge or court paginated, indexed bundle of documents (including respondent's affidavits) together with a skeleton argument containing: (1) a list of issues; (2) a list of propositions of law to be advanced, with authorities relied on; (3) a chronology of events, with references to paginated bundle; (4) where complexity of case warrants, a list of persons involved; Two bundles and two copy skeleton arguments are required where the matter is to be heard by a divisional court.		
21. At least three working days before the hearing counsel for the respondent(s) must lodge a skeleton argument[15].		
22. Parties attend hearing either by counsel or in person[16].		
23. The judge or court may: (1) adjourn and direct that the motion be served on any person who ought to have been served and has not been; (2) allow applicant to amend statement as to grounds or relief or otherwise on such terms, if any, as it thinks fit;		**53,** 5 (7) **53,** 9 (1) **53,** 6 (2)

Steps to be Taken	Form No	RSC
(3) allow further affidavits to be used.		**53**, 6 (2)
24. The judge or court hears counsel for each side and counsel for the applicant in reply and may hear any person in opposition to the motion notwithstanding that he was not served with notice of motion, and (1) may refuse relief sought, in particular where there has been undue delay in making the application; or (2) may grant the relief sought; or (3) where the relief sought is a declaration, an injunction or damages which should not be granted on an application for judicial review, instead of refusing the application, may order the proceedings to continue as if begun by writ.		**53**, 5 (7) **53**, 9 (1) **53**, 9 (5)
25. Where the relief sought is certiorari and the judge or court is satisfied that there are grounds for quashing the decision to which the application relates, in addition to quashing the decision, the judge or court may remit the matter to the court, tribunal or authority concerned to reconsider it in accordance with the findings of the judge or court.		**53**, 9 (4)
26. The judge or court may award damages to the applicant where damages: (1) were claimed in his statement; and (2) could have been awarded in an action begun at the time of the application for judicial review.		**53**, 7 (1)
27. Any order made is drawn up in the Crown Office. The Master of the Crown Office retains custody of all records.		**57**, 6

1 The documents should be prepared and indexed. Where the relief sought includes certiorari to quash an order or other decision, a copy of the order etc must be exhibited to the affidavit.
2 See Atkin's Directory of Costs and Fees.
3 Where interim relief is sought see Paragraph 153 ante.
4 Practice Direction [1994] 1 WLR 1551.
5 Practice Note [1997] 1 All ER 128.
6 Or originating summons to judge in chambers if the court so directs: RSC Ord 53 r 5 (2). See Vol 14 (1996 Issue) title CROWN PRACTICE Forms 41–44.
7 See Atkin's Directory of Costs and Fees.
8 *R v Bow Street Stipendiary Magistrate, ex p Roberts* [1990] 3 All ER 487, [1990] 1 WLR 1317.
9 In criminal causes or matters the application is normally listed before a court.
10 RSC Ord 24.
11 RSC Ord 26.
12 RSC Ord 38 r 2 (3).
13 Supreme Court Fees Order 1980, SI 1980/821, Fee No 5A (as amended).
14 See note 4 above.
15 See note 4 above.
16 Practice Note [1947] WN 218.

Forms

1

NOTICE OF APPLICATION for leave to apply for a range of remedies, including interim relief[1]

(*Royal Arms*)[2]

Applicants' Ref. No. ...   Crown Office Ref. No. ... 19...[3]

The Queen
and
[London Borough] of ....   [Respondent]

Ex parte (*state the names of the applicants*)

This form must be read together with Notes for Guidance obtainable from the Crown Office

---

To the Master of the Crown Office, Royal Courts of Justice, Strand, London WC2A 2LL

Name: (*state the names of the applicants*)
Address: (*state address*)
Description of the Applicants: The Applicants are elderly residents of a residential care home within the Respondents' district.

Judgment etc. (*state clearly the judgment, order, decision or other proceeding in respect of which relief is sought*)

The decisions made by the Social Services Department of the London Borough of ...., on .... 19... that the Applicants' residential care home should be closed and that the same should occur without any consultation of the Applicants.

Relief sought: Judicial review in the form of:
(*state particulars of the relief sought*)

1. An Order of Certiorari to remove into the Queen's Bench Division of the High Court of Justice and to quash the said decisions
[and *or* or]
2. An Order of Mandamus to oblige the Respondent to reconsider its closure decision after consultation with the Applicants in accordance with the law [and *or* or] their legitimate expectations
[and *or* or]
3. A Declaration that the Applicants were and are entitled to be consulted prior to any decision being made, in respect of closure of their residential premises
[and *or* or]
4. Prohibition [and *or* or] Injunction to prevent closure of the said home [and *or* or] removal from the premises of the Applicants
[and *or* or]

5. Interim relief in the form of an injunction restraining the respondents, their servants or agents from altering the Applicants' present accommodation arrangements without their consent.

The Applicant requests an oral application for leave in view of the interim relief sought.

Name and address of the Applicants' Solicitors E. F. & Co,
[Agents for (*name*) of (*address*)]

(Signature)

DATED .... 19 ...

(Second page)

GROUNDS ON WHICH RELIEF IS SOUGHT

(Set out here the grounds for judicial review including an outline of any propositions of law supported by relevant authorities. Grounds must be supported by an affidavit verifying the facts relied on. Where grounds have been settled by counsel, they must be signed by counsel.) (If there has been any delay, include reasons here)

THE FACTS

1. Both the Applicants are aged over 85 years, and are resident in a residential home run by the Respondents (*state address*) that has been selected for closure for reasons of under-use, onerous maintenance requirements and heavy restoration expenditure. The National Assistance Act 1948 Section 21[4] imposes a duty on the Respondents to provide accommodation for the elderly in their area.

2. On .... 19... a working party within the Respondent's social services department looked into the viability of the home in question. It was taken for granted that none of the residents would want to move, most having been there for over .... years. The Applicants have both been resident at (*state address*) for .... years.

3. On .... 19... and on .... 19... the Chair of the Social Services Committee wrote to the Applicants by way of a letter addressed to all the occupants of the home and promised "a full programme of consultation after Christmas" with regard to their future accommodation.

4. On .... 19... the Applicants were informed that the decision to close (*state address*) had been taken, that they would be invited to choose between three other local homes which were to remain open and that they would have to vacate by the end of .... 19... .

THE GROUNDS FOR REVIEW

1. Illegality [and *or* or] Procedural Impropriety

1.1. It is contended that there was a duty to consult the residents before the decision to close (*state address*) was made, either pursuant to statute (National Health Service and Community Care Act 1990 Section 46 (2)[5]) or under the common law, given that a closure decision would inevitably affect what remains of the Applicants' lives in a particularly significant manner. The Applicants will rely on the decision of this Court in *R v Secretary of State for Health, ex p United States Tobacco International Inc* [1992] 1 QB 353[6] for the principle that the Court may infer what is required in order to constitute fairness in any given situation, from all the circumstances of the case.

1.2. Alternatively, if there is merely a discretion on the part of the Respondents whether to consult persons in the position of the Applicants, then the Applicants had a legitimate expectation that they would be consulted in this situation, arising from two letters written by the Chair of the Social Services Committee. The letters are exhibited to the Applicants' verifying affidavit and are capable of only one interpretation that consultation would take place and that it would be full and detailed. Having read the letters the Applicants relied on that promise and did not seek to raise the matter again with any of the staff of the home, or with the Respondents, over the Christmas period. The Applicants will rely on the decisions in *R v Board of Inland Revenue, ex p MFK Underwriting Agencies Ltd* [1990] 1 All ER 91 and *Jockey Club, ex p RAM Racecourses Ltd* [1993] 2 All ER 225[7] for the conditions necessary before a legitimate expectation may be raised.

2. Irrationality

Alternatively, if there be no duty to consult in such circumstances, nor any legitimate expectation on the facts, the Applicants contend that:

2.1. the decision not to consult the residents must be seen to be irrational, in that manifestly relevant considerations, the wishes and views of residents for whose welfare the Respondents were responsible, would not be taken into account in the decision regarding closure of their home of ... years.

2.2. alternatively, the decision to close the home was itself irrational for want of consideration of the manifestly relevant matter set out above.

MISCELLANEOUS MATTERS OF WHICH THE COURT SHOULD BE AWARE:

2.2.1. It might be suggested that there is an alternative remedy open to the Applicants in this case under provisions in the Act, namely, the opportunity to make a complaint to the Minister under Local Authority Social Services Act 1970 Section 7D[8] that the respondents were failing in their statutory duty. However, the Applicants contend that that remedy is neither as convenient nor effective as an application for judicial review. Academic research has shown recently that the Minister has never been known to use these powers to intervene in matters of social services policy, and that the remedy is therefore worthless to individuals

2.2.2. The Applicants contend that in any event the Court's jurisdiction is unaffected by the existence of an alternative remedy in the statute. At most the Court might take its existence into account in its discretion whether to grant a remedy to the Applicants.

INTERIM RELIEF

Since the closure decision is due to take effect at the end of this month the Applicants ask for an interim injunction or a stay of the proceedings under the Rules of the Supreme Court 1965[9] to prevent disturbance of the Applicants' accommodation arrangements pending the full hearing of this application, subject of course to changes to which they might consent.

(If there has been any delay, include reasons here)

(Signature of counsel, after formal parts)

1 See RSC Ord 53 r 3 (2)(a). This form is based on *R v Devon County Council, ex p Baker and R v Durham County Council, ex p Broxon* [1995] 1 All ER 73, CA, where the applicant's appeal in the second case was allowed only on the basis of the facts. See Form 7 post for the affidavit which must support this application.
2 A replica of the royal aArms must be printed or embossed at the first page of every originating process: RSC Ord 1 r 9 (2).
3 The reference number must be included in every pleading: RSC Ord 18 r 6 (1)(a).
4 National Assistance Act 1948 s 21 (as amended) (40 Halsbury's Statutes (4th Edn) SOCIAL SECURITY).
5 National Health Service and Community Care Act 1990 s 46 (2)(as amended) (40 Halsbury's Statutes (4th Edn) SOCIAL SECURITY).
6 *R v Secretary of State for Health, ex p United States Tobacco International Inc* [1992] 1 QB 353, [1992] 1 All ER 212.
7 *Board of Inland Revenue, ex p MFK Underwriting Agencies Ltd* [1990] 1 All ER 91, [1990] 1 WLR 1545; *R v Jockey Club ex p RAM Racecourses Ltd* [1993] 2 All ER 225.
8 Local Authority Social Services Act 1970 s 7D (as inserted) (25 Halsbury's Statutes (4th Edn) LOCAL GOVERNMENT).
9 Rules of the Supreme Court 1965.

2
NOTICE OF APPLICATION for leave to apply for a range of remedies based on legitimate expectation and unreasonableness[1]

(Royal Arms)[2]

Applicants' Ref. No....   Crown Office Ref No. ... 19...[3]

The Queen
and
Commissioners of the Inland Revenue   [Respondents]
Ex parte A. B.   [Applicant]

This form must be read together with Notes for Guidance obtainable from the Crown Office

To the Master of the Crown Office, Royal Courts of Justice, Strand, London WC2A 2LL

Name: *(state the names of the applicants)*
Address: *(state address)*
Description of the Applicant: Businessman, shareholder and director of various public and limited companies

Judgment etc. *(state clearly the judgment, order, decision or other proceedings in respect of which relief is sought).*
The decision made by the Respondents to refuse to treat sales of shares in one of the Applicant's limited companies as a single transaction in accordance with published Revenue policy.

Relief sought: Judicial review in the form of:
(state particulars of the relief sought)
1. An Order of Certiorari to remove into the Queen's Bench Division of the High Court of Justice and to quash the said refusal
[and *or* or]

2. An Order of Mandamus to oblige the Respondents to reconsider their decision in accordance with the law or the Applicant's legitimate expectation
[and or or]
3. A Declaration that the refusal to apply the published policies retrospectively to the Applicant's sales was unlawful
[and or or]
4. A Declaration that the Applicant is entitled to be treated as if he and his wife had sold a single holding of shares
[and or or]
5. A Declaration that the Applicant is entitled to return of £... million in tax paid to the Respondents.

Name and address of the Applicants' Solicitors E. F. & Co of (*address*), [Agents for (*name*) of (*address*)]

(Signature)

DATED .... 19...

(Second page)

GROUNDS ON WHICH RELIEF IS SOUGHT

(Here the grounds for judicial review should be stated, including an outline of any propositions of law, supported by relevant authorities. Grounds must be supported by an affidavit verifying the facts relied on. Where grounds have been settled by counsel they must be signed by counsel)

THE FACTS

1. Up to .... 19... shares in one of the Applicant's limited companies were partly held by the Applicant and his wife; together they owned a majority of the voting shares. The Applicant was advised by a professional advisor that a substantial tax saving could be made if his wife were to transfer her relatively small holding of shares to him before a proposed sale onwards to a purchaser. The advice was subject to the qualification that the "tax avoidance" cases (eg *Furniss v Dawson* [1984] AC 474, [1984] 1 All ER 530[4]) might be applied to the transfer, and as a result, the Applicant and his wife eventually decided to sell the shares separately on .... 19... .

2. On .... 19... the Respondents published an extra-statutory concession and statement of practice. Neither purported to alter the existing practice of the Revenue, but sought instead to clarify the tax position in precisely the sort of transfer that had been proposed between the Applicant and his wife. The clarified practice of the Revenue applicable to such a transfer would have been highly financially advantageous to the Applicant. Neither of the Respondents' publications referred to the "tax avoidance" cases which had led the Applicant and his wife to sell their shares separately.

3. Prior to the decision to sell the shares separately to the proposed purchaser, the Applicant had entered into correspondence with the Revenue mentioning the type of issue raised by the factual situation in which the Applicant found himself, and asking for an indication of Revenue policy. The Respondents' reply made no reference to the relevance of the tax avoidance line of authority to the proposals of the Applicant.

4. The Applicant and his wife would have recovered £... million if the Respondents had treated the sale as a sale of a single holding in accordance with its publications. On .... 19... the Revenue refused to accept that the completed separate sales could be treated as one.

THE LAW

5. The omission on the part of the Respondents to refer to the tax avoidance cases in their publications, if taken together with the emphasis therein that no changes to existing practice were contained in the policy statements means that at the time of the sales of the Applicant's shares, he could have brought what was proposed to be done by him and his wife within a beneficial category of transaction, without fear of the transaction being examined on the basis of *Furniss v Dawson* [1984] AC 474, [1984] 1 All ER 530. He had a legitimate expectation of the Revenue's policy as clarified being applied to his position.

6. In the circumstances it is contended that it is unfair and discriminatory so as to amount to an abuse of power on the part of the Respondents to refuse to treat what was done prior to the publication of the clarification of existing policy as a sale of a single holding. If the clarification of existing practice had been published before the intended sale the Applicant would have had a legitimate expectation of a substantial benefit, namely favourable treatment of a transaction which would have saved him £... million in tax.

(If there has been any delay, include reasons here)

(Signature of counsel, after formal parts)

---

1 See RSC Ord 53 r 3 (2)(a). These grounds are adapted from the case of *R v IRC, ex p Kaye* [1992] STC 581, 65 Tax Cases 82 in which it was held, dismissing the application: (1) it did not follow inevitably from the omission to refer to the tax avoidance authorities in the publications that the Revenue would never seek to challenge a transfer on such grounds; (2) correspondence between the applicants and the Revenue had not raised the specific question whether the relevance of the tax avoidance cases was now negated by the practice statement, so it was not possible to say that there had been a representation or assurance in this case; (3) the applicants had failed to establish that they had been discriminated against, in the sense of being worse off than taxpayers effecting similar transactions after the publication; there was still no assurance by the Revenue of immunity from an avoidance challenge for any taxpayer; (4) a contrary analysis might deter the Revenue from making helpful statements for fear of liability arising. See Form 7 post for the form of the affidavit which must support an application.
2 See Form 1 note 2 ante.
3 See Form 1 note 3 ante.
4 *Furniss v Dawson* [1984] AC 474, [1984] 1 All ER 530, HL.

3

NOTICE OF APPLICATION for leave to apply for a range of remedies based on failure to take account of a relevant consideration [and *or* or] procedural impropriety (prisoners' rights)[1]

(Royal Arms)[2]

Applicants' Ref. No. ...   Crown Office Ref. No. ... 19...[3]

The Queen
and
Deputy Governor of .... Prison   [Respondent]
Ex parte A. B.   [Applicant]

This form must be read together with Notes for Guidance obtainable from the Crown Office

NOTICE OF APPLICATION

To the Master of the Crown Office, Royal Courts of Justice, Strand, London WC2A 2LL

Name: A. B.
Address: (*state address of prison*)
Description of the Applicant: Prisoner with four years of a seven year sentence to serve

Judgment etc. (*state clearly the judgment, order decision or other proceedings in respect of which relief is sought*)
The decisions made by the Respondent
1. to refuse to treat a disciplinary charge against the Applicant for alleged assault occasioning actual bodily harm as an offence meriting investigation by the Crown Prosecution Service;
2. to refuse to allow legal representation of the Applicant at a disciplinary hearing held on the .... 19... and
3. to award the maximum lawful disciplinary award for the alleged offence.

Relief sought: Judicial review in the form of:
(*state particulars of the relief sought*)
1. An Order of Certiorari to remove into the Queen's Bench Division of the High Court of Justice and to quash the said decisions
[and *or* or]
2. An Order of Mandamus to oblige the Respondent to reconsider his decision as to the propriety of treating the alleged offence as a mere disciplinary offence
[and *or* or]
3. An Order of Mandamus to oblige the Respondent to reconsider the question of legal representation in accordance with the law, should his reconsideration of the proper characterisation of the alleged offence still result in a decision to treat it as a disciplinary offence.

Name and address of the Applicants' Solicitors E. F. & Co of (*address*),
[Agents for (*name*) of (*address*)]

(*Signature*)

DATED the .... 19...

(*Second page*)

GROUNDS ON WHICH RELIEF IS SOUGHT

(*Here the grounds for judicial review should be stated, including an outline of any propositions of law supported by relevant authorities. Grounds must be supported by an affidavit verifying the facts relied on. Where grounds have been settled by counsel they must be signed by counsel*)

THE FACTS

1. On .... 19... the Applicant was involved in a fight in .... Prison. He was attacked by another prisoner without provocation and defended himself as was necessary by heaving a tea urn at the aggressor, who was dazed and scalded as a consequence.
2. The Respondent charged the Applicant and the other prisoner involved with disciplinary offences under the Prison Rules 1964[4] (as

amended). The Applicant wrote to the Respondent calling his attention to the Prison Service Guidelines, ... 19..., issued by the Home Office regarding the proper disposition of incidents involving violence in prison, since the decision taken by the UK government that certain offences ought to attract the investigatory powers and procedural protection of criminal proceedings undertaken by the Crown Prosecution Service. The Respondent let it be known to the Applicant that the incident in question was not thought serious enough to justify bothering the Crown Prosecution Service but no reasons were given.

3. On .... 19... the Respondent purported to hear the disciplinary charge and refused an application made by the Applicant at the commencement of the hearing for an adjournment to seek legal advice and representation. The Respondent then purported to determine that the conduct of the Applicant had not occurred by reason of self-defence and that the suitable disciplinary award in this case was confinement in the cells for ... days, the maximum award of that type that the Respondent may lawfully make.

THE LAW

4. It is contended that the decision not to refer the matter to the Crown Prosecution Service was unlawful [and *or* or] irrational by reason of the Respondent's apparent failure to have regard to published guidelines from the Home Office as to appropriate disposition of incidents such as the one in which the Applicant was involved.

5. It is further contended that the very serious disciplinary award meted out is inconsistent with the Respondent's refusal to bring in the Crown Prosecution Service and the decision to deny legal representation, such as to render irrational the award made.

6. It is contended in the alternative that the denial of legal representation in a case requiring skilled cross examination as to the facts of the incident was a breach of natural justice. The Applicant will rely on *R v Secretary of State for the Home Department, ex p Tarrant* [1985] 1 QB 251, [1984] 1 All ER 799[5] in support of his contentions.

(*If there has been any delay, include reasons here*)

(*Signature of counsel, after formal parts*)

1 See RSC Ord 53 r 3 (2)(a). Such a claim could not be used, however, to found a claim for unlawful imprisonment, because of the decision in *R v Deputy Governor of Parkhurst Prison, ex p Hague* [1992] 1 AC 58, [1991] 3 All ER 733, HL. See Paragraph 102 ante. See Form 7 post for the form of the affidavit which must support an application.
2 See Form 1 note 2 ante.
3 See Form 1 note 2 ante.
4 Prison Rules 1964, SI 1964/388 (15 Halsbury's Statutory Instruments (1991 Issue) PRISONS).
5 *R v Secretary of State for the Home Department, ex p Tarrant* [1985] QB 251, [1984] 1 All ER 799.

4
NOTICE OF APPLICATION for leave to apply for a range of remedies based on illegality and unreasonableness (mental health law)[1]

(*Royal Arms*)[2]

Applicants' Ref. No. ...   Crown Office Ref. No. ... 19...[3]

The Queen
and
A. B. District Health Authority   [Respondent]
Ex parte C. D.   [Applicant]

This form must be read together with Notes for Guidance obtainable from the Crown Office

---

To the Master of the Crown Office, Royal Courts of Justice, Strand, London WC2A 2LL

Name: C. D.
Address: (*state address*)
Description of the Applicant: (*state occupation or other description*)
Former hospital porter and presently restricted patient at Broadmoor.

Judgment etc. (*state clearly the judgment, order decision or other proceeding in respect of which relief is sought*)
The decision made by the Respondents to refuse to provide aftercare in the community for the Applicant, in accordance with conditions laid down by a Mental Health Review Tribunal when making a deferred conditional discharge order in respect of the Applicant.

Relief sought: Judicial review in the form of:
(*state particulars of the relief sought*)
1. An Order of Certiorari to remove into the Queen's Bench Division of the High Court of Justice and to quash the said refusal
[and *or* or]
2. An Order of Mandamus to oblige the Respondents to provide aftercare in accordance with Section 117 (2) Mental Health Act 1983[4] or Section 3 (1) National Health Service Act 1977[5]
[and *or* or]
3. A Declaration that the Respondents are in breach of the said section until the said aftercare is provided
[and *or* or]
4. Damages for breach of statutory duty leading to false imprisonment.

Name and address of the Applicants' Solicitors E. F. & Co of (*address*), [Agents for (*name*) of (*address*)]

(*Signature*)

DATED .... 19...

(*Second page*)

GROUNDS ON WHICH RELIEF IS SOUGHT

(*Here the grounds for judicial review should be stated, including an outline of any propositions of law supported by relevant authorities. Grounds must be supported by an affidavit verifying the facts relied on. Where grounds have been settled by counsel they must be signed by counsel*)

THE FACTS

1. The Respondent District Health Authority has refused to supply psychiatric supervision in the community for the Applicant, a patient at .... A Mental Health Review Tribunal considered the Applicant's situation in .... 19... and directed conditional discharge, deferred until it could be satisfied that certain supervision conditions would be met. The Mental Health Review Tribunal expressed the view that any delay in discharge would cause problems in the patient's rehabilitation. The Respondent has however decided that the Applicant should be supervised for ... months in a Regional Secure Unit rather than in the community, because no psychiatrist can be found in the area willing, for reasons of clinical judgment, to take responsibility for the supervision of the Applicant. In the event the Applicant remains at .... against his will.

2. A restriction order without limit of time under Mental Health Act 1983 Section 41[6] was made by the Judge in the Applicant's trial. The Tribunal made its order for deferred conditional discharge with full knowledge of a recent deterioration in the Applicant's condition. One of the conditions of release laid down by the Tribunal was that the supervision of a Responsible Medical Office would be available, which was not in fact possible, because the head of the Regional Secure Unit and his colleagues are not prepared to supervise the Applicant; neither is the consultant psychiatrist, in the area where the Applicant is supposed to live.

THE LAW

3. Although a Mental Health Review Tribunal has no express or implied power to direct a health authority to provide any type of health care, Mental Health Act 1983 Section 117 (2) provides that "it shall be the duty of the District Health Authority and of the local social services authority to provide, in co-operation with relevant voluntary agencies, after-care services for any person". The Applicant contends that doctors are not entitled to substitute their clinical judgments for the decision of the Mental Health Review Tribunal and that Mental Health Act 1983 Section 117 imposes an absolute duty on health authorities. Alternatively it is contended that an absolute duty to provide such aftercare arises under National Health Service Act 1977 Section 3 (1) which demands the provision of a comprehensive range of services. If a medical officer could undermine the powers of the Mental Health Review Tribunal, the order of the Court, the aftercare provisions of Section 117 and the manifest rationale of Mental Health Act 1983 Section 73 (7)[7] providing for discharge would be frustrated.

4. The Court should be aware that the Respondents contend that the said statutory provisions merely require the provision of such aftercare as is considered appropriate by a health authority's officers. There is, furthermore, a remedy for breach of statutory duty by way of intervention by the Secretary of State. The Applicant does not wish to use that avenue of redress since neither he nor his advisors can envisage the Minister intervening in decisions based on clinical judgment and, ultimately, financial resources. The Mental Health Review Tribunal was due to sit again in .... 19... but the Applicant has cancelled the hearing and applies for leave for judicial review instead on the basis that determination of alleged breach of statutory duty is beyond the jurisdiction of such tribunals.

5. It is contended in the circumstances that the failure to provide the aftercare laid down in the decision of the Mental Health Review Tribunal amounts to illegality in that it is based on a misconstruction by the Respondents of the extent of the statutory duty imposed upon them by the Mental Health Act 1983.

(If there has been any delay, include reasons here)

(Signature of counsel, after formal parts)

---

1 See RSC Ord 53 r 3 (2)(a). The grounds in this case are adapted from *R v Ealing District Health Authority, ex p Fox* [1993] 3 All ER 170, [1993] 1 WLR 373 in which it was held, granting the application: (1) although the health authority had fulfilled its general duty to provide facilities considered appropriate by the establishment of a regional secure unit in Ealing, the health authority had a further mandatory duty to provide after care services under Mental Health Act 1983 s 117 (2)(as amended) (28 Halsbury's Statutes (4th Edn) MENTAL HEALTH) for any person to whom the section applied. That duty is a continuing duty in respect of any patient who may be discharged, although the duty to any particular patient is only triggered at the moment of discharge; (2) alternatively, such a duty could arise out of the general statutory framework requiring district health authorities to provide a comprehensive range of hospital and psychiatric services; (3) to fail in this duty amounted to an error of law; (4) the health authority consultants remain free to exercise their clinical judgment but acceptance by the district health authority of those opinions was not a sufficient discharge of its obligations to proceed with reasonable expedition to give effect to the arrangements specified by the mental health review tribunal. If the doctors disagreed with the conditions, the district health authority must endeavour to obtain help from other health authorities, and in the final analysis, refer the matter to the secretary of state so as to enable him to consider exercising his power to refer the case back to the mental health review tribunal under the Mental Health Act 1983 s 71 (1); (5) certiorari would be granted but mandamus compelling provision by Ealing would be withheld. A declaration reflecting the above propositions of law was appropriate in the circumstances. See Form 7 post for the form of the affidavit which must support an application.
2 See Form 1 note 2 ante.
3 See Form 1 note 3 ante.
4 Mental Health Act 1983 s 117 (2)(as amended).
5 National Health Service Act 1977 s 3 (1)(e) (30 Halsbury's Statutes (4th Edn) NATIONAL HEALTH SERVICE).
6 Mental Health Act 1983 s 41 (as amended and as further amended by the Crime (Sentences) Act 1997 s 49 (1), (2)).
7 Mental Health Act 1983 s 73 (7).

5

NOTICE OF APPLICATION for leave to apply for a range of remedies based on unreasonableness, failure to take account of a relevant consideration, fettering of discretion by rigid adherence to a policy [and *or* or] procedural impropriety; giving reasons for delay (education law)[1]

(*Royal Arms*)[2]

Applicants' Ref. No. ...   Crown Office Ref. No. ... 19...[3]

The Queen
and
(1) Governors of A. B. School
(2) The [London Borough of ....]   [Respondents]
Ex parte C. D.   [Applicant]

This form must be read together with Notes for Guidance obtainable from the Crown Office

Description of the Applicant: (*state occupation or other description*) Catering manageress and parent of E. D., a pupil at X. Y. school who hopes to be granted a place at the First Respondents' school for the forthcoming academic season.

Judgment etc. (*state clearly the judgment, order decision or other proceeding in respect of which relief is sought*)

The decision made by the First Respondents to refuse to admit the Applicant's child to their school, on .... 19...; the decision of the Second Respondent to uphold that decision, made on .... 19..., and the decisions of both respondents to conclude thus without giving the Applicant a proper opportunity to be heard.

Relief sought: Judicial review in the form of:

(*state particulars of the relief sought*)

The Applicant seeks an oral hearing of the application for leave[3] and

1. An Order of Certiorari to remove into the Queen's Bench Division of the High Court of Justice and to quash the said decisions

[and *or* or]

2. An Order of Mandamus to oblige the First Respondents to reconsider their decision in accordance with the law or to withdraw their current policy pertaining to children with a history of suspension

[and *or* or]

3. Further or alternatively, a Declaration that the First Respondents' admissions policy regarding children with a history of suspension is unlawful [and *or* or] irrational

[and *or* or]

4. A Declaration that the First [and *or* or] Second Respondents are obliged by the rules of natural justice to afford to the Applicant an opportunity to be heard in person on their reconsideration of the matter.

Name and address of the Applicants' Solicitors E. F. & Co of (*address*), [Agents for (*name*) of (*address*)]

(*Signature*)

DATED .... 19...

(Second page)

GROUNDS ON WHICH RELIEF IS SOUGHT

(Here the grounds for judicial review should be stated, including an outline of any propositions of law supported by relevant authorities. Grounds must be supported by an affidavit verifying the facts relied on. Where grounds have been settled by counsel they must be signed by counsel)

THE FACTS AND LAW

1. The Applicant is the mother of a child, E. D., seeking admission to an aided school, known as ....; it is governed by the Respondent governors, who are the admissions authority for the purposes of the Education Act 1980[4]. That Act provides that the preference as to choice of school on the part of parents of school aged children shall be taken into account by admissions authorities and must be abided by unless compliance would prejudice efficient education or the efficient use of resources.

2. On .... 19... the Applicant indicated her preference that her child should attend the Respondents' school as from the commencement of the .... term 19.... The Respondent governors informed the Applicant on ....19... that E. D. had not been granted a place at the school because the governors were operating a policy of refusing admission to any child who had been suspended from their current schools within the last two years.

3. The Applicant contends that such a policy is unlawful in any event, since if all schools in a particular area adopted such a policy, it would have the effect of precluding access to education for all such children. This would in turn defeat the purpose of the Education Act 1980 by denying parental preference with regard to admissions, in the absence of any evidence whatsoever that the admission of individual pupils would prejudice efficient education in particular schools. The local authority statutorily responsible for the securing of sufficient schools to provide adequate education in the area would be frustrated in its attempts to fulfil that duty. In such circumstances it is contended that the policy is inherently irrational and unlawful by virtue of its consequences being contrary to the general law of educational provision, and to the specific statutory regime concerning parental preference.

4. The Applicant exercised her statutory right of appeal under the Education Act 1996[5], to no avail. The Applicant contends that the existence of the appeal right does not preclude judicial review in this case since her contentions are based primarily upon the inherent unlawfulness of the policy adopted and applied. The appeal committee's written decision dated .... 19... stated that the committee did not see any justification for interfering with the governors' policy, but if the policy is itself unlawful, it is suggested that its upholding by the appeal committee cannot render it lawful.

5. In the alternative, if such a policy is inherently lawful, the Applicant contends that it has been in this case applied to her child in a "blanket" manner, that is to say, without consideration of the special circumstances of her child's case, so as to amount to an unlawful fettering of the admission authority's discretion. Even when the Applicant wrote to the Respondent governors pointing out that her child's very brief suspension had been rescinded when further evidence about the incident leading to it had come to light, the governors maintained that the policy operated in respect of any actual suspension whatsoever. The appeal committee did not permit the Applicant to give evidence about the background to her child's previous suspension. The Applicant will rely on the Code of Practice drawn up by

local authorities in association with the Council on Tribunals, which the Court should be aware is not legally binding. In any event, the Applicant will rely on *R v Greenwich LBC, ex p Governors of John Ball Primary School* [1990] Fam Law 469, CA[6] in support of her contentions under this head.

6. The Applicant contends further and alternatively that the requirements of procedural fairness demand that if such a policy is to be operated by those in the position of the Respondents, then parents such as the Applicant should be given an oral hearing at which to make representations as to why the said policy should be waived in respect of their children. Both the Respondent governors and the appeal committee denied the Applicant any opportunity to address them in person about the grave personal consequences which would arise from rejection of E. D. by the school in question. As such it is contended that the decision is either flawed by procedural unfairness or is vitiated by failure to take into account relevant considerations, namely, the consequences of the decision to the child, E. D. .

(If there has been delay, include the reasons here)

The Applicant has delayed somewhat in making this application for leave in view of her recognition that she might be required to exhaust her statutory remedies before attempting to move this Court. She relies on *R v Northamptonshire County Council, ex p Tebbutt* (CO 322/96, 26 June 1986, unreported) and *Secretary of State for Education and Science and Bedfordshire County Council, ex p Threapleton* [1988] COD 102[7] in support of the contention that it was prudent to defer this application until the hearing of the appeal offered in this case. The month between the appeal committee's decision and this application has been spent applying for legal aid but the Applicant has acted with all possible expedition and co-operated with her legal advisors.

(Signature of counsel, after formal parts)

1 See RSC Ord 53 r 3 (2)(a). The applicant must express such a request or else the application will be dealt with on the papers alone. See Paragraph 141 ante. See Form 7 post for the form of the affidavit which must support an application.
2 See Form 1 note 2 ante.
3 See Form 1 note 3 ante.
4 Education Act 1980 (15 Halsbury's Statutes (4th Edn) EDUCATION).
5 In relation to admissions appeals relating to county and voluntary schools see: Education Act 1996 s 423 and in relation to grant-maintained schools see: Education Act 1996 s 429 (15 Halsbury's Statutes (4th Edn) EDUCATION).
6 *R v Greenwich LBC, ex p Governors of John Ball Primary School* (1990) 88 LGR 589, [1990] Fam Law 469, CA.
7 *R v Northamptonshire County Council, ex p Tebbutt* (CO 322/96, 26 June 1986, unreported) and *R v Secretary of State for Education and Science and Bedfordshire County Council, ex p Threapleton* [1988] COD 102.

6
NOTICE OF APPLICATION for leave to apply for a range of remedies based on failure to take relevant matters into account, taking irrelevant matters into account, error of law and unreasonableness (immigration law)[1]

(*Royal Arms*)[2]

Applicants' Ref. No. ...   Crown Office Ref. No. ... 19...[3]

The Queen

and

Secretary of State for the Home Department   [Respondent]

Ex parte (*state the names of the applicants*)

This form must be read together with Notes for Guidance obtainable from the Crown Office

To the Master of the Crown Office, Royal Courts of Justice, Strand, London WC2A 2LL

Name: (*state the names of the applicants*)
Address: (*state address*)
Description of the Applicants:

Judgment etc. (*state clearly the judgment, order, decision or other proceeding in respect of which relief is sought*)

The refusal of leave of entry to the Applicant, contained in the Notice dated .... 19...

Relief sought: Judicial review in the form of:

(*state particulars of the relief sought*)

An Order of Certiorari to quash the said Notice of Refusal, and an Order of Mandamus to compel the Secretary of State for the Home Department to grant the Applicant leave to enter the United Kingdom

---

Name and address of the Applicants' Solicitors E. F. & Co. of (*address*), [Agents for (*name*) of (*address*)]

(*Signature*)

DATED .... 19...

(*Second page*)

GROUNDS ON WHICH RELIEF IS SOUGHT

(*Set out here the grounds for judicial review including an outline of any propositions of law supported by relevant authorities. Grounds must be supported by an affidavit verifying the facts relied on. Where grounds have been settled by counsel, they must be signed by counsel.*)

THE FACTS

1. The Applicant is a citizen of ....

2. In .... 19... he was given leave to enter the United Kingdom as a student, and undertook an LLB Honours course at ....

3. He was given several extensions of leave, following his failing on a number of occasions, but finally passing his first year examinations. The last such extension was granted on .... 19... and expired on .... 19... .

4. On .... 19... the Applicant was due to take his second year examinations, but was unable to do so because of illness. He was permitted by the .... to sit these examinations the following .... 19... .

5. On .... 19... he returned from a weekend visit to .... On arriving in England he was interviewed by Immigration Officers for the Secretary of State on two occasions on the same day. During the first such interview the Officers telephoned the Secretary to the .... Law Department, and informed the Applicant that they had obtained information on the basis of which they considered it unlikely that he would complete his studies.

6. On .... 19... the Officers served the Applicant with Notice of Refusal the grounds for which were stated to be, inter alia: first, that the Applicant did not have sufficient funds to continue with his course without recourse to public funds or working; and second, that there was no reasonable prospect of his studies finishing.

7. On .... 19... the Applicant was further interviewed by the same Officers, and produced satisfactory documentary evidence of his ability to continue his course without recourse to public funds or working. In addition, he produced evidence of the examinations he had passed.

THE LAW

8. Rule 60 of the Immigration Rules 1990[4] states that a passenger whose stay in the United Kingdom was subject to a time limit and who returns after a temporary absence abroad has no claim to admission as a returning resident, but his application to re-enter should be dealt with in the light of all the relevant circumstances.

GROUNDS

9. Since there had been no change of circumstance since the Applicant was last granted an extension of leave to remain, in .... 19..., save that he had not sat his examination, as intended, in .... 19..., the Immigration Officers must have misdirected themselves as to the relevant Rules.

10. Further or alternatively, the Immigration Officers failed to take into account all relevant factors, inter alia, that the Applicant could support himself without recourse to public funds or working, and had passed and could be expected to pass his examinations.

11. Further or alternatively, the decision to serve a Notice of Refusal of entry was a decision which no reasonable immigration officers properly directing themselves could have taken.

(If there has been any delay, include reasons here)

(Signature of counsel, after formal parts)

1 This draft is based on the facts of *R v Secretary of State for the Home Department, ex p Uzoenyi* [1992] COD 217. It should be noted that the respondent contended that the applicant should have appealed against the decision under the Immigration Act 1971 s 13 (as amended) (31 Halsbury's Statutes (4th Edn) NATIONALITY AND IMMIGRATION); but since two years had passed, and the case was exceptional, the decision was quashed and remitted to the respondent, although no order of mandamus was issued no compel the respondent to grant the applicant leave to enter.
2 See Form 1 note 2 ante.
3 See Form 1 note 3 ante.
4 Statement of Changes in Immigration Rules (H of C Paper (1994) no 395) para 20.

7
AFFIDAVIT of applicant in support of application for leave[1]

Applicant: .... 1st .... 19...G.W.1,2[2]

IN THE HIGH COURT OF JUSTICE   Crown Office Ref No. ... 19...
 Queen's Bench Division
  Crown Office List

IN THE MATTER of an application by (*state name of applicants*) for leave to apply for Judicial Review (Rules of the Supreme Court 1965 Order 53, Rule 3[3])

1. I, (*state name of applicant*), of (*state residence or workplace, and occupation or, if none, description*), the above-named Applicant, make oath and say as follows:

2. I am one of the two Applicants herein, the other being a fellow resident of (*state address*), (*state name of other applicant*). I make this affidavit in support of our application for leave to apply for judicial review of various decisions of the [London Borough] of .... referred to in RSC Appendix A Form No 86A[4].

3. Save as stated herein all facts and matters deposed to hereafter are within my knowledge, information and belief.

4. I have read the Notice of Application prepared by my advisors and confirm that the factual assertions contained therein are true.

5. There is now produced and shown to me marked "G.W.1' a copy of the two letters from the Chair of the Social Services committee referred to in RSC Appendix A Form No 86A. There is now produced and shown to me marked "G.W.2" a copy of the letter addressed to all the occupants of (*state address*) informing us that the decision to close the home had been finally taken, as is explained in RSC Appendix A Form No 86A. That letter was received on .... 19... .

6 I believe that the decision to close the home was actually taken on .... 19... because I have been informed by the warden of (*state address*) and believe that he was summoned to attend a meeting on that day and asked whether he would expect any of the current residents to take legal advice in respect of a closure decision.

7. In all the circumstances I seek leave to apply for judicial review together with the interim relief sought in RSC Appendix A Form No 86A, and thereafter, the substantive relief claimed therein.

SWORN at (*address*) this .... day
 of .... 19...   } (*Deponent's signature*)[5]
Before me,
(*Signature*)
A [*Solicitor or* Commissioner for Oaths][6]

1 See RSC Ord 53 r 3 (1)(b). For examples of applications see Forms 1–6 ante.
2 Every affidavit must be signed by the deponent and the jurat must be completed and signed by the person before whom it is sworn: RSC Ord 41 r 1 (8). See also *Down v Yearley* [1874] WN 158.
3 RSC Ord 53 r 3.
4 RSC Appendix A Form No 86A. See Forms 1–6 ante.
5 Every affidavit must be signed by the deponent and the jurat must be completed and signed by the person before whom it is sworn: RSC Ord 41 r 1 (8). See also *Down v Yearley* [1874] WN 158.
6 Solicitors Act 1974 s 81 (as amended) (41 Halsbury's Statutes (4th Edn) SOLICITORS); Courts and Legal Services Act 1990 s 113 (as amended) (17 Halsbury's Statutes (4th Edn) EVIDENCE); Administration of Justice Act 1985 s 65 (as amended) (35 Halsbury's Statutes (4th Edn) NOTARIES AND LICENSED CONVEYANCERS); Commissioners for Oaths Acts 1889 and 1891 (as amended) (17 Halsbury's Statutes (4th Edn) EVIDENCE).

8
AFFIDAVIT of respondent[1]

Respondents:......... 1st .... 19...[2]

IN THE HIGH COURT OF JUSTICE   Crown Office Ref No.... 19...
Queen's Bench Division
    Crown Office List

IN THE MATTER of an application by (*state names of applicants*) for leave to apply for Judicial Review (Rules of the Supreme Court 1965 Order 53, Rule 3[3])

I, (*state name*), of (*state residence or workplace, and occupation or if none, description*), make oath and say as follows:

1. I am the Director of Social Services for the Respondents herein, the [London Borough] of .... and am duly authorised to make this Affidavit on the Respondents' behalf. I have read a copy of the Affidavit sworn by (*state name*), the First Applicant, and make this Affidavit in reply thereto, and in support of the Respondents' Application that the Leave granted by Mr Justice .... on .... 19... should be set aside. All facts and matters set out in this Affidavit are within my own knowledge, unless otherwise expressly stated to the contrary.

2. (*State address*) is a Residential Care Home owned and operated by the Respondents, and the Applicants are both residents in it. The Respondents have 100 such Homes, several times more than any other local authority, thanks to an exceptionally generous provision dating from the period when the .... were the ruling party. I can confirm that the Applicants have been residents for more than ... years.

3. I set up the Working Party which, in 19..., in view of the impending insolvency of the Respondents, examined the viability of all 100 Residential Care Homes within my Borough. I had visited all of them, including (*state address*), and was informed by many residents, including the Applicants, that they would hate to move from their Homes, which were all furnished and equipped to exceptional standards. Nevertheless, (*state address*) was constructed in 19..., to house ... residents, and the Applicants were by 19... two of only ... remaining. In addition, major works of refurbishment to the wrought iron verandas and conservatory roof were required, at a cost of £... million. The Working Party concluded on .... 19..., that (*state address*) should be closed, and sold to the .... Hotel Group. This decision was not only very fully reported in the local press and on television, but was

communicated, by letter dated .... 19..., to every resident in my authority's Homes. I know the Applicants received the letter, because on .... 19..., in company with ... other aggrieved residents, they arrived at my home and disrupted my Christmas celebrations.

4. I can confirm that on .... 19... and .... 19... (*state name*), the Chairman of the Respondent's Social Services Committee, wrote to the Applicants promising a full programme of consultation; of course, she made it quite clear that such consultation would concern the Applicants' future accommodation only. On .... 19..., pursuant to that letter, I wrote to the Applicants reminding them that the decision to close their Home had been taken in .... 19..., informing them that they would have to leave by the end of .... 19..., and giving them the choice of three equally palatial homes to which to move. I informed the Applicants that the reason they must move by the end of .... 19... was that the Respondents have a contractual obligation to hand (*state address*) over to .... Hotels on .... 19..., and will bear substantial financial penalties if there is any delay, of the order of £...... per day.

5. I am advised by the Borough Solicitor and respectfully submit that there is in law no automatic right to be consulted before administrative decisions are taken by local social services authorities, and that the National Health Service and the Community Care Act 1990 contains no indication that there should be consultation of residents before closure. Section 46 (2) of the Community Care Act 1990[4] does not require consultation of residents. In addition, Section 7D of the Local Authority Social Services Act 1970[5], which provides for complaint to the Secretary of State, by persons aggrieved, would have provided a perfectly adequate remedy for the Applicants. I respectfully submit that there is a presumption that where Parliament has provided a statutory remedy, then that should be taken even if judicial review is not expressly excluded.

6. In any event, however, the Applicants are seeking judicial review long (more than a year) after the decision about which they complain has been taken. This amounts to inordinate and inexcusable delay, for which the Applicants offer no explanation, and in respect of which I respectfully submit that this Honourable Court should not exercise discretion in the Applicants' favour. By their Rules of the Supreme Court Appendix A Form No 86A[6] and Affidavit in support the Applicants are guilty of material non-disclosure of the date and nature of the decision taken as long ago as .... 19..., and seek to obfuscate the nature of the letter sent to them in .... 19... . If Mr Justice .... had been informed of the delay in this case, and of the true facts and circumstances surrounding it, he could not conceivably have granted leave. The Applicants have no excuse by virtue of their age; as recently as last week, they marched with others two miles from (*state address*) and shouted, swore and waved placards at me as I went to work. I also respectfully submit that this is an appropriate case for Counsel and Solicitors to show cause why they should not personally pay the costs incurred to date on an indemnity basis.

SWORN at (*address*) this .... day
of .... 19...
Before me,
(*Signature*)
A [Solicitor *or* Commissioner for Oaths][8]

} (*Deponent's signature*)[7]

1 See RSC Ord 53 r 3 (2)(b). For examples of applications see Forms 1–6 ante.
2 See Form 7 note 2 ante.
3 RSC Ord 53 r 3.
4 National Health Service and Community Care Act 1990 s 46 (2)(as amended) (40 Halsbury's Statutes (4th Edn) SOCIAL SECURITY).
5 Local Authority Social Services Act 1970 s 7D (as inserted) (25 Halsbury's Statutes (4th Edn) LOCAL GOVERNMENT).
6 RSC Appendix A Form No 86A. See Forms 1-6 ante.
7 See Form 7 note 5 ante.
8 See Form 7 note 6 ante.

LAND CHARGES

Practice

1.	Introduction	219
2.	Classes of land charges	220
3.	Registration of land charges	222
4.	Jurisdiction	222
5.	High Court proceedings	223
6.	Procedure in the county court	225
7.	Register of pending actions	225
8.	Bankruptcy petition	226
9.	Register of annuities	226
10.	Register of writs and orders	227
11.	Bankruptcy order	228
12.	Register of deeds of arrangement	228
13.	Register of land charges	228
14.	Compensation for undisclosed land charges	230
15.	Procedure after order vacating registration	232

Forms

1.	Originating summons for vacation of registration of deed of arrangement affecting land	233
2.	Affidavit by trustee under deed of arrangement supporting summons for vacation of registration of deed	234
3.	Order for vacation of registration of deed of arrangement affecting land	235
4.	Originating summons for order vacating land charge	236
5.	Affidavit supporting summons for order vacating land charge: estate contract determined	237
6.	Affidavit supporting summons for order vacating land charge: estate contract never existing	239
7.	Affidavit opposing summons for order vacating land charge: estate contract possibly existing	241
8.	Order for vacation of land charge: contract determined	242
9.	Order for vacation of alleged land charge which never existed	243
10.	Notice of motion in action for order vacating registration of pending action improperly registered	243
11.	Summons for vacation of registration of pending action and for dismissal for want of prosecution	244
12.	Order for vacation of registration of pending action and for dismissal for want of prosecution	245
13.	Originating application to county court for order vacating registration of court order	246

For actions generally . . see title ACTIONS Vol 1 (1992 Issue)
 bankruptcy proceedings . BANKRUPTCY AND INSOLVENCY Vol 7 (1997 Issue)
 compulsory acquisition . COMPULSORY ACQUISITION Vol 12 (1) (1996 Issue)

county court proceedings	COUNTY COURTS Vol 13 (1992 Issue)
deeds of arrangement	BANKRUPTCY AND INSOLVENCY Vol 7 (1997 Issue)
easements	EASEMENTS Vol 17 (1997 Issue)
execution	EXECUTION AND ENFORCEMENT OF JUDGMENTS AND ORDERS Vol 19 (1) (1996 Issue)
originating summonses	ORIGINATING SUMMONSES Vol 29 (1991 Issue)
restrictive covenants	RESTRICTIVE COVENANTS Vol 34 (1) (1994 Issue)
vendor and purchaser summonses	SALE OF LAND Vol 34 (1) (1994 Issue)
writs of execution	EXECUTION AND ENFORCEMENT OF JUDGMENTS AND ORDERS Vol 19 (1) (1996 Issue)

For the substantive law, see 26 Halsbury's Laws (4th Edn) title LAND CHARGES paras 701–900

For statutes, see 37 Halsbury's Statutes (4th Edn) title REAL PROPERTY

For statutory instruments, see 16 Halsbury's Statutory Instruments (1998 Issue) title REAL PROPERTY

LAND CHARGES

Practice

1. Introduction. This title deals with vacation, under an order of the court, of registrations under the provisions of the Land Charges Act 1972[1] of the following:
   1. *pending action*, that is, any action, information or proceeding pending in court[2] relating to land[3] or any interest in or charge on land, a petition in bankruptcy whether or not it affects land[4], a restraint order[5], an acquisition order[6], a property adjustment order[7], an access order[8] and a vesting order[9];
   2. *annuity*[10];
   3. *writs and orders affecting land*, that is, any writ or order affecting land issued or made by any court for the purpose of enforcing a judgment, or recognizance; also any order appointing a receiver or sequestrator of land or a manager of leasehold premises; any bankruptcy order, whether or not the bankrupt's estate is known to include land[11]; any access order[12]; any acquisition order[13]; any restraint order[14]; any charging order[15]; or vesting order[16];
   4. *deed of arrangement affecting land*[17];
   5. *land charge*, that is, a charge on or obligation affecting land of any of the classes[18] set out in the following paragraph.

1 The procedures here described apply equally to registrations (other than registrations of local land charges) made under the provisions of the Land Charges Act 1925 (repealed): Land Charges Act 1972 s 18 (5) (37 Halsbury's Statutes (4th Edn) REAL PROPERTY).
2 "Court" means the High Court or the county court in a case where that court has jurisdiction: Land Charges Act 1972 s 17 (1). As to jurisdiction see Paragraph 4 post.
3 "Land" includes land of any tenure, mines and minerals, buildings and other corporeal hereditaments, a manor, an advowson, a rent and other incorporeal hereditaments, an easement, right, privilege or benefit in, over or derived from land, but not an undivided share in land; "hereditament" means real property which, on an intestacy occurring before 1 January 1926, might have devolved on an heir: Land Charges Act 1972 s 17 (1). See also *Perry v Phoenix Assurance plc* [1988] 3 All ER 60, [1988] 1 WLR 940.
4 Land Charges Act 1972 s 5 (1).
5 Criminal Justice Act 1988 s 77; Prevention of Terrorism (Temporary Provisions) Act 1989 Sch 4 para 6; Drug Trafficking Act 1994 s 26 (12 Halsbury's Statutes (4th Edn) CRIMINAL LAW).
6 Landlord and Tenant Act 1987 s 28 (5) (23 Halsbury's Statutes (4th Edn) LANDLORD AND TENANT).
7 Matrimonial Causes Act 1973 s 24 (as prospectively substituted by the Family Law Act 1996 s 15, Sch 2 paras 1, 6)(27 Halsbury's Statutes (4th Edn) MATRIMONIAL LAW). See *Perez-Adamson v Perez-Rivas* [1987] Fam 89, [1987] 3 All ER 20, CA.
8 Access to Neighbouring Land Act 1992 s 5 (37 Halsbury's Statutes (4th Edn) REAL PROPERTY).
9 Leasehold Reform, Housing and Urban Development Act 1993 ss 26 (1)(as amended and as further amended by Housing Act 1996 s 107 (4), Sch 10 paras 1, 9), 50 (1) (23 Halsbury's Statutes (4th Edn) LANDLORD AND TENANT).

10 Land Charges Act 1972 Sch 1. "Annuity" means a rentcharge or annuity (not created by marriage settlement or will) for one or more life or lives, or for any term of years or greater estate determinable on one or more life or lives, created after 25 April 1855 and before 1 January 1926: Land Charges Act 1972 s 17 (1). No entries have been made in the register of annuities since 1 January 1926: Land Charges Act 1972 Sch 1 para 1.
11 Land Charges Act 1972 s 6 (1)(a)-(c)(as amended). No writ or order affecting an interest under a trust of land may be registered under this section: Land Charges Act 1972 s 6 (1A)(as inserted by the Trusts of Land and Appointment of Trustees Act 1996 Sch 3 para 12 (3)).
12 Land Charges Act 1972 s 6 (1)(d)(as inserted by Access to Neighbouring Land Act 1992 s 5 (1)).
13 Landlord and Tenant Act 1987 s 30 (6).
14 Criminal Justice Act 1988 s 77; Prevention of Terrorism (Temporary Provisions) Act 1989 Sch 4 para 6; Drug Trafficking Act 1994 s 26.
15 Charging Orders Act 1979 s 3 (2) (22 Halsbury's Statutes (4th Edn) JUDGMENTS AND EXECUTION); Criminal Justice Act 1988 ss 78, 79; Drug Trafficking Act 1994 s 27 (12 Halsbury's Statutes (4th Edn) CRIMINAL LAW). A Mareva injunction is not an order made "for the purpose of enforcing a judgment" and may not be registered under Land Charges Act 1972 s 6: *Stockler v Fourways Estates Ltd* [1983] 3 All ER 501, [1984] 1 WLR 25.
16 Leasehold Reform, Housing and Urban Development Act 1993 ss 26 (1)(as so amended), 50 (1).
17 Land Charges Act 1972 s 7 (1).
18 Land Charges Act 1972 s 2 (as amended and as further amended by Trusts and Appointment of Trustees Act 1996 s 25 (1), Sch 3 para 12 (1), (2) and Family Law Act 1996 s 66 (1), Sch 8 para 47).

2. Classes of land charges.

Class A: A rent, annuity or principal money payable by instalments or otherwise, with or without interest, not including a rate, being a charge (otherwise than by deed) upon land created pursuant to the application of some person before or after 1 January 1926:
　1. under the provisions of any Act, for securing to any person either the money spent by him or the costs, charges and expenses incurred by him under the Act, or the money advanced by him for repaying the money spent, or the costs, charges and expenses incurred by another person under the authority of an Act[1]; or
　2. in respect of the commutation by the Environmental Agency or an internal drainage board of obligations to repair banks or maintain watercourses[2]; or
　3. on an agricultural holding in respect of compensation[3]; or
　4. in respect of the redemption of a tithe rentcharge[4]; or
　5. in respect of the apportionment of a tithe redemption annuity[5]; or
　6. in respect of redemption of corn rents[6]; or
　7. in respect of improvements to business premises[7]; or
　8. in respect of Civil Defence works[8] or
　9. in respect of a scheme for the apportionment on redemption of corn rents or other payments in lieu of tithes[9].

Class B: A charge on land, not being a local land charge, of any of the kinds described in *Class A*, created otherwise than pursuant to the application of any person, either created before 1 January 1926 but acquired under a conveyance made on or after that date, or created after that date[10].

CLASSES OF LAND CHARGES

Class C: A mortgage charge or obligation affecting land of any of the following kinds, created either before 1 January 1926 but acquired under a conveyance made after that date, or created after that date:
1. a puisne mortgage[11];
2. a limited owner's charge;[12]
3. a general equitable charge[13]; and
4. an estate contract[14].

Class D: A charge or obligation affecting land of any of the following kinds[15]:
1. any charge acquired by the Inland Revenue Commissioners for estate duty leviable or payable on any death on or after 1 January 1926, for capital transfer tax payable on any death after 12 March 1975 or for inheritance tax on any death on or after 18 March 1986[16]; and
2. a covenant or agreement (other than between lessor and lessee) restrictive of the user of land entered into on or after 1 January 1926; and
3. an equitable easement created or arising on or after 1 January 1926.

Class E: An annuity[17] created before 1 January 1926 and not registered in the register of annuities.

Class F: A charge affecting any land by virtue of the Matrimonial Homes Act 1983[18] or Part IV of the Family Law Act 1996[19].

---

1 Land Charges Act 1972 s 2 (2)(a) (37 Halsbury's Statutes (4th Edn) REAL PROPERTY).
2 Land Drainage Act 1991 s 34 (2) (as amended by the Environment Act 1995 s 120 (1), Sch 22 para 191), (3) (22 Halsbury's Statutes (4th Edn) LAND DRAINAGE).
3 Agricultural Holdings Act 1986 ss 85, 86 (1 Halsbury's Statutes (4th Edn) AGRICULTURE)
4 Tithe Act 1918 ss 4, 6 (repealed) (14 Halsbury's Statutes (4th Edn) ECCLESIASTICAL LAW).
5 Tithe Annuities Apportionment Act 1921 s 1 (as amended) (14 Halsbury's Statutes (4th Edn) ECCLESIASTICAL LAW).
6 Tithe Act 1936 s 30 (1) (14 Halsbury's Statutes (4th Edn) ECCLESIASTICAL LAW).
7 Landlord and Tenant Act 1927 Sch 1 para 7 (23 Halsbury's Statutes (4th Edn) LANDLORD AND TENANT).
8 Civil Defence Act 1939 ss 18 (4)(repealed), 19 (1)(repealed).
9 Corn Rents Act 1963 s 1 (5)(as amended by Arbitration Act 1996, s 107 (1), Sch 3 para 17) (14 Halsbury's Statutes (4th Edn) ECCLESIASTICAL LAW).
10 Land Charges Act 1972 s 2 (3)(as amended), (8). Local land charges are no longer within the scope of the land charges legislation, following the repeal of the remaining parts of the Land Charges Act 1925 and its replacement by the Local Land Charges Act 1975: see Local Land Charges Act 1975 s 1 (as amended and as further amended by the Water Act 1989 s 190 (1), Sch 25 para 52; the Norfolk and Suffolk Broads Act 1988 s 21, Sch 6 para 14 and the Environment Act 1995 s 98, Sch 10 para 14). As to their enforceability and their effect on a purchaser without notice, see Local Land Charges Act 1975 s 10 (as amended by SI 1991/724, art 2 (8), Schedule).
11 Land Charges Act 1972 s 2 (4)(i). That is, any legal mortgage not being one protected by a deposit of documents relating to the legal estate affected.
12 Land Charges Act 1972 s 2 (4) (ii). That is, an equitable charge acquired by a tenant for life or statutory owner by reason of the discharge by him of estate duty or capital transfer tax (now inheritance tax).
13 Land Charges Act 1972 s 2 (4) (iii). That is, any other equitable charge not secured by deposit of documents and not arising, or affecting an interest arising, under a trust of land or settlement, and not included in any other class of land charge. A charge by way of indemnity against rents equitably apportioned or charged exclusively on land in exoneration of other land and against the breach or non-observance of covenants or conditions is not, however, deemed to be a general equitable charge and is not registrable as a land charge.

14 Land Charges Act 1972 s 2 (4)(iv). That is, any contract by an estate owner or person entitled at the date of the contract to have a legal estate conveyed to him to convey or create a legal estate, including a contract conferring a valid option of purchase, a right of pre-emption, an option to renew in a lease or any other like right. See *Phillips v Mobil Oil Co Ltd* [1989] 3 All ER 97, [1989] 1 WLR 888, CA, and *Pritchard v Briggs* [1980] Ch 338, [1980] 1 All ER 294, CA.
15 Land Charges Act 1972 s 2 (5).
16 Finance Act 1986 ss 100, 101, Sch 19 (as amended) (42 Halsbury's Statutes (4th Edn) TAXATION).
17 Land Charges Act 1972 s 2 (6). For the meaning of "annuity" see Paragraph 1 note 10 ante.
18 Matrimonial Homes Act 1983 ss 1 (repealed), 2 (repealed). Although these sections were repealed by the Family Law Act 1996 (27 Halsbury's Statutes (4th Edn) MATRIMONIAL LAW) pre-existing charges are not affected.
19 Land Charges Act 1972 s 2 (7)(as so amended). For the circumstances in which such a charge arises see the Part IV of the Family Law Act 1996 ss 30 (as amended by SI 1997/74 art 2, Schedule para 10 (a)), 31 (27 Halsbury's Statutes (4th Edn) MATRIMONIAL LAW); see also *Watts v Waller* [1973] QB 153, [1972] 3 All ER 257, CA.

3. Registration of land charges. Registration is effected by applying in the prescribed form[1] for the appropriate entry to be made by the Chief Land Registrar in one of the five registers kept by him at the Land Charges Department of Her Majesty's Land Registry, namely the registers of pending actions, of annuities, of writs and orders affecting land, of deeds of arrangement affecting land, and of land charges[2]. Where a person has died and a pending land action, writ or order or a land charge would apart from his death have been registered in his name, it is to be so registered notwithstanding his death[3].

The Land Charges Act 1972[4] does not apply to instruments or matters required to be registered or re-registered after 1925, if and so far as they affect registered land and can be protected under the Land Registration Act 1925[5]. Neither does the Act apply to any charge created by an instrument executed on or after 27 July 1971 which requires compulsory registration of the title to the land affected[6]. The Chief Land Registrar is under no obligation to ascertain whether or not an instrument or matter affects registered land[7].

1 Land Charges Act 1972 s 1 (2) (37 Halsbury's Statutes (4th Edn) REAL PROPERTY). For the forms and the particulars which must be given see the Land Charges Rules 1974, SI 1974/1286, Sch 2 Forms K1–K5 (as amended by SI 1986/2001; SI 1990/485; SI 1995/1355).
2 Land Charges Act 1972 s 1 (1).
3 Law of Property (Miscellaneous Provisions) Act 1994 s 15 amending the Land Charges Act 1972 by inserting new sections 3 (1A), 5 (4A) and 6 (2A). Note that the amendments do not apply in relation to applications for registration made before 1 July 1995 but without prejudice to a person's right to make a new application after that date.
4 See Paragraph 1 note 1 ante.
5 Land Charges Act 1972 s 14 (1).
6 Land Charges Act 1972 s 14 (3)(as prospectively amended by Land Registration Act 1997 s 4 (1), Sch 1 para 3). For instruments which induce compulsory registration of title, see the Land Registration Act 1925 ss 123, 123A (as substituted by Land Registration Act 1997 s 1) (37 Halsbury's Statutes (4th Edn) REAL PROPERTY).
7 Land Charges Act 1972 s 14 (2).

4. Jurisdiction. The courts having jurisdiction under the Land Charges Act 1972 are the High Court and, where that court has jurisdiction, the county court[1].

The jurisdiction of the county court is limited territorially[2] and is further limited by the nature of the matter, the amount of the capital sum secured or the value of the land affected[3]. A county court has jurisdiction:
1. in the case of a land charge of Class C (i), C (ii) or D (i) if the amount does not exceed £30,000[4];
2. in the case of a land charge of Class C (iii), if it is for a specified capital sum of money not exceeding £30,000 or, where it is not for a specified capital sum, if the capital value of the land affected does not exceed £30,000[5];
3. in the case of a land charge of Class A, Class B, Class C (iv), Class D (ii), Class D (iii) or Class E, if the capital value of the land affected does not exceed £30,000[6];
4. in the case of a land charge of Class F, if the land affected by it is the subject of an order made by the court under Section 1 of the Matrimonial Homes Act 1983, or Section 33 of the Family Law Act 1996[7] or an application for an order under those Acts relating to that land has been made to the court[8];
5. in a case where an application under Section 23 of the Deeds of Arrangement Act 1914[9] could be entertained by the court[10].

The parties to certain proceedings which would otherwise fall outside the jurisdiction of the county court may, however, by written memorandum signed by them or their respective solicitors, agree that a specified county court shall have jurisdiction[11]. A county court has jurisdiction to order the vacation of a registration in the register of pending actions where the action was brought or the petition in bankruptcy was filed in that court[12].

1 Land Charges Act 1972 s 17 (1) (37 Halsbury's Statutes (4th Edn) REAL PROPERTY).
2 County Courts Act 1984 s 1 (as amended by Civil Procedure Act 1997 s 10, Sch 2 para 2 (1), (4)) (11 Halsbury's Statutes (4th Edn) COUNTY COURTS).
3 County Courts Act 1984 s 23 (c). Land Charges Act 1972 s 1 (6A)(as inserted by SI 1991/724 art 2 (8), Schedule, and as further amended by Family Law Act 1996 s 66 (1), Sch 8 para 46)). As to the classes of land charges and other matters capable of registration under the Land Charges Act 1972, see Paragraphs 1, 2, 3 ante.
4 Land Charges Act 1972 s 1 (6A)(a)(as so inserted).
5 Land Charges Act 1972 s 1 (6A)(b)(as so inserted).
6 Land Charges Act 1972 s 1 (6A)(c)(as so inserted).
7 Matrimonial Homes Act 1983 s 1 (repealed); Family Law Act 1996 s 33 (27 Halsbury's Statutes (4th Edn) MATRIMONIAL LAW).
8 Land Charges Act 1972 s 1 (6A)(d)(as so inserted and amended).
9 Deeds of Arrangement Act 1914 s 23 (as amended) (4 Halsbury's Statutes (4th Edn) BANKRUPTCY AND INSOLVENCY).
10 Land Charges Act 1972 s 1 (6A)(e)(as so inserted).
11 County Courts Act 1984 s 24 (as amended); Vol 13 (1992 Issue) title COUNTY COURTS Paragraph 31.
12 Land Charges Act 1972 s 5 (10), (11)(as inserted).

5. High Court proceedings. Applications under the Land Charges Act 1972[1] are made by summons. An originating summons[2] in the Chancery Division will be appropriate[3]. The making of orders to vacate entries in the register of land charges under Section 1 (6) of the Act is dealt with by judges in the Chancery Division and only by masters in plain cases[4]. Where the application is made in pending proceedings, the application should be made by ordinary summons[5] in the action, in whatever division the proceedings are pending or, if the pending proceedings are in bankruptcy, by the form of application appropriate to the application concerned[6].

In certain circumstances it is incorrect to apply summarily for an order for the vacation of a registration, and an ordinary action is necessary in the first place to determine whether the interest alleged to be protected by the registration in fact exists. In such a case an order for vacation is only an ancillary relief. Thus, where there is an arguable case as to whether a binding contract for sale of land, protected by registration as an estate contract as defined by Class C (iv)[7], has been effectively determined, that substantive point must be decided at the trial of an action before application to the court for vacation of the registration[8]. Where, however, there is no reasonably arguable case in favour of a binding contract or other registrable interest having been created or remaining enforceable, summary application to the court is in order[9]. Where proceedings in which substantive relief is sought in relation to the subject matter of the registration have been commenced by writ or originating summons applications for the vacation of the registration may in a clear case be made by interlocutory motion or summons to the master[10].

If the person entitled to the benefit of the registration is unwilling, though able, to apply for the cancellation of the registration[11], and is also unwilling to specify the grounds for his refusal, it may be difficult to gauge the strength of the possible defence; but this clearly has to be attempted at the initial stage when the form which the proceedings are to take is decided.

Although the principal authorities relate to estate contracts and pending land actions, which give rise to most of the litigation on vacation of registrations, there is no reason to believe that the court would not apply similar principles to other registrations under the Act.

1   Land Charges Act 1972 (37 Halsbury's Statutes (4th Edn) REAL PROPERTY).
2   RSC Ord 5 r 3; see Form 4 post.
3   See Form 1 post.
4   Land Charges Act 1972 s 1 (6). Chancery Division Practice Directions No 13B (A)(i)(j): Supreme Court Practice 1997 para 854. It is suggested that application is made to the master in the first instance who will exercise his discretion as to whether the application should be referred to the judge.
5   See Form 11 post. As to cases in which application by motion for interlocutory relief is appropriate, see text to note 10 above.
6   Insolvency Rules 1986, SI 1986/1925, r 7.2 (3 Halsbury's Statutory Instruments (1995 Issue) BANKRUPTCY AND INSOLVENCY).
7   See Paragraph 2 ante for definition of Class C land charge.
8   *Re Engall's Agreement* [1953] 2 All ER 503, [1953] 1 WLR 977, where VAISEY J complained that the originating summons was an attempt to use the machinery of the Land Charges Act 1925 to obtain adjudication on the existence or non-existence of the contract; he concluded that such was not an appropriate way in which to approach what was a difficult question. Either party could bring an action for specific performance or rescission; it was wrong to apply for removal of the charges from the register before the existence of the contract had been decided by action; it was dealing with the shadow, not the substance, it was starting at the wrong end. See now, however, the cases cited in notes 9 and 10 below. Precedents are not given in this title for the vacation of each instrument or matter which can be registered under the Land Charges Act 1972. The forms given, can however, be adapted to the different circumstances.
9   *Heywood v BDC Properties Ltd (No 1)* [1963] 2 All ER 358, [1963] 1 WLR 634; on appeal [1963] 2 All ER 1063, [1963] 1 WLR 975, CA.
10 *Boobyer v Thornville Properties Ltd* (1968) 19 P & CR 768; *Thomas v Rose* [1968] 3 All ER 765, [1968] 1 WLR 1797; *Hooker v Wyle* [1973] 3 All ER 707, [1974] 1 WLR

235; *Calgary and Edmonton Land Co Ltd v Dobinson* [1974] Ch 102, [1974] 1 All ER 484. For a form of motion which may be adapted, see Form 10 post. The application should be made by summons, not motion, unless there is a sufficient degree of urgency or other good reason to justify proceeding by motion: Chancery Division Practice Directions No 15G: Supreme Court Practice 1997 para 856.
11 See Paragraph 13 post.

6. Procedure in the county court. Proceedings in a county court to lead to the vacation of bankruptcy and deeds of arrangement registrations follow similar lines to those laid down for the High Court[1]. Where the county court has jurisdiction to order the vacation of other entries registered under the Land Charges Act 1972[2], the proceedings are begun by originating application[3].

1 Insolvency Rules 1986, SI 1986/1925, rr 7.1–7.10 (3 Halsbury's Statutory Instruments (1995 Issue) BANKRUPTCY AND INSOLVENCY), apply a common code of procedure to all courts having bankruptcy jurisdiction.
2 Land Charges Act 1972 (37 Halsbury's Statutes (4th Edn) REAL PROPERTY).
3 CCR Ord 3 r 4; see Form 13 post. For the cases in which the county court has jurisdiction see Paragraph 4 ante.

7. Register of pending actions. A pending action[1] may be registered in the register of pending actions[2], which gives particulars, in the name of the estate owner or other person whose estate or interest is intended to be affected by the action, of the court in which the action was begun, the title of the action and day when it was begun[3]. A pending action does not bind a purchaser without express notice of it unless it is registered[4]. A petition in bankruptcy does not bind a purchaser of a legal estate in good faith for money or money's worth unless it is registered as a pending action[5].

The registration ceases to have effect after five years, but may be renewed from time to time for further periods of five years[6], and a pending action, other than a bankruptcy petition, may be cancelled on the application of the person having the benefit of the registration, without any court order[7].

The court[8] may, if it thinks fit, on the determination of proceedings protected by registration in the register of pending actions or while proceedings are pending, if satisfied that the proceedings are not prosecuted in good faith, by order vacate the registration and direct the party on whose behalf the registration was made to pay all or any of the costs and expenses occasioned by the registration and vacation[9]. Where the registration is improperly made the court may order vacation even where the proceedings are still pending and are being prosecuted in good faith[10].

1 For the meaning of "pending action" see Paragraph 1 ante. See also *Calgary and Edmonton Land Co Ltd v Dobinson* [1974] Ch 102, [1974] 1 All ER 484; *Whittingham v Whittingham* [1979] Fam 9, [1978] 3 All ER 805, CA; *Selim Ltd v Bickenhall Engineering Ltd* [1981] 3 All ER 210, [1981] 1 WLR 1318; *Sowerby v Sowerby* (1982) 44 P & CR 192; *Haslemere Estates Ltd v Baker* [1982] 3 All ER 525, [1982] 1 WLR 1109; *Regan & Blackburn Ltd v Rogers* [1985] 2 All ER 180, [1985] 1 WLR 870; *Perez-Adamson v Perez-Rivas* [1987] Fam 89, [1987] 3 All ER 20, CA and *Willies-Williams v The National Trust* (1993) 65 P & CR 359.
2 Land Charges Act 1972 s 5 (1) (37 Halsbury's Statutes (4th Edn) REAL PROPERTY).
3 Land Charges Act 1972 s 5 (2), (3).

4   Land Charges Act 1972 s 5 (7). "Purchaser" means any person (including a mortgagee or lessee) who for valuable consideration takes any interest in land or in a charge on land: Land Charges Act 1972 s 17 (1).
5   Land Charges Act 1972 s 5 (8)(as amended).
6   Land Charges Act 1972 s 8. By Land Charges Act 1972 s 16 (2)(as amended), rules may be made under the Insolvency Act 1986 s 412 (4 Halsbury's Statutes (4th Edn) BANKRUPTCY AND INSOLVENCY) relating, inter alia, to the re-registration of a bankruptcy petition or bankruptcy order. In practice, such registrations are seldom, if ever, renewed and, since no rules have been made, their renewal might not be authorised: see *Re a Receiving Order (in Bankruptcy)* [1947] Ch 498, [1947] 1 All ER 843.
7   For an application see the Land Charges Rules 1974, SI 1974/1286, Sch 2 Form K 11.
8   For the meaning of "court" see Paragraph 1 note 2 ante.
9   Land Charges Act 1972 s 5 (10). For a summons and order see Forms 11, 12 post. The county court's jurisdiction is limited to cases where the action was brought or the bankruptcy petition was filed in that county court: Land Charges Act 1972 s 5 (11)(as inserted).
10 Land Charges Act 1972 s 1 (6); *Calgary and Edmonton Land Co Ltd v Dobinson* [1974] Ch 102, [1974] 1 All ER 484. In this case the application will be by motion; see Form 10 post or by summons; see *Taylor v Taylor* [1968] 1 All ER 843, [1968] 1 WLR 378, CA and Paragraph 5 note 10 ante.

8. Bankruptcy petition. A bankruptcy petition is registrable in the register of pending actions[1]. On the filing of the petition the bankruptcy registrar must immediately send notice of it to the Chief Land Registrar, requesting that it be registered[2]. The registration can be vacated only by order of the court[3]. Such an order must be made if the petition is dismissed or withdrawn[4], or if a bankruptcy order made on the petition is annulled[5].

The order is in every case permissive; it is for the debtor or other person affected by the proceedings to apply for cancellation of the relevant registration[6].

1   Land Charges Act 1972 s 5 (1)(b) (37 Halsbury's Statutes (4th Edn) REAL PROPERTY); Insolvency Rules 1986, SI 1986/1925, rr 6.13, 6.43 (3 Halsbury's Statutory Instruments (1995 Issue) BANKRUPTCY AND INSOLVENCY).
2   Insolvency Rules 1986 rr 6.13 (creditor's petition), 6.43 (debtor's petition), Sch 4 Form 6.14.
3   A county court has jurisdiction only if the bankruptcy petition was filed in that court: Land Charges Act 1972 s 5 (11)(as inserted).
4   Insolvency Rules 1986 r 6.27.
5   Insolvency Act 1986 s 282 (as prospectively amended by the Criminal Justice Act 1988 s 170 (2), Sch 16) (4 Halsbury's Statutes (4th Edn) BANKRUPTCY AND INSOLVENCY); Insolvency Rules 1986 r 6.213 (1)(as amended).
6   For the form of application for cancellation, see the Land Charges Rules 1974, SI 1974/1286, Sch 2 Form K 11. The application must be supported by an office copy of the relevant order of the court see Land Charges Rules 1974, SI 1974/1286, r 10 (16 Halsbury's Statutory Instruments (1998 Issue) REAL PROPERTY).

9. Register of annuities. The register of annuities[1] has been closed for the purpose of fresh registrations since 31 December 1925[2], although annuities are now registrable as land charges of Class E if created before 1926 and Class C (iii) if created after 1925[3]. An annuity capable of registration before 1926 is void as against a creditor or a purchaser of any interest in the land charged unless the annuity is registered in the register of annuities or the register of land charges[4].

Existing registrations in the register of annuities can be cancelled without recourse to the court by lodging a form of satisfaction, cesser or discharge with the Chief Land Registrar[5]. Normally the registration will be cancelled at the instance of the personal representatives of the deceased annuitant. A registration may be vacated pursuant to an order of the court[6].

1   For the meaning of "annuity" see Paragraph 1 note 10 ante.
2   Land Charges Act 1925 s 4 (1)(repealed); Land Charges Act 1972 Sch 1 para 1 (37 Halsbury's Statutes (4th Edn) REAL PROPERTY).
3   Land Charges Act 1972 s 2 (4)(as amended and as further amended by Trust of Land and Appointment of Trustees Act 1996 s 25 (1), Sch 3 para 12 (1), (2)), (6); for the meaning of "purchaser", see Land Charges Act 1972 s 17 (1) and Paragraph 7 note 4 ante.
4   Land Charges Act 1972 Sch 1 para 4.
5   Land Charges Act 1972 Sch 1 para 2.
6   Land Charges Act 1972 s 1 (6).

10. Register of writs and orders. Writs or orders affecting land, including bankruptcy orders whether or not the bankrupt's estate is known to include land[1], may be registered in the register of writs and orders[2] in the name of the estate owner or other person whose land, if any, is affected by the writ or order[3]. A registrable writ or order, and a delivery in execution or other proceeding taken pursuant to it or in obedience to it, is void as against a purchaser of the land unless the writ or order is registered[4], although in respect of a bankruptcy order the protection applies only in favour of a purchaser for money or money's worth of a legal estate in good faith[5]. The registration ceases to have effect after five years, but may be renewed from time to time for further periods of five years[6].

The registration may be vacated pursuant to an order of the court[7] or, except in the case of bankruptcy proceedings, may be cancelled without a court order at the instance of the person in whose favour it was effected[8].

Following the vacation of an entry, application may be made to the Registrar for a certificate that the entry has been cancelled[9].

1   Land Charges Act 1972 s 6 (1)(c)(as amended) (37 Halsbury's Statutes (4th Edn) REAL PROPERTY). As to these writs and orders see Paragraph 1 text and notes 10–14 ante. "Writ" here does not, of course, include a writ of summons. No writ or order affecting an interest under a trust of land may be registered under the Land Charges Act 1972 s 6 (1): Land Charges Act 1972 s 6 (1A)(as inserted by Trusts of Land and Appointment of Trustees Act 1996 s 25 (1), Sch 3 para 12 (1), (3)). Amongst the writs and orders affected are charging orders on the land of a judgment debtor under the Charging Orders Act 1979 (22 Halsbury's Statutes (4th Edn) JUDGMENTS AND EXECUTION), charging orders under RSC Ord 50, or CCR Ord 31, writs of possession, orders of foreclosure or sale (in an action for redemption or foreclosure, or in reference to an equitable mortgage, or allowing a creditor to follow the assets of a deceased person), orders appointing a receiver by way of equitable execution or under the Mental Health Act 1983 s 99 (28 Halsbury's Statutes (4th Edn) MENTAL HEALTH), and orders authorising Settled Land Act trustees to exercise the powers of a tenant for life and access orders under the Access to Neighbouring Land Act 1992. A Mareva injunction is not a writ or order for enforcing a judgment and is not capable of registration under the Land Charges Act 1972 s 6 (1): *Stockler v Fourways Estates Ltd* [1983] 3 All ER 501, [1984] 1 WLR 25.
2   Land Charges Act 1972 s 6 (1)(as amended and as further amended by Access to Neighbouring Land Act 1992 s 5 (1)).
3   Land Charges Act 1972 s 6 (2).
4   Land Charges Act 1972 s 6 (4)(as amended). For the meaning of "purchaser" see Land Charges Act 1972 s 17 (1) and Paragraph 7 note 4 ante.

5   Land Charges Act 1972 s 6 (5)(as substituted).
6   Land Charges Act 1972 s 8. As to the renewal of a bankruptcy order see, however, Paragraph 7 note 6 ante.
7   Land Charges Act 1972 s 1 (6).
8   For an application for cancellation see the Land Charges Rules 1974, SI 1974/1286, Sch 2 Form K11.
9   For an application for such a certificate see Land Charges Rules 1974 Sch 2 Form K20.

11. Bankruptcy order. When a bankruptcy order is made the bankruptcy registrar sends copies of it to the Official Receiver[1], who forthwith sends notice of it to the Chief Land Registrar with a request that it be registered in the register of writs and orders[2]. The registration can be vacated only by order of the court[3].

1   Insolvency Rules 1986, SI 1986/1925, rr 6.34 (1) (order made on creditor's petition), 6.46 (1) (order made on debtor's petition) (3 Halsbury's Statutory Instruments (1995 Issue) BANKRUPTCY AND INSOLVENCY). See Insolvency Rules 1986 Sch 4 Form 6.26 (as substituted by SI 1987/1919, r 3, Schedule).
2   Insolvency Rules 1986 rr 6.34 (2)(a), 6.46 (2)(a), Sch 4 Form 6.26 (as amended by SI 1991/495).
3   Land Charges Act 1972 s 1 (6) (37 Halsbury's Statutes (4th Edn) REAL PROPERTY).

12. Register of deeds of arrangement. A deed of arrangement affecting land may be registered in the register of deeds of arrangement in the name of the debtor, on the application of a trustee of the deed or of a creditor assenting to or taking the benefit of the deed[1]. A deed of arrangement is void as against a purchaser of any land comprised in it or affected by it unless the deed is so registered[2]. The registration ceases to have effect after five years, but may be renewed from time to time for further periods of five years[3].

The registration may be vacated pursuant to an order of the court[4], but it cannot be cancelled by application to the Chief Land Registrar without a court order.

1   Land Charges Act 1972 s 7 (1) (37 Halsbury's Statutes (4th Edn) REAL PROPERTY).
2   Land Charges Act 1972 s 7 (2). For the meaning of "purchaser" see Land Charges Act 1972 s 17 (1) and Paragraph 7 note 4 ante.
3   Land Charges Act 1972 s 8.
4   Land Charges Act 1972 s 1 (6). For an originating summons, supporting affidavit and order see Forms 1–3 post. The county court has jurisdiction in a case where it could entertain an application under the Deeds of Arrangement Act 1914 s 23 (as amended) (4 Halsbury's Statutes (4th Edn) BANKRUPTCY AND INSOLVENCY): Land Charges Act 1972 s 1 (6A)(e)(as substituted by SI 1991/724, art 2 (8), Schedule).

13. Register of land charges. Land charges[1] may be registered in the register of land charges[2] in the name of the estate owner whose estate is intended to be affected[3].

A land charge of Class A created after 31 December 1888, or of Class B, C, D or F created or arising after 1925, is void as against a purchaser of the land charged or any interest in it unless the land charge is registered before completion[4]; although as respects a Class D land charge and an estate contract the protection applies only in favour of a purchaser for money or money's worth of a legal estate[5]. Further, after the expiration of a year from the first conveyance on or after 1 January 1889 of a Class A land charge created before that date, or from the first conveyance after 1925 of a Class B or C land charge created before 1926, the person entitled to it cannot recover the land charge or any part of it as against a purchaser of the land or any interest in it unless the land charge is registered before completion[6].

Where a land charge, other than a land charge of Class F, ceases or is overreached[7] it will normally be cancelled on the application of the person entitled to the benefit of it supported, if he is not the person on whose behalf the land charge was registered, by sufficient evidence of his title to it[8].

An application to cancel the registration of a land charge of Class F must, unless the application is signed by the person on whose behalf the application for registration was made, be accompanied either by a written release of the rights of occupation to which the charge relates, or by sufficient evidence of the event which has brought such rights to an end[9]. The registration of a land charge of any class may, however, be vacated pursuant to an order of the court[10], but the court should not be asked for an order if the registration can be cancelled in the normal way. A special procedure exists for the cancellation of an entry other than a land charge of Class F in a case where the Chief Land Registrar has first been consulted and is satisfied that the applicant for cancellation would suffer exceptional hardship or expense if he were required to comply with the normal provisions governing cancellation[11]. The registration of a restrictive covenant affecting freehold land or land let for a term of more than 40 years of which 25 years or more have expired, but not let on a mining lease[12], may be vacated if the Lands Tribunal wholly discharges the covenant under its statutory powers[13]. This provision has, however, only a limited application to the registration of restrictive covenants as land charges because a covenant between lessor and lessee is excluded from the definition of restrictive covenant[14]. Further, since registration merely operates as notice and there is no provision for recording devolution in title, it is not possible to give effect on the register to an order that merely modifies or partially discharges a covenant, although it is otherwise if part of the land originally affected is wholly freed from the covenant.

1   For the six classes of land charges see Paragraph 2 ante.
2   Land Charges Act 1972 s 2 (1) (37 Halsbury's Statutes (4th Edn) REAL PROPERTY).
3   Land Charges Act 1972 s 3 (1). Registrations should be effected and searches made against the estate owners' names as appearing in the title deeds: *Standard Property Investment plc v British Plastics Federation* (1985) 53 P & CR 25. Where a person has died and a land charge created before his death would apart from his death have been registered in his name it shall be so registered notwithstanding his death: Land Charges Act 1972 ss 3 (1A), 5 (4A), 6 (2A)(as inserted by Law of Property (Miscellaneous Provisions) Act 1994 s 15). The amendments do not apply to applications for registration made before 1 July 1995 but without prejudice to a person's right to make a fresh application after that date.
4   Land Charges Act 1972 s 4 (2), (5)–(8)(as amended). For Class A land charges see also Land Charges Act 1972 s 4 (3). For the meaning of "purchaser" see Paragraph 7 note 4 ante.
5   Land Charges Act 1972 s 4 (6).
6   Land Charges Act 1972 s 4 (3), (7). For the meaning of "purchaser" see Land Charges Act 1972 s 17 (1) and Paragraph 7 note 4 ante.

7 The registration of any charge, annuity or other interest does not prevent its being overreached under any other Act, except where otherwise provided by that other Act (Land Charges Act 1972 s 13 (1)), and the registration of a puisne mortgage or charge as a land charge does not operate to prevent its being overreached in favour of a prior mortgagee or person deriving title under him where, by reason of a sale, foreclosure or otherwise, the right of the puisne mortgagee or subsequent chargee to redeem is barred (Land Charges Act 1972 s 13 (2)).
8 Land Charges Rules 1974, SI 1974/1286, r 10 (16 Halsbury's Statutory Instruments (1998 Issue) REAL PROPERTY). For an application for cancellation see Land Charges Rules 1974 Sch 2 Form K11.
9 Land Charges Rules 1974 r 11. For the relevant form of application, see Land Charges Rules 1974 Sch 2 Form K13. For the evidence required to establish that the rights of occupation have come to an end, see Family Law Act 1996 Sch 4 para 4 (27 Halsbury's Statutes (4th Edn) MATRIMONIAL LAW). If the charge was registered or the registration was renewed pursuant to Family Law Act 1996 Sch 4 para 4 (3) evidence must be lodged to satisfy the Chief Land Registrar that the order of the court referred to in the application for registration or renewal has ceased to have effect (Family Law Act 1996 Sch 4 para 4 (1), (2)).
10 Land Charges Act 1972 s 1 (6). For an originating summons, supporting and opposing affidavits, and orders, see Forms 4–9 post. See Paragraph 5 ante. The county court has jurisdiction to vacate a land charge in cases where the value of the subject matter falls within its jurisdiction: Land Charges Act 1972 s 1 (6A)(as substituted by SI 1991/724, art 2 (8), Schedule and Family Law Act 1996 s 66 (1), Sch 8 para 46).
11 Land Charges Rules 1974 r 10 proviso. For the relevant form of application see Land Charges Rules 1974 Sch 2 Form K12, which may be used only with the prior approval of the Chief Land Registrar and must be supported by sufficient evidence that the charge has been discharged or overreached and is of no effect. The Chief Land Registrar will not permit the use of this procedure as an alternative to an application to the court in a case where the person entitled to the benefit of the charge refuses to release the charge but is available to be sued.
12 Law of Property Act 1925 s 84 (12)(as amended) (37 Halsbury's Statutes (4th Edn) REAL PROPERTY).
13 That is, under the Law of Property Act 1925 s 84 (1)(as amended); see generally Vol 34 (1) (1994 Issue) title RESTRICTIVE COVENANTS.
14 Land Charges Act 1972 s 2 (5)(as amended); *Dartstone Ltd v Cleveland Petroleum Co Ltd* [1969] 3 All ER 668, [1969] 1 WLR 1807.

14. Compensation for undisclosed land charges. Provision is made for the payment of compensation to a purchaser of any estate or interest in land who suffers loss by reason that the estate or interest is affected by a registered land charge[1] of which he had no actual knowledge on the date of completion of the purchase[2]. The following conditions must be satisfied:
1. the date of completion of the purchase must have been after 1 January 1970[3]; and
2. the charge must have been registered against the name of an owner of an estate in the land who was not as owner of any such estate a party to any transaction, or concerned in any event, comprised in the relevant title[4].

Any compensation for loss under this provision is to be paid by the Chief Land Registrar and is to include the amount of any expenditure reasonably incurred by the claimant for the purpose either of securing that the estate or interest is no longer affected by the registered land charge or is so affected to a lesser extent, or of obtaining compensation[5]. The cause of action is deemed to accrue at the time when the registered land charge in question comes to the notice of the purchaser[6]. Any proceedings for the recovery of compensation under this provision must be commenced in the High Court[7]. If the claim is dismissed the purchaser may not be ordered to pay the Chief

Land Registrar's costs unless the court considers that it was unreasonable for the purchaser to commence the proceedings[8]. Where compensation has been claimed under this provision the Registrar is required to make such entries in or amendments and additions to the relevant register and index as he deems necessary in order to bring the charge to the notice of any person who inspects the register or makes a search in the index, in relation to the estate or interest affected[9].

Apart from the provision described above, there is no express provision in the Land Charges Act 1972 for the payment of indemnity comparable to the indemnity provisions applicable to registered land[10]. Nevertheless, it would appear that the Chief Land Registrar would be liable in damages to a chargee who suffered loss because his charge, although properly registered as a land charge, was not disclosed due to an error in an official certificate of search and was thus rendered unenforceable against a purchaser of the land affected[11].

1   This includes any instrument or matter registered in the registers maintained under the Land Charges Act 1972 s 1 (as amended by SI 1991/724, art 2 (8), Schedule and Family Law Act 1996 s 66 (1), Sch 8 para 46): Law of Property Act 1969 s 25 (10); Land Charges Act 1972 s 18 (5) (37 Halsbury's Statutes (4th Edn) REAL PROPERTY).
2   Law of Property Act 1969 s 25 (1). As to the types of dispositions to which the section applies, see Law of Property Act 1969 s 25 (9). Whether the purchaser had knowledge of the charge is to be determined without regard to the Law of Property Act 1925 s 198: Law of Property Act 1969 s 25 (2) (37 Halsbury's Statutes (4th Edn) REAL PROPERTY). A vendor could not rely on the Law of Property Act 1925 s 198 (1) to relieve her from her obligation to make a full and frank disclosure of the existence of a registered charge before relying on the conditions of sale, see *Rignall Developments Ltd v Halil* [1988] Ch 190, [1987] 3 All ER 170. Any knowledge acquired in the course of a transaction by a person who is acting therein as counsel, or as solicitor or other agent, for another is to be treated as the knowledge of that other: Law of Property Act 1969 s 25 (11).
3   That is, the date of commencement of the Law of Property Act 1969. See further as to the date of completion Law of Property Act 1969 s 25 (10).
4   The relevant title means (i) in relation to a disposition made under a contract, the title to which the purchaser was, apart from any acceptance by him (by agreement or otherwise) of a shorter or an imperfect title, entitled to require; or (ii) in relation to any other disposition, the title which he would have been entitled to require if the disposition had been made under a contract to which the Law of Property Act 1925 s 44 (1) applied and that contract had been made on the date of completion: Law of Property Act 1969 s 25 (10).
5   Law of Property Act 1969 s 25 (4).
6   Law of Property Act 1969 s 25 (5)(as amended).
7   The making of final orders on application under Law of Property Act 1969 s 25 (6) is not dealt with by the masters of the Chancery Division: Chancery Division Practice Directions No 13B (A)(i)(m): Supreme Court Practice 1997 para 854, but see Paragraph 5 note 4 ante.
8   Law of Property Act 1969 s 25 (6). At the time of writing no such proceedings have yet been brought.
    It may be supposed, however, that the procedure would approximate closely to that for the recovery of indemnity in relation to registered land under the Land Registration Act 1925 s 83 (as substituted by Land Registration Act 1997 s 2). See title LAND REGISTRATION Paragraph 33 and Forms 46, 47 post, which may be adapted as necessary.
9   Land Charges Rules 1974, SI 1974/1286, r 15 (1) (16 Halsbury's Statutory Instruments (1998 Issue) REAL PROPERTY). Exactly how this would be achieved in practice is by no means clear, in view of the fact that the index is an index of the names of estate owners and not of parcels of land.
10 See title LAND REGISTRATION Paragraph 31 post.
11 *Ministry of Housing and Local Government v Sharp* [1970] 2 QB 223, [1970] 1 All ER 1009, CA; but see also the Land Charges Act 1972 s 10 (6), which, in the absence of fraud, excludes liability for any loss which may be suffered (1) by reason of any discrepancy between (i) the particulars which are shown in a certificate of the result of search as being

the particulars in respect of which the search for entries was made; and (ii) the particulars in respect of which the search for entries was required by the person who made the requisition for the search; or (2) by reason of any communication of the result of a search made otherwise than by issuing an official certificate.

15. Procedure after order vacating registration. Having obtained an order vacating a registration[1], the applicant must lodge an office copy of the order, together with the appropriate application form[2], with the Superintendent, Land Charges Department, Burrington Way, Plymouth, Devon PL5 3LP[3]. The application must be accompanied by the prescribed fee[4] unless that fee is debited by the Chief Land Registrar to a credit account[5]. Application may also be made for an official certificate that an entry has been cancelled[6].

1 That is, under the Land Charges Act 1972 s 1 (6) (37 Halsbury's Statutes (4th Edn) REAL PROPERTY).
2 Land Charges Rules 1974, SI 1974/1286, Sch 2 Form K11.
3 Land Charges Rules 1974 r 2 (2) (16 Halsbury's Statutory Instruments (1998 Issue) REAL PROPERTY). The application may be sent by prepaid post or delivered by hand: Land Charges Rules 1974 r 20 (1).
4 Land Charges Fees Rules 1990, SI 1990/327 (16 Halsbury's Statutory Instruments (1998 Issue) REAL PROPERTY).
5 Land Charges Rules 1974 r 20 (2). For the regulations governing credit accounts, see the Land Charges Fees Rules 1990 r 4 (as amended).
6 Land Charges Rules 1974 r 12, Sch 2 Form K20. For the fee see the Land Charges Fees Rules 1990, present fee £1.00.

Forms

1

ORIGINATING SUMMONS for vacation of registration of deed of arrangement affecting land[1]

(*Royal Arms*)[2]

IN THE HIGH COURT OF JUSTICE   Ch 19... B. No. ...
Chancery Division

Between   A. B.   ...   Plaintiff
                 and
                 C. D.   ...   Defendant

To C. D. of (*address*).

LET the Defendant, within [14 days] after service of this summons on him, counting the day of service, return the accompanying Acknowledgment of Service to the appropriate Court Office.

By this summons, which is issued on the application of the Plaintiff A. B. of (*address*), the Plaintiff claims against the Defendant the following relief pursuant to Section 1 (6) of the Land Charges Act 1972, namely:

1. An order that the registration of the deed of arrangement dated .... 19... and made between A. B. of the first part, C. D. (the trustee) of the second part, and the several creditors of A. B. who should execute the same deed of the third part, and registered on .... 19... under the provisions of the Land Charges Act 1972 in the register of deeds of arrangement affecting land kept at HM Land Registry in the name of A. B. (under reference number ...) be vacated.

2. An order that the costs of and occasioned by this application and of the vacation of the registration be paid by the Defendant.

If the Defendant does not acknowledge service, such judgment may be given or order made against or in relation to him as the Court may think just and expedient.

DATED .... 19...

NOTE: This summons may not be served later than [4 *or, if leave is required to effect service out of the jurisdiction* 6] calendar months beginning with the above date unless renewed by order of the Court.

This summons was taken out by E. F. & Co of (*address*), [Agents for (*name*) of (*address*),] Solicitors for the Plaintiff, whose address is (*address*).

IMPORTANT

Directions for Acknowledgment of Service are given with the accompanying form.

1 RSC Appendix A Form No 8; Land Charges Act 1972 s 1 (6) (37 Halsbury's Statutes (4th Edn) REAL PROPERTY); Paragraph 12 ante. For a supporting affidavit see Form 2 post; for an order see Form 3 post.
2 A replica of the Royal Arms must be printed or embossed at the first page of every originating process: RSC Ord 1 r 9.

2
AFFIDAVIT by trustee under deed of arrangement supporting summons for vacation of registration of deed[1]

Defendant: C. D.: 1st: .... 19... C.D.1[2]

IN THE HIGH COURT OF JUSTICE   Ch 19... B. No. ...
Chancery Division

Between	A. B.	...	Plaintiff
	and		
	C. D.	...	Defendant

I, C. D. of (*state residence or workplace, and occupation or, if none, description*), make oath and say as follows:

1. By a deed of arrangement for the benefit of creditors dated .... 19... and made between A. B. of the first part, myself (C. D.), (as trustee) of the second part, and those creditors of A. B. who executed or assented in writing to the deed of the third part ("the creditors"), after reciting that A. B. was indebted to the creditors who claimed from A. B. the sums of money set out opposite their respective names in the schedule to the deed or were mentioned or referred to in the assents signed by them respectively, and that, upon the agreement to convey and assign all of his property and effects mentioned in the deed for the benefit of his creditors who agreed to release him from his debts, the debtor A. B. as beneficial owner appointed, conveyed and assigned to me all his real estate and property and the goodwill of his business, plant, stock-in-trade and other assets upon the trusts declared in the deed. The deed is now produced and shown to me marked "C.D.1".

2. The assignment provided that, if and when the debts and the costs, charges and expenses incurred under the terms of the deed were paid and discharged, I at A. B.'s expense reconvey the trust estate or so much of it as remained vested in me to him or by his direction, freed and discharged from the debts.

3. On .... 19... the deed was registered under the provisions of the Land Charges Act 1972 in the name of A. B. in the register of deeds of arrangement affecting land kept at HM Land Registry (under reference number ...) in respect of his freehold property known as (*insert name of property*) in the county of ....[3].

4. A. B. has paid or caused to be paid to me as his trustee all debts, costs and charges due and payable under the deed of arrangement and by a deed of release dated .... 19..., and made between myself and A. B. I acknowledged his payment to me of £...... being the debts due to the creditors together with my charges and expenses in connection with the deed of arrangement. The release also contained my conveyance, assignment and release to A. B. of the freehold property and all of his other real estate and property comprised in the deed and including the goodwill of his business, plant, stock-in-trade and other assets set out in the deed.

5. The solicitors of A. B. have informed me and I believe that they are applying to this Honourable Court for an order vacating the registration of the deed as a deed of arrangement affecting land, and I confirm my consent to such order being made.

SWORN at (*address*) on
.... 19...
Before me,
(*Signature*)
A [Solicitor *or* Barrister *or* Notary Public *or* Commissioner for Oaths][5]

(*Deponent's signature*)[4]

---

1 Land Charges Act 1972 s 1 (6) (37 Halsbury's Statutes (4th Edn) REAL PROPERTY); Paragraph 12 ante. For the originating summons see Form 1 ante.
2 Practice Note [1983] 3 All ER 33, sub nom Practice Direction [1983] 1 WLR 922 (as amended by Practice Note [1995] 2 All ER 511, sub nom Practice Direction [1995] 1 WLR 510) and Chancery Division Practice Directions No 8A(i)(a): Supreme Court Practice 1997 para 820.
3 The property affected should be referred to if it is specified in the registration. Where practicable the register must specify the county and district in which the land is situated, together with a short description of the land affected: Land Charges Rules 1974, SI 1974/1286, Sch 1 item 4 (iv) (16 Halsbury's Statutory Instruments (1998 Issue) REAL PROPERTY).
4 Every affidavit must be signed by the deponent and the jurat must be completed and signed by the person before whom it is sworn: RSC Ord 41 r 1 (8). See also *Down v Yearley* [1874] WN 158.
5 Solicitors Act 1974 s 81 (as amended) (41 Halsbury's Statutes (4th Edn) SOLICITORS); Courts and Legal Services Act 1990 s 113 (as amended) (17 Halsbury's Statutes (4th Edn) EVIDENCE); Administration of Justice Act 1985 s 65 (as amended) (31 Halsbury's Statutes (4th Edn) NOTARIES AND LICENSED CONVEYANCERS); Commissioners for Oaths Acts 1889 and 1891 (as amended) (17 Halsbury's Statutes (4th Edn) EVIDENCE).

3
ORDER for vacation of registration of deed of arrangement affecting land[1]

IN THE HIGH COURT OF JUSTICE   Ch 19... B. No. ...
Chancery Division
   Master[2] ....
      .... 19...

Between   A. B.   ...   Plaintiff
                  and
                  C. D.   ...   Defendant

UPON THE APPLICATION by originating summons of the Plaintiff
AND UPON HEARING Counsel for the Plaintiff
AND UPON READING the documents in the Court File recorded as having been read

IT IS ORDERED that the registration of a deed of arrangement dated .... 19... and made between A. B. of the first part C. D. of the second part and the several creditors of A. B. who should execute the same deed of the third part and registered in the register of deeds of arrangement affecting land kept at HM Land Registry on .... 19... in the name of A. B. under reference number ... be vacated.

1 Adapted from the order made on 20 July 1948 in *Re Trent Bridge Buildings, Hallam v Burrows* (unreported 1948/H/No 2020): see the Land Charges Act 1972 s 1 (6) (37 Halsbury's Statutes (4th Edn) REAL PROPERTY) and Paragraph 12 ante. For a summons and supporting affidavit see Forms 1, 2 ante.
2 Masters of the Chancery Division shall not make orders to vacate entries in the register under the Land Charges Act 1972 (other than in plain cases): Chancery Division Practice Directions No 13B (A)(i)(j): Supreme Court Practice 1997 para 854; but see Paragraph 5 note 4 ante.

4
ORIGINATING SUMMONS for order vacating land charge[1]
(Royal Arms)[2]

IN THE HIGH COURT OF JUSTICE Ch 19... B. No. ...
Chancery Division

Between   A. B.   ...   Plaintiff
               and
               C. D.   ...   Defendant

To C. D. of (*address*)

LET the Defendant, within [14 days] after service of this summons on him, counting the day of service, return the accompanying Acknowledgment of Service to the appropriate Court Office.

By this summons, which is issued on the application of the Plaintiff A. B. of (*address*), the Plaintiff claims against the Defendant the following relief pursuant to Section 1 (6) of the Land Charges Act 1972, namely:

[**Either**, *where it is claimed that the registration, though originally either authorised or required, is now unnecessary by reason of the determination of the interest or matter claimed by it*[3]:

1. An order that the registration of the land charge of Class [C (iv)] in respect of [an estate contract] imposed or created by an instrument dated .... 19... made between A. B. of the one part and C. D. of the other part and then affecting the property above mentioned, which was registered on .... 19... on behalf of C. D. in the register of land charges at HM Land Registry in the name of A. B. as estate owner of the property under reference number ... be vacated.

Or, *where it is claimed that the original registration was, ab initio, neither authorised nor required*[4]:

1. An order that the registration of the land charge of Class [C (iv)] in respect of [an estate contract] claimed by C. D. to have been imposed or created by an instrument dated .... 19... made between A. B. of the one part and C. D. of the other part and alleged to affect the property above mentioned, which was registered on .... 19... on behalf of C. D. in the register of land charges at HM Land Registry in the name of A. B. as estate owner of the property under reference number ... be vacated.]

2. An order that the costs of and occasioned by this application and of the vacation of the registration be paid by the Defendant.

If the Defendant does not acknowledge service, such judgment may be given or order made against or in relation to him as the Court may think just and expedient.

DATED .... 19...

AFFIDAVIT 237

NOTE: This summons may not be served later than [4 *or, if leave is required to effect service out of the jurisdiction* 6] calendar months beginning with the above date unless renewed by order of the Court.

This summons was taken out by E. F. & Co of (*address*), [Agents for (*name*) of (*address*),] Solicitors for the Plaintiff, whose address is (*address*).

IMPORTANT

Directions for Acknowledgment of Service are given with the accompanying form.

1 RSC Appendix A Form No 8; Land Charges Act 1972 s 1 (6) (37 Halsbury's Statutes (4th Edn) REAL PROPERTY); Paragraph 13 ante. For supporting affidavits see Forms 5, 6 post. For an opposing affidavit see Form 7 post. For orders see Forms 8, 9 post.
2 See Form 1 note 2 ante.
3 For a supporting affidavit and an order see Forms 5, 8 post. This alternative is also appropriate where the continuation of a properly made registration is now unwarrantable.
4 For a supporting affidavit and an order see Forms 6, 9 post. Where there is no reasonably arguable case as to whether the interest or matter alleged to be protected by the registration ever existed or is still subsisting, application may be made by interlocutory motion in the proceedings for an order for the vacation of the registration: *Doobyer v Thornville Properties Ltd* (1968) 19 P & CR 768; *Calgary and Edmonton Land Co Ltd v Dobinson* [1974] Ch 102, [1974] 1 All ER 484. For a form of notice of motion, which may be adapted, see Form 10 post. See also Paragraph 3 ante. It should be noted that the duties of the Chief Land Registrar in regard to applications for registration are purely ministerial. Save in the case of applications for cancellation or rectification he is not concerned to inquire into or otherwise verify the accuracy or validity of any matter or thing stated or appearing in any application: Land Charges Rules 1974, SI 1974/1286, r 22 (16 Halsbury's Statutory Instruments (1998 Issue) REAL PROPERTY); as to misconceived applications relating to registered land, see Land Charges Rules 1974 r 13.

5
AFFIDAVIT supporting summons for order vacating land charge: estate contract determined[1]

Plaintiff: A. B.: 1st: .... 19... A.B.1, 2, 3, 4, 5, 6[2]

IN THE HIGH COURT OF JUSTICE   Ch 19... B. No. ...
Chancery Division

Between   A. B.   ...   Plaintiff
                and
                C. D.   ...   Defendant

I, A. B. of (*state residence or workplace, and occupation or, if none, description*), the above-named Plaintiff, make oath and say as follows:

1. I am the freehold owner of (*specify property*) ("the property").

2. At the date of the agreement referred to below, the Defendant C. D. held a monthly tenancy of the property.

3. By an agreement in writing dated .... 19... and made between myself and C. D., the following matters, among others were agreed:

(1) that the property should be sold by me to the Defendant C. D. for £......;

(2) that a deposit of ...% of the purchase price paid at exchange of contracts should be held by my solicitors, E. F. & Co, as stakeholders;

(3) that the Defendant's tenancy of the property should continue unaffected until actual completion of his purchase;

(4) that an abstract or epitome of title should be delivered to the Defendant at least ... weeks before the date fixed for completion; and

(5) that if either party rescinded the agreement as provided for in it the deposit should be repaid to the Defendant without interest and the Defendant should return the abstract or epitome of title and other documents sent to him. The agreement is now produced and shown to me marked "A.B.1".

4. On .... 19... my solicitors delivered the epitome of title and associated papers to G. H. & Co, the solicitors for the Defendant.

5. On or about .... 19... the Defendant visited my home and told me that owing to financial difficulties he was unable to complete his purchase.

6. On .... 19... my solicitors wrote to the Defendant's solicitors offering on my behalf to rescind the agreement on or before .... 19... when the Defendant should give up possession of the property, and having done so the deposit would be returned to the Defendant according to the terms of the agreement, my solicitors' reasonable costs having been deducted from it.

7. On .... 19... the Defendant's solicitors confirmed in writing that the Defendant accepted the terms offered for rescission of the agreement.

8. On .... 19... the Defendant left the property, paid me in cash the rent due and handed the keys of the property to me at my house.

9. On .... 19... my solicitors sent to the Defendant's solicitors their receipted bill of costs amounting to £...... and their cheque of the same date being made payable to the Defendant for the balance of the deposit (£......). A true copy of my solicitors' bill and their presented and paid cheque are now produced and shown to me marked "A.B.2" and "A.B.3" respectively.

10. On .... 19... the Defendant's solicitors returned to my solicitors the epitome of title and associated papers which are now produced and shown to me, their covering letter is marked "A.B.4", and the epitome and papers are contained in a bundle marked "A.B.5".

11. On or about .... 19... I let the property to a new tenant and from that date, I have been in receipt of the rents and profits of the property. The Defendant has not since the rescission made, nor I to him, any claim or representation except as mentioned below, that the agreement was still in existence.

12. During .... 19... I negotiated a sale of the property to P. Q., but he will not exchange contracts until the registration of the land charge mentioned in the originating summons to these proceedings has been vacated.

13. The land charge was registered by the Defendant on .... 19... to protect the agreement, but the existence of the registration was unknown to me and, so they inform me, to my solicitors, until disclosed by an official certificate of search issued to P. Q. .

14. My solicitors wrote to the Defendant on .... 19... to demand the cancellation of the registration on the ground that the agreement has been rescinded, but this has not been done and his solicitors replied on .... 19..., asserting that the agreement is still binding and enforceable.

15. The bundle now produced and shown to me marked "A.B.6" contains letters received by my solicitors from the Defendant's solicitors and verified copies of letters sent by my solicitors to the Defendant's solicitors and to the Defendant which relate to those issues.

SWORN at (*address*) on
.... 19...
Before me,
(*Signature*)
A [Solicitor *or* Barrister *or* Notary Public *or* Commissioner for Oaths][4]

(*Deponent's signature*)[3]

1 Land Charges Act 1972 s 1 (6) (37 Halsbury's Statutes (4th Edn) REAL PROPERTY); Paragraph 13 ante. For an originating summons see Form 4 ante. This form illustrates circumstances in which, although the land charge was properly registered in the first place, there is no arguable case for asserting that the interest originally protected (in this instance an estate contract) is still subsisting. In such circumstances an order for vacation of the registration may be sought by interlocutory motion: *Boobyer v Thornville Properties Ltd* (1968) 19 P & CR 768; *Calgary and Edmonton Land Co Ltd v Dobinson* [1974] Ch 102, [1974] 1 All ER 484. For a form of notice of motion, which may be adapted, see Form 10 post. See also Paragraph 5 ante.
2 See Form 2 note 2 ante.
3 See Form 2 note 4 ante.
4 See Form 2 note 5 ante.

6
AFFIDAVIT supporting summons for order vacating land charge: estate contract never existing[1]

Plaintiff: J. K.: 1st: .... 19... J.K.1, 2[2]

IN THE HIGH COURT OF JUSTICE
Chancery Division

Ch 19... B. No. ...

Between   A. B. Ltd   ...   Plaintiff
                and
                C. D.   ...   Defendant

I, J. K., of (*address*), Managing Director of A. B. Ltd ("the Company"), the Plaintiff Company, make oath and say as follows:

1. The Company is the freehold owner of (*specify property*) ("the property") which is let on 3 occupational leases, at rents totalling £...... all expiring on .... 19... .

2. On .... 19... following a resolution of the Company's Board of Directors, I instructed R. S. & Co of (*address*), estate agents, to sell the property subject to and with the benefit of the leases at a price of £...... .

3. By letter dated .... 19... R. S. & Co informed the Company that they had found a purchaser, namely, the Defendant. They had received a deposit of £...... but the Defendant, before exchanging contracts, wished to obtain planning permission for a new building on the site for business office purposes having an internal floor area of at least ... square metres.

4. On .... 19... E. F. & Co, the Company's solicitors, wrote to G. H. & Co, the Defendant's solicitors, informing them that they had been instructed in the sale of the property to the Defendant, subject to contract, at a price of £...... . They added that they understood the proposed purchaser was making an immediate application for outline planning permission for its proposed development. With their letter the Company's solicitors enclosed a draft agreement for sale and purchase for approval by the Defendant's solicitors. The draft agreement is now produced and shown to me marked "J.K.1".

5. By correspondence between the respective solicitors from .... 19... to .... 19... the usual preliminary inquiries before contract were raised and answered, and the draft agreement was agreed without amendment.

6. By letter dated .... 19... the Defendant's solicitors informed the Company's solicitors that outline planning permission for the proposed development had been granted. Conditions attached to the permission, relating to the position of the new building line and the provision of additional car parking facilities, reduced the internal floor area available for office purposes to ... square metres. The purchase price should therefore be proportionately reduced to £....... .

7. By letter dated .... 19... the Company's solicitors notified the Defendant's solicitors that the proposed reduced purchase price was not agreed and, since the Defendant was not prepared to pay the purchase price of £......, the negotiations for sale to the Defendant were to be considered at an end. A cheque for £...... in repayment of the deposit was forwarded with the letter.

8. On .... 19... the land charge Class C (iv) the subject of these proceedings was registered by the Defendant's solicitors on behalf of the Defendant. The registration alleges that an estate contract was created by correspondence between the solicitors for the parties during the period from .... 19... to .... 19... (both dates inclusive).

9. By letter to the Defendant's solicitors dated .... 19... the Company's solicitors demanded the cancellation of the registration on the ground that no estate contract within the meaning of Section 2 (4) of the Land Charges Act 1972[3] was created between the parties by the correspondence or at all, but this has not been done, and by letter from his Solicitors dated .... 19... the Defendant maintains that a binding contract for sale and purchase exists between the parties and that the Defendant reserves the right to enforce it against the Company.

10. The bundle now produced and shown to me marked "J.K.2" contains letters received by the Company from R. S. & Co and by the Company's solicitors from the Defendant's solicitors and verified copies of letters sent by the Company's solicitors to the Defendant's solicitors with reference to these issues and, in particular, the originals or verified copies (*as the case may be*) of all the correspondence referred to in the registration.

SWORN at (*address*) on
.... 19...
Before me,
(*Signature*) } (*Deponent's signature*)[4]

A [Solicitor *or* Barrister *or* Notary Public *or* Commissioner for Oaths][5]

1 Land Charges Act 1972 s 1 (6) (37 Halsbury's Statutes (4th Edn) REAL PROPERTY); Paragraph 13 ante. For an originating summons see Form 4 ante and note 3 thereto ante. This form illustrates circumstances in which there is no arguable case for asserting that a land charge ever existed, so that it would be open to the plaintiff by motion to seek an interlocutory order for the vacation of the registration: *Boobyer v Thornville Properties Ltd* (1968) 19 P & CR 768; *Calgary and Edmonton Land Co Ltd v Dobinson* [1974] Ch 102, [1974] 1 All ER 484. For a form of notice of motion which may be adapted, see Form 10 post. See also Paragraph 5 ante.
2 See Form 2 note 2 note.
3 Land Charges Act 1972 s 2 (4). The Law Commission's report "Transfer of Land: Formalities for Contracts for Sale etc of Land" (Law Comm No 164) commenting on

the Bill subsequently enacted as the Law of Property (Miscellaneous Provisions) Act 1989 suggests in para 4.15 that it is still possible to create contracts by correspondence so that it may remain desirable for the parties to use the formula "subject to contract" on letters which contain or refer to documents containing the terms of the contract if the letters are signed by a party to the contract. Note also, however, that the Bill as drafted by the Law Commission, was materially different from that enacted by Parliament, see the comments of STUART-SMITH LJ, *Commission for the New Towns v Cooper (Great Britain) Ltd* [1995] 2 All ER 929 at 952, 953.

4 See Form 2 note 4 ante.
5 See Form 2 note 5 ante.

7
AFFIDAVIT opposing summons for order vacating land charge: estate contract possibly existing[1]

Defendant: C. D.: 1st: .... 19...[2]

IN THE HIGH COURT OF JUSTICE   Ch 19... B. No. ...
Chancery Division

Between   A. B.   ...   Plaintiff
                and
                C. D.   ...   Defendant

I, C. D. of (*state residence or workplace, and occupation or, if none, description*), the above-named Defendant, make oath and say as follows:

1. I have read a copy of an affidavit of the above-named Plaintiff, A. B., filed with the Court on .... 19... .

2. The agreement mentioned in paragraph ... of the affidavit provided that the root of title to (*specify property*) ("the property") was a conveyance on sale dated .... 19..., and made between J. K. and L. M. . The epitome delivered as alleged in paragraph ... of the affidavit showed the root of title as a deed dated .... 19... and made between those parties, but this deed neither complied with the contractual provision nor was itself a good root of title, since, after recitals showing that the parties were entitled to the said property and other property in equal shares as part of their partnership property, J. K. conveyed for value the whole of his undivided freehold share in the property to L. M. . A requisition was raised on my behalf as alleged in paragraph ... of the affidavit, requesting deduction of a full 15 years title and I refused to accept the epitome delivered as sufficient, but the Plaintiff has never deduced title as requested. In the circumstances I maintain that an adequate epitome of title has yet to be delivered by the Plaintiff, and I deny that I have accepted or ought to be deemed to have accepted such title to the said property as the Plaintiff has so far deduced. The Plaintiff has never informed me or my solicitors, G. H. & Co, that the deeds and documents from which he could supply such an epitome as I requested are unavailable.

3. A notice to complete on or before .... 19... was given as alleged in paragraph ... of the affidavit, but this notice was, I contend, unreasonably short and, for this reason and those already mentioned the notice was invalid.

4. The issue in dispute between the Plaintiff and myself is the present existence or non-existence of a binding contract for sale of the property to me, and I have therefore today arranged for a writ to be issued beginning an action in which I am Plaintiff and the Plaintiff in this action is Defendant to

determine that matter, and an application has been made on my behalf to register the action as a pending action under the Land Charges Act 1972. I intend to proceed vigorously with that action and I therefore respectfully request that no order be made in these proceedings pending the trial of the action.

SWORN at (*address*) on
.... 19...
Before me,
(*Signature*)
A [Solicitor *or* Barrister *or* Notary Public *or* Commissioner for Oaths][4]

(*Deponent's signature*)[3]

1. Land Charges Act 1972 s 1 (6) (37 Halsbury's Statutes (4th Edn) REAL PROPERTY); Paragraph 13 ante. This affidavit illustrates facts quite unconnected with those in Forms 5, 6 ante. It would be appropriate where there was a truly arguable question whether a binding contract exists, so that the substantive issue ought to be decided at the trial of the action, rather than on motion; see Paragraph 5 ante.
2. See Form 2 note 2 ante.
3. See Form 2 note 4 ante.
4. See Form 2 note 5 ante.

8
ORDER for vacation of land charge: contract determined[1]

IN THE HIGH COURT OF JUSTICE   Ch 19... B. No. ...
Chancery Division
Master[2] ....
.... 19...

Between   A. B.   ...   Plaintiff
and
C. D.   ...   Defendant

UPON THE APPLICATION of the Plaintiff

AND UPON HEARING Counsel for the Plaintiff and for the Defendant

AND UPON READING the documents in the Court File recorded as having been read

IT IS ORDERED that the registration of the land charge Class [C (iv)] created on .... 19... and registered in the register of land charges kept at HM Land Registry on .... 19... in the name of A. B. and numbered ... in such register be vacated.

AND IT IS ORDERED that the costs of and occasioned by this application [be paid by the Defendant].

1. Land Charges Act 1972 s 1 (6) (37 Halsbury's Statutes (4th Edn) REAL PROPERTY); Paragraph 13 ante. For an originating summons see Form 4 ante. This form would be appropriate in the circumstances referred to in the supporting affidavit, where the interest or matter which was originally the subject of an authorised registration has ceased to exist, so that the continued registration is unwarranted; see Form 5 ante.
2. See Form 3 note 2 ante.

9

ORDER for vacation of alleged land charge which never existed[1]

IN THE HIGH COURT OF JUSTICE   Ch 19... B. No. ...
　Chancery Division
　　Master[2] ....
　　　......... 19...

Between   A. B.   ...   Plaintiff
                           and
                           C. D.   ...   Defendant

UPON THE APPLICATION of the Plaintiff
AND UPON HEARING Counsel for the Plaintiff and for the Defendant
AND UPON READING the documents in the Court File recorded as having been read
THE COURT being satisfied that the land charge alleged to have been created by the Plaintiff in favour of J. K. on .... 19... which was registered on behalf of J. K. in the register of land charges at HM Land Registry on .... 19... under reference number ... against the name .... was not a land charge and that there is not and never has been any such land charge in existence at any material time
IT IS ORDERED pursuant to Section 1 (6) of the Land Charges Act 1972 that the registration of the land charge alleged to have been created and registered as aforesaid be vacated
AND IT IS ORDERED that the costs of and occasioned by this application [be paid by the Defendant].

1　Land Charges Act 1972 s 1 (6) (37 Halsbury's Statutes (4th Edn) REAL PROPERTY); Paragraph 13 ante. For an originating summons see Form 4 ante. This order is appropriate where there is no arguable case for asserting that any land charge ever existed: see Form 6 ante.
2　See Form 3 note 2 ante.

10

NOTICE OF MOTION in action for order vacating registration of pending action improperly registered[1]

IN THE HIGH COURT OF JUSTICE   Ch 19... B. No. ...[2]
　Chancery Division

Between   A. B.   ...   Plaintiff
                           and
                           C. D.   ...   Defendant

TAKE NOTICE that Mr Justice .... will be moved on .... 19... at ... [am *or* pm], or so soon thereafter as Counsel can be heard, by Counsel on behalf of the Plaintiff for an order under Section 1 (6) of the Land Charges Act 1972[3] that the registration by the Defendant of the writ of summons in this action in the register of pending actions at HM Land Registry under reference number ... be vacated.

AND that the costs of the application be the Plaintiff's costs in any event.
DATED .... 19...

(*Signature*)

of (*address*), [Agents for (*name*) of (*address*),] Solicitors for the Plaintiff[4]

To the Defendant and to G. H. & Co of (*address*), his Solicitors

1   Under the Land Charges Act 1925 (repealed) there was no clear power for the court to order vacation of a pending action registration in these circumstances, so that the practice was to apply for an order under the general jurisdiction of the court: see *Heywood v BDC Properties Ltd (No 2)* [1964] 2 All ER 702, [1964] 1 WLR 971, CA. The court's power to order vacation under the Land Charges Act 1972 s 1 (6) (37 Halsbury's Statutes (4th Edn) REAL PROPERTY) is, however, wider in its terms than the former provisions and it is therefore no longer necessary for the order to be made under the general jurisdiction: see *Calgary and Edmonton Land Co Ltd v Dobinson* [1974] Ch 102, [1974] 1 All ER 484. See also Paragraph 7 ante. Under the current practice, the making of orders is dealt with by the judges in the Chancery Division, and only by masters in plain cases: Chancery Division Practice Directions No 13B (A)(i)(j): Supreme Court Practice 1997 para 854. It is suggested that the application should be made by summons to the master, as he, in the first instance, will exercise his discretion as to whether the application should be referred to a judge. If the case is urgent or there is other good reason to justify it proceedings can be commenced by motion; Chancery Division Practice Directions No 15G: Supreme Court Practice 1997 para 856, but see also Paragraph 5 note 4 ante.
2   The reference number must be included in every pleading: RSC Ord 18 r 6 (1)(a).
3   Land Charges Act 1972 s 1 (6) (37 Halsbury's Statutes (4th Edn) REAL PROPERTY).
4   RSC Ord 8 r 3 (3) (applying RSC Ord 6 r 5).

11
SUMMONS for vacation of registration of pending action and for dismissal for want of prosecution[1]

IN THE HIGH COURT OF JUSTICE   19... B. No. ...
   Queen's Bench Division

Between   A. B.   ...   Plaintiff
                   and
                   C. D.   ...   Defendant

LET ALL PARTIES attend before the Judge in Chambers, in Room No. ..., Central Office, Royal Courts of Justice, Strand, London WC2A 2LL, on .... 19... at ... [am *or* pm], on the hearing of an application on the part of the Defendant for an order:

1. That this action be dismissed with costs to be taxed and paid to the Defendant by the Plaintiff for want of prosecution, the Plaintiff not having [served a statement of claim *or* issued a summons for directions *or as the case may be*].

2. That the registration by the Plaintiff of the writ of summons in this action in the register of pending actions in HM Land Registry under reference number ... be vacated pursuant to Section 5 (10) of the Land Charges Act 1972.

3. That, pursuant to Section 5 (10) of the Land Charges Act 1972, the costs and expenses occasioned by the said registration and by its vacation be paid by the Plaintiff.

DATED .... 19...

This summons was taken out by G. H. & Co of (*address*), [Agents for (*name*) of (*address*),] Solicitors for the Defendant.

To the Plaintiff, and to E. F. & Co, his Solicitors

---

1   Land Charges Act 1972 ss 1 (6), 5 (10) (37 Halsbury's Statutes (4th Edn) REAL PROPERTY); See Paragraphs 5, 7 ante. For an order see Form 12 post.

12

ORDER for vacation of registration of pending action and for dismissal for want of prosecution[1]

IN THE HIGH COURT OF JUSTICE   19... B. No. ...
  Queen's Bench Division
    The Honourable Mr Justice .... Judge in Chambers
      .... 19...

Between   A. B.   ...   Plaintiff
                    and
                   C. D.   ...   Defendant

UPON HEARING Counsel for the Plaintiff and for the Defendant

AND UPON READING the affidavit of A. B. sworn on .... 19... and the affidavit of C. D. sworn on .... 19...

IT IS ORDERED

(1) that this action be, for want of prosecution, dismissed with costs including the costs of this application to be taxed and paid by the Plaintiff to the Defendant

(2) that the registration of the writ of summons herein in the register of pending actions at HM Land Registry effected on ....., 19,,, under reference number ... against the name .... be vacated and that the Plaintiff do pay the costs and expenses occasioned by the registration and vacating thereof such costs to be taxed if not agreed

---

1   Land Charges Act 1972 s 5 (10) (37 Halsbury's Statutes (4th Edn) REAL PROPERTY); see Paragraph 7 ante. For a summons see Form 11 ante.

13

ORIGINATING APPLICATION to county court for order vacating registration of court order[1]

(*Royal Arms*)[2]

IN THE .... COUNTY COURT　　　　　　No. of Matter ....[3]
In the Matter of the Land Charges Act 1972
And in the Matter of freehold property at (*address*)

Between　　　　　　　A. B.　　　　...　　　Plaintiff
　　　　　　　　　　　and
　　　　　　　　　　　C. D.　　　　...　　　Respondent

　　　A. B. of (*address and description*), applies to the Court for an order in the following terms under Section 1 (6) of the above-named Land Charges Act 1972 that the registration of an Order of the Court made on .... 19... in an action entitled (*set out title*) and registered under the above-named Act in the register of writs and orders affecting land kept at HM Land Registry on .... 19... under reference number ... against the name .... be vacated.

　　　The grounds on which the Applicant claims to be entitled to the order are: (*specify the grounds in numbered paragraphs, showing that the applicant is the proper person to apply and that the court has jurisdiction*[4]).

　　　The name and address of the person on whom it is intended to serve this application is C. D. of (*address*)[5].

　　　The Applicant's address for service is (*address*)[6].

　　　DATED .... 19...

　　　　　　　　　　　　　　　　　　　(*Signature*)[7]
　　　　　　　　　　　　　　　　　　　[Solicitor for the] Applicant

1　Land Charges Act 1972 s 1 (6), (6A)(as substituted by SI 1991/724 art 2 (8), Schedule and amended by Family Law 1996 s 66 (1), Sch 8 para 46) (37 Halsbury's Statutes (4th Edn) REAL PROPERTY); see Paragraphs 4, 6 ante.
2　Every form in the County Court Forms Schedule marked with the word "Royal Arms" shall have a replica of the Royal Arms printed or embossed by an officer of the court at the head of the first page: County Court (Forms) Rules 1982, SI 1982/586, r 2 (4).
3　Every document filed, served or issued must bear the title of the action or matter and the distinguishing number allotted to it by the court: CCR Ord 3 r 7.
4　The wording of the Land Charges Act 1972 s 1 (6A)(as so substituted and amended) should be followed, especially if the application is to vacate a land charge, compare with Form 11 ante.
5　An originating application must state the names and addresses of any persons to be served: CCR Ord 3 r 4 (2)(b).
6　An originating application must state the applicant's address for service: CCR Ord 3 r 4 (2)(c).
7　If the application is settled by counsel it must be signed by him: CCR Ord 50 r 6.

LAND REGISTRATION

Practice

A: INTRODUCTION

1.	Scope of title	251
2.	The Registrar	251
3.	Summary of matters coming before courts	252
4.	Summary of matters heard by Registrar	253

B: COURT PROCEEDINGS

5.	Courts with jurisdiction	253
6.	Court procedure	254
7.	References by Registrar to High Court	254
8.	Appeals from Registrar	255
9.	Procedure on appeals and references to High Court	256
10.	Application direct to the court	257
11.	Proceedings where registration of title is only incidental	258
12.	Production of evidence in court	260

C: PROCEEDINGS BEFORE THE REGISTRAR

13.	Matters heard by Registrar	261
14.	Procedure prior to hearing	262
15.	Witnesses	263
16.	Conduct of hearing	264
17.	Registrar's order	265

D: OBJECTIONS AND CAUTIONS

18.	Objections to registration	266
19.	Caution against first registration	267
20.	Objections to dealings and entries on the register	269
21.	Caution against dealings and against conversion	270
22.	Unregistered mortgages	274
23.	Notice of deposit of certificate	274

E: RESTRICTIONS AND INHIBITIONS

24.	Restrictions	275
25.	Inhibitions	277
26.	Bankruptcy affecting proprietor	278

F: RECTIFICATION OF THE REGISTER

27.	Rectification of the register generally	280
28.	When register may be rectified	280
29.	Where rectification is not possible	282
30.	Application for rectification	283
31.	Correction of error in registration	283

G: INDEMNITY FOR LOSS

32.	Entitlement to indemnity for loss	284
33.	Where indemnity is not payable	286
34.	Payment of indemnity	287

H: COSTS

35.	Costs of proceedings in Land Registry	289
36.	Costs on application to the court	290

Forms

A: FIRST REGISTRATION

1.	Objection to first registration	291
2.	Reply to objection to first registration	292
3.	Notice of hearing of matter arising on objection to first registration	293
4.	Witness summons	294
5.	Order by Solicitor to HM Land Registry on hearing of objection to first registration	295
6.	Originating motion on appeal from Registrar's order on objection to first registration	296
7.	Affidavit supporting originating motion on appeal from order on objection to first registration	297
8.	Order by Registrar extending period for first registration in compulsory area	298
9.	Caution against first registration of land	299
10.	Notice to cautioner against first registration of application to register land	300
11.	Consent by cautioner to application for first registration	301
12.	Objection by cautioner to cancellation of caution against first registration	302
13.	Reply by applicant to cautioner's objection to cancellation of caution against first registration	303
14.	Order by Registrar referring to court matter arising on cautioner's objection to first registration	304

B: DEALINGS

15.	Application for entry on register of appurtenant right of way	305
16.	Notice to servient owner of proposed entry of appurtenant right of way	307
17.	Objection to entry of appurtenant right of way	308
18.	Application for service of notice warning off caution against dealings	309
19.	Notice to cautioner against dealings on application to warn off cautioner or to register dealing	310
20.	Objection by cautioner to cancellation of caution against dealings	311
21.	Reply to objection by cautioner to cancellation of caution against dealings	313
22.	Notice of hearing in connection with caution against dealings	315
23.	Order on hearing in connection with caution against dealings	316
24.	Order by Registrar referring to the court matter arising on objection by cautioner against dealings	317
25.	Originating summons on reference by Registrar to court	318
26.	Affidavit supporting originating summons on reference by Registrar to court	319

C: RESTRICTIONS

27.	Application for order under restriction in anticipation of proposed dealing	332
28.	Order by Registrar under restriction as to registration of proposed dealing	323
29.	Originating summons for cancellation of restriction	324

D: BANKRUPTCY PROCEEDINGS

30.	Inquiry of registered proprietor as to whether bankruptcy proceedings affect him	326
31.	Notice of registration of a creditor's notice	328

32.	*Notice to registered proprietor of registration of bankruptcy inhibition*	329
33.	*Notice of application to cancel bankruptcy inhibition* .	330
34.	*Application by trustee in bankruptcy for registration in place of registered proprietor and rectification of register*	331

E: RECTIFICATION OF THE REGISTER

35.	*Application for Registrar's consent to taking of proceedings for rectification*	332
36.	*Consent by Registrar to defending of proceedings for rectification*	333
37.	*Originating summons for rectification of register*	334
38.	*Affidavit supporting originating summons for rectification of register*	335
39.	*Order for rectification of register*	337
40.	*Application for rectification by excluding land from adjoining owner's title and including it in applicant's title*	338
41.	*Notice to registered proprietor of application to rectify register*	340
42.	*Objection by registered proprietor to rectification of register*	341
43.	*Order by Registrar for rectification of register*	343
44.	*Originating motion on appeal from order by Registrar for rectification of the register*	344
45.	*Order by Registrar referring to court matter arising on application for rectification*	345

F: INDEMNITY FOR LOSS

46.	*Claim for indemnity for loss*	347
47.	*Originating summons for the determination of questions as to right to or amount of indemnity*	349
48.	*Affidavit supporting originating summons for the determination of questions as to indemnity*	350

For bankruptcy . . . see title	BANKRUPTCY AND INSOLVENCY Vol 7 (1997 Issue)
easements . . .	EASEMENTS Vol 17 (1997 Issue)
land charges . .	LAND CHARGES ante
leases . . .	LANDLORD AND TENANT Vols 24 (1), (2) (1995 Issue)
mortgages . . .	MORTGAGES Vol 28 (1997 Issue)
originating summonses .	ORIGINATING SUMMONSES Vol 29 (1991 Issue)
recovery of land . .	LANDLORD AND TENANT Vols 24 (1), (2) (1995 Issue)
restrictive covenants . .	RESTRICTIVE COVENANTS Vol 34 (1) (1994 Issue)
sale of land . .	SALE OF LAND Vol 34 (1) (1994 Issue)
settled land . .	TRUSTS AND SETTLEMENTS Vol 41 (1991 Issue)

For the substantive law, see 26 Halsbury's Laws (4th Edn) title LAND REGISTRATION paras 901-1490
For statutes, see 37 Halsbury's Statutes (4th Edn) title REAL PROPERTY
For statutory instruments, see 16 Halsbury's Statutory Instruments (1998 Issue) title REAL PROPERTY

Practice

A: INTRODUCTION

1. Scope of title. This title deals with judicial proceedings under the Land Registration Acts 1925[1], 1936[2], 1966[3], 1971[4], 1986[5], 1988[6] and 1997[7] and the rules made thereunder[8] before the courts[9] and before the Registrar[10] and with other matters principally in connection with the exercise of the Registrar's judicial powers[11]. Conveyancing matters are dealt with in THE ENCYCLOPAEDIA OF FORMS AND PRECEDENTS.

1 Land Registration Act 1925 (37 Halsbury's Statutes (4th Edn) REAL PROPERTY).
2 The Land Registration Act 1936 amended procedure under the Land Registration Act 1925 relating to the land registration insurance fund and included other amendments concerning fees and determination of value.
3 The Land Registration Act 1966 altered the provisions of the 1925 Act relating to areas of compulsory registration and the registration of unregistered land. The whole Act has now been repealed following the extension of compulsory registration throughout England and Wales.
4 The Land Registration and Land Charges Act 1971 amended the Acts of 1925 and 1966 and relates primarily to rights to indemnity and the registers kept under the Land Registration Act 1925.
5 The Land Registration Act 1986 amended the 1925 Act in relation to conversion of title, leases which induce compulsory registration and which are overriding interests, the minor interests index and related matters.
6 The Land Registration Act 1988 made provision for an open register amending the 1925 Act to increase rights of inspection of the register.
7 The Land Registration Act 1997 amended the 1925 Act by introducing new triggers for compulsory first registration of unregistered land and altering the provisions relating to indemnity.
8 The main rules are the Land Registration Rules 1925, SR & O 1925/1093 (as amended) (16 Halsbury's Statutory Instruments (1998 Issue) REAL PROPERTY), but specific sets of rules have been made to deal with such matters as fees and official searches.
9 As to the courts see Paragraph 5 post.
10 See Paragraph 2 post.
11 A few of the forms which follow relate to action taken by the Registrar in an administrative capacity but which might lead to judicial proceedings before him or before the courts.

2. The Registrar. This term is used throughout this title to mean the Chief Land Registrar. The former stipulation that the Chief Land Registrar be a barrister or solicitor of at least ten years' standing has been abolished[1]. Accordingly, provision was made for the post of Solicitor to HM Land Registry to be established (and legally qualified registrars to act as his deputies) with power to exercise the judicial and quasi judicial functions of the Chief Land Registrar[2]. The Solicitor is a qualified registrar nominated by the Chief Land Registrar[3] and must be a barrister or solicitor with a 10 year general qualification[4]. His main powers relate to rectification of the register, the hearing of disputes and other issues arising out of litigation[5]. Powers relating to the hearing of disputes are also exercisable by any qualified registrar who is directed by the Chief Land Registrar to conduct a hearing[6]. Accordingly, the expression "the Registrar" is therefore also used in this title to include the Solicitor to HM Land Registry in relation to those matters involving the exercise of the Registrar's judicial or quasi judicial functions[7].

The Lord Chancellor has power to create district registries and to appoint district registrars[8]. District land registrars have in general the same powers as regards land within their jurisdiction as registrars in the Land Registry[9].

1 See the Courts and Legal Services Act 1990 s 125 (7), Sch 20 (11 Halsbury's Statutes (4th Edn) COURTS AND LEGAL SERVICES) which repealed Administration of Justice Act 1956 s 53.
2 Land Registration (Conduct of Business) Regulations 1997, SI 1997/713, regs 3, 4.
3 Land Registration (Conduct of Business) Regulations 1997 reg 3 (1).
4 Land Registration (Conduct of Business) Regulations 1997 reg 2 (b). For the definition of general qualification, see the Courts and Legal Services Act 1990 s 71 (3) (11 Halsbury's Statutes (4th Edn) COURTS AND LEGAL SERVICES).
5 Land Registration (Conduct of Business) Regulations 1997 reg 4, Schedule.
6 Land Registration (Conduct of Business) Regulations 1997 reg 6.
7 Such as the Land Registration Rules 1925, SR & O 1925/1093, rr 220, 298 (16 Halsbury's Statutory Instruments (1998 Issue) REAL PROPERTY).
8 Land Registration Act 1925 s 132 (1). These are Birkenhead, Coventry, Croydon, Durham (Boldon House), Durham (Southfield House), Gloucester, Harrow-on-the-Hill, Kingston upon Hull, Leicester, Lytham St Annes, Nottingham (East), Nottingham (West), Peterborough, Portsmouth, Stevenage, Swansea (Cofrestrfa Tir Ddosbarthol Abertawe), Telford, Tunbridge Wells, District Land Registry for Wales (Cofrestrfa Tir Ddosbarthol Cymru), Weymouth and York: Land Registration (District Registries) Order 1998, SI 1998/140.
9 Land Registration Act 1925 s 133.

3. Summary of matters coming before courts. The principal occasions on which the courts may be asked to decide matters under the legislation are:
1. where a matter is referred for the decision or opinion of the court by the Registrar[1];
2. where there is an appeal from a decision or order of the Registrar[2]; or
3. where an application is made direct to the court without a prior hearing or reference by the Registrar[3].

In addition there are court proceedings which happen to relate to registered land but in which the fact of registration is purely incidental[4].

1 See Paragraph 7 post.
2 See Paragraph 8 post.
3 See Paragraph 9 post.
4 See Paragraph 11 post.

4. Summary of matters heard by Registrar. There are two main provisions under which the Registrar may hear and determine matters judicially. The first is general and extends to questions and disputes arising before the Registrar on any application or during any investigation of title[1]. The second relates more specifically to disputes arising in connection with cautions against dealings where a cautioner, after having been served with the prescribed notice, has shown cause why his caution should continue to have effect or why a dealing referred to in the notice should not be registered[2].

1 Land Registration Rules 1925, SR & O 1925/1093, r 298 (16 Halsbury's Statutory Instruments (1998 Issue) REAL PROPERTY). See Paragraph 13 post.
2 Land Registration Rules 1925 r 220. See Paragraph 19 post.

B: COURT PROCEEDINGS

5. Courts with jurisdiction. When "the court" is referred to in the Land Registration Acts[1] and Rules[2], the reference is to the High Court or to the county court[3], where it has jurisdiction by virtue of rules made for that purpose[4]. Since no such rules have been made[5], the county court possesses an original jurisdiction only in cases where it would do so[6], apart from the Land Registration Acts, and in which the question whether title to particular land is registered or unregistered is immaterial. The county court has, therefore, no jurisdiction at present over matters in respect of which particular jurisdiction is conferred by the Land Registration Acts; thus it may not hear appeals from or references by the Registrar or applications under those Acts made direct to the court, though it has power to order rectification of the register in an appropriate case where the fact of registration of the title is only incidental[7]. Since December 1990 it has no longer been necessary to invoke the powers of the High Court or county court to order the inspection and production of copies of registers and other documents in the custody of the Registrar as the register is now open to the public[8]. Any person aggrieved by an order made by the High Court in the exercise of its jurisdiction under the Land Registration Acts (otherwise than on appeal from a county court) may appeal within the prescribed time and in the same manner and with the same incidents as an appeal from an order made by the High Court in the exercise of its ordinary jurisdiction[9]. In the absence of jurisdiction under the Acts being vested in the county court[10], the provisions with regard to appeals from the county court[11] are not yet applicable.

1 Land Registration Acts 1925–1997 (37 Halsbury's Statutes (4th Edn) REAL PROPERTY). See Paragraph 1 ante.
2 Land Registration Rules 1925, SR & O 1925/1093, r 298 (16 Halsbury's Statutory Instruments (1998 Issue) REAL PROPERTY).
3 Land Registration Act 1925 s 3 (ii)(as substituted).
4 Any such rules would be made under the Land Registration Act 1925 s 138 (1)(as substituted).

5   No such rules had been made at the date of going to press. When the county court has jurisdiction under the Land Registration Acts, it will have all the powers of the High Court for the purpose of that jurisdiction: Land Registration Act 1925 s 138 (3)(as substituted).
6   The county court's jurisdiction is sometimes limited by the nature of the matter and by the amount of the capital sum secured or the value of the land affected: County Courts Act 1984 ss 21 (as amended), 23 (11 Halsbury's Statutes (4th Edn) COUNTY COURTS). The parties may agree by written memorandum that a specified county court shall have jurisdiction: County Courts Act 1984 s 24 (1)(as amended).
7   *Watts v Waller* [1973] QB 153, [1972] 3 All ER 257, CA. See Paragraph 8 note 3 post.
8   Land Registration Act 1925 s 112 (as substituted by the Land Registration Act 1988 s 1). Leases or charges referred to in the register which are in the custody of the Registrar are excluded from this right. Documents in the custody of the Registrar which are not referred to in the register may be inspected in prescribed cases or at the Registrar's discretion.
9   Land Registration Act 1925 s 143 (3)(as amended). Notice of any such appeal which is delivered to the registry must be entered on the register; see the Land Registration Rules 1925 r 301.
10 See the text to notes 5, 6 above.
11 Land Registration Act 1925 s 143 (1), (2).

6. Court procedure. All matters within the jurisdiction of the High Court under the Land Registration Acts are assigned to the Chancery Division[1], and are heard and determined by a single Chancery judge[2]. Procedure is generally by originating summons[3] or, in the case of an appeal from a decision of the Registrar, by originating motion[4].

Where the county court has original jurisdiction, proceedings will be commenced, as a rule, by plaint and summons in the ordinary manner[5].

1   Land Registration Act 1925 s 138 (2)(as substituted) (37 Halsbury's Statutes (4th Edn) REAL PROPERTY).
2   RSC Ord 93 r 10 (2). The Lord Chancellor may from time to time assign the duties vested in the High Court in relation to all or any matters under the Land Registration Acts to a particular judge: Land Registration Act 1925 s 138 (4)(as substituted).
3   RSC Ord 5 r 3.
4   RSC Ord 55 r 3 (1). For a notice of originating motion and supporting affidavit see Forms 6, 7 post.
5   CCR Ord 3 r 1. As to the lack of jurisdiction under the Land Registration Acts see Paragraph 5 ante.

7. References by Registrar to High Court. The Registrar has wide powers to refer matters to the High Court in the following circumstances instead of determining them himself:
1. if any question, doubt, dispute, difficulty or complaint arises before him on any application or during any investigation of title which he has power to hear, he may, if he thinks fit, instead of deciding the question himself, refer the matter[1] at any stage, or any question thereon, for the court's decision[2], whether or not he has actually commenced a hearing himself;
2. where notice has been served on a cautioner in respect of a caution against dealings[3], and the cautioner has objected[4], the Registrar may, instead of determining the matter himself, at any stage refer it[5], or any question arising on it, for the court's decision[6];

3. where any person interested has applied to the Registrar to determine whether a claim to statutory priority for a charge is well founded, the Registrar may either himself determine all questions as to the priorities and relative rights of the parties or may require the matter to be brought before the court for decision[7];
4. if, on the examination of any title, the Registrar considers that whilst it is open to objection it is nevertheless a title the holding under which will not be disturbed, he may either approve it or require the applicant to apply to the court, on a statement signed by the Registrar, for its sanction to the registration[8];
5. if, on the examination of any title, the Registrar entertains a doubt as to any matter of law or fact arising, he may, on the application of any party interested, refer a case for the opinion of the High Court[9].

An order of the Registrar referring a matter to the court[10] is addressed to the applicant and requires him to begin court proceedings within a specified period[11] for the determination of the matter by taking out an originating summons or other appropriate originating process and to serve such process within a further specified period[12].

1 For orders see Forms 14, 45 post.
2 Land Registration Rules 1925, SR & O 1925/1093, r 298 (2) (16 Halsbury's Statutory Instruments (1998 Issue) REAL PROPERTY). See for example Form 24 post.
3 See generally Paragraph 21 post.
4 See Form 20 post.
5 For an order see Form 24 post.
6 Land Registration Rules 1925 r 220 (4).
7 Land Registration Rules 1925 rr 157, 158.
8 Land Registration Act 1925 s 13 proviso (c) (37 Halsbury's Statutes (4th Edn) REAL PROPERTY). In practice the Registrar's discretion of approving a good holding title has been exercised so freely and with such satisfactory results that this power of reference has proved almost superfluous.
9 Land Registration Act 1925 s 140 (1). In practice this power has also proved unnecessary in view of the wide powers of reference already mentioned.
10 See Forms 14, 24, 45 post.
11 The period may be extended on application to the Registrar if reasonable grounds are shown.
12 For an originating summons and supporting affidavit see Forms 25, 26 post. See further Paragraph 8 post.

8. Appeals from Registrar. When the Registrar has determined the issue or issues after a hearing before him and has made such order in the matter as he considers just[1], any person aggrieved by his decision or order may appeal to the court within 28 days of the Registrar's decision[2]. Notice of the intention to appeal should be given in writing to the registry as soon as possible so that an appropriate note may be made on the register. No appeal from a decision or order of the Registrar or, unless otherwise ordered, of the court, will affect any dealing for valuable consideration which has been duly registered before such a notice has been delivered[3].

Provision is also made in a number of other specific instances for appeal to the court where a person is aggrieved by an order of the Registrar, or by his refusal to make an order, or in certain other particular circumstances[4]. It has been held that no appeal lies to the court arising out of the Registrar's refusal to register as absolute a title about which he is not satisfied[5]. Any wrongful refusal or failure by the Registrar to grant an absolute title might, however, be challenged by judicial review[6].

1   Land Registration Rules 1925, SR & O 1925/1093, rr 220 (3), 298 (1) (16 Halsbury's Statutory Instruments (1998 Issue) REAL PROPERTY). As to hearings generally see Paragraph 13 post. As to orders of the Registrar in such circumstances see, for example Forms 5, 23, 43 post.
2   Land Registration Act 1925 ss 13 proviso (b), 56 (1) (37 Halsbury's Statutes (4th Edn) REAL PROPERTY); Land Registration Rules 1925 r 299. As to the meaning of "court" see Paragraph 5 ante.
3   Land Registration Rules 1925 r 301. The requirement to enter notice of appeal applies to appeals from the High Court: *Belcourt v Belcourt* [1989] 2 All ER 34, [1989] 1 WLR 195.
4   These include an appeal against an order for production of deeds (Land Registration Act 1925 s 15 (2)); against an order as to costs (Land Registration Act 1925 s 17 (1) proviso); against any act done by the Registrar in relation to a caution (Land Registration Act 1925 s 56 (1), see Form 6 post), or in relation to an application for an inhibition (Land Registration Act 1925 s 57 (3)); an appeal in respect of an order made under a restriction (Land Registration Act 1925 s 58 (3)); an appeal against rectification of the register by the Registrar (Land Registration Act 1925 s 82 (1)).
    Some of these instances may, of course, occur in connection with a hearing by the Registrar. See *Quigly v Chief Land Registrar* [1992] 3 All ER 940, [1992] 1 WLR 834, in which the court held that it had no jurisdiction to hear an appeal against the Registrar's discretion to refuse to allow inspection of documents in his custody. Land Registration Act 1925 s 83 (7), which formerly provided for appeals against determinations by the Registrar as to indemnity, has been repealed and is replaced by the Land Registration and Land Charges Act 1971 s 2 (1) (37 Halsbury's Statutes (4th Edn) REAL PROPERTY), and which now provides that if any question arises as to whether any person is entitled to an indemnity under any provision of the Land Registration Act 1925 or as to the amount of any such indemnity, he may apply to the court to have that question determined. The Registrar's right to settle claims by agreement is, however, expressly preserved (Land Registration and Land Charges Act 1971 s 2 (5)). As to applications to the court in respect of claims for indemnity, see generally Paragraph 33 post and Forms 46–49 post.
5   *Dennis v Malcolm* [1934] Ch 244; *MEPC Ltd v Christian-Edwards* [1978] Ch 281, [1978] 3 All ER 795, CA.
6   See RSC Ord 53.

9. Procedure on appeals and references to High Court. With the exception of an appeal from a county court, which is heard by a divisional Court of the Chancery Division, any appeal to, and case stated or question referred for the opinion of the High Court under the Land Registration Act 1925[1] must be heard and determined by a single judge of the Chancery Division[2]. No appeal lies from the judge's decision on an appeal except with his leave or that of the Court of Appeal[3].

Proceedings are begun by originating motion (in the case of an appeal) or originating summons[4], which should be entitled in the usual way. The fact that the proceedings are issued under the Land Registration Acts 1925 to 1986[5], should be specified in the body thereof together with the section or sections under which the relief is sought[6], and in the case of an appeal must specify the grounds of the appeal[7].

Except with the court's leave no grounds other than those so stated may be relied on, though the court may amend the grounds[8]. The bringing of the appeal does not operate as a stay of proceedings on the Registrar's decision unless the court or the Registrar so orders[9].

The originating motion or originating summons must be served on the Registrar and on every party to the proceedings before the Registrar (other than the appellant)[10], and the appeal entered, within 28 days after the date on which notice of the Registrar's decision was given to the appellant[11]. Unless the court otherwise orders, the appeal may not be heard sooner than 21 days after service of the originating motion[12].

Whilst the appeal is by way of rehearing[13] and is not a trial de novo enabling the case to be presented differently, the court may allow or require further evidence on questions of fact[14], and it may draw any inferences of fact which might have been drawn in the proceedings before the Registrar[15]. The evidence is not reheard by the court, which proceeds on the Registrar's note of evidence or an official shorthand note, supplemented by any additional notes of evidence exhibited to the appellant's affidavit supporting his originating summons and stating the general nature of the case[16]. The Registrar should, in his decision, state his view of the facts. Any additional evidence sought to be given on the appeal should be by affidavit. Where the whole of the documents and facts are on common ground no affidavit will be necessary on the appeal, but copies of the agreed statement of facts and relevant documents should be produced on the hearing of the appeal[17].

1 Land Registration Act 1925 (37 Halsbury's Statutes (4th Edn) REAL PROPERTY).
2 RSC Ord 93 r 10 (1), (2)(f). For the Lord Chancellor's power to nominate a particular judge to hear Land Registration Act matters see Paragraph 6 note 2 ante.
3 RSC Ord 93 r 10 (3).
4 RSC Ord 5 r 3; RSC Ord 55 rr 1 (1), 3 (1); see Forms 6, 25, 48 post. See also Paragraph 5 note 3 ante.
5 See Paragraph 1 ante.
6 Chancery Division Practice Directions No 23: Supreme Court Practice 1997 para 865.
7 RSC Ord 55 rr 1 (4), 3 (2).
8 RSC Ord 55 r 6 (3).
9 RSC Ord 55 r 3 (3). As to the notice of intention to appeal which must be given to the registry, and its effect, see Paragraph 8 ante.
10 RSC Ord 55 r 4 (1)(b).
11 RSC Ord 55 r 4 (2), (4). For calculating the period see *Minister of Labour v Genner Iron & Steel Co (Wollescote) Ltd* [1967] 1 WLR 1386; *Minister of Labour v Dyons and Fowle Ltd (No 2)* [1967] 1 WLR 1390. The appeal is entered by lodging a copy of the originating motion, with a copy for the judge, at Chancery Chambers: RSC Ord 57 rr 1 (1)(c), 2.
12 RSC Ord 55 r 5.
13 RSC Ord 55 r 3 (1).
14 RSC Ord 55 r 7 (2); and see *Re Gilbert's Application* [1961] 2 All ER 313, [1961] 1 WLR 822, CA.
15 RSC Ord 55 r 7 (3).
16 *Re Gilbert's Application* [1961] 2 All ER 313, [1961] 1 WLR 822, CA, where RUSSELL J dealt with the practice at some length. For affidavits see Forms 7, 26, 49 post.
17 *Re Gilbert's Application* [1961] 2 All ER 313, [1961] 1 WLR 822, CA.

10. Application direct to the court. In some circumstances application may be made direct to the court without a prior hearing or reference by the Registrar[1]. Original applications concerning rectification[2], cautions[3], restrictions[4], inhibitions[5] and indemnity[6] are dealt with separately in this title. Application may also be made with regard to the acquisition of title to land by adverse possession[7] or easements by prescription[8], questions arising on title when a person under disability, or outside the jurisdiction of the High

Court, or yet unborn, is interested[9], and a number of other matters[10]. In this connection it is important to note that no indemnity is payable on account of costs incurred in taking or defending any legal proceedings without the consent of the Registrar[11]. Proceedings by or against the Registrar do not rank as Crown proceedings[12].

1   For the meaning of "court" see Paragraph 5 ante. As to procedure generally see Paragraph 6 ante.
2   Land Registration Act 1925 s 82 (as amended) (37 Halsbury's Statutes (4th Edn) REAL PROPERTY). See Paragraph 20 post.
3   See Paragraph 11 text to notes 16, 17 post.
4   Land Registration Act 1925 s 58. See Paragraph 24 post.
5   Land Registration Act 1925 s 57. See Paragraph 25 post.
6   Land Registration Act 1925 s 83 (as substituted by the Land Registration Act 1997 s 2); Land Registration and Land Charges Act 1971 s 2 (1) (37 Halsbury's Statutes (4th Edn) REAL PROPERTY).
7   Land Registration Act 1925 s 75 (3).
8   Land Registration Act 1925 s 75 (5); Land Registration Rules 1925, SR & O 1925/1093, r 250 (16 Halsbury's Statutory Instruments (1998 Issue) REAL PROPERTY).
9   Land Registration Act 1925 ss 141, 142.
10 For example in connection with the description of registered land (Land Registration Act 1925 s 76), but see the Land Registration Rules 1925 rr 281, 285; and entry of notice of a lease of registered land without the lessor's consent (Land Registration Act 1925 s 48 (2)) although his concurrence is immaterial if the lease is binding upon him. See also the Land Registration Rules 1925 rr 46, 186 and *Strand Securities Ltd v Caswell* [1965] Ch 958, [1965] 1 All ER 820, CA.
11 Land Registration Act 1925 s 83 (5)(c)(as substituted by the Land Registration Act 1997 s 2). See Paragraph 33 post.
12 Crown Proceedings Act 1947 s 23 (3)(f) (13 Halsbury's Statutes (4th Edn) CROWN PROCEEDINGS).

11. Proceedings where registration of title is only incidental. There are many kinds of proceedings, both contentious and non-contentious, relating to land in which the fact that the title to the land is registered is merely incidental. The procedure in an instance of this kind will be the normal procedure applicable to the case, and only after judgment has been given or an order has been made will the Chief Land Registrar be concerned. The following are examples of court orders and proceedings consequent upon which the register may need to be adjusted:

1. a vesting order made on the appointment or discharge of a trustee or otherwise[1];
2. an order appointing a substitute, or special, or additional personal representative[2];
3. a vesting order, or an order appointing a person to convey, whereby certain minor interests are disposed of or created[3];
4. an order authorising Settled Land Act trustees to exercise powers in the name of the tenant for life[4];
5. any order by virtue of which the power of disposing of registered land has become vested in some person other than the proprietor[5];
6. an order for rectification consequent on a decision of the court that some person is entitled to any estate, right or interest in or to any registered land or charge[6];
7. an order in an action for specific performance[7];
8. an order discharging or modifying a restrictive covenant[8];

COURT PROCEEDINGS 259

9. an order appointing a receiver for a mental patient[9];
10. an order for foreclosure[10], or directing sale of mortgaged premises[11];
11. bankruptcy proceedings generally[12], including an order for administration of the estate of a deceased insolvent[13], and a vesting order following the disclaimer of a registered lease by the trustee in bankruptcy[14];
12. an order appointing an administrator or liquidator of a company[15];
13. an order directing the vacation of a caution against dealings[16] made on an interlocutory motion in an action in which substantive relief is sought in respect of the interest or alleged interest in land protected by the caution[17]; and
14. an order appointing a manager of leasehold premises[18].

Service on the Registrar of any order or office copy of any order of any court is made by delivering it at the registry[19]. When the order directs rectification of the register to be made or any other act to be done, an application to this effect must be delivered at the same time and the matter will then be proceeded with as the Registrar directs[20].

1 Land Registration Act 1925 s 47 (1) (37 Halsbury's Statutes (4th Edn) REAL PROPERTY); Trustee Act 1925 ss 40 (as amended by the Trusts of Land and Appointment of Trustees Act 1996 s 25 (1), Sch 3 para 3 (1), (14)), 41 (as amended), 44 (48 Halsbury's Statutes (4th Edn) TRUSTS AND SETTLEMENTS); Land Registration Rules 1925, SR & O 1925/1093, r 302 (16 Halsbury's Statutory Instruments (1998 Issue) REAL PROPERTY); *Re Strathblaine Estates Ltd* [1948] Ch 228, [1948] 1 All ER 162; Vol 41 (1991 Issue) title TRUSTS AND SETTLEMENTS Paragraph 13.

2 Land Registration Act 1925 s 41 (1); Administration of Estates Act 1925 s 23 (2) (17 Halsbury's Statutes (4th Edn) EXECUTORS AND ADMINISTRATORS); Administration of Justice Act 1985 s 50 (17 Halsbury's Statutes (4th Edn) EXECUTORS AND ADMINISTRATORS).

3 Land Registration Act 1925 s 103 (1)(as amended by the Trusts of Land and Appointment of Trustees Act 1996 s 25 (1), Sch 3 para 5 (1), (10)). "Minor interests" means interests not capable of being disposed of or created by registered dispositions and capable of being overridden (whether or not a purchaser has notice of them) by the proprietor unless protected under the Act, and all rights and interests which are not registered or protected on the register and are not overriding interests: see Land Registration Act 1925 s 3 (xv)(as amended by the Trusts of Land and Appointment of Trustees Act 1996 s 25 (1), Sch 3 para 5 (1), (2)). See also *Williams and Glyn's Bank Ltd v Boland* [1981] AC 487, [1980] 2 All ER 408, HL, cited and distinguished in *City of London Building Society v Flegg* [1988] AC 54 , [1987] 3 All ER 435, HL. "Overriding interests" means all the incumbrances, interests, rights and powers not entered on the register but subject to which registered dispositions take effect: Land Registration Act 1925 s 3 (xvi). Most overriding interests are listed in Land Registration Act 1925 s 70 (1)(as amended). See *Ashburn Anstalt v Arnold* [1989] Ch 1, [1988] 2 All ER 147, CA for the extent to which an overriding interest was created by an agreement that tenants giving up occupation for redevelopment would be offered a new lease; *Kemmis v Kemmis (Welland Intervening)* [1988] 1 WLR 1307, [1988] 2 FLR 223, CA; *Abbey National Building Society v Cann* [1991] 1 AC 56, [1990] 1 All ER 1085, HL which held that the benefit of Land Registration Act 1925 s 70 (1)(g) may not be claimed where the claimants were not in actual occupation at the date of completion of the purchase; *Lloyds Bank plc v Rosset* [1991] 1 AC 107, [1990] 1 All ER 1111, HL where the relevant date for being in actual occupation was the date of the creation of the bank's charge. An option to purchase has been held not to amount to a "minor interest": *Murray v Two Strokes Ltd* [1973] 3 All ER 357, [1973] 1 WLR 823.

4 Land Registration Act 1925 s 87 (5); Settled Land Act 1925 s 24 (1) (48 Halsbury's Statutes (4th Edn) TRUSTS AND SETTLEMENTS). See Vol 41 (1991 Issue) title TRUSTS AND SETTLEMENTS.

5 Land Registration Rules 1925 r 131 (as amended).

6 Land Registration Act 1925 s 82 (1)(a), (5). See Paragraph 28 post.
7 In an action for specific performance of a contract relating to registered land, or a registered charge, the court may cause any party who has registered interests or rights in the land or charge, or who has entered any notice, caution, restriction, or inhibition, against it, to appear in the action and show cause why the contract should not be specifically performed, and may direct that any order made in the action shall be binding on any such party: Land Registration Act 1925 s 139. As to actions for specific performance generally see Vol 37 (1995 Issue) title SPECIFIC PERFORMANCE.
8 Land Registration Act 1925 s 50 (3)(as amended); Law of Property Act 1925 s 84 (1)(as substituted) (37 Halsbury's Statutes (4th Edn) REAL PROPERTY). See Vol 34 (1) (1994 Issue) title RESTRICTIVE COVENANTS.
9 Land Registration Act 1925 s 111 (5)(as amended); Vol 26 (1996 Issue) title MENTAL HEALTH: COURT OF PROTECTION Paragraph 35.
10 Land Registration Act 1925 s 34 (3); Law of Property Act 1925 ss 88 (2), 89 (2); Land Registration Rules 1925 r 147. See Vol 28 (1997 Issue) title MORTGAGES Paragraphs 2, 45. See also Practice Note [1932] WN 6, and note 1 above.
11 Land Registration Act 1925 s 34 (4); Law of Property Act 1925 ss 88 (1), 89 (1), 91 (1), (2). See Vol 28 (1997 Issue) title MORTGAGES Paragraph 2.
12 Land Registration Act 1925 ss 42 (1)(as amended), 43 (as amended), 61 (as amended and as further amended by the Land Registration Act 1988 ss 1, 2, Schedule), 62 (as amended); Land Registration Rules 1925 rr 174–184 (as substituted). See generally Vol 7 (1997 Issue) title BANKRUPTCY AND INSOLVENCY.
13 Insolvency Act 1986 s 421 (4 Halsbury's Statutes (4th Edn) BANKRUPTCY AND INSOLVENCY); and see note 12 above.
14 Land Registration Act 1925 s 42 (2)(as amended); and see the authorities cited in note 12 above.
15 Land Registration Rules 1925 r 185. See Vol 10 (1995 Issue) title COMPANIES WINDING-UP Paragraph 61.
16 As to cautions against dealings, see Paragraph 21 post.
17 *Lester v Burgess* (1973) 26 P & CR 536; *Calgary and Edmonton Land Co Ltd v Dobinson* [1974] Ch 102, [1974] 1 All ER 484. See also as to cases in which such an order will be made: *Rawlplug Co Ltd v Kamvale Properties Ltd* (1968) 20 P & CR 32; *Calgary and Edmonton Land Co Ltd v Discount Bank (Overseas) Ltd* [1971] 1 All ER 551, [1971] 1 WLR 81; *Tiverton Estates Ltd v Wearwell Ltd* [1975] Ch 146, [1974] 1 All ER 209, CA; *Clearbrook Property Holdings Ltd v Verrier* [1973] 3 All ER 614, [1974] 1 WLR 243; and *Norman v Hardy* [1974] 1 All ER 1170, [1974] 1 WLR 1048.
18 Landlord and Tenant Act 1987 s 24 (1)(as amended) (23 Halsbury's Statutes (4th Edn) LANDLORD AND TENANT).
19 Land Registration Rules 1925 r 302 (1).
20 Land Registration Rules 1925 r 302 (2). No such rectification or act may, however, be completed until the expiration of 4 clear days from the date of the order: Land Registration Rules 1925 r 302 (2) proviso.

12. Production of evidence in court. Any land certificate or charge certificate is admissible as evidence of the several matters therein contained[1], and office copies of and extracts from the register and of and from documents filed in the registry are admissible in evidence in all actions and matters, and between all persons or parties, to the same extent as the originals would be[2]. Any document bearing the registry seal is similarly admissible[3].

When a party desires to produce evidence in court with regard to any register, plan or document filed in the registry it should normally be sufficient to produce the land or charge certificate, or an office copy. Only when he is unable to arrange for production of the certificate or office copy[4], or, in exceptional circumstances, when the authenticity of an original document is in question[5], should it be necessary to subpoena the Registrar for the production in court of the register, plan or document itself[6].

Any person is entitled to apply for office copies of the register and title plan or a certificate of inspection of the title plan[7] or an office copy of a document referred to in the register (not being a lease or charge or a copy of a lease or charge)[8].

1 Land Registration Act 1925 s 68 (37 Halsbury's Statutes (4th Edn) REAL PROPERTY), extended by the Land Registration Rules 1925, SR & O 1925/1093, rr 264, 275 (16 Halsbury's Statutory Instruments (1998 Issue) REAL PROPERTY), to include office copies of entries and filed documents annexed thereto. For the contents of certificates see Land Registration Rules 1925 rr 261, 262 (as amended), 263. The certificate will only evidence the state of the register as at the date it was last compared with the register. Accordingly it may be lodged at the registry again for some comparison with the register as shortly before the proceedings as possible if it is to be safely relied on as reflecting the current state of the register. In practice most parties will find it more convenient to hold on to the certificate and apply for up-to-date office copies as authentic evidence of the current state of the register.
2 Land Registration Act 1925 s 113 (as amended by the Land Registration Act 1988 s 2). As to indemnity for loss by reason of inaccuracy in an office copy or extract, see Paragraph 32 post.
3 Land Registration Act 1925 ss 126 (7), 132 (4).
4 As to office copies see notes 7, 8 below.
5 For example where it is claimed that fraud has occurred in connection with the execution or attestation of a document or otherwise in relation to it.
6 All subpoenas must be addressed to the Chief Land Registrar, who deputes an officer of the registry to accept service of them and to attend in answer to them. Inquiry should be made at the registry or a district registry for an appointment for service, which is effected by delivery of a copy and production of the original writ. A subpoena duces tecum is not in order unless it clearly defines the particular document or documents required to be produced. In any case where more than mere production of documents is required a detailed indication should be given in writing of the matters as to which evidence is required to be given. In appropriate cases the applicant will be called upon to submit a proof of evidence.
7 Land Registration Act 1925 s 112 (as substituted by the Land Registration Act 1988 s 1) and Land Registration (Open Register) Rules 1992, SI 1992/122, r 2 (16 Halsbury's Statutory Instruments (1998 Issue) REAL PROPERTY).
8 Land Registration (Open Register) Rules 1992 r 3.

C: PROCEEDINGS BEFORE THE REGISTRAR

13. Matters heard by Registrar. Provision is made for the Registrar to hear and determine the matter where any question, doubt, dispute, difficulty or complaint arises before him upon any application or during any investigation of title:
1. as to the registration of a title, incumbrance or charge[1];
2. as to any dealing with any registered title, incumbrance or charge or any matter entered or noted in or omitted from the register[2];
3. as to the amendment or withdrawal from the register or production to the Registrar of any certificate or other document[3]; or
4. as to any registration or other proceeding in the registry[4].

This applies whether the question relates to the construction[5], validity or effect of an instrument, or the persons interested, or the nature or extent of their interests or powers, or as to order of priority[6], or the mode in which an entry should be made or dealt with in the register or otherwise[7], or arises on a conflict between the verbal particulars on the register and the filed plan or general map[8].

Subject to appeal to the court[9], the Registrar makes such order[10] in the matter as he thinks just[11], although he may, if he thinks fit, instead of deciding the question himself, refer the matter at any stage, or any question thereon, for the decision of the court[12].

If a caution against dealings has been registered and the cautioner on receipt of a notice[13] shows cause why his caution should not be cancelled or why a dealing should not be registered, the Registrar may appoint a time for the persons interested to appear before him so that he may hear the matter[14].

It is noteworthy that, with regard to the matters which come before the Registrar in this way, there is no limitation on his jurisdiction whether on account of the value or on account of the nature of the land concerned.

1 Land Registration Rules 1925, SR & O 1925/1093, r 298 (1)(a) (16 Halsbury's Statutory Instruments (1998 Issue) REAL PROPERTY). As to objections to registration, see Land Registration Rules 1925 r 35 and the Land Registration Act 1925 s 13 (37 Halsbury's Statutes (4th Edn) REAL PROPERTY).
2 Land Registration Rules 1925 r 298 (1)(b).
3 Land Registration Rules 1925 r 298 (1)(c).
4 Land Registration Rules 1925 r 298 (1)(d).
5 *Re Dances Way, West Town, Hayling Island* [1962] Ch 490, [1962] 2 All ER 42, CA.
6 See the Land Registration Rules 1925 r 158.
7 Land Registration Rules 1925 r 298 (1).
8 Land Registration Rules 1925 r 285.
9 For the meaning of "court" see Paragraph 5 ante.
10 For examples see Forms 5, 24, 45 post; and, generally, see Paragraph 17 post.
11 Land Registration Rules 1925 r 298 (1).
12 Land Registration Rules 1925 r 298 (2). For a similar power on the hearing of a caution, see Land Registration Rules 1925 r 220 (4). As to references to the court generally see Paragraph 7 ante.
13 See Paragraph 18 post.
14 Land Registration Rules 1925 r 220 (2). See also note 12 above.

14. Procedure prior to hearing. Most of the disputes heard by the Registrar are the outcome of objections[1] that have been lodged in respect of applications made to the registry and brought to the notice of the objector by the service of notice, advertisement or other means.

Thus, in the case of applications for first registration[2], for conversion of title[3], or for the replacement of a lost land certificate[4], there are provisions, where appropriate, for advertisement and for the service of notice. Similarly there are provisions as to the service of notices in the case of applications to register dealings[5].

Any objection[6] must state the grounds on which it is based, and if it prima facie shows cause why effect should not be given to the application, the Registrar will send a copy or full particulars of the objection to the applicant so as to give him an opportunity to reply to it. When the reply[7] is received, details will be transmitted to the objector and, if the issues are still not clear or if it appears that agreement may be reached between the parties, further correspondence may take place.

Once, however, the points at issue have been defined and remain unresolved, the Registrar will, if he is going to hear the matter himself[8], appoint a time for a hearing[9], and will then serve notice on all persons appearing to be interested notifying them of the time and place of the hearing[10] and stating that they may attend before him at that time in person or by solicitor or counsel[11]. Further copies of the notice will also be sent to the respective solicitors, who will be requested to provide information as to counsel, witnesses and authorities to be referred to. The plaintiff will also be expected to produce an agreed bundle of documents and statement arguments setting out the basis of the respective cases.

1 For example the Land Registration Rules 1925, SR & O 1925/1093, rr 34, 35 (16 Halsbury's Statutory Instruments (1998 Issue) REAL PROPERTY) (objection to registration), and Land Registration Rules rr 219, 220 (1) (objection by cautioner to registration of dealing).
2 As to notices and advertisements on the examination of the title, see the Land Registration Act 1925 s 13 (37 Halsbury's Statutes (4th Edn) REAL PROPERTY), the Land Registration Rules 1925 rr 25, 31 (as amended), 32 and Paragraph 16 post. For the service of the prescribed notice where an application is made for the registration of land in respect of which a caution against first registration has been entered see the Land Registration Act 1925 s 53 and Paragraph 19 post.
3 As to conversion of title, see the Land Registration Rules 1925 r 48 (as substituted), and Paragraph 21 post.
4 As to lost certificates, see the Land Registration Act 1925 s 67(2), and the Land Registration Rules 1925 r 271.
5 For examples of the service of notices in particular cases see Paragraph 18 post. As to the service of the prescribed notice where there is a caution against dealings on the register, see the Land Registration Act 1925 s 55, the Land Registration Rules 1925 r 218 and Paragraph 19 post.
6 See Forms 1, 12, 17, 20, 42 post.
7 See Forms 2, 13, 21 post.
8 He may at any stage refer the matter for the decision of the court: see Paragraph 7 ante.
9 Land Registration Rules 1925 rr 35, 220, 298. The Registrar may do this of his own accord or at the request of an interested party.
10 Such hearings normally take place at the offices of the Land Registry Headquarters, 32 Lincoln's Inn Fields, London WC2A 3PA. The notice will specify the nature of the dispute with reference to the relevant rules and will state that the persons notified may attend before the Registrar either in person or by their solicitor or counsel, that it is not obligatory to attend but that if they do not attend such order will be made and proceedings taken as the Registrar shall think just. The Registrar may, at the request of the parties, however, be prepared to hear the matter more locally and generally at the location of the most conveniently situated district land registry.
11 Land Registration Rules 1925 r 300. For notice of hearing see Forms 3, 22 post. A corporation, including a limited company, may appear only by solicitor or counsel.

15. Witnesses. The Registrar may by summons[1] under the seal of the registry require the attendance of all such persons as he may think fit to give evidence on oath in relation to the registration of any title or in any proceedings in the registry, or may require any person having the custody of any map, survey or book made or kept in pursuance of any Act, or any land or charge certificate, to produce it for his inspection[2].

He may allow to every person summoned by him the reasonable charges of his attendance[3], and no person may be required to attend in obedience to any summons unless the reasonable charges of his attendance and of the production of documents are paid or tendered to him[4]. Failure to obey a summons may result in prosecution and a fine[5].

When any such summons has been issued by the Registrar for service on a person not bound to attend or produce documents at his own expense[6], the declaration verifying the service of the summons must prove that the reasonable charges of attendance or production have been paid or tendered to him[7].

On an application for registration of title to land (or in other proceedings in the registry[8]) the Registrar may require a person to show cause why he should not produce deeds or documents relating to or affecting the title which that person has in his possession or custody and to the production of which the applicant for registration or his trustee is entitled[9]. Unless cause is shown to the Registrar's satisfaction within the time specified, the Registrar may order the deeds or documents to be produced as he thinks fit at the applicant's expense[10].

1   Any party to the hearing may apply to the Registrar to issue such a summons, see Form 4 post. As to the preparation and service of summons see the Land Registration Rules 1925, SR & O 1925/1093, r 311 (16 Halsbury's Statutory Instruments (1998 Issue) REAL PROPERTY).
2   Land Registration Act 1925 ss 64 (2), 128 (1) (37 Halsbury's Statutes (4th Edn) REAL PROPERTY); Land Registration Rules 1925 r 320.
3   Land Registration Act 1925 s 128 (1). Any such charges allowed by the Registrar are deemed to be charges incurred in or about proceedings for registration and may be dealt with accordingly: Land Registration Act 1925 s 128 (2). As to costs see Land Registration Act 1925 s 17 and Paragraph 16 note 3 post. There may be some doubt as to whether the expenses of a person producing a document which he is bound to produce at his own expense are to be regarded as a reasonable charge: see notes 6, 7 below.
4   Land Registration Act 1925 s 128 (1) proviso.
5   Land Registration Act 1925 s 128 (3)(as amended).
6   For an example of a person being under an obligation to produce a document at his own expense see Land Registration Act 1925 s 110 (6).
7   Land Registration Rules 1925 r 319. As to service of summonses, see Land Registration Rules 1925 r 311.
8   Land Registration Rules 1925 r 320.
9   Land Registration Act 1925 s 15 (1). An aggrieved person may appeal to the court, which may annul or confirm the Registrar's order with or without modification: Land Registration Act 1925 s 15 (2). If the person disobeys any order of the Registrar under this section, the Registrar may certify the disobedience to the court and that person may be punished by the court as if the order made by the Registrar were an order of the court: Land Registration Act 1925 s 15 (3).
10 Land Registration Act 1925 s 15 (1).

16. Conduct of hearing. The conduct of proceedings before the Registrar is not governed by rules but is within the discretion and under the control of the Registrar, who in actual practice follows the normal rules of procedure. The Registrar is attended by an official, who is also legally qualified, and who had prior responsibility for the conduct of the matter. This official administers oaths, takes notes, and prepares and transmits the final order. The proceedings are also recorded verbatim by a shorthand writer[1]. After evidence[2] and argument before him at the hearing, which is open to the public, the Registrar determines the issues and makes his order[3].

The Registrar has wide discretionary powers: he may in any particular case for any purpose extend the time limit or relax the regulations made by general rules, and he may also at any time adjourn any proceedings and make a new appointment[4]. If at any time he is of opinion that the production of further documents or evidence or the giving of further notices is necessary or desirable, he may refuse to complete or proceed with a registration or to do any act or make any entry until such further documents, evidence or notices have been supplied or given[5].

1   A transcript is available on application by any party to the proceedings on payment of its cost. As to the use of a transcript on an appeal to the court see *Re Gilbert's Application* [1961] 2 All ER 313, [1961] 1 WLR 822, CA.
2   The Registrar may require evidence to be given on oath: Land Registration Act 1925 s 128 (1) (37 Halsbury's Statutes (4th Edn) REAL PROPERTY); Land Registration Rules 1925, SR & O 1925/1093, r 316 (4) (16 Halsbury's Statutory Instruments (1998 Issue) REAL PROPERTY).
3   See Paragraph 17 post.
4   Land Registration Rules 1925 r 322 (1).
5   Land Registration Rules 1925 r 322 (2).

17. Registrar's order. After deciding the issues before him at the hearing, the Registrar will make such order[1] as he thinks just[2], including an order as to costs[3]. The decision is regarded as a final determination and the doctrine of res judicata applies[4].

Apart from hearings, the Registrar may make orders for a number of widely differing purposes. He may, for example, by order extend the period for applying for first registration[5], or authorise the registration of an intended dealing for the purpose of compliance with a restriction[6], or require the production of a deed[7], or require or excuse the production of a land certificate[8].

1   See Forms 5, 23, 43, 47 post.
2   Land Registration Rules 1925, SR & O 1925/1093, rr 220 (3), 298 (1) (16 Halsbury's Statutory Instruments (1998 Issue) REAL PROPERTY). Land Registration Rules 1925 r 220 (3), which deals with hearings in respect of cautions against dealings, gives examples of various orders that may then be appropriate, see Form 23 post. When the order has been made after the conclusion of the hearing, office copies of it will be sent to the parties or their solicitors.
3   See Paragraph 35 post.
4   Confirmed by MADDOCKS J in *Bradford and Bingley Building Society v Darin* (15 May 1996, Manchester district registry, unreported).
5   Land Registration Act 1925 s 123A (3)(as inserted by the Land Registration Act 1997 s 1) (37 Halsbury's Statutes (4th Edn) REAL PROPERTY). See Form 8 post.
6   Land Registration Rules 1925 r 237. See Form 28 post.
7   Land Registration Act 1925 s 15 (1).
8   Land Registration Act 1925 ss 82 (6), 103 (2); Land Registration Rules 1925 r 15.

D: OBJECTIONS AND CAUTIONS

18. Objections to registration. When an application has been made for a first registration or for conversion of title[1] it is necessary in appropriate cases to make searches and inquiries[2], to issue advertisements[3] and serve notices[4], in order to enable the Registrar to obtain a full disclosure of any interests or claims affecting the land which may not have been revealed by the evidence of title supplied to him.

Having served notices or issued advertisements, the Registrar must afford sufficient opportunity to any person wishing to object[5].

Any person[6] may object to the registration by delivering at the registry, before the completion of the registration, a written objection[7], signed by himself or his solicitor[8], stating concisely the grounds of the objection and giving an address in the United Kingdom to which notices may be posted to him[9].

The Registrar gives notice of any objection to the applicant[10] and invites him to comment in reply. The reply[11] should contain the substance of the applicant's case and should assist in defining the issues between the parties. The Registrar sends a copy or full particulars of the reply to the objector, and, if he feels that the issues are still not clearly defined or that there is a possibility of reaching a settlement once the issues are clearly defined, if they remain unresolved, will continue to correspond with the parties. Once the issues are clearly defined, if they remain unresolved the Registrar either refers the matter to the court[12] or hears and determines it himself, subject to a right of appeal to the court[13].

The Registrar has, however, power to overlook mere technical defects: if, upon the examination of any title[14], he is of opinion that it is open to objection but that it is nevertheless a title the holding under which will not be disturbed, he may approve it or may require the applicant to apply to the court, upon a statement signed by the Registrar, for the court's sanction to the registration[15]. No such reference has yet been ordered.

1 As to the conversion of a possessory title into an absolute or good leasehold title, see the Land Registration Act 1925 s 77 (as substituted) (37 Halsbury's Statutes (4th Edn) REAL PROPERTY); and the Land Registration Rules 1925, SR & O 1925/1093, r 48 (as substituted) (16 Halsbury's Statutory Instruments (1998 Issue) REAL PROPERTY).
2 All searches and inquiries which the Registrar considers necessary in the examination of, in relation to, the title must be made or obtained by such person and in such manner as the Registrar directs: Land Registration Rules 1925 r 27. Where as is usually the case, land is proposed to be registered with absolute or good leasehold title the title shown by the documents accompanying the application is examined by or under the superintendance of the Registrar, who may make such searches and inquiries as he deems expedient: Land Registration Rules 1925 r 25.
3 Before registration of an absolute or good leasehold title is completed an advertisement, giving the name and address of the person to be registered, a short description of the land, and requiring any objections to be made within a specified period, must be inserted in the London Gazette and in such local or other newspapers as the Registrar in each case decides: Land Registration Rules 1925 rr 31 (as amended), 32. When, however, the original lessee is registered as first proprietor, or the applicant is a purchaser on a sale completed within the previous year, an advertisement is not posted unless the Registrar thinks it is necessary or advises such.

4   When land is to be registered with absolute or good leasehold title the Registrar may give such notices to tenants, occupiers and other persons as he deems expedient: Land Registration Rules 1925 r 25. Where a lease affecting registered land is registered, notice of the registration will be given to the proprietor of the freehold land or of the superior lease out of which the lease is derived, unless his consent accompanies the application or is signified by the deposit of the land certificate to meet the application: Land Registration Rules 1925 rr 46 (1), 186 (3). For other examples of when notice may be served see the Land Registration Rules 1925 r 276 (notice to adjoining owner as to fixed boundaries), Land Registration Rules 1925 r 23 and the Land Registration Act 1925 s 97 (as amended) (notices on registration of foreshore), and Land Registration Act 1925 s 77 (as substituted); and the Land Registration Rules 1925 r 48 (as substituted) (conversion of title). As to the preparation and service of notices see Land Registration Rules 1925 rr 311–315 (as amended); for the Registrar's power to require further notices to be given if he thinks them necessary or desirable, to extend time limits or to relax the regulations, see Land Registration Rules 1925 r 322.
5   Land Registration Act 1925 s 13 proviso (a). These are objections arising otherwise than out of cautions against first registration or against conversion (see Paragraphs 19, 21 post).
6   That is, where he has been served with a notice under for example the Land Registration Rules 1925 r 25.
7   See Form 1 post.
8   Land Registration Rules 1925 r 34 (1).
9   Land Registration Rules 1925 r 34 (2).
10 Land Registration Rules 1925 r 35 (1). He also gives notice of the grounds of objection
11 See Form 2 post.
12 Land Registration Rules 1925 r 298 (2).
13 Land Registration Act 1925 s 13 proviso (b). The objector must be given at least seven clear days' notice of hearing: Land Registration Rules 1925 r 35 (2), see Form 3 post. As to hearings see Paragraph 13 ante. As to appeals see Paragraph 8 ante.
14 The Registrar may modify his examination if the land has been sold or purchased under a court order or if it appears to him that the title has been sufficiently investigated on a transaction for value (Land Registration Rules 1925 r 28 (as substituted)), and in certain cases he may and does act on a solicitor's certificate as to title: see Land Registration Rules 1925 r 29 (as substituted).
15 Land Registration Act 1925 s 13 proviso (c). For the Registrar's power to refer a case for the court's opinion where he entertains a doubt arising on the examination of a title see Land Registration Act 1925 s 140; and see Paragraph 9 ante.

19. Caution against first registration. Any person having or claiming such an interest in land not already registered as entitles him to object to any disposition[1] of it without his consent may lodge a caution[2] with the Registrar to the effect that the cautioner is entitled to be served with notice of any application that may be made for the registration of an interest in the land affecting his right[3].

This is a safeguard which should always be considered where the title to land is not registered but where there is nevertheless a possibility that an application for the registration of the title may be made either:
   1. by a person who is not entitled to apply[4]; or
   2. by a person who is entitled to apply but who may fail to disclose in the application rights or interests to which the land is subject and which are not overriding interests[5].

The caution must contain an address for service in the United Kingdom and give sufficient particulars to identify on the Ordnance map or the Land Registry General Map the land to which it relates[6]. The caution is in prescribed form containing a statutory declaration[7] stating the nature of the cautioner's interest in the land affected by the caution[8].

Any person may apply for an office copy[9] of a caution against first registration which will include a copy of the document prepared by the Land Registry which records details of the caution and a copy of the plan prepared by the Land Registry identifying the extent of the land affected by the caution.

Registration of an estate in respect of which a caution has been lodged cannot be effected until notice[10] has been served on the cautioner giving him an opportunity to appear and oppose the registration, and 14 days[11] have elapsed since the date of the service of the notice, or the cautioner has entered an appearance, whichever happens first[12].

If an application has been so made for registration which has resulted in a notice being served on a cautioner, the caution will only be cancelled to enable the registration to proceed either if the time prescribed elapses without the cautioner taking due action to oppose the registration, or if the cautioner consents to the registration unconditionally or subject to the condition of some special entry being made on the register which is acceptable to the applicant[13], or else if, after the cautioner has opposed the registration and, if necessary, the matter has been heard[14], the Registrar or the court orders the registration to proceed and the caution to be cancelled.

If the cautioner proposes to oppose the registration and object to cancellation of the caution, he is required by the notice served upon him to enter an appearance by lodging a written objection[15] stating fully the grounds of his objection so as to show cause to the Registrar and to provide the applicant with sufficient details of the cautioner's case. If the grounds are insufficient the Registrar may allow reasonable time for amendment and further particulars. If no prima facie cause can be shown the objection will be dismissed and the application will proceed. If, however, sufficient grounds are given the Registrar will send a copy or full particulars of the objection to the applicant, and invite his reply. The applicant will already have been shown the caution and supporting statutory declaration.

The reply[16] should be drawn so as to provide the cautioner with sufficient details of the applicant's case and to define the issues between the parties. The Registrar will then send a copy or full particulars of the reply to the cautioner.

If the Registrar is not satisfied that the issues are yet fully defined, or if it appears that a settlement may not be yet reached, he may continue corresponding with the parties. When, however, the issues are clear and remain unresolved without realistic prospect of the parties reaching a negotiated settlement, he will either hear and determine the matter himself[17] or refer it for the decision of the court[18].

A caution against first registration may at any time be withdrawn in respect of the whole or any part of the land to which it relates pursuant to an application[19] signed by the cautioner or the person entitled to the benefit of the caution, or their respective solicitors[20].

Any person aggrieved by anything done by the Registrar in relation to the caution may appeal to the court[21].

1   "Disposition" is taken to mean a disposition free from incumbrances and other rights and interests in the land.
2   See Form 9 post.
3   Land Registration Act 1925 s 53 (1) (37 Halsbury's Statutes (4th Edn) REAL PROPERTY). If any person lodges a caution without reasonable cause he is liable to pay compensation for any damage caused, to be recovered as a debt by the person sustaining the damage from the cautioner, see Land Registration Act 1925 s 56 (3).

4 As to the persons who may apply for registration see Land Registration Act 1925 ss 4 (1), 8 (1).
5 As to the effect of first registration see Land Registration Act 1925 ss 5–7, 9–12.
6 Land Registration Rules 1925, SR & O 1925/1093, r 64 (as substituted) (16 Halsbury's Statutory Instruments (1998 Issue) REAL PROPERTY).
7 Land Registration Rules 1925 Sch 1 Form CT1 (as inserted by SI 1997/3037).
8 Land Registration Act 1925 s 53 (2).
9 Land Registration (Open Register) Rules 1992, SI 1992/122, r 8 (1) (16 Halsbury's Statutory Instruments (1998 Issue) REAL PROPERTY).
10 See Form 10 post. Notice is sent not only of every application for the registration of the interest mentioned in the caution but also of any interest affecting it adversely. Thus, on a caution relating to freehold land, notice will be sent of applications to register the freehold, any leasehold not clearly subsidiary to any existing registered lease, and a rent or other incorporeal hereditament issuing out of or otherwise affecting the land; and on a caution relating to leasehold land, notice is sent of applications to register the leasehold interest referred to in the caution and any inferior leasehold not clearly subsidiary to an existing registered sub-lease.
11 This is the usual period, though the Registrar may in special circumstances direct a different one being not less than seven days: Land Registration Rules 1925 r 67; see also, as to the calculation of time under notices, Land Registration Rules 1925 r 313 (as substituted).
12 Land Registration Act 1925 s 53 (3).
13 Land Registration Rules 1925 r 69. See also Form 11 post.
14 Land Registration Rules 1925 r 298; See Paragraph 13 ante.
15 See Form 12 post.
16 See Form 13 post.
17 Land Registration Rules 1925 r 298 (1): see Paragraph 13 ante.
18 Land Registration Rules 1925 r 298 (2); see Paragraph 7 ante.
19 Land Registration Rules 1925 Sch 2 Form 16 (as amended by SI 1997/3037).
20 Land Registration Rules 1925 r 68 (1).
21 Land Registration Act 1925 s 56 (1). For an originating motion see Form 6 post.

20. Objections to dealings and entries on the register. Where a caution against dealings[1], a mortgage caution[2] or a notice of deposit or intended deposit[3] is entered on the register and a subsequent application is made to register a dealing affecting the land or charge concerned, the Registrar will serve a notice[4] on the cautioner or depositee[5]. Notices are also served when an application is made to register a dealing or to make an entry on the register and the particular circumstances warrant the taking, in the Registrar's discretion[6], of such additional precautions.

A notice may thus, for example, be served where a person claiming to have acquired title to registered land under the Limitation Acts[7] applies to be registered as the proprietor[8]; or where a proprietor applies, whether on first registration or at any other time, to have an appurtenant right entered on the register[9]; or where application is made to enter notice of an overriding interest or of a claim thereto on the register[10]; or where an application has been made to the Registrar to rectify the register[11]; or where application has been made in connection with the acquisition of title paramount to the registered estate[12].

Having served the notice, the Registrar will, unless it is a mere courtesy notice, allow a sufficient opportunity for an objection to be made[13], and this may lead to the matter being heard by the Registrar[14] or being referred by him to the court[15].

1   See Paragraph 21 post.
2   See Paragraph 22 post.
3   See Paragraph 23 post.
4   See Form 19 post.
5   For example see the Land Registration Act 1925 s 55 (37 Halsbury's Statutes (4th Edn) REAL PROPERTY) and the Land Registration Rules 1925, SR & O 1925/1093, r 218 (16 Halsbury's Statutory Instruments (1998 Issue) REAL PROPERTY).
6   Land Registration Rules 1925 r 322.
7   Limitation Act 1980 s 17 (24 Halsbury's Statutes (4th Edn) LIMITATION OF ACTIONS).
8   Land Registration Act 1925 s 75 (as amended).
9   Where the proprietor wishes to have a specific entry on the register of any appurtenant right capable of subsisting as a legal estate he may apply to the Registrar for such an entry to be made: Land Registration Rules 1925 rr 252, 257; see Form 15 post. The Registrar thereupon gives such notice to the person in possession of the land affected as he deems advisable and, if the land affected is registered, he must give notice to the proprietor and every person appearing by the register to be interested: Land Registration Rules 1925 r 253; see Form 16 post. An objection may be lodged; see Form 17 post. If satisfied that the right is capable of subsisting as a legal estate and appurtenant to the land, the Registrar may enter it as part of the description of the land in the property register, or, if he is not so satisfied, he must enter it with such qualification as he deems advisable or may merely enter notice of the fact that the proprietor claims it: Land Registration Rules 1925 r 254. The effect of the full entry as part of the description of the land is to confer an absolute, good leasehold, qualified or possessory title to the right, according to the nature of the title to the land: Land Registration Rules 1925 r 254. A mere note on the register that a right is expressed to be granted does not guarantee the title to it. As to the vesting of appurtenances on registration of a proprietor see Land Registration Rules 1925 rr 251, 256 and the Land Registration Act 1925 ss 5, 9, 20 (1)(as amended), 23 (1)(as amended), 72. As to the need to complete by registration a grant of an easement affecting registered land see Land Registration Act 1925 ss 19 (as amended), 22 (as amended). If, however, application is made for first registration of a transfer of registered land and the conveyance or transfer to the applicant grants or refers to the grant of an appurtenant legal easement, the Registrar, if satisfied as to the title to it, will normally, without any specific application, enter the benefit of this right in the property register.
10 Land Registration Act 1925 s 70 (3); Land Registration Rules 1925 rr 197, 198.
11 Land Registration Act 1925 s 82 (1). See Forms 40, 41 post.
12 Land Registration Rules 1925 rr 131 (as amended), 266.
13 Land Registration Rules 1925 r 312 (2).
14 Land Registration Rules 1925 r 298 (1). See Paragraph 13 ante.
15 Land Registration Rules 1925 r 298 (2). See Paragraph 13 ante.

21. Caution against dealings and against conversion. Any person interested under any unregistered instrument, or interested as a judgment creditor, or otherwise howsoever, in any land or charge registered in the name of any other person may lodge a caution[1] with the Registrar to the effect that no dealing with that land or charge on the part of the proprietor is to be registered until notice has been served upon the cautioner[2]. Where land is registered with a possessory or good leasehold or qualified title it is also possible to apply for a caution against conversion[3]. The lodging of a caution does not prejudice any person's claim or title[4].

The application to register a caution must be supported by a statutory declaration[5] containing a reference to the land or charge to which the caution relates and to the title number, and stating the nature of the interest claimed by the cautioner[6].

Thus, the cautioner may claim to be entitled as being the beneficial owner, or as tenant for life under the Settled Land Act 1925, as purchaser under a contract, as plaintiff in an action in the Chancery Division, as equitable mortgagee by virtue of a charge under hand[7], as a beneficial tenant in common under a trust of land[8], or as a judgment creditor in whose favour a charging order has been made by the court affecting the interest of one of two or more joint proprietors of land[9]. The interest must be one that is enforceable by the courts, and it must not be a right or claim arising prior to and conflicting with the grant of either an absolute title or a good leasehold title[10]. Furthermore, a person whose interest has been registered or protected by notice[11] or restriction[12] is not, except with the consent of the Registrar, entitled to lodge a caution in respect of his interest[13]. If any person lodges a caution without reasonable cause he will be liable to compensate any person sustaining damage[14].

Once a caution against dealings has been lodged the Registrar may not, without the cautioner's consent[15], register any dealing by the proprietor with the land or charge affected by the caution until he has served notice[16] on the cautioner, warning him that his caution will cease to have any effect after the expiration of 14 days[17] after service of the notice unless an objection[18] is made by the cautioner or his solicitor within that period showing good cause why the caution should continue to have effect or why the dealing should not be registered[19]. A similar notice must be served on the cautioner on the written application at any time of the proprietor of the land or of a charge to which a caution relates[20].

The following courses are open to the cautioner after the notice has been served:

1. he may unconditionally consent to the cancellation of his caution[21];
2. he may consent to the cancellation of the caution or to the registration of the dealing giving rise to the service of the notice, but only upon certain specified conditions[22];
3. he may at any time apply for withdrawal of the caution[23];
4. he may make no response within the period prescribed (or any extension of it) in which case, where the notice has been given in respect of the whole of the land or charge affected by the caution, the caution is deemed, unless the Registrar otherwise directs, to be exhausted and will be cancelled[24], whereupon the land or charge may be dealt with in the same manner as if no caution had been lodged[25];
5. at any time before the expiration of the period prescribed by the notice (or any extension of it), he or his personal representative may show cause why the caution should continue to have effect or why the dealing should not be registered[26]; cause may be shown by the cautioner or his legal representative appearing before the Registrar or, as is normal, delivering a written statement[27] signed by himself or his solicitor setting forth the grounds of his objection[28].

If the cautioner can show no prima facie grounds for maintaining his caution or his objection to the registration of the dealing the Registrar may order that the caution be cancelled[29].

If, however, prima facie cause is shown the Registrar will write to the applicant or his solicitors sending a copy or full particulars of the cautioner's objection and inviting a reply. On receipt of the reply[30], which should be so drawn as to provide sufficient details of the applicant's case and to define the issues between the parties, the Registrar, if satisfied that the issues are sufficiently defined and that there is no immediate possibility of a settlement, may appoint a time for the proprietor or the applicant for registration (as the case may be) and the cautioner or his personal representative, and such other persons as he may deem expedient, to appear before him[31]. Notice of the hearing[32] will be served on all persons concerned, who may then appear at the appointed time either in person or by counsel or solicitor[33].

After hearing the parties and serving such notices (if any) as he considers necessary, the Registrar will make such order[34] as he thinks just; for instance, he may order that the caution shall continue to have effect, or that it be cancelled, or that the registration be refused either with or without an inhibition against registration at any future time, or that the registration be completed forthwith, or after an interval, or conditionally, or with some modification, or subject to the prior registration of a dealing in favour of the cautioner, or subject to some notice, restriction or other entry[35].

If sufficient grounds of objection are shown and no settlement is reached, the Registrar will not necessarily hear the matter himself; he may instead, at any stage, refer it, or any question arising on it, for the decision of the court[36].

1   Land Registration Rules 1925, SR & O 1925/1093, r 215 (1) (16 Halsbury's Statutory Instruments (1998 Issue) REAL PROPERTY). See Land Registration Rules 1925 Sch 2 Form 63.
2   Land Registration Act 1925 s 54 (1)(as amended) (37 Halsbury's Statutes (4th Edn) REAL PROPERTY).
3   Land Registration Rules 1925 r 215 (2). See Land Registration Rules 1925 Sch 2 Form 69 (as amended by SI 1997/3037). As to conversion see the Land Registration Act 1925 s 77 (as substituted) and the Land Registration Rules 1925 r 48 (as substituted).
4   Land Registration Act 1925 s 56 (2); *Re White Rose Cottage* [1964] Ch 483, [1964] 1 All ER 169, affd in part [1965] Ch 940, [1965] 1 All ER 11, CA; *Barclays Bank Ltd v Taylor* [1974] Ch 137, [1973] 1 All ER 752, CA; *Clark v Chief Land Registrar* [1994] Ch 370, [1994] 4 All ER 96, CA.
5   Land Registration Rules 1925 Sch 2 Form 14 (as amended by SI 1997/3037), which gives examples of interests which may give rise to such an application.
6   Land Registration Rules 1925 r 215 (4).
7   See also the Land Registration Act 1925 s 41 (2) (lodgment of caution by person intending to apply to court for appointment as special or additional personal representative); Land Registration Act 1925 s 59 (1), (2) (protection by caution of various interests which could be protected by registration of land charge if land was unregistered); Land Registration Act 1925 s 106 (3) (as substituted) (protection by caution of unregistered charge); Land Registration Act 1925 s 111 (4) (lodgment of caution in name or on behalf of infant); Land Registration Rules 1925 r 57 (persons interested in settled land); Land Registration Rules 1925 r 238 (Church Commissioners). This is not, however, intended as an exhaustive list. Provision for payment of sum additional to purchase price in event of purchaser developing property would not be protected by caution: *Woolf Project Management Ltd v Woodtrek Ltd* (1987) 56 P & CR 134, [1988] 1 EGLR 179.
8   *Elias v Mitchell* [1972] Ch 652, [1972] 2 All ER 153. Prior to 1 January 1997, the Land Registration Act 1925 s 3 (viii)(as amended) expressly excluded an undivided share in land (the share of a tenant in common under a trust for sale) from its definition of land. Nevertheless, in this case it was held that such an undivided share in registered land amounted to a minor interest which, since it was an interest in land, qualified for protection by caution. This definition of "land" in the Land Registration Act 1925 s 3 (viii)(as amended) was further amended from 1 January 1997 by the Trusts of Land and Appointment of Trustees Act 1996 s 25, Sch 4, by the repeal of the words "excluding an undivided share" so removing this inconsistency.
9   Charging Orders Act 1979 s 2 (1)(a), (2)(a) (22 Halsbury's Statutes (4th Edn) JUDGMENTS AND EXECUTION).
10 Land Registration Act 1925 ss 5, 9, 10. In such a case an application for rectification may be an appropriate remedy.
11 For the effect of notices, see Land Registration Act 1925 s 52.
12 Land Registration Act 1925 s 58.

OBJECTIONS AND CAUTIONS

13 Land Registration Act 1925 s 54 (1) proviso (as amended). Rights of occupation under the Matrimonial Homes Act 1983 or Family Law Act 1996 may not be protected by caution but only by notice: Matrimonial Homes Act 1983 s 2 (8), (9)(repealed subject to transitional provisions by the Family Law Act 1996 s 66 (2), (3), Sch 9 paras 11, 12, Sch 20); Family Law Act 1996 s 31 (10), (11) (27 Halsbury's Statutes (4th Edn) MATRIMONIAL LAW).

14 Land Registration Act 1925 s 56 (3); see also *Clearbrook Property Holdings Ltd v Verrier* [1973] 3 All ER 614, [1974] 1 WLR 243.

15 See note 21 below.

16 See Form 19 post.

17 This is the usual period, but the Registrar may direct a different one, being not less than seven days, in special circumstances: Land Registration Rules 1925 r 218 (2). After notice has been served application may be made to the Registrar to extend the period stated in the notice if good reason can be shown.

18 See Form 20 post.

19 Land Registration Act 1925 s 55 (1); Land Registration Rules 1925 rr 218–220. It is important, however, to note that a caution registered against the proprietor of the land will not affect dealings by the proprietor of a registered charge in respect of the same land, and vice versa.

20 Land Registration Rules 1925 r 218 (1). When a caution is registered a notice is served on the proprietor telling him the nature of the interest claimed by the cautioner.

21 The personal representative of a deceased cautioner may consent on his behalf: Land Registration Act 1925 s 56 (4). Any consent must be signed by the cautioner or personal representative, or by his solicitor: Land Registration Rules 1925 r 217. For a consent see Form 19 post.

22 See note 21 above. The condition might be, for example, that notice of the interest protected by the caution is entered on the register with priority over the dealing or that the dealing be registered subject to the caution remaining on the register.

23 The application must be signed by the cautioner or his personal representative, or by his solicitor: Land Registration Rules 1925 r 222, Sch 2 Form 71 (as amended by SI 1997/3037). A caution may be withdrawn at any time and this course of action should be pursued once the purpose for registering the caution is at an end: to leave one on the register without justification may expose the caution to an action for damages. Any statutory liability previously incurred to indemnify or to make compensation is not, however, affected by the withdrawal; see the Land Registration Act 1925 s 56 (3).

24 Land Registration Rules 1925 r 221. If notice is served as to only part of the land affected by the caution, and there is no response, the caution will be cancelled as to that part only.

25 Land Registration Act 1925 s 55 (1).

26 Land Registration Rules 1925 r 219. For example there has been fraud or a mistake, or the dealing which it is sought to register is inconsistent with a prior dealing or with some adverse right or minor interest which would not be overridden if the land were not registered.

27 See Form 20 post.

28 Land Registration Act 1925 s 55 (2); Land Registration Rules 1925 r 220 (1). The Registrar may require the cautioner to give security to indemnify every party against any damage that may be sustained by reason of the delay caused: the Land Registration Act 1925 s 55 (2). There is, however, no prescribed form of bond.

29 Land Registration Rules 1925 r 220 (2).

30 See Form 21 post.

31 Land Registration Rules 1925 r 220 (2).

32 See Form 22 post.

33 Land Registration Rules 1925 r 300. Note that in this rule "solicitor" does not include a reference to "a licenced conveyancer", see Land Registration Rules 1925 r 1 (5C) (as inserted).

34 See Form 23 post.

35 Land Registration Rules 1925 r 220 (3). Any person aggrieved by any act done by the Registrar in relation to a caution may appeal to the court: Land Registration Act 1925 s 56 (1). For the procedure see Paragraph 9 ante.

36 Land Registration Rules 1925 r 220 (4). For the Registrar's order see Form 24 post; for an originating summons and supporting affidavit see Forms 25, 26 post.

22. Unregistered mortgages. The proprietor of any registered land may, subject to any entry to the contrary on the register, mortgage, by deed or otherwise, the land or any part of it in any manner which would have been permissible if the land had not been registered and with the same effect[1]. The land must, however, be described by reference to the register or in such other way as is sufficient to enable the Registrar to identify it without reference to any other document[2]. Unless and until the mortgage becomes a registered charge[3] it takes effect only in equity and is capable of being overridden as a minor interest[4] unless it is protected either

    1.   by the entry of notice on the register[5]; or
    2.   by the entry of such other notice as may be prescribed[6]; or
    3.   by the entry of a caution against dealings[7].

The former provision for the protection of mortgages by cautions in a specially prescribed form[8] which has been obsolete for many years was repealed in 1977[9].

1   Land Registration Act 1925 s 106 (1)(as substituted) (37 Halsbury's Statutes (4th Edn) REAL PROPERTY).
2   Land Registration Act 1925 s 25 (2)(a).
3   That is under Land Registration Act 1925 s 26.
4   Land Registration Act 1925 s 106 (2). As to minor interests, see Land Registration Act 1925 ss 3 (xv)(as amended by the Trusts of Land and Appointment of Trustees Act 1996 s 25 (1), Sch 3 para 5 (1), (2)), 101. See also *Williams and Glyn's Bank Ltd v Boland* [1981] AC 487, [1980] 2 All ER 408, HL cited and distinguished in *City of London Building Society v Flegg* [1988] AC 54, [1987] 3 All ER 435, HL.
5   That is under Land Registration Act 1925 s 49 (as amended and as further amended by the Criminal Justice Act 1988 s 170 (1), Sch 15 para 6, the Landlord and Tenant Act 1987 s 61 (1), Sch 4 para 1, the Community Charges (Administration and Enforcement) Regulations 1989, SI 1989/438, reg 45 (5), the Access to Neighbouring Land Act 1992 s 5 (2), the Council Tax (Administration and Enforcement) Regulations 1992, SI 1992/613, reg 51 (5), the Leasehold Reform, Housing and Development Act 1993 s 187 (1), Sch 21 para 1, the Drug Trafficking Act 1994 ss 65 (1), 67 (1), Sch 1 para 1, Sch 3, and the Trusts of Land and Appointment of Trustees Act 1996 s 25 (1), Sch 3 para 5 (1), (5)).
6   For example a notice of deposit of the land certificate under Land Registration Rules 1925, SR & O 1925/1093, r 239 (as substituted) (16 Halsbury's Statutory Instruments (1998 Issue) REAL PROPERTY). Note that it is no longer possible to apply for entry of a notice of deposit or intention to deposit, see Paragraph 23 post.
7   That is under the Land Registration Act 1925 s 54 (as amended); see Paragraph 20 ante.
8   That is the procedure under Land Registration Act 1925 s 106 as originally enacted.
9   By the Administration of Justice Act 1977 s 26 (1).

23. Notice of deposit of certificate. It is provided that the proprietor of any registered land or charge may create a lien on the registered land or charge by the deposit of the land certificate or charge certificate. The lien is subject to any overriding interests, if any, and to any estates, interests, charges, or rights registered or protected on the register. It is also provided that the lien so created shall be equivalent to a lien created in the case of unregistered land by the deposit of documents of title or of the mortgage deed by an owner entitled for his own benefit to the registered estate or a mortgagee beneficially entitled to the mortgage, as the case may be[1].

The Land Registration Rules formerly included provisions to enable a person with whom a land or charge certificate was deposited to give notice to the Registrar and for such notices to be entered on the register[2]. However, since September 27 1989, when Section 2 of the Law of Property

(Miscellaneous Provisions) Act 1989 came into force, the deposit alone of a land or charge certificate, or title deeds in the case of unregistered land, is no longer sufficient to create an equitable charge or lien on the land to which it relates; it is now only possible to create a lien by the deposit of title documents if there is a satisfactory agreement in writing between the parties[3]. Nevertheless, until April 3 1995, it was still permissible to enter notice of deposit, though the entry gives no guarantee that it protects a genuine interest[4]. Since that date it is no longer possible to apply for the entry of a notice of deposit[5], but protection by registration of a notice will still be available where a lien has been validly created and the lender has the land or charge certificate in his possession[6].

1 Land Registration Act 1925 s 66 (37 Halsbury's Statutes (4th Edn) REAL PROPERTY).
2 Land Registration Rules 1925, SR & O 1925/1093, rr 239–243 (as originally made).
3 Law of Property (Miscellaneous Provisions) Act 1989 s 2 (37 Halsbury's Statutes (4th Edn) REAL PROPERTY).
4 Land Registration Act 1925 s 52. Where there is an existing notice of deposit on the register, it gives notice of the deposit and operates as a caution against dealings; Land Registration Rules 1925, SR & O 1925/1093, r 239 (1) (as substituted) (16 Halsbury's Statutory Instruments (1998 Issue) REAL PROPERTY). See Paragraph 21 ante.
5 Land Registration Rules 1995, SI 1995/140, r 4. See also *United Bank of Kuwait plc v Sahib* [1996] 3 All ER 215, CA.
6 Land Registration Act 1925 s 49 (as amended and as further amended by the Criminal Justice Act 1988 s 170 (1), Sch 15 para 6, the Landlord and Tenant Act 1987 s 61 (1), Sch 4 para 1, the Community Charges (Administration and Enforcement) Regulations 1989, SI 1989/438, reg 45 (5), the Access to Neighbouring Land Act 1992 s 5 (2), the Council Tax (Administration and Enforcement) Regulations 1992, SI 1992/613, reg 51 (5), the Leasehold Reform, Housing and Development Act 1993 s 187 (1), Sch 21 para 1, the Drug Trafficking Act 1994 ss 65 (1), 67 (1), Sch 1 para 1, Sch 3, and the Trusts of Land and Appointment of Trustees Act 1996 s 25 (1), Sch 3 para 5 (1), (5)).

E: RESTRICTIONS AND INHIBITIONS

24. Restrictions. A restriction is an entry on the register which restrains or limits the otherwise wide and unfettered powers of a proprietor[1]. It may be entered on the application of the registered proprietor of any registered land or charges[2] or some other person[3], or by the Registrar[4].

The proprietor may apply[5] to the Registrar to make an entry in the register that no disposition is to be registered unless the following things, or such of them as the proprietor determines, are done:

1. unless notice of any application for the disposition is posted to a specified address;
2. unless the consent to the disposition of some named person or persons is given;
3. unless some such other matter or thing is done as the applicant requires and the Registrar approves[6].

The application may be made either voluntarily or because of a duty to do so[7].

If satisfied of the applicant's right to give the directions, the Registrar enters the restrictions on the register unless he deems them unreasonable or calculated to cause inconvenience[8].

The Registrar will enter a restriction where he is specifically required to do so[9] or where it appears that a proprietor does not have full and unlimited powers and that the register should be made to reflect this[10].

Virtually every restriction is framed to include the saving words "except under an order of the Registrar", or words to that effect.

Application may be made to the Registrar for an order[11] under a restriction in anticipation of an intended dealing, and he may in his discretion, notwithstanding any restriction on the register, order that the dealing be registered either unconditionally or subject to such limitations or conditions as he thinks fit[12].

In the case of settled land the Registrar may, on a similar application, notwithstanding any restriction on the register, grant a certificate that an intended disposition is authorised by a settlement or otherwise, and will be registered, and a purchaser who obtained such a certificate is not concerned to see that the disposition is authorised, although where capital money is paid to the persons to whom it is required to be paid by a restriction, or into court, no such certificate is required[13].

No land held by or in trust for a charity may be sold, leased or otherwise disposed of unless certain requirements are complied with or the consent of the court or the Charity Commissioners is obtained[14] and where any such disposition will be registered, the instrument effecting the disposition must contain the relevant restriction[15].

It is usually possible in practice either to comply with the terms of a restriction without involving the Registrar or to adopt some simple expedient to avoid bringing a restriction into operation. Thus, with the joint proprietorship restriction, a simple transfer by a sole surviving proprietor appointing a new trustee obviates the need for any order.

Any voluntary restriction may at any time be withdrawn or modified on application signed by all the persons appearing by the register to be interested, or their solicitors[16], and may also be set aside by order of the court[17] obtained on originating summons[18].

1   That some such restraint is necessary in the case of limited or fiduciary owners and the like is apparent from reference for example to the Land Registration Act 1925 ss 18 (as amended), 21 (as amended), 25 (as amended) (37 Halsbury's Statutes (4th Edn) REAL PROPERTY).
2   Land Registration Act 1925 s 58 (1).
3   Land Registration Act 1925 s 58 (5). Because the land or charge certificate must be produced before a restriction is entered on the register (Land Registration Act 1925 s 64 (1)(c)(as amended) a person other than the proprietor can rarely have a restriction entered without the proprietor's consent. Note, however, exceptionally that Land Registration Rules 1925, SR & O 1925/1093, r 236 (as substituted) (16 Halsbury's Statutory Instruments (1998 Issue) REAL PROPERTY) permits those beneficially interested in land to apply where the land is subject to a trust of land and where a restriction should have been entered either because the proprietor or the survivor of the proprietors is not solely beneficially entitled or by virtue of the provisions of the Trusts of Land and Appointment of Trustees Act 1996 ss 6, 8 (37 Halsbury's Statutes (4th Edn) REAL PROPERTY).
4   Text to note 9 below.
5   As to the application see the Land Registration Rules 1925 r 235 (as substituted), Sch 2 Form 75 (as substituted by SI 1996/2975 and amended by SI 1997/3037). See also Form 27 post.
6   Land Registration Act 1925 s 58 (1). The Land Registration Rules 1925 r 128 (as substituted) provides that no disposition of charity land is to be registered unless the instrument contains a certificate complying with Charities Act 1993 s 37 (as amended

by the Trusts of Land and Appointment of Trustees Act 1996 s 25 (2), Sch 4, and the Land Registration Act 1997 s 4 (1), Sch 1 Pt I para 6 (1)) (5 Halsbury's Statutes (4th Edn) CHARITIES) or the disposition is authorised by the trusts of the charity. See Land Registration Rules 1925 Sch 2 Form 12 (as substituted by SI 1993/1704 and amended by SI 1996/2975).

7   Restrictions are obligatory where, for example, settled land is involved: see Land Registration Act 1925 ss 86 (3), 91 (1); Land Registration Rules 1925 rr 56–58, 99, 100, 102, 104, 170 (as amended), 171 (as amended), Sch 2 Forms 9 (as amended by SI 1996/2975), 10 (as amended by SI 1996/2975), 11. See paragraph 1 of Form 27 post. See also Land Registration Rules 1925 rr 59A (as inserted), 106A (as inserted) giving effect to the Trusts of Land and Appointment of Trustees Act 1996 to protect beneficiaries when trustees powers of disposition are limited.
8   Land Registration Act 1925 s 58 (2); see also the Land Registration Rules 1925 r 78.
9   For example where there are joint proprietors and the Registrar is not satisfied that they are entitled for their own benefit or can give a valid receipt for capital money or that one of them is a trust corporation: see the Land Registration Act 1925 s 58 (3); and the Land Registration Rules 1925 rr 213 (as amended), 214. The Registrar is required to enter a restriction where the charity trustees, the official custodian or any other trustees for the charity apply to be registered as proprietor: Land Registration Rules 1925 r 123 (1)(as substituted).
10 See for example, Land Registration Rules 1925 r 259 (as amended).
11 See Form 27 post.
12 Land Registration Rules 1925, r 237 (1). See Form 28 post.
13 Land Registration Act 1925 s 89; Land Registration Rules 1925 r 237 (1).
14 Charities Act 1993 ss 37 (as amended by the Trusts of Land and Appointment of Trustees Act 1996 s 25 (2), Sch 4, and the Land Registration Act 1997 s 4 (1), Sch 1 Pt I para 6 (1)), 39 (as amended by the Trusts of Land and Appointment of Trustees Act 1996 s 25 (2), Sch 4, and the Land Registration Act 1997 s 4 (1), Sch 1 Pt I para 6 (2), (3)).
15 Land Registration Rules 1992 rr 60 (as substituted and amended), 123 (as substituted).
16 Land Registration Act 1925 s 58 (4); Land Registration Rules 1925 r 235 (2)(as substituted).
17 Land Registration Act 1925 s 58 (4).
18 See Form 29 post.

25. Inhibitions. An inhibition is an extreme measure to prevent a registered proprietor effectively disposing of or dealing with his land or charge, whether absolute or to some limited extent.

The court[1] or, subject to an appeal to the court, the Registrar, upon the application[2] of any person interested in relation to any registered land or charge, may, after directing such inquiries (if any) to be made and notices to be given and hearing such persons as the court or Registrar thinks expedient, issue an order or make an entry inhibiting for a time, or until the occurrence of an event to be named in the order or entry, or generally until further order or entry, the registration or entry of any dealing with any registered land or registered charge[3].

The court and the Registrar have in fact wide discretionary powers in connection with the application and any orders or entries resulting from it; the court or Registrar may make or refuse any such order or entry, may annex to it any terms or conditions, may discharge the order or cancel the entry when granted, with or without costs, may order a notice or restriction to be placed on the register and may generally act in such manner as justice requires[4].

Generally speaking, however, the entry of a notice, restriction or caution will provide adequate protection, and it is only in the most exceptional circumstances[5] that an application for an inhibition is appropriate, as, perhaps, in a suspected case of fraud, before taking any other step, or, if proceedings have begun, by way of interlocutory relief.

Apart from any express application, there are circumstances in which the Registrar must, of his own accord, enter an inhibition on the register. For example, he must enter an inhibition against the title of any proprietor of any registered land or charge which appears to be affected by a bankruptcy order registered under the Land Charges Act 1972[6] or where a manager of premises has been appointed by court order under the Landlord and Tenant Act 1987[7] or where land is transferred to the incumbent of a benefice[8]. There are also circumstances in which the Registrar may of his own accord enter an inhibition on the register, as, for instance, pending the result of a hearing before him if for any reason he thinks it desirable[9].

Any person aggrieved by an inhibition may apply to the Registrar for its removal unless it was originally entered under a court order, in which case the aggrieved person must apply to the court for its cancellation[10]. It is also possible to apply to the Registrar for an order under an inhibition in anticipation of an intended dealing[11].

1 For the meaning of "court" see Paragraph 5 ante.
2 Application to the court is by originating summons: RSC Ord 5 r 3. If the issues involve facts, the proceedings should be started by writ: *Re 462 Green Lane Ilford, Gooding v Borland* [1971] 1 All ER 315, [1971] 1 WLR 138 but see also *Re Deadman (decd)* [1971] 2 All ER 101. The form of an application to the Registrar is not prescribed, but it must either be accompanied by the proprietor's written consent or be supported by the applicant's statutory declaration and any other evidence the Registrar deems necessary: Land Registration Rules 1925, SR & O 1925/1093, r 230 (1) (16 Halsbury's Statutory Instruments (1998 Issue) REAL PROPERTY).
3 Land Registration Act 1925 s 57 (1), (3) (37 Halsbury's Statutes (4th Edn) REAL PROPERTY).
4 Land Registration Act 1925 s 57 (2), (4).
5 Exceptional circumstances might be the enforcement of a restraint order under the Drug Trafficking Act 1994 s 26 (12), (13), the Criminal Justice Act 1988 s 77 (12), (13), or the Prevention of Terrorism (Temporary Provisions) Act 1989 s 13 (8), Sch 4 para 6 (12 Halsbury's Statutes (4th Edn) CRIMINAL LAW), the application for an acquisition order under the Landlord and Tenant Act 1987 s 28 (5), (6) (23 Halsbury's Statutes (4th Edn) LANDLORD AND TENANT), or for a vesting order under the Leasehold Reform, Housing and Urban Development Act 1993 ss 26 (as amended), 50.
6 Land Registration Act 1925 s 61 (3)(as amended), (4), (6)(as amended). Such an inhibition is known as a bankruptcy inhibition. Notice of entry must be given to the registered proprietor: see the Land Registration Rules 1925 r 180 (as substituted) and Form 32 post. See further Paragraph 26 post and the Land Charges Act 1972 ss 6 (as amended by the Access to Neighbouring Land Act 1992 s 5 (1), the Law of Property (Miscellaneous Provisions) Act 1994 s 15 (1), (4), and the Trusts of Land and Appointment of Trustees Act 1996 s 25 (1), Sch 3 para 12 (1), (3)), 18 (6) (37 Halsbury's Statutes (4th Edn) REAL PROPERTY).
7 Landlord and Tenant Act 1987 s 24 (as amended).
8 Land Registration Act 1925 s 99 (1)(as amended); Land Registration Rules 1925 r 232.
9 Land Registration Rules 1925 r 230 (2).
10 Land Registration Rules 1925 r 231. See the Land Registration Act 1925 s 57 (2) and Paragraph 9 ante. An application to the court will be made by originating summons: RSC Ord 5 r 3.
11 Land Registration Rules 1925 r 237.

26. Bankruptcy affecting proprietor. When a bankruptcy petition is filed, the bankruptcy registrar or district judge of the county court must send notice of it to the Chief Land Registrar with a request that it be registered as a pending action[1], whereupon the Chief Land Registrar, having registered it accordingly, must register a creditors' notice against the title of any proprietor of any registered land or charge which appears to be affected[2]. When a bankruptcy order is made the Official Receiver must send the Chief Land Registrar notice of it with a request that it be entered in the register of writs and orders affecting land[3], whereupon, having done so, he must register a bankruptcy inhibition against the title of any proprietor of any registered land or charge which appears to be affected[4].

Where any doubt arises as to the identity of the debtor which is often the case given that the courts frequently only supply limited particulars or cases of reasonable doubt, the Registrar is always prepared to consider written evidence of mistaken identity. The Registrar must, as soon as practicable, after making such inquiry and giving such notice as he deems necessary, take such action as he thinks advisable[5].

On the bankruptcy of the proprietor, his registered estate or interest, if belonging to him beneficially, vests in the trustee in bankruptcy[6]. On production to the Registrar of an office copy of the bankruptcy order with a certificate by the Official Receiver that the registered land is part of the bankrupt's estate, the Official Receiver may be registered as proprietor in the bankrupt's place[7]. If the Official Receiver is registered as proprietor and another person is later appointed trustee, that trustee can apply for registration on production of an office copy of the certificate of his appointment[8]. If the Official Receiver is not registered as proprietor, the trustee in bankruptcy may be so registered on producing office copies of the bankruptcy order and of the certificate of his appointment and a certificate of the trustee that the land is part of the bankrupt's estate[9]. The existing bankruptcy entries relating to the petition and order will be cancelled when the Official Receiver or trustee in bankruptcy is registered as proprietor.

Where the registration of a pending action in respect of a bankruptcy petition is vacated, application may be made to cancel any ensuing creditors' notice[10]. Where a bankruptcy order has been rescinded or the bankruptcy annulled or the bankruptcy proceedings do not affect or have ceased to affect the bankrupt's statutory powers, application may be made to cancel any related bankruptcy inhibition[11]. The Registrar then usually serves notice on the Official Receiver or trustee in bankruptcy[12].

1 That is, under the Land Charges Act 1972 s 5 (1), (6) (37 Halsbury's Statutes (4th Edn) REAL PROPERTY), see title LAND CHARGES ante; Insolvency Rules 1986, SI 1986/1925, rr 6.13 (creditor's petition), 6.43 (debtor's petition) (3 Halsbury's Statutory Instruments (1995 Issue) BANKRUPTCY AND INSOLVENCY).
2 Land Registration Act 1925 s 61 (1) (37 Halsbury's Statutes (4th Edn) REAL PROPERTY). See Form 31 post.
3 That is under the Land Charges Act 1972 s 6 (1)(c)(as substituted), see title LAND CHARGES Paragraph 8 ante; Insolvency Rules 1986, SI 1986/1925, rr 6.34 (2)(a) (order made on creditor's petition), 6.46 (2)(a) (order made on debtor's petition).
4 Land Registration Act 1925 s 61 (3)(as amended). See Form 32 post. This also applies to an order appointing a manager of premises made under the Landlord and Tenant Act 1987 s 24 (8) (23 Halsbury's Statutes (4th Edn) LANDLORD AND TENANT).
5 Land Registration Rules 1925, SR & O 1925/1093, r 181 (as substituted) (16 Halsbury's Statutory Instruments (1998 Issue) REAL PROPERTY). See Form 32 post.
6 Land Registration Act 1925 ss 42 (1)(as amended), 43, 61 (5).
7 Land Registration Rules 1925 rr 174 (1)(as substituted), 177 (as substituted).
8 Land Registration Rules 1925 r 175 (as substituted).
9 Land Registration Rules 1925 r 176 (as substituted). See also Form 34 post.
10 Land Registration Rules 1925 r 181 (as substituted). The application should normally be

supported by an office copy of the court order directing vacation of the registration of the pending action.
11 Land Registration Rules 1925 r 181 (as substituted by SI 1986/2116). Where a registered chargee, whose charge has priority over the bankruptcy entries, exercises his power of sale, the creditors' notice and bankruptcy inhibition will be cancelled: see also the Land Registration Act 1925 s 61 (4).
12 See Form 33 post. As to the entry and vacation of the creditors' notice and bankruptcy inhibition see further 26 Halsbury's Laws (4th Edn) paras 1382–1390.

F: RECTIFICATION OF THE REGISTER

27. Rectification of the register generally. An application for rectification is closely allied to a claim for indemnity[1] since, where such an application fails, a claim for indemnity may offer an alternative remedy, and, where such an application succeeds, a claim for compensation from any person suffering loss as a result may then follow[2].

Rectification is not considered here in its widest sense and thus does not include the making of an entry in or a correction of the register so as to give effect to the vesting in some person other than the proprietor of the power of disposition of the land whether by operation of any statute or statutory power, by order of the court or by paramount title[3]. Nor does it include entries made to give effect to the transitional provisions of the 1925 property legislation as to the divesting and vesting of legal estates[4], or formal changes of names and addresses[5], or amendments made on the register where a mistake has occurred in a bankruptcy order or the amendments have been notified by the Official Receiver[6], or the correction of plans or verbal descriptions of registered land on an application for that purpose by the proprietor[7].

1 See Paragraph 32 post.
2 Compare with the Land Registration Act 1925 s 83 (1), (2)(as substituted by the Land Registration Act 1997 s 2) (37 Halsbury's Statutes (4th Edn) REAL PROPERTY). See Paragraph 32 post.
3 Land Registration Rules 1925, SR & O 1925/1093, r 131 (as amended)(16 Halsbury's Statutory Instruments (1998 Issue) REAL PROPERTY).
4 Land Registration Act 1925 ss 2 (1), 78 (as amended by the Trusts of Land and Appointment of Trustees Act 1996 s 25 (1), Sch 3 para 5 (1), (6)); Land Registration Rules 1925 rr 211, 248.
5 Land Registration Rules 1925 r 249.
6 Land Registration Rules 1925 r 182 (as substituted).
7 Land Registration Rules 1925 r 284; *Lee v Barrey* [1957] Ch 251, [1957] 1 All ER 191, CA.

28. When register may be rectified. Subject to an important exception mentioned hereafter, the register of title may be rectified pursuant to a court order[1] or, subject to an appeal to the court[2], by the Registrar in any of the following cases:
 1. where a court of competent jurisdiction[3], having decided[4] that a person is entitled to any estate, right or interest in or to any registered land or charge, and that as a consequence rectification is required, makes an order to that effect[5];

2. where the court[6], on the application[7] of any person aggrieved by an entry in, or omission from, the register, or by default or unnecessary delay in the making of an entry, orders rectification[8];
3. in any case and at any time with the consent of all persons interested[9];
4. where the court or Registrar is satisfied that any entry has been obtained by fraud[10];
5. where two or more persons are, by mistake, registered as proprietors of the same estate or charge[11];
6. where a mortgagee has been registered as proprietor of the land instead of as proprietor of a charge and a right of redemption is subsisting[12];
7. where a legal estate has been registered in the name of a person who, if the land had not been registered, would not have been the estate owner[13];
8. in any other case where, by reason of any error or omission in the register, or by reason of any entry made under a mistake, it may be deemed just to rectify the register[14].

The register may be so rectified notwithstanding that the rectification may affect any estates, rights, charges or interests acquired or protected by registration, or by any entry on the register, or otherwise[15].

1   For the meaning of "court" see Paragraph 5 ante.
2   As to the procedure on appeal to the court see Paragraph 9 ante.
3   This term is wider than "the court" as defined in Paragraph 5 ante. It thus includes the county court where that court has jurisdiction to decide a question relating to the land or charge and where the fact that the title to the land is registered is only incidental: see *Watts v Waller* [1973] QB 153, [1972] 3 All ER 257, CA; *Argyle Building Society v Hammond* (1984) 49 P & CR 148, CA; *Proctor v Kidman* (1986) 51 P & CR 67, CA. If the court, on reaching its decision, then considers that rectification of the register is required, it may make an order for rectification which the Registrar must obey: Land Registration Act 1925 s 82 (5) (37 Halsbury's Statutes (4th Edn) REAL PROPERTY); Land Registration Rules 1925, SR & O 1925/1093, r 302 (16 Halsbury's Statutory Instruments (1998 Issue) REAL PROPERTY). The power of the court is, of course, limited by the provisions of the Land Registration Act 1925 s 82 (3)(as amended), referred to hereafter.
4   In view of the use of the word "decided" the court's power under this provision is not exercisable in interlocutory proceedings: see *Lester v Burgess* (1973) 26 P & CR 536.
5   Land Registration Act 1925 s 82 (1)(a).
6   Note the difference in wording between this and the last provision.
7   For the procedure see Paragraph 30 post.
8   Land Registration Act 1925 s 82 (1)(b).
9   Land Registration Act 1925 s 82 (1)(c).
10 Land Registration Act 1925 s 82 (1)(d); see Form 34 post. Subject to the provisions of the Land Registration Acts with respect to indemnity and to registered dispositions for valuable consideration, any disposition of land or a charge which, if registered, would be fraudulent and void, is fraudulent and void notwithstanding registration: see the Land Registration Act 1925 s 114 and *Re Leighton's Conveyance* [1936] 1 All ER 667; on appeal [1937] Ch 149, [1936] 3 All ER 1033, CA; compare with *Argyle Building Society v Hammond* (1984) 49 P & CR 148, CA. See also *Norwich and Peterborough Building Society v Steed (No 2)* [1993] Ch 116, [1993] 1 All ER 330, CA, where SCOTT LJ averred that where a proprietor was registered as a result of a forged transfer or where the doctrine of non est factum applied, the register could be rectified not only against the proprietor of the land but also any registered chargee for value without notice.
11 Land Registration Act 1925 s 82 (1)(e).
12 Land Registration Act 1925 s 82 (1)(f). See Forms 37, 38 post.
13 Land Registration Act 1925 s 82 (1)(g). See *Chowood Ltd v Lyall (No 2)* [1930] 1 Ch 426; affd [1930] 2 Ch 156, CA; *Bridges v Mees* [1957] Ch 475, [1957] 2 All ER 577;

Re 139 Deptford High Street [1951] Ch 884, [1951] 1 All ER 950; Re Sea View Gardens, Claridge v Tingey [1966] 3 All ER 935, [1967] 1 WLR 134; and Form 25 post.
14 Land Registration Act 1925 s 82 (1)(h); see Capital and Counties Bank Ltd v Rhodes [1903] 1 Ch 631 at 657, CA. The Registrar may rectify the register by cancelling a note as to an exception and reservation in respect of a right of way: Re Dances Way, West Town, Hayling Island [1962] Ch 490, [1962] 2 All ER 42, CA. See also Chowood Ltd v Lyall (No 2) [1930] 2 Ch 156, CA; and Re 139 Deptford High Street [1951] Ch 884, [1951] 1 All ER 950.
15 Land Registration Act 1925 s 82 (2). This power to rectify is an express power and applies to entries made in the register under the Land Transfer Acts 1875 and 1897 (38 & 39 Vict c 87; 60 & 61 Vict c 65), notwithstanding their repeal by the Land Registration Act 1925 s 147 (1)(as amended), see Chowood Ltd v Lyall (No 2) [1930] 1 Ch 426 at 439; affd [1930] 2 Ch 156, CA.

29. Where rectification is not possible. The register cannot, however, be rectified in any of the cases above referred to, except for the purpose of giving effect to an overriding interest[1] or an order of the court, so as to affect the title of a registered proprietor who is in possession[2] unless:
1 the proprietor has caused or substantially contributed to the error or omission by fraud or lack of proper care[3]; or
2. in any particular case it is considered for any other reason that it would be unjust not to rectify the register against him[4].

These provisions with regard to possession[5] apply whether the proposed rectification relates to the extent of the registered land or otherwise affects the title. Accordingly an application to the Registrar or the court to rectify, for example, a registered title to land which is in the proprietor's possession by entering on the register notice of a restrictive covenant omitted from it on first registration will fail unless the applicant can show that the rectification is for the purpose of giving effect to an overriding interest or an order of the court or that the case falls within one of the two instances referred to above in which possession is no bar to rectification[6].

1 See *Abbey National Building Society v Cann* [1991] 1 AC 56, [1990] 1 All ER 1085, HL, followed in *Lloyds Bank plc v Rosset* [1990] 1 All ER 1111, [1991] 1 AC 107, HL.
2 "Possession" includes receipt of rent and profits or the right to receive them: Land Registration Act 1925 s 3 (xviii) (37 Halsbury's Statutes (4th Edn) REAL PROPERTY). Where a person is in possession of registered land in right of a minor interest for example a beneficiary under a trust of land, he is deemed for the purpose of Land Registration Act 1925 s 82 to be in possession as agent for the proprietor: Land Registration Act 1925 s 82 (4). In neither *Chowood Ltd v Lyall (No 2)* [1930] 2 Ch 156, CA, nor *Bridges v Mees* [1957] Ch 475, [1957] 2 All ER 577, was the proprietor in possession of the land. As to minor interests see Paragraph 11 note 3 ante.
3 Land Registration Act 1925 s 82 (3)(a)(as amended); *Re 139 Deptford High Street* [1951] Ch 884, [1951] 1 All ER 950; *Re Sea View Gardens Claridge v Tingey* [1966] 3 All ER 935, [1967] 1 WLR 134.
4 Land Registration Act 1925 s 82 (3)(c); *Hodges v Jones* [1935] Ch 657. See also *Re 139 Deptford High Street* [1951] Ch 884 at 892, [1951] 1 All ER 950 at 954 and *Re Sea View Gardens Claridge v Tingey* [1966] 3 All ER 935, [1967] 1 WLR 134.
5 The Land Registration Act 1925 s 82 (3)(b) formerly provided that the register might be rectified against a registered proprietor who was in possession if the immediate disposition to him, or the disposition to any person through whom he claimed otherwise than for valuable consideration, was void. This provision was repealed by the Administration of Justice Act 1977 s 24.
6 *Hodges v Jones* [1935] Ch 657. The person or persons entitled to the benefit of the covenant may have a right of indemnity, see Paragraph 30 post.

30. Application for rectification. An application for rectification may be made either to the Registrar, from whom appeal lies to the court[1], and who may, if he thinks fit, at any stage refer the matter, or any question on it, for the court's decision[2], or direct to the court[3]. No special form is prescribed for such an application to the Registrar[4], but it should set out concisely the grounds of the application and refer, where appropriate, to a plan. It may be possible to resolve the matter without a judicial hearing. An opportunity to object to the application will be given to all persons appearing from the register to be interested in the land or charge[5], and the applicant will be given particulars of any objections made. If necessary there will be a hearing[6], and the Registrar will make his order[7]. Alternatively he may refer the matter to the court[8]. Application to the court is generally by originating summons[9]. It should be remembered that generally no indemnity is payable on account of costs incurred inter alia in taking or defending legal proceedings without the Registrar's consent[10].

The Registrar must obey any court order on being served with it, or an official copy of it[11]. On every rectification the land certificate and any charge certificate affected must be produced to the Registrar unless he otherwise orders[12]. In rectification proceedings the parties are generally the registered proprietor and any person with rival claims. If, however, any question arises as to whether a person is entitled to an indemnity under any provision of the Land Registration Act 1925 or as to the amount of any such indemnity, the proper parties to any proceedings which may be necessary to determine such questions will be the claimant and the Chief Land Registrar[13].

1 Land Registration Act 1925 s 82 (1) (37 Halsbury's Statutes (4th Edn) REAL PROPERTY). As to appeals to the court see Paragraph 9 ante.
2 Land Registration Rules 1925, SR & O 1925/1093, r 298 (2) (16 Halsbury's Statutory Instruments (1998 Issue) REAL PROPERTY).
3 Land Registration Act 1925 s 82 (1).
4 See Form 40 post.
5 See Forms 41, 42 post.
6 As to hearings before the Registrar see Paragraph 13 ante.
7 See Form 43 post.
8 Land Registration Rules 1925 r 298 (2). See Paragraph 7 ante and Form 45 post.
9 For an originating summons, supporting affidavit and order see Forms 37–39 post.
10 Land Registration Act 1925 s 83 (5)(c)(as substituted by the Land Registration Act 1997 s 2); see Paragraph 33 post. For an application and a consent see Forms 35, 36 post.
11 Land Registration Act 1925 s 82 (5). The order is served by leaving it, with an application for rectification, at the registry: Land Registration Rules 1925 r 302 (1), (2). The rectification must not, however, be completed until the expiration of four clear days from the day on which the order is made: Land Registration Rules 1925 r 302 (2) proviso.
12 Land Registration Act 1925 s 82 (6).
13 Land Registration and Land Charges Act 1971 ss 1 (1), 2 (1) (37 Halsbury's Statutes (4th Edn) REAL PROPERTY). The Chief Land Registrar's power to settle claims for indemnity by agreement is expressly preserved (Land Registration and Land Charges Act 1971 s 2 (5)). As to indemnity, see generally Paragraph 32 post.

31. Correction of error in registration. Where any clerical or error of a like nature is discovered in the register, or in any plan or document referred to therein, which can be corrected without detriment to any registered interest, the Registrar may, if he thinks fit, after giving any notices and calling for any evidence or obtaining any consent he deems proper, cause the necessary correction to be made[1].

Where it is proved to his satisfaction that the whole of the land comprised in a title, or too large a part to be properly dealt with under the foregoing rule, has been registered in error, the Registrar may enter notice of the fact in his register; he may also cancel the registration wholly or to the extent required, either with the consent of the proprietor and all other persons appearing by the register to be interested in that land[2] or, after notice to those persons and any inquiry he considers proper and upon the production of such evidence as he deems necessary[3].

1 Land Registration Rules 1925, SR & O 1925/1093, r 13 (16 Halsbury's Statutory Instruments (1998 Issue) REAL PROPERTY).
2 Land Registration Rules 1925 r 14 (a).
3 Land Registration Rules 1925 r 14 (b). LUXMOORE J observed in *Chowood Ltd v Lyall (No 2)* [1930] 1 Ch 426 at 439, apparently obiter, that no limitation is placed on this power. Nevertheless it seems improbable that it could be held as overriding the express protection afforded by the Land Registration Act 1925 s 82 (3)(as amended) (37 Halsbury's Statutes (4th Edn) REAL PROPERTY) to a proprietor in possession. See Forms 40–43 post.

G: INDEMNITY FOR LOSS

32. Entitlement to indemnity for loss. Persons who suffer actual, as distinct from contemplated, loss in the following circumstances are in general[1] entitled to be indemnified by the Registrar out of moneys provided by Parliament[2]:

1. *Loss on rectification*: Any person suffering loss[3] by reason of any rectification of the register is entitled to indemnity[4]. Equally, if, notwithstanding the rectification the person in whose favour the register is rectified suffers loss by reason of an error or omission in the register in respect of which it is so rectified, he also will be entitled to be indemnified[5]. A proprietor of any registered land or charge claiming in good faith under a forged disposition is, where the register is rectified, deemed to have suffered loss by reason of the rectification[6].
2. *Loss on unrectified error or omission*: Where an error or omission has occurred in the register but it is not rectified, any person suffering loss by reason of the error or omission is entitled to indemnity[7]. Statutory applications of this rule include the following:
    2.1. Where the estate or assets of a bankrupt proprietor suffer loss either:
        2.1.1. by reason of the Registrar's omission to register a creditors' notice or bankruptcy inhibition[8]; or
        2.1.2. on account of the execution or registration of a disposition after a bankruptcy petition or bankruptcy order is registered[9] under the Land Charges Act 1972, and before the registration of a creditors'

notice or bankruptcy inhibition[10]; the trustee in bankruptcy is entitled to indemnity as a person suffering loss by reason of an error or omission in the register[11].

2.2. Any person, other than the proprietor, who suffers loss by reason of any entry on the register made on the conversion of a title[12] is entitled to indemnity as if a mistake had been made in the register[13].

2.3. The proprietor of a charge made for securing further advances who, by reason of any failure on the part of the Registrar or the Post Office with reference to the prescribed notice of a subsequent entry on the register[14], suffers loss in relation to a further advance is entitled to indemnity as if a mistake had occurred in the register, but if the loss arises by reason of an omission to register or amend the chargee's address for service, no indemnity is payable[15].

3. *Loss from inaccurate copy document*: Any person suffering loss by reason of the inaccuracy of any office copy of or extract from the register or of and from documents filed in the registry is entitled to indemnity, and no solicitor, trustee, personal representative or other person in a fiduciary position is answerable for any loss occasioned by relying on any such copy or extract[16].

4. *Loss on loss or destruction of document*: Any person suffering loss by reason of the loss or destruction of any document lodged at the registry for inspection or safe custody is entitled to indemnity[17].

5. *Loss on error in search:* Any person suffering loss by reason of an error in any official search is entitled to indemnity[18].

6. *Loss on error or omission in filed abstract*: Any person suffering loss by reason of an error or omission in a filed abstract, copy of, or extract from, a deed or other document which is referred to on the register is entitled to indemnity, the abstract or extract being assumed, as between vendor and purchaser, to be correct and to contain all material portions of the original[19].

---

1 For important exceptions see Paragraph 33 post.
2 Land Registration and Land Charges Act 1971 s 1 (1) (37 Halsbury's Statutes (4th Edn) REAL PROPERTY), this provision replaces the former provisions relating to the Land Registry insurance fund, which has been abolished.
3 Where the register is rectified to give effect to existing overriding interests, the rectification puts the proprietors in no worse position than they had been in before, so there is no loss: see *Re Chowood's Registered Land* [1933] Ch 574. In *Re Boyle's Claim* [1961] 1 All ER 620, [1961] 1 WLR 339, the relevant date for considering whether there was a person in actual occupation of the disputed land whose rights were an overriding interest under the Land Registration Act 1925 s 70 (1)(g) (37 Halsbury's Statutes (4th Edn) REAL PROPERTY), was held to be the date when the person prejudiced by the rectification acquired his registered title. See also *Hodgson v Marks* [1971] Ch 892, [1971] 2 All ER 684, CA.
4 Land Registration Act 1925 s 83 (1)(a)(as substituted by the Land Registration Act 1997 s 2).
5 Land Registration Act 1925 s 83 (1)(b)(as substituted by the Land Registration Act 1997 s 2). This effectively reverses the dictum of WALTON J in *Freer v Unwins Ltd* [1976] Ch 288, [1976] 1 All ER 634.
6 Land Registration Act 1925 s 83 (4)(as substituted by the Land Registration Act 1997 s 2).
7 Land Registration Act 1925 s 83 (2)(as substituted by the Land Registration Act 1997 s 2).
8 As to bankruptcy inhibitions see Paragraph 24 ante. For the circumstances in which the Registrar must register such notices and inhibitions see the Land Registration Act 1925 s 61 (1), (3)(as amended). See Forms 46, 47 post.

9 Land Charges Act 1972 ss 5 (1), (4), 6 (1)(as amended and as further amended by the Access to Neighbouring Land Act 1992 s 5 (1)), (2) (37 Halsbury's Statutes (4th Edn) REAL PROPERTY). See Paragraph 8 ante.
10 See note 7 above.
11 Land Registration Act 1925 s 61 (7)(as amended).
12 That is under Land Registration Act 1925 s 77 (as substituted).
13 Land Registration Act 1925 s 77 (6)(as substituted).
14 When a registered charge is made for securing further advances the Registrar must, before making any entry on the register which would prejudicially affect the priority of any further advance thereunder, give notice of the intended entry to the chargee, and in respect of any further advance the chargee will not be affected by the entry unless the advance is made after the date when the notice ought to have been received by post: Land Registration Act 1925 s 30 (1).
15 Land Registration Act 1925 s 30 (2).
16 Land Registration Act 1925 s 113 (as amended by the Land Registration Act 1988 s 2 Schedule). The effect of the amendment was to exclude plans from the benefit of this provision.
17 Land Registration Act 1925 s 83 (3)(as substituted by the Land Registration Act 1997 s 2).
18 Land Registration Act 1925 s 83 (3)(as substituted by the Land Registration Act 1997 s 2). Application can be made on the appropriate prescribed form for an official search of the register with priority by a purchaser or without priority by any other person: Land Registration (Official Searches) Rules 1993, SI 1993/3276, rr 3–9 (16 Halsbury's Statutory Instruments (1998 Issue) REAL PROPERTY). An official search may be made by delivering the application at the proper office by several means of communication, including telephone, facsimile or direct access from a remote terminal to the Land Registry's computer system; operation of the direct access services is subject to limitations set out in directions and notices issued by the Chief Land Registrar.

Any person may apply for an official search of the index map, parcels index and list of pending applications for first registration by any of the prescribed means of communication: Land Registration (Open Register) Rules 1992, SI 1992/122, r 9 (16 Halsbury's Statutory Instruments (1998 Issue) REAL PROPERTY).
19 Land Registration Act 1925 s 110 (4).

33. Where indemnity is not payable. No indemnity is payable:

1. on account of any loss suffered by a claimant wholly or partly as a result of his own fraud or wholly as a result of his own lack of proper care[1];
2. on account of any mines or minerals, or rights to work or obtain them, unless a note is entered on the register that they are included in the title[2];
3. by reason of a purchaser acquiring any interest under a registered disposition from a company which is registered as proprietor of any estate or charge already registered[3], free from any mortgage, charge, debenture, debenture stock, trust deed for securing the same, or other incumbrance created or issued by the company, whether or not it has been registered under the Companies Acts[4], unless it is registered or protected by caution or otherwise under the Land Registration Act[5];
4. by reason of an alteration in the register to give effect to a court vesting order on the disclaimer of a registered lease by a trustee in bankruptcy[6];
5. on account of costs or expenses (of whatever nature) incurred without the Registrar's consent unless:
    5.1. by reason of urgency it was not practicable to apply for the Registrar's consent before they were incurred and
    5.2. the Registrar subsequently approves them for the purpose of this provision[7].

It is, for this reason, most important, in cases where a claim for indemnity may arise to registered land, to consider whether an approach should first be made to obtain the Registrar's consent[8].

1   Land Registration Act 1925 s 83 (5)(a)(as substituted by the Land Registration Act 1997 s 2) (37 Halsbury's Statutes (4th Edn) REAL PROPERTY). As to cases where the loss arises partly as a result of the claimant's own lack of proper care see Land Registration Act 1925 s 83 (6)(as substituted by the Land Registration Act 1997 s 2).
2   Land Registration Act 1925 s 83 (5)(b)(as substituted by the Land Registration Act 1997 s 2). Since "land" includes mines and minerals (Land Registration Act 1925 s 3 (viii)(as amended by the Trusts of Land and Appointment of Trustees Act 1996 s 25 (2), Sch 4)), they will be included impliedly in a registration except where expressly excepted (see the Land Registration Rules 1925, SR & O 1925/1093, r 196 (16 Halsbury's Statutory Instruments (1998 Issue) REAL PROPERTY)). Nevertheless there is no statutory guarantee as to their inclusion under these indemnity provisions unless the note referred to is entered in the property register (see Land Registration Rules 1925 r 195). As to rights to mines and minerals in the case of land registered under the earlier Acts being overriding interests see the Land Registration Act 1925 s 70 (1)(l).
3   If the company had been registered as first proprietor, this provision would not apply to debentures, etc, created before first registration because they should be noted as incumbrances under the Land Registration Rules 1925 r 40.
4   Companies Acts 1985–1989 (8 Halsbury's Statutes (4th Edn) COMPANIES).
5   Land Registration Act 1925 s 60.
6   Land Registration Act 1925 s 42 (2)(as amended).
7   Land Registration Act 1925 s 83 (5)(c)(as substituted by the Land Registration Act 1997 s 2). See Forms 35, 36 post. This substantial provision which came into effect on 27 April 1997 creates a major change extending the former requirement for consent which applied only to costs incurred in bringing or defending court proceedings. The new s 83 applies equally to any claim for indemnity made before 27 April 1997 which has not been settled or finally determined by that date, as well as claims made subsequently, but the need to obtain a consent under the new provision only applies to costs and expenses incurred in respect of proceedings, negotiations or other courses of action begun after 27 April 1997.
    This provision does not apply to proceedings under the Land Registration and Land Charges Act 1971 s 2 (1) (37 Halsbury's Statutes (4th Edn) REAL PROPERTY) for the determination of any question as to whether a person is entitled to an indemnity or as to the amount of such indemnity (Land Registration and Land Charges Act 1971 s 2 (2)).
8   When an application is made for such consent the Registrar will always consider whether it would be more appropriate to seek to facilitate a settlement of the dispute rather than allowing the applicant unnecessarily to incur the costs of litigation in respect of which he may or may not be entitled to an indemnity at the conclusion of the proceedings. Whilst an absence of a consent precludes a claim for indemnity, nevertheless the giving of such consent does not mean that the costs of the person applying or any other sum will be recoverable as a matter of course. In order to succeed a claim for indemnity must arise from a loss for which indemnity is payable under the provisions of the Land Registration Acts.

34. Payment of indemnity. Any claim for indemnity should be lodged with the Registrar at the earliest opportunity once the claim has been established and in event within the prescribed period of limitation. Liability to pay indemnity is a simple contract debt, and for the purposes of the Limitation Act 1980[1] the cause of action is deemed to arise at the time when the claimant knows, or but for his own default might have known, of the existence of his claim[2].

The Registrar, on behalf of the Crown, is entitled to recover the amount of any indemnity paid for a loss from any person who has caused or substantially contributed to the loss by his fraud[3]. The Registrar is also entitled for the purpose of recovering the amount paid from any person to enforce any right of action (of whatever nature and however arising) which the claimant would have been entitled to enforce had the indemnity not been paid, and, where the register has been rectified, any right of action (of whatever nature and however arising) which the person in whose favour the register has been rectified would have been entitled to enforce had it not been rectified[4].

Where an indemnity is paid in respect of the loss of an estate or interest in or charge on land, the amount paid must not exceed, where the register is not rectified, the value of the estate, interest or charge at the time when the error or omission which caused the loss was made[5] or, where the register is rectified, the value (if there had been no rectification) of the estate, interest or charge immediately before the time of rectification[6]. An indemnity is to include such amount, if any, as may be reasonable in respect of any costs or expenses properly incurred by the applicant in relation to the matter, and an applicant for indemnity may be entitled to an indemnity of such amount, if any, as may be reasonable in respect of any such costs or expenses, notwithstanding that no other indemnity money is payable[7].

The claim for indemnity[8] should give the full grounds for and details of the claim and be supported by evidence such as, for example, valuers' reports and bills of costs when necessary. The claim should in the first instance be sent to the Registrar, who is empowered to settle claims by agreement[9]. If, exceptionally, however, agreement cannot be reached, either immediately, or following negotiations, as to whether the claimant is entitled to indemnity or as to the amount, the claimant may apply to the court to have the outstanding questions determined[10]. On such an application the court may not order the applicant, even if unsuccessful, to pay any costs except his own unless it considers that the application was unreasonable[11].

Indemnity in respect of settled land, as distinct from indemnity in respect of any particular estate, remainder or reversion therein, is paid to the trustees of the settlement and held by them as capital money arising from the settled land[12].

Where the incumbent of a benefice is entitled to indemnity the money is paid to the Church Commissioners and appropriated by them to the benefice[13].

1 Limitation Act 1980 s 5 (24 Halsbury's Statutes (4th Edn) LIMITATION OF ACTIONS).
2 Land Registration Act 1925 s 83 (12)(as substituted by the Land Registration Act 1997 s 2) (37 Halsbury's Statutes (4th Edn) REAL PROPERTY). Under the former provisions a claim could, when the loss arose from registration of absolute or good leasehold title become statute barred six years after the relevant registration whether or not the claimant had any means of knowing that the registration had occurred.
3 Land Registration Act 1925 s 83 (9), (10)(a)(as substituted by the Land Registration Act 1997 s 2).
4 Land Registration Act 1925 s 83 (10)(b)(as substituted by the Land Registration Act 1997 s 2). This does not prejudice any other rights of recovery which by virtue of an enactment were exercisable by the Registrar when he has made a payment of indemnity: Land Registration Act 1925 s 83 (11)(as substituted by the Land Registration Act 1997 s 2).
5 Land Registration Act 1925 s 83 (8)(a)(as substituted by the Land Registration Act 1997 s 2).
6 Land Registration Act 1925 s 83 (8)(b)(as substituted by the Land Registration Act 1997 s 2).
7 Land Registration Act 1925 s 83 (9)(as substituted). This provision takes effect subject

to the Land Registration Act 1925 s 83 (5)(c)(as substituted by the Land Registration Act 1997 s 2) as restricted in its application by the Land Registration and Land Charges Act 1971 s 2 (2), which excludes liability for indemnity on account of costs or expenses (of whatever nature) incurred without the consent of the Registrar: see Paragraph 33 note 6 ante.
8 See Form 46 post.
9 Land Registration and Land Charges Act 1971 s 2 (5) (37 Halsbury's Statutes (4th Edn) REAL PROPERTY).
10 Land Registration and Land Charges Act 1971 s 2 (1). For an originating summons, see Form 48 post.
11 Land Registration and Land Charges Act 1971 s 2 (3).
12 Land Registration Act 1925 s 84.
13 Land Registration Act 1925 s 99 (3)(as amended).

H: COSTS

35. Costs of proceedings in Land Registry. All costs incurred in any proceedings in the registry are in the Registrar's discretion which is exercised having regard to the provisions as to costs contained in the Land Registration Act 1925 and the Land Registration Rules 1925[1].

In particular, all costs, charges and expenses incurred by any parties in or about any proceedings for registration must, unless the parties otherwise agree, be taxed by the taxing officer of the court[2], but the persons by whom and the proportions in which the costs are to be paid are in the Registrar's discretion and must be determined according to his orders, having regard to the general principle that any applicant under the Land Registration Act 1925 is, subject to certain exceptions[3], liable prima facie to pay all costs, charges and expenses incurred by or in consequence of his application[4]. Any charges allowed by the Registrar in connection with the attendance of any person or the production of documents in obedience of any summons he has issued are deemed to be charges incurred in or about proceedings for registration and may be dealt with accordingly[5]. When a request is made for costs the Registrar will treat each case on its merits, carefully considering all the facts, arguments and principles involved before making his order.

Any party aggrieved by any order of the Registrar as to costs may appeal to the court, which may annul or confirm the Registrar's order, with or without modification[6]. If any person disobeys any order of the Registrar as to costs, the Registrar may certify the disobedience to the court, whereupon that person, subject to a right of appeal to the court, may be punished by the court as if the Registrar's order were a court order[7].

1 Land Registration Rules 1925, SR & O 1925/1093, r 321 (1) (16 Halsbury's Statutory Instruments (1998 Issue) REAL PROPERTY).
2 Land Registration Rules 1925 r 321 (2). As to taxation of costs generally see RSC Ord 62 r 29.
3 These are: in a case where parties object whose rights are sufficiently secured without their appearance; and where any costs, charges or expenses are incurred unnecessarily or improperly: Land Registration Act 1925 s 17 (1) (37 Halsbury's Statutes (4th Edn) REAL PROPERTY).
4 Land Registration Act 1925 s 17 (1).
5 Land Registration Act 1925 s 128 (2).

6 Land Registration Act 1925 s 17 (1) proviso.
7 Land Registration Act 1925 s 17 (2); Land Registration Rules 1925 r 321 (3). See generally Vol 12 (1) (1996 Issue) title CONTEMPT OF COURT.

36. Costs on application to the court. On any application to the court under the Land Registration Acts 1925 to 1986[1], both in the High Court and in the county court, the court's powers to award costs is discretionary[2].

Where in an action to enforce against a vendor specific performance of his contract to sell registered land or a registered charge, the court may cause any persons who have registered interests or rights therein, or have notices, cautions, restrictions or inhibitions entered against the land or charge, to appear in the action and show cause why the contract should not be specifically performed, all costs incurred by persons so appearing must be taxed and, unless the court otherwise orders, paid by the vendor[3].

1 Land Registration Act 1925 (37 Halsbury's Statutes (4th Edn) REAL PROPERTY).
2 RSC Ord 62 r 2 applying the Supreme Court Act 1981 s 51 (as substituted) (11 Halsbury's Statutes (4th Edn) COURTS AND LEGAL SERVICES); CCR Ord 31 r 1. It should however be noted that on an application to the court to determine any question as to indemnity under the Land Registration and Land Charges Act 1971 s 2 (1) (37 Halsbury's Statutes (4th Edn) REAL PROPERTY), the court may not order the applicant, even if unsuccessful, to pay any costs except his own, unless it considers that the application was unreasonable: Land Registration and Land Charges Act 1971 s 2 (3).
3 Land Registration Act 1925 s 139. See, as to taxation of costs generally, Vol 13 (1992 Issue) title COSTS.

Forms

A: FIRST REGISTRATION

1
OBJECTION to first registration[1]

HM LAND REGISTRY

Land Registration Acts 1925 to 1986[2]

(*Quote reference if known*)
        County and District ....
        Title No. (*if known*) ....
        Property: (*address*)

We, X. Y. & Co of (*address*), as Solicitors for J. K., of (*address*) (hereinafter called "the Objector"), give notice[3] to the Chief Land Registrar that we object to the pending application for registration of A. B., of (*address*) (hereinafter called "the Applicant") as first proprietor of the above-mentioned land unless notice is entered on the register pursuant to Rule 40 of the Land Registration Rules 1925 of an equitable mortgage in favour of the Objector secured by the deposit of the title deed in respect of the above-mentioned land on the following grounds:

    1. By a letter dated .... 19... the Applicant wrote to the Objector requesting a loan of £...... free of interest to be secured on the said land for which purpose the Applicant proposed to deliver as security a conveyance dated ....19... made between (1) P. Q. and (2) the Applicant, which was the only deed stated to be in his possession relating thereto. On ....19... the parties entered into a written agreement recording the terms and in which the Objector acknowledged receipt of the conveyance and forwarded the Applicant the sum of £......[4].

    2. The sum of £......, a part of the sum of £......, has been repaid but the balance of £...... remains outstanding.

    3. The Objector still holds the conveyance dated .... 19... and has the benefit of an equitable mortgage on the said land for the sum of £...... which remains owing to him.

4. However, provided that notice of this equitable mortgage is to be entered in the charges register of the Applicant's title, the Objector will be willing to forward the conveyance to the Registrar and to withdraw his objection.

Dated .... 19...

(*Signature*)

of (*address*), Solicitors for the Objector.

1 Land Registration Rules 1925, SR & O 1925/1093, rr 34, 40 (16 Halsbury's Statutory Instruments (1998 Issue) REAL PROPERTY). See Paragraph 18 ante. There is no prescribed form, but it is advisable to use the formal heading and to set out the objection in numbered paragraphs, as in this example. For a reply see Form 2 post.
2 Land Registration Acts 1925–1986 (37 Halsbury's Statutes (4th Edn) REAL PROPERTY). See Paragraph 1 ante.
3 The notice of objection must give an address in the United Kingdom of the person objecting to which all notices and other communications for him may be sent through the post: Land Registration Rules 1925 r 34 (2).
4 It is now settled that a mere deposit of title documents is insufficient to create an equitable charge on the land or charge to which they relate: Law of Property (Miscellaneous Provisions) Act 1989 s 2; *United Bank of Kuwait plc v Sahib* [1995] 2 All ER 973, [1995] 2 WLR 94.

2

REPLY to objection to first registration[1]

HM Land Registry

Land Registration Acts 1925 to 1986[2]

(*Quote reference if known*)
County and District ....
Title No. (*if known*) ....
Property: (*address*)

We, E. F. & Co of (*address*), Solicitors for A. B. of (*address*), the Applicant for registration as first proprietor of the land described above (hereinafter called "the Applicant"), reply as follows to the notice of objection to registration[3] dated .... 19... given by X. Y. & Co of (*address*), Solicitors for J. K. (hereinafter called "the Objector"):

1. The Applicant admits that by way of an agreement recorded in writing the Objector lent him the sum of £...... on .... 19... and that the land was agreed to be treated as security for the loan, and that for such purpose he deposited the conveyance dated .... 19... with the Objector.

2. The Applicant denies that any part of the loan still remains outstanding. On .... 19... he repaid to the Objector the sum of £...... and in the following year on .... 19... he repaid to the Objector the balance of £...... that was still owing. On each occasion the Objector forwarded a proper receipt, and these receipts dated .... 19... and .... 19... respectively, are held by the Applicant. No steps were, however, taken to obtain the return of the conveyance dated .... 19... when the balance of the loan was repaid.

3. When the Applicant recently decided to sell the land and attempted to find the conveyance it could not be traced. The Applicant genuinely believed that it had been lost in the circumstances described in the

application for registration, and had forgotten that it had been deposited with the Objector as security for the loan which had long since been repaid.

4. The Applicant is accordingly entitled to the land free and discharged from any equitable mortgage in favour of the Objector, and he requests the Registrar to exercise his powers to enforce the production[4] of the conveyance dated .... 19... .

DATED .... 19...

(*Signature*)
of (*address*), Solicitors for the Applicant

1 See Paragraph 18 ante. There is no prescribed form, but it is advisable to use the formal heading and to divide the reply into numbered paragraphs as in this example.
2 See Form 1 note 2 ante.
3 See Form 1 ante.
4 Land Registration Act 1925 s 15 (1) (37 Halsbury's Statutes (4th Edn) REAL PROPERTY); see Paragraph 18 ante.

3
NOTICE of hearing of matter arising on objection to first registration[1]

HM LAND REGISTRY

Land Registration Acts 1925 to 1986[2]

Land Registration (Conduct of Business) Regulations 1997

NOTICE OF HEARING under Rule 298 of the Land Registration Rules 1925
    Title No. ....
    County and District ....
    Property: (*address*)

In the Matter of the application of A. B. for registration as first proprietor of the land referred to above and the objection by J. K. to such registration

WHEREAS a [question *or* doubt *or* dispute *or* difficulty *or* complaint] has arisen within the meaning of Rule 298 of the Land Registration Rules 1925 as to the right of A. B. to apply for registration in respect of the said land

TAKE NOTICE that the [Chief Land Registrar *or* Solicitor to HM Land Registry] will hear and determine the matter at [HM Land Registry, Lincoln's Inn Fields, London WC2A 3PH *or as the case may be*], at ...[am *or* pm] on .... 19... and make such order in the matter as he shall think just or refer the matter for the decision of the Court

AND FURTHER TAKE NOTICE that you may attend before the [Chief Land Registrar *or* Solicitor to HM Land Registry] at that time either in person or by your Solicitor or Counsel.

It is not obligatory to attend, but if you do not, such order will be made and proceedings taken as the [Chief Land Registrar *or* Solicitor to HM Land Registry] may think just and expedient.

DATED .... 19...
To (*name*) of (*address*)

(*Land Registry Official Stamp*)

1 Land Registration Rules 1925, SR & O 1925/1093, r 35 (2) (16 Halsbury's Statutory Instruments (1998 Issue) REAL PROPERTY); Land Registration (Conduct of Business) Regulations 1997, SI 1997/713, regs 3, 4. See Paragraph 18 ante. As to notice of hearing generally see the Land Registration Rules 1925 rr 298, 300 and Paragraph 14 ante. For the objection and reply see Forms 1, 2 ante.
2 See Form 1 note 2 ante.

4
WITNESS SUMMONS[1]

HM LAND REGISTRY

Land Registration Acts 1925 to 1986[2]

Land Registration (Conduct of Business) Regulations 1997

County and District ....
Title No. ....

In the Matter of the [freehold *or* leasehold] land known as (*address*) [in the course of being] registered under Title No. ....
And in the Matter of (*description of matter*[3])

Between	A. B.	...	Plaintiff
	and		
	C. D.	...	Defendant

LET L. M. of (*address*), attend before the Solicitor to HM Land Registry at HM Land Registry, Lincoln's Inn Fields, London WC2A 3PH, on .... 19..., at ... [am *or* pm] to give evidence on behalf of [A. B.], of (*address*), [add, *in the case of a summons to produce documents*[4]: and to produce to him at the time and place aforesaid the following documents, namely: (*give full description of documents*)].

To L. M. of (*address*)
DATED .... 19...

This Summons was taken out by E. F. & Co of (*address*), [Agents for (*name*) of (*address*),] Solicitors for the above-named A. B.

(*Land Registry Seal*)

NOTE—This Summons is issued pursuant to Section 128 of the Land Registration Act 1925 and Rule 320 of the Land Registration Rules 1925, and if the person summoned wilfully neglects or refuses to attend [and produce the documents] as aforesaid he will be liable to a fine not exceeding £......(*the current amount representing level 2 on the standard scale*[5]).

1 Land Registration Act 1925 ss 64 (2), 128 (1) (37 Halsbury's Statutes (4th Edn) REAL PROPERTY); Land Registration Rules 1925, SR & O 1925/1093, r 320 (16 Halsbury's Statutory Instruments (1998 Issue) REAL PROPERTY). See Paragraph 14 ante. This form illustrates the two forms of summons obtainable from HM Land Registry: Form 98A, requiring attendance to give evidence and to produce maps, official documents, and land and charge certificates, and Form 98C, requiring attendance to give evidence. As to preparation and service of summons see Land Registration Rules 1925 r 311. For the powers of the Solicitor to HM Land Registry see Land Registration (Conduct of Business) Regulations 1997, SI 1997/713, regs 3, 4.
2 See Form 1 note 2 ante.
3 The description should correspond with the wording of the Land Registration Rules 1925 r 298 (that is, indicate whether the nature of the matter is a "question, doubt, dispute, difficulty or complaint" within the meaning of the rule).

4 Omit this if the witness is not summoned to produce documents. Before this summons can be issued prima facie evidence should be produced to the Registrar that the person summoned is in possession of the documents of which production is required.
5 Land Registration Act 1925 s 128 (3)(as amended).

5
ORDER by Solicitor to HM Land Registry on hearing of objection to first registration[1]

HM LAND REGISTRY

Land Registration Acts 1925 to 1986[2]

Land Registration (Conduct of Business) Regulations 1997

ORDER BY THE SOLICITOR TO HM LAND REGISTRY

Title No. ....
County and District ....
Property: (*address*)

In the Matter of the application by A. B., of (*address*), to be registered as proprietor with an absolute title to the above-mentioned [freehold *or* leasehold] land and the objection thereto made by J. K., of (*address*)

UPON HEARING [Counsel for the Applicant and for the Objector *or* the Applicant and the Objector in person *or as the case may be*]

IT IS ORDERED that [the Applicant be registered as proprietor with an absolute title to the [freehold *or* leasehold] land and the caution against the registration thereof registered on .... 19... in favour of the Objector be cancelled *or* the application for registration of the Applicant be cancelled and that the caution against the registration of the freehold land registered on .... 19... in favour of the Objector shall continue to have effect *or as the case may be*]

AND that the costs of and incidental to the hearing[3] be borne by the [Objector *or* Applicant] and such costs be taxed on the standard basis if not agreed

DATED .... 19...

(*Signature*)
[Solicitor to HM Land Registry]
(*Land Registry Seal*)

1 Land Registration Rules 1925, SR & O 1925/1093, r 298 (1) (16 Halsbury's Statutory Instruments (1998 Issue) REAL PROPERTY); Land Registration (Conduct of Business) Regulations 1997, SI 1997/713, regs 3, 4. See Paragraphs 8, 17 ante. For an example of an order referring the matter to the court see Form 14 post; for an originating motion on appeal see Form 6 post.
2 See Form 1 note 2 ante.
3 As to costs see Paragraph 35 ante. As to the basis of taxation of costs see RSC Ord 62 r 12.

6
ORIGINATING MOTION on appeal from Registrar's order on objection to first registration[1]

(*Royal Arms*)[2]

IN THE HIGH COURT OF JUSTICE　　　　　　　　　　　Ch 19... No. ...[3]
Chancery Division[4]
　　[......... District Registry[5]]

And in the Matter of the Land Registration Acts 1925 to 1986[6]

TAKE NOTICE that the High Court of Justice, Chancery Division, at the Royal Courts of Justice, Strand, London WC2A 2LL, will be moved before the Honourable Mr Justice .... at the expiration of ... days[7] from the date of service upon you of this notice or so soon thereafter as Counsel can be heard, by Counsel on behalf of A. B. for the following relief, namely:

　　1. An order that the order dated .... 19... of the [Chief Land Registrar[8] *or* Solicitor to HM Land Registry] that (*set out shortly the terms of the order*) may be discharged and an order that (*specify the order required*).

　　2. An order that the costs and expenses of A. B. properly incurred in [opposing before the [Chief Land Registrar *or* Solicitor to HM Land Registry] the objection made by C. D. *or* maintaining before the [Chief Land Registrar *or* Solicitor to HM Land Registry] A. B.'s objection] and the costs of and incidental to this appeal may be provided for[9].

AND FURTHER TAKE NOTICE that the grounds of this appeal are: (*state the grounds*)

　　DATED .... 19...[10]

　　　　　　　　　　　　　　　　　　　　　　　(*Signature*)[11]

　　E. F. & Co of (*address*), [Agents for (*name*) of (*address*),] Solicitors for the above named A. B. whose address is (*address*)[12]

　　To C. D. of (*address*)

1　Land Registration Act 1925 ss 53, 56 (1) (37 Halsbury's Statutes (4th Edn) REAL PROPERTY); Land Registration Rules 1925, SR & O 1925/1093, r 299 (16 Halsbury's Statutory Instruments (1998 Issue) REAL PROPERTY). See Paragraph 20 ante. As to appeals to the court generally see Paragraph 9 ante. The notice of motion must be served on the Chief Land Registrar and on every party to the proceedings (other than the appellant) in which the decision appealed against was given: RSC Ord 55 r 4 (1)(b). The notice must be served and the appeal entered within 28 days after the date of the order appealed against: RSC Ord 55 r 4 (2). The period of 28 days is to be calculated from the date on which notice of the order was given to the appellant: RSC Ord 55 r 4 (4). For the Registrar's order see Form 5 ante. For a supporting affidavit see Form 7 post.
2　A replica of the Royal Arms must be printed or embossed on the first page of every originating process: RSC Ord 1 r 9.
3　See RSC Appendix A Form No 13.
4　Proceedings relating to land registration are allocated to the Chancery Division: RSC Ord 93 r 10 (2)(f).
5　A notice of originating motion commencing proceedings assigned to the Chancery Division may be issued out of a Chancery district registry: RSC Ord 8 r 3 (5).
6　Land Registration Acts 1925 to 1986 (37 Halsbury's Statutes (4th Edn) REAL PROPERTY).
7　Unless the court otherwise directs, the appeal cannot be heard sooner than 21 days after service of the notice of motion by which the appeal is brought: RSC Ord 55 r 5.
8　See Form 5 ante.
9　Land Registration Act 1925 s 17. See Paragraph 36 ante.
10　See RSC Appendix A Form No 13.
11　See RSC Appendix A Form No 13.
12　RSC Ord 8 r 3 (3) applying RSC Ord 6 r 5.

7
AFFIDAVIT supporting originating motion on appeal from order on objection to first registration[1]

Appellant: A. B.: 1st: .... 19...[2]

IN THE HIGH COURT OF JUSTICE   Ch 19... No. ...[3]
Chancery Division[4]
[........ District Registry[5]]

And in the Matter of the Land Registration Acts 1925 to 1986[6]

I, A. B. of (*state residence or workplace, and occupation or, if none, description*), make oath and say as follows:

1. I am the Appellant in this appeal from an order[7] of the [Chief Land Registrar *or* Solicitor to HM Land Registry] dated .... 19... that (*state the terms of the order*).

2. (*Exhibit any notes of evidence required to supplement the official Land Registry transcript or note of evidence.*)

3. (*Exhibit any documents which are not officially marked as exhibits by the Registrar, or which do not prove themselves, or which are not agreed documents.*)

4. The [Chief Land Registrar's *or* Solicitor to HM Land Registry's] view, as expressed in his decision given at the hearing before him at HM Land Registry at (*address*), on .... 19... of the facts adduced in evidence before him was that (*state view*) but I claim that such view is wrong in that (*state reasons*).

5. I claim to be entitled [to be registered *or* to object to the registration of the Defendant] as first proprietor of the above-mentioned land and that accordingly [the caution registered on .... 19... in favour of the Defendant against first registration of the above-mentioned land ought to be cancelled and that my application for first registration should be duly completed *or* the application for first registration by the Defendant of the above-mentioned land should be cancelled and the caution registered on .... 19... in my favour against first registration of the above-mentioned land should remain in full force and effect.]

SWORN at (*address*), on
.... 19...
Before me,
(*Signature*)
A [Solicitor *or* Barrister *or* Notary Public *or* Commissioner for Oaths][9]

(*Deponent's signature*)[8]

---

1 Land Registration Act 1925 ss 53, 56 (1) (37 Halsbury's Statutes (4th Edn) REAL PROPERTY); Land Registration Rules 1925, SR & O 1925/1093, r 299 (16 Halsbury's Statutory Instruments (1998 Issue) REAL PROPERTY). See Paragraph 8 ante. As to the contents of the affidavit see *Re Gilbert's Application* [1961] 2 All ER 313 at 317, CA, [1961] 1 WLR 822 at 826, per RUSSELL J. For the originating motion see Form 6 ante.
2 Chancery Division Practice Directions No 8A (i)(a): Supreme Court Practice 1997 para 820 and Practice Note [1983] 3 All ER 33, sub nom [1983] 1 WLR 922 (as amended by Practice Note [1995] 2 All ER 511, sub nom Practice Direction [1995] 1 WLR 510).
3 See Form 6 note 3 ante.
4 See Form 6 note 4 ante.
5 See Form 6 note 5 ante.
6 See Form 6 note 6 ante.
7 See Form 5 ante.
8 Every affidavit must be signed by the deponent and must be completed and signed by the person before whom it is sworn: RSC Ord 41 r 2 (1).

9 Solicitors Act 1974 s 81 (as amended) (41 Halsbury's Statutes (4th Edn) SOLICITORS); Courts and Legal Services Act 1990 s 113 (17 Halsbury's Statutes (4th Edn) EVIDENCE); Administration of Justice Act 1985 s 65 (31 Halsbury's Statutes (4th Edn) NOTARIES AND LICENSED CONVEYANCERS); Commissioners for Oaths Act 1889 and 1891 (as amended) (17 Halsbury's Statutes (4th Edn) EVIDENCE).

8
ORDER by Registrar extending period for first registration in compulsory area[1]

HM LAND REGISTRY

Land Registration Acts 1925 to 1986[2]

ORDER BY THE CHIEF LAND REGISTRAR

Property: (*brief description*) ("the land")
WHEREAS

1. By [a Conveyance *or as the case may be*] dated .... 19... made between (1) A. B. and (2) C. D. ("the applicant") the land was transferred to the applicant.

2. The applicant failed to apply to be registered as the proprietor of the land within the period of 2 months mentioned in Section 123A (2) of the Land Registration Act 1925.

3. On .... 19... the applicant by his solicitors E. F. & Co of (address) showed cause why no application for first registration of the land was made within the said period of 2 months.

NOW IT IS HEREBY ORDERED in pursuance of the provisions of Section 123A (3) of the Land Registration Act 1925 that the period within which the applicant shall be entitled to apply for first registration of his title to the land be extended until .... 19...

AND that the costs of and incidental to the hearing be borne by the [objector *or* applicant] and such costs be taxed on the standard basis if not agreed

DATED .... 19...

(*Signature*)

[Chief Land Registrar *or* Solicitor to HM Land Registry]

(*Land Registry Seal*)

1 Land Registration Act 1925 s 123A (2), (3)(as inserted by the Land Registration Act 1997 s 1) (37 Halsbury's Statutes (4th Edn) REAL PROPERTY). See Paragraph 17 ante. The period may be extended if the application for first registration cannot be made within 2 months from the date of the deed inducing the registration, or can only be made by then incurring unreasonable expense, or has not been made by then by reason of some accident or other sufficient cause. The Registrar is always prepared to extend the period on simple grounds without the submission of an elaborate case. A reason must, however, be given even though the explanation amounts in fact to no more than that it was an oversight. In non-contentious cases, the order is indorsed on the

conveyance, grant or assignment or other deed inducing registration on completion of the registration. In contentious cases, where, for example, there is an objection to first registration and the objector contends that the period for first registration ought not to be extended, the order, if made, will be in this form and a note of it will be indorsed on the deed inducing first registration. The application for extension may be made before the application for registration. In practice, however, it is usual to include an application for extension of the period with the late application for registration itself.

2   See Form 6 note 6 ante.

9
CAUTION against first registration of land[1]
HM LAND REGISTRY

Land Registration Acts 1925 to 1986[2]

County and District ....

I, G. H., Solicitor, of (*address*), apply that notice[3] of any application for the first registration of the [freehold land *or* leasehold land held under a lease short particulars of which are set out below] described hereunder, [and shown and edged with red on the plan annexed hereto and signed by me *or* comprising parcels numbered ... on the Land Registry General Map, (*county*), Sheet ..., Section ...], should be served on C. D.[4] of (*address*)[5].

Short description of land. ....

[Short particulars of the lease under which the land is held: (*date, parties, term and date of commencement of term*)]

DATED .... 19...

(*Signature of cautioner's solicitor*)

1   Land Registration Act 1925 s 53 (1) (37 Halsbury's Statutes (4th Edn) REAL PROPERTY); Land Registration Rules 1925, SR & O 1925/1093, r 64 (as substituted) (16 Halsbury's Statutory Instruments (1998 Issue) REAL PROPERTY). See Paragraph 19 ante. It must be supported by a statutory declaration. Although a conveyancing form, this form is included here to indicate the general nature of a caution.
2   See Form 6 note 6 ante.
3   See Form 10 post.
4   That is the cautioner.
5   An address for service in the United Kingdom must be given.

10
NOTICE to cautioner against first registration of application to register land[1]

HM LAND REGISTRY

Land Registration Acts 1925 to 1986[2]

Any communication in reply to this notice should be addressed to: The Chief Land Registrar, The .... District Land Registry, (*address*)[3], quoting (*reference*)

To C. D.[4], of (*address*)
Caution Title No. ....
County and District ....
Property (*address*) [*add, if leasehold*: held under a lease dated .... 19... for ... years from .... 19...]

The Chief Land Registrar hereby gives notice that A. B., of (*address*), has applied to be registered as proprietor of the [freehold *or* leasehold] property described above, which property is affected by the caution dated .... 19... lodged by you at HM Land Registry. If you intend to appear and oppose such registration you are to enter an appearance[5] for the purpose by lodging an objection to the registration in accordance with the provisions of Section 53 of the Land Registration Act 1925 and with Rule 67 of the Land Registration Rules 1925[6] at HM Land Registry, (*address of appropriate district land registry*) before the expiration of ... days[7] from the date of the service of this notice. Unless you appear the registration will be proceeded with in your absence.

DATED .... 19...

(*Land Registry Official Stamp*)

1 Adapted from the Land Registration Rules 1925, SR & O 1925/1093, Sch 2 Form 15 (as amended by SI 1997/3037). This is the official notice served by the Registrar on a cautioner when application is made to register the land protected by the caution: see the Land Registration Act 1925 s 53 (3) (37 Halsbury's Statutes (4th Edn) REAL PROPERTY) and Paragraph 19 ante.
2 See Form 6 note 6 ante.
3 As to district land registries, see Paragraph 1 note 8 ante.
4 That is, the cautioner.
5 An appearance is entered by lodging an objection; see Form 12 post.
6 See note 7 below.
7 That is, 14 days or such period (not being less than 7 days) as the Registrar under special circumstances directs: Land Registration Rules 1925 r 67 (16 Halsbury's Statutory Instruments (1998 Issue) REAL PROPERTY). The Registrar will always consider granting an extension of time if reasonable cause is shown. As to the date when the notice is deemed to have been received see Land Registration Rules 1925 r 313 (as substituted).

11
CONSENT by cautioner to application for first registration[1]

HM LAND REGISTRY

Land Registration Acts 1925 to 1986[2]

(*Reference given in notice to cautioner*)
Caution Title No. ....
County and District ....
Property: (*address*)

[I *or* C. D.[3]] of (*address*), on whom notice[4] was served pursuant to Section 53 (3) of the Land Registration Act 1925 on .... 19... in respect of the caution[5] dated .... 19... [do *or* does] hereby consent to the registration of the [freehold *or* leasehold] property referred to in the notice dated .... 19... [but only on condition[6] that notice of the equitable mortgage, the terms of which are set out in an agreement dated .... 19... referred to in the statutory declaration lodged in support of the caution is entered on the register with priority over all other charges entered thereon whether legal or equitable] and request that [, provided the Registrar enters notice of the equitable mortgage as aforesaid,] the caution be cancelled [as to the part thereof comprised in the registration].

DATED .... 19...

(*Signature of cautioner or his solicitors*)

1 Land Registration Rules 1925, SR & O 1925/1093, r 69 (16 Halsbury's Statutory Instruments (1998 Issue) REAL PROPERTY). See Paragraph 19 ante. The personal representative of a deceased cautioner may consent in the same manner as the cautioner: Land Registration Act 1925 s 56 (4) (37 Halsbury's Statutes (4th Edn) REAL PROPERTY).
2 See Form 6 note 6 ante.
3 That is, the cautioner.
4 See Form 10 ante.
5 See Form 9 ante.
6 If the condition is not accepted by the applicant for first registration, the consent will be of no effect and the objection procedure will apply.

12

OBJECTION by cautioner to cancellation of caution against first registration[1]

HM LAND REGISTRY

Land Registration Acts 1925 to 1986[2]

(*Reference given in notice to cautioner*)
Caution Title No. ....
County and District ....
Property: (*address*)

We, G. H. & Co of (*address*), as Solicitors[3] for C. D. of (*address*) (hereinafter called "the Cautioner"), give notice to the Chief Land Registrar that the Cautioner objects to the registration of A. B.[4] of (*address*), as proprietor of the land at the rear of 10 .... Lane, ... (hereinafter called "the land in dispute") referred to in the notice[5] dated .... 19... served on the Cautioner pursuant to Section 53 of the Land Registration Act 1925[6] and coloured red on the plan annexed thereto.

The grounds for objection are as follows[7]:

1. By a conveyance dated .... 19... and made between J. K. of the one part and L. M. of the other part, 10 .... Lane, ..., and the land in dispute were conveyed to L. M. in fee simple, and in the conveyance L. M. covenanted with J. K. for the benefit of 12 .... Lane that no erections of any kind save a garden shed would be erected on the land in dispute.

2. By a conveyance dated .... 19... and made between L. M. and the Cautioner, L. M. conveyed 10 .... Lane and the land in dispute to the Cautioner subject to the covenant contained in the conveyance.

3. On .... 19... the Cautioner conveyed 10 .... Lane to one N. O. . The land in dispute was not included in this conveyance.

4. By a Deed of Release dated .... 19... and made between P. Q. of the one part and the Cautioner of the other part, P. Q., as owner of 12 .... Lane, in consideration of the sum of £...... released the Cautioner and the land in dispute from the covenant contained in the conveyance dated .... 19... .

5. The Cautioner cultivated the land in dispute as part of the garden ground of 10 .... Lane from .... 19... until .... 19... when 10 .... Lane was conveyed to N. O. . Soon after, the Cautioner moved to (*address*) and although he did not continue to cultivate the land in dispute he has since paid T. U., a local gardener, to cut down the weeds and brambles from time to time and to maintain the gate and fences in case the land should eventually be required for building purposes.

6. The Cautioner is entitled as owner in fee simple of the land in dispute as previously declared in the statutory declaration dated .... 19... made by .... in support of the caution against first registration, and he accordingly objects to the registration of A. B. as the proprietor thereof.

DATED .... 19...

(*Signature*)
of (*address*), Solicitors for the Cautioner

1 See Paragraph 19 ante. Although no form is prescribed for such an objection and it may accordingly be given by letter, it is advisable to use the formal heading as in this example. For a reply see Form 13 post.
2 See Form 6 note 6 ante.
3 The objection may be made by the cautioner or his solicitor. The personal representative of a deceased cautioner may object in the same manner as the cautioner: Land Registration Act 1925 s 56 (4) (37 Halsbury's Statutes (4th Edn) REAL PROPERTY).
4 That is the applicant for registration.
5 See Form 10 ante.
6 Land Registration Act 1925 s 53 (37 Halsbury's Statutes (4th Edn) REAL PROPERTY).
7 The full ground should be summarised so as to show cause to the Registrar and to provide the applicant with concise details of the objector's case; see Paragraph 18 ante.

13
REPLY by applicant to cautioner's objection to cancellation of caution against first registration[1]

HM LAND REGISTRY

Land Registration Acts 1925 to 1986[2]

(*Reference given in notice to cautioner*)
 Caution Title No. ....
 County and District ....
 Property: (*address*)

We, E. F. & Co of (*address*), Solicitors for A. B., the Applicant for registration (hereinafter called "the Applicant"), reply as follows to the notice of objection[3] dated .... 19... given by [G. H. & Co as Solicitors for] the Cautioner C. D. (hereinafter called "the Cautioner"):

 1. The Applicant admits the statements contained in clauses 1–4 of the said notice, and also admits that between .... 19... and .... 19... the Cautioner cultivated the land in dispute (being the land in respect of which the Applicant applies for registration) as part of the garden ground of 10 .... Lane, ...

 2. On .... 19... the Applicant acquired the freehold of premises in .... Street, ..., which back on to the land in dispute, and since that date has carried on business at those premises as a builder and decorator.

 3. In the month of .... 19... the boundary between the land in dispute and the premises was marked by the remains of a fence which was in such a state of disrepair that access could be obtained between the two properties at a number of places.

 4. In the month of .... 19... the land in dispute was vacant and overgrown, and the Applicant, being short of space, began to use it for depositing materials, and entered upon it with the intention of taking possession.

 5. From that time until .... 19... the Applicant continuously used the land in dispute as part of his business premises by stacking timber and bricks and parking lorries and plant on it. Throughout that period he maintained the fences on all sides save on the side abutting his premises, where the fence has now completely disappeared, and kept the gate on the southern side locked so that the only access was through his .... Street premises. At no time did the Cautioner or anyone authorised by him enter or attempt to enter the land in dispute to cut down wood or brambles or for any other

purpose, and during the whole period the Applicant remained in undisputed possession of the land without acknowledging the title of the Cautioner or any other person.

6. The first notification of any claim by the Cautioner was on .... 19... when G. H. & Co wrote to the Applicant demanding that he clear his materials from the site. By this date, however, the Applicant had already acquired title by adverse possession against the Cautioner under the provisions of the Limitation Act 1980[4].

7. The Applicant accordingly contends that he is entitled to be registered with title absolute and that the caution against first registration should be cancelled as the Cautioner no longer has any interest in the land in dispute.

DATED .... 19... .

(*Signature*)

of (*address*), Solicitors for the Applicant

1 See Paragraph 18 ante. Although no form is prescribed for such a reply and it may be given by letter, it is advisable to use the formal heading as in this example.
2 See Form 6 note 6 ante.
3 See Form 12 ante.
4 Limitation Act 1980 s 15 (24 Halsbury's Statutes (4th Edn) LIMITATION OF ACTIONS).

14

ORDER by Registrar referring to court matter arising on cautioner's objection to first registration[1]

HM LAND REGISTRY

Land Registration Acts 1925 to 1986[2]

Land Registration (Conduct of Business) Regulations 1997

Caution Title No. ....
Title No. ....
County and District ....
Property: (*address*)

WHEREAS.

1. C. D. is the Cautioner in respect of a caution registered pursuant to Section 53 of the Land Registration Act 1925[3] against the first registration of the [freehold *or* leasehold] land [known as (*describe the property*) *or* shown and coloured [red] on the attached plan *or* held under a lease (*give date and particulars of lease*) *or as the case may be*] and claims to be [the freehold owner of the land *or as the case may be*].

2. A. B. has applied for first registration of the [freehold *or* leasehold] land and the Cautioner has objected thereto.

IT IS ORDERED that the matter be referred for the decision of a Judge of the Chancery Division of the High Court of Justice, pursuant to the Rules of the Supreme Court Order 93 Rule 10[4], in accordance with the provisions in that behalf contained in Rule 298 (2) of the Land Registration Rules 1925 as affected by the Land Registration (Conduct of Business) Regulations 1997, and that A. B., within [6] weeks of the date hereof, do take out an originating summons or such other originating process as may be appropriate[5] and do serve each originating process upon C. D within a further 2 weeks therefrom for the purpose of bringing the matter before the Court[6] and, in particular, for the purpose of determining whether the caution shall continue to have effect or be cancelled.

AND IT IS FURTHER ORDERED that the costs be dealt with as directed by the Court.

DATED .... 19...

(*Signature*)
[Solicitor to HM Land Registry]
(*Land Registry Seal*)

To A. B., of (*address*)

1 Land Registration Rules 1925, SR & O 1925/1093, r 298 (2) (16 Halsbury's Statutory Instruments (1998 Issue) REAL PROPERTY). See Paragraph 9 ante. For an order made by the Registrar deciding the matter himself see Form 5 ante.
2 See Form 6 note 6 ante.
3 Land Registration Act 1925 s 53 (37 Halsbury's Statutes (4th Edn) REAL PROPERTY). As to cautions against first registrations see Paragraph 18 ante.
4 RSC Ord 93 r 10 (2)(f).
5 Where fraud is alleged the proceedings should be commenced by writ; see RSC Ord 5 r 2 and *Re 462 Green Lane, Ilford, Gooding v Borland* [1971] 1 All ER 315, [1971] 1 WLR 138.
6 For the procedure on a reference to the court see Paragraph 9 ante. For an originating summons, see Form 25 post, which may be adapted.

B: DEALINGS

15

APPLICATION for entry on register of appurtenant right of way[1]

HM LAND REGISTRY

Land Registration Acts 1925 to 1986[2]

County and District: ....
Title No. ....
Property: (*address*) ....

A. B. of (*address*), hereby applies to the Registrar for an entry to be made on the register of the title mentioned above of the right of way hereafter described as appurtenant to the land in such title. The application is made on the following grounds:

1. By a conveyance dated .... 19... made between J. K. and L. M., the above-mentioned property and other house plots in (*name of street and county*), lying to the north and south thereof were conveyed to L. M., together with a right of way for the benefit of land thereby conveyed and every part thereof for L. M. and his successors in title to pass and repass at all times and for all purposes over the passageway leading from the rear of the plots into .... Lane, ... On .... 19... L. M. was registered as proprietor of the land thereby conveyed with an absolute freehold title under

Title No. .... and a note was made in the Property Register of the title that by the conveyance dated .... 19... a right of way was expressed to be granted as aforesaid.

2. For many years before and up to the date of the transfer next mentioned L. M. and his predecessors in title had continuously and openly enjoyed the right as appurtenant to his and their land and every part thereof.

3. A. B. was on .... 19... registered as proprietor of (*address*) under Title No. .... (being part of the land formerly comprised in Title No. ....) pursuant to a transfer thereof to him by L. M. dated .... 19... and A. B. has ever since enjoyed the right as appurtenant to this property[3].

4. Although the transfer dated .... 19... did not expressly refer to the right of way, A. B. nevertheless claims that, on his registration as proprietor of the land comprised in Title No. .... by virtue of the provisions of Section 20 (1) of the Land Registration Act 1925 and Rule 251 of the Land Registration Rules 1925[4], there was vested in him, together with the land, the right of way which is now enjoyed with and appurtenant to the said premises. A. B. therefore applies under Rule 252 of the Land Registration Rules 1925[5] for an entry to be made on the register of Title No. .... that there is appurtenant[6] to the land in the title a right of way at all times and for all purposes over the passageway leading from the rear of (*address*) to .... Lane, ...

DATED .... 19...

(*Signature*)

Solicitors for A. B.

1 Land Registration Rules 1925, SR & O 1925/1093, rr 251, 252 (1) (16 Halsbury's Statutory Instruments (1998 Issue) REAL PROPERTY). See Paragraph 20 ante. The application must state the nature of the right and must furnish evidence of its existence: Land Registration Rules 1925 r 252 (2). There is no prescribed form, but it is convenient to use the heading and set out the facts in numbered paragraphs as in this example. For notice to the servient owner and an objection to the entry see Forms 16, 17 post. As to an application for an entry to be made against a title of the existence of an overriding interest see the Land Registration Act 1925 s 70 (3) (37 Halsbury's Statutes (4th Edn) REAL PROPERTY) and the Land Registration Rules 1925 rr 197 (1), 250 (2)(a). If the grant of an easement is a disposition of registered land (see the Land Registration Act 1925 ss 18 (1), 21 (2)) the disposition must be completed by registration if the grantee is to obtain a legal estate: Land Registration Act 1925 ss 19 (as amended), 22 (as amended).
2 See Form 6 note 6 ante.
3 As to the acquisition by prescription of easements, rights or privileges affecting registered land see the Land Registration Act 1925 s 75 (5) and the Land Registration Rules 1925 r 250.
4 When registered, a disposition of registered land vests in the transferee or grantee the estate transferred or created together with all rights, privileges and appurtenances belonging or appurtenant to it, including, subject to any entry on the register, the appropriate rights and interests which would have been transferred under the Law of Property Act 1925 s 62 (37 Halsbury's Statutes (4th Edn) REAL PROPERTY) if the land had not been registered; see the Land Registration Act 1925 ss 20 (1)(as amended), 23 (1)(as amended) and the Land Registration Rules 1925 rr 251, 256.
5 Reference might also be made to Land Registration Rules 1925 r 250 (2)(b).
6 The benefit of an easement, right or privilege cannot be entered on the register except as appurtenant to a registered estate, and then only if capable of subsisting as a legal estate: Land Registration Rules 1925 rr 252, 257. As to the form of entry see Land Registration Rules 1925 rr 254, 255.

16
NOTICE to servient owner of proposed entry of appurtenant right of way[1]

HM LAND REGISTRY

Land Registration Acts 1925 to 1986[2]

County and District: ………
Title No. ………
Property: (*address*)

Any communication in reply to this notice should be addressed to: The Chief Land Registrar, The ……… District Land Registry, (*address*), quoting (*reference*)

To P. Q. of (*address*)

The Chief Land Registrar hereby gives notice that an application has been made by E. F. & Co of (*address*), as Solicitors on behalf of A. B. of (*address*), under Rule 252 of the Land Registration Rules 1925[3] for entry to be made in the register of Title No. ……… that there is appurtenant to the land in that title, which is shown on the plan annexed hereto and edged with red, a right of way for A. B. and others the owners of the land in the title to pass and repass at all times and for all purposes over the passageway tinted brown on such plan [of which passageway you are [understood to be] the owner *or* which passageway is registered under Title No. ……… of which you are the registered proprietor *or as the case may be*].

If you have no objection to the application please sign the form of consent at the bottom of the enclosed copy of this notice and return, together with the [Land *or* Charge] certificate[4] which will be dealt with without fee. An addressed envelope which requires no stamp is enclosed for this purpose.

If you have any objection to the [registration *or* making of any corresponding entry in the register of Title No. ……… that this passageway is subject to the aforesaid rights[5]], notice of the objection setting out the grounds on which it is based should be delivered at the District Registry at the above address within a period of [14] days from the date of the service of this notice, after which period, in the absence of any objection, the registration may be completed.

DATED ……… 19…

NOTE: Your attention is directed to Rule 313 (as amended) of the Land Registration Rules 1925[6] which is as follows:

Every notice sent through the post shall, unless returned by the Post Office, be deemed to have been received by the person addressed 7 days after its issue exclusive of the day of posting, and the time fixed by the notice for taking any step thereunder is to be calculated accordingly.

(*Enclose copy notice and an addressed envelope*)

CONSENT

I hereby consent to the registration of the right of way referred to above [and to the making of a corresponding entry against Title No. ………].

DATED ……… 19…

(*Signature of servient owner*)

1 Land Registration Rules 1925, SR & O 1925/1093, r 253 (16 Halsbury's Statutory Instruments (1998 Issue) REAL PROPERTY). See Paragraph 20 note 8 ante. For the application see Form 15 ante; for an objection to the entry see Form 17 post.
2 See Form 6 note 6 ante.
3 Land Registration Rules 1925 r 252. See Paragraph 19 note 8 ante.
4 Subject to the prescribed exceptions the certificate, if outstanding, must be produced whenever notice is to be entered on the register adversely affecting the title: Land Registration Act 1925 s 64 (1)(c)(as amended) (37 Halsbury's Statutes (4th Edn) REAL PROPERTY).
5 Land Registration Rules 1925 r 253 (2); Land Registration Act 1925 s 70 (3).
6 Under the Land Registration Rules 1925 r 313 (2) the Registrar may, as an alternative to setting out the rule itself, give an explanation as to its effect.

17
OBJECTION to entry of appurtenant right of way[1]

HM LAND REGISTRY

Land Registration Acts 1925 to 1986[2]

County and District: ………
Title No. ………
Property: (*address*) ………

To the Chief Land Registrar (*address*)

P. Q., of (*address*), hereby gives notice that he objects to the entry of the right of way referred to in the notice[3] addressed to him by the Chief Land Registrar dated ……… 19… as appurtenant to the land therein described [and to any corresponding entry being made against Title No. ………, of which he is the registered proprietor *or as the case may be*] for the following reasons:

1. He is and has been since ……… 19… [the freehold owner *or* registered as proprietor] [with absolute title under Title No. ………] of the soil of the passageway tinted brown on the plan attached to such notice. The passageway is not subject to a right of way for the benefit of the land edged red on the plan or at all.

2. He denies that A. B. or his predecessors in title or any of them have at any time used the passageway continuously as of right.

3. If in fact the passageway has been used by A. B. or his predecessors in title at any time then (subject to what is stated in clause 4 hereof) such user has been:

(1) occasional, intermittent and dependent at all times upon the will of P. Q.;

(2) secret without the knowledge or consent of P. Q. and without his having the means of knowing thereof or consenting thereto.

4. By an agreement dated ……… 19… and made between P. Q. of the one part and R. S. (a former owner of land edged red and adjoining land) of the other part P. Q. granted to R. S. licence and permission to use the passageway for … years from the date thereof for the sole purposes and upon the conditions therein mentioned.

5. The entry on the register of Title No. ……… relating to a right of way expressed to be granted by a conveyance dated ……… 19… was only notice of the claim of L. M. to such right and it is denied that J. K. (a party to the conveyance) had any title to make the purported grant of this right in such conveyance.

DATED ……… 19…

(*Signature*)
Solicitors for P. Q.

1 This is an objection to a notice served under the Land Registration Rules 1925, SR & O 1925/1093, r 253 (16 Halsbury's Statutory Instruments (1998 Issue) REAL PROPERTY); see Paragraph 20 ante and Form 16 ante. It is assumed that, before this formal objection is lodged, details of the grounds on which the applicant claims will be supplied to the objector. As to objections generally and the procedure leading up to a hearing see Paragraph 20 ante. The Registrar may decide to hear the matter himself (Land Registration Rules 1925 r 298 (1)) or he may at any stage refer the matter to the court (Land Registration Rules 1925 r 298 (2)). He has, however, some discretion under Land Registration Rules 1925 r 253 (2) and the Land Registration Act 1925 s 70 (3) (37 Halsbury's Statutes (4th Edn) REAL PROPERTY) as to whether he enters the burden of the right, which is an overriding interest (see Land Registration Act 1925 s 70 (1)(a) and the Land Registration Rules 1925 r 258), on the register of any servient title affected and, if not satisfied that the right is appurtenant, may enter it with qualifications, or merely enter notice of the fact that the proprietor claims it. It would seem, therefore, that if, without a hearing, the Registrar refused an application to enter a right as part of the description of the land so as to confer an absolute title, no appeal would lie; see *Dennis v Malcolm* [1934] Ch 244; although, if the refusal was wrongful, it might be challenged by judicial review, see title JUDICIAL REVIEW ante. If the dominant owner then wanted to establish his right he might apply to the court for a declaration that he was entitled to it; if, on the other hand, the servient owner wanted to settle the question conclusively, he might apply to the court for a declaration that no right of way existed and also, if need be, for an injunction.
2 See Form 6 note 6 ante.
3 See Form 16 ante.

18
APPLICATION for service of notice warning off caution against dealings[1]

HM LAND REGISTRY

Land Registration Acts 1925 to 1986[2]

County and District ....
Title No. ....
Property: (*address*)
[No. of charge ....[3]]

Date: .... 19...

I, A. B., of (*address*), the registered proprietor of the [land *or* charge] above mentioned, hereby apply that notice[4] under Section 55 of the Land Registration Act 1925 may be served on C. D., of (*address*) in respect of a caution registered in his favour on .... 19... against the [title *or* charge].

(*Signature of registered proprietor or his solicitor*)

1 Land Registration Act 1925 s 55 (1) (37 Halsbury's Statutes (4th Edn) REAL PROPERTY); Land Registration Rules 1925, SR & O 1925/1093, r 218 (1) (16 Halsbury's Statutory Instruments (1998 Issue) REAL PROPERTY). See Paragraph 21 ante.
2 See Form 6 note 6 ante.
3 Include this where the caution relates to a charge.
4 See Form 19 post.

19

NOTICE to cautioner against dealings on application to warn off cautioner or to register dealing[1]

HM LAND REGISTRY

Land Registration Acts 1925 to 1986[2]

County and District ....
Title No. ....
Property: (*address*)
[No. of charge ....[3]]

Any communication in reply to this notice should be addressed to: The Chief Land Registrar, The .... District Land Registry, (*address*), quoting (*reference*)

To C. D. of (*address*)

The Chief Land Registrar hereby gives notice that the caution lodged by you in this office on .... 19... requiring that no dealing with the [land *or* charge] above referred to should be registered until notice had been served on the Cautioner will cease to have any effect [as to so much of the land as is comprised in a [transfer *or* charge] dated .... 19... by the registered proprietor to L. M., of (*address*), being the land known as 10 .... Lane, ...] after the expiration of [14] days[4] next ensuing the date at which this notice is served, in the absence of objection[5] by you within that period.

DATED .... 19...

[The land [transferred *or* charged] will be registered under Title No. ....]

[This notice is given in respect of a [transfer *or* charge] by A B.[6] to L. M. of the land in the above-mentioned title affected by the caution. The transaction was lodged for registration by E. F. & Co, Solicitors of (*address*), *or, where the notice is served on the application of the person against whom the caution was lodged*: This notice is given in respect of an application[7] lodged by E. F. & Co, Solicitors of (*address*), on behalf of A. B., the registered proprietor of the [land in the above title *or* above charge] for the cancellation on the register of the caution under the provisions of Rule 218 of the Land Registration Rules 1925][8].

If you have no objection to the [dealing *or* application] you are requested to sign the consent below and to return it forthwith, using the accompanying addressed label, which requires no stamp.

If you object to the [registration *or* cancellation of the caution] a statement giving concisely the ground of your objection[9], signed by yourself or your solicitor, should be lodged within the prescribed period.

NOTE: Your attention is directed to Rule 313 (as amended) of the Land Registration Rules 1925[10] which is as follows:

Every notice sent through the post shall, unless returned by the Post Office, be deemed to have been received by the person addressed 7 days after its issue exclusive of the day of posting, and the time fixed by the notice for taking any step thereunder is to be calculated accordingly.

(*Enclose copy notice and an addressed envelope*)

CONSENT

I[11] hereby consent to the [registration of the dealing referred to above and] [cancellation of the caution on the register [as to so much of the land as is comprised in the dealing]] [registration of the dealing referred to above on condition that [the caution registered in my name against the title is continued on the register *or as the case may be*][12]].

DATED .... 19...

(Signature of cautioner or his solicitor)

1 Land Registration Act 1925 s 55 (1) (37 Halsbury's Statutes (4th Edn) REAL PROPERTY); Land Registration Rules 1925, SR & O 1925/1093, r 218 (16 Halsbury's Statutory Instruments (1998 Issue) REAL PROPERTY). See Paragraph 21 ante. This notice is served by the Registrar on a cautioner either when a dealing is presented for registration without his consent or on the application (Form 18 ante) of the proprietor of the land or charge to which the caution relates. The notice will be modified as appropriate if served in respect of some dealing other than a transfer or charge.
2 See Form 6 note 6 ante.
3 Include this where the caution relates to a charge.
4 See Paragraph 21 note 17 ante.
5 See Form 20 post.
6 The registered proprietor.
7 See Form 18 ante.
8 If only part of the land is concerned modify the description in this paragraph.
9 See Form 20 post.
10 See Form 16 note 6 ante.
11 As to who may consent see Paragraph 21 ante.
12 The nature of the interest protected by caution and that of the dealing will determine whether or not consent can be given unconditionally.

20

OBJECTION by cautioner to cancellation of caution against dealings[1]

HM LAND REGISTRY

Land Registration Acts 1925 to 1986[2]

County and District ....
Title No. ....
Property: (*address*)
[No. of charge ....[3]]

To the Chief Land Registrar, (*address*)

We, G. H. & Co of (*address*), as Solicitors for C. D. of (*address*) (hereinafter referred to as "the Cautioner"), hereby give you notice that he objects to the cancellation of the caution registered in his favour on .... 19... and referred to in the notice[4] dated .... 19... addressed to him on the following grounds[5]:

1. The caution was lodged in respect of an agreement in writing dated .... 19... made between A. B. (the registered proprietor of the land in the above-mentioned title, hereinafter referred to as "the Registered Proprietor") of the one part and the Cautioner of the other part whereby it

was agreed that the Registered Proprietor should sell and the Cautioner should purchase with vacant possession the land comprised in the title at the price of £......, of which £...... was then paid to the Registered Proprietor by way of deposit.

2. The agreement stated that the premises were sold subject to all overriding interests within the meaning of Section 70 of the Land Registration Act 1925[6] affecting the same but that the Registered Proprietor was not aware of any such overriding interests.

3. In spite of the provisions of the agreement on .... 19... the Cautioner ascertained that parts of the premises, namely (*specify the parts*), were in the occupation of persons who claimed that they were the tenants of the Registered Proprietor.

4. On .... 19... the Cautioner by letter addressed by G. H. & Co to E. F. & Co, the Solicitors acting for the Registered Proprietor, complained of the facts stated in the above Paragraph and stated that the Cautioner required vacant possession of the premises on completion, which by the agreement was fixed for .... 19... .

5. E. F. & Co replied to this letter on .... 19... to the effect that the Registered Proprietor would adhere to his contract and that vacant possession would be given as agreed. On the faith of this statement G. H. & Co on behalf of the Cautioner delivered requisitions on title and (subject thereto) a draft form of transfer for approval to E. F. & Co. In the requisitions it was reiterated that vacant possession was required on completion.

6. The requisitions have not been answered and the draft transfer has not been approved in spite of 2 further letters addressed by G. H. & Co to E. F. & Co. On .... 19... E. F. & Co gave notice on behalf of the Registered Proprietor to G. H. & Co on behalf of the Cautioner purporting to rescind the contract pursuant to the terms thereof, and returned the deposit.

7. The Cautioner thereupon lodged the caution on .... 19... and the same was duly registered.

8. The Cautioner has ascertained that the whole of the premises the subject of the agreement for sale and purchase are now vacant and he believes that if the registration of the caution is cancelled the Registered Proprietor will immediately sell the land to another purchaser at a higher price.

9. The Cautioner has been at all material times and still is willing to perform his part of the agreement, but he contends that the Registered Proprietor, though able, is not willing to perform his part thereof.

10. The Cautioner maintains that he is entitled to the benefit of a valid contract for sale and that accordingly the caution should not be cancelled.

DATED .... 19...

(*Signature*)

of (*address*), Solicitors for the Cautioner

1 Land Registration Act 1925 s 55 (2) (37 Halsbury's Statutes (4th Edn) REAL PROPERTY); Land Registration Rules 1925, SR & O 1925/1093, rr 219, 220 (1) (16 Halsbury's Statutory Instruments (1998 Issue) REAL PROPERTY). See Paragraph 21 ante. The form is not prescribed, but it is advisable to use the formal heading and set out the objection in numbered paragraphs as in this example. For a reply see Form 21 post.
2 See Form 6 note 6 ante.
3 Include this where the caution relates to a charge.
4 See Form 19 ante.

5   The nature of the cautioner's interest in the land or charges will have been indicated in the statutory declaration supporting the caution; see the Land Registration Rules 1925 r 215 (4). That statement must be amplified to show the precise circumstances of his claim which would justify the Registrar in ordering that the caution shall continue to have effect.
6   For the meaning of "overriding interests" see Paragraph 11 ante. They include the rights of every person in actual occupation of the land or in receipt of the rents and profits thereof, save where inquiry is made of such person and the rights are not disclosed: Land Registration Act 1925 s 70 (1)(g). See also *Williams and Glyn's Bank Ltd v Boland* [1981] AC 487, [1980] 2 All ER 408, HL; *Ashburn Anstalt v Arnold* [1989] Ch 1, [1988] 2 All ER 147, CA; *Kemmis v Kemmis (Welland Intervening)* [1988] 1 WLR 1307, [1988] 2 FLR 233, CA; *Abbey National Building Society v Cann* [1991] 1 AC 56, [1990] 1 All ER 1085, HL; *Lloyds Bank plc v Rosset* [1991] 1 AC 107, [1990] 1 All ER 1111, HL; and *Woolwich Building Society v Dickman* [1996] 3 All ER 204, CA. Note that the words "unless the contrary is expressed on the register" should not be interpreted as indicating the existence of any category of overriding interest can be negated by entry on the register.

21
REPLY to objection by cautioner to cancellation of caution against dealings[1]

HM LAND REGISTRY

Land Registration Acts 1925 to 1986[2]

County and District ....
Title No. ....
Property: (*address*)
[No. of charge ....[3]]

To the Chief Land Registrar, (*address*)

We, E. F. & Co of (*address*), as Solicitors for A. B. of (*address*), the Registered Proprietor of the land comprised in the title above mentioned (hereinafter called "the Applicant") in reply to the objection[4] dated .... 19... by C. D. (the Cautioner under the caution registered on .... 19...) submit that the caution should not have been lodged in the first instance and ought now to be cancelled on the register for the following reasons: (*state the grounds on which the registered proprietor claims that the caution should forthwith cease to have effect, eg*)

1   The Cautioner was not at the date of lodgment of the caution and has not been since and is not now a person interested in the land in the title referred to above within the meaning of Section 54 of the Land Registration Act 1925[5].

2. The Applicant admits that an agreement was entered into as alleged in Paragraph 1 of the Cautioner's objection dated .... 19... and that such agreement contained a clause to the effect set out in Paragraph 2 of that objection.

3. The agreement was also made subject to an express condition contained therein that if the Cautioner should make and insist upon any requisition in respect of the Applicant's title with which the Applicant was unable to comply, the Applicant should be at liberty to rescind the sale by notice in writing to the Cautioner, who should thereupon be entitled to receive back the amount of his deposit without interest or expenses.

4. The Applicant admits that a letter dated .... 19... was sent as stated in Paragraph 4 of the Cautioner's objection.

5. In their reply dated .... 19... to the last-mentioned letter (which reply is referred to in Paragraph 5 of the Cautioner's objection) E. F. & Co stated that the top floor of the premises was then being occupied by the Cautioner's father, who would be leaving the premises within a week or thereabouts; that the ground floor was then occupied under the terms of the will of a relative of the Cautioner by a beneficiary but without any arrangement for a tenancy and without payment of rent, but that the Cautioner was arranging for the occupier in question to move out before completion and that it was intended to give vacant possession in accordance with the contract. It is contended that the material facts of these occupations were known to the Cautioner before contract.

6. It is admitted that the Cautioner's Solicitors subsequently delivered their client's requisitions on title and a draft transfer as stated in Paragraph 5 of the objection. Although the Applicant believed and had reason to believe, both at the date of the contract as well as the date of the letter referred to in Paragraph 5 hereof, that he would be able to give vacant possession of the entire premises on completion, he subsequently became unable to do so. In the requisitions the Cautioner again stipulated for vacant possession on completion and in two further letters dated .... 19... and .... 19... his Solicitors insisted upon compliance with this requisition. The Applicant, being unable to comply with such requisition, rescinded the contract on .... 19... by notice given by his Solicitors as stated in Paragraph 6 of the objection and also then returned the deposit.

7. Save for the admissions herein expressed or implied the Applicant denies the allegations in the objection by the Cautioner.

8. For the reasons stated the Applicant maintains that the agreement was duly rescinded in accordance with the terms thereof and that it is at an end.

DATED .... 19... .

(*Signature*)

of (*address*), Solicitor for the Applicant

1 Land Registration Act 1925 s 55 (37 Halsbury's Statutes (4th Edn) REAL PROPERTY). See Paragraph 21 ante. Although the form is not prescribed it is advisable to use the heading and set out the reply in numbered paragraphs as in this example.
2 See Form 6 note 6 ante.
3 Include this where the caution relates to a charge.
4 Land Registration Act 1925 s 54 (as amended). See Form 20 ante.
5 See Paragraph 21 ante.

22
NOTICE of hearing in connection with caution against dealings[1]

HM LAND REGISTRY

Land Registration Acts 1925 to 1986[2]

Land Registration (Conduct of Business) Regulations 1997

NOTICE OF HEARING under Rule 220 of the Land Registration Rules 1925
Title No. ....
County and District ....
Property: (*address*)

In the Matter of the Application[3] of [A. B. of (*address*), the Registered Proprietor of the land, to warn off a caution under Rule 218 of the Land Registration Rules 1925[4] *or* J. K. of (*address*), to register a transfer dated .... 19... by A. B. to J. K. of the land in the above-mentioned title *or as the case may be*]

And in the Matter of the notice[5] served on .... 19... pursuant to Section 55 of the Land Registration Act 1925[6] and Rule 218 of the Land Registration Rules 1925 on C. D., the Cautioner, of (*address*), in respect of the caution registered in his favour on .... 19... against the title

WHEREAS cause has been shown[7] under Rule 220 of the Land Registration Rules 1925[8] why the [caution registered on .... 19... against the above title in favour of C. D., the Cautioner, of (*address*), shall continue to have effect *or* the transfer dated .... 19... should not be registered]

NOW THEREFORE TAKE NOTICE that the [Chief Land Registrar *or* Solicitor to HM Land Registry] will hear and determine the matter at [HM Land Registry, Lincoln's Inn Fields, London WC2A 3PH *or as the case may be*], at ...[am *or* pm] on .... 19... and make such order in the matter as he shall think just or refer the matter for the decision of the Court

AND FURTHER TAKE NOTICE that you may attend before the [Chief Land Registrar *or* Solicitor to HM Land Registry] at that time either in person or by your Solicitor or Counsel.

It is not obligatory to attend, but if you do not, such order will be made and proceedings taken as the [Chief Land Registrar *or* Solicitor to HM Land Registry] may think just and expedient.

DATED .... 19...
To (*name*) of (*address*)

(*Land Registry Official Stamp*)

---

1 Land Registration Rules 1925, SR & O 1925/1093, rr 218, 220 (2)–(4) (16 Halsbury's Statutory Instruments (1998 Issue) REAL PROPERTY); Land Registration Act 1925 s 55 (37 Halsbury's Statutes (4th Edn) REAL PROPERTY). See Paragraph 20 ante. For the jurisdiction of the Solicitor to HM Land Registry, see Land Registration (Conduct of Business) Regulations 1997, SI 1997/713, regs 3, 4. As to notice of hearing generally see the Land Registration Rules 1925 r 300 and Paragraph 13 ante.
2 See Form 6 note 6 ante.
3 See Form 18 ante.
4 See Paragraph 21 ante.
5 See Form 19 ante.
6 See Paragraph 21 ante.
7 See Form 20 ante.
8 See Paragraph 21 ante.

23

ORDER on hearing in connection with caution against dealings[1]

HM LAND REGISTRY

Land Registration Acts 1925 to 1986[2]

Land Registration (Conduct of Business) Regulations 1997

ORDER BY THE SOLICITOR TO HM LAND REGISTRY

Title No. ....
County and District ....
Property: (*address*)

In the Matter of the application [by A. B. of (*address*) (the Applicant), for the cancellation of the caution registered on .... 19... against the above-mentioned title in favour of C. D. of (*address*) (the Objector) *or* by J. K. of (*address*) (the Applicant), to register a transfer dated .... 19... by A. B. to the Applicant of the land in the above-mentioned title *or as the case may be*] and the objection by [the Objector *or* C. D. of (*address*) (the Objector)]

AFTER HEARING [Counsel for the Applicant and for the Objector *or as the case may be*]

IT IS ORDERED that the caution registered on .... 19... in favour of the Objector shall [continue to have effect [and the application to register the transfer dated .... 19... be cancelled] *or* cease to have effect and that the entry thereof on the register of the above-mentioned title be cancelled [and that the registration of the transfer dated .... 19... in favour of the Applicant be completed forthwith] *or as the case may be*[3]]

AND that the costs of and incidental to the hearing[4] be borne by the [Objector *or* Applicant] and such costs be taxed on the standard basis if not agreed

DATED .... 19...

(*Signature*)
[Solicitor to HM Land Registry]
(*Land Registry Seal*)

1 Land Registration Rules 1925, SR & O 1925/1093, r 220 (3) (16 Halsbury's Statutory Instruments (1998 Issue) REAL PROPERTY). See Paragraph 21 ante. As to orders by the Registrar see generally Paragraph 17 ante. For the jurisdiction of the Solicitor to HM Land Registry, see Land Registration (Conduct of Business) Regulations 1997, SI 1997/713, regs 3, 4.
2 See Form 6 note 6 ante.
3 For examples of orders the Registrar may make see Paragraph 20 ante. It should be noted that under the Land Registration Rules 1925 r 220 (2) the Registrar may order that a caution be cancelled without a formal hearing, but that he may only order that it should continue to have effect after a hearing. In either case, the unsuccessful party may appeal to the court under Land Registration Rules 1925 r 299. For a form of originating motion, see Form 44 post, which may be adapted. Where the order is made otherwise than following a hearing it will contain recitals setting out the Registrar's reasons for ordering that the caution be cancelled.
4 See Form 5 note 2 ante.

24
ORDER by Registrar referring to the court matter arising on objection by cautioner against dealings[1]

HM LAND REGISTRY

Land Registration Acts 1925 to 1986[2]

Land Registration (Conduct of Business) Regulations 1997

ORDER BY THE SOLICITOR TO HM LAND REGISTRY

Title No. ....
County and District ....
Property: (*address*)

In the Matter of the application [by A. B. of (*address*) (the Applicant), for the cancellation of the caution registered on .... 19... against the above-mentioned title in favour of C. D. of (*address*) (the Objector) *or* by J. K. of (*address*) (the Applicant), to register a transfer dated .... 19... by A. B. to the Applicant of the land in the above-mentioned title *or as the case may be*] and the objection by [the Objector *or* C. D. of (*address*) (the Objector)]

WHEREAS:

1. A. B. (in these recitals called "the Proprietor") is the registered proprietor of the freehold land comprised in the above-mentioned title.

2. C. D. (in these recitals called "the Cautioner") is the Cautioner in respect of a caution registered against the above-mentioned title pursuant to Section 54 of the Land Registration Act 1925[3] on .... 19... and the statutory declaration in support of the caution states that the Cautioner is interested in the land as purchaser under a contract for sale dated .... 19... made between the Proprietor and the Cautioner.

3. The Proprietor by his Solicitors applied[4] pursuant to Rule 218 of the Land Registration Rules 1925[5] for notice[6] under Section 55 of the Act[7] to be served on the Cautioner for the purpose of warning off the caution, and such notice was duly served by the Chief Land Registrar.

4. The Cautioner has objected[8] to the cancellation of the caution on the grounds that it protects an enforceable contract for sale between the parties which the Proprietor denies.

IT IS ORDERED that the matter be referred for the decision of a Judge of the Chancery Division of the High Court of Justice pursuant to the Rules of the Supreme Court, Order 93, Rule 10, in accordance with the provisions in that behalf contained in Rule 220 (4) of the Land Registration Rules 1925[9], and that A. B. within [6] weeks from the date hereof do take out an originating summons[10] and do send such originating summons within a further 2 weeks therefrom for the purpose of bringing the matter before the Court and in particular for the purpose of determining whether the caution shall continue to have effect or be cancelled.

AND IT IS FURTHER ORDERED that the costs be dealt with as directed by the Court.

DATED .... 19...

(*Signature*)
[Solicitor to HM Land Registry]
(*Land Registry Seal*)

To A. B., of (*address*)

1 Land Registration Rules 1925, SR & O 1925/1093, rr 218, 220 (4) (16 Halsbury's Statutory Instruments (1994 Issue) REAL PROPERTY). See Paragraphs 7, 21 ante, and the Land Registration Act 1925 ss 54 (as amended), 55 (37 Halsbury's Statutes (4th Edn) REAL PROPERTY). For the jurisdiction of the Solicitor to HM Land Registry, see Land Registration (Conduct of Business) Regulations 1997, SI 1997/713, regs 3, 4.
2 See Form 6 note 6 ante.
3 See Paragraph 21 ante.
4 See Form 18 ante.
5 See Paragraph 21 ante.
6 See Form 19 ante.
7 See Paragraph 21 ante.
8 See Form 20 ante.
9 See note 1 above.
10 RSC Ord 93 r 10. See Form 25 post.

25

ORIGINATING SUMMONS on reference by Registrar to court[1]

(*Royal Arms*)[2]

IN THE HIGH COURT OF JUSTICE   Ch 19... B. No. ...[3]
   Chancery Division[4]
   [......... District Registry[5]]

Between   A. B.   ...   Plaintiff
                   and
                   C. D.   ...   Defendant

To C. D. of (*address*)

LET the Defendant within ... days after service of this summons on him, counting the day of service, return the accompanying Acknowledgment of Service[6] to the appropriate Court Office.

By this summons, which is issued on the application of the Plaintiff A. B. of (*address*), the Plaintiff seeks the determination of the following matters which have been referred to this Honourable Court by [HM Chief Land Registrar *or* the Solicitor to HM Land Registry] by an order dated .... 19... made under the provisions in that behalf contained in Rule 220 (4) of the Land Registration Rules 1925, namely:

1. Whether C. D. was at the date of registration of the caution registered against Title No. ... and is now a person interested in the land comprised in the above-mentioned title within the meaning of Section 54 of the Land Registration Act 1925[7] by reason of [the existence of an enforceable contract between A. B. and C. D. for the sale of the land][8];

2. Whether the caution shall continue to have effect or be cancelled[9];

3. That the costs of this application may be provided for.

This application is made under Section 138 of the Land Registration Act 1925[10] and Rule 220 of the Land Registration Rules 1925[11].

If the Defendant does not acknowledge service, such judgment may be given or order made against or in relation to him as the Court may think just and expedient.

DATED .... 19...

NOTE—This Summons may not be served later than [4, *or if leave is required to effect service out of the jurisdiction,* 6] calendar months beginning with the above date unless renewed by order of the Court.

This Summons was taken out by E. F. & Co of (*address*), [Agents for (*name*) of (*address*),] Solicitors for the said Plaintiff whose address is as stated above[12].

IMPORTANT

Directions for acknowledgment of service are given with the accompanying form[13].

1 Land Registration Rules 1925, SR & O 1925/1093, r 220 (4) (16 Halsbury's Statutory Instruments (1998 Issue) REAL PROPERTY), under which the particular reference is made. See Paragraphs 9, 21 ante. As to references to the court generally, and other cases where references may be made, see Paragraph 7 ante. For the Registrar's order on which the reference is made see Form 24 ante; for other orders referring matters to the court see Form 14 ante and Form 45 post. For a supporting affidavit see Form 26 post.
2 A replica of the Royal Arms must be printed or embossed on the first page of every originating process: RSC Ord 1 r 9.
3 See RSC Appendix A Form No 8.
4 Proceedings relating to land registration are allocated to the Chancery Division: RSC Ord 93 r 10 (2)(f).
5 An originating summons commencing proceedings assigned to the Chancery Division may be issued out of a Chancery district registry: RSC Ord 7 r 5 (2).
6 See Vol 6 (1998 Issue) title ACKNOWLEDGMENT OF SERVICE Form 4.
7 See Paragraph 21 ante.
8 As to the nature of cautionable interests see Paragraph 21 ante.
9 This paragraph follows the wording of the Registrar's order; see Form 24 ante.
10 Land Registration Act 1925 s 138 (as substituted).
11 See note 1 above.
12 RSC Ord 7 r 3 (2) applying RSC Ord 6 r 5.
13 See note 6 above.

26
AFFIDAVIT supporting originating summons on reference by Registrar to court[1]

Plaintiff: A. B.: 1st; .... 19...A.B.1,2,3,4,5[2]

IN THE HIGH COURT OF JUSTICE   Ch 19... B. No. ...[3]
   Chancery Division[4]
   [......... District Registry[5]]

Between   A. B.   ...   Plaintiff
                and
                C. D.   ...   Defendant

I, A. B. of (*state residence or workplace, and occupation or, if none, description*), make oath and say as follows:

1. I was registered as proprietor of the freehold land comprised in the above-mentioned title on .... 19... and I hold the same free from incumbrances other than certain restrictive covenants, notice whereof is registered in the charges register of the title.

2. The land is a vacant plot of land in respect of which the .... Council as planning authority granted outline planning permission under the Town and Country Planning Act 1990[6] for the erection of 10 pairs of semi-detached private dwelling-houses.

3. In the month of .... 19... I entered into negotiations with the Defendant for the sale of land to him, and on .... 19... I wrote to the

Defendant offering to sell the land to him at a purchase price of £...... on condition that the sale was completed within 4 weeks. I asked the Defendant to indorse his agreement to these terms by signing the duplicate copy of the letter which I had agreed and sent to him and to return the signed duplicate to me. A copy of the letter is now produced and shown to me marked "A.B.1".

4. The Defendant did not return the said duplicate letter and by letter to me dated .... 19... the Defendant replied that he accepted my offer but added that he considered the purchase price to be excessive having regard to the limitation on the number of dwelling-houses imposed by the outline planning permission mentioned above. The Defendant suggested that the initial purchase price should be £......, but that, in the event of his obtaining within 5 years planning permission for a greater number of dwelling-houses, an additional sum of £...... should be payable in respect of each pair of dwelling-houses in excess of 10 for which planning permission should be given, with a maximum total purchase price of £....... . The letter is now produced and shown to me marked "A.B.2".

5. Between .... 19... and .... 19... further correspondence passed between the Defendant and myself in an attempt to reach agreement as to the terms of the proposed sale. A bundle of correspondence, comprising the originals of all the letters sent by the Defendant to me and copies of all the letters sent by me to the Defendant within that period, is now produced and shown to me marked "A.B.3".

6. The negotiations between myself and the Defendant did not result in any agreement between us and no contract for sale complying with the provisions of Section 2 of the Law of Property (Miscellaneous Provisions) Act 1989[7] was exchanged between us. By letter to the Defendant dated .... 19... I informed him that I considered the negotiations at an end.

7. By letter to me dated .... 19... the Defendant alleged that the letters dated .... 19... and .... 19... created a binding contract between us for the sale of the land[8]. He claimed that the suggestions made by him in the letter dated .... 19... with regard to the purchase price and the subsequent correspondence between us had amounted only to an abortive negotiation for the variation of that contract. The letter is now produced and shown to me marked "A.B.4".

8. On .... 19... I entered into a binding contract for sale of the land with another person, and shortly before completion thereof, which was due to take place on .... 19... I was informed by my Solicitors, E. F. & Co, that an official certificate of result of search of the register of the above title obtained by the purchaser's Solicitors had revealed that the Defendant had caused the above-mentioned caution to be registered on .... 19... . The statutory declaration in support of the caution stated that the Defendant was interested in the land as a purchaser under a contract of sale dated .... 19... made between myself and the Defendant.

9. On .... 19... I applied[9] by my Solicitors to the Chief Land Registrar pursuant to Rule 218 of the Land Registration Rules 1925[10] for notice[11] under Section 55 of the Land Registration Act 1925[12] to be served on the Defendant for the purpose of warning off the caution, and such notice was served by the Chief Land Registrar.

10. The Defendant, through his Solicitors, G. H. & Co in reply gave notice of objection[13] to the cancellation of the caution to the Chief Land Registrar on the ground that it protected an enforceable contract for sale between us, which I have, by my Solicitors, denied.

11. By order[14] dated .... 19... under Rule 220 (4) of the Land Registration Rules 1925[15], the Chief Land Registrar has referred this matter to this Honourable Court and has required me to begin these proceedings. An office copy of the order is now produced and shown to me marked "A.B.5".

SWORN at (*address*), on
.... 19...
Before me,
(*Signature*)
A [Solicitor *or* Barrister *or* Notary Public *or* Commissioner for Oaths][17]

(*Deponent's signature*)[16]

1   Land Registration Rules 1925, SR & O 1925/1093, r 220 (4) (16 Halsbury's Statutory Instruments (1998 Issue) REAL PROPERTY). See Paragraphs, 9, 21 ante. For the originating summons see Form 25 ante.
2   Chancery Division Practice Directions No 8A (i)(a): Supreme Court Practice 1997 para 820 and Practice Note [1983] 3 All ER 33, sub nom [1983] 1 WLR 922 (as amended by Practice Note [1995] 2 All ER 511, sub nom Practice Direction [1995] 1 WLR 510).
3   See Form 25 note 3 ante.
4   See Form 25 note 4 ante.
5   See Form 25 note 5 ante.
6   Town and Country Planning Act 1990 s 92 (46 Halsbury's Statutes (4th Edn) TOWN AND COUNTRY PLANNING).
7   Law of Property (Miscellaneous Provisions) Act 1989 s 2 (37 Halsbury's Statutes (4th Edn) REAL PROPERTY).
8   The Law Commission's report "Transfer of Land: Formalities of Contracts for Sale etc., of Land" (Law Comm No 164) comments in para 4.15 that it is still possible to create contracts by correspondence despite the Law of Property (Miscellaneous Provisions) Act 1989 so it may be advisable for the parties to use the formula "subject to contract" on letters which contain or refer to documents containing the terms of the contract or if the letters are signed by a party to the contract. Note also, however, that the Bill as drafted by the Law Commission was materially different from that enacted by Parliament, and see the comments of STUART-SMITH LJ in *Commission for the New Towns v Cooper* (*Great Britain*) *Ltd* [1995] Ch 259, [1995] 2 All ER 929, CA where it was held that the final offer and its acceptance in two separate letters could not without more amount to an exchange of contracts. Only an exchange of letters which acknowledged the existence of an already concluded contract would be sufficient.
9   See Form 18 ante.
10 Land Registration Rules 1925 r 218. See Paragraph 21 ante.
11 See Form 19 ante.
12 Land Registration Act 1925 s 55 (37 Halsbury's Statutes (4th Edn) REAL PROPERTY). See Paragraph 21 ante.
13 See Form 20 ante.
14 See Form 24 ante.
15 See note 1 above.
16 See Form 7 note 8 ante.
17 See Form 7 note 9 ante.

C: RESTRICTIONS

27

APPLICATION for order under restriction in anticipation of proposed dealing[1]

HM LAND REGISTRY

Land Registration Acts 1925 to 1986[2]

(*Quote reference if known*)
        County and District ....
        Title No. (*if known*) ....
        Property: (*address*)

We, E. F. & Co of (*address*), as Solicitors for A. B. of (*address*), the tenant for life under a settlement arising under a trust deed dated .... 19... and made between X. Y. of the one part and R. S. and T. U. of the other part, and L. M., of (*address*), and N. O., of (*address*), the trustees of the settlement, hereby apply to the Solicitor to HM Land Registry for an order under the hereinafter mentioned restriction that the under-mentioned disposition will, when presented, be registered unconditionally. The circumstances are:

1. By a transfer dated .... 19... X. Y. of (*address*), as settlor, transferred the land in the above title to A. B., and it was thereby declared that the land was vested in A. B. upon trusts from time to time affecting it by virtue of the trust deed, and the entry of the following restriction was requested:

    "No disposition under which capital money arises is to be registered unless the money is paid to L. M. of (*address*), and N. O. of (*address*) (the trustees of a settlement of whom there must be not less than 2 nor more than 4 trustees, unless a trust corporation is the sole trustee), or into court. Except under an order of the Registrar no disposition is to be registered unless authorised by the Settled Land Act 1925[3]."

2. On .... 19... A. B. was registered as proprietor of the land and the restriction was duly entered on the register as requested.

3. The following powers were declared by the above-mentioned transfer to be expressly conferred on the tenant for life by the trust deed dated .... 19... a copy of which [accompanies this application *or* is filed in HM Land Registry[4]] in extension of those conferred by the Settled Land Act 1925[5]:

    3.1. power to make any lease or contract for the same without previous notice of intention being given to any trustee or any solicitor of any trustee[6];

    3.2. power to grant any lease wholly in consideration of a fine or without a fine being taken and reserving only a peppercorn or nominal rent[7];

    3.3. power, subject to Section 149 (3) of the Law of Property Act 1925, to grant any lease to take effect in possession at the expiration of any existing lease or at any future time[8].

4. A. B. proposes [in consideration of a premium of £......] to execute a lease of the land in the above-mentioned title in favour of P. Q. for [200] years from .... 19... at a [nominal] rent of £......[9].

[5. L. M. and N. O. will be joined as parties to the lease for the purpose of receiving the premium.]

DATED .... 19... .

(*Signature*)
of (*address*), Solicitor for the Applicant

1 Land Registration Rules 1925, SR & O 1925/1093, r 237 (16 Halsbury's Statutory Instruments (1998 Issue) REAL PROPERTY). See Paragraph 24 ante. For the jurisdiction of the Solicitor to HM Land Registry, see Land Registration (Conduct of Business) Regulations 1997, SI 1997/713, regs 3, 4. No form of application is prescribed.
2 See Form 5 note 6 ante.
3 This restriction is that set out in the Land Registration Rules 1925 Sch 2 Form 9 (as amended by SI 1996/2975). References in a restriction to powers under the Settled Land Act 1925 (48 Halsbury's Statutes (4th Edn) TRUSTS AND SETTLEMENTS) are deemed to include extended powers conferred by the settlement, but the existence of such extended powers will not be apparent from the register, see Land Registration Rules 1925 r 58. The real reason for this application arises from the latter part of the above restriction.
4 The settlement or a copy may be filed in the registry for safe custody and reference: Land Registration Rules 1925 r 59 (1).
5 Settled Land Act 1925 ss 108, 109 (48 Halsbury's Statutes (4th Edn) TRUSTS AND SETTLEMENTS).
6 See the Settled Land Act 1925 s 101.
7 See the Settled Land Act 1925 s 42 (1).
8 See the Settled Land Act 1925 s 42 (1), and the Law of Property Act 1925 s 149 (3) (37 Halsbury's Statutes (4th Edn) REAL PROPERTY).
9 Two copies of the draft lease should be lodged.

28

ORDER by Registrar under restriction as to registration of proposed dealing[1]

HM LAND REGISTRY

Land Registration Acts 1925 to 1986[2]

Land Registration (Conduct of Business) Regulations 1997

ORDER BY THE SOLICITOR TO HM LAND REGISTRY

Title No. ....
County and District ....
Property: (*address*)

In the Matter of the restriction registered against the above-mentioned title on .... 19... to the effect that (*state the terms of the restriction*)

And in the Matter of an application by E. F. & Co, of (*address*), Solicitors on behalf of A. B., of (*address*) [and L. M., of (*address*), and N. O., of (*address*)]

UPON READING a copy of the trust deed dated .... 19... and made between (*state the parties*) and a draft of a lease proposed to be entered into between A. B. of the first part L. M. and N. O. of the second part and P. Q. of the third part for [200] years from .... 19... at a rent of £...... a year

It is Ordered pursuant to Rule 237 (1) of the Land Registration Rules 1925 under the restriction that on presentation within [one month] of the date hereof of a lease in the form of the filed draft duly executed and stamped such lease be completed by registration as a disposition[3] and that notice thereof be entered against the title referred to above provided that such lease shall not be inconsistent with any entry that may be made on the register after the date of this order and before the presentation for registration of the lease [and provided that the premium of £...... payable under the lease has been paid to L. M. and N. O. as trustees of the settlement].

Dated .... 19...

(*Signature*)
[Solicitor to HM Land Registry]
(*Land Registry Seal*)

1 Land Registration Rules 1925, SR & O 1925/1093, r 237 (1) (16 Halsbury's Statutory Instruments (1998 Issue) REAL PROPERTY). See Paragraph 24 ante. For the application see Form 27 ante. The order may be entered on the register. It must be filed and, so long as it remains in force, will be shown to anyone searching the register: Land Registration Rules 1925 r 237 (2). An office copy will be supplied to the applicant. If the order is not entered on the register it should be referred to when the dealing is lodged for registration.
2 See Form 5 note 6 ante.
3 Land Registration Act 1925 ss 18 (1)(e), (5), 20 (1)(as amended), 21 (1)(d), (5), 23 (1)(as amended) (37 Halsbury's Statutes (4th Edn) REAL PROPERTY); Land Registration Rules 1925 r 46. If application is made to register a lease with a good leasehold title where the lessor's title is registered and there is a restriction on the register, the lease is a disposition of the land by the proprietor and notwithstanding the Land Registration Act 1925 s 10, it is therefore necessary to consider the effect of the restriction which is on the lessor's title.

29
ORIGINATING SUMMONS for cancellation of restriction[1]
(*Royal Arms*)[2]

IN THE HIGH COURT OF JUSTICE　　　　　　　　　　Ch 19... B. No. ...[3]
　Chancery Division[4]
　　[......... District Registry[5]]

Between	A. B.	...	Plaintiff
	and		
	C. D.	...	Defendant

To C. D. of (*address*)

Let the Defendant within ... days after the service of this summons on him, counting the day of service, return the accompanying Acknowledgment of Service[6] to the appropriate Court Office.

By this summons, which is issued on the application of the Plaintiff A. B. of (*address*), the Plaintiff, who is the registered proprietor of the property comprised in registered Title No ...., seeks the following relief, namely:

1. An order under Section 58 (4) of the Land Registration Act 1925 that the restriction registered on .... 19... in the proprietorship register of the said title to the effect that except under an Order of the Registrar no disposition of the property comprised in the above-mentioned title should be registered without the consent of the Defendant be vacated;

2. That the costs of and occasioned by this application may be provided for;
3. Such further or other relief as may be requisite.

This application is made under Sections 58 and 138 of the Land Registration Act 1925[7].

If the Defendant does not acknowledge service, such judgment may be given or order made against or in relation to him as the Court may think just and expedient.

DATED .... 19...

NOTE—This Summons may not be served later than [4, *or if leave is required to effect service*, 6] calendar months beginning with the above date unless renewed by order of the Court.

This Summons was taken out by E. F. & Co of (*address*), [Agents for (*name*) of (*address*),] Solicitors for the said Plaintiff whose address is as stated above[8].

IMPORTANT

Directions for acknowledgment of service are given with the accompanying form[9].

1 Adapted from RSC Appendix A Form No 8. See the Land Registration Act 1925 s 58 (4) (37 Halsbury's Statutes (4th Edn) REAL PROPERTY) and Paragraph 24 ante. If all parties agree to the withdrawal of the restriction, application should be made instead to the Registrar under the Land Registration Rules 1925, SR & O 1925/1093, r 236B (as inserted) (16 Halsbury's Statutory Instruments (1998 Issue) REAL PROPERTY).
2 A replica of the Royal Arms must be printed or embossed on the first page of every originating process: RSC Ord 1 r 9.
3 See RSC Appendix A Form No 8.
4 Proceedings relating to land registration are allocated to the Chancery Division: RSC Ord 93 r 10 (2)(f).
5 An originating summons commencing proceedings assigned to the Chancery Division may be issued out of a Chancery district registry: RSC Ord 7 r 5 (2).
6 See Vol 6 (1998 Issue) title ACKNOWLEDGMENT OF SERVICE Form 4.
7 Land Registration Act 1925 ss 58, 138 (as substituted).
8 RSC Ord 7 r 3 (2) applying RSC Ord 6 r 5.
9 See note 6 above.

D: BANKRUPTCY PROCEEDINGS

30
INQUIRY of registered proprietor as to whether bankruptcy proceedings affect him[1]

HM LAND REGISTRY

The .... District Land Registry
Fax: ....

PRIVATE
(*Address*)

Telephone ....
This matter is being
dealt with by ....
Date: ....

County: .... District/London Borough: ....
Title number(s): ....
Property ....

Dear ....

This letter is written to you and to others with a name similar to you, to seek your help and co-operation in identifying a person concerned with recent proceedings in the Bankruptcy Court.

If you are not the person referred to in Panel 1 I should be most grateful if you would simply complete the panel below with your signature and return this letter to me by .... 19... in the enclosed pre-paid envelope (no stamp needed). No further inquiry will then be made. If the address as shown above, under the word "PRIVATE", is incorrect or incomplete, please amend it as necessary. I will then correct the register entry accordingly.

If you are the person referred to in Panel 1 I should be most grateful if you would complete Panel 2 and likewise return this letter.

I am sorry if you have been troubled unnecessarily. I am, however, required to make these inquiries under the Land Registration Acts and Rules. Please do not hesitate to contact me by telephone or by letter if you would like any further explanation or information. I am most grateful for your co-operation in this aspect of the administration of justice.

Yours sincerely
(*Signature*)

For the Chief Land Registrar

I am not the person referred to in Panel 1
   Signature ....
   Name ....
   Date .... 19...

PANEL 1

Details of Bankruptcy proceedings

Debtor's name ....
Debtor's address ....
Debtor's occupation ....
Bankruptcy proceedings of the .... Court
Court Reference No. .... of 19...
Petition in Bankruptcy and/or Bankruptcy Order under number(s): ....

PANEL 2

I am the person referred to above to whom bankruptcy proceedings apply and
I am the proprietor of the registered title referred to on the previous page.

My address is: ....
* the address shown under the word "PRIVATE" on the previous page.
* that shown against 'property' on the previous page.
* as follows ....

(* Please delete as appropriate or insert new address in the space provided above.)

Signature ....
Name ....
Date .... 19...

(The following need not be returned with your reply)

WHY HAS THIS LETTER BEEN SENT?

When bankruptcy proceedings are commenced against a debtor, the Bankruptcy Court informs the Chief Land Registrar who is required (*) to record a note of the proceedings as soon as possible against all property which appears to belong to the debtor. The purpose of this is to protect people to whom money is owed by preventing the debtor from disposing of his or her assets and to protect prospective purchasers of the property which might be affected by the bankruptcy proceedings.

Debtors often change their addresses or are sometimes known by various names. The details known to creditors are often limited. There are often many people who have the same, or similar, names with addresses in one geographical area and the Chief Land Registrar has to make inquiries of all of them. Inquiries such as this are part of the process of administering justice and of protecting those who are owed money.

(*) under Section 61 of the Land Registration Act 1925, and Rules 179-182 of the Land Registration Rules 1925 as substituted by the Land Registration (Companies and Insolvency) Rules 1986.

WHAT HAPPENS IF YOU DO NOT REPLY TO THIS LETTER?

If you are unable for any reason to confirm within 28 days that you are NOT the person referred to, the Chief Land Registrar will have to enter notice of the proceedings on the register of your property. However, the note made on the register will be removed immediately once a letter is received from you confirming that you are not the person named in the proceedings. In these circumstances, no record would remain on the register to suggest that such an entry had ever been made.

LAND REGISTRATION: FORMS

YOUR ADDRESS ON THE REGISTER

It is always important for the register to show your current address. If this letter was not sent to your present address, but has been forwarded to you, please give your new address when you reply to this letter. You may use the same envelope.

1 Land Registration Rules 1925, SR & O 1925/1093, rr 179–182 (as substituted) (16 Halsbury's Statutory Instruments (1998 Issue) REAL PROPERTY). See Paragraph 26 ante. This inquiry enables the Registrar to decide what action to take in the case of doubt. As to the effect of registration or failure to register a creditors' notice or bankruptcy inhibition; see the Land Registration Act 1925 s 61 (as amended and as further amended by the Land Registration Act 1988 s 2, Schedule) (37 Halsbury's Statutes (4th Edn) REAL PROPERTY). For notice of entry of a creditor's notice, see Form 31 post.

31
NOTICE of registration of a creditor's notice[1]

HM LAND REGISTRY

The .... District Land Registry
Fax: ....

PRIVATE
To A.B[2].

Telephone ....
This matter is being
dealt with by ....
Date: .... 19...

NOTICE of the registration of a Creditors' Notice

Important - This letter is not a circular. Please read it carefully. If you do not know what to do, you should consider taking legal advice.

County: .... District/London Borough: ....
Title number(s): ....
Property ....
Dear ....
Your title to the property referred to above appears to be affected by a petition in bankruptcy so a Creditors' Notice has been entered on the register of your property.

Details of the petition are included in the entry, a copy of which is set out below:

.... 19... CREDITORS' NOTICE entered under Section 61 (1) of the Land Registration Act 1925 to protect the rights of all creditors, as the title of the proprietor of the land appears to be affected by a petition in bankruptcy against .... presented in the ....Court (Court Reference Number ....)(Land Charges Reference Number ....

A fuller explanation of why this entry has been made is set out below.

If further information about this petition is required you should make inquiry to the Court quoting the Court Reference Number.

No action or reply on your part is necessary unless you are not the person who is the subject of the petition in bankruptcy in which case you should contact the Land Registry without delay.

Yours sincerely
(*Signature*)

Explanatory notes

Following notification by the Bankruptcy Court, notice of a petition in bankruptcy is registered at the Land Charges Department in the debtor's name. The Chief Land Registrar must, as soon as practicable after registration of the petition, enter a Creditors' Notice in the register of every title which appears to be affected by the petition (Section 61 (1) of the Land Registration Act 1925). A Creditors' Notice is normally entered where it seems that the owner of the property is the debtor named in the petition.

The purpose of entering a Creditors' Notice is twofold: first to protect people to whom money is owed by preventing the debtor from disposing of his or her assets and secondly to protect prospective purchasers of the debtor's property.

Please note that the date inside the brackets at the beginning of the copy register entry set out above is the date on which the entry was made in the register.

1 Land Registration Act 1925 s 61 (1) (37 Halsbury's Statutes (4th Edn) REAL PROPERTY). Land Registration Rules 1925, SR & O 1925/1093, r 179 (as substituted) (16 Halsbury's Statutory Instruments (1998 Issue) REAL PROPERTY). See Paragraph 26 ante.
2 That is the address for service: Land Registration Rules 1925 r 315 (1)

32
NOTICE to registered proprietor of registration of bankruptcy inhibition[1]

HM LAND REGISTRY

The .... District Land Registry
Fax ....

PRIVATE
To A. B.[2]

Telephone ....
This matter is being dealt with by ....
Date: .... 19...

Notification of the registration of a Bankruptcy Inhibition

Important - This letter is not a circular. Please read it carefully. If you do not know what to do, you should consider taking legal advice.

County. .... District/London Borough: ....
Title number(s): ....
Property ....
Dear ....

Your title to the property referred to above appears to be affected by a bankruptcy order so a Bankruptcy Inhibition has been entered on the register of your property.

Details of the Bankruptcy order are included in the entry, a copy of which is set out below:

.... 19... BANKRUPTCY INHIBITION entered under Section 61 (3) of the Land Registration Act 1925, as the title of the proprietor of the land appears to be affected by a bankruptcy order made by the .... Court (Court Reference Number ....) against .... (Land Charges Reference Number ....).

No disposition by the proprietor of the land or transmission is to be registered until the trustee in bankruptcy of the property of the bankrupt is registered.

If further information about this petition is required you should make inquiry to the Court quoting the Court Reference Number.

No action or reply on your part is necessary unless you are not the person who is the subject of the bankruptcy order in which case you should contact the Land Registry without delay.

1 Land Registration Act 1925 s 61 (3)(as amended) (37 Halsbury's Statutes (4th Edn) REAL PROPERTY). Land Registration Rules 1925, SR & O 1925/1093, r 180 (as substituted) (16 Halsbury's Statutory Instruments (1998 Issue) REAL PROPERTY). See Paragraph 26 ante.
2 That is the address for service: Land Registration Rules 1925 r 315 (1).

33
NOTICE of application to cancel bankruptcy inhibition[1]

HM LAND REGISTRY

Land Registration Acts 1925 to 1986[2]

County and District: ....
Title No. ....
Property: (*address*) ....

To the [Official Receiver *or* Trustee in Bankruptcy] of the estate of A. B. (No. .... of 19...).

The Chief Land Registrar hereby gives notice that application has been made to him by E. F. & Co of (*address*), Solicitors, on behalf of (*name of registered proprietor or other applicant*) to cancel the bankruptcy inhibition registered in pursuance of Section 61 (3) of the Land Registration Act 1925 against the title above referred to.

If you have any objection to the proposed cancellation such objection should be made in writing to the Chief Land Registrar, HM Land Registry, Lincoln's Inn Fields, London WC2A 3PH[3], within 7 days from the date of the service of this notice, otherwise the cancellation will be duly effected.

NOTE: Your attention is directed to Rule 313 (as amended) of the Land Registration Rules 1925[4] which is as follows:

Every notice sent through the post shall, unless returned by the Post Office, be deemed to have been received by the person addressed 7 days after its issue exclusive of the day of posting, and the time fixed by the notice for taking any step thereunder is to be calculated accordingly.

DATED .... 19...

(*Land Registry Official Stamp*)

1 Land Registration Rules 1925, SR & O 1925/1093, r 181 (as substituted) (16 Halsbury's Statutory Instruments (1998 Issue) REAL PROPERTY); Land Registration Act 1925 s 61 (3) (37 Halsbury's Statutes (4th Edn) REAL PROPERTY). See Paragraph 26 ante.
2 See Form 6 note 6 ante.
3 In district registry cases the address of the district registry will be used.
4 Land Registration Rules 1925 r 313 (as substituted).

34
APPLICATION by trustee in bankruptcy for registration in place of registered proprietor and rectification of register[1]

HM LAND REGISTRY

Land Registration Acts 1925 to 1986[2]

County and District: ....
Title No. ....
Property: (*address*) ....

To the Chief Land Registrar

TAKE NOTICE that T. B. of (*address*), the trustee of the property of A. B., a bankrupt, hereby applies to be registered as proprietor of the land in the above-mentioned title and for rectification of the register for the following reasons:

1. A. B. is the registered proprietor of the land in the above-mentioned title.

2. The charge (hereinafter called "the registered charge") dated .... 19... registered on .... 19... affecting the land in the above title is expressed to secure £...... and interest and to be made in favour of C. D. who was registered as proprietor thereof on .... 19... aforesaid.

3. On .... 19... a bankruptcy order was made against A. B., and an office copy of that order is annexed hereto.

4. On .... 19... T. B. (as appears from the annexed certified office copy of his certificate of appointment by a meeting of A. B.'s creditors) was appointed trustee of the property of A. B.[3]

5. The land in the above-mentioned title is comprised in A. B.'s estate.

6. By an order of the .... Court dated .... 19... made pursuant to Section 340 of the Insolvency Act 1986, an office copy of which order is annexed to this application, it was ordered that the registered charge should be discharged and cease to have effect and that the registered charge and all other deeds and documents relating to the land in the above title in the possession of C. D. should be surrendered and delivered up to T. B. .

7. The charge certificate containing the registered charge has been delivered up to T. B. in accordance with the said order and accompanies this application.

And T. B. accordingly applies to the Chief Land Registrar:

(1) for registration of himself as proprietor of the land comprised in the above title and;

(2) for rectification of the register of the above title under Section 82 (1) (a) and (d) of the Land Registration Act 1925 by the cancellation of the registered charge and of the entries in the register relating thereto.

DATED .... 19...

(*Signature*)

Solicitors for T. B.

---

1   Land Registration Rules 1925, SR & O 1925/1093, r 176 (as substituted) (16 Halsbury's Statutory Instruments (1998 Issue) REAL PROPERTY). See Paragraph 27 ante. Notice of the application would be served on the proprietor of the charge, although it is difficult to see, in the circumstances described in the form, on what basis he could effectively object to rectification of the register. As to rectification generally see the Land Registration Act 1925 s 82 (as amended) (37 Halsbury's Statutes (4th Edn) REAL PROPERTY) and Paragraph 28 ante. See the Insolvency Act 1986 s 340 (4 Halsbury's Statutes (4th Edn) BANKRUPTCY AND INSOLVENCY).

2   See Form 6 note 6 ante.

3   The registered estate of the bankrupt belonging to him beneficially vests in the trustee without any amendment to the register: Land Registration Act 1925 s 61 (5). Although at this stage it is not essential for the trustee to apply for registration, it is necessary that the application should establish his title.

E: RECTIFICATION OF THE REGISTER

35

APPLICATION for Registrar's consent to taking of proceedings for rectification[1]

HM LAND REGISTRY

Land Registration Acts 1925 to 1986[2]

County and District: ....
Title No. ....
Property: (*address*) ....

We, G. H. & Co of (*address*), as solicitors for C. D. of (*address*), beg to inform you that we have been instructed to begin proceedings[3] in the High Court of Justice against A. B. of (*address*) (the registered proprietor of the land referred to above), with a view to obtaining an order for rectification of the register of the said title. In the event of C. D. failing in his action it may become necessary for us to advise him to claim to be indemnified under Section 83 of the Land Registration Act 1925. We therefore beg to apply for your formal consent to proceedings being taken as aforesaid for the purpose of Section 83 (5)(c) of the Land Registration Act 1925. The nature of the relief and the grounds upon which it will be sought are: (*set out shortly the nature of the claim and the reasons for making it*).

(*Signature*)

of (*address*), Solicitors for C. D.

1 Land Registration Act 1925 s 83 (5)(c)(as substituted by the Land Registration Act 1997 s 2) (37 Halsbury's Statutes (4th Edn) REAL PROPERTY). See Paragraphs 29, 33 ante. No form is prescribed; this form may readily be adapted for an application for consent to defend legal proceedings. Note also that the substituted subsection now provides that no indemnity is to be payable on account of costs *of whatever nature* incurred without the consent of the Registrar; see Paragraph 33 ante. An exception to this general rule is made when, by reason of urgency it is not practicable to apply for consent before any costs are incurred provided the Registrar subsequently approves the costs. For a consent adapt Form 36 post. No consent is required to take proceedings for the determination of questions as to the right of any person to be indemnified or as to the amount of such indemnity under the Land Registration and Land Charges Act 1971 s 2 (1) (37 Halsbury's Statutes (4th Edn) REAL PROPERTY): Land Registration and Land Charges Act 1971 s 2 (2).
2 See Form 6 note 6 ante.
3 For an originating summons see Form 37 post.

36
CONSENT by Registrar to defending of proceedings for rectification[1]

HM LAND REGISTRY

Land Registration Acts 1925 to 1986[2]

County and District: ....
Title No. ....
Property: (*address*) ....

To G. H. & Co of (*address*)

For the purpose of Section 83 (5)(c) of the Land Registration Act 1925 the Chief Land Registrar hereby consents to your clients defending the action in the Chancery Division of the High Court of Justice between A. B. and C. D. (Ch 19... B. No...).

Your attention is drawn to the fact that, whereas the absence of a consent such as is given above is a bar to a successful claim for indemnity on account of costs, nevertheless the giving of such consent does not mean that the costs of the person so applying or any other sum will be recoverable as a matter of course. In order to succeed a claim must arise from a loss for which indemnity is payable under the provisions of the Land Registration Acts 1925 to 1986[3].

DATED .... 19...

(*Signature*)

[Assistant] Land Registrar[4]

---

1 Land Registration Act 1925 s 83 (5)(c)(as substituted by the Land Registration Act 1997 s 2) (37 Halsbury's Statutes (4th Edn) REAL PROPERTY). See Paragraphs 29, 33 ante. For an application for consent, see Form 35 ante.
2 See Form 6 note 6 ante.
3 For cases where indemnity is payable see Paragraph 32 ante.
4 The modern practice is for the consent to be embodied in a formal letter signed by a land registrar or assistant land registrar acting under the authority of the Chief Land Registrar. Consent may in practice be made conditional for example upon the person to whom it is given lodging copies of all subsequent pleadings as they are served, or it may be limited to the taking of certain steps as to the incurring of expenditure up to a certain limit.

37
ORIGINATING SUMMONS for rectification of register[1]
(Royal Arms)[2]

IN THE HIGH COURT OF JUSTICE   Ch 19 ... B. No. ...[3]
Chancery Division[4]
[......... District Registry[5]]

Between	A. B.	...	Plaintiff
	and		
	C. D.	...	Defendant

To C. D. of (address)

LET the Defendant within ... days after service of this summons on him, counting the day of service, return the accompanying Acknowledgment of Service[6] to the appropriate Court Office.

By this Summons, which is issued on the application of the Plaintiff A. B. of (address), the Plaintiff seeks as against the Defendant, who is registered as the proprietor of the land comprised in the registered Title No ..., the following relief, namely:

1. An order under Section 82 of the Land Registration Act 1925 that the proprietorship register of the above-mentioned title be rectified by the reinstatement of the Plaintiff as proprietor of the land in place of the Defendant and that the charges register of the title be rectified by the reinstatement of the registration of a charge dated .... 19... and the registration of the Defendant as proprietor thereof on the ground that a right of redemption is subsisting in favour of the Plaintiff under the charge;

2. That the costs of this application may be provided for; and

3. Such further or other relief as may be requisite.

This application is made under Sections 82 and 138 of the Land Registration Act 1925[7].

If the Defendant does not acknowledge service, such judgment may be given or order made against or in relation to him as the Court may think just and expedient.

DATED .... 19...

NOTE—This Summons may not be served later than [4, *or if leave is required to effect service out of the jurisdiction*, 6] calendar months beginning with the above date unless renewed by order of the Court.

This Summons was taken out by E. F. & Co of (address), [Agents for (name) of (address),] Solicitors for the said Plaintiff whose address is as stated above[8].

IMPORTANT

Directions for acknowledgment of service are given with the accompanying form[9].

---

1 Land Registration Act 1925 s 82 (1)(f) (37 Halsbury's Statutes (4th Edn) REAL PROPERTY); Paragraph 28 ante. If he has not already done so, the plaintiff would be advised to register a caution against dealings under the Land Registration Act 1925 s 54 (as amended) but in any event, upon receipt of such an application the Registrar will see that it is entered on the registry's day list which contains details of all pending applications so ensuring that it will come to the attention of any person who conducts a search against the title for any reason; see Paragraph 20 ante and Forms 18–23 ante. For supporting affidavit and an order see Forms 38, 39 post.

2 A replica of the Royal Arms must be printed or embossed on the first page of every originating process: RSC Ord 1 r 9.

3 See RSC Appendix A Form No 8.
4 Proceedings relating to land registration are allocated to the Chancery Division: RSC Ord 93 r 10 (2)(f).
5 An originating summons commencing proceedings assigned to the Chancery Division may be issued out of a Chancery district registry: RSC Ord 7 r 5 (2).
6 See Vol 6 (1998 Issue) title ACKNOWLEDGMENT OF SERVICE Form 4.
7 Land Registration Act 1925 s 138 (as substituted).
8 RSC Ord 7 r 3 (2) applying RSC Ord 6 r 5.
9 See note 6 above.

38
AFFIDAVIT supporting originating summons for rectification of register[1]

Plaintiff: A. B.: 1st: .... 19...A.B.1[2]

IN THE HIGH COURT OF JUSTICE   Ch 19 ... B. No. ...[3]
Chancery Division[4]
[......... District Registry[5]]

Between   A. B.   ...   Plaintiff
and
C. D.   ...   Defendant

I, A. B. of (*state residence or workplace and occupation or, if none, description*), the Plaintiff in this action, make oath and say as follows:

1. By a charge dated .... 19... I charged the land comprised in the registered Title No ..., of which I was then the registered proprietor and to which I was then beneficially entitled, as security for the sum of £...... then advanced to me by J. K. together with interest at the rate of ... % per annum and the said charge was duly registered[6] on .... 19... with the said J. K. as proprietor thereof.

2. The charge contained a covenant by me for repayment of the sum of £...... on .... 19... and for payment of the interest until such repayment by weekly payments of £....... .

3. Owing to financial difficulties caused by illness, for the treatment of which I was admitted to hospital on .... 19..., I ceased to make the weekly payments of interest to J. K. at that date.

4. On or about .... 19... J. K. entered into possession of the land and thereafter let the same and received the rents and profits thereof.

5. On or about .... 19... I paid to J. K. a sum of £...... on account of the interest then in arrear under the charge and his receipt therefor is now produced to me and marked "A.B.1".

6. On .... 19... J. K. died, and on .... 19... probate of his will was granted to the Defendant out of the .... Probate Registry.

7. On .... 19... the Defendant applied to the Chief Land Registrar for registration of himself as proprietor of the land[7]. Such application was based upon a deed poll of the Defendant C. D. dated .... 19... whereby he declared as to the default in the payment of interest under the charge, the entry of J. K. into possession as aforesaid and the receipt of rents and profits from the land by J. K. and subsequently by the Defendant as his personal representative, and as to his belief that neither I nor any other person claiming through me was entitled to redeem the charge. The application was supported by evidence by way of statutory declaration by one M. N. as to the entry upon the land, receipt of the rents and profits and as to the

possession having been continuous and undisputed. The evidence produced to the Chief Land Registrar did not, however, reveal the aforesaid payment of £...... made by me on account of interest. The registration of the Defendant as proprietor of the land and the cancellation of the entries relating to the charge was completed as at the date of the application, namely, ... 19... aforesaid.

8. On .... 19... I was discharged from hospital, having been continuously under treatment there since my admittance as aforesaid, and I thereupon sought possession of the land from the Defendant and offered to resume the weekly payments of interest under the charge and to pay the arrears of interest thereunder by additional weekly payments of £......, but the Defendant alleged that I had no further interest in the land and refused to give me possession thereof or to accept my offer regarding interest and the arrears thereof.

> SWORN at (address), on
> .... 19...
> Before me,
> (Signature)

(Deponent's signature)[8]

A [Solicitor or Barrister or Notary Public or Commissioner for Oaths][9]

1 Land Registration Act 1925 s 82 (1)(f) (37 Halsbury's Statutes (4th Edn) REAL PROPERTY). See Paragraph 29 ante. For an originating summons see Form 37 ante.
2 See Form 7 note 2 ante.
3 See Form 6 note 3 ante.
4 See Form 6 note 4 ante.
5 See Form 6 note 5 ante.
6 The charge was created under the Land Registration Act 1925 s 25 (as amended) and registered under Land Registration Act 1925 s 26.
7 The application for registration was made on a declaration under Land Registration Act 1925 s 34 (2). See also Land Registration Act 1925 s 34 (4), (5), the Limitation Act 1980 s 16 (24 Halsbury's Statutes (4th Edn) LIMITATION OF ACTIONS) and the Land Registration Rules 1925, SR & O 1925/1093, r 149 (16 Halsbury's Statutory Instruments (1998 Issue) REAL PROPERTY). The basis of this allegation is that the payment of interest referred to in paragraph 5 prevented the acquisition of title by the chargee (J. K.) and his successor in title (C. D.) under the Limitation Act 1980.
8 Every affidavit must be signed by the deponent and must be completed and signed by the person before whom it is sworn: RSC Ord 41 r 2 (1).
9 Solicitors Act 1974 s 81 (as amended) (41 Halsbury's Statutes (4th Edn) SOLICITORS); Courts and Legal Services Act 1990 s 113 (17 Halsbury's Statutes (4th Edn) EVIDENCE); Administration of Justice Act 1985 s 65 (31 Halsbury's Statutes (4th Edn) NOTARIES AND LICENSED CONVEYANCERS); Commissioners for Oaths Acts 1889 and 1891 (as amended) (17 Halsbury's Statutes (4th Edn) EVIDENCE).

39
ORDER for rectification of register[1]

IN THE HIGH COURT OF JUSTICE   Ch 19 ... B. No. ...[2]
Chancery Division[3]
[......... District Registry[4]]
Mr Justice ....
.... 19...

Between	A. B.	...	Plaintiff
	and		
	C. D.	...	Defendant

UPON THE APPLICATION of the Plaintiff by Originating Summons
AND UPON HEARING Counsel for the Plaintiff and for the Defendant
AND UPON READING the documents on the Court File recorded as having been read
[AND UPON HEARING oral evidence]
AND IT APPEARING by the evidence aforesaid that a right of redemption under the above-mentioned charge is subsisting in favour of the Plaintiff and that the Defendant has been registered in error as proprietor of the above-mentioned land[5]
IT IS ORDERED
1. that the register of the above-mentioned title be rectified by cancelling in the proprietorship register the registration of the Defendant as proprietor of the land and registering the Plaintiff as proprietor of the land as at the date upon which he was formerly registered as such proprietor and by registering in the charges register the above-mentioned charge as at the date upon which it was formerly so registered and by registering in the same register the Defendant as proprietor of the charge as at the date upon which he was formerly registered as proprietor of the land
2. that the Defendant do within [7] days from the date of the entry of this Order deliver up to the Chief Land Registrar the land certificate in respect of the title [and the charge] for the before-ordered rectification to be carried into effect[6]

(*Add order as to costs and otherwise as appropriate*)

---

1 Land Registration Act 1925 s 82 (1) (37 Halsbury's Statutes (4th Edn) REAL PROPERTY). See Paragraph 30 ante. For an originating summons see Form 37 ante.
2 See Form 6 note 3 ante.
3 See Form 6 note 4 ante.
4 See Form 6 note 5 ante.
5 Land Registration Act 1925 s 34 (2). See Form 38 note 3 ante.
6 Land Registration Act 1925 s 82 (6). See Paragraph 29 ante. The original charge, if available, will be required in order for it to be taken into the fresh charge certificate. Land Registration Rules 1925, SR & O 1925/1093, r 262 (as amended) (16 Halsbury's Statutory Instruments (1998 Issue) REAL PROPERTY).

40
APPLICATION for rectification by excluding land from adjoining owner's title and including it in applicant's title[1]

HM LAND REGISTRY

Land Registration Acts 1925 to 1986[2]

County and District: ....
Title Nos. .... and ....
Properties: .... and ....

We, E. F. & Co of (*address*), as Solicitors for A. B. of (*address*) (hereinafter called "the Applicant"), hereby apply to the Chief Land Registrar to rectify the register of Title No. .... above mentioned by excluding therefrom and from the filed plan thereof the strip of land ... metres wide which is tinted blue on the plan annexed hereto (hereinafter called "the blue land") and to rectify the register of Title No. .... above mentioned by including therein and in the filed plan thereof the blue land. This application is made on the following grounds:

1. On 1 February 1984 the Applicant applied for registration as first proprietor with absolute title of the freehold land and dwelling-house known as "Mayfield", (*address*) (which premises include the blue land and which with the blue land are hereinafter referred to as "Mayfield"). Registration with absolute title under Title No. .... was duly completed, subject only to certain incumbrances that are not material to this application. It is clear from an inspection of the filed plan of Title No. .... that that title does not include the blue land, and the Applicant was informed when the land certificate was issued to him that the blue land was not included because it had been previously registered with possessory title under Title No. .... aforesaid.

2. The following is a summary of the title of the Applicant which was examined by the Registrar and which induced first registration of the Applicant:

14 January 1919	Conveyance (1) J. K.; (2) L. M.
28 February 1923	Conveyance (1) L. M.; (2) N. O.
24 August 1956	Probate of will of N. O. granted to X. O. and Y. O.
12 April 1957	Conveyance (1) X. O. and Y. O.; (2) P. Q.
12 April 1957	Mortgage (1) P. Q.; (2) R. S.
19 January 1984	Receipt indorsed on mortgage
19 January 1984	Conveyance (1) P. Q.; (2) the Applicant

3. The conveyances of 14 January 1919 and 28 February 1923 comprised Mayfield and also other land which was conveyed by reference to the respective plans drawn thereon. The conveyance of 12 April 1957 conveyed Mayfield by reference to the plan drawn thereon, and that deed and those subsequent to it were produced to the Registrar at the time of the before-mentioned application for first registration.

4. From the date of the conveyance of 19 January 1984 until the date of the happening of the events mentioned in the next Paragraph hereof the Applicant was continuously in actual and undisputed possession of the whole of Mayfield and he is still in actual and undisputed possession of the whole

of Mayfield except for the blue land and he claims that he is still in actual (though not undisputed) possession of the blue land[3].

5. On or about 16 November 1997 the Applicant found that one C. D. (whom he had known as the ostensible owner of the land and dwellinghouse situate on the east side of Mayfield and known as "Lamorna", (*address*) had begun to erect a brick-built garage upon part of the blue land. The Applicant immediately informed C. D. that the blue land belonged to the Applicant and that C. D. was trespassing, and required C. D. to remove all bricks, building materials and tools from the land, but C. D. claimed that the blue land belonged to him. Subsequently the Applicant and C. D. consulted their respective solicitors; copies of all letters sent by E. F. & Co, the Applicant's solicitors, to C. D., and to G. H. & Co, his solicitors, as well as those received by E. F. & Co, accompany this application.

6. The Applicant has now learnt that the title of C. D. to Lamorna aforesaid is registered with possessory freehold title[4] at HM Land Registry under Title No. .... and that such title includes the blue land, as is apparent from the inspection of the filed plan thereof. The Applicant understands that the title of C. D. was registered merely upon the strength of a statutory declaration that he was in possession of Lamorna aforesaid at the time of applying for registration.

The Applicant accordingly applies to the Chief Land Registrar to rectify the register and filed plans of Titles Nos. .... and .... respectively in manner aforesaid pursuant to Section 82 (1)(g) and (h) of the Land Registration Act 1925[5] and Rule 14 of the Land Registration Rules 1925[6] on the grounds that he is the only person entitled thereto and that C. D. has not acquired any title in respect thereof by adverse possession.

7. The land certificate relating to Title No. .... is enclosed with this application[7].

(*Signature*)
of (*address*), Solicitors for
A. B.

To the Chief Land Registrar of (*address*)

1 Land Registration Act 1925 s 82 (1) (37 Halsbury's Statutes (4th Edn) REAL PROPERTY); Land Registration Rules 1925, SR & O 1925/1093, r 14 (16 Halsbury's Statutory Instruments (1998 Issue) REAL PROPERTY). See Paragraphs 28, 30, 31 ante. The form is not prescribed, but it is advisable to use the heading and set out the grounds in numbered paragraphs as in this example. Notice of the application will be given to all persons appearing from the register to be interested; see Form 41 post.
2 See Form 6 note 6 ante.
3 As to the significance of possession see the Land Registration Act 1925 s 82 (3)(as amended) and Paragraph 29 ante. For the effect of a first registration with a possessory title to the freehold see the Land Registration Act 1925 s 6 and Paragraph 19 ante.
4 See note 3 above.
5 Land Registration Act 1925 s 82 (1)(g), (h). See Paragraph 28 ante.
6 See Paragraph 30 ante.
7 Land Registration Act 1925 s 82 (6). See Paragraph 30 ante.

41
NOTICE to registered proprietor of application to rectify register[1]

HM LAND REGISTRY

Land Registration Acts 1925 to 1986[2]

County and District: ....
Title Nos. .... and ....
Properties: .... and ....

To C. D. of (*address for service entered on register*[3])

NOTICE

E. F. & Co of (*address*), as solicitors for A. B. of (*address*) (hereinafter called "the Applicant"), have applied to the Chief Land Registrar for rectification of the register of the above-mentioned title, of which you are registered as proprietor with a possessory freehold title, by the removal from the filed plan thereof of the land which is tinted blue on the plan annexed hereto (hereinafter referred to as "the blue land"). The application is made pursuant to Section 82 (1)(g), (h) of the Land Registration Act 1925[4] and Rule 14 of the Land Registration Rules 1925[5].

The grounds on which the application has been made are as follows: (*set out the grounds of the application*).

If you have no objection to the application you are requested to deliver immediately to the Chief Land Registrar the land certificate in respect of the above title[6]. A pre-paid addressed envelope which requires no stamp is enclosed for this purpose.

If, however, you have any objection to the application, notice of the objection[7] setting out fully the grounds on which it is based should be delivered at the Registry within a period of **[14]** days from the date of the service of this notice. If no objection is received within this period, the application may be completed and the blue land removed from the filed plan of Title No. ....

DATED .... 19...

NOTE: Your attention is directed to Rule 313 (as amended) of the Land Registration Rules 1925[8] which is as follows:

Every notice sent through the post shall, unless returned by the Post Office, be deemed to have been received by the person addressed 7 days after its issue exclusive of the day of posting, and the time fixed by the notice for taking any step thereunder is to be calculated accordingly.

1 Land Registration Act 1925 s 82 (1) (37 Halsbury's Statutes (4th Edn) REAL PROPERTY); Land Registration Rules 1925, SR & O 1925/1093, r 14 (16 Halsbury's Statutory Instruments (1998 Issue) REAL PROPERTY). See Paragraphs 20, 31 ante.
2 See Form 6 note 6 ante.
3 Land Registration Rules 1925 r 315.
4 See Paragraph 28 ante.
5 See Paragraph 31 ante.
6 Land Registration Act 1925 s 82 (6). See Paragraph 30 ante.
7 See Form 42 post.
8 See Form 16 note 6 ante.

42

OBJECTION by registered proprietor to rectification of register[1]

HM LAND REGISTRY

Land Registration Acts 1925 to 1986[2]

County and District: ....
Title Nos. .... and ....
Properties: .... and ....

We, G. H. & Co of (*address*), as Solicitors for C. D. of (*address*) (hereinafter called "the Objector"), in answer to the Application by A. B. (hereinafter called "the Applicant") for rectification of the register and filed plan of the Objector's Title No. .... above-mentioned object to such rectification because:

1. The Objector is legally and beneficially entitled to the land shown and tinted blue on the plan attached to the Chief Land Registrar's notice dated .... 19... (hereinafter called "the blue land").

2. The Objector has enjoyed possession of the blue land openly without interruption or objection by any person and without permission from any person for nearly 20 years[3].

3. The Applicant is not and has never been in possession of the blue land. For these reasons and in reliance upon the facts stated in the Schedule hereto, the Objector claims that the register and filed plan of Title No. .... of which the Objector is the registered proprietor should not be rectified by the exclusion of the blue land therefrom.

SCHEDULE

STATEMENT OF FACTS

1. The Objector purchased the freehold land of which he is now registered as proprietor with possessory title[4] under Title No. .... aforesaid on or about .... 19... from X. O. and Y. O., who conveyed it to him as personal representatives of N. O. deceased.

2. The conveyance to the Applicant contained a plan from which (as well as from the parcels) it was apparent that such conveyance comprised the blue land as part of the messuage and premises known as Lamorna, (*address*), now comprised in the Objector's title. The blue land and the remainder of Lamorna are hereinafter together referred to as "Lamorna".

3. The earlier title of the Objector's vendors to Lamorna is a common title with the earlier title of the Applicant to the adjoining property known as Mayfield, as disclosed in his application.

4. From the date of his purchase in .... 19... until .... 19... the Objector remained continuously in undisputed possession of Lamorna, but at no time during that period had there been a wall, fence, hedge or ditch marking the boundary between Lamorna and Mayfield. The houses on both plots were erected during the summer of the year 19..., and at some time in the year 19... the Objector and one P. Q. (who was then the occupier of Mayfield and with whom the Objector was on friendly terms) agreed orally that for the purpose of maintaining an unhindered aspect from the rear of their respective houses no hedge should be grown or fence or wall erected between their properties.

5. In or about the month of .... 19... the Objector built a tool shed on part of the blue land which remained there until he removed it and erected it in another part of the garden of Lamorna in the year 19... . The Objector did not seek permission from any person before erecting this shed, nor did P. Q. at any time object to its being erected or kept on the blue land.

6. In the autumn of the year 19... the Objector (wishing to refer to his title deeds of Lamorna in connection with restrictive covenants affecting the same) was unable to find them or any of them in spite of exhaustive search and inquiries, and he could not then and cannot now account for their loss. Further, he was unable to obtain secondary evidence of their contents because the offices of his Solicitors, G. H. & Co, at (*address*) (where a completed draft of the conveyance to him and other papers relevant to his title had been kept), were with all the contents thereof, totally destroyed by fire on the night of .... 19... .

7. As a result of the circumstances described in the preceding Paragraph hereof the Objector by his Solicitors applied on .... 19... for registration of his title to Lamorna at HM Land Registry with absolute title and then lodged in support of his application two statutory declarations[5], which were filed in the Registry. The Chief Land Registrar declined to register the Objector with absolute title but subsequently granted the Objector a possessory title[6].

8. On .... 19... the Objector began to erect a brick-built garage upon part of the blue land and the Applicant then for the first time informed the Objector that he claimed the blue land as part of Mayfield.

DATED .... 19...

(*Signature*)

of (*address*), Solicitors for the Objector.

1   Land Registration Act 1925 s 82 (1) (37 Halsbury's Statutes (4th Edn) REAL PROPERTY). See Paragraph 30 ante. There is no prescribed form but it is desirable to use the heading and set out the grounds in numbered paragraphs as in this example. The use of a schedule may be found convenient. For the application and notice see Forms 40, 41 ante.

2   See Form 6 note 6 ante.

3   As to the significance of possession see the Land Registration Act 1925 s 82 (3)(as amended) and Paragraph 29 ante.

4   For the effect of registration of freehold land with a possessory title see the Land Registration Act 1925 s 6 and Paragraph 19 ante.

5   Where an applicant for registration has no title deeds in his possession a statutory declaration may be accepted as prima facie evidence of his right to apply if the Registrar is satisfied on inquiry or otherwise that the applicant is in possession: Land Registration Rules 1925, SR & O 1925/1093, r 37 (as amended) (16 Halsbury's Statutory Instruments (1998 Issue) REAL PROPERTY).

6   Land Registration Act 1925 s 4; *Dennis v Malcolm* [1934] Ch 244.

43
ORDER by Registrar for rectification of register[1]
HM LAND REGISTRY

Land Registration Acts 1925 to 1986[2]

Land Registration (Conduct of Business) Regulations 1997

ORDER BY THE SOLICITOR TO HM LAND REGISTRY

Title No. ………
County and District ………
Property: (*address*)

In the Matter of the application by A. B. of (*address*) (the Applicant), pursuant to Section 82 (1) (g) and (h) of the Land Registration Act 1925 and Rule 14 of the Land Registration Rules 1925, to rectify the register of Title No. ……… above-mentioned by removing therefrom and from the filed plan thereof a certain strip of land and to rectify the register of Title No. ……… by including therein and in the filed plan thereof the strip of land, to which application C. D., of (*address*) (the Objector) made objection

AFTER HEARING Counsel for the Applicant and for the Objector

IT IS ORDERED that the register of Title No. ……… be rectified by removing therefrom and from the filed plan thereof the strip of land of even width … metres lying immediately to the east of and co-extensive with the common boundary of the land in that title and in Title No. ……… and that the register of Title No. ……… be rectified by including therein and in the filed plan thereof the strip of land

AND IT IS FURTHER ORDERED that the Applicant and the Objector do produce to the Chief Land Registrar the land certificates of Title Nos. ……… and ……… respectively within a period of 21 days from the date of this order[3]

AND IT IS FURTHER ORDERED that the costs of and incidental to this hearing be borne by the Objector and that in default of agreement such costs be taxed on the standard basis[4].

DATED ……… 19…

(*Signature*)

Chief Land Registrar

(*Land Registry Seal*)

---

1 Land Registration Act 1925 s 82 (1) (37 Halsbury's Statutes (4th Edn) REAL PROPERTY); Land Registration Rules 1925, SR & O 1925/1093, r 14 (16 Halsbury's Statutory Instruments (1998 Issue) REAL PROPERTY). See Paragraphs 28, 30, 31 ante. This is the form of order following a hearing by the Registrar. Where the Registrar makes an order for rectification without a hearing the order will contain recitals setting forth the relevant facts and the Registrar's reasons for rectifying the register including the view that there is not a sustainable objection to the rectification application. Whether or not there has been a hearing, any party aggrieved by the order may appeal to the court under Land Registration Rules 1925 r 299. For the application and an objection see Forms 40, 42 ante. For a reference to the court see Form 45 post. For an originating motion on appeal to the court, see Form 44 post.
2 See Form 6 note 6 ante.
3 Land Registration Act 1925 s 82 (6). See Paragraph 30 ante.
4 As to costs see Paragraph 34 ante.

44

ORIGINATING MOTION on appeal from order by Registrar for rectification of the register[1]

(*Royal Arms*)[2]

IN THE HIGH COURT OF JUSTICE   Ch 19... No. ...[3]
   Chancery Division[4]
      [......... District Registry[5]]

In the Matter of the Land Registration Acts 1925 to 1986[6]

And in the Matter of an Order of the [Chief Land Registrar *or* Solicitor to HM Land Registry] made thereunder on .... 19...

TAKE NOTICE that the High Court of Justice, Chancery Division, at the Royal Courts of Justice, Strand, London WC2A 2LL, will be moved before the Honourable Mr Justice .... at the expiration of ... days[7] from the service upon you of this notice or so soon thereafter as Counsel can be heard, by Counsel on behalf of A. B., for the following relief, namely:

   1. An order that the order[8] dated .... 19... of the [Chief Land Registrar *or* Solicitor to HM Land Registry] that the register of Title No. .... be rectified by removing therefrom and from the filed plan thereof the strip of land of even width ... metres lying immediately to the east of and co-extensive with the common boundary of the land in that title and in Title No. .... and that the register of Title No. .... be rectified by including therein and in the filed plan thereof the strip of land may be discharged.

   2. A declaration that A. B. has acquired a title by adverse possession to the strip of land more particularly described in the order of the Chief Land Registrar pursuant to the provisions of the Limitation Act 1980[9].

   3. An order that the costs and expenses properly incurred by A. B. in relation to the application to the [Chief Land Registrar *or* Solicitor to HM Land Registry] and the costs of and incidental to this appeal may be provided for.

This application is made under Section 138 of the Land Registration Act 1925 and Rule 299 of the Land Registration Rules 1925[10].

And further take notice that the grounds of this appeal are[11]:

   (1) The [Chief Land Registrar *or* Solicitor to HM Land Registry] was wrong in deciding as a fact that A. B. had not by himself and his predecessors in title enjoyed uninterrupted possession of the land adversely to C. D. and his predecessors in title for upwards of 20 years.

   (2) The [Chief Land Registrar *or* Solicitor to HM Land Registry] was wrong in deciding as a fact that A. B. had acknowledged C. D.'s title to the land.

   (3) The [Chief Land Registrar *or* Solicitor to HM Land Registry] was wrong in deciding as a matter of law that A. B. had not acquired a title to the land by adverse possession pursuant to the provisions of the Limitation Act 1980.

   (4) The order dated .... 19... of the [Chief Land Registrar *or* Solicitor to HM Land Registry] was in all other respects wrong in giving effect to C. D.'s application for rectification of the register.

   DATED .... 19...[12]

                                           (*Signature*)[13]

   E. F. and Co of (*address*), [Agents for (*name*) of (*address*),] Solicitors for the above named A. B. whose address is (*address*)[14]

   To C. D. of (*address*)

1   For the form of the order appealed against, see Form 43 ante. For the practice see Paragraphs 28, 29, 30, 31 ante. See also the Land Registration Act 1925 s 138 (as substituted) (37 Halsbury's Statutes (4th Edn) REAL PROPERTY); Land Registration Rules 1925, SR & O 1925/1093, r 299 (16 Halsbury's Statutory Instruments (1998 Issue) REAL PROPERTY). Notice of the motion should be served on the Chief Land Registrar: RSC Ord 55 r 4 (1)(b).
2   A replica of the Royal Arms must be printed or embossed on the first page of every originating process: RSC Ord 1 r 9.
3   See RSC Appendix A Form No 13.
4   Proceedings relating to land registration are allocated to the Chancery Division: RSC Ord 93 r 10 (2)(f).
5   A notice of originating motion commencing proceedings assigned to the Chancery Division may be issued out of a Chancery district registry: RSC Ord 8 r 3 (5).
6   Land Registration Acts 1925–1986 (37 Halsbury's Statutes (4th Edn) REAL PROPERTY).
7   Unless the court otherwise directs, the appeal may not be heard sooner than 21 days after the service of notice of the motion by which the appeal is brought: RSC Ord 55 r 5. The notice must be served and the appeal entered within 28 days after notice of the order appealed against has been received by the appellant: RSC Ord 55 r 4 (2), (4). A notice of motion is entered in the Crown Office, Royal Courts of Justice, Strand, London WC2A 2LL, together with two copies and the requisite fee. For the fee see the current Atkin's Directory of Costs and Fees.
8   For the order appealed against, see Form 43 ante. The originating motion will be supported by an affidavit setting out the relevant facts which were stated in Forms 40, 42 ante, and exhibiting an office copy of the Registrar's order. For a form of affidavit which may be adapted for this purpose, see Form 7 ante.
9   For the application of the Limitation Act 1980 (24 Halsbury's Statutes (4th Edn) LIMITATION OF ACTIONS) to land the title to which is registered see the Land Registration Act 1925 s 75 (as amended).
10 See note 1 above.
11 The grounds of appeal set out here are merely examples and are not necessarily the grounds which would be relied upon by a party who had objected in the terms of Form 42 ante. However, the court may allow or require further evidence to be adduced on questions of fact, see Paragraph 9 ante.
12 See RSC Appendix A Form No 13.
13 See RSC Appendix A Form No 13.
14 RSC Ord 8 r 5 (3) applying RSC Ord 6 r 5.

45
ORDER by Registrar referring to court matter arising on application for rectification[1]

HM LAND REGISTRY

Land Registration Acts 1925 to 1986[2]

Land Registration (Conduct of Business) Regulations 1997

ORDER BY THE SOLICITOR HM LAND REGISTRY

Title No. ....
County and District ....
Property: (*address*)

WHEREAS:

1. On .... 19... C. D. was registered as first proprietor with possessory title of the freehold property known as (*address*) under Title No. ....

2. A. B. claims that he is the owner in fee simple of a strip of land of even width ... metres lying immediately to the east of and co-extensive with the

common boundary of the land in the title and the land in Title No. ....
and has accordingly applied, under Section 82 (1) (g) and (h) of the Land Registration Act 1925 and Rule 14 of the Land Registration Rules 1925[3], to the Chief Land Registrar to rectify the register of Title No. .... by removing therefrom and from the filed plan thereof the strip of land and to rectify the register of Title No. .... of which A. B. is registered as proprietor with title absolute by adding thereto and to the filed plan thereof the strip of land.

3. C. D. has objected to the application.

NOW THEREFORE IT IS HEREBY ORDERED that the matter be referred for the decision of a Judge of the Chancery Division of the High Court of Justice pursuant to the Rules of the Supreme Court, Order 93, Rule 10, in accordance with the provisions in that behalf contained in Rule 298 (2) of the Land Registration Rules 1925 as applied by the Land Registration (Conduct of Business) Regulations 1997 and that A. B., within [6] weeks from the date hereof, take out an originating summons or such other originating process as may be appropriate[4] and do serve such originating process upon C. D within a further 2 weeks thereafter for the purpose of bringing the matter before the Court[5] and in particular for the purpose of determining whether the register of Title No. .... and the Register of Title No. .... should be rectified in accordance with the application of A. B. as aforesaid.

AND IT IS FURTHER ORDERED that the costs be dealt with as directed by the Court.

DATED .... 19...

(Signature)
Solicitor HM Land Registry
(Land Registry Seal)

To A. B., of *(address)*

1 Land Registration Rules 1925, SR & O 1925/1093, r 298 (2) (16 Halsbury's Statutory Instruments (1998 Issue) REAL PROPERTY). See Paragraphs 7, 30 ante. For the jurisdiction of the Solicitor to HM Land Registry, see Land Registration (Conduct of Business) Regulations 1997, SI 1997/713, regs 3, 4. As to rectification see the Land Registration Act 1925 s 82 (1) (37 Halsbury's Statutes (4th Edn) REAL PROPERTY), the Land Registration Rules 1925 r 14 and Paragraphs 28, 30, 31 ante. For an order made by the Registrar himself see Form 43 ante. In an appropriate case rectification may be sought direct from the court; see Form 37 ante.
2 See Form 6 note 6 ante.
3 See note 1 above.
4 If fraud is alleged the proceedings must be commenced by writ: *Re 462 Green Lane, Ilford, Gooding v Borland* [1971] 1 All ER 315, [1971] 1 WLR 138.
5 For the procedure on a reference to the court, see RSC Ord 93 r 10 and Paragraph 7 ante. For an originating summons see Form 25 ante, which may be adapted.

F: INDEMNITY FOR LOSS

46
CLAIM for indemnity for loss[1]
HM Land Registry

Land Registration Acts 1925 to 1986[2]

County and District: ………
Title No. ………
Property: (*address*) ………

We, E. F. & Co of (*address*), as Solicitors for the Official Receiver who is the trustee of the property of A. B., a bankrupt, hereby give notice that the estate and assets of the bankrupt have suffered a loss by reason of the failure of the Chief Land Registrar to register a creditors' notice [and a bankruptcy inhibition] against the title above mentioned whereby the Official Receiver claims that he is entitled to be indemnified.

We accordingly hereby apply to the Chief Land Registrar for the Official Receiver as trustee aforesaid to be indemnified for such a loss under the provisions of Sections 61 (7) and 83 of the Land Registration Act 1925[3].

This application is made on the following grounds:

1. A. B. of (*address and occupation*), was registered as a proprietor of the title above mentioned on ……… 19… .

2. A petition in bankruptcy was presented by his creditors against A. B., who was therein described as A. B. (male) of (*address and description*) in the [High Court of Justice] on ……… 19… . An application to register the petition as a pending action was sent by the Registrar in Bankruptcy of the High Court of Justice on ……… 19… to the Land Charges Superintendent at HM Land Registry and was acknowledged to have been received on ……… 19… .[4]

3. On ……… 19… the petition was registered in the register of pending actions kept under the Land Charges Act 1972[5], but the Chief Land Registrar did not then and has not since registered a creditors' notice against the title above mentioned[6].

[*Add if appropriate.*

4. A bankruptcy order was made on the said petition on ……… 19… and was sent at once by the Registrar in Bankruptcy of the High Court of Justice to the Official Receiver. An application to register the Order in the register of writs and orders affecting land was sent by the Official Receiver on ……… 19… to the Land Charges Superintendent at HM Land Registry and was acknowledged to have been received on ……… 19… .[7]

5. On ……… 19… the Order was registered in the register of writs and orders affecting land kept under the Land Charges Act 1972, but the Chief Land Registrar did not then and has not since registered an inhibition against the title above mentioned[8].]

6. G. H. & Co of (*address*), as Solicitors on behalf of one C. D. to whom A. B. had agreed to sell the above-mentioned land, applied for an official search of the title referred to above on ……… 19… . The official certificate of the result thereof dated ……… 19… disclosed no entries relating to the bankruptcy proceedings against the said A. B. .

7. The sale to C. D. was completed on .... 19... in consideration of £...... then paid as to £...... to P. Q. (the proprietor of a charge dated .... 19... and registered on .... 19...) and as to £...... to A. B. . The transfer to C. D. was completed by registration on .... 19... pursuant to the priority conferred by the search[9], and the entry of the registered charge, which had been duly discharged, was cancelled on the register.

8. By reason of P. Q. being a fully secured creditor the estate and assets of A. B. divisible amongst his creditors have suffered loss to the extent of no more than £...... paid to the bankrupt as aforesaid, no part of which has been recovered by or on behalf of the Official Receiver.

9. The loss has arisen because of the failure of the Registrar to register a creditors' notice [and a bankruptcy inhibition] prior to the date of the official search pursuant to Section 61 of the Land Registration Act 1925[10].

10. The estate and assets in the bankruptcy aforesaid have also suffered loss to the extent of £...... (as shown by the annexed bill of costs[11]) in respect of the costs and expenses of and incidental to the investigation by the Official Receiver of the circumstances set out above, and claim is also made for such costs and expenses as well as the costs of this present application[12].

DATED .... 19...

(Signature)
Solicitors for the Official Receiver

1 Land Registration Act 1925 ss 61 (7), 83 (as substituted by the Land Registration Act 1997 s 2) (37 Halsbury's Statutes (4th Edn) REAL PROPERTY); Land Registration and Land Charges Act 1971 s 2 (5) (37 Halsbury's Statutes (4th Edn) REAL PROPERTY). See Paragraph 32 ante. The form is not prescribed, but it is advisable to use the heading and set out the grounds in numbered paragraphs as in this example. If the Registrar agrees the claim, he will authorise the payment of indemnity accordingly. If in an exceptional case, there is no agreement, the applicant may apply to the court for the outstanding questions to be determined under the Land Registration and Land Charges Act 1971 s 2 (1).
2 See Form 6 note 6 ante.
3 See note 1 above.
4 Insolvency Rules 1986, SI 1986/1925, rr 6.13 (creditor's petition), 6.43 (debtor's petition) (3 Halsbury's Statutory Instruments (1995 Issue) BANKRUPTCY AND INSOLVENCY). See Paragraph 26 ante.
5 Land Charges Act 1972 s 5 (1) (37 Halsbury's Statutes (4th Edn) REAL PROPERTY). See title LAND CHARGES Paragraph 5 ante; and Paragraph 26 ante.
6 Land Registration Act 1925 s 61 (1). The Registrar must, as soon as practicable after the registration under the Land Charges Act 1972, register a creditors' notice against a title that appears to be affected by a petition in bankruptcy. If he is not completely satisfied as to the identity of the debtor (as he might well not be on the facts stated in the above form) he will serve a notice in Form 30 ante, on the registered proprietor with a view to establishing his identity. If, for example through failure of the proprietor to note a change of his address on the register, this notice is not delivered, the Registrar will have to decide whether in all the circumstances a creditors' notice should be entered.
7 Insolvency Rules 1986, SI 1986/1925, rr 6.34 (2)(a) (order made on creditor's petition), 6.46 (2)(a)(as amended) (order made on debtor's petition); Land Charges Act 1972 s 6 (1)(c)(as substituted). See Paragraph 25 ante.
8 Land Registration Act 1925 s 61 (3)(as amended). See Form 30 ante.
9 As to this search see the Land Registration (Official Searches) Rules 1993, SI 1993/3276, rr 2 (as amended), 3. The priority period expires 30 days after the application for search is deemed to have been delivered at the appropriate district land registry.
10 See note 1 above.
11 An itemised bill of costs should be lodged with the application. If the claimant is registered for VAT purposes, the registry will indemnify the VAT exclusive amount only as the claimant will in those circumstances be able to obtain an input tax credit.
12 Land Registration Act 1925 s 83 (9)(as substituted by the Land Registration Act 1997 s 2). See Paragraph 34 ante.

47
ORIGINATING SUMMONS for the determination of questions as to right to or amount of indemnity[1]

(*Royal Arms*)[2]

IN THE HIGH COURT OF JUSTICE   Ch 19 ... B. No. ...[3]
Chancery Division[4]
[......... District Registry[5]]

Between   A. B.   ...   Plaintiff
                   and
         The Chief Land Registrar   ...   Defendant

To: The Chief Land Registrar, HM Land Registry, Lincoln's Inn Fields, London WC2A 3PH.

LET the Defendant within ... days after service of this summons on him, counting the day of service, return the accompanying Acknowledgment of Service[6] to the appropriate Court Office.

By this Summons, which is issued on the application of the Plaintiff A. B. of (*address*), the Plaintiff seeks against the Defendant the following relief, namely:

1. A declaration pursuant to Section 2 (1) of the Land Registration and Land Charges Act 1971[7] that the Plaintiff is entitled to an indemnity under Section 83 of the Land Registration Act 1925[8] of £...... to be paid by the Defendant out of moneys provided by Parliament;

2. An order that the costs and expenses properly incurred by the Plaintiff in relation to this matter may be provided for[9].

This application is made under Section 83 of the Land Registration Act 1925[10] and Section 2 (1) of the Land Registration and Land Charges Act 1971[11].

If the Defendant does not acknowledge service, such judgment may be given or order made against or in relation to him as the Court may think just and expedient.

DATED .... 19...

NOTE—This Summons may not be served later than [4, *or if leave is required to effect service out of the jurisdiction,* 6] calendar months beginning with the above date unless renewed by order of the Court.

This Summons was taken out by E. F. & Co of (*address*), [Agents for (*name*) of (*address*),] Solicitors for the said Plaintiff whose address is as stated above[12].

IMPORTANT

Directions for acknowledgment of service are given with the accompanying form[13].

---

1   See Paragraph 34 ante. Any claim for indemnity should in the first instance be made in writing to the Chief Land Registrar, and may be addressed to him either at the appropriate district land registry or at the headquarters office HM Land Registry, Lincoln's Inn Fields, London WC2A 3PH (see Form 46 ante). Only if the Chief Land Registrar refuses to settle the claim for indemnity under the Land Registration Act 1925 s 83 (as substituted by Land Registration Act 1997 s 2) (37 Halsbury's Statutes (4th Edn) REAL PROPERTY) by agreement under the Land Registration and Land Charges Act 1971 s 2 (5) (37 Halsbury's Statutes (4th Edn) REAL PROPERTY) on grounds which the applicant considers to be ill-founded, or if no agreement can be reached as to the amount of the indemnity, will the need to consider the commencement of proceedings for the

determination of the outstanding questions under Land Registration and Land Charges Act 1971 s 2 (1) arise. For a supporting affidavit see Form 48 post. It is not unknown for the defendant in proceedings in which rectification of the register is sought to issue a third party notice claiming an indemnity against the Registrar under RSC Ord 16. This, however, is not generally a convenient procedure for the determination of questions under the Land Registration and Land Charges Act 1971 s 2 (1), because, except in the clearest cases, (when the Registrar will not seek to resist the claim), the outstanding questions as to indemnity (for example as to whether the claimant lacked proper care) cannot be determined until the full facts emerge at the trial of the main action.

2   A replica of the Royal Arms must be printed or embossed on the first page of every originating process: RSC Ord 1 r 9.
3   See RSC Appendix A Form No 8.
4   Proceedings relating to land registration are allocated to the Chancery Division: RSC Ord 93 r 10 (2)(f).
5   An originating summons commencing proceedings assigned to the Chancery Division may be issued out of a Chancery district registry: RSC Ord 7 r 5 (2).
6   See Vol 6 (1998 Issue) title ACKNOWLEDGMENT OF SERVICE Form 4.
7   See note 1 above.
8   See note 1 above.
9   As to indemnity in respect of costs or expenses see the Land Registration Act 1925 s 83 (9)(as substituted by Land Registration Act 1997 s 2).
10 See note 1 above.
11 See note 1 above.
12 RSC Ord 7 r 3 (2) applying RSC Ord 6 r 5.
13 See note 6 above.

48

AFFIDAVIT supporting originating summons for the determination of questions as to indemnity[1]

Plaintiff: A. B.: 1st: .... 19...[2]

IN THE HIGH COURT OF JUSTICE   Ch 19 ... B. No. ...[3]
Chancery Division[4]
    [......... District Registry[5]]

Between   A. B.   ...   Plaintiff
                                  and
                    The Chief Land Registrar   ...   Defendant

I, A. B. of (*state residence or workplace, and occupation or, if none, description*), make oath and say as follows:

1. I am the Plaintiff in these proceedings in which I seek a declaration that I am entitled to an indemnity of £...... to be paid by the Chief Land Registrar out of moneys provided by Parliament in respect of loss suffered by me in circumstances hereinafter appearing.

2. On .... 19... I purchased from one P. Q. the freehold land and premises known as .... at a price of £......, and on .... 19... I was registered as first proprietor thereof with absolute title under the Title No .... and no restrictive covenants or other incumbrances were entered on the register[6]. I was at the time of registration and have since remained in possession of the land.

[3. In or about the month of .... 19... I began to build upon the land 10 shops with flats thereover.]

4. In the month of .... 19... and subsequently G. H. & Co, acting on behalf of one C. D., by letters addressed to me claimed that the land in the above-mentioned title was subject to certain restrictive covenants imposed by a deed dated .... 19... and made between (*state the parties*); that the deed created a building scheme[7]; that the covenants operated to prevent me (inter alia) from building shops and flats on my land; and that C. D., as owner of the neighbouring land for the benefit of which the covenants were imposed was entitled to enforce them and intended to take all reasonable steps to do so.

5. Proceedings were then begun against me on behalf of C. D. on .... 19... claiming [damages and an injunction and] rectification of the register of the above-mentioned title [as a result of which I asked the Chief Land Registrar for consent to defend the proceedings in accordance with the provisions of Section 83 (5)(c) of the Act[8]. This consent was granted by the Chief Land Registrar by letter dated .... 19...[9]. On the service of the writ I suspended my building work.]

6. At the trial of the action [an injunction was granted and], notwithstanding the provisions of Section 82 (3) of the Act[10], an order for rectification of the register by the entry of notice of the restrictive covenants was made. The register of the above-mentioned title was accordingly rectified on .... 19...[11].

7. On .... 19... a claim to the Chief Land Registrar was accordingly made by E. F. & Co, solicitors on my behalf, for indemnity in respect of the loss which I had suffered and would suffer by reason of the omission of the Chief Land Registrar to enter notice of the covenants on the register of title and by reason of the subsequent rectification, and in respect of which I had not received any compensation or indemnity from any source[12].

8. In a letter dated .... 19... addressed to my solicitors, the Chief Land Registrar admitted in principle that I was entitled to be indemnified under Section 83 (1) of the Land Registration Act 1925. However, despite prolonged negotiations and correspondence between my solicitors and the Chief Land Registrar no agreement has been reached with the Chief Land Registrar under Section 2 (5) of the Land Registration and Land Charges Act 1971 as to the amount of such indemnity[13].

9. The amount of the loss in respect of which I claim indemnity is £...... as set out below:

(1) Loss of the value of the land for the building purposes aforesaid	£......
(2) Interest thereon for ... years at ... % per annum	£......
(3) Deterioration of plant upon the land	£......
(4) Solicitor's costs and charges relative to the proposed development	£......
(5) Surveyor's costs and charges similarly	£......
(6) The Applicant's taxed costs incurred in the defence of the action[14]	£......
Total	£......

SWORN at (*address*), on
.... 19...
Before me,
(*Signature*)
A [Solicitor *or* Barrister *or* Notary Public *or* Commissioner for Oaths][16]

(*Deponent's signature*)[15]

1 For a form of originating summons, see Form 47 ante. This affidavit assumes that a claim for indemnity has already been submitted to the Chief Land Registrar (see Form 46 ante) and has been admitted in principle but that no agreement has been reached with the Registrar under the Land Registration and Land Charges Act 1971 s 2 (5) (37 Halsbury's Statutes (4th Edn) REAL PROPERTY) as to the amount of the loss suffered by the applicant. In matters of property valuation the Registrar normally seeks the advice of the District Valuer and Valuation Officer.
2 See Form 7 note 2 ante.
3 See Form 6 note 3 ante.
4 See Form 6 note 4 ante.
5 See Form 6 note 5 ante.
6 Land Registration Act 1925 ss 5, 50 (as amended) (37 Halsbury's Statutes (4th Edn) REAL PROPERTY); Land Registration Rules 1925, SR & O 1925/1093, r 40 (16 Halsbury's Statutory Instruments (1998 Issue) REAL PROPERTY).
7 As to the effect of the creation of a building scheme see *Elliston v Reacher* [1908] 2 Ch 665, CA.
8 Land Registration Act 1925 s 83 (5)(c)(as substituted by Land Registration Act 1997 s 2). See Paragraph 34 ante and Form 35 ante.
9 Compare with Form 36 ante.
10 Land Registration Act 1925 s 82 (3)(as amended). See Paragraph 29 ante. In this case it is assumed that the circumstances specified in the sub-section were present, so that rectification could be ordered.
11 Land Registration Act 1925 s 82 (5); Land Registration Rules 1925 r 302.
12 The several headings of the claim should be supported by evidence, showing how the figures are arrived at. Thus the valuer's report, itemised bills of costs etc should be exhibited. See also the Land Registration Act 1925 s 83 (9)(as substituted by the Land Registration Act 1997 s 2).
13 The extent (if at all) to which it will be appropriate to exhibit the correspondence between the claimant and the Registrar will of course depend on whether or not that correspondence has been conducted on a "without prejudice" basis.
14 Land Registration Act 1925 s 83 (5)(c)(as substituted by the Land Registration Act 1997 s 2). See Paragraph 34 ante.
15 Every affidavit must be signed by the deponent and must be completed and signed by the person before whom it is sworn: RSC Ord 41 r 2 (1).
16 Solicitors Act 1974 s 81 (as amended) (41 Halsbury's Statutes (4th Edn) SOLICITORS); Courts and Legal Services Act 1990 s 113 (17 Halsbury's Statutes (4th Edn) EVIDENCE); Administration of Justice Act 1985 s 65 (31 Halsbury's Statutes (4th Edn) NOTARIES AND LICENSED CONVEYANCERS); Commissioners for Oaths Acts 1889 and 1891 (as amended) (17 Halsbury's Statutes (4th Edn) EVIDENCE).

Index

ISSUES

AFFIDAVIT
  Order 14A application, supporting, 23
APPEAL
  Order 14A, under, 24
CASE STATED
  meaning, 29
  application of opinion, motion for, [64]
  availability under statutes and rules, 31
  Commonwealth court, for, 33
  form of, 31
  Scottish court, for—
    form, [62]
    memorandum identifying, [63]
    notice of motion, [61 64]
    practice, 33
CHANCERY DIVISION
  trial of preliminary issue or point of law, 17
COMMONWEALTH COURT
  case stated for, 33
CONSTRUCTION (INTERPRETATION)
  Order 14A, under. *See* ORDER 14A PROCEEDINGS
COSTS
  written offer on liability, as to, 11
COUNTY COURT
  questions and issues in, 34 [65 66]
DAMAGES
  assessment—
    practice, 9
    summons for directions, 9 [42]
  separate trial of issue of, 8 [37 38]
DEFENDANT
  issue—
    another party, between, 28
    non-party, between, 29
DISCOVERY
  issue of liability, as to, 8
  question or issue for, 25
DISMISSAL OF ACTION
  Order 14A, under, summons for, [54]
  Order 18 Rule 19, under, summons for, [54]
  trial of preliminary issue, on, 18 [48]
DISTRICT JUDGE
  reference of question to—
    notice of application, [65]
    order for, [66]
    practice, 34
    report on, [66]
EVIDENCE
  Order 14A application, supporting, 23
  trial of preliminary issue or point of law, on, 18

FOREIGN JUDGMENT
  issue as to setting aside registration of, 28 [57]
GARNISHEE PROCEEDINGS
  question in, 27
INSPECTION
  issue of liability, in, 8
INTERLOCUTORY PROCEEDINGS
  issues. *See* ISSUE
INTERPLEADER
  question or issue in, 25 [56]
ISSUE
  assessment of damages. *See under* DAMAGES
  case stated. *See* CASE STATED
  construction, of. *See* ORDER 14A PROCEEDINGS
  county court—
    practice generally, 34
    reference to district judge or referee, 34 [65 66]
  damages—
    assessment. *See under* DAMAGES
    separate trial, 8 [37]
  defendant and non-party, between, 29
  defendant and party, between, 28
  discovery, for, 25
  execution, as to, 28
  interpleader proceedings—
    judgment, [56]
    order to be stated and tried, 26
    summary determination, 25
  liability, of—
    costs, 11
    discovery and inspection, 8
    garnishee proceedings, 27
    interlocutory judgment, summons for, [40]
    judgments after separate trial, [41]
    partner or firm, [46]
    personal injuries actions, 8–9
    separate trial, 8 [37 38]
    written offer—
      acceptance, 11 [39]
      contents, 10
      costs, 11
      form of, 11 [39]
      judgment by consent, 11
      notice of acceptance, [39]
      practice, 10
      refusal to accept, 11
      third party proceedings, 11
      time for, 10
  Order 14A. *See* ORDER 14A PROCEEDINGS
  partnership issue, order directing trial of, 29 [46]

Page numbers in square brackets refer to forms

INDEX TO ISSUES

ISSUES—*continued*
ISSUE—*cont.*
  preliminary, trial of—
    appeal to Court of Appeal, 17
    Chancery Division, 17
    conditions for, 12
    court's powers, 12
    directions for, 16
    dismissal of action on, 18 [48]
    evidence, 18
    examples of, 13
    judgment after, [49]
    order after, [48 49]
    order for, [45 46]
    pleadings, on—
      order, for, [44]
      summons for, [43]
    refusal of, examples, 13
    summons for, [43 44]
    trial of action, treated as, 18 [49]
  preliminary point of law—
    meaning, 14
    evidence on trial of, 18
    Order 14A. *See* ORDER 14A PROCEEDINGS
    trial of—
      availability, 14
      cases where ordered, 15
      determination distinguished, 14
      directions for, 16
      jurisdiction, 17
      order disposing of whole action, [50]
      order for, 16 [47]
      summons for, 16 [47]
  question distinguished, 6
  registration of foreign judgment, as to setting aside, 28 [57]
  scope of title, 15
  separate trial of—
    availability, 16
    court's powers, 7n
    damages, 8 [37]
    different places or modes of trial, 6
    judgment after, [41]
    order for, 7 [38]
    personal injuries actions, 8–9
    summons for, [37]
    time for making order, 7
    types of order, 7
    See also liability, of *supra*
  special case. *See* SPECIAL CASE
  split trial, 9n
  terminology, 5
JUDGMENT
  interlocutory, on written offer on liability, summons for, [40]
  Order 14A, under. *See under* ORDER 14A PROCEEDINGS
  trial of issue, on—
    interpleader proceedings, [56]
    preliminary issue, [49]

JUDGMENT—*cont.*
  trial of issue, on—*cont.*
    separate trial of issue of liability, [41]
JUDGMENT BY CONSENT
  written offer on liability, on, 11
LIABILITY
  garnishee proceedings, question in, 27
  issue of. *See under* ISSUE
MEMORANDUM
  case stated for Scottish court, identifying, [63]
MOTION
  Order 14A, under, 22
NON-PARTY
  issue between defendant and, 29
NOTICE
  acceptance of offer on liability, 11 [39]
NOTICE OF APPLICATION
  reference of question to district judge or referee, for, 34 [65]
NOTICE OF MOTION
  case for opinion of Scottish court, as to, [61 64]
OFFER
  liability, as to, 10 [39]
OFFICIAL REFEREE
  meaning, 17n
  trial of preliminary issue or point of law, 17
ORDER
  action, dismissing, on trial of preliminary issue, 18 [48]
  interpleader issue to be stated and tried, 26
  leave to formulate special case, for, [59]
  reference of question to district judge or referee, for, [66]
  special case, on, [60 61]
  trial of issue, for—
    general form, [45]
    partnership issue, [46]
    pleadings, on, [44]
    separate trial, 17 [38]
  trial of preliminary issue, after [48–50]
  trial of preliminary point of law, for, 16 [47]
ORDER 14 PROCEEDINGS
  summons for judgment, [53]
ORDER 14A PROCEEDINGS
  affidavit evidence, 23
  appeal, 24
  application, mode of, 22
  consent of parties, 21
  construction of document, summons for judgment, [52]
  court's powers to dispose of case, 19 21
  dismissal of action on point of law, summons for, [54]
  evidence, 23
  finality of determination on point of law, 24
  formulation of point of law, 20
  hearing of parties, 21
  judgment—
    defendant, for, [55]

Page numbers in square brackets refer to forms

INDEX TO JUDICIAL REVIEW

ISSUES—*continued*
ORDER 14A PROCEEDINGS—*cont.*
  judgment—*cont.*
    oral application, on, [56]
    plaintiff, for, [55]
  leave to defend, 20–21
  motion under, 22
  point of law, summons for judgment on, [53]
  scope of, 19
  suitable question of law or construction, 20
  summons, 22 [54 55]
PARTNER
  question as to liability of, 29 [46]
PARTNERSHIP
  trial of issue as to, order for, 29 [46]
PARTY TO ACTION
  issue between defendant and, 28
PERSONAL INJURY
  issues of liability and damages, 8–9
  written offer on liability, 10 [39]
PLEADING
  trial of preliminary issue on, [43 44]
POINT OF LAW
  Order 14A proceedings on. *See* ORDER 14A PROCEEDINGS
  preliminary, trial of. *See under* ISSUE
QUEEN'S BENCH DIVISION
  trial of preliminary issue or point of law, 17
QUESTION
  county court, in, 34 [65 66]
  discovery, for, 25
  execution, as to, 28
  garnishee proceedings, in, 27
  issue distinguished, 6
  liability of partner or firm, as to, 29 [46]
  preliminary. *See under* ISSUE
  scope of title, 5
REPORT
  reference to district judge or referee, on, [66]

SCOTLAND
  case stated for Scottish court, 33 [61–63]
SPECIAL CASE
  meaning, 29
  court's powers, 32
  form of, 30 [59]
  leave—
    order giving, [59]
    summons for, [58]
  order on, [60 61]
SUMMONS
  dismissal of action under Order 14A or Order 18, for, [54]
  interlocutory judgment for agreed proportion of liability, for, [40]
  Order 14A, application under, 22 [53 54]
  summary judgment under Order 14, for, [53]
  trial, for—
    preliminary issue on the pleadings, [43]
    preliminary issues or questions, [44]
    preliminary point of law, 16 [47]
    separate trial of issue, [37]
SUMMONS FOR DIRECTIONS
  assesment of damages, for, 9 [42]
  trial of preliminary point of law, 16
SUMMONS FOR LEAVE
  special case, as to, [58]
THIRD PARTY PROCEEDINGS
  garnishee proceedings, question in, 27
  written offer of contribution, 11
TRIAL
  issue, of. *See under* ISSUE
WITNESS
  trial of preliminary issue or point of law, 18
WRIT OF EXECUTION
  issue or question on application for, 28

JUDICIAL REVIEW

AFFIDAVIT
  leave for judicial review, as to—
    applicant's, 175 [213]
    respondent's, 184 [214]
APPEAL
  asylum cases, 118
  judicial review substantive hearing, from, 188
  special educational needs, as to, 128
BAIL
  judicial review, pending—
    generally, 181
    immigration cases, 119
BREACH OF STATUTORY DUTY
  Inland Revenue, claim against, 149
  prisoners' rights, and, 136

CERTIORARI
  discretion as to, 79
  nature of, 77
  no-certiorari clauses, 155
  use of, 77
CIVIL SERVICE
  judicial review, availability, 88
COMPROMISE AND SETTLEMENT
  judicial review applications, 185
COSTS
  judicial review applications, of, 177 188
CRIMINAL PROCEEDINGS
  judicial review, public/private law divide, 96
  renewal of judicial review application, 180
CROSS-EXAMINATION
  judicial review, on, 185

Page numbers in square brackets refer to forms

JUDICIAL REVIEW—continued

CROWN COURT
  judicial review of decisions, 90
CROWN SERVANT
  judicial review, availability, 87
DAMAGES
  false imprisonment under mental health provisions, 140
  housing duties, as to, 121
  judicial review generally, 81
DECLARATION
  judicial review, on. *See under* JUDICIAL REVIEW
DISCOVERY
  judicial review applications, 184
EDUCATION
  Funding Agency, 122
  judicial review of decisions. *See under* JUDICIAL REVIEW
  legislation, 122
ESTOPPEL
  judicial review, and, 116 187
EUROPEAN COMMISSION OF HUMAN RIGHTS
  prisoners' applications to, 135
EUROPEAN COURT OF JUSTICE
  judicial review of community institutions, 173
  member states, actions against, 174
EXTENSION OF TIME
  judicial review application, for, 164
FALSE IMPRISONMENT
  mental health provisions, under, 140
HABEAS CORPUS
  mental health applications, 140
HOMELESS PERSON
  judicial review of decisions as to. *See under* JUDICIAL REVIEW
HOUSING
  judicial review of rehousing decisions. *See under* JUDICIAL REVIEW
IMMIGRATION
  asylum cases, 118
  judicial review. *See under* JUDICIAL REVIEW
INJUNCTION
  court's powers, 81
  mandatory, meaning, 81
  restrictive, meaning, 81
INLAND REVENUE
  breach of statutory duty claim as alternative to judicial review, 149
  judicial review of taxation matters. *See under* JUDICIAL REVIEW
JUDICIAL REVIEW
  amenability—
    civil service, 88
    commercial matters, 144
    conditions for, 82
    contract as source of respondent's powers, 82
    Crown Court, 90
    Crown employment, 87
    Crown prerogative, 84

JUDICIAL REVIEW—*cont.*
  amenability—*cont.*
    'domestic' bodies, 87
    education, 124 129
    'functions' test, 85 86
    homeless persons cases, 120 121
    immigration cases, 118
    inferior courts and tribunals, 89
    informal tribunals, 87
    mental health cases, 137
    prisoners' rights, 131
    public employment, 87
    public law body, 83
    social security decisions, 151
    source of power, 83
    statutory duties and employment law, 89
    taxation matters, 144
  appeal from substantive hearing, 188
  application for—
    leave, *See* leave, application for *infra*
    procedural table, 191
    substantive, *See* substantive hearing *infra*
  asylum cases, 118
  bail, 181
  bias and natural justice, 105
  breach of statutory duty as alternative, 136 149
  certiorari, nature and use of, 77
  chartered bodies, 84
  civil service, 88
  collateral defences, 94
  collateral public law issues, 93
  commercial matters—
    availability of review, 144
    grounds for review, 146
    illegality, 146
    procedural impropriety, 146
    restrictions on review, 148
    unreasonableness, 147
  compromise and settlement, 185
  conditions for challenge by, 82
  consent and exclusivity rule, 96
  construction of statutes, and illegality, 98
  consultation—
    education, in, 130n
    failure to perform, 102
    fair, meaning, 102
  contract as source of respondent's powers, 85
  costs—
    leave application of, 177
    security for, 183
    substantive hearing, 188
  criminal proceedings, 96
  cross-examination of deponents, 185
  Crown Court decisions, of, 90
  Crown employment, 87
  Crown prerogative, and availability, 84
  damages—
    court's powers, 81
    homeless persons, 121

Page numbers in square brackets refer to forms

356

INDEX TO JUDICIAL REVIEW

JUDICIAL REVIEW—*continued*
JUDICIAL REVIEW—*cont.*
  damages—*cont.*
    notice of application, [205]
  declaration—
    matters to consider, 80
    nature of, 80
    notice of application, [197 201 205 208]
  discontinuance, 186
  discretionary remedies, 79
  documents to be lodged, 186
  'domestic' bodies, availability of review, 87
  EC law—
    European Court of Justice, review in, 173
    legal analysis, 169
    member states, action against, 174
    principles generally, 167
    relevance in domestic courts, 168
    remedies, 170
    special relevance for review, 171
  education—
    admission policies etc, 125
    appeal arrangements, 125
    assessment of special educational needs, 127
    availability of review, 124 129
    complaints procedures, 125
    consultation, 130n
    discrimination, 126
    exclusions, 127
    Funding Agency, 122
    legislation, 122
    local education authorities' duties, 123
    notice of application for leave to apply, [208]
    reforms, 122
    school governors' duties, 123
    special educational needs, 127–129
  employment law and statutory duties, 89
  estoppel—
    illegality, and, 101 116
    issue estoppel, 187
    legitimate expectation, and, 116
    principles of, 116
  European Convention on Human Rights, 174
  European Court of Justice, in, 173 174
  exclusivity of procedure, 91
  exhaustion of other remedies—
    exhaustion rule, 165
    non-application of rule, 166
    practice of courts in general, 167
    principles of, 165
  expedition, directions for, 181
  extension of the time limits for, 164
  fettering of discretion—
    nature of, 115
    notice of application based on, [208]
  function of, 75
  'functions' test, 85 86
  grounds—
    amendment of, 185
    commercial matters, 146

JUDICIAL REVIEW—*cont.*
  grounds—*cont.*
    estoppel, 116
    fettering discretion, 115
    illegality. *See* illegality *infra*
    irrationality. *See* irrationality *infra*
    legitimate expectation, 116
    principles generally, 97
    procedural impropriety. *See* procedural impropriety *infra*
    proportionality principle, 112
    unlawful delegation, 114
    unreasonableness. *See* unreasonableness *infra*
  historical development, 75
  homelessness—
    application for review, 121
    availability of review, 120
    Code of Guidance for Local Authorities, 120
    damages, 121
    reasoned decision, 121
    rehousing duty, 120
    review of local housing authority's decision, 120
  illegality—
    meaning, 97 98
    commercial matters, 146
    estoppel, 101 116
    fettering of discretion, 101
    improper purposes, 99
    legitimate expectation, 101
    matters of law, 100
    nature of, 97
    statutory construction, 98
    ultra vires acts, 101
  immigration cases—
    asylum decisions, 118
    availability, 118
    bail, 119
    exhaustion rule, 118
    legitimate expectation, 119
    notice of application for leave, [211]
    procedural impropriety, 119
    unreasonableness, 118
  improper conduct, 99
  informal tribunals, review of, 87
  injunction and stay—
    special directions as to, 181
    use of, 81
  interim relief, notice of application for, [197]
  irrationality—
    meaning, 107
    concept of, 107
    examples of, 109
    ground of, 106
    irrelevancies, 109
    mixed grounds for review, 110
    'no evidence' cases, 109
    qualifications to doctrine of, 111
    unreasonableness, and, 107

Page numbers in square brackets refer to forms

INDEX TO JUDICIAL REVIEW

JUDICIAL REVIEW—*continued*
JUDICIAL REVIEW—*cont.*
  irrationality—*cont.*
    Wednesbury unreasonableness, 106 107
    See also unreasonableness *infra*
  jurisdiction, 175
  Law Commission's reforms, 75
  leave, application for—
    affidavit—
      applicant's, 175 [213]
      respondent's, 184 [214]
    bail, 181
    challenge of leave, 183
    choice between paper or oral application, 176
    conditional grant of leave, 177 183
    costs, 177
    delay, 163
    documents required, 175
    education, [208]
    expedition, 181
    extension of time, 164
    housing, 121
    immigration, [211]
    injunction and stay, 181
    internal appeal or review, as to, time limits, 176
    limited or conditional leave, 177 183
    mental health, [205]
    need for, 175
    notice. *See* notice of application *infra*
    oral applications, 176
    paper applications, 176
    practice, 175
    prisoner's rights, as to, [202]
    procedural table, 191
    renewal applications, 180
    respondent, service on, 177
    security for costs, 183
    service, 177 181
    setting aside, 183 184
    special directions, 181
    taxation, as to, [200]
    test for leave, 177
    time estimates, 176
    time limits, 163 175–176
    venue, 175
  legitimate expectation—
    conditions, 103
    consultation duties, 102
    estoppel, 116
    immigration cases, 119
    nature of, 116
    notice of application based on, [200]
    procedural impropriety, 103
  Lloyd's of London, 145
  locus standi—
    associations or groups, 161
    future of, 163
    inadequate, 161
    'open' and 'closed' systems, 163

JUDICIAL REVIEW—*cont.*
  locus standi—*cont.*
    principles generally, 158
    relevance of strength of the case, 162
    statutory, 161
    sufficient interest, 158
    two-stage test, 162
    type of interest, 159
  mandamus, nature and use of, 78
  matters of law—
    exclusivity of procedure, 94
    illegality, ground of, 100
  mental health cases—
    advantages of review, 137n
    authorised detention, 138
    availability of review, 137
    discharge from hospital—
      bodies other than tribunal, by, 141
      Mental Health Review Tribunal, by, 141
    exhaustion rule, 167
    mental disorder, meaning, 139n
    notice of application for leave to apply, [205]
    procedural provisions, 143
    remedies for unauthorised detention, 140
    unreasonable use of provisions for detention, 138
  natural justice—
    bias, 105
    content of, 104
    procedural impropriety, 103
  'no evidence' cases and irrationality, 109
  notice of application—
    affidavit supporting, 175 [213]
    consideration of irrelevant matters, as to, [211]
    damages, [205]
    error of law, as to, [211]
    fettering of discretion, based on, [200]
    general form, [197]
    interim relief, [197]
    legitimate expectation, based on, [200]
    practice, 175
    procedural impropriety, based on, [202 208]
    relevant consideration, as to—
      education, [208]
      immigration, [211]
      prisoners' rights, [202]
    unreasonableness, based on—
      education, [208]
      immigration, [211]
      mental health, [205]
      taxation, [200]
  ouster and finality clauses—
    effect of *Anisminic* case, 156
    finality clauses, 155
    historical development, 155
    position before *Anisminic* case, 155
    time-limit ouster clauses, 157
    void and voidable errors, 155

Page numbers in square brackets refer to forms

JUDICIAL REVIEW—continued

JUDICIAL REVIEW—cont.
- parole decisions, of, 133
- prisoners' rights—
  - availability of review, 131
  - Boards of Visitors, 130 131
  - breach of statutory duty, 136
  - disciplinary hearings, 132
  - governors' decisions, 131
  - international aspects, 135
  - managerial decisions, 132
  - notice of application for leave to apply, [202]
  - parole decisions etc, 133
  - private law claims, 135
  - reform proposals, 135
  - unreasonableness, 134
- procedural impropriety—
  - bias, 105
  - commercial matters, 146
  - consultation duties, 102
  - exclusions, 104
  - immigration cases, 119
  - legitimate expectation, 103
  - natural justice and fairness, 103 104
  - nature of, 97 101
  - notice of application based on, [202 208]
  - statutory procedures, 102
- procedural table, 191
- prohibition, use of, 78
- proportionality, 112
- public employment, 87
- public law body—
  - *meaning*, 83
  - employment decisions, 87
  - 'functions' test, 85 86
  - source of power, 83
- public/private law divide—
  - collateral defences, 94
  - collateral public law issues, 93
  - consent, 96
  - criminal proceedings, 96
  - dual public and private elements within single statutory provision, 93
  - exceptions, 92
  - exclusivity of challenge procedures, 92
  - history of, 91
  - matters of law, 94
  - transfer of proceedings, 93
  - *Winder* doctrine, use of, 95
- relevant consideration, notice of application as to failure to take into account. *See under* notice of application *supra*
- remedies—
  - availability, 76
  - certiorari, 77
  - damages, 81
  - declaration, 80
  - discretion as to, 79
  - EC law, 170
  - injunction and stay, 81

JUDICIAL REVIEW—cont.
- remedies—*cont.*
  - mandamus, nature of, 78
  - prohibition, nature of, 78
  - respondent's affidavit, 184 [214]
  - scope of title, 76
  - security for costs, 183
- self-regulatory bodies, 144
- social security—
  - availability of review, 151
  - commissioners' decisions, 153
  - decision-makers, 150
  - exhaustion of other appeals and other remedies, 151
  - legislation, 150
  - social fund, 154
  - tribunal decisions, review of, 151
- statutory provisions with dual public and private elements, 93
- stay of execution pending, 81
- substantive hearing—
  - amendment of Form 86A, 185
  - appeal from, 188
  - costs, 188
  - cross-examination of deponents, 185
  - discontinuance, 186
  - discovery, 184
  - entering motion for, 182
  - further evidence of applicant, 185
  - issue estoppel, 187
  - listing, 180 186
  - originating notice of motion, 182–183
  - preparation of documents, 182
  - procedural provisions, 183
  - procedural table, 191
  - procedure, 187
  - respondent's reply, 184 [214]
  - service, 182
  - settlement and compromise, 185
  - standing out of lists, 186
  - time provisions, 183
- sufficient interest test, 158
- taxation—
  - availability of review, 144
  - breach of statutory duty as alternative remedy, 149
  - notice of application for leave to apply, [200]
  - restrictions on review, 148
- time limits—
  - extension, 164
  - leave application, for, 163
  - mandamus, 164
- transfer of proceedings, 93
- tribunals, availability, 87 89
- ultra vires acts, ground of illegality, 101
- uncontested applications, 185
- unlawful delegation, ground of, 114
- unreasonableness—
  - *meaning*, 107

Page numbers in square brackets refer to forms

INDEX TO LAND CHARGES

JUDICIAL REVIEW—*continued*
JUDICIAL REVIEW—*cont.*
  unreasonableness—*cont.*
    application of concept of, 107
    commercial matters, 147
    examination by courts, 108
    immigration cases, 118
    irrationality, 107
    notice of application. *See under* notice of application *supra*
    prisoners' rights, 134
    proportionality, 134
    pure unreasonableness, examples, 110
    Wednesbury unreasonableness, 106 107
    See also irrationality *supra*
  VAT cases, 144
  Winder doctrine, use by public law defendants, 95
JURISDICTION
  judicial review applications, 175
LAW COMMISSION
  judicial review recommendations, 75
LOCAL EDUCATION AUTHORITY
  general duties of, 123
  judicial review. *See under* JUDICIAL REVIEW
LOCAL HOUSING AUTHORITY
  judicial review. *See under* JUDICIAL REVIEW
MANDAMUS
  discretion as to, 79
  nature and use of, 78
  running of time, 164
MENTAL HEALTH
  damages for false imprisonment, 140
  habeas corpus, 140
  judicial review of decisions. *See under* JUDICIAL REVIEW
MENTAL HEALTH REVIEW TRIBUNAL
  appeal from, 137
  discharge procedure, 141
  judicial review. *See under* JUDICIAL REVIEW
  procedural rules, 143
NOTICE OF APPLICATION
  judicial review, as to. *See under* JUDICIAL REVIEW
ORIGINATING NOTICE OF MOTION
  judicial review substantive hearing, for, 182–183
PRISON GOVERNOR
  judicial review. *See under* JUDICIAL REVIEW

PRISONER
  European Human Rights Commission, application to, 135
  judicial review and rights of. *See under* JUDICIAL REVIEW
  reform proposals for prisons, 135
  UN Mimimum Standards Rules and Body of Principles, 135
PROCEDURAL TABLES
  judicial review, 191
PROHIBITION
  discretion as to, 79
  nature and use of, 78
RACIAL DISCRIMINATION
  education, in, 126
SCHOOL GOVERNOR
  duties of, 123
SECURITY FOR COSTS
  judicial review applications, as to, 183
SERVICE (PROCESS)
  judicial review applications, 181 182
  leave application for judicial review, of, 177 181
SEX DISCRIMINATION
  education, in, 126
SOCIAL SECURITY
  judicial review. *See under* JUDICIAL REVIEW
SOCIAL SECURITY APPEAL TRIBUNAL
  judicial review, 151
SOCIAL SECURITY COMMISSIONER
  judicial review, 153
STAY OF EXECUTION
  judicial review, pending, 81
TAX
  judicial review of decisions. *See under* JUDICIAL REVIEW
TRIBUNAL
  informal, availability of judicial review, 87
  judicial review, availability, 89
  special educational needs appeals, 128
UNITED NATIONS
  prisoners and detainees, minimum standards rules etc, 135
VALUE ADDED TAX
  judicial review, 144
VENUE
  judicial review applications, 175

LAND CHARGES

AFFIDAVIT
  vacation of registration—
    opposing, estate contract possibly existing, [241]
    supporting—
      deed of arrangement, as to, [234]
      estate contract determined, [237]
      estate contract never existing, [539]

ANNUITY
  meaning, 220n
  cancellation of existing entries in register, 227
  Class A or B land charge, 220
  Class C land charge, 226
  Class E land charge, 221
  registration of, 227

Page numbers in square brackets refer to forms

INDEX TO LAND CHARGES

LAND CHARGES—*continued*
BANKRUPTCY ORDER
  registration and vacation, 228
BANKRUPTCY PETITION
  registration and cancellation of registration, 226
COMPENSATION
  land charges undisclosed, as to, 232
COUNTY COURT
  land charges—
    jurisdiction, 222
    originating application for vacation of registration of court order, [246]
    procedure, 225
DAMAGES
  land charge unenforceable due to official error, 231
DEED OF ARRANGEMENT
  registration where affecting land, 228
  vacation of registration—
    affidavit supporting, by trustee, [234]
    order for, [235]
    originating summons, [233]
    powers, 228
DISMISSAL OF ACTION
  vacation of registration of pending action, on, [244 245]
ESTATE CONTRACT
  meaning, 222n
  Class C land charge, 221
  determined, vacation of registration, [237 243]
  never existing, vacation of registration, [239 243]
  possibly existing, affidavit opposing vacation of registration, [241]
  registration, 228
INDEMNITY
  undisclosed land charges, 230
JURISDICTION
  land charges, as to, 222
LAND CHARGE
  meaning, 219
  annuities, 227
  application to register, 223
  bankruptcy order, 228
  bankruptcy petition, 226
  cancellation of registration, 229
  Class A, 220
  Class B, 220
  Class C—
    meaning, 221
    annuities registrable as, 226
  Class D, 221
  Class E—
    meaning, 221
    annuities registrable as, 226
  Class F—
    meaning, 221
    cancellation, 229
  compensation where undisclosed, 230
  county court. *See under* COUNTY COURT

LAND CHARGE—*cont.*
  damages where charge unenforceable due to official error, 231
  deed of arrangement—
    registration, 228
    vacation of registration, 228 [233–235]
  determination as to existence of alleged interest, 224
  excluded matters and instruments, 222
  High Court procedure, 223
  jurisdiction, 222
  land, meaning, 219n
  local land charges, 221n
  matrimonial home, as to, 221 223
  pending action. *See* PENDING ACTION
  registered land, exclusions, 222
  registers, 222
  registration, 222 228
  restrictive covenants, 229
  scope of title, 219
  undisclosed, compensation for, 232
  vacation of registration—
    availability, 228–229
    bankruptcy order, 228
    bankruptcy petition, 226
    deed of arrangement, 228 [233–235]
    determined interest, [237 242]
    interest never existing, [239 243]
    interest possibly existing, [241]
    interlocutory motion for, [243]
    originating application for, [246]
    originating summons for, [233]
    pending action, 225 [243–245]
    practice, 223–224
    procedure after, 232
    restrictive covenants, 229
    scope of title, 219
    special procedure where hardship etc, 229
    summary applications, 224
    writs and orders, 227
  writs and orders—
    registrable, 219 227n
    registration and cancellation, 227
MATRIMONIAL HOME
  Class F land charge, 221 223
MORTGAGE
  Class C land charge, 221
NOTICE OF MOTION
  vacation of registration of pending action improperly registered, [243]
ORDER
  dismissal of action where pending action improperly registered, [245]
  registration of, where affecting land, 227
  vacation of registration, for—
    deed of arrangement affecting land, [235]
    land charge—
      contract determined, [242]
      never existing, [243]

Page numbers in square brackets refer to forms

INDEX TO LAND REGISTRATION

LAND CHARGES—*continued*
ORDER—*cont.*
  vacation of registration, for—*cont.*
    pending action, [245]
ORIGINATING APPLICATION
  vacation of registration of court order affecting land, for, [246]
ORIGINATING SUMMONS
  vacation of registration, for—
    deed of arrangement, [233]
    land charge, [236]
PENDING ACTION
  meaning, 219
  dismissal for want of prosecution, [244 245]
  registration of, 225
  vacation of registration—
    improperly registered, notice of motion, [243]
    order for, [245]

PENDING ACTION—*cont.*
  vacation of registration—*cont.*
    practice, 225
    summons for, [244]
REGISTERED LAND
  land charges, exclusions, 222
RESTRICTIVE COVENANT
  vacation of registration, 229
SUMMONS
  vacation of registration of pending action and dismissal for want of prosecution, [244]
TRUSTEE
  vacation of registration of deed of arrangement, affidavit supporting, [234]
WRIT
  registration where affecting land, 219 227

LAND REGISTRATION

ADVERTISEMENT
  first registration of title to land, of, 266n
AFFIDAVIT
  appeal from Chief Land Registrar, supporting, [297]
  indemnity as to land registration, as to, [350]
  rectification of land register, supporting, [335]
  reference to court by Chief Land Registrar, on, [319]
APPEAL
  land registration, as to. *See under* LAND REGISTRATION
BANKRUPTCY ORDER
  inhibition. *See under* LAND REGISTRATION
  rectification of land register, [331]
BANKRUPTCY PETITION
  creditor's notice—
    cancellation of, 279
    registration, 278 [328]
CAUTION
  land registration, as to. *See under* LAND REGISTRATION
CHARITY LAND
  restriction on land register, 276
CHIEF LAND REGISTRAR
  meaning, 251–252
  affidavit on appeal from, [297]
  appeal from, 255 256 [296 297]
  consent to legal proceedings, [332 333]
  district registrars, 252
  hearing by—
    adjournment etc, 265
    conduct of, 264
    costs, 289
    extension of time, 265
    jurisdiction, 253 261
    notice of hearing, [293 315]

CHIEF LAND REGISTRAR—*cont.*
  hearing by—*cont.*
    order, 265
    powers, 262
    procedure prior to, 262
    production of deeds etc, 263
    shorthand note, 264
    witnesses, 263 [294]
  inhibition, entry of, 277–278
  jurisdiction, 253 261
  matters for hearing by, 261
  order—
    caution against dealings, as to, [317]
    extension of period for first registration, [298]
    intended dealing where inhibition, as to, 277
    powers, 262 265
    rectification of register, [343]
    reference to court, for, 254 [304 317 345]
    registration of proposed dealing under restriction, [323]
  originating motion on appeal from, [296]
  power to refer matters to court, 254
  restriction, entry of, 276
  witnesses, 263 [294]
CLAIM
  indemnity as to land registration, for, 287 [347]
COMMENCEMENT OF PROCEEDINGS
  land registration, as to, 254
COMPENSATION
  caution against first registration, as to, 268n
CONSENT
  cautioner by, to application for registration, [301]
  proceedings for rectification of land register, to, [332 333]
COSTS
  land registration proceedings, of, 289 290

Page numbers in square brackets refer to forms

INDEX TO LAND REGISTRATION

LAND REGISTRATION—*continued*
COUNTY COURT
  land registration proceedings—
    appeal from, 256
    commencement, 254
    jurisdiction, 253
COURT OF APPEAL
  land registration appeals to, 256
CREDITOR'S NOTICE
  cancellation, 278–279
  notice of registration of, 278n [328]
EVIDENCE
  appeal from Chief Land Registrar, on, 257
  Land Registry documents as, 260
EXTENSION OF TIME
  Chief Land Registrar's powers, 265
  first registration in compulsory area, for, [298]
INDEMNITY
  land registration, as to. *See under* LAND REGISTRATION
INHIBITION
  land register, on. *See under* LAND REGISTRATION
INQUIRY
  bankruptcy proceedings affecting registered proprietor of land, as to, [326]
INSOLVENCY ADMINISTRATION ORDER
  rectification of land register, 259
JUDGMENT CREDITOR
  caution against dealings, 270
JURISDICTION
  Chief Land Registrar, 253 261
  land registration matters, 252 253
LAND CERTIFICATE
  admissibility as evidence, 260
  notice of deposit, 274
  rectification of register, 283
LAND REGISTRATION
  appeal—
    costs, as to, 289
    county court, from, 256
    Court of Appeal, to, 256
    jurisdiction, 256
    Registrar, from—
      affidavit supporting, [297]
      caution against first registration, as to, 268
      entitlement, 255
      first registration, as to, [296 297]
      notice of intention, 255
      originating motion, 256 [296]
      practice, 255
      procedure, 256
      rectification of register, as to, [344]
      time limits, 255
  applications direct to court, 257
  bankruptcy proceedings—
    creditors' notice, 278–279 [328]
    inhibition—
      meaning, 278n
      cancellation, 279 [330]
      notice of registration, 278n [329]

LAND REGISTRATION—*cont.*
  bankruptcy proceedings—*cont.*
    inhibition—*cont.*
      practice, 278–279
    inquiry whether proceedings affect registered proprietor, [326]
    notice of petition, 278
    notice of registration of creditor's notice, [328]
    official receiver, registration as proprietor, 279
    procedure, 278–279
    rectification of register, [331]
    trustee in bankruptcy, registration as proprietor, 279 [331]
  caution—
    conversion, against, 270
    dealings, against. *See under* dealings *infra*
    first registration, against. *See under* first registration *infra*
  Chancery Division, assignment to, 254
  charge certificate. *See* land certificate *infra*
  charity land restriction, 276
  clerical errors, 283
  commencement of proceedings, 254
  conversion of title—
    caution against, 270
    effect of caution, 271
    objection to, 266
    persons able to lodge caution, 270
    procedure prior to hearing, 271
  costs—
    appeal as to, 289
    court proceedings, 290
    indemnity proceedings, 288
    Land Registry proceedings, 289
  county court proceedings, 253 254
  court proceedings—
    commencement, 254
    direct applications, 257
    evidence, 260
    jurisdiction, 252 253
    reference by Registrar. *See* reference to court *infra*
  dealings—
    caution against—
      affidavit on reference to court, [319]
      application for service of notice on cautioner, [309]
      effect, 269
      notice of hearing, 272 [315]
      notice to cautioner, 269 [310]
      objection to cancellation, 271 [311]
      order, 271 [316 317]
      originating summons on reference to court, [318]
      persons able to lodge, 270
      procedure after service of notice on cautioner, 271

Page numbers in square brackets refer to forms

LAND REGISTRATION—*continued*
LAND REGISTRATION—*cont.*
  dealings—*cont.*
    caution against—*cont.*
      reply to objection to cancellation, 271 [313]
      statutory declaration supporting, 270
      withdrawal, 273n
    inhibition. *See* inhibition *infra*
    objection to, 269
    restriction. *See* restriction *infra*
    entry on register of appurtenant right—
      application for, 270n [305]
      effect, 270n
      notice to servient owner, [307]
      objection to, 269 [308]
  evidence of, admissibility, 260
  first registration—
    advertisement as to, 266n
    caution against—
      appeal, 268
      cancellation, 268 [302 303]
      circumstances for, 267
      compensation where unreasonable, 268n
      consent to application for registration, [301]
      contents of, 267
      disposition, meaning, 268n
      form of, [299]
      notice to cautioner, 268 [300]
      objection to cancellation, 268 [302]
      order for reference to court, [304]
      persons able to lodge, 267
      practice, 267
      reply to objection to cancellation, 268 [303]
      statutory declaration supporting, 268
      withdrawal, 268
    compulsory, extension of period for, [298]
    notice of, 266n 267n
    objection to—
      affidavit supporting appeal, [297]
      appeal from Registrar, [296 297]
      cautioner, by, 268 [302]
      form of, [291]
      notice of hearing, [293]
      order, [295 304]
      originating motion on appeal, [296]
      practice, 266
      reply, 266 [303]
      witness summons, [294]
    searches and inquiries, 266n 267n
    service of notices, 267n
    technical defects in title, 266
  indemnity—
    affidavit on application to court, [350]
    amount of, 288
    benefice, as to, 288
    claim for, 287 [347]
    costs, 288

LAND REGISTRATION—*cont.*
  indemnity—*cont.*
    entitlement, 284
    error in search, 285
    evidence, 288
    exclusions, 286
    filed abstract etc, error in, 285
    inaccurate copy document, 285
    lost etc documents, 285
    originating summons for determination as to, [349]
    payment of, 287
    recovery by Registrar where fraud, 287
    rectification, loss on, 284
    running of time, 287
    settled land, 288
    unrectified error or omission, 284
  inhibition—
    meaning, 277
    application for, 278n
    bankruptcy. *See* bankruptcy proceedings *supra*
    mandatory, 278
    power to enter, 277–278
    removal or cancellation, 278
  jurisdiction—
    court, 252 253
    Registrar, 253 261
  land certificate—
    admissibility as evidence, 260
    notice of deposit, 274
    rectification, production on, 283
  legislation, 251
  minor interests, meaning, 259n
  mortgages, 270 274
  notice of deposit, 274
  office copies, 261
  order—
    caution against dealings, as to, [316]
    first registration, as to, [295]
    rectification of register, [337]
    reference to court, for, [304 317 345]
    Registrar's. *See under* CHIEF LAND REGISTRAR
  overriding interests, meaning, 259n
  proceedings where registration of title incidental, 258
  production of evidence in court, 260
  rectification—
    affidavit supporting, [335]
    alternative remedy, 280
    appeal from Registrar, [344]
    application for, 283 [338]
    bankruptcy, on, [331]
    consent to proceedings for, [332 333]
    clerical etc errors, 283
    excluded cases, 282
    grounds, 280
    indemnity—
      alternative remedy, 280
      grounds, 284

Page numbers in square brackets refer to forms

INDEX TO LAND REGISTRATION

LAND REGISTRATION—*continued*
LAND REGISTRATION—*cont.*
  rectification—*cont.*
    notice to proprietor of application, [340]
    objection to, 283 [341]
    order for, [337]
    originating summons for, [334]
    parties to proceedings, 283
    procedure, 283
    reference to court, 283 [345]
    scope of section, 280
    service of order, 283n
    trustee in bankruptcy, application by, 279 [331]
  reference to court—
    caution against dealings, [317]
    caution against first registration, [304]
    circumstances for, 254
    procedure, 256
    rectification of register, 283 [345]
  Registrar. *See* CHIEF LAND REGISTRAR
  restriction—
    meaning, 275
    application as to proposed dealing, [322]
    avoidance of operation, 276
    cancellation, originating summons for, [324]
    charity land, 276
    effect, 275
    order for registration of proposed dealing, [323]
    persons able to apply, 275
    Registrar's powers, 276
    settled land, 276
    withdrawal or modification, 276
  scope of title, 251
  Solicitor to HM Land Registry—
    caution against dealings, order as to, [316]
    objection to first registration, order on, [295]
    powers, 252
    qualifications, 252
  title deeds etc, production of, 263
  unregistered mortgages, 274
LIMITATION PERIOD
  indemnity as to land registration, 287
MORTGAGE
  caution against dealings, 270
  unregistered, 274
NOTICE
  cautioner, to—
    application to warn off or to register dealing, [310]
    registration application, of, 268 [300]
  deposit of land or charge certificate, of, 274
  rectification of land register, as to, [340]
  registration, of—
    bankruptcy inhibition, [329]
    creditor's notice, [328]
  servient owner, to, as to entry of appurtenant right on land register, [307]

NOTICE OF APPLICATION
  cancellation of bankruptcy inhibition, for, 279 [330]
NOTICE OF HEARING
  caution against dealings, as to, 272 [315]
  Chief Land Registrar, before, [293 315]
  first registration of title, as to, [293]
NOTICE OF INTENTION
  appeal from Chief Land Registrar, 255
OBJECTION
  cancellation of caution, to—
    dealings, against, 271 [311]
    first registration, against, 268 [302]
  entries on land register, to, 270n [308]
  first registration of title, to, 268 [291]
  rectification of land register, to, [341]
OFFICIAL RECEIVER
  registration in place of registered proprietor, 279
ORDER
  land registration, as to. *See under* CHIEF LAND REGISTRAR; LAND REGISTRATION
ORIGINATING MOTION
  appeal, on—
    Chief Land Registrar, from, 256 [296 344]
    rectification of land register, as to, [344]
ORIGINATING SUMMONS
  cancellation of restriction on land register, for, [324]
  indemnity as to land registration, as to, [349]
  inhibition, for entry of, 268n
  rectification of land register, for, [334]
  reference to court by Chief Land Registrar, on, [318]
REGISTERED LAND
  direct applications to court, 257
  proceedings where registration of title incidental, 258
  unregistered mortgages, 274
REPLY
  objection, to—
    cancellation of caution against dealings, 271 [313]
    cancellation of caution against first registration, 268 [303]
    first registration of title, 266 [292]
RESTRICTION
  land register, on. *See under* LAND REGISTRATION
RIGHT OF WAY
  entry on land register—
    application for, 270n [305]
    effect, 270n
    notice to servient owner, [307]
    objection to, [308]
SERVICE (PROCESS)
  notice as to first registration of title, 267n
  notice warning off cautioner against dealings, [309]
  rectification of land register, as to, 283n

Page numbers in square brackets refer to forms

LAND REGISTRATION—*continued*
SETTLED LAND
   indemnity as to land registration, 288
   registration of dealings where restriction on register, 276
SOLICITOR
   Land Registry, to. *See under* LAND REGISTRATION
STATUTORY DECLARATION
   caution, supporting—
     dealings, against, 270
     first registration, against, 268

TITLE
   land to, registration. *See* LAND REGISTRATION
TRUSTEE IN BANKRUPTCY
   registration of title in place of registered proprietor, 279 [331]
VESTING ORDER
   rectification of land register consequent on, 258
WITNESS
   Chief Land Registrar, hearing by, 263 [294]
WITNESS SUMMONS
   first registration of title, as to, 263 [294]

Page numbers in square brackets refer to forms